PENGUIN  CLASSICS

ANNALS

TACITUS, born in about 56 CE in southern Gaul (modern Provence) under the Emperor Nero, was probably the son of a civil servant. He was in Rome by 75, training as an orator. As Tacitus tells us in the *Histories*, his own political career flourished under the Flavian emperors Vespasian (69–79), Titus (79–81) and Domitian (81–96). When that dynasty ended, Tacitus began a career as a writer. In quick succession he published the *Agricola*, a biography of his father-in-law, and the *Germania*, an ethnographical study of the peoples of Germany, both in 98. There followed (some time early in the second century) his *Dialogue on Orators*. Today Tacitus is best known as a historian. His debut in the genre, the *Histories*, is a gripping narrative of the turbulent civil war that brought the Flavian dynasty to power in 69; it originally covered the whole Flavian period up to Domitian's assassination in 96. His next work, the *Annals*, moves further back in time to cover the Julio-Claudian emperors from Tiberius (14–37) to Nero (54–68). Neither narrative survives complete, but both preserve Tacitus' uniquely compelling historical voice and offer a chilling denunciation of the corrupting force of power in the Roman Empire. His strong moralizing ethos, together with brilliant techniques of literary artistry, combine to create a powerful and enduring portrait of imperial Rome at its best and worst. Tacitus' public career reached its culmination when he won the prestigious post of proconsul of Asia (112/13). He died at some point after 115 and probably lived into the reign of Hadrian (117–38), but there is no evidence for his later life or the date of his death.

CYNTHIA DAMON received her PhD from Stanford University in 1990 and taught at Harvard University and at Amherst College before moving to the University of Pennsylvania in 2007. She is the author of *The Mask of the Parasite*, a commentary on Tacitus' *Histories* 1, and, with Will Batstone, *Caesar's Civil War*. Current projects include a critical edition of Caesar's *Bellum civile* and a study of the reception of Pliny's *Natural History*.

T0200817

TACITUS

Annals

Translated and with an Introduction by
CYNTHIA DAMON

PENGUIN BOOKS

PENGUIN CLASSICS

Published by the Penguin Group
Penguin Books Ltd, 80 Strand, London WC2R ORL, England
Penguin Group (USA) Inc., 375 Hudson Street, New York, New York 10014, USA
Penguin Group (Canada), 90 Eglinton Avenue East, Suite 700, Toronto, Ontario, Canada M4P 2Y3
(a division of Pearson Penguin Canada Inc.)
Penguin Ireland, 25 St Stephen's Green, Dublin 2, Ireland (a division of Penguin Books Ltd)
Penguin Group (Australia), 707 Collins Street, Melbourne, Victoria 3008, Australia
(a division of Pearson Australia Group Pty Ltd)
Penguin Books India Pvt Ltd, 11 Community Centre, Panchsheel Park, New Delhi – 110 017, India
Penguin Group (NZ), 67 Apollo Drive, Rosedale, Auckland 0632, New Zealand
(a division of Pearson New Zealand Ltd)
Penguin Books (South Africa) (Pty) Ltd, Block D, Rosebank Office Park,
181 Jan Smuts Avenue, Parktown North, Gauteng 2193, South Africa

Penguin Books Ltd, Registered Offices: 80 Strand, London WC2R ORL, England

www.penguin.com

This translation first published in Penguin Classics 2012

021

Translation and editorial material © Cynthia Damon, 2012
All rights reserved

The moral right of the translator has been asserted

Set in 10.25/12.25pt Postscript Adobe Sabon
Typeset by Jouve (UK), Milton Keynes

Printed and bound in Great Britain by Clays Ltd, Elcograf S.p.A.

ISBN: 978-0-140-45564-9

Contents

THE ANNALS

Acknowledgements

Of the many translations I consulted as I worked on this project, two deserve special mention. First, the version of Alfred John Church and William Jackson Brodribb, first published in 1888, which succeeds so well in rendering the dignity of Tacitus' prose. After more than a hundred years its language has acquired an old-fashioned patina that diverts attention onto itself, and the Latin text it renders is out of date. But the words of the Church and Brodribb Tacitus have weight, as they should. And second, the 2004 version by Tony Woodman. No one can fail to admire the skill, care and precision with which he Englished Tacitus' Latin, but his fellow translators, present and future, must be his greatest admirers. Some have the additional good fortune of knowing Tony himself, a peerless friend, and, if very lucky, of having heard Tony read from his translation. Giving voice, literally, to Tacitus, Tony reminds us that this text – and its translations – should be read aloud.

Over the years I have asked many students to read parts of this translation and to tell me what they liked – and what they didn't. Somehow it was always the latter category that elicited the more detailed and lively response. Particular thanks are due to the students in my 2010 Writing History class, who read a penultimate draft and demanded changes for the final draft: Eric Banecker, Zach Dann, Hannah Keyser, Noreen Sit and Matthew Sommer. I listened. Graduate students who read drafts in tandem with Tacitus' Latin performed a different, and difficult, service. I like to think that it helped them enjoy Tacitus more: Talia Hudelson, Kyle Mahoney and Jake Morton. It certainly helped me. Special thanks in this category are due to

Ginna Closs, who discussed the problem of Tacitus' long indirect quotations with me and pushed for a solution. Ginna also read and helped refine my early attempts at one. Carrie Mowbray stepped up to vet the notes.

This translation was the first major project I undertook after moving to Penn, and I have profited immensely from the department's collegiality and intellectual vivacity. So the volume is dedicated to my colleagues with thanks.

Chronology 1:
Principal events referred to in the *Annals*

Regal period (traditional dates) BCE

Republic BCE

100   Second tribunate and death of Saturninus; birth of
        Julius Caesar

91   Tribunate and death of Livius Drusus

91–88   War between Rome and her Italian allies

88   Sulla's first consulship; first march on Rome;
        Marius is outlawed

87–84   Cinna's first, second, third and fourth consulships
        and death

86   Marius' last consulship and death

83   Sulla returns to Italy, renews civil war; second
        march on Rome

82   Sulla is appointed dictator, reforms Roman
        constitution

80   Sulla's second consulship

78   Death of Sulla; revolt of the consul Lepidus

70   Pompey and Crassus consuls for the first time;
        some Sullan reforms are dismantled

63   Birth of Augustus

59   Caesar's first consulship

58–50   Caesar's command in Gaul

55   Pompey and Crassus consuls for the second time

52   Pompey's third consulship

49–48   Civil war between Pompey and Caesar, ending at
        Pharsalus

48   Death of Pompey; Caesar is appointed dictator;
        Caesar's second consulship

47–45   Civil war between Caesar and senatorial opponents

47   Caesar is appointed dictator

46   Caesar consul for the third time and dictator for
        ten years

45   Caesar consul for the fourth time

44	Caesar consul for the fifth time, with Antony; Caesar dictator for life; assassination of Caesar; adoption of Octavian
43	Battle of Mutina: Octavian vs Antony; Octavian's first consulship; formation of triumviral government (Octavian, Antony, Lepidus)
42	Battle of Philippi: Octavian and Antony vs Brutus and Cassius; birth of Tiberius
40	Marriage of Antony and Octavia
38–36	Civil war: Octavian vs Sextus Pompey
38	Octavian marries Livia; birth of Drusus
37	Renewal of triumvirate for another five-year term
33	Octavian's second consulship; Agrippa is aedile
31	Octavian's third consulship; battle of Actium: Octavian vs Antony and Cleopatra
30	Octavian's fourth consulship; deaths of Antony and Cleopatra
29–27	Octavian consul for the fifth, sixth and seventh times
27	Octavian takes the name Augustus
26–23	Augustus consul for the eighth, ninth, tenth and eleventh times
23	Augustus receives tribunician power for life; death of Augustus' nephew Marcellus
21	Agrippa marries Augustus' only child Julia
20	Tiberius' mission to the East; Parthians return Roman standards
18	Augustus' legislation on adultery, marriage and luxury
17	Augustus adopts his grandsons Gaius and Lucius Caesar; Secular Games
15	Birth of Drusus' son Germanicus

14	Birth of Augustus' granddaughter Agrippina
13	Tiberius' first consulship; birth of Tiberius' son Drusus
12	Augustus becomes Pontifex Maximus; death of Agrippa; birth of Agrippa Postumus
11	Tiberius marries Julia
10	Birth of Drusus' son Claudius
9	Death of Tiberius' brother Drusus
7	Tiberius' second consulship
6	Tiberius withdraws to Rhodes
5	Augustus consul for the twelfth time; Gaius Caesar is consul-designate
2 BCE	Augustus consul for the thirteenth time; Lucius Caesar is consul-designate; Augustus is proclaimed 'father of his country'; Julia is exiled for adultery
2 CE	Death of Lucius Caesar; Tiberius returns from Rhodes
4	Death of Gaius Caesar; Augustus adopts Tiberius and Agrippa Postumus; Tiberius adopts Germanicus; Tiberius receives tribunician power
6	Agrippa Postumus is disgraced and exiled to Planasia
8	Augustus' granddaughter Julia is exiled for adultery
9	Revolt in Germany; Quinctilius Varus is defeated by Arminius
10–12	Tiberius' campaigns in Germany
12	Germanicus' first consulship; birth of Germanicus' son Gaius
14	Death of Augustus; Tiberius becomes emperor; death of Agrippa Postumus; army mutinies in Pannonia and Germany; Sejanus becomes Guard commander

15   Drusus' first consulship; Germanicus' first cam-
        paign in Germany; first treason trials

16   Germanicus' victory over Arminius at Idistaviso;
        destruction of Germanicus' fleet; trial and suicide
        of Libo; false Agrippa Postumus

17   Germanicus' German triumph; Germanicus'
        Eastern mission begins; Piso is appointed governor
        of Syria; revolt of Tacfarinas in Africa

18   Germanicus' second consulship; Germanicus
        crowns Artaxias in Armenia

19   Germanicus travels to Egypt; Drusus' victory over
        Maroboduus in Germany; death of Germanicus;
        civil war in Syria; Agrippina returns to Rome

20   Trial and suicide of Piso; modifications to Augus-
        tus' marriage legislation

21   Drusus' second consulship; death of Arminius;
        Sacrovir revolt in Gaul

22   Triumphal honours for Sejanus' uncle Blaesus over
        Tacfarinas; death of Junia

23   Death of Drusus

24   Final defeat of Tacfarinas in Africa

25   Treason trial of Cremutius Cordus

26   Sejanus begins the destruction of Agrippina;
        Sejanus saves Tiberius' life at Sperlonga; Tiberius
        withdraws from Rome, eventually settling on Capri

28   Death of Augustus' exiled granddaughter Julia;
        revolt in Frisia

29   Death of Livia; exile of Agrippina

31   Fall and death of Sejanus; Macro becomes Guard
        commander; death of Germanicus' son Nero

33   Death of Germanicus' son Drusus; death of
        Agrippina

64   Nero's first stage appearance; fire in Rome; Golden
        House is begun

65   Pisonian conspiracy; death of Seneca; death of
        Lucan; death of Poppaea

66   Nero crowns Tiridates king of Armenia; revolt in
        Judaea; death of Petronius; trial and death of
        Thrasea Paetus

67   Nero's tour of Greece

68   Revolt of Vindex in Gaul; Galba is proclaimed
        emperor; Nero's suicide

69   Year of the four emperors (Galba, Otho, Vitellius,
        Vespasian)

Chronology 2:
Principal events of Tacitus' lifetime

56?	Birth of Tacitus
68	End of Julio-Claudian dynasty with suicide of Nero in June
69	Beginning of Flavian dynasty with accession of Vespasian in July
75	Tacitus in Rome, studying oratory
c.77	Tacitus marries daughter of Agricola, embarks on a senatorial career
77–84	Agricola's governorship of Britain
79	Death of Vespasian; Titus becomes emperor
81?	Tacitus holds the office of quaestor
81	Death of Titus; Domitian becomes emperor
88	Tacitus holds the office of praetor and a major public priesthood
88	Secular games
89–93	Tacitus is away from Rome, perhaps as a provincial governor
93	Death of Agricola
96	Assassination of Domitian
97	Tacitus holds a suffect consulship; delivers funeral oration for Verginius Rufus
98	Tacitus begins to write: *Agricola*, *Germania* and eventually the *Dialogue on Orators*

Introduction

The *Annals* is a history of Rome under its first imperial dynasty by Rome's greatest historian. Tacitus begins as he means to go on, with the confrontation between autocracy and liberty: 'The city of Rome was originally in the hands of kings; liberty and the consulship were instituted by Lucius Brutus' (*Annals* 1.1.1). The re-establishment of autocratic rule in Rome under the Emperor Augustus, after five centuries of the republican government instituted by Brutus, brought fundamental changes to many areas of life, including the writing of history. Tacitus is the first surviving historian to confront the resulting problems squarely as problems. Others either went along with the requisite changes or resorted to posthumous publication. Tacitus, however, challenges the emperors for control over history. Of course, the Julio-Claudians themselves were long dead by the time Tacitus was writing in the early second century CE, so his challenge may be thought rather tardy, but his theme is autocratic power as much as it is the emperors themselves, and the nature of the power wielded by subsequent dynasties, including that under which he himself was writing, was essentially the same as that of Tiberius and Gaius, Claudius and Nero. Readers of the *Annals* will find each detail from the period between Augustus' death in 14 CE and Nero's suicide in 68 CE pregnant with universal significance about the nature and use of absolute power.

TACITUS' POLITICAL AND
LITERARY CAREER

Tacitus was born, it seems, during the principate of Nero, perhaps in 56 or 57 CE; this is deduced from the dates of his known political offices. Nothing is known about the earliest years of his life, but by the mid-70s CE he was in Rome, training himself for a senatorial career by attending on the leading speakers of the day (*Dialogue on Orators* 2.1). That career was 'initiated', as Tacitus tells the readers of his *Histories*, by Vespasian, who marked Tacitus out as a future senator (*Histories* 1.3.3). The first, unattested, stages of his political career must have been a minor magistracy at Rome, followed by military service as a junior officer. Around *c.*77 CE he married into the senatorial family of Gnaeus Julius Agricola (*Agricola* 9.6). His career was somehow 'advanced by Titus' in this period, but no details are known (*Histories* 1.3.3). Tacitus next surfaces under Domitian, by whom, he tells us, his career was 'carried further' (ibid.). In 88 CE he was praetor and a member of a priesthood that, along with Domitian, organized the Secular Games in that year (*Annals* 11.11.1). Abroad on public service when Agricola died on 23 August 93 CE (*Agricola* 45.5), Tacitus returned to Rome after an absence of some three years to hold a consulship in the second half of 97 CE. An inscription informs us that Tacitus reached the summit of a senatorial career under Trajan as governor of Asia in 112/13 CE. In *Annals* 2.61.2 he may refer to the extension of Roman dominion to the Red Sea, territory first conquered on Trajan's Parthian campaigns of 115/16. How long Tacitus lived into Hadrian's principate (117–38 CE) is a matter of scholarly dispute.

During Tacitus' first two decades of service to the state, the Flavian peace established itself and imperial power passed from father to son and brother to brother. As a senator Tacitus had a share in governance: in elections, legislation, trials, religious business and provincial affairs. But despite all of this apparent activity these were years of intellectual and moral inertia by his account (*Agricola* 3.1–2). The political landscape changed drastically in 96 CE with Domitian's assassination. The choice of a new emperor devolved on the senate, which chose the elderly Nerva, a man from their own ranks. Tacitus weathered the transition to a new dynasty well, emerging as consul one year into Nerva's reign.

While fulfilling his political, military and religious responsibilities in these years Tacitus also built himself a reputation as an orator. Surviving details are sparse but significant.[1] Both pertain to the post-Flavian period and to issues prominent in his later writings. As consul Tacitus gave the official eulogy for a man named Verginius Rufus, an important, if enigmatic, figure in the civil war that brought the Flavian house to power in 68/9 CE: Rufus' refusal to accept the imperial power offered him by his troops became a symbol of the principle that the senate, not soldiers, should choose the Emperor (*Histories* 1.8.2, 2.51; Pliny, *Letters* 2.1.6). Crises such as these were fortunately rare, but the other situation that we know to have occasioned a speech from Tacitus was commonplace: extortion by a provincial governor. In 100 CE Tacitus was part of a team that successfully prosecuted an extortionate governor of Africa, Marius Priscus (Pliny, *Letters* 2.11). Priscus, like all important provincial governors, was a senator and was tried in the senate, which was notoriously reluctant to convict its own members (see, for example, *Annals* 1.2.2). But extortion was a crime that threatened the stability of the provinces, as Tacitus shows repeatedly in the *Annals* (see p. xxxii). A responsible senate would punish this crime, and did punish it at the instigation of Tacitus and others in the case of Priscus.

Domitian's assassination freed Tacitus' pen. In 98 CE he published the *Agricola*, a biography of his father-in-law which tries to salvage something from the moral wasteland of Domitian's principate. In close sequence, before or after, came the *Germania*, part ethnography of the Germans, Rome's most troublesome neighbours, part meditation on the ills besetting Rome herself. A third short work, the *Dialogue on Orators*, was written some time between 96 and 103 CE. Though the format of this work distances the *Dialogue* from its author – it is ostensibly the report of a discussion heard by a young and silent Tacitus – it is, in fact, one of his most personal works and marks a crucial stage in his literary development.

Tacitus announces the *Dialogue* as a vehicle for explaining the decline of Roman oratory, a trend that prompted comment from his contemporaries as well. The problem with oratory as a genre at the end of the first century CE was fundamentally a problem of audience. To whom could one speak? Or, more precisely, given the possible audiences, what was worth saying? The citizen body, the 'Roman people' of the famous phrase 'the senate and the Roman people' (SPQR), was no longer called upon to decide anything, and was better addressed by benefactions such as the 'bread and circuses' rendered proverbial by Juvenal (*Satire* 10.78–81). The senate did retain a semblance of authority, but often refused to decide matters that came before it; it quickly became a self-censoring body. An emperor was swayed not by rhetorical skill but by associates – freedmen, family members, advisers, informers – equipped with a keen sense of psychology. The courtroom remained a venue for speech-making, but if Tacitus' contemporary Pliny is an accurate guide it elicited a sadly diminished product.

Various explanations for this state of affairs are offered over the course of the *Dialogue*, but the final explanation is a political one: oratory flourishes in a state in which decisions are collective, because the orator's art enables him to sway assemblies, but it is empty in a state in which important decisions are made by a ruler who is both 'very wise' and 'one man' (*Dialogue* 41.4: *'sapientissimus et unus'*). Substantive contributions to public affairs required a new literary form.

Tacitus chose history. In the preface to his first historical work, the *Histories*, Tacitus maintains that the present is 'a happy age in which it is permitted to feel what you wish and say what you feel' (1.1.4). Yet he was not so rash as to test the limits of permissibility by writing about the immediate present, the principates of Nerva and Trajan. Instead, he wrote a history of the period that coincided with his own youth and rising career, the brief reigns of Galba, Otho and Vitellius, and the longer span of Flavian dominance, twenty-eight years all told (69 to 96 CE), covered in some twelve or fourteen books. (The

surviving part of the *Histories* treats only the civil wars of 69
CE and the first few months of Vespasian's reign.) We surmise
from Pliny's letters on the eruption of Vesuvius in 79 CE, which
were written at Tacitus' request, that Tacitus was at work on
the *Histories* around 106 CE.

TACITUS' *ANNALS*

Scope and perspective

After Tacitus finished his account of the principates of Vespasian, Titus and Domitian (when that was, we do not know) he
moved back in time, not forward, for his next project. In the
Annals he treats the Julio-Claudian period, starting well before
his own birth and concluding with events that occurred during
his teenage years. This temporal distance allows him to claim
that he writes with greater objectivity than he was able to do in
the *Histories*, which told the story of emperors who advanced
his political career. 'My plan is to report a few final things about
Augustus, then Tiberius' principate and the rest, without anger
or favour, from whose causes I consider myself distant.' Tacitus
reserved the full tale of Augustus' principate for a still later
work, one that seems never to have been begun (see *Annals*
3.24.3). His focus is thus on the development of the autocratic
regime created more or less from scratch by Augustus, and on
its effect on state and individuals in the Roman world.

The story is a painful one, and many readers have felt that
Tacitus' tone in telling it belies his opening assertion of objectivity. Alongside the expected historical narrative and analysis,
one finds outrage, anger and sorrow, a disconcerting mix. Ever
the orator, Tacitus aims both to inform and to move his reader,
and even to please. Is he objective? Yes, in the sense that he is
indifferent to the reaction of the powerful men whose history
he records. And no: he believes passionately in the importance
of what he is recording and the act of recording it. Tacitus
'glows with inner fervour' according to one eminent historian
of style, and his *Annals* will provoke you.

The *Annals* will also teach you much about the nature of the Roman Empire in the first century CE. Not everything, however. Tacitus' interests are not identical with those of modern students of empire. Like us, he is interested in military power, political ties between centre and periphery, laws and revenue. But he pays almost no attention to local conditions, to family and social relations at any level below the very highest, to the physical environment or the economy or culture. The historian writes as a member of the Roman senate, with all the insights and limitations that such a perspective entails: insider knowledge of the military and political systems, up to a point, but also a blindness to the contributions of others. These limitations are compounded by the damage done by time. Tacitus' entire account of the principate of Gaius has been lost, as has the beginning of his account of Claudius' reign. There is also a substantial gap in the text near the end of the Tiberian books (see 5.6 and note 1 to Book 6) and the work breaks off incomplete in the middle of 66 CE, although Tacitus surely planned to continue the narrative to the end of Nero's life in June 68, if not to the end of 68 to effect the junction with his *Histories*, which begin on 1 January 69 CE. Perhaps the *Annals* were never finished.

History writing in Rome traditionally focused on military and political affairs, and the political and military dominance of the emperors meant that historians began to focus on these figures. The detail with which Tacitus reports the actions, relationships and characters of imperial family members is incomprehensible to a modern reader hoping to make sense of the Roman Empire as a whole. But such details were essential to Tacitus' original readers, who were trying to shape lives and careers for themselves within that empire. Not under the Julio-Claudians themselves, it is true, but in comparable conditions.

Aims

Tacitus engages in a running dialogue with these readers, explaining his historiographical policies on, for example, the use of sources and the selection of episodes, instructing them on how to read historical narratives and history itself, and

providing encouragement when tedium threatens. Above all he
wants to communicate his aims in writing the *Annals*. First, he
aims to be useful. This is traditional in ancient historiography,
and has both practical and moral dimensions. The practical one
involves understanding historical processes, especially causes
and effects. Thus, when Tacitus defends the presence of apparently trivial material in the narrative he does so on the grounds
that 'from these, great events' stirrings often arise' (4.32.2). As
for the moral dimension, Tacitus expects readers to see their
own actions reflected, sometimes uncomfortably, in his history:
'you will find people who think, their characters being similar,
that others' bad behaviour is a reproach to themselves. Even
glory and virtue have haters – for too nearly accusing their
opposites' (4.33.4). In both of these passages the idea that 'history is good for you' is used to help the reader swallow
unpalatable aspects of the text, and allows Tacitus to align himself with the reader's experience. He does this even more
effectively when pondering the career of an influential senator
named Marcus Lepidus, who managed to retain Tiberius'
favour while also resisting the political system's incentives to
immoral behaviour. 'This makes me wonder,' says Tacitus. 'Are
fate and one's birth-lot the source, as of other things, also of an
emperor's inclination towards some and grievance against
others? Or is it something in our choices? Can one forge,
between craggy defiance and degrading deference, a path clear
of favour-seeking and danger?' (4.20.3). Presumably, he hopes
his readers will wonder with him and aspire to emulate Lepidus
themselves. Lepidus was, after all, says Tacitus encouragingly,
a 'consequential and wise man' (4.20.2).

  Praise like this, and blame, too, are the essence of another of
Tacitus' historiographical aims: he intends to do his part to ensure
that 'everyone receives due honour from posterity' (4.35.3). In
the phrase 'due honour' the emphasis is on 'due' not 'honour', as
is clear from a programmatic statement in Book 3 (3.65.1):

My policy is to trace proposals in detail only if conspicuously
honourable or of noteworthy disgrace, for in my view the principal obligation of histories is that manifestations of excellence not

go unspoken and, for perverse words and deeds, to generate fear from posterity and infamy.

Given the prevalence of bad behaviour over good in the *Annals*, Tacitus is much occupied with generating fear in those readers who might be likely to figure in a future history of Rome, emperors included. The curse on Tiberius that Tacitus puts in the mouth of Germanicus' moribund son Drusus is extreme only in its tone: '*As you have filled our house with deaths, so you must pay retribution to ancestral name and family, and to posterity!*' (6.24.2; for the significance of the italics see p. liii). The political and military elite are likewise subjected to punishment in the historian's court. Their obsequiousness and failures of nerve are requited with mockery, while the accusations they initiate and the treacheries they perpetrate incur withering invective.

There are no heroes in the annals. At best there are rare individuals like Marcus Lepidus who make things turn out better than they might have done. Tacitus' claims about his own contribution, therefore, are understandably muted (4.32.1–2):

> No one should compare my *Annals* with the writing of those who narrated the past history of the Roman people. Huge wars, successful assaults on cities, routed and captured kings, or, when they turned to internal affairs, disputes of consuls against tribunes, land-holding and welfare laws, conflicts between the commons and the 'best men' – these were the things they recorded, free to roam. My work is in a narrow field and inglorious.

Tacitus is not after glory, but impact. Both content and form contribute. But before considering these elements in more detail we need to ask where Tacitus found his information.

Sources

In composing a history of the principates of Tiberius and his Julio-Claudian successors Tacitus drew on prior histories of the period, some of them written by contemporaries of the events themselves. These are his authorities, whose consensus he generally follows, as at 11.31.1: 'All accounts show Claudius so overwhelmed by panic that questions kept coming. *Am I the Empire's master? Is Silius my subject?*' On a few occasions Tacitus names some of his authorities while observing discrepancies between them, but in general he is silent about the works on which he based his history. In any case, none of them survives. Tacitus criticizes these earlier histories on various grounds, including error, bias, fabrication and incompleteness, and hopes to better them. Where possible he weighs one authority against another (see, for example, 13.20.2), but he is also proud to have discovered and included material that does not appear in written histories before his *Annals*. 'I am aware that most writers omit the full tally of perils and punishments. They flag at the supply, and fear that material they found excessive and grim may affect readers with like fatigue. But many matters worth knowing have come to my notice, even if unheralded by others' (6.7.5). As this passage suggests, Tacitus is no more helpful in identifying his new sources, either, but we do get some clues.

Memoirs, for example. Tacitus cites the memoirs of Agrippina's daughter, 'who recorded her life and her family's disasters for posterity' (4.53.2), as the source for a private encounter between Tiberius and his daughter-in-law Agrippina. Scholars have surmised that Tacitus also drew on the memoirs of the Neronian general Corbulo for his very full account of Corbulo's military achievements (see the Index of Names for the full list of passages, and especially 15.16.1). Tacitus was clearly also familiar with the writings of another author prominent in his narrative, the philosopher Seneca, and he seems to have used these in constructing his memorable portrait of the man (see 15.63.3). Biographies are not mentioned in the *Annals*, but in the *Agricola* Tacitus refers to the biography of Thrasea Paetus, who, like Corbulo, appears in an extended series of episodes in the *Annals* (*Agricola* 2.1). Individuals' careers also survived in family memory, not necessarily written, but still perhaps accessible to Tacitus. At 4.33.4 he cites the danger of such memories as one of the challenges

of history writing. Another informal source of information
cited in the *Annals* is rumour, which is handled with appropriate caution (4.11.3; see p. xxxvii) though not discounted
entirely (3.16.1; 12.52.2): a reminder of (and perhaps a protest
against) the limits on information imposed by the regime.

But where an official version of events was on record, particularly events involving the senate, Tacitus seems to have
consulted it. Explicit references to the senate's archives are
quite rare (5.4.1; 6.47.3), but the archives' significance as a
source for the *Annals* is evident from the regular presence of
senatorial business in Tacitus' account of events in Rome:
debates and legislation, trials and verdicts, celebrations and
more. Our presumption that Tacitus availed himself of this
material is reinforced by a letter from Pliny the Younger, who,
responding to Tacitus' request for information about a trial in
which Pliny had participated, observes that the historian can
find all the information he needs in the official records (*Letters*
7.33.1). These records were probably the source for the detail
that forty-four speeches were delivered in the senate in the
aftermath of Sejanus' downfall in 31 CE (5.6.1), for example.

Tacitus also mentions another form of public records: the
inscriptions in which the government published official decisions. There are few explicit references to these, though he does
mention visible evidence of a curiosity from Claudius' reign:
the three letters Claudius added to the Roman alphabet. 'In use
while he was in power, afterwards forgotten, they are seen even
now on the official bronzes used for publishing senatorial
decrees to the populace and affixed in public squares and
temples' (11.14.3; see also 12.24.2, 12.53.3). However, Tacitus
dismisses another type of public record, 'the city's daily gazette', as containing material unworthy of being dignified as
history (13.31.1).

One other category of source requires further discussion.
The *Annals* contain many long speeches, apparently quoted
verbatim: speeches from senatorial debates (3.53–54), trial
speeches (4.34–35, 16.22.2–5), generals' exhortations (pas-
sim), speeches addressed to assemblies (1.43) and the Emperor
(12.37), as well as private conversations (14.53–56). In these

speeches Tacitus is following a long-standing historical tradition, rather alien to our modern conception of history, in
which the historian produced his own versions of historical
speeches heard by himself or his informants, and had licence to
compose speeches that neither he nor anyone else could have
heard. For Claudius' speech to the senate urging that Gaul's
nobility be eligible for senatorial office (11.24), for example,
substantial remains of the original survive in inscriptional
form, so that we have a relatively good sense of the relationship
between what Claudius said (or the official version of what he
said) and what Tacitus has him say: the speech was a historical
fact and Tacitus accurately represents its overall argument, but
the words and rhetoric are his own. The quotation marks that
surround such speeches in this translation must not be taken to
indicate authenticity. On the other hand, these speeches
shouldn't be dismissed as fictions, either, since Tacitus was
familiar with the speeches of Tiberius and Claudius, and with
those written for Nero by Seneca, to name only the most frequently cited. (On the further distinction between speeches in
the work that are 'quoted' verbatim and those that are para-
phrased, and the graphic distinction between these in this
translation, see p. liii.)[2]

Tacitus' willingness to compose speeches for his characters is
an example of the more general licence an ancient historian
enjoyed in writing up the past. From sources such as those
already mentioned Tacitus will have borrowed a basic outline
of events and some elements of their treatment. How much
Tacitus owes to his literary predecessors it is hard to say, since
his borrowings only come into focus when our other accounts
of the period – primarily those written by Suetonius and Dio,
who drew on the same sources as Tacitus – are closely aligned
with what we find in the *Annals*. A more important point for
understanding the narrative presented here is that Tacitus
would not have felt the need to have a source for every detail.
For a battle, for instance, all he needed from his sources was
the participants, a rough date, a place and an outcome. If his
sources provided further information, such as a description of
the terrain, a clever stratagem or a casualty count, he might use

that, too. But for the rest – the generals' exhortations, the emotions of the troops, vignettes of valour or cowardice, climatic conditions and so on – he was drawing on his literary sense, not on his sources.

Themes

In the *Annals* Tacitus tells the history of the half-century after Augustus' death, so the content is hugely varied, even with the limitations imposed by his perspective and aims. Here only a few of the principal themes can be considered.

1. *Military affairs*

The narrative is Roman, almost to a fault. (There are processes of universal significance here, but their context and operation are deeply and sometimes infuriatingly Roman.) This means, among other things, that military affairs are well represented, indeed strangely prevalent in a history of the period often referred to as the Pax Augusta. Such campaigns as there were, and the military discipline that made them successful, formed an important link to Rome's past, and, in Tacitus' view, ought to inform Rome's future. It is no accident that the first major event recorded in the *Annals* after Tiberius' succession is a mutiny involving some eleven legions. Tacitus devotes nearly half of Book 1 to the aims, psychology and eventual suppression of this uprising, which was a serious challenge to the very institution of the principate. The placement and prominence of this episode make the role of the military central to the remainder of the work, as Tacitus presents a series of episodes addressing such questions as: what makes the legions effective? What does the commander contribute? How do these campaigns measure up to past glories? What is the relationship between military strength and political stability? Or between military achievement and social standing? Tacitus records significant military successes in nearly every book of the *Annals* (the depressing Book 16 being an exception) and makes a point of explaining the strategies and admiring the valour and discipline underpinning them. Almost none of the conquests was accomplished by an emperor, although Tiberius was responsible for substantial military successes under Augustus, and Claudius buttressed his legitimacy by 'conquering' Britain in a lightning campaign in 43 CE. Instead, military victory was one area in which Rome's elite, Tacitus' peers, could still contribute to the commonwealth and to their own legacy. There were risks involved, sometimes large ones. Corbulo's military career, for example, in which Tacitus invests some forty chapters spanning the principates of Claudius and Nero, concluded in disaster: forced suicide consequent on a trumped-up charge of treason.[2] And, on a larger scale, the dominant role of the army in Roman affairs was most fully realized in the series of events that toppled the Julio-Claudians from power in 68 CE, in which military forces and their commanders determined the course of Roman history. In the *Histories* Tacitus had summarized the lesson of the traumatic civil wars of 68–9 CE with the observation that 'one of the hidden truths of the imperial system had been divulged: that an emperor could be made elsewhere than in Rome' (*Histories* 1.4.2): it was to be the soldiers based in the provinces rather than the senators and imperial family in Rome who established Rome's second dynasty in power.

Besides victory and defeat, discipline and disorder, and individual valour with its attendant risks, military affairs included the more mundane elements of ruling an empire, such as revenue collection and provincial governance. None of this makes for stirring history, but Tacitus, who had himself been a provincial governor, pays regular attention to imperial administration at all levels. So he shows Tiberius making a prudent reduction in a tax rate after acquiring through conquest a new revenue stream (2.42.4), and, as a contrasting example, Nero's startling suggestion of abolishing all indirect taxes: '*Shall I give this loveliest of gifts to the human race?*' (13.50.1). Nero's advisers talk him out of it, but Tacitus takes the opportunity to review the history of this kind of taxation and the more sober measures that were eventually passed on that occasion (13.50.2–51). There are frequent references to imperial largesse towards provincial beneficiaries, particularly after natural disasters such as earthquakes and fires (see 2.47.1–3 and note 53 to Book 2, and 16.13.3), and to the incorporation of local elites into the senatorial class (3.55.3, 11.23-4). But also, lower down the administrative scale, illustrations of government gone wrong. Rebellions in Thrace (4.46), Germany (4.72), Cappadocia (6.41) and Britain (14.31-8) arise at the point where revenue is extracted, often owing to the abuses of fairly low-level military authorities. An outbreak of revolt in Germany is typical (4.72):

> That same year [28 CE] the Frisians, a people living beyond the Rhine, shed their quietude, more from our greed than because compliance was intolerable. The tribute Drusus had ordered from them was modest, appropriate to their pinched resources: their payment was oxhides for military use. No one paid attention to how sturdy or how big until Chief Centurion Olennius, imposed on the Frisians as ruler, chose aurochs hide as the standard for acceptance. (2) Difficult, this, even for other peoples, but harder for Germans to bear since – though the woods teem with huge beasts – their domestic livestock is modest. At first whole oxen, then fields, finally wives' and children's bodies were delivered into slavery. (3) This led to rage and protest and, when no help arrived, a remedy in war.

Tacitus' reference to 'our greed' even though this incident occurred thirty years before he was born is one indication among many that he was writing about the past with one eye on the imperial present and future. Getting the revenues right, as Tiberius' brother Drusus seems to have done, was important not just for the well-being of the Frisians. These revenues, collected empire-wide, paid for the legions that kept the Emperor in power.

2. *Governance and politics*

To Roman thinking, an account of foreign (usually military) affairs represented only one part of the historian's responsibilities. What was also required was an account of politics in Rome. In the *Annals* the most significant elements of domestic politics are the role of the senate and the actions of individual senators, but, also, even more significant is the behaviour of the imperial family. Obviously, this latter category was absent

from republican-era historiography, which makes its prevalence in the *Annals* especially striking. In minute detail Tacitus
scrutinizes the actions and psychology of members of the
imperial household: the Emperor and his family, but also his
advisers, freedmen and close companions. And when he is baf-
fled by their actions, he tells us so. He also includes many
episodes concerned with the affairs of royal households in
Parthia and Armenia, which act as a mirror image to dynastic
politics in Rome. This close study of court life underpins Tacitus' judgements, as when he describes Tiberius' corruption by
absolute power (6.48.2) or the surprising fact of Claudius' succession (3.18.4):

> But the more I reflect on events recent and past, the more I am
> struck by the element of the absurd in everything humans do. For
> judging by people's talk, expectation and expressions of respect,
> anyone was more 'destined to rule' than the future emperor For-
> tune was hiding.

As this quotation suggests, one of the principal themes related
to the imperial family was that of succession.

Tacitus' treatment of the senate is deep-dyed with chagrin
and disgust: chagrin at the senate's insignificance and disgust at
the behaviour of the senators, careerists whose actions only
exposed and increased the senate's insignificance. An episode
that occurs early in Tiberius' reign reveals some of the mechan-
isms at play (2.35):

> Public business was postponed that year, which I would not
> report except that the contrasting opinions of Gnaeus Piso and
> Asinius Gallus on the matter are worth knowing. Piso, when
> Tiberius had said he would be absent, recommended: *All the
> more reason to act, so that the ability of senate and equestrians
> to uphold their responsibilities in the Emperor's absence will
> reflect well on the republic.* (2) Gallus, since a show of independ-
> ence had been preempted by Piso, said: *Nothing is sufficiently
> notable or consistent with the dignity of the Roman people
> unless it is done before Tiberius and under his eyes. Accordingly,*

Italy's assembly and the provinces' converging should be saved
for his presence. With Tiberius listening in silence, great disputatiousness was used by both sides, but business was deferred.

The complex mix of senatorial independence (Piso's position),
individual ambition (Gallus' motivation) and the Emperor's
reticence results in a kind of paralysis. It was not intentional or
even perhaps inevitable, but it was humiliating, nonetheless.
Whenever the opportunity arises, Tacitus highlights moments
when the senate claimed or forfeited effectiveness as a partner
in running the Empire (see 3.52, 3.60–61, 15.20–22).

Much more numerous are passages that focus on the actions
of individual senators, both those who were models of virtue,
sensible and prudent, and capable of good acts – and those
who were not. As one might expect in a history as dark as the
Annals, harmful behaviours predominate. A notable example
is delation, the bane of the senatorial class in this period.

The Roman judicial system had always depended on individuals to initiate prosecutions; there was no equivalent for the
office of the Attorney General. In earlier times to prosecute a
senator, usually an eminent senator, required carefully weighing
the political pros and cons: friends and enemies could be won
as a result. But under the Empire the enmity and friendship of
one man, the Emperor, mattered so much more than any other
relationship that the traditional calculus was badly skewed. If a
prosecution served the Emperor's ends – making his position
more secure or removing those who had offended him – there
was little reason not to go ahead with the case. True, each case
eroded the collective well-being of the senatorial class, but delation could be hugely profitable to the individual (see, for
example, 1.74.2, 12.59.2). Tacitus' narrative redresses the balance by adding eternal ignominy to the counter-arguments.
This he dispenses to individuals and, as in the following passage, to the whole class of *delatores* (6.7.3):

This was the most pernicious development of those times: leading senators practising the vilest delation, some openly, others in
secret. It was impossible to separate outsiders from connections,

friends from strangers, recent events from those obscured by
time. Accordingly, whatever people said in the Forum or at parties led to censure, so that everyone hurried to get ahead and
target a defendant. Some aimed to help themselves, but more
were infected, so to speak, by sickness and contagion.

Comments such as this appear throughout the text. As a senator himself, Tacitus attacks the self-degradation of the senate
and the diseased morals of individual senators. He is sensitive
to the pressures under which senators acted, but also painfully
aware of the consequences for his class: 'The human capacity
for fellowship perished from fear's violence, and as brutality
grew stronger compassion was kept at bay' (6.19.3).

3. Oratory

Delation also threatened the art with which Tacitus had made
his name: oratory. Like so much else in the period he wrote
about, oratory suffered under the new political system. It was
deployed for trivial ends (see 16.2.2) as well as harmful ones,
and sought obscurity and obfuscation as often as clarity and
persuasion (see 13.3.2). Tacitus fights back by showing the cultural value of oratory, keeping a record of oratorical successes,
and by paying attention to rhetorical style both in the speeches
he writes for the *Annals* and the speeches he reports.

Early in the *Annals* oratory gets a surprising defender:
Tiberius himself, whose talents as a speaker Tacitus discusses
and whose speeches he cites. Of the various honours proposed
for the recently dead imperial heir Germanicus, Tiberius took
exception to one and only one: a tribute to Germanicus' eloquence, 'distinctive for gold and size'. It was to have been a
likeness in gold displayed in the senate house itself, where a
number of silver likenesses of the 'leaders of eloquence' were
already present. But Tiberius circumvented this proposal by
promising to dedicate an ordinary silver likeness himself, on
the grounds that '*Distinction in eloquence is not based on fortune. It is renown enough if Germanicus is ranked with the
ancient writers*' (2.83.3). This episode does not redound entirely
to Tiberius' credit, since his scaling down of the proposed

honour may have been motivated by hostility to Germanicus as well as by respect for oratory, but at the very least the pretext for his action was a respect for oratory.

'Distinction in eloquence is not based on fortune,' said Tiberius, a view reinforced by an episode in the *Annals* that reveals that oratorical excellence is not inheritable, either. In 16 CE the grandson of the Quintus Hortensius who was one of the Late Republic's most eminent orators and the man Cicero regarded as his only real rival was reduced to pleading for a financial subvention from the senate (2.37–8). As he made the case that he was 'prevented by changed times from getting or earning money, popular favour, and eloquence – an heirloom of our house,' he gestured again and again to his grandfather's silver likeness on display. The speaker is a fairly pathetic figure, and his performance raises the question of whether eloquence can really be an heirloom.

In the *Annals* oratorical prowess still functions, as it did under the Republic, as an engine of social mobility (Tacitus' own career was a case in point). Tacitus includes an extended debate on the question of whether courtroom speakers should be paid for their efforts (11.5–7). Monetary compensation was forbidden by a law dating back to the Republic (see 11.5.3 and note 9 to Book 11); speakers were presumably rewarded by other forms of gratitude, including the 'fame and posterity' mentioned here. The pragmatic argument against the ban – that only the wealthy can devote themselves to oratory under current conditions – is advanced for Claudius' consideration (11.7.3): '*We are ordinary senators in quiet times, seeking only the advantages of peace. Consider the commoner splendid in his toga: if arts' rewards are removed, arts themselves will perish.*' Claudius agreed and proposed a compromise of limited payments.

Tacitus also shows the power of a good speech. Perhaps the most striking example is the defence speech of Marcus Terentius, who managed 'to utter what everyone was thinking' and carry such conviction with his audience that his prosecutors were punished in his stead (6.9.1). Tacitus introduces this episode with particular fanfare, as having been neglected by his predecessors but 'worth knowing' (6.7.5). Other noteworthy speeches he marks out as effective even under the difficult conditions imposed by an autocratic regime (see 3.36.2–3, 13.27, 14.48–9).

Towards the end of *Annals* 4 Tacitus offers a new criterion by which to assess oratorical merit: longevity (4.61). He comments on the style of a man of 'celebrated eloquence – while alive':

> The monuments of his talent do not enjoy commensurate reten-
> tion. In impact, no doubt, rather than study lay his potency, and
> although other men's thought and effort gain vigour with poster-
> ity, Haterius' melodious and fluent style was extinguished with
> himself.

On this criterion the genre in which Tacitus himself was now investing his study, thought, and effort – historiography – outstripped even the best oratory.[4]

4. *Historical memory*

Under an autocratic regime the important truths are not going to be easy to see or to speak about. Insight and conjecture are constantly called for. There are limits to what these can achieve, of course, but Tacitus wants his readers to push up against the limits rather than rest content with the official line. He gives an illustration of how to go about this in connection with a per-sistent rumour concerning the death of Tiberius' son Drusus in 23 CE. First Tacitus reports, then contradicts the rumour by assessing it against the historical record and gauging its psy-chological plausibility. Then he explains the larger purpose of the exercise.

> Why do I relay and challenge rumour? To rebut in a clear instance
> false hearsay, and to request from those into whose hands my
> work comes that they not give the widespread and incredible – so
> greedily received! – priority over things true and not tainted with
> the marvellous (4.11.3).

In this way Tacitus shows readers how to deal with the threat that rumours pose to historical memory, but the task of penetrating the deceptive or baffling façade with which Tiberius, say, screens the truth requires much more intensive tutelage. To provide this, Tacitus makes Tiberius' contemporaries the readers' proxies. Senators in particular are constantly confronted with the problem of deciphering Tiberius' intentions. The first major political event of the *Annals*, the accession of Tiberius, is replete with examples (1.8–14). Numerous obstacles between the historian and the truth are a fundamental element of the history of the period as Tacitus tells it. He thematizes the problem early on in the first bit of advice given to the newly powerful Livia and Tiberius after Augustus' death, when a veteran of Augustus' court

> warned Livia against making household mysteries, friends' advice and soldiers' services common knowledge. *Tiberius must not relax the regime's strength by bringing everything to the senate. It is a condition of absolute power that its account only balances if rendered to one man* (1.6.3).

The historian fights a running battle against official obfuscation.

For example, when an exiled adulterer of Tiberius' former wife Julia is executed on his lonely island off the coast of North Africa, Tacitus' sources differ on who was responsible. Tacitus claims it was Tiberius, who killed first Julia then her lover fourteen years after Augustus exiled them (1.53.2–5). But this is not the end of Tacitus' account. He also explains the existence of a discrepancy:

> The soldiers were sent not from Rome but from Africa's governor Lucius Asprenas, according to some reports. Tiberius was their source; he had hoped in vain that talk about the murder could be deflected onto Asprenas (1.53.6).

Tacitus does not take Tiberius' bait.

He also resists the official erasure from the historical record of Claudius' disgraced wife Messalina. In 48 CE the senate decreed the 'removal of her name and likenesses from places public and private' (11.38.3). This instance of memory sanction seems to have been carried out with particular thoroughness, since very few representations of Messalina survive. But Tacitus gives a long and circumstantial account of her end (11.25–38). Claudius and his contemporaries wanted the world to forget Messalina, but Tacitus' readers never will.

The republican heroes Brutus and Cassius are also remembered in the *Annals*, along with a historian who wrote about them. Like those of Messalina and others who fell foul of the principate, images of Brutus and Cassius were banned from public and private display. But people remembered the men nevertheless. At the funeral of Junia, Cassius' wife and Brutus' sister, sixty-four years after the battle of Philippi in which they perished, 'twenty portrait-masks from the most illustrious families preceded her: Manlii, Quinctii and other names of equal renown. But Brutus and Cassius outshone the rest precisely because their likenesses were not on display' (3.76.2). Their memory survived because a succession of historians told of their deeds (4.34–35). The latest of these was Cremutius Cordus, who was accused of treason under Tiberius because he praised Brutus and called Cassius the last of the Romans. Cordus died and his books were burned in 25 CE, but Tacitus tells the tale nearly a century later, concluding, with sardonic glee, 'All the more pleasurable, then, to mock the witlessness of those who believe that with present power it is possible to extinguish the future's memory' (4.35.5).

Structure

Annals, the title by which the work is known at present, is generic not specific.[5] When Tacitus refers to the work as 'my annals' (4.32.1) he is alluding to one of its defining features, the year-by-year structure of the narrative. Each year between 15 and 68 CE is, for the most part, a self-contained tale. This is the traditional structure of Roman historiography, and is based on a tight functional connection between the Roman political and military calendars and Roman histories with their focus on political and military events. The form is evoked in the text every year by a 'year-beginning' formula, and frequently by a closing

formula as well. Most of the 'year-beginning' notices take the
form found in republican histories and official documents. For
example, 'Gaius Pompeius, Quintus Veranius, consuls' for 49
CE (12.5.1). Against this regularity, unusual year-beginnings
such as that for 21 CE – 'Next, Tiberius' fourth consulship,
Drusus' second. Father and son as colleagues? Striking' (3.31.1) –
show the traditional formula to be a façade sacrificed, when
necessary, to political expediency or other pressures (see, for
example, 3.2.3, 15.48.1). A similar point is made by the occasional breaches of year boundaries, when Tacitus combines the
events of several years into a single coherent episode (see
6.38.1, 12.40.4, 13.53.1 and note 79 to Book 13). In annalistic
histories there were also patterns within a year's narrative,
including a regular alternation between affairs at Rome (usually politics) and affairs abroad (usually war). By employing
and deforming these fundamental structures of earlier Roman
historiography Tacitus makes it clear that (appearances to the
contrary) under the principate neither political office nor military conquest was at all comparable to its republican model.

Life under the principate was organized in larger structures
than the republican year. The largest of these were the reigns of
individual emperors. To Tiberius' twenty-three years of power
(14–37 CE) Tacitus devotes a neatly structured six-book section
or hexad within the *Annals*. Gaius' four years (37–41 CE) and
Claudius' fourteen (41–54 CE) are covered in two and four
books respectively, and together constitute a second hexad. The
structure given to Nero's reign (54–68 CE) is harder to see
because of the loss of its conclusion; some scholars think there
were six Nero books, too, but four is more likely. For both
Tiberius and Nero we can also see internal divisions within
these larger structures. At the beginning of Book 4, for example,
Tacitus marks the year 23 CE, the ninth of Tiberius' reign, as a
turning point for Tiberius: 'that year initiated for Tiberius a
regime changed for the worse' (4.6.1). Nero's murder of his
mother in 59 CE has a similar articulating function, after which,
according to Tacitus, he 'poured himself into every barely
checked debauch that mother-respect, such as it was, had
delayed' (14.13.2). The Tiberian hexad is neatly concluded with

an overview of Tiberius' whole career, a conclusion in which
Tacitus adapts the annalistic practice of ending a year with brief
obituaries for notable men who died during the year (see, for
example, 3.30, 4.61, 6.27.2, etc.), but enlarges the form to
reflect the much greater notability of an emperor, whose death
brings not a year but an era to a close (6.51).

Within these multi-book sections the narrative is divided into
the smaller units of books, episodes and serial stories. Book
divisions were, in part, a concession to practicality: there was a
limit to the amount of text one could put on a papyrus book
roll. But Tacitus puts the formal imperative to good use by giving each book a clear and often striking ending: Arminius'
obituary for Book 2, the funeral of Junia Calvina for Book 3,
the marriage of Nero's parents for Book 4, the suicide of Messalina for Book 11, and so on. Most books also have a striking
beginning. Book 3 starts with the elder Agrippina's return to
Italy with the ashes of Germanicus; Book 5 with Livia's death;
Book 12 with the marriage of Claudius and Agrippina the
younger; Book 14 with her murder; and, on a more light-hearted
note, Book 16 begins with Nero's ridiculous treasure hunt.

Among the *Annals*' major episodes are the army mutiny that
occupies a large part of Book 1 (1.16–52) and the conspiracy to
murder Nero in Book 15 (15.48–74). The large compass of
these episodes is particularly striking since both the mutiny and
the conspiracy were, in the end, failures. But both also illus-
trate the kind of action that would eventually bring about the
collapse of the Julio-Claudian dynasty and contribute to Tacitus' analysis of imperial power. As do, in a different way,
shorter episodes such as the murder of Britannicus (13.15–17)
and the elimination of Octavia (14.60–64). Most of the serial
stories involve Rome's conflicts with external enemies, such as
Tacfarinas in Africa and the Parthians in the East.

The *Annals* are thus characterized by a high degree of structural artistry, but you have to stand back from the text to see it.
The reading experience is of a much more particulate tale.
Most units of narrative are quite small, two to three paragraphs in length, from which the reader must assemble an
understanding of Julio-Claudian history. Tacitus sometimes

provides connections between these building blocks through thematic continuity or verbal echo, but more often he simply juxtaposes them and expects his reader – moved by the outrage he has aroused – to make the connections. For a reader not swept along on a wave of indignation, the *Annals* can be hard work: there is a lot of raw material here.[6] The infrequency of explicit authorial synthesis is deliberate. As we saw earlier, Tacitus wants to train readers to think for themselves.

NOTES

1. The other contemporary references to Tacitus' high reputation as an orator are laudatory but unspecific (Pliny, *Letters* 1.20.24, 7.20.4, 9.23.2).
2. Tacitus also uses the indirect quotation construction to paraphrase senatorial decrees and earlier histories. These passages are here rendered with English indirect quotation rather than with italics, to avoid giving the impression that the wording of these important historical sources is exact.
3. Corbulo's death occurs in 67 CE, after the end of what survives of the *Annals*.
4. An explicit contrast between these literary forms is drawn by Tacitus' contemporary and correspondent Pliny, who saw history as the genre most likely to yield its author lasting fame (*Letter* 5.8.3; see also 9.27).
5. The work's original title is not known for certain, but the most likely title preserved in the manuscript tradition is *From the Death of the Deified Augustus*, which reflects the form of Livy's *From the Foundation of the City*.
6. For this succinct formulation of the problem I am grateful to Matthew Sommer, a student in my 2010 Writing History class at Penn.

Further Reading

Readers who want to delve further into the world depicted by
Tacitus in the *Annals* will find a rather different view of the
same period in *The Twelve Caesars*, trans. Robert Graves,
revised by J. B. Rives (London: Penguin, 2007), written by Tacitus' younger contemporary Suetonius. A lively picture of the
world in which Tacitus himself lived is available in *The Letters
of the Younger Pliny*, trans. Betty Radice (Harmondsworth:
Penguin, 1963), which includes letters addressed to Tacitus.
Dio's much later history of the period, though incomplete,
helps fill in some of the major gaps in Tacitus' narrative, especially the fall of Sejanus and the reign of Caligula: *Dio Cassius:
Roman History, Volume VII, Books 56–60*, trans. Earnest
Cary (Cambridge, MA.: Harvard University Press (Loeb Classical Library), 1924). Those who want to read more of Tacitus
himself can explore his history of the Flavian period: *The Histories*, trans. Kenneth Wellesley, revised by Rhiannon Ash
(London: Penguin, 2009) or *The Histories*, trans. W. H. Fyfe,
revised by D. S. Levene (Oxford: Oxford University Press,
2008). These two translations, both good, are very different in
style. For works in genres other than history, readers might like
to try Tacitus' *Agricola and the Germania*, trans. Harold Mat-
tingly, revised by J. B. Rives (London: Penguin, 2010) and
Tacitus' Agricola, Germany and Dialogue of Orators, trans.
Herbert W. Benario (Oklahoma, OK: Haworth Press, 1991).
   The body of secondary literature on Tacitus and the Julio-
Claudian period is rich; only a tiny selection can be mentioned
here. Ronald Syme's two-volume *Tacitus* (Oxford: Clarendon
Press, 1958) is still fundamental on the historian's life and

times. Re-evaluations of some of the evidence for Tacitus' career can be accessed in Anthony Birley's article 'The Life and Death of Cornelius Tacitus' (*Historia*, 2000). Among the older discussions of Tacitus' literary achievement, those by Ronald Martin in *Tacitus* (London: Batsford Academic, 1981), B. Walker in *The Annals of Tacitus* (New York: Arno Press, 1981) and Judith Ginsburg in *Tradition and Theme in the Annals of Tacitus* (New York: Arno Press, 1981) are still excellent guides, as are the introductions of commentaries on the Latin text, including H. Furneaux's (Oxford: Clarendon Press, 1896) and F. R. D. Goodyear's (Cambridge: Cambridge University Press, 1972, 1981). More recent treatments, which ask different questions of the work, include Patrick Sinclair's *Tacitus the Sententious Historian: A Sociology of Rhetoric in Annales 1–6* (University Park, PA.: Pennsylvania State University Press, 1995), Ellen O'Gorman's *Irony and Misreading in the Annals of Tacitus* (Cambridge: Cambridge University Press, 2000) and Francesca Santoro L'Hoir's *Tragedy, Rhetoric and the Historiography of Tacitus' Annales* (Ann Arbor, MI: University of Michigan Press, 2006). A. J. Woodman's work on the *Annals*, which is spread over a large number of individual discussions, deserves special mention for its sustained and stimulating study of the principles and methods of Tacitean historiography. His *Rhetoric in Classical Historiography: Four Studies* (London: Croom Helm, 1988) and *Tacitus Reviewed* (Oxford: Clarendon Press, 1998) are good starting places, while his translation of the *Annals* (Indianapolis, IN: Hackett Publishing, 2004) gives Latin-less readers the closest possible access to Tacitean Latin. He has also put together a useful collection of studies by other scholars in the *Cambridge Companion to Tacitus* (Cambridge: Cambridge University Press, 2009). A recent arrival is Ronald Mellor's synthetic essay on *Tacitus' Annals* (Oxford: Oxford University Press, 2010), a successor to *Tacitus* (London: Routledge, 1993), his earlier book on the historian, and *Tacitus: The Classical Heritage* (London: Garland, 1995), his edited collection on Tacitus' reception. Another fine collection on reception is *Tacitus and the Tacitean Tradition* (Princeton, NJ: Princeton University Press, 1993), edited by

T. J. Luce and A. J. Woodman. On Tacitus' sources for the *Annals*, Olivier Devillers's *Tacite et les sources des Annales: enquêtes sur la méthode historique* (Leuven: Peeters, 2003) is indispensable. Several recent studies on Tacitus' earlier works shed indirect light on the *Annals*; see especially Rhiannon Ash's *Ordering Anarchy: Armies and Leaders in Tacitus' Histories* (London: Duckworth, 1999), Holly Haynes's *The History of Make-Believe: Tacitus on Imperial Rome* (Berkeley, CA.; London: University of California Press, 2003) and Dylan Sailor's *Writing and Empire in Tacitus* (Cambridge: Cambridge University Press, 2008). For the historiographical tradition in which Tacitus was writing, see the recent *Cambridge Companion to the Roman Historians* (Cambridge: Cambridge University Press, 2009), edited by Andrew Feldherr; and for a more focused treatment see *Latin Historians* (Oxford: Oxford University Press, 1997) by C. S. Kraus and A. J. Woodman. For a broad overview of the role of the historian in Ancient Greece and Rome see John Marincola's *Authority and Tradition in Ancient Historiography* (Cambridge: Cambridge University Press, 1997).

A few of the many books on the Julio-Claudian period of Roman history may be singled out for their particular relevance to Tacitus' treatment of the period. On the role of the senate during the principate Richard J. A. Talbert's *The Senate of Imperial Rome* (Princeton, NJ: Princeton University Press, 1984) is invaluable, as is Fergus Millar's magisterial study of the role of the Roman emperor, *The Emperor in the Roman World (31 BC–AD 337)* (London: Duckworth, 1977). On the control of historical memory, see Harriet Flower's *The Art of Forgetting: Disgrace and Oblivion in Roman Political Culture* (Chapel Hill, NC: University of North Carolina Press, 2006). On delation and treason trials, see Steven Rutledge's *Imperial Inquisitions: Prosecutors and Informants from Tiberius to Domitian* (London: Routledge, 2001). The political climate of Nero's principate in particular is well evoked by Vasily Rudich's *Political Dissidence under Nero: The Price of Dissimulation* (London: Routledge, 1993) and Shadi Bartsch's *Actors in the Audience: Theatricality and Doublespeak from Nero to Hadrian* (Cambridge, MA.: Harvard University Press, 1994). Chaim

Wirszubski's *Libertas as a Political Ideal at Rome during the
Late Republic and Early Principate* (Cambridge: Cambridge
University Press, 1950) remains a good introduction to a theme
of central interest to Tacitus. And Greg Rowe's *Princes and
Political Cultures: The New Tiberian Senatorial Decrees* (Ann
Arbor, MI.: University of Michigan Press, 2002) offers an entry
point to the recently discovered inscriptions that shed light on
Tacitus' narrative of dynastic conflict under Tiberius.

There are valuable biographies for each of the Julio-Claudian
emperors and some of their consorts. See, for example, Anthony
Barrett's *Livia: First Lady of Imperial Rome* (New Haven, CT;
London: Yale University Press, 2002) and *Caligula: The Corruption of Power* (London: Batsford, 1989), as well as Barbara
Levick's *Tiberius the Politician* (rev. ed. London: Batsford,
1990) and *Claudius* (London: Batsford, 1990). On the princi-
pate of Claudius, Josiah Osgood's *Claudius Caesar: Image and
Power in the Early Roman Empire* (Cambridge: Cambridge
University Press, 2011) is a particularly good complement to
Tacitus' narrative because he tries to elicit the history of these
years from sources other than Tacitus and Suetonius. Other
biographical studies that read successfully against the grain of
the ancient sources are Edward Champlin's *Nero* (Cambridge,
MA.: Harvard University Press, 2003) and Judith Ginsburg's
*Representing Agrippina: Constructions of Female Power in the
Early Roman Principate* (Oxford: Oxford University Press,
2006).

Note on the Translation

Of all the devices that Tacitus employs to impose his will on the history of the Julio-Claudian period and to move his readers, perhaps the most effective is his Latin style. Although this is not the place for a full account of his achievement in using style to convey meaning, doing Tacitus' style justice has been a primary objective of this translation. An impossible one, perhaps. But before looking in more detail at some aspects of his style, I should mention an expedient adopted in this translation that affects every page of it.

NAMES

The personal names in any account of Roman history are a problem for modern readers. Roman naming practices as reflected in literature (inscriptions are somewhat different) make it very difficult to distinguish between different generations of one family and even individuals from different families, especially over a narrative covering many decades. In the *Annals* this difficulty is compounded by Tacitus' practice of referring to a single person by several forms of his or her name. Because Tacitus refers to so many people in this narrative – more than a thousand – I have privileged clarity over every other consideration.

Tacitus' general policy in naming people is to give a fuller form of a person's name at his or her first introduction and to use a shorter form thereafter. Thus, the Neronian-era general

Gnaeus Domitius Corbulo is introduced at 3.31.3 with a stand-
ard-format family name Domitius, followed by his surname
or cognomen Corbulo (Tacitus never uses his personal name
Gnaeus), but in later appearances he is often called just
Corbulo. However, Tacitus employs many variations of this
pattern. The Guard commander prominent in the Pisonian
conspiracy is sometimes called Faenius Rufus, sometimes Rufus
Faenius, sometimes Faenius, and sometimes Rufus. And Rufus
is attached as a surname to thirteen other family names in the
Annals. Homonymy is most prevalent with reference to the
emperors and their sons, whom Tacitus frequently calls Caesar.
These variations presumably had significance for Tacitus' original readers, and even now scholars intimately familiar with
Roman nomenclature can make sense of some of his variations,
but for most readers they are irrelevant and confusing. My policy is to give the full name at a character's first appearance
(family name, then surname; like Tacitus I omit personal
names) and then to use either that or one shorter form thereafter, regardless of what appears in Tacitus' text. Readers
who want to know where Augustus' wife Livia, say, is called
Augusta or Julia instead of Livia will find that information in
the Index of Names. For each member of the imperial household, which had a limited number of names, I have where
possible used a distinctive name. Tiberius' daughter-in-law, for
example, always appears as Livilla in this translation, although
Tacitus always calls her Livia, which invites confusion with
Augustus' wife. However, there aren't enough names to go
around, so three different men are called Drusus (Tiberius'
brother, Tiberius' son and the second son of Germanicus) and
two are called Nero (Germanicus' eldest son and the Emperor).
In this translation Caesar refers to Julius Caesar, except when
it appears in direct address to an emperor, where the reference
is to that emperor. For the overlap in names of Roman elite
families, where necessary, clarification is provided in the notes.
Finally, for individuals who are likely to be known to modern
readers from sources other than the *Annals* – especially Latin
authors – I have used the most familiar form of the name.
Lucan, for example, whom Tacitus calls Annaeus Lucanus and

Lucanus Annaeus, I call Lucan. The forms actually used by Tacitus are recorded in the Index of Names.

STYLE

As befits a work of supreme literary artistry and historical importance the *Annals* have enjoyed a long history of fine translations. Each of them succeeds in some aspects of the task of rendering Tacitus into English, but none succeeds in all. Neither does this one. It is a humbling experience to ponder the work of a writer like Tacitus, who uses the resources of his own language so masterfully and pushes them to the limit. His innovations are especially hard to render, since novel expressions in a translation may baffle understanding or offend taste. Be that as it may, my aim has been to replicate the special qualities of Tacitean Latin in English, insofar as this is possible, while also producing a clear and accurate narrative of events.

Brevity

Reproducing the brevity that is an essential and distinctive feature of Tacitus' style has been a particular concern, and a challenge. Translating Latin always results in English that is wordier than the original Latin. For example, if rendered completely the Latin phrase *discurrunt mutati* (1.44.2) yields something like 'They ran off in different directions in a new frame of mind.' Twelve English words for Latin's two. The relative verbosity of English is particularly evident when rendering Tacitus' spare Latin style. To communicate what the Latin prefix *dis-* accomplishes when added to *currere* ('to run') English adds both the adverb 'off' and the prepositional phrase 'in different directions'. The particularly Tacitean compression of this phrase comes from *mutati*, a participle that means 'having been changed' and modifies the subject of *discurrunt*. Tacitus doesn't specify the nature of the change, nor does he need to since it is clear from the context that Germanicus' speech has changed the soldiers' mutinous attitude into one of remorseful eagerness to please. But 'they ran off in different directions having been changed' is impossible English. Other translators have rendered the phrase as follows: 'Away they hurried hither and thither, altered men' (Church and Brodribb); 'Changed men, they hastened round' (Grant); 'Now transformed, they ran everywhere' (Woodman); 'Changed men now, they ran off in different directions' (Yardley). All convey the sense adequately, but with more than double the number of words needed by Tacitus. The briefest possible translation would be 'they scattered, transformed', but the inappropriately random sense of 'scattered' and the awkwardness of using forms ending in identical *-ed* endings but with different syntax work against this. In translating *discurrunt mutati* as 'They ran off transformed' I rely on the subsequent description of atomized activity ('tied up the most seditious and dragged them') to suggest 'in different directions', and on the cultural associations of 'transformation' to supply a reference to the soldiers' attitude. (On the value of preserving the word order, see below.)

Rendering Tacitus' pithy Latin in equally pithy English requires a different solution for almost every phrase, but several expedients were adopted wherever possible. Double negatives are simplified into positive expressions, unless the negativity has a particular point. Past tense verbs of various forms are rendered with simple past forms, provided the sequence of events remains clear; this eliminates a great number of uninteresting auxiliary verbs in English. Forms of the verb 'to be' are omitted where Tacitus omits them and English permits. Instead of explanatory conjunctions ('since', 'because') a colon is sometimes substituted between effect and cause. Asyndeton (the omission of conjunctions, especially 'and') is very common in Tacitus' Latin and occasionally adopted here, but English is much less tolerant of this device. It is particularly prevalent in character descriptions (such as that of Sejanus at 4.1.3) and at the high point of battle narratives (see 4.50).

The technical terms for Roman institutions offer a special challenge when it comes to brevity in translation. Since no English equivalents exist, clarity invites a gloss rather than a translation. But glosses are wordy, so I have simplified instead. I use 'exile' to describe people who are barred from Italian soil, rather than Tacitus' 'forbidden water and fire', which reflects the wording of the judicial sentence. Even worse than single expressions such as this are passages full of lists. So at 15.25.3 I give 'governors' instead of the phrase 'prefects, procurators, propraetors' with which Tacitus specifies different categories of provincial governor. Similarly, where possible I use 'officers' instead of 'tribunes and centurions', 'horns' instead of 'tubas and trumpets', and so on. The details underlying my simple expressions are explained in the notes.

Word order

The patterns of word arrangement in Latin and English sentences are very different. Most obviously, Latin clauses and sentences regularly end with the verb, as a kind of punctuation. (Classical Latin used punctuation marks very sparingly.) In Tacitus' Latin the placement of words and their juxtapositions produce some very striking effects, which I have tried to reproduce in English, at some cost to syntactic fidelity. For example, when Tacitus uses a powerful verb to close a sentence, the punctuating effect can sometimes only be reproduced in English by changing the voice of the verb. Consider 15.68.1 where the literal translation of *tum poenam iussam subiit* is 'he then underwent the ordered punishment'. But this reverses the sequence in which Tacitus (and history) arranged events, which emerges better in 'Punishment was ordered and met.' Replicating Tacitus' word order also reduces the readability of the English, so I reserve it for passages where the gain in meaning outweighs the awkwardness of arrangement.

Another device, less frequently used but somewhat disconcerting when encountered, is a very brief question without syntax. For example, in Tacitus' report of the aftermath of Germanicus' most noteworthy victory in Germany he describes the celebration of the Roman army and their erection of a trophy listing the tribes they had defeated, then considers the enemy (2.19.1): 'The Germans? Wounds, losses and annihilation all caused them less pain and anger than this display.' Putting 'The Germans?' at the front like this preserves the Latin word order, which puts *Germanos* in the object case at the beginning of the sentence. In my view it also replicates the experience of readers of Tacitus' complex Latin sentences, who are often presented with a topic before they get the syntax that integrates it into the sentence. This must constitute a kind of puzzle, where one has to hold the idea of 'Germans as direct object' in one's head until the syntax catches up with it.

Focalization

Focalization is crucial to the inner world that Tacitus creates for his characters, especially (but not only) emperors, and I have made conveying it accurately a priority. Consider Tacitus' report of Nero's response to being thwarted in his first plan for eliminating a consul named Vestinus (15.69.1):

> Turning, accordingly, to the power of mastery, he dispatched the officer Gerellanus with a cohort of soldiers. He ordered him to anticipate the consul's attempts, to seize his 'citadel', to crush his 'picked men'. (Vestinus had a residence overlooking the Forum and attractive slaves all of an age.)

Many translators render the object of the initial participial phrase, *vim dominationis*, with some form of 'despotism' or 'tyranny', but if Tacitus is reflecting Nero's thoughts here – as I think he is, since he quotes Nero's terms for what he himself calls 'residence' and 'slaves all of an age' – Nero didn't think to himself, 'I'm a despot' but rather something like 'I'm the boss.' Accordingly, I use 'mastery' here for a term that I elsewhere render with 'regime' and other more negatively tinged words. The Emperor's power looks different to different observers and requires different labels. Similarly, the term *severitas* is rendered as 'austerity' when it is a lifestyle choice, but 'severity' when it describes punishments and is contrasted with leniency, and 'strictness' when it is a broader policy and equated with inflexibility. Using different English expressions for a single Latin word obviously makes it impossible for the reader to track Tacitus' use of a term like *dominatio* or *severitas*, but reflecting an utterance's perspective seemed the higher priority.

Another policy adopted in aid of focalization is that of printing reported speech and thought – in both short and much longer passages – in italics. Direct quotations or 'quotations' (see p. xxxv on Tacitus' speeches) are enclosed within quotation marks. However, the much more numerous passages in which Tacitus uses the indirect quotation construction – writing, for example, about Octavia, that Nero 'insisted that she was barren' instead of ' "She is barren," he insisted' (14.60.1) – are given in italics. In Latin the construction's syntax makes it more visually distinct from its narrative surroundings than it is in English: subjects appear in the object case and verbs are infinitive. Indirect quotations strike the eye in Tacitus' Latin and because he uses them so often and to such good effect they should do so in English as well. As they do in the following rendering of the thoughts of a victorious Roman army, faced with a choice between accepting a surrender or finding some other way to prevent the enemy from causing trouble again (12.17.1): 'This [the surrender] the victors rejected, since slaughtering the surrendered seemed brutal, and guarding a great multitude toilsome. *Better they fall to the law of war.*' Over the course of long passages of reported speech or thought the gain in clarity through the use of italics is considerable. But the primary gain is the immediacy they give to the words and thoughts of Tacitus' memorable characters.

NOTES

I supply notes as follows:

1. On named entities (persons, places, buildings, rituals, etc.) if mentioned elsewhere by Tacitus in a relevant context. A cross reference is supplied. Other references can be found via the Index of Names.

2. On aspects of the Roman world as necessary for comprehension of the text. A brief explanation is supplied. Information

about Roman history more generally should be sought elsewhere. The Further Reading section is a good starting place.

3. On matters relevant to the composition of the *Annals*.

4. On the Latin text when the text underlying the translation
is corrupt or when its meaning is obscure or when a feature of
Tacitus' Latin is particularly resistant to translation.

TEXT

The Latin text underlying this translation is H. Heubner's
Teubner edition of the *Annals* (Stuttgart, 1983). Divergences
are listed in the Appendix. For each of the two surviving parts
of the *Annals* (Books 1–6, Books 11–16) the text rests on a single manuscript. The readings of these two precious survivors
are occasionally mentioned in the notes and in the Appendix.
Such mentions should be regarded as the tip of an editorial ice-
berg. These two manuscripts, one written in the ninth century
CE, the other in the eleventh, transmit a text that has suffered
much damage since Tacitus put pen to papyrus in the second
century CE.

Both manuscripts are referred to by the abbreviation 'M',
which indicates their current location in the Biblioteca Medicea
Laurenziana in Florence. The shelf marks are Plut. 68.1 for the
ninth-century manuscript of *Annals* 1–6, and Plut. 68.2 for
the eleventh-century manuscript of *Annals* 11–16. Both are
now readable in their entirety online in the fine digital images
hosted by the Laurentian library website (http://teca.bmlon-
line.it). The text transmitted by the later of the two manuscripts
is, as one would expect, the most corrupt. What this means for
the reader of the *Annals* can be seen in the Appendix, where the
textual uncertainties listed for Books 11–16 greatly outnumber
those for Books 1–6.

Nothing can be done to repair the major damage to the text,
the loss of most of Book 5, all of Books 7–10 and some of Book
11, but repairs can be attempted where the text has suffered
lesser damage such as the omission of single words or the garb-
ling of spelling or the intrusion of material not in the original.

Copyists and readers and editors have been working for centuries to find sense where the manuscripts transmit nonsense or the wrong sense. The text of Heubner's edition is the product of this long labour and brings us about as close as we can get with the evidence available to Tacitus' original Latin. There are inevitably places where no one repair has won universal acceptance. For these I give a brief indication of the problem and possible solutions in the Appendix.

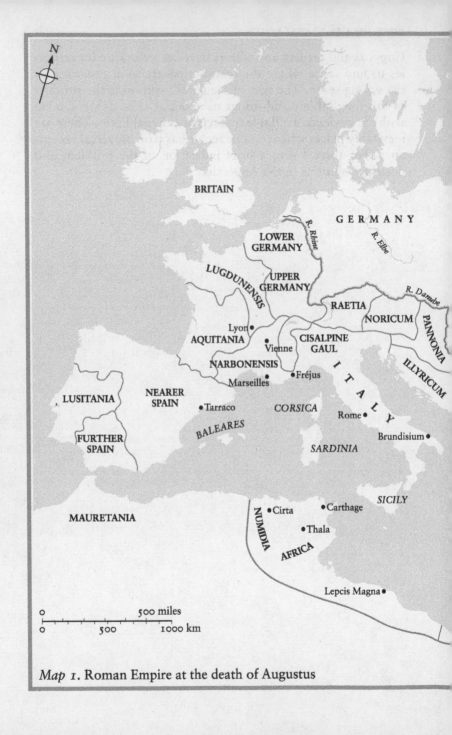

Map 1. Roman Empire at the death of Augustus

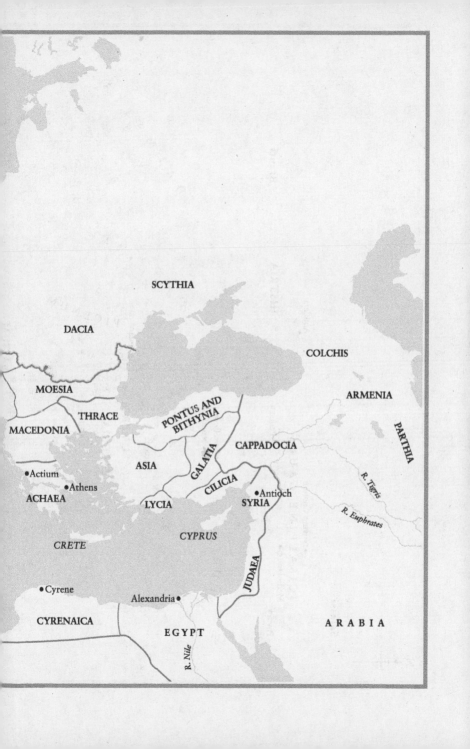

SCYTHIA

DACIA

COLCHIS

MOESIA

ARMENIA

THRACE

PONTUS AND
BITHYNIA

MACEDONIA

PARTHIA

CAPPADOCIA

GALATIA

ASIA

R. Tigris

CILICIA

•Actium

LYCIA

•Antioch

•Athens

SYRIA

ACHAEA

R. Euphrates

CYPRUS

CRETE

JUDAEA

•Cyrene

Alexandria •

CYRENAICA

ARABIA

EGYPT

R. Nile

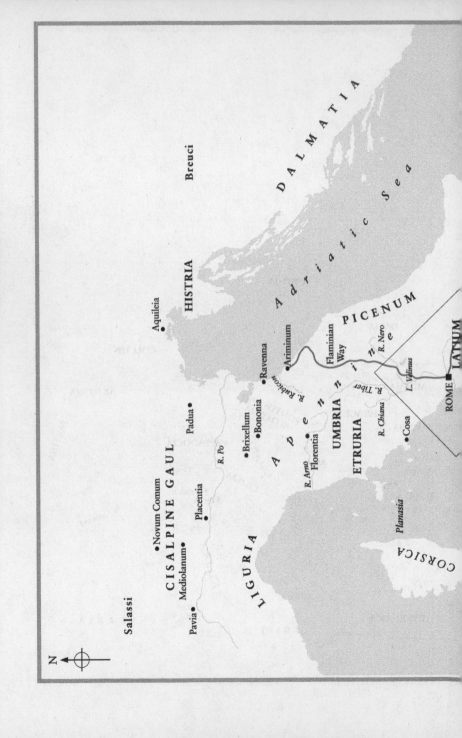

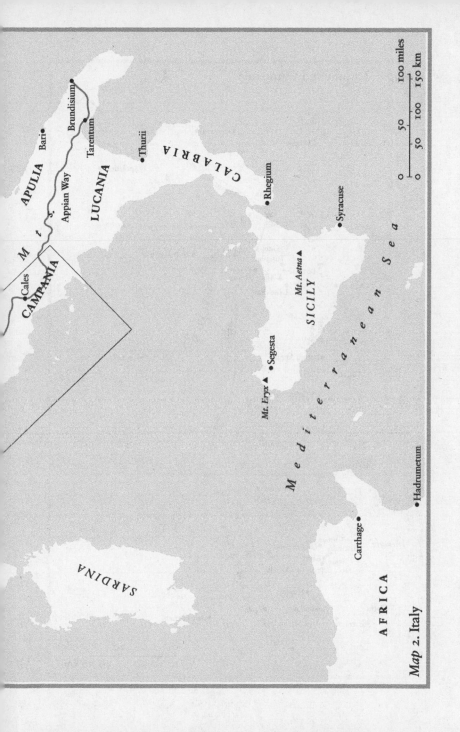

Map 2. Italy

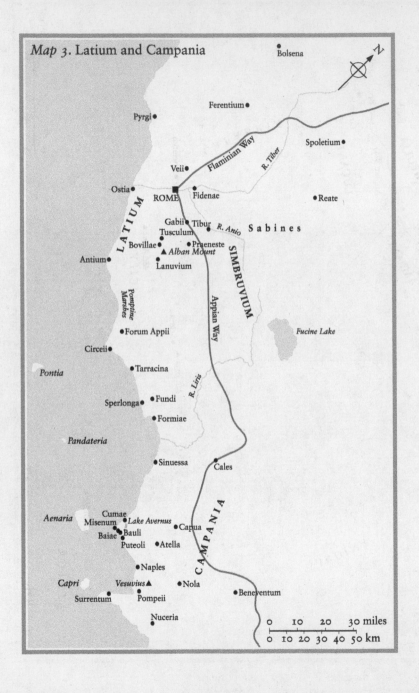

Map 3. Latium and Campania

Bolsena

N

Ferentium

Pyrgi

Flaminian Way

R. Tiber

Spoletium

Veii

Ostia

ROME

Fidenae

Reate

LATIUM

Gabii Tibur

R. Anio

Sabines

Tusculum

Bovillae

Praeneste

Alban Mount

SIMBRUVIUM

Antium

Lanuvium

Pompine
Marshes

Appian Way

Fucine Lake

Forum Appii

Circeii

Tarracina

Pontia

R. Liris

Sperlonga Fundi

Formiae

Pandateria

Sinuessa

Cales

CAMPANIA

Aenaria

Cumae

Misenum Lake Avernus

Baiae Bauli

Puteoli

Capua

Atella

Naples

Capri

Vesuvius

Nola

Beneventum

Surrentum

Pompeii

Nuceria

0   10   20   30 miles

0   10 20 30 40 50 km

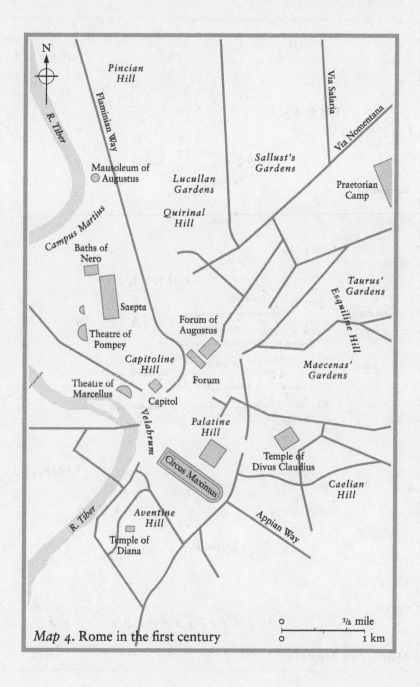

N

*Pincian
Hill*

Flaminian Way

Via Salaria

Via Nomentana

R. Tiber

*Sallust's
Gardens*

Mausoleum of
Augustus

*Lucullan
Gardens*

Praetorian
Camp

Campus Martius

*Quirinal
Hill*

Baths of
Nero

*Taurus'
Gardens*

Saepta

Forum of
Augustus

Esquiline Hill

Theatre of
Pompey

*Capitoline
Hill*

Forum

*Maecenas'
Gardens*

Theatre of
Marcellus

Capitol

Velabrum

*Palatine
Hill*

Temple of
Divus Claudius

Circus Maximus

*Caelian
Hill*

R. Tiber

*Aventine
Hill*

Appian Way

Temple of
Diana

o   ½ mile

o   1 km

Map 4. Rome in the first century

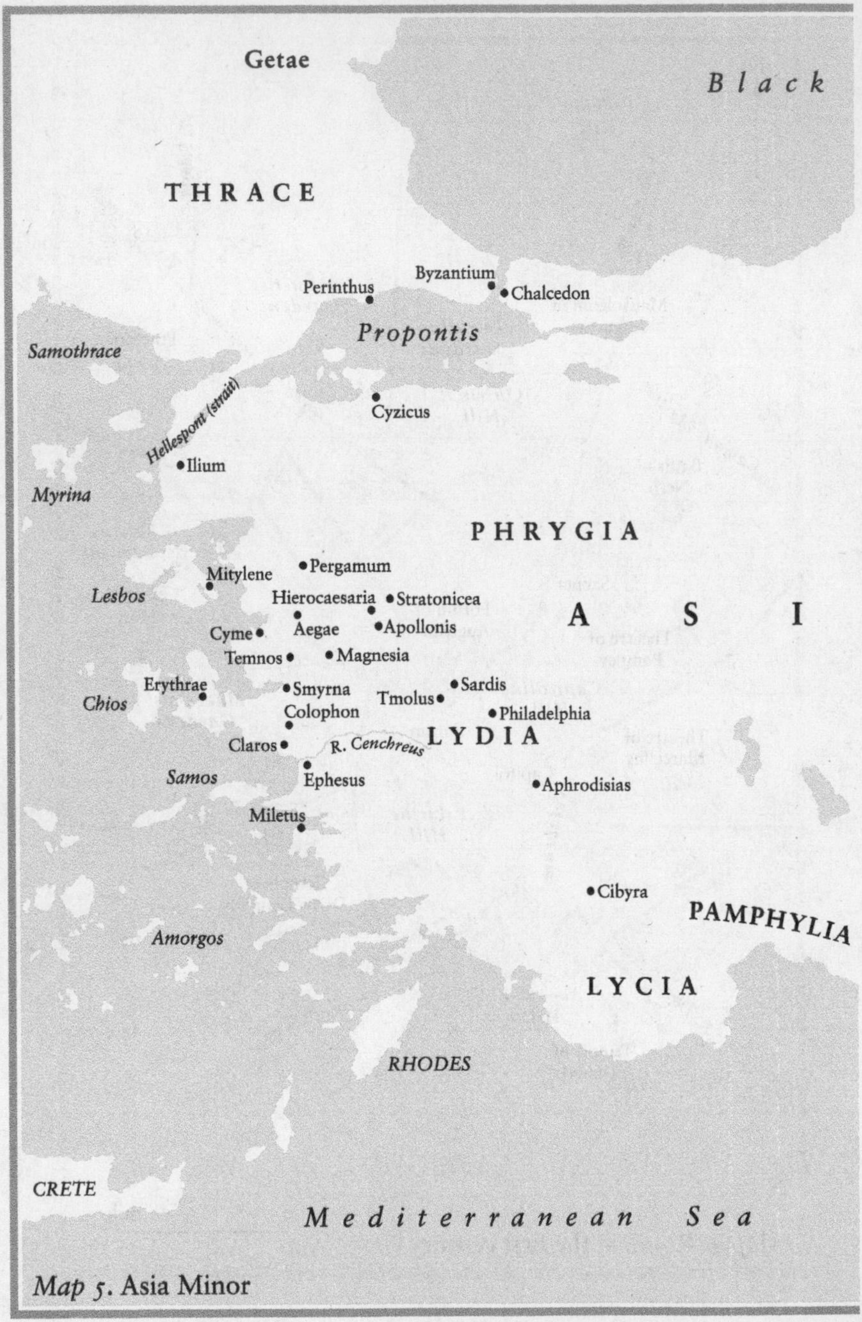

Getae

Black

THRACE

Perinthus
Byzantium
Chalcedon

Propontis

Samothrace

Cyzicus

Hellespont (strait)

Ilium

Myrina

PHRYGIA

Lesbos

Mitylene
Pergamum
Hierocaesaria
Stratonicea

A **S** **I**

Cyme
Aegae
Apollonis

Temnos
Magnesia

Chios

Erythrae
Smyrna
Sardis

Colophon
Tmolus
Philadelphia

Claros
R. Cenchreus

LYDIA

Samos

Ephesus

Aphrodisias

Miletus

Cibyra

PAMPHYLIA

Amorgos

LYCIA

RHODES

CRETE

M e d i t e r r a n e a n   S e a

Map 5. Asia Minor

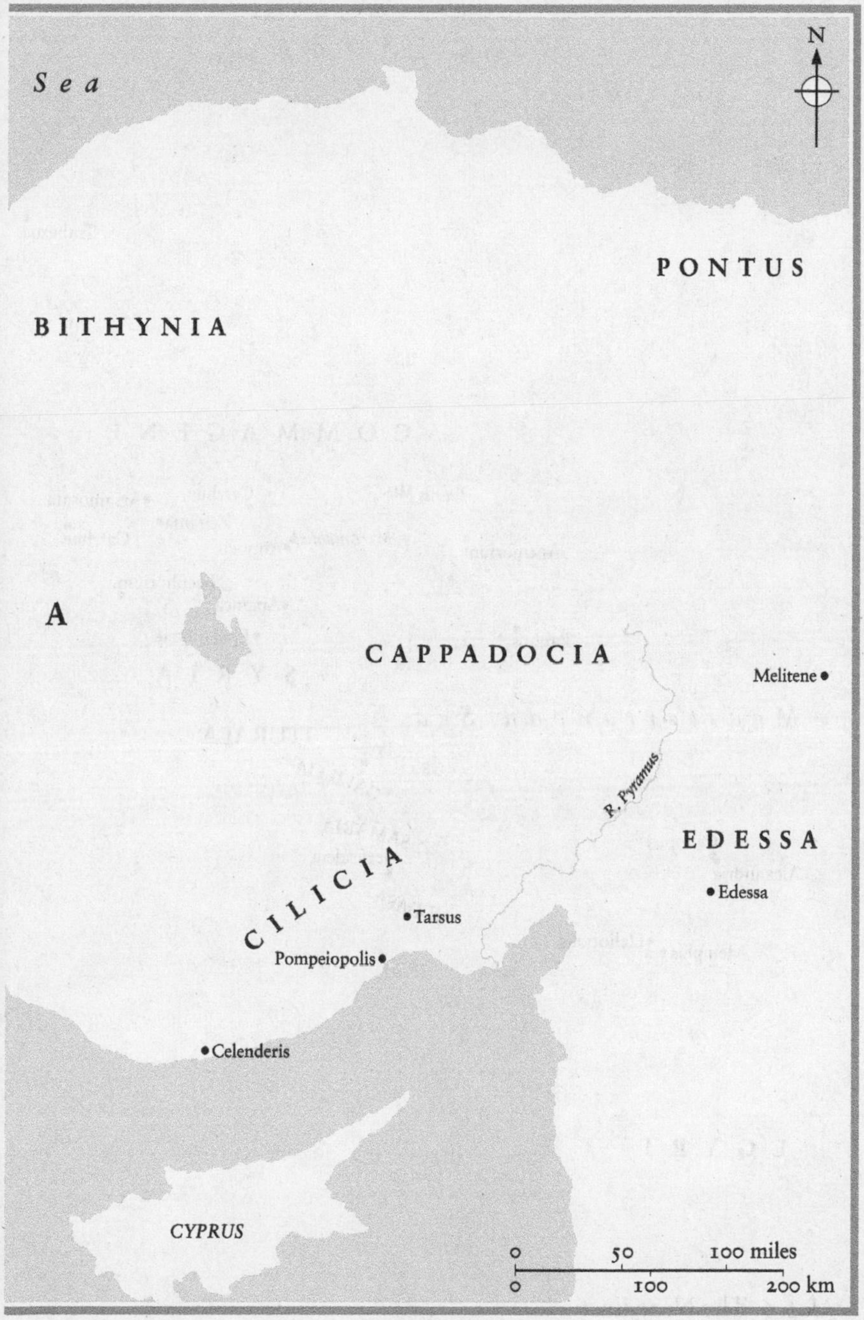

Sea

PONTUS

BITHYNIA

A

CAPPADOCIA

Melitene •

R. Pyramus

EDESSA

CILICIA

• Edessa

• Tarsus

Pompeiopolis •

• Celenderis

CYPRUS

0   50   100 miles

0   100   200 km

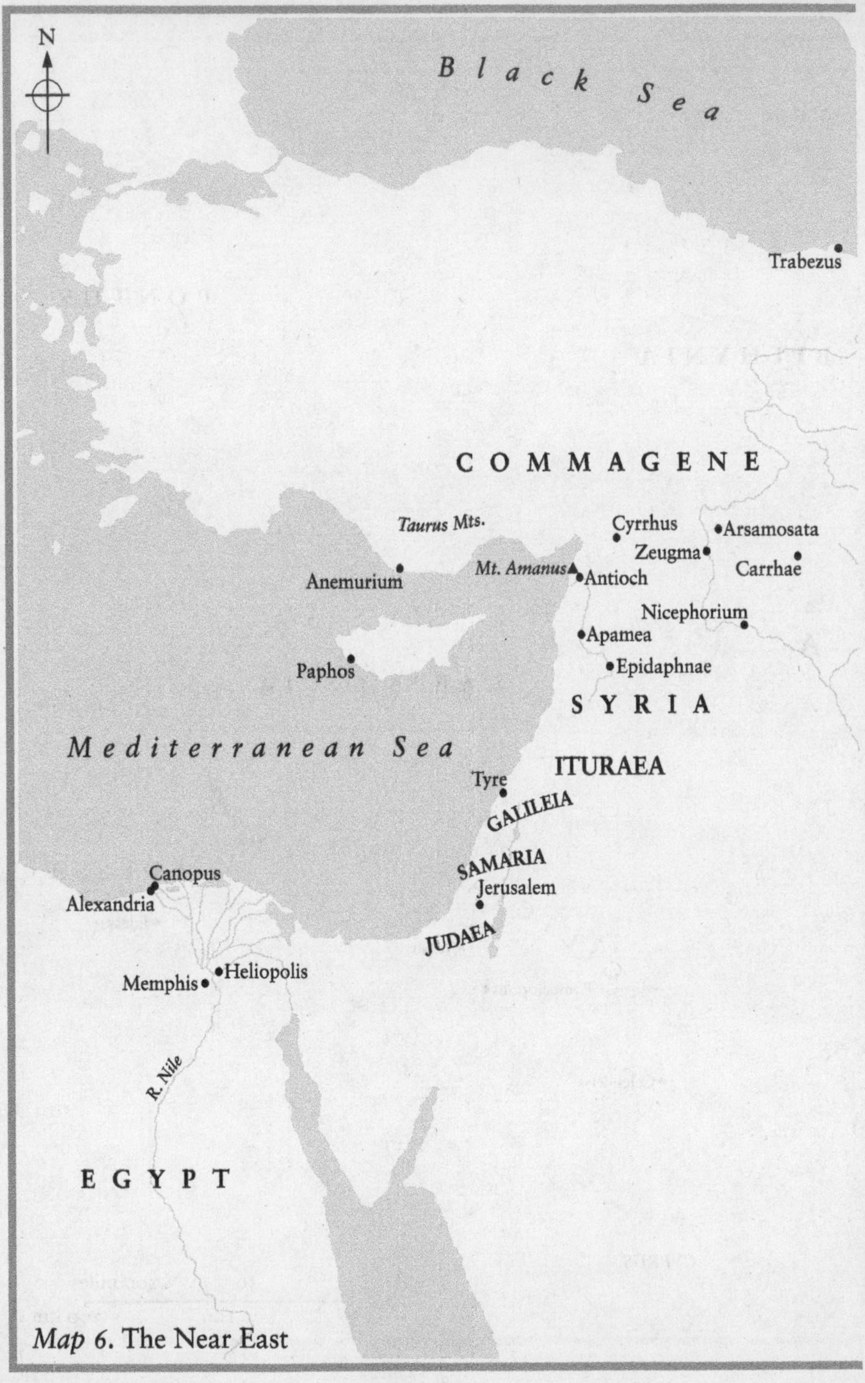

N

Black Sea

Trabezus

COMMAGENE

Taurus Mts.

Cyrrhus
Arsamosata
Zeugma
Carrhae

Anemurium
Mt. Amanus Antioch

Nicephorium

Apamea

Paphos

Epidaphnae

SYRIA

Mediterranean Sea

Tyre ITURAEA

GALILEIA

Canopus

SAMARIA

Alexandria

Jerusalem

JUDAEA

Memphis Heliopolis

R. Nile

EGYPT

Map 6. The Near East

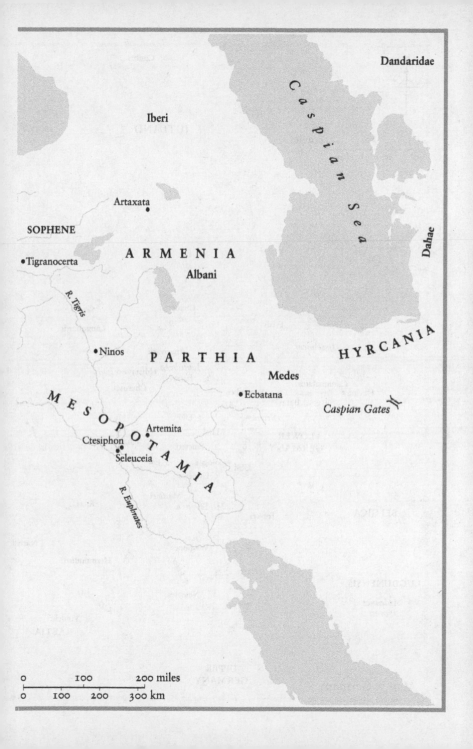

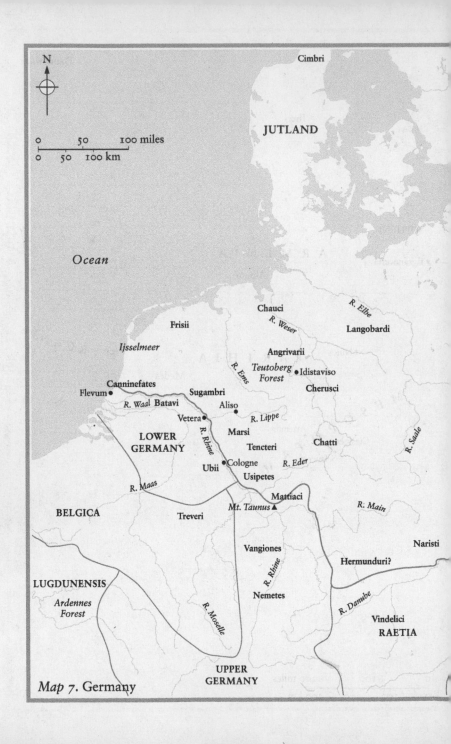

N

0　　50　　100 miles
0　50　100 km

Ocean

Cimbri

JUTLAND

Chauci   *R. Elbe*
Frisii   *R. Weser*   Langobardi

Ijsselmeer   Angrivarii
R. Ems   *Teutoberg* •Idistaviso
                 Forest
Canninefates   Sugambri   Cherusci
Flevum •   *R. Waal* Batavi   Aliso •
                 Vetera •   *R. Lippe*
LOWER   Marsi
GERMANY   Tencteri   Chatti   *R. Saale*
          Ubii •Cologne   *R. Eder*
          Usipetes
R. Maas   Mattiaci
                 Mt. Taunus ▲   *R. Main*
BELGICA   Treveri
                 Vangiones   Naristi
LUGDUNENSIS   Hermunduri?
Ardennes   *R. Rhine*
Forest   Nemetes
                 R. Danube   Vindelici
          R. Moselle   **RAETIA**

          UPPER
          GERMANY

Map 7. Germany

SCANDINAVIA

Suebian Sea

Gotones

R. Vistula

Veneti?

Semnones

Lugii

R. Oder

R. Elbe

GERMANY

Hermunduri?

R. Morava

Marcomani

R. Vltava

Boihaemum

R. Danube

Quadi

NORICUM

UPPER
PANNONIA

Dacians

LOWER
PANNONIA

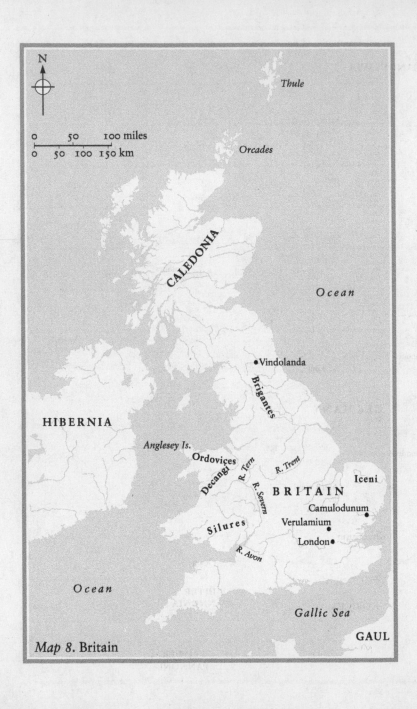

N

0   50   100 miles
0   50 100 150 km

Thule

Orcades

CALEDONIA

Ocean

•Vindolanda

Brigantes

HIBERNIA

Anglesey Is.

Ordovices

Decangi

R. Tern

R. Trent

Iceni

BRITAIN

R. Severn

Camulodunum

Silures

Verulamium
•
London•

R. Avon

Ocean

Gallic Sea

Map 8. Britain

GAUL

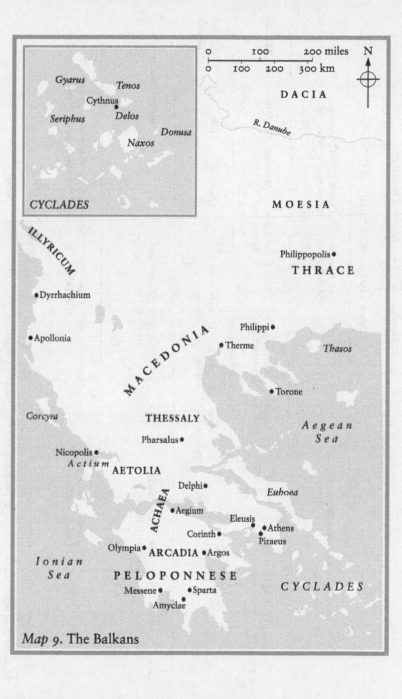

Map 9. The Balkans

A: The Family of Augustus

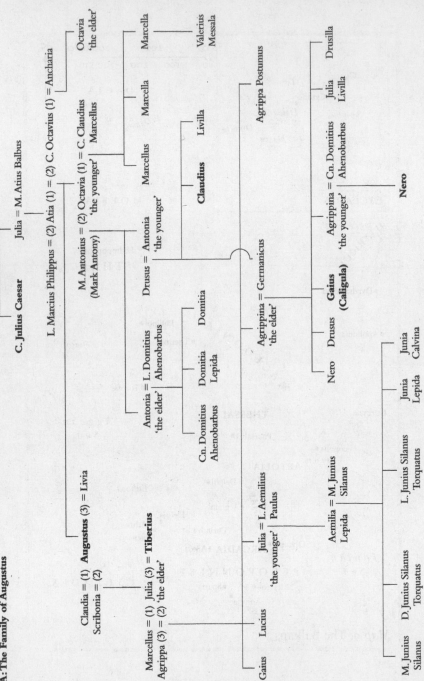

B: The Julio-Claudian Emperors

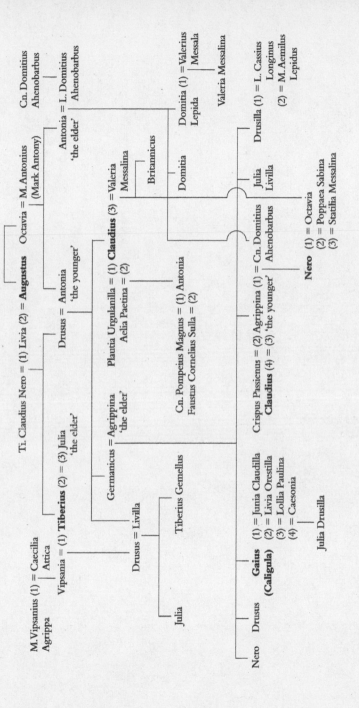

ANNALS

BOOK 1

1. The city of Rome[1] was originally in the hands of kings; liberty and the consulship were instituted by Lucius Brutus. Dictatorships were assumed temporarily. The Board of Ten did not exercise control beyond a two-year period, nor was the military tribunes' consular authority long prevalent. Neither Cinna's regime nor Sulla's was lengthy. The power of Pompey and Crassus quickly gave way to Caesar, likewise the armies of Lepidus and Antony to Augustus, who as 'first citizen'[2] received everything, weary as it was from civil strife, into his command.

(2) For the Roman people of old – their successes and misfortunes – writers of renown produced a record, and the tale of Augustus' times did not lack reputable talents until the spread of flattery proved a deterrent. The affairs of Tiberius and Gaius, Claudius and Nero, in their prosperity, were falsified through fear and after their fall were written with hatreds still fresh. (3) Thus my plan is to report a few final things about Augustus, then Tiberius' principate and the rest, without anger or favour,[3] from whose causes I consider myself distant.

2. After Brutus and Cassius were killed, the state was no longer armed. Sextus Pompey was crushed in Sicily and, with Lepidus discarded and Antony dead, the only Julian faction-leader left was Octavian, who then dropped the 'triumvir' title. *I am a consul*, he proclaimed, *content with tribunician authority for protecting the populace.* When he had enticed the army with gifts, the people with subsidized food and everyone with the sweetness of repose he rose up gradually and absorbed the functions of senate, magistrates and laws, without opposition:

the most spirited men had perished in battle or through pro-
scription and the rest of the elite – the readier each was for
servitude – were exalted with wealth and office, and, once bet-
tered by revolution, preferred a safe present to former perils.
(2) Nor did provinces protest this state of affairs: the rule of
senate and people was feared because of powerful men's rival-
ries and magistrates' greed, and the protection of the laws was
feeble, given their constant disruption by violence, lobbying
and finally cash.

3. Augustus marked out reinforcements for his mastery:
Marcellus, his sister's son, still quite young, with a priesthood
and aedileship, and Agrippa, low in origin but good at soldiering and his ally in victory, with repeated consulships. After
Marcellus' death Augustus took Agrippa as son-in-law. Stepsons Tiberius and Drusus he advanced with independent
commands although his own household was still unscathed.
((2) Augustus had brought Agrippa's sons Gaius and Lucius
into the imperial family and was ablaze with desire – although
he made a show of refusing – for them to be called 'leaders of
the youth' while still in boyhood's toga, and marked out for
consulships.) (3) Then Agrippa passed away. Lucius Caesar, en
route to Spain's armies, and Gaius Caesar, returning from
Armenia wounded and weak, were taken either by premature
but fated death or by the guile of their stepmother Livia. Since
Drusus was already gone, Tiberius alone of Augustus' stepsons
remained and everything converged on him. He was adopted as
son, partner in rule and partaker of tribunician power, and shown
throughout the armies, not, as before, through his mother's
unseen artifice but at her open urging. ((4) Livia had bound the
elderly Augustus so tightly that he banished his only grandson
Agrippa Postumus to Planasia. A man without virtue's attainments, to be sure, with physical strength the basis of his senseless
bravado, but discovered in no wrongdoing.) (5) And yet Augustus put Germanicus, Drusus' son, at the head of eight legions on
the Rhine and ordered his adoption into the family by Tiberius –
although Tiberius had an adult son at home – to multiply the
defences providing support.

(6) No war remained then except against the Germans, more

to dispel the disgrace of losing an army with Varus than from desire of extending the Empire or for any worthwhile prize.

(7) At home the situation was calm. For magistracies there was no change to the terminology. The younger men were born after Actium and most of the elderly were born during the civil wars. How many were left who had seen a republic?[4]

4. Given the upheaval in the community's disposition nowhere did former morality survive unscathed. Everyone discarded equality and looked to the Emperor's orders – without alarm at the time, since Augustus' age was vigorous and he sustained himself, his house and the peace. (2) But when advanced age grew weary in a body now frail and the end with its new hopes was near, a few made pointless speeches about liberty's benefits; more feared war and some desired it. The majority drew distinctions between impending masters with varied talk. (3) *Agrippa Postumus is grim and furious at his belittlement. In neither age nor experience is he equal to so huge a burden. Tiberius is mature in years and tried in war, but has the old inborn Claudian arrogance. Many signs of brutality, though repressed, are emerging. (4) Raised from first infancy in the ruling house, in his prime he was heaped with consulships and triumphs. Even when, apparently retired, he lived at Rhodes in exile, anger and pretence and secret lusts were his sole preoccupations. (5) There is also his mother with her female unruliness. This means servitude to a woman and two young men besides, who will oppress the state in the interim and eventually dismember it!*

5. With these things and their like in the air, Augustus' condition deteriorated. Some suspected his wife's crime, for a rumour had started. *A few months earlier Augustus, with select accomplices and Fabius Maximus his sole companion, sailed to Planasia to see Agrippa Postumus. There were many tears on both sides and signs of affection, and the expectation that Agrippa would be restored to his grandfather's household. Maximus told this to his wife Marcia, she to Livia. (2) This was known to Augustus and soon thereafter Maximus was dead. By choice? Uncertain. At Maximus' funeral people heard*

Marcia's laments: she blamed herself as responsible for her husband's ruin. (3) Whatever the reality was, Tiberius had scarcely reached Illyricum when he was summoned by a hurried letter from his mother. It has not been ascertained whether he found Augustus still breathing at Nola or lifeless. (4) For a strict cordon was placed around the house and its approaches by Livia and happy news was occasionally broadcast. Once provision was made for the occasion's demands, word went out simultaneously that Augustus was gone and Tiberius in control.

6. The first action of the new regime was killing Agrippa Postumus. He was unaware and unarmed, but the centurion, though mentally braced, had trouble finishing him. Tiberius did not address the senate on this subject. His father's orders, he pretended. *Augustus instructed the senior guard officer not to delay killing Agrippa when his own days were done.* (2) True, with his many cruel complaints about the man's character Augustus achieved ratification for Agrippa's exile by senatorial decree. But he never went so far as to murder any of his own. Death inflicted on a grandson for a stepson's security? Not credible. Closer to truth: Tiberius and Livia – he from fear, she from stepmotherly hostility – hastened the killing of a man suspect and hated. (3) When the centurion, following military protocol, reported that what Tiberius ordered was done, Tiberius responded: *I gave no orders. You must render an account of your deed to the senate.* When this was discovered by Sallustius Crispus,[5] who shared Tiberius' secrets and had sent a document to the commanding officer, Crispus feared being put on trial himself. Thinking it equally dangerous to produce fiction or truth he warned Livia against making household mysteries, friends' advice and soldiers' services common knowledge. *Tiberius must not relax the regime's strength by bringing everything to the senate. It is a condition of absolute power that its account only balances if rendered to one man.*

7. In Rome people rushed into servitude: consuls, senators, equestrian-ranked. The more distinguished, the more false and frenzied – with faces composed not to seem happy at an emperor's departure or too gloomy for a beginning – in mixing tears and joy, protest and flattery. (2) Sextus Pompeius and

Sextus Appuleius, the consuls, were the first to swear allegiance
to Tiberius. With them were Seius Strabo and Gaius Turranius,
superintendent of the Guard cohorts and grain supply, respectively. Then came the senate, soldiers and people. (3) For
Tiberius began everything with the consuls, as if the old constitution was in force and he uncertain about ruling. Even his
edict summoning the senate was issued under the heading of
tribunician power, which he held under Augustus. (4) Its words
were few and quite limited in scope. *I will consult you about
my parent's honours. I am staying with his corpse and that is
now my sole public function.* (5) But after Augustus' death
Tiberius gave the Guard its watchword as emperor. He had
sentries – armed – and everything else pertaining to a court.
With him into the Forum came soldiers, into the senate, soldiers. He wrote to the armies as if the principate were his,
hesitant nowhere except when addressing the senate. (6) His
particular fear was lest Germanicus, who had numerous legions
plus a vast quantity of allied troops and remarkable support
among the people, prefer holding absolute power to expecting
it. (7) Tiberius meant to benefit his reputation, too: he would
seem to have been summoned, to be the official choice, rather
than to have crept in through wifely ambition with a senile
adoption. Later, people realized that he feigned hesitation to
scrutinize the attitudes of leading men, whose language and
looks he gave a criminal twist to – and stored up.

8. At that initial meeting Tiberius only allowed discussion of
final arrangements for Augustus. Augustus' will, brought by
the Vestals, had Tiberius and Livia as heirs. Livia was taken
into the Julian family and Augustus' name.[6] As secondary heirs
Augustus listed grandsons and great-grandsons, in the third
place Rome's leading men, many of whom he hated – a form of
boasting and strutting for posterity. (2) Augustus' legacies were
not beyond a citizen's measure, except that he gave the people
and urban populace 43,500,000 sesterces, Guard soldiers
1,000 coins each, and legionaries and Roman citizen auxiliaries 300 per man.

(3) Then came the question of honours. These seemed the
most notable: that Augustus' funeral pass through the

triumphal gate, as Asinius Gallus recommended, and that the titles of laws he passed and the names of peoples he conquered lead the way, as Lucius Arruntius recommended. (4) Valerius Messala added that the oath of allegiance to Tiberius should be renewed annually.[7] When asked by Tiberius whether his own instructions prompted this proposal, Messala replied: *I spoke spontaneously. And in matters pertaining to the state I will use no counsel but my own, even at risk of offending* – the only type of flattery as yet untried. (5) Senators exclaimed that Augustus' body should be carried to the pyre on senators' shoulders. Tiberius excused them with pretentious moderation and issued the people an edict of admonition. *Long ago your excesses of favour disrupted Caesar's funeral, but this should not make you want Augustus cremated in the Forum rather than in the Campus Martius, the site he intended.*

(6) On the occasion, soldiers were in position, apparently as protection, causing much ridicule from those who had themselves seen or knew from their parents that day when, with servitude still unripe and liberty's reclamation unsuccessful, Caesar's assassination seemed to some the worst of deeds, to others the finest. *Now an elderly emperor, after a lengthy rule and the provision of abundant heirs against a republic,[8] needs military protection for his burial to pass calmly!*

9. This led to much talk about Augustus himself. Most marvelled at meaningless things: the same date[9] for his initial long-ago assumption of command and for life's end, his finishing life at Nola in the house and room where his father Octavius died. (2) Even the number of his consulships came up, in which he equalled Valerius Corvus and Marius together, and the unbroken thirty-seven years of tribunician power, and earning a 'victorious general' salutation twenty-one times, and other honours numerous and new.

(3) Among the insightful, however, Augustus' life was variously extolled or criticized. *Duty towards parent and the needs of the state – where, at that time, laws had no place – drove him to take up arms against fellow citizens, and these cannot be either acquired or wielded with rectitude.* (4) *To Antony he conceded much, while pursuing vengeance against his father's*

*killers, likewise to Lepidus. After Lepidus grew old in idleness
and Antony was ruined by debauches the only remedy for our
discordant country was one-man rule.* (5) *Neither royalty,
however, nor dictatorship, but rather a 'first citizen' is the basis
of our state. Ocean and distant rivers fence the Empire, as do
legions, provinces and fleets, all connected. Justice applies with
citizens, restraint with allies. Rome herself is splendidly adorned.
A very few things have been handled with violence to give the
remainder quiet.*

10. Contrarily: *Duty towards parent and the state's situation were adopted as a screen. Desire for dominance caused
the mobilization of veterans through largesse, an adolescent
civilian's acquisition of an army, the bribery of consular legions
and the pretence of favour for the Pompeian cause.* (2) *Then,
by senatorial decree, he appropriated the insignia and authority of a praetor. Then came the deaths of Hirtius and Pansa.*
(Either the enemy had killed them or else, for Pansa, poison
applied to his wound did, and for Hirtius, his own soldiers and
Octavian as plot's strategist.) *He seized the troops of both,
extorted a consulship from an unwilling senate and turned
weapons given for Antony against the state. For the proscrip-
tion of citizens and the land reallocations not even those
responsible had praise.* (3) *Removing Cassius and the two Bru-
tuses was no doubt a concession to inherited antagonism,
although propriety would waive personal hatreds for public
advantage. But Sextus Pompey was tricked by the appearance
of peace, Lepidus by a show of friendship. Afterwards, Antony:
agreements at Tarentum and Brundisium, and marriage with
Octavian's sister, seduced him and the penalty he paid for this
duplicitous marriage connection was death.* (4) *True, there was
peace thereafter – bloody peace, with the Lollian and Varian
calamities, and the murders at Rome of men like Varro and
Egnatius and Jullus.* ((5) Not even domestic matters were off-
limits: taking Nero's wife, consulting priests – a mockery! – as
to whether, with a child conceived but not yet born, her marriage would be correct. *** and Vedius Pollio's extravagance.[10]
Finally, Livia: troubling to the state as mother and troubling
in the imperial house as stepmother.) (6) *No honours remain*

*for gods if Augustus wants worship for himself with temples
and divine likenesses and conducted by priests.* (7) *Not even
Tiberius' adoption as successor was motivated by affection or
concern for the state: having observed Tiberius' arrogance and
brutality, Augustus sought glory for himself from a comparison
with someone vastly inferior.* (A few years earlier, when Augustus requested from the senate renewal of Tiberius' tribunician
power, although his speech honoured Tiberius, he also made
certain comments on character, style and habits that, while
excusing, criticized.)

(8) After a traditional funeral, a temple and divine cult were
decreed.

11. Reorientation followed: entreaties were directed to
Tiberius. He contrasted the Empire's magnitude and his own
restraint. *Only Augustus' mind was sufficient to so huge a burden. I myself, having entered into some of his responsibilities at
his request, know from experience how toilsome and vulnerable to Fortune is the task of ruling everything. Accordingly,
since the community's props include so many notable men, do
not confer the totality on one. A larger number will more easily
accomplish the duties of government by combined effort.* (2) A
speech like this was more impressive than reliable. Tiberius'
language, even on matters he was not trying to hide, was
always, from either nature or habit, equivocal and obscure, but
on that occasion, when he exerted himself to bury his feelings
deep, it was especially layered with uncertainty and ambiguity.
(3) The senators, whose one fear was lest they seem to understand, let loose with protests, tears and prayers: towards the
gods, towards Augustus' likeness, towards the knees of Tiberius
himself they stretched hands. Then he ordered a document
brought forward and read. (4) In it the state's resources were
enumerated: citizens and allies in arms, fleets, kingdoms and
provinces, taxes and other revenues, the state's obligations and
grants. All of this Augustus had written himself. And he had
added the advice that the Empire be kept within limits. Was
fear his motive? Or was this jealousy?

12. Meanwhile the senate grovelled, reduced to abject
appeals. Tiberius chanced to say: *Though unequal to the*

totality of the state, I will assume a protectorate over whatever
portion is entrusted to me. (2) Then Asinius Gallus: 'A question, Caesar. What portion do you want entrusted to you?'
Upset by the unexpected query, Tiberius fell briefly silent. Then,
collecting his wits, he responded. *It does not suit my sense of*
decency to choose – or avoid – some of what I would rather be
entirely excused from. (3) In return, Gallus, inferring offence
from Tiberius' expression, said: *My question did not mean to*
divide what cannot be split, but to show by your own confes-
sion that the body of the state is one and must be ruled by one
man's mind. He added praise of Augustus and reminded
Tiberius of his victories and outstanding acts as civilian over so
many years, (4) but did not assuage anger thereby. Gallus was
long since hated: after marrying Vipsania (Agrippa's daughter,
formerly Tiberius' wife) his behaviour exceeded citizen-like
limits and in him his father Asinius Pollio's spirit survived.

13. After this, Lucius Arruntius, with a speech very like Gallus', produced comparable offence, although Tiberius had no
long-standing hatred towards him. But he was suspicious of a
wealthy and active man of outstanding attainments and comparable fame. (2) For in Augustus' final conversations, when
discussing who would refuse to take the Emperor's role though
adequate to it, who of the unqualified would want it, who had
both the ability and the desire, Augustus had said: *Marcus Lepi-*
dus is capable but reluctant, Asinius Gallus eager and deficient.
Lucius Arruntius is not unworthy and, if he gets a chance, will
risk it. (3) About the first names accounts agree; in Arruntius'
place some give Piso.[11] All except Lepidus were later overtaken
by various charges laid by Tiberius.

(4) Even Quintus Haterius and Mamercus Scaurus grated on
a suspicion-filled mind, Haterius when he said 'How long, Caesar, will you allow the absence of a head of state?' Scaurus for
saying *There is hope that the senate's prayers will be effective*
in your not having used the prerogative of tribunician power to
veto the consuls' proposal. Against Haterius, Tiberius protested immediately. Scaurus, for whom his anger was more
implacable, he silently bypassed. (5) Wearied by the general
outcry and individuals' demands, Tiberius gradually changed

course. Not that he admitted to holding power, but he did stop his denials and their requests. (6) People agree that when Haterius went to the palace to excuse himself and tumbled down before Tiberius' knees as he walked, he was nearly killed by soldiers because Tiberius, either by chance or tripped by Haterius' grasp, fell forward. Nor did the danger of such a man appease him. Finally, Haterius petitioned Livia and gained her most attentive entreaties' protection.

14. Senators showed significant obsequiousness towards Livia, too. Some were proposing that she be called the country's 'parent', others, its 'mother', more, that to Tiberius' name be added 'son of Livia'. (2) Tiberius: *Honours for women need limits and I will apply equal restraint in honours accorded myself,* he maintained. Anxious about resentment[12] and taking female prominence as a slight to himself, he did not allow her even a lictor by decree and refused an 'Altar to Adoption' and other such things. (3) For Germanicus he sought a proconsular command and envoys were sent to confer it, as well as to console Germanicus' sorrow at Augustus' departure. (Tiberius didn't ask the same for Drusus, since Drusus was consul-designate and at hand.) (4) He nominated twelve candidates for the praetorship, the number traditional since Augustus, and when the senate urged an increase, he pledged on oath not to exceed it.

15. An innovation: elections were transferred from assembly to senate. (Until then, although the most important elections went according to the Emperor's decision, some were decided by citizen support.) The people did not protest their lost prerogative except with empty murmuring, and the senate, released from outlay and sordid pleading, grasped it willingly, since Tiberius limited himself to recommending no more than four candidates whose appointment – without rejection, without lobbying – was obligatory.

(2) The plebeian tribunes asked to put on at their own expense the festival, new to the calendar, called 'Augustalia' from Augustus' name. But money from the Treasury was decreed and permission to wear triumphal robes in the procession, but not conveyance in a chariot. (3) Later the annual

event was transferred to the praetor with jurisdiction over cases between citizens and foreigners.

16. Such was the state of affairs in Rome when sedition overtook Pannonia's legions, for no new reasons, except that the change of emperor opened up mob licence and, from civil war, an expectation of profits. (2) Three legions were together in summer quarters with Junius Blaesus[13] in charge. At news of Augustus' death and Tiberius' inauguration – cause for public mourning or rejoicing – he suspended ordinary duties. This was the beginning of carousing among the soldiers, of squabbling and paying heed to every reprobate, and finally of desiring luxury and leisure and rejecting discipline and toil.

(3) In the camp was a certain Percennius, formerly head of a theatre claque and later a regular-grade soldier, wayward of tongue and practised at engaging crowds in fan fervour. Naive souls were uncertain about the terms of military service after Augustus. He gradually set them moving with night-time conversations or, at the turn of day to evening after the better men slipped away, he would bring the worst together.

17. Eventually, having in readiness other agents, too, for sedition, he asked, as if addressing an assembly, *Why do you obey a few centurions and fewer tribunes, slave-like? When will you dare to demand redress, if you don't approach a new and still precarious emperor with entreaties – or weapons?* (2) *Enough cowardly mistakes have been made these many years: you tolerate thirty and forty years of service, old men now, most with hacked and wounded bodies.* (3) *Even discharge doesn't end a soldier's career, when quartered in a detachment he endures under a different name the same toil. If any outlive these numerous hazards they are hauled to remote lands where they receive as 'fields' boggy marsh or mountainous wilderness.* (4) *Moreover, military service is burdensome in itself and unprofitable: ten small coins per day is the value of soul and body. And from these come payments for clothing, weapons and tents, and for centurion brutality and exemption from fatigues. But – heavens! – floggings and wounds, harsh winters, busy summers, grim war and barren peace are perennial.* (5) *The only remedy is enlistment on fixed terms: a denarius a day,*

the sixteenth year of service as the last, no quartering with detachments thereafter, and the discharge bonus paid in camp in cash. (6) *Do Guard cohorts, which get two denarii and are restored to their homes after sixteen years, undergo more dangers? No disrespect to sentry duty in Rome, but here among wild peoples we can see the enemy from our tents.*

18. Cheers from the crowd, variously prompted: these exclaimed about the marks of beatings, those about white hair, most about threadbare garments and exposed bodies. (2) They finally went so far in madness as to discuss mixing three legions into one. Deterred by rivalry, with everyone demanding distinction for his legion, they changed course and put the three eagles and the cohort standards together. Meanwhile, heaping turves, they raised a tribunal as a more conspicuous base, working quickly. (3) Blaesus arrived. Berating and grabbing individuals, he cried: 'Dirty your hands with my death instead! The scandal will be less if you kill your commander than if you defect from your emperor. I, unharmed, will maintain my legions' loyalty or, throat slit, will hasten their regret.'

19. Additions continued to the earthwork, nevertheless. It was already chest high when at last, overcome by Blaesus' persistence, they abandoned the project. (2) Using great rhetorical artistry he said that mutiny and mobs were not appropriate for conveying soldiers' desires to Tiberius. *Such novel requests were not made by veteran soldiers to past commanders, nor by you yourselves to Augustus, and it is bad timing to increase a new emperor's burden of cares.* (3) *If, however, you aim to attempt in peacetime what not even civil-war winners demanded, why, contrary to your habitual obedience and proper discipline, is violence your plan? You should choose envoys and instruct them in my presence.* (4) Shouting followed: *Your officer son, Blaesus, must perform this mission, and request discharge for soldiers after sixteen years! We will give other instructions when the first have succeeded.* (5) After young Blaesus left there was moderate calm, but pretentiousness filled the soldiers. *The commander's son serving as envoy for our common cause is proof enough that things have been extorted by necessity that we did not get through moderation!*

20. Meanwhile, units sent to Nauportus before the mutiny to see to roads and bridges and other needs heard about disturbances in camp. They uprooted their standards and, after plundering nearby villages and town-sized Nauportus itself, applied to centurions attempting containment first ridicule and insults and eventually a flogging. (There was particular anger at the camp superintendent Aufidienus Rufus. Pulling him from his vehicle they loaded on packs and drove him at the head of the column, asking in mockery: *How do you like enduring outsize burdens, long marches?* (2) For Rufus was long a private, later a centurion, and eventually camp superintendent. He brought back old-fashioned and harsh soldiering: he was strict about work and toil, and the more merciless for having suffered himself.)

21. When these units arrived, the mutiny revived. Roaming, they pillaged the surrounding area. Blaesus ordered a few – the most booty-laden – flogged and jailed as a terror to the rest. (The legate was still obeyed by centurions and the best regulars.) (2) Struggling against the men dragging them off, they clasped bystanders' knees, invoked now the names of individuals, now their unit or cohort or legion. *This same thing threatens you all!* they cried. At the same time they heaped abuse on Blaesus, called heaven and gods to witness and left nothing undone for stirring antipathy, pity, fear and anger. (3) Everyone rushed up and, after breaking open the jail, unfastened shackles. Deserters and men condemned to death were now mixed in with them.

22. Violence blazed hotter then and the mutiny had more leaders. A certain Vibulenus, a private, was hoisted up before Blaesus' tribunal on bystanders' shoulders. In the presence of agitated men curious about what he was planning, he said 'You restored daylight and life to these innocent wretches, but who can restore life to my brother, my brother to me? He was sent to you by the army of Germany for your common interests, but last night Blaesus slit his throat using the gladiators he keeps and arms to eliminate soldiers. (2) Tell me, Blaesus, where did you discard the body? Not even the enemy begrudges burial! When I have satisfied my grief with kisses and tears, order my

slaughter, too, so long as these men can bury us who were killed for no crime but because we took thought for the legions' advantage.'

23. He set these words on fire with his lament, beating his breast and face. When they scattered, those whose shoulders held him up, he fell headlong and grovelled at the feet of individuals, stirring up so much apprehension and ill will that some soldiers tied up the gladiators in Blaesus' service, and others the rest of his household. Still others poured out to look for a corpse. (2) Had it not quickly become known that no body was found, that Blaesus' slaves – despite torture – were denying the murder and that Vibulenus never had a brother, they were not far from eliminating their commander. (3) They did expel officers and the camp superintendent and ransacked the fugitives' packs. There was even a killing: the centurion Lucilius, to whom in military jest they had given the name 'Hand me another!' (After breaking his staff on a soldier's back he used to demand another in a loud voice, and another.) (4) The rest found shelter in hiding. One was detained: Julius Clemens, who was considered suitable, given his innate alacrity, for transmitting the soldiers' instructions. (5) Moreover, the Eighth and the Fifteenth were readying weapons against one another: the Eighth demanded a centurion named Sirpicus for death, the Fifteenth protected him. But the Ninth's soldiers interjected entreaties and, meeting rejection, threats.

24. This news drove Tiberius, despite his secretive nature and concealment especially of whatever was most irksome, to send Drusus with civic leaders and two Guard cohorts. His instructions were quite flexible. *The situation will determine your decisions.* Picked soldiers made the cohorts unusually reliable. (2) Added to these were most of the Guard cavalry and the core of the German bodyguards that used to attend the Emperor. Likewise the Guard commander Sejanus,[14] who had been made his own father's colleague and had great authority with Tiberius: a guide for Drusus and, for the rest, a broker of dangers and rewards.

(3) When Drusus approached, the legions met him 'dutifully'. Not happily, as was customary, nor with insignia gleaming, but

unwashed, unsightly, and with an expression, despite their
sorrowful act, closer to defiance. 25. After he entered the fortifications, they secured the gates with sentries and ordered armed
bands to wait at set locations in the camp. The rest surrounded
the tribunal in daunting ranks. Drusus stood demanding silence
with his hand. (2) With eyes on the multitude they clamoured
brazenly, but seeing Drusus, trembled. There was vague grumbling, ruthless shouting and suddenly silence. With emotions
divergent they were both fearful and frightening. (3) Finally, interrupting the chaos, Drusus read a letter from his father filled
with Tiberius' particular concern for the surpassingly brave
legions with which he had endured numerous wars. *As soon as
my mind rests from grief I will bring your demands before the
senate. Meanwhile, I have sent my son to concede directly what
can be given immediately. The remainder must be kept for the
senate, which is rightly considered deficient in neither indulgence nor strictness.*

26. The response from the assembly: *Instructions were given
to the centurion Clemens and he should carry them out!* Clemens spoke about discharge after sixteen years and rewards upon
completion of service, that a denarius should be the daily pay
and that veterans not be quartered with a detachment. When
Drusus offered an excuse – *the decision rests with the senate
and my father* – shouting caused disruption. (2) *Why have you
come if not to increase soldiers' pay or alleviate toil, without
permission to do any good? But everyone – heavens! – is allowed
to flog and kill. Tiberius habitually frustrated the legions' desires
with Augustus' name, the same tactics that Drusus has acti-
vated. Will no one but underage sons[15] come to us?* (3) *It is truly
strange for an emperor to defer to the senate only concerning
the soldiers' interests. Must the senate therefore be consulted
whenever punishments or battles are indicated? Or are rewards
a matter for masters, but anyone can decide penalties?*

27. Finally they abandoned the tribunal. Encountering
Guard soldiers or Drusus' friends they gestured threateningly,
which led to strife and the start of violence. People were particularly hostile to Gnaeus Lentulus:[16] superior in age and
military glory to the others, he was stiffening Drusus, so they

believed, and led the rejection of 'outrages to the military'.
(2) Eventually he left Drusus and – danger foreseen – headed
for winter quarters. They surrounded him, asking: *Where are
you heading? To the Emperor or to senators? Will you oppose
the legions' interests there, too?* while pressing closer and hurling rocks. Lentulus was already bloodied by a stone's blow and
expecting death when the hurried arrival of the contingent that
had come with Drusus brought protection.

28. Night's menace, liable to erupt into crime, was assuaged
by chance. For the moon in a suddenly clear sky grew visibly
faint. Soldiers ignorant of the reason thought this an omen
about the present, likening the planet's defection to their own
difficulties. *Our aims will be reached successfully if the moon
recovers her light and brilliance!* (2) Accordingly, with bronze
resounding and a chorus of horns[17] they raised a din. As the
moon appeared brighter or darker they rejoiced or mourned.
When clouds arose blocking sight, people believed the moon
buried among the shades – so prone to superstition are minds
once stricken. *Eternal toil is portended for us, and our actions
are opposed by the gods!* they lamented.

(3) *We must take advantage of this new orientation,* Drusus
thought, *and convert accident's gift into wisdom.* He ordered
men to go tent-to-tent. Clemens was roused, and other men of
rectitude and influential with the crowd. (4) These mingled with
the night watch, sentries and gate guards, offering hope and
intensifying fear. 'How long will we keep the Emperor's son
besieged? Where will our struggles end? Will we take a loyalty
oath to Percennius and Vibulenus? Will Percennius and Vibulenus dispense pay to soldiers and land to veterans? Are they to
replace men like Tiberius and Drusus in running the Roman
people's empire? (5) Better that we, as we came last to guilt, be
first in repentance. It is a slow process to make collective
demands. For immediate service your return is immediate.'
(6) After minds were shaken by these words and became mutually
suspicious, Drusus' men began to separate recruit from veteran
and legion from legion. Love of compliance gradually returned.
They abandoned the gates and returned the standards – grouped
in one spot when the mutiny began – to their proper places.

29. At daybreak an assembly was called. Drusus, though inexperienced at speaking, showed innate nobility in rebuking past and praising present behaviour. *Neither terror nor threats sway me. If I see your course changed towards restraint, if I hear you suppliant, I will write to my father suggesting that he receive the legions' entreaties appeased.* (2) When they begged him, he sent young Blaesus again, with Lucius Aponius, an equestrian-ranked man from his retinue, and Catonius Justus, a chief centurion, to Tiberius. (3) Conflicting opinions followed. One proposal was to await the envoys and meanwhile use affability to soothe the soldiers, the other, to take stronger remedial action. *Nothing is moderate in a crowd. They terrorize if not afraid, but once intimidated are despised with impunity. Superstition is applying pressure. We must add danger from their commander by removing those responsible for the mutiny.* (4) Drusus' character being inclined to harsher measures, he ordered Vibulenus and Percennius summoned and killed. Most report them buried inside the General's tent; others say the bodies were discarded outside the rampart for show.

30. Then every conspicuous agitator was sought out. Part were killed wandering outside the camp by Guard centurions or soldiers, some were betrayed by regular army units – loyalty's proof. (2) Adding to the soldiers' worries was an early winter with storms so continuous and cruel that they couldn't leave their tents or congregate; they could barely secure the standards that gust and flood kept trying to grab. (3) Also persistent was fear of heaven's wrath. *It is not coincidental for the impious when stars grow dull and storms descend. The only relief for our ills is for everyone to abandon this unlucky and tainted camp and, absolved now by expiation, to be restored to their own winter quarters.* (4) First the Eighth, then the Fifteenth went back. The Ninth's soldiers protested that they should wait for Tiberius' letter, but then, forsaken by the others' departure, they voluntarily anticipated impending necessity. (5) Drusus, without awaiting the envoys' return, since present conditions were sufficiently settled, returned to Rome.

31. At about the same time and for the same reasons Germany's legions were disturbed, in bigger numbers and more

violently, and with a great hope that Germanicus would be
unable to endure another's command and would offer himself
to legions whose power would carry everything along.

(2) There were two armies on the Rhine. The Upper army[18]
was under the legate Gaius Silius; for the Lower, Aulus Caecina
was responsible. Overall control was with Germanicus, then
busy conducting a census of the Gallic provinces. (3) Those
under Silius' direction were watching undecided for the fate of
sedition elsewhere. The Lower army's soldiers slid into a frenzy,
starting with those of the Twenty-first and Fifth, and carrying
along the First and Twentieth. For they were together in summer quarters in Ubian territory, at leisure or light tasks.
(4) Upon hearing of Augustus' end, the home-bred multitude
from a recent levy in Rome – habituated to carousing, impatient
of toil – filled the naive minds of the rest. *The time has come for
veterans to demand timely discharge, for military-age men to
demand more generous pay, and for everyone to demand an
end to misery and punish centurion brutality.* (5) This was not
said by one man, like Percennius among Pannonia's legions, or
in the fearful hearing of soldiers wary of other, stronger armies:
sedition had many faces and voices. *Rome's affairs have been
placed in our hands. The commonwealth grows with our victories. Victorious generals have our name by association.*[19]

32. Caecina did not confront them: the outnumbering madness stripped him of constancy. Suddenly, crazed men drew
swords and attacked centurions, long a fuel for soldiers' hatred
and for violence a spark. Face down, the centurions were bat-
tered with sixty lashes apiece to match their number, then
thrown torn, gashed and in some cases lifeless before the rampart or into the Rhine. (2) Although Septimius escaped to the
tribunal and fell at Caecina's feet, howls for him persisted until
he was surrendered for destruction. Cassius Chaerea[20] – who
later, by killing Gaius, gained posterity's remembrance – was
then in his prime, high-spirited; amidst men resisting and armed
he used his sword to open a path. (3) No longer did an officer's
or camp superintendent's authority obtain: the night watch,
sentry duty, and whatever else present need indicated, were
allocated by the men themselves. There was striking evidence,

for those assessing soldier mentality more thoroughly, of a
great and implacable upheaval in the fact that the men were
equally – not here and there or at the prompting of a few –
ablaze, equally silent, with so much uniformity and constancy
that you would have thought they had a ruler.

33. Meanwhile Germanicus, who, as I said, was taking a
census in Gaul, got word that Augustus was dead. He had
Augustus' granddaughter Agrippina as his wife and several
children from her. He himself, son of Tiberius' brother Drusus
and Livia's grandson, was nevertheless anxious about hidden
antipathy towards himself in uncle and grandmother, its causes
sharper because unfair. (2) For Drusus had a substantial remembrance among the Roman people and, it was believed, intended
to restore liberty if he gained power. This generated goodwill
for Germanicus – and the same hope. The man had a citizen-like
character and remarkable affability, quite different from Tiberius'
words and looks, arrogant and obscure. (3) Plus there were
female grievances from stepmotherly provocations, Livia's to
Agrippina, and Agrippina herself somewhat too excitable,
except that purity and love of husband helped her turn a still
untamed character to the good.

34. The closer Germanicus was to exalted hope the more
unstinting were his exertions for Tiberius. He administered the
loyalty oath to himself, his entourage and Belgae communities.
Hearing thereafter of chaos among the legions he set out
quickly[21] and encountered them outside the camp, their eyes
lowered as if in remorse. (2) After he entered the fortifications
a confusion of complaints became audible. Some men, taking
his hand apparently for a kiss, inserted his fingers into their
mouths to show their lack of teeth. Others displayed limbs bent
with age. (3) When they assembled there in an obvious jumble
he ordered them to separate into their units – *we will hear you
better this way*, was the response – and the standards brought
forward so that this at least would make the cohorts distinct.
They complied, slowly. (4) After beginning with veneration for
Augustus, Germanicus changed course to Tiberius' victories
and triumphs, mustering particular praise for Tiberius' finest
achievements in Germany with those very legions. Then he

extolled Italy's consensus and the loyalty of the Gallic provinces. *Nowhere is there trouble or disaffection.* Silence or a restrained murmur was the reception.

35. Then Germanicus touched on the mutiny. *Where is soldierly self-control? Where is traditional discipline, your glory? Where have you put your tribunes, your centurions?* he kept asking. Every man bared his body, angrily showing wound scars and marks of flogging. Soon a confusion of voices berated exemption-payments, meagre pay and hard jobs, specifying rampart and ditches, fodder, timber and firewood in heaps, and everything else procured of necessity or to combat leisure in camp. (2) The sharpest outcry came from veterans counting out thirty or more campaigns. *Give relief to weary men! Instead of death in unchanging toil,* they pleaded, *a time-limit for military service – so exhausting! – and retirement without want.* (3) Some even demanded Augustus' cash legacy. There were expressions propitious for Germanicus and even a declaration. *If you want power, we are ready!* (4) Then, however, as if contaminated by crime, Germanicus leapt headlong from the tribunal. They blocked his departure with weapons, threatening him unless he went back up. *I will die rather than shed my loyalty!* he exclaimed and grabbed the sword at his side. It was out and heading for his chest, except that those closest took and forcefully restrained his right hand. (5) The furthest edge of the assembly, a mixed bunch, and – difficult to credit! – some individuals came closer urging him to strike. A soldier named Calusidius even drew and offered his sword, adding: *It's sharper.* This seemed brutal and wrong even to raving men and there was a lull in which Germanicus was hurried by friends into his tent.

36. There they discussed remedies. For reports kept arriving. *Envoys are being arranged for bringing the Upper army into the cause. The Ubian capital is designated for destruction,*[22] *and hands steeped in booty will burst free to ransack Gaul.* (2) Another fear was the enemy, aware of the Roman mutiny, and if the riverbank was abandoned, likely to invade. *But if auxiliary and allied troops are armed against defecting legions it means civil war. Strictness is dangerous, indulgence scandalous.*

*Whether nothing or everything is conceded to soldiers, the
state's position is precarious.* (3) So after comparing arguments
the decision was to write a letter in the Emperor's name. *Discharge is granted to men with twenty years' service. Those who
have done sixteen get a release; they remain in detachments,
exempt from everything but repelling the enemy. Augustus'
legacy* – which they had demanded – *is payable and doubled.*

37. The soldiers saw these terms as emergency fabrications
and demanded them immediately. Discharges were handled
quickly by officers; largesse was postponed for winter quarters.
Men of the Fifth and Twenty-first did not leave until, still in
summer quarters, the money – assembled from the travel allow-
ances of Germanicus himself and his friends – was paid in full.
(2) The First and Twentieth were led back to the Ubii by the
legate Caecina in a disgraceful column: money chests seized
from the commander rode among standards and eagles. (3) Germanicus set out for the Upper army. The Second, Thirteenth and
Sixteenth did not hesitate when he administered the military
oath; the Fourteenth delayed a little. Cash and discharges – even
though these legions did not insist – were delivered.

38. In Chaucan territory a mutiny was begun by a garrison
of detachments from disaffected legions. The immediate execution of two men brought some constraint. The order was given
by Manius Ennius, the camp superintendent, from fine precedent rather than actual authority. (2) With commotion still
swelling he fled but was found. Since hiding places were unreliable, he borrowed protection from boldness. *It is not a
superintendent but your general Germanicus and your Emperor
Tiberius that you are violating.* This dismayed his opponents,
and he immediately seized a standard and turned it towards the
Rhine. *Anyone who leaves the column will be considered a
deserter!* he shouted and led them back to winter quarters, disruptive but daring nothing.

39. Meanwhile the senate's envoys reached Germanicus
back at Cologne.[23] Two legions, the First and Twentieth, were
wintering there, plus, in detachments, their recently discharged
veterans. (2) Apprehensive and guilt-maddened, they were
open to fear. *They have come with the senate's instructions to*

nullify what we extorted by sedition! (3) As crowds regularly supply a 'defendant' even for false charges, they blamed Munatius Plancus, former consul, leader of the delegation, author of the senatorial decree.[24] Early that night they began to demand the standard in Germanicus' residence. With a rush to the entrance they worked open the doors, dragged him from his bedroom and, brandishing a death threat, forced him to surrender it. (4) Later, wandering the streets they encountered the envoys who, hearing about the scare, headed for Germanicus. The soldiers loaded them with insults and were preparing a killing, for Plancus especially, whose status impeded flight. The only recourse for the endangered man was the First's camp, where, as he clung to the standards and eagle, reverence provided security. Had the eagle-bearer Calpurnius not warded off violence verging on a rarity even between enemies, an envoy of the Roman people, in a Roman camp, would have stained the gods' altars with his blood. (5) Only at daybreak, when general and soldier recognized one another and what had been done, did Germanicus enter the camp. He ordered Plancus brought and received him onto the tribunal. (6) Then berating their blind frenzy – *its resurgence is due to the gods' anger, not the soldiers'* – he revealed why the envoys had come, expressing eloquent sorrow about embassy privilege and Plancus' serious and undeserved misfortune. *How much disgrace the legion has incurred!* The assembly stood stunned, not quiet, when he dismissed the envoys with a guard of auxiliary cavalry.

40. In that dangerous situation everyone criticized Germanicus for not going to the Upper army, where there was compliance and help against rebels. *Enough – more than enough! – mistakes were made with discharges and payments and mild measures.* (2) *Even if you hold your own well-being cheap, why keep your little son and pregnant wife among crazed men, violators of every human law? Restore them at least to their grandfather and the state.* (3) Germanicus hesitated long over his wife's refusal. *I am Augustus' descendant, not someone worthless in the face of danger!* she declared. Finally, embracing her pregnant belly and their common son and lamenting much, he got her to leave.

(4) They set out, a female and pitiable column: the General's
wife a refugee with her little son in her lap, in tears around her
his friends' wives, who were also taken away. And there was no
less gloom in those who stayed. 41. The sight was unlike that
of a prosperous Caesar or of a Caesar's camp: more like a captured city. The groaning and wailing attracted the ears and eyes
of the soldiers, even, who emerged from their tents. *What is
this tearful sound? This journey, so dismal? Notable women
have no centurion for protection, no soldier, nothing appropriate to a commander's wife, nothing of the customary entourage.
They are heading for the Treveri and the good faith of foreigners!* (2) Then came shame and compassion and the memory of
her father Agrippa and grandfather Augustus. *Drusus was her
father-in-law. She herself is a woman of impressive fecundity
and pre-eminent purity. Her child was born in camp and
brought up sharing the legions' tents.* (They called him – a soldier's word – 'Little Boot',[25] that being the footwear he generally
wore, to win crowd favour.) (3) But nothing so changed them
as resentment of the Treveri. Pleading and obstructing – *Come
back! Stay!* – some rushed up to Agrippina, most returned to
Germanicus. He, still fresh to grief and anger, began thus to the
men flocking round:

42. 'Wife and child are not dearer to me than father and
state, but my father will have the protection of his majesty and
Rome's empire that of other armies. I am removing my spouse,
my children – whom I would willingly offer up for destruction
if that served your glory – to somewhere far from madmen, so
that whatever crime impends is expiated by my blood only, so
that Augustus' great-grandson murdered and Tiberius'
daughter-in-law dead do not increase your guilt. (2) These
days, what have you left undared or undefiled? What name
shall I give to this gathering? Shall I call you soldiers, blockad-
ing your emperor's son with rampart and weapons? Or citizens,
so despising the senate's authority? You have shattered combat's rules, the sanctity of embassies and the law of nations.
(3) Caesar curbed an army mutiny with a single word by calling men refusing the military oath "civilians". Augustus
dismayed the legions at Actium with face and look. I am not

their like, but I am their descendant and if a soldier from Spain or Syria were rejecting me it would be strange and unwarranted. But the First and Twentieth! The Twentieth received its standards from Tiberius and you joined him in numerous battles – from which numerous rewards accrued! It's a fine thanks you give your general. (4) Am I to send this report to my father, who hears wholly happy news from other provinces? "Your own recruits, your own veterans are not satisfied with discharges and cash payments! Only here are centurions killed, officers cast out, envoys shut in. Camp and river are polluted with blood and I myself live on sufferance among men who hate me."

43. 'At that assembly, O my short-sighted friends, why did you take away the sword with which I intended to pierce my heart? He did a finer and fonder thing, the man who offered one: at least I would have fallen not yet complicit in my army's numerous crimes! And you would have chosen a general who would leave my death, perhaps, unpunished, but would avenge those of Varus and his three legions. (2) May the gods not allow the Belgae to have the honour and renown – although the offer stands – of rescuing the Roman name and subduing Germany's peoples! (3) May it be your spirit, Augustus, whose place is now heaven, and your image, Drusus my father, and the memory of you in these soldiers of yours, who are now open to decency and glory, that washes away this stain and turns citizen wrath towards enemy destruction! (4) And you too, men, in whom I now see new faces, new feelings, if you are now restoring to the senate their envoys, to your emperor your obedience, and to me my wife and child, move away from contagion, separate the troublemakers. This will be a foundation for remorse, and loyalty's tie.'

44. Suppliant at this, and declaring his reproaches true, they pleaded. *Punish the guilty, forgive the misguided, and lead us against the enemy! Recall your wife, let the legions' darling return! He should not be given to Gauls as hostage!* Agrippina's return Germanicus excused with the imminence of birth and winter. *But my son will return. The rest is for you to do.*

(2) They ran off transformed, tied up the most seditious and dragged them to the legate of the First, Gaius Caetronius, who determined verdict and punishment for each like this. The legions stood assembly-fashion but with drawn swords. The accused was brought forward on a platform by an officer. If they shouted 'Guilty!' he was sent headlong and slaughtered. (3) The soldiers rejoiced at the killings. *We are clearing ourselves!* And Germanicus did not stop them, since without orders from him both the deed's brutality and its resentment would be theirs.

(4) The veterans followed this example, and were then sent to Raetia. The pretext was defending the province against threatening Suebi, but the purpose was to extricate them from a camp still grim because of the remedy's harshness and likewise the memory of crime.

(5) Germanicus then reviewed the centurions. When called by the commander each stated his name, rank, birthplace, years of service, deeds of valour in battle and decorations, if any. If officers and legion affirmed his industry and innocence, he kept his rank. Whenever reproaches of greed or cruelty were unanimous, he was discharged.

45. The immediate problems settled thus, there remained one equally vast in the bravado of the Fifth and Twenty-first, which were wintering at the sixtieth milestone, a place called Vetera.[26] (2) These were the first to mutiny,[27] their hands committed the worst atrocities. Neither dismayed by the punishment of fellow-soldiers, nor moved by their remorse, they remained angry. Accordingly, Germanicus prepared to send weapons, fleet and allies down the Rhine. *If they refuse my command, I will decide the issue by war.*

46. In Rome the outcome in Illyricum was still unknown when news of the German legions' uprising arrived. A frightened community criticized Tiberius. *While he teases senate and people – powerless and weaponless! – with mock hesitation, soldiers mutiny! The still-immature authority of two young men cannot curb them.* (2) *He should have gone himself and confronted them with his imperial majesty. They would have*

yielded if they had seen an emperor with long experience,
supreme in both severity and generosity. (3) *Wasn't Augustus,*
even in weary age, capable of numerous trips to Germany? And
yet Tiberius, in his prime, sits among the senators, playing word
games. He has done enough for Rome's servility; the soldiers'
morale needs patching up so they are willing to endure peace.

47. Unmoved by such talk, indeed fixed, was Tiberius' intention not to leave the capital or put himself and the state at risk.
For he had many countervalent worries. *The army spread*
around Germany is stronger, the army in Pannonia is closer.
The former relies on Gaul's resources, the latter threatens Italy.
So which do I put first? I don't want those put second to be
provoked by the slight. The approach by my sons is even-
handed and avoids harm to my majesty, which gets greater
reverence from a distance. And it's excused in young men if
they refer some things to their father. Soldiers who stand up to
Germanicus or Drusus can be appeased or broken by me, but
what other help is there if they defy the Emperor? Still, as if just
on the point of departure, he chose companions, collected
supplies, equipped ships. Later, with winter or business as con-
tradictory excuses, he fooled first the insightful, then the people,
then the provinces for a very long time.

48. Germanicus, though having an army in hand and punishment ready for the defectors, thought the men should still
have time[28] to show whether, following recent precedent, they
would see to their own affairs. He wrote to Caecina: *I am com-*
ing with a strong force. If they don't punish evildoers first, I
will use indiscriminate killing. (2) Caecina read this secretly to
eagle- and standard-bearers and to the soundest element in
camp. *Free everyone from infamy and yourselves from death,*
he urged. *In peacetime, issues of responsibility and justice get*
consideration, but under war's pressure innocent and guilty
perish equally. (3) After testing individuals they deemed suitable and seeing the majority of the troops obedient, they set a
time, on Caecina's recommendation, *for an armed attack on*
those who are the worst disgraces, eager for sedition. A signal
was exchanged, then they burst into tents and butchered men

unawares. Only the plotters knew the origin of the killing – and its endpoint.

49. The sight was different from that of any civil war anywhere. Not in battle, not from opposing camps, but in their own quarters, the men – together by day at meals, together by night at rest – took sides and wielded weapons. Shouting, wounds and blood were there to see, but the reason was hidden. Chance ruled the rest. Some good men were killed, too, after the worst offenders, seeing the targets of violence, armed themselves. (2) Neither general nor officer was present as a restraint. The masses were given licence – and vengeance to the full. Later Germanicus entered the camp. *That was not a cure*, he said tearfully, *but a calamity*. He ordered the bodies burnt.

(3) Morale was still grim when desire possessed them of marching against the enemy – expiation for madness. *There is no other way to appease the shades of our fellow-soldiers, except by taking honourable wounds on our guilty chests.* (4) Germanicus went along with his soldiers' fervour. Via a bridge connection he crossed 12,000 men from the legions, 26 allied infantry cohorts,[29] and 8 cavalry units. (In this mutiny their restraint remained inviolate.)

50. The Germans were happily active nearby, while first mourning for the loss of Augustus then discord held us in its grip. The Roman general, marching rapidly, breached the Caesian Forest, a frontier road begun by Tiberius. He established camp on the road, fortifying front and back with a rampart, the sides with felled trees. (2) From there Germanicus was going through dark woods and of two routes debated whether to take the usual short one or the more difficult one, untried and therefore unattended to by the enemy. (3) The longer was chosen and everything sped up: scouts had reported a German holiday that night, an entertainment with ceremonial feasting. Caecina's orders were to go ahead with unencumbered units and clear the forest obstacles. Legions followed at a short distance. (4) Night helped with brilliant stars. Arriving at Marsian villages they took positions surrounding men still lying abed or beside tables – without fear and without posting guards.

Everything was carelessly chaotic. There was no fear of war
and even peace is languid and lax among drunkards.

51. Germanicus divided his avid legions into four wedges to
widen the plundering. With sword and flames he ravaged a
fifty-mile swath. Neither sex nor age won compassion. Things
profane, things sacred – including those nations' most celebrated sanctum, 'Tanfana's' – were levelled to the ground.
Unscathed, his soldiers had cut down men half-asleep, weaponless or wandering. (2) The carnage roused the Bructeri, Tubantes
and Usipetes to occupy the woods on the army's retreat. This
was known to Germanicus and he proceeded with march – and
battle. Half the cavalry and the auxiliary cohorts led, then the
First and around the baggage the Twenty-first sealed the left
flank, the Fifth the right. The Twentieth secured the rear and
behind them the remaining allies. (3) The enemy remained
motionless until the column was strung out through the woods.
Then, while making limited feints on front and flanks, they
attacked the rearguard full force. Confusion ensued among the
rapid-deployment cohorts at the dense German hordes, but
then Germanicus rode up to the Twentieth. *This is your opportunity to obliterate the mutiny!* he shouted. *Go ahead, make
haste to convert guilt into glory!* (4) Afire, they broke through
the enemy with a concerted thrust, drove them into the open
and cut them down. Meanwhile the troops at the column's head
escaped the forest and fortified a camp. Thereafter the journey
was quiet. Optimistic, given recent events – earlier ones they
forgot – the soldiers were placed in winter quarters.

52. The news caused Tiberius joy and worry. He rejoiced
that sedition was suppressed. But the fact that, with extravagant expenditure and early discharge, Germanicus had sought
the soldiers' goodwill, and Germanicus' martial glory, too,
made him anxious. (2) He nevertheless reported Germanicus'
achievements to the senate with many a reference to his valour
and too much showy verbal decoration for people to believe
the sentiments deeply felt. (3) He praised Drusus and the end of
the Illyricum uprising in fewer words, but more earnestly and
with a credible speech. And upheld all of Germanicus' indul-
gences in Pannonia's armies, too.

53. That same year Julia reached her final day. She was shut away for unchastity by her father Augustus, first on Pandateria, then in the town of the Regini,[30] who live beside the Sicilian strait. She was wife to Tiberius when Gaius and Lucius Caesar were flourishing and despised him as an inferior. (This was the fundamental reason for Tiberius' withdrawal to Rhodes.) (2) Once he was in power and she an outcast – disgraced and, after Agrippa Postumus' death, destitute of all hope – he killed her with poverty and long decay. *The murder will be obscured by her lengthy exile,*[31] he thought. (3) The same motivation for brutality obtained against Sempronius Gracchus, a man of noble family, clever of wit and perversely eloquent, who violated Julia during her marriage to Agrippa. Nor was that the end of their affair. Passed on to Tiberius, she was kept ablaze by her persistent lover with defiance and hatred of her husband. A letter critical of Tiberius that Julia wrote to her father was, people thought, written by Gracchus. (4) Banished, accordingly, to Cercina, an island off Africa, he tolerated exile for fourteen years. (5) The soldiers then sent for killing found him on a promontory with no happy prospects. At their arrival he requested a brief moment for writing final instructions to his wife Alliaria, and offered his neck to the assassins: in the constancy of his death not unworthy of the Sempronian name, in life a disgrace. (6) The soldiers were sent not from Rome but from Africa's governor Lucius Asprenas, according to some reports. Tiberius was their source; he had hoped in vain that talk about the murder could be deflected onto Asprenas.

54. The year likewise acquired new ceremonies. A priesthood, the Augustan Brotherhood, was added, just as Titus Tatius once instituted the Titius Brotherhood to preserve Sabine rituals. They were chosen by lot, twenty-one of Rome's elite, plus Tiberius, Drusus, Claudius and Germanicus. (2) The Augustan Games initiated then were disturbed by strife in the actors' contest. (Augustus was indulgent to that competition to gratify Maecenas' effusive love for Bathyllus. He did not distance himself from such pursuits and thought it citizen-like to engage in the crowd's pleasures. Tiberius' character was otherwise. But

the populace had been pampered for many years and Tiberius did not yet dare[32] divert it to tougher conditions.)

55. (15 CE) Drusus Caesar, Gaius Norbanus, consuls.

Germanicus was decreed a triumph, but still had a war. Though making full-scale preparations for the summer, he anticipated at spring's beginning with a sudden raid against the Chatti. For hope had arisen that the enemy was split between Arminius and Segestes, notable men both – for perfidy towards us, or loyalty.

((2) Arminius was an agitator in Germany; Segestes disclosed rebellion preparations, especially at the last feast before the fight, and urged Varus to arrest him and Arminius and the other leading men. *The populace won't dare anything if their leaders are removed, and you will have time to distinguish between crimes and innocent men.* (3) But Varus fell to fate and Arminius' might. Segestes, though dragged into war by his people's consensus, remained a dissenter, his hatred the stronger on personal grounds, since Arminius had seized his already betrothed daughter. The son-in-law was hated by his hostile father-in-law: ties of affection in congenial men, spurs to anger in hostile ones.)

56. Accordingly, Germanicus gave Caecina four legions, 5,000 auxiliary troops and some emergency levies of Germans from our side of the Rhine. He himself led as many legions and double the number of allies. Establishing a stronghold on the traces of his father's garrison on the Taunus, he hurried his unencumbered army against the Chatti. Lucius Apronius[33] was left for construction work on road and river. (2) A rarity in that climate, a drought, and low rivers made the march unimpeded and swift; rain and river increases were a worry for the return. (3) He reached the Chatti so unforeseen that people of non-combatant age and sex were immediately captured or slain. The men had crossed the Eder by swimming and parried the Romans beginning their bridge. Then, driven back by artillery and arrows, they tried in vain for peace terms. When some deserted to Germanicus, the rest, abandoning settlements and villages, dispersed into the forests. (4) Germanicus, after burning their capital Mattium and pillaging open terrain, returned towards the Rhine.

The enemy did not dare harass the rearguard, which is their habit when strategy rather than fear has caused them to yield. (5) The Cherusci had intended to help the Chatti, but Caecina deterred them by showing arms here and there. The Marsi dared an engagement, but with a successful battle he checked them.

57. Envoys arrived from Segestes begging help against the violence of his countrymen, by whom he was besieged, Arminius being more influential with them because he urged war: to barbarians, the readier a man is for bold action the more reliable and effective he is considered in troubled times.

((2) Segestes had added to the delegation his son Segimundus. Conscious of guilt, Segimundus hesitated. (In the year of Germany's revolt, a priest at the Altar of the Ubii, he tore up his priestly insignia and fled to the rebels.) Induced to hope, nevertheless, for Roman clemency, he brought his father's instructions. He was kindly received and sent under guard to the Rhine's Gallic bank.)

(3) For Germanicus, diverting his march paid off. They fought the besiegers and extracted Segestes with a large group of relatives and dependants, (4) including nobly born women, among them Arminius' wife, Segestes' daughter. More like her husband in character than her father, she was neither reduced to tears nor suppliant: hands firmly in her lap, she kept her eyes on her pregnant belly. (5) Spoils, too, were brought, items from the Varian disaster given as booty to several of those surrendering. Plus Segestes himself, huge to see and, remembering a virtuous alliance, unafraid.

58. His words were of this sort: 'For me, today is not the first day of loyalty and constancy towards the Roman people. Ever since I was given citizenship by Augustus I have chosen friends and enemies by your advantage. Not from hatred of my country (for traitors are hateful – even to the side they privilege) but because in my view Roman and German interests are the same: peace, not war. (2) So I denounced the man who stole my daughter and violated your treaty, Arminius, to Varus, who was then at the army's head. Kept waiting by the General's indolence, and since laws were no help, I demanded that he arrest me and Arminius and his conspirators. That night is my

witness – would that it was my last! (3) Subsequent events can better be decried than defended. But I both put Arminius in chains and suffered chains from his supporters. And as soon as your help was available I chose old over new, quiet over trouble. Not for any reward, but to clear myself of perfidy, and likewise as a suitable mediator for the German people, in case regret rather than ruin is their choice. (4) For my son's youthful error I ask forgiveness. My daughter, I admit, was brought under compulsion. Yours to determine which prevails: that she carries Arminius' child or is a child of mine.'

(5) Germanicus' response was merciful: for Segestes' children and relatives he promised security, and for Segestes a home in the old province. He led his army back and received the 'Victorious General' title on Tiberius' authority.

(6) Arminius' wife produced offspring of the male sex. The boy was raised at Ravenna. The derision that he contended with I will report[34] in time.

59. The story spread of Segestes' surrender and kind welcome, meeting with hope or offence according to people's unwillingness or desire for war. Arminius, maddened beyond his innate violence by the seizure of his wife and the subjection of her progeny to slavery, rushed among the Cherusci demanding arms against Segestes, arms against Germanicus, (2) not refraining from insult. *A fine father! A great commander! A powerful army! So many hands carrying off one young woman!* (3) *Three legions and three legates succumbed to me. I wage war not by betrayal or against pregnant women, but in the open against armed men. You can still see in Germany's groves the Roman standards that I hung up to our ancestral gods.* (4) *Segestes can live on a conquered shore, restore a priesthood[35] to his son – Germans will never live down the sight of rods and axes and toga[36] between Elbe and Rhine.* (5) *To other peoples, ignorant of the Roman Empire, executions are unfamiliar, taxes unknown. But since we shed these things – and Augustus withdrew thwarted, that Augustus now among the gods, as did his picked man, Tiberius – let's not be scared of an inexperienced youth, a mutinous army!* (6) *If you prefer country, parents and ancient ways to masters and new settlements,*

*follow Arminius to glory and freedom, not Segestes to shame-
ful enslavement.*

60. He roused with these words not only the Cherusci but
also bordering peoples and drew into his cause Inguiomerus,
his uncle, a man of long-standing authority with the Romans.
This increased Germanicus' fear. (2) Lest war encroach massed
and single, he sent Caecina with forty Roman cohorts through
the Bructeri to the Ems, to divide the enemy. An auxiliary
officer, Pedo, led the cavalry through Frisian territory. Germanicus himself embarked four legions and went by water. Infantry,
cavalry and fleet converged simultaneously at the pre-determined
river. When the Chauci promised auxiliaries, they were added
as fellow-soldiers. (3) As the Bructeri began burning their possessions, Lucius Stertinius and an unencumbered unit sent by
Germanicus routed them. Amidst the carnage and booty he
found the Nineteenth's eagle, lost with Varus. The column was
then led to the furthest Bructeri and everything between Ems
and Weser pillaged. Nearby was the Teutoberg Forest, in which
the remains of Varus and his legions were said to lie unburied.

61. A desire assailed Germanicus: to pay final respects to
soldiers and general. The universal feeling in the army was
compassion, for kinfolk, for friends, for wars' fortunes and
human destiny. Caecina was sent ahead to investigate the
wood's secrets and raise causeways in the marshy wetness and
treacherous terrain. Then they entered the gloomy place, hideous in appearance and memory. (2) Varus' first camp, with a
wide perimeter road and demarcated headquarters, showed the
handiwork of three legions. From a low-heaped rampart and
shallow ditch one could see the base of the survivors' thinned
ranks. At the battlefield's centre, bones lay whitening, scattered
or heaped where men had fled or resisted. (3) Alongside were
fragments of weapons and the limbs of horses and, affixed to
tree trunks, skulls. In nearby groves were the barbarian altars
where they sacrificed officers and chief centurions. (4) Survivors of that disaster (they had slipped away from battle or
captivity) gave the report. *Here the legates fell; there the eagles
were seized.* They told where Varus was first wounded, where,
with his unlucky right hand, he found self-inflicted death. And

what platform Arminius spoke from, how many stocks there were for captives, and pits, and how, in his arrogance, Arminius mocked the standards and eagles.

62. The entire army, present six years after the disaster, began to inter the bones of three legions. No one knew whether he was burying the remains of stranger or friend. But everyone, as if these were relatives and blood kin, and with his anger at the enemy augmented, was both sorrowful and hostile. The first of the turves for building the mound was placed by Germanicus, a pleasing tribute to the dead by one allied in grief with those present. ((2) Tiberius did not approve, either interpreting everything of Germanicus' for the worse, or else he believed that the sight of unburied casualties made an army slower for battle and more cowardly towards enemies. *A commander responsible for augury and our most ancient rites should not have handled dead remains.*)

63. Germanicus followed Arminius withdrawing into trackless parts. At the first opportunity he ordered the cavalry to charge and take an enemy-occupied field. Arminius' men had instructions to mass near the trees. He turned them suddenly and gave the sally-signal to men hidden in the woods. (2) The cavalry was disrupted by the new front. Cohorts sent in support but broken by a line of fleeing men increased everyone's panic. They were being forced into a marsh familiar to the winning side and unfavourable to the inexperienced, except that Germanicus led out and deployed the legions, bringing the enemy terror, the soldiers confidence. The fight was a draw and they disengaged.

(3) Germanicus withdrew the army to the Ems, then transported his legions by ship, as they had come. Some cavalry were ordered to the Rhine via the Ocean shore.

Caecina led his own troops. He was returning by a known route, but was nevertheless instructed to pass the long causeways as soon as possible. (4) This narrow track amidst vast marshes was built up long ago by Lucius Domitius.[37] The rest was mudflat, clinging with heavy clay or hazardous with streams. Surrounding it were gently sloping forests – filled by Arminius. Using shortcuts and forced marches he had arrived ahead of soldiers burdened with baggage and weapons. (5) Caecina worried about how to rebuild the age-shattered causeways while repelling the enemy. He decided to lay out camp there, so that construction could start while others fought.

64. The barbarians, struggling to break through the outposts and press the workers, harried, encircled and attacked to the mingled shouting of labourers and fighters. (2) Everything was uniformly unfavourable to the Romans: their position in a deep bog, shifting underfoot and slippery for movement, their bodies weighed down by armour; and they couldn't wield pikes in water. But the Cherusci were accustomed to marsh battles. They had long limbs and huge lances for wounding even from a distance. (3) Night finally freed the failing legions from an unequal fight. The Germans, with the energy of success, did not rest even then, diverting all the springs in the surrounding heights onto the bottomland. The flooded ground and submerged work doubled the soldiers' task. (4) This was Caecina's fortieth campaign under or in command and, knowing success as well as uncertainty, he was undismayed. Pondering the future, the only plan he found was to keep the enemy among the trees while the wounded and heavier part of his column went ahead. For between the hills and swamps was a stretch of level ground permitting a slender line. (5) He chose the Fifth for the right flank, the Twenty-first for the left, the First to lead the column, the Twentieth against the pursuit.

65. Night was restless on both sides. The barbarians' celebratory feasts, happy singing and implacable noise filled valley bottoms and echoing woods. In the Roman camp the fires were feeble, voices halting. Men rested near the rampart or wandered among the tents, sleepless rather than watchful. (2) The General was terrified by a ghastly dream: Varus, blood-smeared and risen from the marsh. He seemed to see and hear him beckoning, but did not follow and pushed away the outstretched hand. (3) At daybreak the legions dispatched to the flanks, either afraid or defiant, deserted their position and quickly seized level ground beyond the wet. (4) Arminius, though free to attack, did not make an immediate sally. But when the baggage was stuck in the mud, with the soldiers in confusion

around it, the standards in disarray and, as happens at such moments, everyone quick for himself with ears slow to orders, then he ordered the Germans to go in, shouting 'It's Varus and his legions again, caught by the same fate!' With picked men he cut through the column, wounding horses especially. (5) Sliding in their own blood and the marsh slipperiness, they threw their riders, then scattered those nearby and trampled the fallen. The worst trouble was around the eagles, which couldn't be carried against the press of weapons or planted in muddy ground. (6) Caecina was holding the line until, with his horse run through, he fell and was surrounded, except that the First intervened. Help came from the enemy's greed: killing was forgotten while pursuing booty. The legions struggled out, as day turned to evening, onto open and solid ground. (7) Nor was this the end of their misery. A rampart had to be built and the material for it found, but most of the earth-moving and turf-cutting tools were lost. No tents for the troops, no bandages for the wounded. Sharing out food filthy with mud and blood, they lamented the death-like darkness. *So many thousands of men with only one day left!*

66. A horse chanced to break free. Roaming terrified by the shouting, it caused havoc among those converging. So great was the consternation – *The Germans have broken in!* people believed – that everyone rushed the gates, especially the gate away from the enemy and safer for men in flight. (2) Caecina discovered the fear to be groundless, and when neither authority nor pleas nor even grabbing hold enabled him to block or stop his soldiers, he flung himself onto the gate threshold. Compassion finally – since going out required stepping over their commander's body – closed the way, while officers explained: *False alarm*.

67. The men were assembled at headquarters and ordered to hear Caecina's words in silence. *It is a critical moment*, he warned them. *Safety lies in weapons alone – together with a plan. We must stay inside the rampart until the enemy, in the hope of storming it, comes closer. Then, a sally on all sides. A sally gets us to the Rhine.* (2) *But if you flee, you face more forests, deeper swamps and enemy brutality. Victors get*

honour and glory, he reminded them, and spoke of things loved at home and honourable in camp. He was silent about failure. (3) Legates' and officers' horses, beginning with his own, he gave – without favouritism – to the bravest fighters; these first, then the infantry, were to attack the enemy.

68. The Germans were no less restless with hope, desire and leader disagreements. *Let's allow them to leave, and once they are out, surround them again stuck in the wet*, urged Arminius. Inguiomerus urged more vigorous action, which barbarians like. *Let's take arms and encircle the rampart! Storming it will be easy. More captives for us and booty intact.* (2) So at dawn they demolished the ditches, tossed bundled branches in and seized the rampart's summit, where the infrequent soldiers were apparently transfixed by fear. (3) When the enemy was slowed by the defences, the signal was given to the troops; horns[38] chorused. Then with a shout and a rush they surrounded the Germans from behind, jeering. *No forests and swamps here! Our positions are equally favourable, as are our gods!* (4) To the enemy – *easy killing, a few men and poorly armed*, they thought – the sound of horns and flash of arms were unexpected, their impact the greater. Men fell, greedy in successes but careless in reverses. (5) Arminius left the fight unscathed, Inguiomerus after a grievous wound. The masses were slaughtered while anger and daylight lasted. At night, finally, the legions turned back. Although more wounds and the same want of food caused suffering, they had strength, health, supplies – everything! – in victory.

69. Meanwhile word of the surrounded army had spread. *A hostile column of Germans is heading for Gaul!* Had Agrippina not prevented them breaking the Rhine bridge, there were men brazen enough, in their alarm, for that outrage. But a woman huge of spirit assumed the leader's role then, and to soldiers destitute or wounded she distributed clothing and bandages. (2) Pliny,[39] author of *German Wars*, says that she stood at the bridgehead praising and thanking the returning legions. This made its way deep into Tiberius' consciousness. (3) *These attentions are not ingenuous, nor is the soldiers' favour sought for opposing foreigners.* (4) *Nothing is left for*

commanders when a woman inspects troops, approaches standards, tests largesse. As if there wasn't enough favour-seeking in showing off the general's son in military garb, and wanting a Caesar to be called 'Little Boot'. Agrippina now has more power among the armies than do legates and generals. A mutiny that the Emperor's name could not stop – suppressed by a woman! (5) Thoughts that were inflamed and aggravated by Sejanus, with his knowledge of Tiberius' character, sowing hatreds far afield to cover, and then, when grown, bring forth.

70. Germanicus handed the Second and Fourteenth (of the legions he had transported by boat) to Publius Vitellius[40] to take by land, so that a lighter fleet would sail shallow waters and run aground when they ebbed. (2) Vitellius' journey, at first, on dry ground or with limited wave encroachment, was calm. Later, with the north wind gusting, as well as the equinox (when Ocean's swelling is greatest), his column was pulled and pushed and the land was swamped. Sea, shore and field had the same appearance, nor could uncertain ground be distinguished from solid, shallow water from deep. (3) They were toppled by waves, swallowed by whirlpools. Animals, baggage and lifeless bodies floated among and against them. Units were mingled, above water sometimes only as far as chest or face, and occasionally, when the ground fell away, scattered and drowned. Voices didn't help, nor mutual exhortations, against the waves. Valiant men or cowards, wise or foolish, plans or chance – it made no difference. Everything was equally enveloped in violence. (4) Finally, Vitellius struggled onto higher ground and drew up there. They spent the night without supplies, without fire, the majority with bodies naked and bruised, scarcely less wretched than men surrounded by an enemy: there, honourable death is possible, but these faced inglorious destruction. (5) Light brought the land back and they pushed through to the river that Germanicus had reached with the fleet. The legions were then embarked, although spreading rumour had them drowned. Nor did people believe in their safety until they saw Germanicus and his army returning.

71. Stertinius, dispatched for the surrender of Segimerus, Segestes' brother, escorted him and his son to Cologne. Each

was pardoned, Segimerus easily, his son with more reluctance. *He molested Varus' corpse!* people said. (2) Replenishing the army's losses became a contest between Gaul, Spain and Italy, each offering what it had available: arms, horses, gold. Germanicus praised their zeal, but accepted only arms and horses for the war. The soldiers' financial assistance he provided himself. (3) To ease the memory of the disaster by affability, too, he visited the wounded, extolled the deeds of each with eyes on the man's wounds. He made them resolute for himself and for battle, one man with hope, another with glory, all with conversation and attention.

72. Decreed that year: honorary triumphs for Caecina, Apronius and Silius for their achievements with Germanicus. The title 'Father of his Country', frequently pressed on him by the people, Tiberius rejected. Nor did he allow oaths of obedience, despite the senate's urging. *Everything mortals have is uncertain, and the more I get, the more precarious my position is,* he maintained. (2) But he did not thereby gain credit for a citizen-like attitude, for he had brought back the treason law.

(Its name was the same in the past, but the cases before the court were different: men who damaged the army by betrayal or the populace with seditions or, by conducting state business improperly, diminished the majesty of the Roman people. Deeds were accused, words had impunity. (3) Augustus was the first to hold a hearing about libellous pamphlets under this law's pretext. He was dismayed by Cassius Severus'[41] wantonness, which prompted defamatory attacks on notable men and women. Then Tiberius, when asked by the praetor Pompeius Macer whether to hear treason cases, replied: *Laws are to be used.* (4) He, too, was provoked by poems, published under dubious names, about his brutality and arrogance and misunderstandings with his mother.)

73. I am not averse to reporting the preliminary charges attempted against Faianius and Rubrius, men of modest equestrian rank, so that people know from what beginnings and with what strategy on Tiberius' part an utterly ruinous affliction crept in, was checked, then blazed forth and took hold of everything. (2) Faianius' accuser reproached him for having

included among his 'Augustus-attendants' (they existed in
every household, like priesthoods) a certain mime actor Cassius of bodily disrepute. And for having transferred ownership
of a statue of Augustus when selling his park. Rubrius' charge
was having offended Augustus' divinity by perjury. (3) When
these came to Tiberius' attention, he wrote to the consuls.
*Divine status for my father was not decreed for the honour to
be diverted into fellow citizens' ruin. The actor Cassius, like
others of that profession, participated in the festival my mother
devoted to Augustus' memory. And it is not sacrilege if Augustus' likenesses, like other divine representations, accrue to the
sale of parks and houses. (4) As for the oath, the same applies
as if Rubrius had sworn falsely by Jupiter: injuries to gods are
the gods' concern.*

74. Shortly thereafter Granius Marcellus, Bithynia's governor, was indicted for treason by his quaestor Caepio
Crispinus. (Caepio was supported by Romanius Hispo, who
initiated a livelihood that the misery of the period and human
brazenness later made widespread. (2) Needy, unknown, and
restless, using secret petitions to access the Emperor's brutality,
then exposing the most eminent to danger, he achieved power
with one man and hatred with the rest, and set the pattern
according to which poor men became rich and contemptible
men formidable, devising ruin for others – and eventually for
themselves.) (3) Caepio pretended that Marcellus spoke un-
favourably about Tiberius, an inescapable charge, since the
accuser selected the foulest of Tiberius' habits for his indictment: since they were true, they were also uttered, people
believed. Hispo added that a statue of Marcellus sat higher
than those of Caesars, and that in another, the head of Augustus had been cut off and replaced by a likeness of Tiberius.
(4) At this, Tiberius blazed so hot that, shattering his taciturnity,
he proclaimed: *I, too, will give an opinion about this case,
openly and under oath.* His aim was that the rest feel obliged to
do likewise. (5) But there were still traces of dying liberty.
Gnaeus Piso said, 'In what order, Caesar, will you give your
opinion? If first, I will have a lead to follow. But if after everyone's, I fear I may unwittingly disagree.' (6) Troubled, and with

patience commensurate with the rashness of his flare-up, Tiberius tolerated the defendant's acquittal on the treason charge. An extortion charge went forward to assessors.

75. Not sated by senate hearings, Tiberius sat in courtrooms, too, at the tribunal's edge so as not to displace the presiding magistrate. Many of the decisions made in his presence countered bribery and powerful men's pleas – but in the service of truth liberty was impaired.

(2) Meanwhile the senator Aurelius Pius brought a complaint – *The construction of a public road and aqueduct has ruined my house* – and appealed to the senate. Treasury officials resisted, but Tiberius provided relief and paid the house price to Aurelius, since expenditures for honourable ends gave him pleasure, a virtue he long retained while shedding the rest. (3) When the ex-praetor Propertius Celer requested a poverty exemption from senatorial rank, Tiberius gave him a million sesterces after ascertaining that Celer inherited his predicament. (4) Others attempting the same thing he ordered to get the senate's approval: in his desire for strictness he seemed, even when acting properly, harsh. So the rest preferred silence and poverty to confession and charity.

76. That same year the Tiber, raised by continuous rains, flooded Rome's low ground. Its receding brought material and human wreckage. Asinius Gallus therefore proposed consulting the Sibylline Books. Tiberius refused, a man given to concealing divine and human matters alike. But remediation – controlling the river – was assigned to Ateius Capito and Lucius Arruntius.

(2) Achaea and Macedonia protested their tax burden. Temporary relief from senatorial administration and transfer to the Emperor was the decision.

(3) At a gladiatorial show offered in the name of Germanicus and Drusus, Drusus presided. (Blood, however worthless, was too much his delight, which inspired fear in the crowd and, people said, his father's criticism.) (4) Why Tiberius himself stayed away was variously interpreted. For some, it was due to his aversion to company, for others, to a sour character and worry about comparison with Augustus, whose attendance

showed affability. I am not inclined to credit this: *He gave his son an opportunity to show his brutality and arouse popular grievances.* But it, too, was said.

77. The theatre-related licence[42] that began the previous year broke out more seriously, with deaths in the audience and for soldiers and a centurion, and a Guard officer wounded during their attempt to prevent insults to magistrates and strife in the crowd. (2) In the senate discussion about this seditiousness, the motion that praetors should have the authority to flog actors (3) was vetoed by Haterius Agrippa,[43] a plebeian tribune. He was berated in a speech by Asinius Gallus, to silence from Tiberius, who used to provide the senate with these semblances of liberty. But the veto stood, since Augustus once ruled that actors were exempt from flogging and, to Tiberius, it was wrong to break Augustus' pronouncements. (4) About salary caps and impediments to fan carousing there were many decrees, the most significant being: no senator to enter a mime actor's house, men of equestrian rank not to escort them in public, shows to be given only in the theatre, and punishing spectator excess with exile to be within the praetors' power.

78. Permission to build an Augustus temple at Tarraco, sought by Spain, was granted, setting an example for every province. (2) The 1 per cent sales tax[44] instituted after the civil wars (the people were protesting it) was, Tiberius decreed, the foundation of the military treasury. Plus: *The state cannot support veteran discharges except after twenty years' service.* So the mistakes made during the recent mutiny, through which a sixteen-year term was extorted, were nullified for the future.

79. Next, a discussion was started in the senate by Arruntius and Ateius. *In order to control the Tiber's overflows, should the rivers and lakes that strengthen it be diverted?* There were hearings for municipal delegations.[45] Florentines pleaded that the Chiana not be moved from its customary bed into the Arno. *Ruinous for us!* (2) Comparable statements came from Interamnates. *It means destruction for Italy's most fertile fields, if the Nera* – as was planned – *is split into channels and overflows.* (3) Nor did Reatines stay silent, refusing a dam at Lake Velinus where it empties into the Nera, since it would burst

into adjoining areas. *The best arrangements for human affairs are nature's.*[46] *She has given rivers their outlets and beds, their source as well as their endpoints. Consideration should be given, too, to religion: your allies consecrated rites and groves and altars to the streams of their ancestors. Moreover, Tiber himself does not want to flow, bereft of his neighbour rivers, with diminished glory.* (4) Either the towns' pleas or the task's difficulty or religious belief prevailed and Piso's[47] opinion was accepted. *Nothing should be changed*, he had moved.

80. Extended: Poppaeus Sabinus'[48] governorship in Moesia, with Achaea and Macedonia added. This, too, was characteristic of Tiberius: prolonging commands and keeping people – some until life's end! – in the same armies and judicial posts. (2) Various explanations are given. For some, it was from his aversion to any new responsibility that arrangements once decided were preserved in perpetuity. For others, from jealousy, lest there be more beneficiaries. There are also people who judge him, despite his innate cunning, to have been anxious about decisions. For he did not seek outstanding virtues and yet shunned vices. *The best men are a source of danger for me, the worst, of disgrace for the state*, he feared. (3) Such paralysis eventually brought him to the point of entrusting provinces to men whom he would not allow to leave Rome.

81. Concerning consular elections, as held first then under Tiberius and subsequently, I scarcely dare affirm anything, so conflicting are my findings in both historians and Tiberius' own speeches. (2) Sometimes, omitting the candidates' names, he sketched their background, life and military service to identify them. (3) Occasionally he omitted these indications, too, and urged candidates not to disturb the elections with vote-getting. *I will see to that*, he promised. (4) Generally, he just said that the candidates who registered with him were those whose names he gave to the consuls. *Others, too, can register if they are confident of influence or merit.* Fine words, but in reality empty or duplicitous: the more elaborate the façade of liberty covering them, the more potential they had to erupt into menacing servitude.

BOOK 2

1. (16 CE) Statilius Taurus Sisenna, Lucius Libo, consuls.

Trouble in Eastern kingdoms and Roman provinces originated with the Parthians: after requesting and receiving from Rome a king, although he was Arsacid by birth, they rejected him as foreign. (2) This was Vonones, a hostage given to Augustus by Phraates. (Phraates,[1] although he repelled Roman armies and leaders, employed every form of homage towards Augustus and sent some offspring to consolidate their friendship – less from fear of us than distrusting his population's loyalty.)

2. After the death of Phraates and subsequent kings, internal carnage brought to Rome envoys from Parthia's leading men with a summons for Vonones, eldest of Phraates' children. This enhanced his own eminence, Augustus believed, and he strengthened Vonones financially. The barbarians received him rejoicing – the usual response to new regimes. (2) Then came shame. *Decadent Parthians! Seeking from an alien world a king infected with enemy ways! The Arsacid throne is now held and bestowed as one of Rome's provinces! Where is the glory of Crassus' killers and Antony's evicters if Augustus' lackey – so many years of servitude endured! – gives the Parthians orders?* (3) Inflaming their scorn was Vonones himself, divergent from ancestral practices: the infrequency of his hunting, his listless attention to horses, the litter-conveyance he generally used in cities, his contempt for traditional feasts. Other sources of ridicule: Greek companions and safe-keeping for supplies of trivial value. (4) Ready access and outgoing affability were unfamiliar to Parthians as virtues, strange as vices. And since

his ways were foreign to their customs, hatred accrued equally
to the perverse and the honourable.

3. Accordingly, Artabanus,[2] an Arsacid by blood, raised
among the Dahae, was encouraged. Routed in the first encounter, he repaired his forces and gained royal power. Defeated
Vonones had Armenia as refuge. It was rulerless then and,
though located between Parthian and Roman forces, untrustworthy[3] because of Antony's crime: Artavasdes, the Armenians'
king, was lured out by him with a show of friendship, then
loaded with chains and finally killed. (2) Artavasdes' son
Artaxias, remembering his father and hostile to us, used Arsacid
might for his own and his kingdom's security. After Artaxias
was killed by kinfolk plotting, Tigranes was bestowed by
Augustus on the Armenians and escorted to his kingdom by
Tiberius. Tigranes did not have longlasting dominion, nor did
his children, despite their being joined – foreign ways! – in both
matrimony and royal power.

4. Then on Augustus' order Artavasdes was imposed. His
ejection involved calamity for us. At this point Gaius Caesar
was chosen to organize Armenia. He put Ariobarzanes – Median
by origin – over Armenians well-disposed because of his striking physical beauty and pre-eminent genius. (2) When accidental
death removed Ariobarzanes, they had scarce tolerance for his
line. After trying a woman ruler – Erato by name, soon
expelled – they were aimless and adrift, more rulerless than free,
and welcomed the fleeing Vonones to royal power. (3) This
brought threats from Artabanus. The Armenians were an inadequate prop and for our might to be Vonones' defence required
beginning a war against the Parthians. So Creticus Silanus,[4]
Syria's governor, sent for him and supplied guards, leaving him
his dissipation and royal title. A mockery that Vonones struggled to escape. How? I will pay that debt where due.[5]

5. To Tiberius the troubled East brought some gratification. With this pretext he could detach Germanicus from
familiar legions and, once he was imposed on new provinces,
expose him to plot and accident alike. (2) Germanicus, however, the more vigorous was his soldiers' support and his uncle's

aversion, was the more intent on hastening victory. He reviewed routes to battle and the events – painful or successful – of his campaigns; this was his third. (3) *Germans are routed in battle and on proper battlefields, but helped by forests, bogs, short summer and early winter. My troops? They succumb less to wounds than to distance travelled and loss of weapons. Gaul is weary of supplying horses. My long baggage column is susceptible to ambush, a liability for defenders. (4) But suppose a sea voyage: a foothold quickly established unbeknownst to the enemy, plus an earlier start to the war, and legions and supplies using the same transport. Fresh cavalry and horses via rivers' mouths and channels, in the middle of Germany!*

6. Accordingly, he applied himself to this. Sending Publius Vitellius and Gaius Antius for the Gauls' census, he made Silius, Anteius and Caecina responsible for building a fleet.[6] (2) A thousand ships seemed sufficient. They were quickly made: some shallow, with narrow prow and stern and wide belly to facilitate coping with the waves, some flat-bottomed for running aground harm-free. Most had steering-tackle at both ends so that with a quick crew switch they could land in either direction. Many had decks to carry catapults and were likewise suitable for transport of horses or supplies. Under sail they were handy and quick under oar, and the soldiers' enthusiasm fortified them for show and intimidation. (3) The Batavians' 'Island' was the designated assembly point: its easy landings made it convenient for welcoming troops and as a staging place for war. (4) (The Rhine, after a long stretch in one bed or going around modestly sized islands, practically splits into two rivers at the start of Batavian territory, retaining its name and violent current where it runs alongside Germany before mingling with Ocean. On the Gallic bank it flows wider and calmer with a different name – locals call it the Waal – and eventually exchanges that name, too, with the Maas; through that river's gigantic mouth it pours into the same Ocean.)

7. Germanicus during the ship muster ordered his legate Silius to take unencumbered units and raid the Chatti.[7] He himself, hearing that a stronghold beside the Lippe was besieged, led six legions there. (2) Silius' accomplishments,

owing to unexpected storms, were nothing but seizing limited plunder and the wife and daughter of Arpus, a Chattan headman. Nor was Germanicus given an opportunity for battle: at word of his arrival the besiegers slipped away after demolishing the mound recently built for Varus' legions and the old Drusus altar. (3) Germanicus restored the altar, and to honour his father filed past at the head of his legions. He decided not to duplicate the mound. Everything between the stronghold of Aliso and the Rhine was fortified by new roads and causeways.

8. Then the fleet arrived. Supplies were sent ahead, ships distributed to legions and allies. Entering the canal called Drusiana, Germanicus[8] prayed to Drusus that, as he himself was making the same venture, his father, pleased and appeased, assist by example and the memory of his plans and works. From there they went through estuary and Ocean as far as the Ems, easy sailing. (2) They left the fleet on the western bank – it was a mistake[9] not to take troops heading east to that side. Many days were spent making bridges. (3) For cavalry and legions the crossing at the edge of the tidal zone, water not yet in flood, was worry-free. The end of the auxiliary column and the Batavians there, bobbing about and demonstrating the art of swimming, experienced trouble; some drowned. (4) Germanicus was laying out defences[10] when a defection by the Angrivarii in the rear was announced. Stertinius[11] was dispatched immediately with cavalry and rapid-deployment troops. Fire and slaughter were perfidy's punishment.

9. The Weser flowed between Romans and Cherusci. On its bank stood Arminius with the other leading men. To his question whether Germanicus had come, 'He is here,' was the response. Arminius then begged permission to speak with his brother. This man was in the army, Flavus by name, notable for loyalty and for the loss of an eye to a wound a few years earlier under Tiberius' command. (2) With permission he came forward and was greeted by Arminius,[12] who dismissed his attendants and requested that the archers arrayed on our bank withdraw. When they left, he asked: *Where did that ugliness on your face come from?* (3) The other named place and battle.

What reward did you get? Flavus mentioned promotion, torque and crown and other military decorations, while Arminius mocked slavery's worthless recompense.

10. There followed contrasting speeches. Flavus' was on Rome's greatness, Germanicus' resources. *For the defeated, punishments are severe, for anyone surrendering, there is ready mercy. Your wife*[13] *and son are not treated as enemies.* Arminius' was on duty to country, the liberty they inherited, Germany's household gods, their mother his ally in entreaty. *Do not choose being the deserter and betrayer of friends and kinfolk, indeed of your own people, over being their ruler.* (2) They gradually lapsed into abuse. Actual fighting not even the intervening river was going to prevent, except that Stertinius ran up and restrained a wrathful Flavus demanding weapons and horse. (3) Visible opposite was a threatening Arminius, announcing battle. (Most of his interjections were in Latin: he had served in Roman camps as a native leader.)

11. Next day the German line stood ready across the Weser. Germanicus, thinking that sending legions into battle without establishing bridges and garrisons was not general-like, had cavalry cross at a ford. The leaders were Stertinius and a chief centurion Aemilius, attacking different locations to divide the enemy. Where the river was swiftest, Chariovalda, the Batavian commander, erupted. (2) The Cherusci, feigning flight, drew him into a forest clearing. Arising and pouring out from every direction they drove their adversaries and pressed them yielding. The Batavians circled, the Cherusci harried, some hand-to-hand, others from a distance. (3) Chariovalda withstood enemy brutality for a long time, then urged his troops to break through the oncoming masses as one. He went in against the densest. Weapons converged, his horse was hit, he fell; likewise many nobles roundabout. The rest their own strength or cavalry reinforcements with Stertinius and Aemilius removed from danger.

12. Germanicus crossed the Weser. From deserter information he learned the place Arminius chose for battle. *Other nations, too, have assembled in the forest sacred to Hercules. They will risk a night assault on your camp.* The informant was

thought reliable. Campfires were spotted and scouts who crept closer reported the noise of horses and a huge disorganized column's rumbling. (2) With a decisive battle at hand, Germanicus thought he should investigate the soldiers'. attitude. He pondered. *How can I get it unadulterated?* (3) *Officers' reports are more often optimistic than well-informed, freedmen are servile, and in friends, flattery is inherent. Suppose I summon an assembly? There, too, whatever a few begin the rest cheer. I need to know their inner thinking, when secluded and unguarded around the mess they divulge hope and fear.*

13. As night began he left headquarters. On hidden paths unknown to the watch, with one companion and his shoulders under an animal pelt, he travelled the camp's streets, stood beside the tents and enjoyed the talk about himself. One would praise their general's birth, his looks another, most his tolerance and affability, his even temper in work and play. *We must thank him in battle!* and *Traitors and peace-breakers must fall as victims to vengeance and glory!* (2) Meanwhile one of the enemy – he knew Latin – rode near the rampart and spoke loudly: wives and fields and pay (100 sesterces per day throughout the war) were promised to whoever deserted, in Arminius' name. (3) This insult intensified the legions' anger. *Let daylight come and battle be given! We soldiers will take the Germans' fields, haul away their wives! We accept the omen and designate the enemy's marriages and money as booty!* (4) After midnight a feint was made on the camp. No weapons were thrown, there being numerous units guarding the fortifications and no slackness, as the enemy saw.

14. The same night brought Germanicus happy repose. He saw himself after sacrificing – consecrated blood spattered his robe – in possession of another sacrifice, more beautiful, from the hands of his grandmother Livia. Exalted by the portent and with auspices concurring, he summoned an assembly. Sensible forecasts and matters suited to imminent battle were his themes. (2) *Open fields, for Roman soldiers, are not the only good battle terrain. If you think about it, forests and woods are good, too. The barbarians' gigantic shields and prodigious spears are less handy amidst tree trunks and undergrowth than pikes and*

swords and close-fitting body armour. (3) *Multiply your cuts,
go for faces, stabbing. A German has no breastplate, helmet or
even shield reinforced by iron or thong: just wickerwork or
thin, painted boards. The first line does carry spears, but the
rest have fire-sharpened or short weapons. The German's body,
though grim to see and effective in a short attack, lacks tolerance for wounds. They have no shame at bad behaviour, no
worry about leaders in retreat or flight. They take fright at
resistance; amidst success they pay to divine and human law no
heed.* (4) *If weary of road and sea you desire an end, it is available in this battle. The Elbe is now closer than the Rhine. No
war remains, provided you establish me here, as I tread the
footsteps of father and uncle, as victor.*

15. The general's speech carried the soldiers' enthusiasm
with it and the signal for battle was given.

Nor did Arminius and the other German leaders deprive
their men of a declaration. *These Romans are the quickest runaways from Varus' army! To avoid war's suffering they involved
themselves in sedition. The backs of some are a mass of scars,
some have limbs broken by waves or storms. With these they
face hostile enemies again and contrary gods, having no good
hope.* (2) *To fleet and trackless Ocean they had recourse lest
anyone block them approaching or harry them once beaten,
but after an engagement the losers will find in wind and oars
empty help.* (3) *Just remember their greed, their cruelty, their
arrogance. What else is there for us but holding on to freedom
or dying before enslavement?*

16. They led the men thus ablaze and demanding battle to an
open field called Idistaviso. It lay between river and hills. Where
riverbanks receded or mountain spurs stood firm, it had irregu-
lar curves. Behind rose forest: high-reaching branches, clear
ground between trunks. (2) The field and the woods' edge were
held by the barbarian line. The Cherusci occupied the ridges
alone; once the Romans were fighting they would run down
from above. (3) Our army advanced thus: Gallic and German
auxiliaries in front, after them, archers on foot. Then four legions
and, with two headquarters units and picked riders, Germanicus. Next, an equal number of legions and rapid-deployment

troops with mounted archers and the remaining allied units. The
men were alert and ready for marching order to become battle
position.

17. Then they saw Cheruscan hordes bursting forth high
spirited. *The strongest cavalry rush the flank, Stertinius and the
rest circle around and attack their backs,* Germanicus ordered. *I
will arrive on time.* (2) Meanwhile, a splendid omen: eight eagles
headed for the woods and entered. The sight caught the commander's attention and he called out. *Follow Rome's birds,*[14] *the
legions' own gods!* (3) Simultaneously, the infantry line made
contact and the cavalry, sent earlier, fell upon the hindmost and
flanks. Wonderful to tell: there were two enemy columns fleeing
in opposite directions. Those holding the forest rushed into the
open, those with field positions into the forest. (4) In between,
the Cherusci were forced from the hills, Arminius conspicuous
among them – fighting, shouting, wounded – prolonging the
fight. Bearing down on archers, he meant to break through
there, except that auxiliary cohorts opposed.[15] (5) But bodily
effort and his horse's speed got him through, face smeared with
his own blood to prevent recognition. Some report him recognized by the Chauci active among Rome's auxiliaries, and
released. The same valour – or stratagem – got Inguiomerus out.
(6) For the rest? Wholesale slaughter. Many tried to swim the
Weser. Weapons hurled, or the river's force overwhelmed them,
and finally the mass of onrushing men and riverbank collapse.
Some – shameful flight! – climbed to the treetops, using branches
for concealment. Up came archers who amused themselves
shooting. Or else their trees, uprooted, crushed them.

18. It was a great victory for us, and not bloody. From late
morning until night the enemy was killed, filling ten miles with
corpses and weapons. Among the spoils were found chains
intended, as if the outcome were secure, for Romans. (2) The
soldiers acclaimed Tiberius 'victorious general' on the battlefield and built a mound. On it they set, like trophies, weapons
above the defeated nations' names.

19. The Germans? Wounds, losses and annihilation all
caused them less pain and anger than this display. Prepared,
before this, to abandon home and withdraw across the Elbe,

they now wanted battle, seized weapons. Commoners, leaders, young men and old suddenly rushed the Roman column, causing chaos. (2) At length they chose a spot hemmed by river and woods. It contained flat ground, narrow and wet. The woods themselves were surrounded by deep water, except the side the Angrivarii had raised with broad earthworks to separate themselves from the Cherusci. This was the infantry position. The cavalry was in nearby groves under cover: once the legions entered the forest it would be behind them.

20. None of this was unknown to Germanicus. Plans, positions, the obvious, the hidden: he knew, and would turn enemy stratagems to their ruin. To his legate Seius Tubero he gave cavalry and field, and he deployed his infantry so that part entered the forest on a flat approach, part climbed the earthwork obstacle. Difficult jobs he assigned to himself, others to legates. (2) Those with a level approach burst in easily. Those who had to attack the earthwork – it was like scaling a wall – found heavy overhead blows troublesome. The General perceived the disadvantage of close-quarters fighting. Withdrawing the legions a little he ordered slingers[16] to hurl their bullets and dislodge the enemy. Spears were shot from catapults. The more conspicuous the defender, the more wounded he fell. (3) Germanicus with headquarters units captured the rampart, then led the charge into the woods, where each step was contested, the enemy's back to the water, Romans hemmed in by river and hills. For both, their position was intractable. Hope lay in valour, salvation in victory.

21. The Germans' spirit was no less, but fighting style and weaponry brought them down. They were a huge multitude in narrow positions with too-long spears that they could not extend or retract. Unable to use feints and physical speed, they were forced into a stationary battle. Opposite, our soldiers – shields chest-hugging, hands on hilts – gouged the barbarians' broad limbs and naked faces, and opened a passage, routing the enemy. Arminius now proved remiss owing to serial dangers, or else his recent wound slowed him. But Inguiomerus appeared everywhere in the battle; Fortune left him, not courage. (2) Germanicus, to be more recognizable, had removed his

head's protection. He entreated his men to pursue the carnage. *No need for captives! Only a massacre of the tribe will end the war.* Late that day he withdrew a legion from battle to make camp. The rest, until nightfall, sated themselves with enemy gore. The cavalry contest was inconclusive.

22. After his speech praising the victors, Germanicus had a weapon mound built, its inscription proud. *After conquering the nations between Rhine and Elbe the army of Tiberius Caesar consecrated this monument to Mars, Jupiter and Augustus.* About himself he made no addition, from fear of envy or deeming awareness of the deed enough. (2) The war against the Angrivarii he entrusted then to Stertinius, except that they surrendered hurriedly. The suppliants, by refusing nothing, received a full pardon.

23. Summer was now ending. Some legions were sent back to winter quarters by land, but most Germanicus embarked: down Ems to Ocean their voyage. (2) At first the sea was calm; a thousand ships[17] splashed oars or sailed before the wind. Then from a black cloud mass streamed hailstones, while with squalls from different directions confusing the waves visibility was reduced and steering hindered. The soldiers, frightened and ignorant of ocean hazards, disrupted the sailors or offered ill-timed assistance and undermined the experts' work. (3) Then sky and sea alike surrendered wholly to the south wind. From Germany's swollen terrain and deep rivers came an immense tract of clouds. The wind, which was strong and more stinging from the chill of its northern vicinity, seized and scattered the ships onto open ocean or islands dangerous with broken rocks or hidden shallows. (4) These were avoided narrowly, with difficulty – then the tide changed and set in the wind's direction. Impossible to stay anchored or empty out the swamping waves. Horses, oxen, baggage, even weapons were jettisoned to relieve hulls wet from leaks and overtopping waves.

24. Ocean being more violent than other seas, and Germany pre-eminent for grim climate, that calamity was accordingly extreme in its strangeness and size, with hostile shores encircling and waters so extensive as to be thought the last and

landless sea. (2) Some ships sank; more were cast up on distant islands. Soldiers, there being no human cultivation there, were consumed by hunger, except those whom horse carcasses – fellow castaways – sustained. Only Germanicus' warship put in at Chauci territory. He spent those days and nights on clifftop and headland, proclaiming himself guilty of the huge disaster. Friends struggled to keep him from plunging into the same sea. (3) Eventually, with the swell subsiding and the wind favouring, limping ships returned with a few rowers, or clothing spread for sails, some towed by the stronger. These were immediately repaired and dispatched to scour the islands. Most men were rounded up by this effort. Many the Angrivarii, recent allies, ransomed from the interior and returned. Some, carried to Britain, were sent back by its rulers. (4) The further away their return started, the more marvels they told: violent whirlwinds, unheard-of birds, sea monsters, equivocal bodies – *man? beast?* – were seen, or believed, from fear.

25. The rumour of the fleet's destruction roused Germans to hope for war and Germanicus to repress it. Silius with 30,000 infantry and 3,000 cavalry was ordered against the Chatti. Germanicus himself with a larger force invaded the Marsi, whose leader Mallovendus – his surrender had recently been accepted – provided information. *In a nearby grove is buried a Varus-legion eagle under a modest garrison's protection.* (2) One group was immediately sent to tempt the enemy from the front. Others, circling behind, would dig. Both met good fortune. All the more eagerly did Germanicus proceed inland, laying waste and uprooting an enemy that didn't venture engagement or, whenever it resisted, was immediately defeated and never – captives told him – more afraid. (3) *You Romans are not beaten and no disasters will overcome you!* they declared. *Fleet destroyed, weapons lost, shores strewn with the bodies of horses and men, and you still have the same courage, matching spirit, and apparently greater numbers for invading!*

26. Back to winter quarters, soldiers happy inside. *Misfortunes at sea? Successful campaign? Equal, on balance.* Plus there was Germanicus' generosity: whatever sum anyone declared as a loss he reimbursed. People were sure that the

enemy was faltering and making peace-seeking plans. *One more summer and the war can be finished!* (2) Many letters arrived from Tiberius with advice. *Come home! A triumph has been decreed:*[18] *enough results, enough disasters. Successful and significant battles are to your credit, but remember, too, what winds and waves – through no leader fault – have brought: heavy, painful losses.* (3) *Nine times Augustus sent me to Germany and I accomplished more by policy than by force: capitulation by the Sugambri, the constraints of peace for the Suebi and King Maroboduus. You can leave the Cherusci and other rebel tribes – now that Roman vengeance has been served – to internal strife.*[19] (4) When Germanicus begged a year to complete his undertakings, Tiberius applied a sharper spur to forbearance by offering a second consulship,[20] whose duties required Germanicus' presence. With a rider: *If warfare is still necessary, leave something for your brother Drusus' renown. There is no other enemy. Only in Germany can he achieve a victorious name and bring home laurels.* (5) Germanicus delayed no longer, but understood. *Excuses! Envy is the reason – glory all but won – I am being wrenched away.*

27. Around this time one of the Scribonius household, Libo Drusus, was reported for attempting revolution. The affair's beginning, course and end I will discuss with particular care, since things first came to light then that consumed the state for many years.

(2) Firmius Catus,[21] a senator from Libo's inner circle, urged the unwary and gullible man towards astrologers' promises, fortune-tellers' rites and even dream interpreters, exhibiting Pompey as his great-grandfather, Scribonia – once wife to Augustus – as his great-aunt, the Caesars as his cousins, a house full of ancestor-busts. Catus encouraged him towards dissipation and debt, and acted as his partner in pleasure and insolvency to have more evidence for entrapment.

28. Catus found enough witnesses and slaves to corroborate, then demanded access to the Emperor. (Disclosure of the charge and the accused was done by equestrian-ranked Vescularius Flaccus,[22] who had closer acquaintance with Tiberius.) (2) Though not rejecting the evidence, Tiberius declined contact.

Conversational exchange can continue with Flaccus as inter-mediary. Meanwhile, Tiberius honoured Libo with a praetorship and invited him to meals, showing no estrangement of face, no disturbance while speaking, so thoroughly was his anger buried. Libo's every utterance and action, although he could have prevented them, Tiberius preferred to know, until a certain Junius, who was solicited to raise the dead with spells, delivered evidence to Fulcinius Trio.[23] ((3) Celebrated, among accusers, was Trio's talent, and hungry for notoriety.) Trio immediately seized the defendant, approached the consuls, demanded a senate hearing. Senators got a summons, plus this: *We need to discuss a serious and shocking matter.*

29. Libo, meanwhile, mourning-clad and in the company of leading women, paid calls, pleaded with connections, sought a voice to pit against his peril. Everyone refused – with different excuses, the same alarm. (2) On the trial day, weary with fear and anguish – or, as some record, shamming illness – he was brought by litter to the senate house doors. He leaned on his brother, stretched hands and pleas to Tiberius. A fixed expression met him. Then Tiberius recited statements and sources, controlling his delivery so as to seem neither to mitigate nor aggravate the charges.

30. Supplementing Trio and Catus as accusers were Fonteius Agrippa and Vibius Serenus.[24] They competed for the privilege of making the big speech. Finally Serenus, since no one was yielding and Libo was there with no defender, declared that he would present the charges singly. He brought forth such crazy statements as: *Libo enquired whether he would have the resources to cover the Appian Way to Brundisium with coins.* (2) There were others of this sort, senseless, pointless and – taken more mildly – pitiful. In one, however, the accuser showed, in Libo's handwriting, the names of imperial family members and senators, plus alarming or mysterious marks. (3) The defendant denied it. Knowledgeable slaves were to be questioned under torture, it was decided. And since a long-standing senate decree forbade interrogations potentially deadly to a master, Tiberius, a clever inventor of legal novelties, ordered specific slaves sold to an official[25] – plainly intending that the investigation of Libo

through his slaves not infringe the senatorial decree. (4) In consequence, the defendant requested adjournment and went home. Final entreaties he gave to his relative Publius Quirinius[26] for the Emperor.

31. The response? *Ask the senate.* There was a cordon around Libo's house meanwhile, and even uproar in his foyer. Soldiers were audible and visible. Libo, at the meal intended as his final pleasure, was in agony, calling for a killer, clasping slave hands, introducing a sword. (2) They panicked and backed away, overturning the table lamp. Deadly darkness ensued and two blows to the gut by his own hand. His groan as he fell brought freedmen running. The soldiers, after inspecting the butchery, withdrew. (3) The accusation before senators was nevertheless – and with unchanged vehemence – completed. Tiberius, under oath, said: *I would have petitioned you for his life, however guilty, had he not hurried on a voluntary death.*

32. Libo's property was divided[27] among the accusers. Expedited praetorships were given to those of senatorial rank. Next came Cotta Messalinus' proposal that Libo's likeness[28] not escort his posterity's funerals. And Gnaeus Lentulus' that no Scribonius take the name Drusus. (2) Public thanksgivings were arranged on Pomponius Flaccus' motion. Gifts to Jupiter, Mars and Concordia; and also that the Ides of September, the date of Libo's suicide, be a holiday: thus decreed Lucius Plancus, Asinius Gallus, Papius Mutilus, Lucius Apronius. (I record their proposals and flatteries to make it known that this is a long-standing evil in our state.) (3) There was also a senatorial decree on expelling astrologers and fortune-tellers from Italy. One of them, Lucius Pituanius, was hurled from the cliff.[29] Publius Marcius the consuls took outside the Esquiline Gate and, after the bugle-call was sounded by their order, inflicted on him an ancient punishment.

33. At the next senate meeting much was said against the community's extravagance by ex-consul Quintus Haterius and former praetor Octavius Fronto. Decreed: no solid-gold dinner services, no silk clothing to sully men. Fronto brought another motion, demanding limits on silverware, furniture, households.

(It was still common then that senators, if they thought something was in the public interest, expressed it when consulted.) (2) Asinius Gallus spoke against it. *With the Empire's increase, private resources, too, have grown. No novelty this, but a longstanding pattern. For the Fabricii 'money' meant one thing, for the Scipios another. Everything reflects the state. When it was small, narrowness characterized citizen homes, but after it reached its magnificence, individuals spread themselves. (3) In households and silverware and items acquired for use, nothing is excessive or moderate except with reference to the owner's fortune. Senatorial and equestrian classes are distinct not because they are naturally different, but so that those who have priority in seating, rank and status likewise have it in items acquired to rest the spirit or for bodily health. Unless perhaps our most illustrious men must undertake more cares and greater dangers, but do without things that ease cares and dangers!* (4) Ready assent accrued to Gallus under these respectable headings – from his admission of failings to an audience like him. Plus Tiberius had said: *There is no census underway now. If morals begin to slip, correction will have a sponsor.*

34. Meanwhile, Lucius Piso[30] berated lobbying in the Forum, tainted trials and the brutality of pleaders threatening accusation. *I am going away, leaving Rome to live in some secluded and distant countryside,* he declared. He was also abandoning the senate. Tiberius, shaken, although he applied mild words to calming Piso, also urged Piso's friends to use influence or pleas to detain departure. (2) Comparable proof of aggrieved independence was soon given. Piso sent a summons[31] to Urgulania, a woman placed above the laws by Livia's friendship. Urgulania did not obey. (She went to Tiberius' house, ignoring Piso.) Nor did Piso relent, despite Livia's complaints. *I am being harassed and belittled!* (3) Thinking some indulgence to his mother citizen-like – *I will go to the courtroom and support Urgulania* – Tiberius left the Palace. His soldiers had orders to follow at a distance. It was a sight to see: people crowding up as, with settled expression and varied conversation, he took his time along the route. Finally, when friends were unsuccessful in restraining Piso, Livia ordered payment of the money at issue.

(4) Thus ended an affair from which Piso emerged quite glorious and Tiberius with reputation enhanced. (Urgulania's potency in civic business was so excessive that once, when witness in a trial conducted in the senate, she did not bother to go. A praetor was sent to question her at home, although hearing Vestals in Forum and courtroom whenever they gave evidence was a long-standing custom.)

35. Public business was postponed that year, which I would not report except that the contrasting opinions of Gnaeus Piso and Asinius Gallus[32] on the matter are worth knowing. Piso, when Tiberius had said he would be absent, recommended: *All the more reason to act, so that the ability of senate and equestrians to uphold their responsibilities in the Emperor's absence will reflect well on the republic.* (2) Gallus, since a show of independence had been pre-empted by Piso, said: *Nothing is sufficiently notable or consistent with the dignity of the Roman people unless it is done before Tiberius and under his eyes. Accordingly, Italy's assembly and the provinces' converging[33] should be saved for his presence.* With Tiberius listening in silence, great disputatiousness was used by both sides, but business was deferred.

36. Another contest – Gallus vs Tiberius – began. Gallus recommended that magistrates for a five-year period be elected,[34] that legionary legates serving before their praetorships become praetors-designate immediately, and that the Emperor name twelve candidates per year. Everyone realized that this proposal went quite far. *The mysteries of command are being tested.* (2) But Tiberius, as if it was an increment to his power, said: *It weighs heavily on my moderation to choose and defer so many. Avoiding grievances even yearly is difficult, although defeat has ensuing hope as consolation. How much hatred will arise from candidates put off for more than five years? How can one foresee over so long anyone's state of mind, family or fortune? Pretentiousness accrues even with one-year designations: what if an office is flaunted for five? It means a five-fold increase in magistracies, and subversion of the laws by which the periods for exercising candidatorial industriousness and for seeking and holding office were established.* An apparently

favour-seeking speech, with which Tiberius kept command's force in his grasp.

37. Tiberius also provided property-qualification help to certain senators. There was, therefore, more surprise that he listened quite aloof to the pleas of Marcus Hortalus, a nobly born man in obvious want. The grandson of the orator Hortensius, Hortalus had been enticed by Augustus' million sesterces gift to marry and raise children, lest a most illustrious family fail. (2) Accordingly, with four sons on the senate-house threshold,[35] at his turn to speak during a meeting on the Palatine, looking now at Hortensius' likeness among the orators, now at Augustus', Hortalus began thus: 'Senators, these boys, whose age and youth you see, I raised not by choice but at Augustus' prompting. (And my ancestors *did* deserve descendants.) (3) For, prevented by changed times from getting or earning money, popular favour and eloquence – an heirloom of our house – I was satisfied if my slender means neither shamed me nor burdened anyone else. But bidden by the Emperor, I married. Behold the stock and offspring of numerous consuls, numerous dictators! (4) Envy is not my aim in mentioning these things, but winning pity.[36] In their prime, Tiberius, these boys will achieve such offices as you bestow. Meanwhile, protect Hortensius' great-grandsons, Augustus' foster-children, from want!'

38. The senate's inclination spurred Tiberius to readier resistance in approximately these words: 'If everyone impoverished begins to come here and seek money for his children, individuals will never be satisfied and the state will run short. This was not the purpose of our ancestors' concession that senators may occasionally digress from the motion at their turn and make proposals beneficial to the community – for us to advance private interests and our own holdings along with antipathy towards senate and emperors, whether they indulge in generosity or refuse. (2) It is not entreaty but importunity – inconvenient and unexpected when the senate has convened on other matters – to rise and inflict the number and age of one's children on the senate's forbearance, and to transfer like compulsion onto me and practically break down Treasury doors. If

we exhaust the Treasury by courting favour, crimes will be needed to replenish it. (3) Augustus gave you money, Hortalus, but not upon request nor on condition that money always be given. Otherwise industriousness will flag and idleness intensify, if fear and hope rest not in oneself, and everyone awaits others' help carefree, timid for himself, burdensome for us.' (4) These and like words, though heard with nods by men accustomed to praise everything of an emperor's, respectable or not, most people received in silence or with covert grumbling, as Tiberius perceived. After a short silence: *I have made my response to Hortalus. But if you senators approve, I will give his children* 200,000 *sesterces each – the boys, that is.* (5) Others expressed gratitude, Hortalus said nothing – from alarm or else retaining inherited nobility even in Fortune's straits. Nor did Tiberius show compassion thereafter, although the house of Hortensius slipped into shameful want.

39. That same year a single slave's audacity – had rescue not been quick – would have felled the state with discord and civil conflict.

A slave of Postumus Agrippa named Clemens, learning of Augustus' end, went to Planasia. *Subterfuge or force to get hold of Agrippa, then transport to the Germany-based armies,* the plan of no servile mind. (2) His bold actions were prevented by cargo-boat tardiness. Meanwhile, Agrippa's murder[37] was accomplished. Bigger and riskier actions his new intent, Clemens stole the ashes, sailed to Cosa, an Etruria promontory, and stowed himself in hiding so hair and beard could grow, for in age and build he was not unlike his master. (3) Then, through appropriate agents who shared his secret, the story was repeated – *Agrippa is alive!* – in secret conversations at first, as is usual for things forbidden, and later with rumour ranging into the ready ears of the naive, or indeed among men disruptive and therefore revolution-hungry. (4) He himself would approach towns at dark and was not seen publicly or long in one place. But since truth gains strength from visibility and duration, and falsehoods from haste and uncertainty, he would leave rumour behind or anticipate it.

40. Word spread, meanwhile, across Italy – *Preserved by the*

gods' gift! Agrippa! – and was believed in Rome. Clemens went by boat to Ostia. He was fêted by a huge multitude, and likewise in the city by clandestine gatherings. Tiberius was torn by twofold worry. *Use military force to check my own slave? Or leave insubstantial belief to time's fading? Nothing should be disregarded,* he reflected at some times, *Wholesale fear is not needed,* at others. Undecided between shame and fear, he finally handed the business to Sallustius Crispus.

(2) Crispus chose two of his dependants – soldiers, some report – and urged: *Simulate complicity and get close. Offer money. Promise loyalty and risk-taking.* They followed orders, then watched for an unguarded night and took a suitable few. Clemens was tied up, gagged, hauled to the palace. (3) To Tiberius' question, *How did you become Agrippa?* Clemens responded, they say, 'Same way you became Caesar.' He could not be compelled to reveal his associates. Tiberius, since public execution was too risky, ordered him killed in a secluded part of the palace and his body secretly removed. Although many people – members of the imperial household, men of equestrian and senatorial rank – were said to have provided financial support and helpful advice, there was no investigation.

41. To conclude the year: dedications. An arch beside Saturn's temple commemorating the recovery – under Germanicus' leadership and Tiberius' auspices – of standards lost with Varus. A temple of Fors Fortuna Tiber-side in the Gardens Caesar bequeathed to the Roman people. A shrine to the Julian family and statue of Augustus at Bovillae.[38]

(2) (17 CE) Gaius Caelius, Lucius Pomponius, consuls.

On 26 May Germanicus celebrated a triumph[39] over Cherusci, Chatti, Angrivarii and other nations as far as the Elbe, parading plunder, prisoners and representations of mountains, rivers and battles. The war, since finishing it was forbidden, was considered finished. (3) Increased onlooker attention[40] came from the exceptional beauty of the man himself, and from the chariot, five children its load. But underneath there was hidden alarm, as people reflected. *No success attended the crowd's favour for his father Drusus. And his uncle Marcellus, despite the blaze of popular enthusiasm, was snatched away still young. Brief and unlucky are the Roman people's love affairs.*

42. Tiberius, in Germanicus' name, gave 300 sesterces apiece to the citizen body and named himself as colleague for Germanicus' consulship. Even so, belief in sincere affection was not achieved. He decided, therefore, to remove Germanicus with specious honour. He engineered reasons – or seized what chanced to hand.

(2) King Archelaus, in his fiftieth year as Cappadocia's ruler, was hated by Tiberius, during whose stay on Rhodes Archelaus did not pay court. *Nary a favour!* Insolence was not what caused Archelaus' omission: he had been warned by Augustus' intimates. *While Gaius Caesar is alive and an envoy for Eastern affairs, Tiberius' friendship is dangerous*, they believed. (3) When, after the Caesars' line was overthrown, Tiberius took control, he coaxed Archelaus out with a letter from Livia, who, not hiding her son's grievances, offered clemency if Archelaus came to plead for it. Ignorant of the plot, or else fearing compulsion if they thought he understood, he hastened to Rome. His reception was a merciless emperor, then accusation before the senate. It wasn't owing to the fabricated charges but to anguish – he was exhausted by age, and kings find equality strange, let alone humiliation – that his lifetime's limit was reached by choice or fate. (4) His kingdom became a province again. *With this revenue*, Tiberius declared, *the 1 per cent tax*[41] *can be lowered.* He set it at half that for the future. (5) In this same period, kings' deaths – Antiochus of Commagene, Philopator of Cilicia – disrupted their countries: many people wanted rule by Rome, others, by king. And the provinces of Syria and Judaea, exhausted by their burdens, were begging for tribute-reduction.

43. Accordingly, Tiberius addressed the senate on these matters and about Armenia – what I reported above[42] – and said: *The troubled East can only be settled by Germanicus' good sense. My vitality is sinking; Drusus' has not yet matured.* A senatorial decree entrusted to Germanicus the overseas provinces and authority, wherever he went, outranking that of governors.[43] (2) Tiberius, however, had removed from Syria

Creticus Silanus,[44] a marriage-connection of Germanicus' (Silanus' daughter was pledged to Nero, Germanicus' eldest son).
He appointed Gnaeus Piso, a man innately impetuous and
unacquainted with deference. Piso's spirit was ingrafted from
his father, who, during the civil war when the Pompeian cause
was resurgent in Africa provided staunch service against Caesar,
then, after following Brutus and Cassius, received permission
to return, but abstained from office-seeking until spontaneously solicited to accept a consulship offered by Augustus.
(3) Besides inherited defiance, Piso's wife Plancina's[45] noble birth
and wealth were incitements. He hardly deferred to Tiberius;
Tiberius' children – *Far beneath me!* – he despised. (4) Piso held
this certain: *I have been chosen as Syria's ruler to check Germanicus' hopes.* Some believed that he had secret instructions
from Tiberius. Plancina was certainly advised by Livia – female
rivalry![46] – to harass Agrippina.

((5) The court was divided and discordant with unspoken
backing for Drusus or Germanicus. Tiberius favoured Drusus –
My own son and bloodline! – but for Germanicus his uncle's
aversion increased affection in others, also because the renown
of his maternal line gave him priority – *Antony my grandfather,
Augustus my great-uncle,* was his boast. (6) Drusus, by contrast, had as great-grandfather the equestrian-ranked Pomponius
Atticus. *A disgrace to Claudian busts,* people felt. And Germanicus' spouse Agrippina outstripped Livilla, Drusus' wife, in
fecundity and fame. But the brothers were extremely concordant. Their relatives' struggles did not shake them.)

44. Soon thereafter Drusus[47] was sent to Illyricum to get
used to soldiering and to gain army backing. *A man given to
city dissipation's carouses[48] will be under better control in
camp,* thought Tiberius, *and I will be safer with both sons
controlling legions.* (2) But Suebi were the pretext, begging
help against Cherusci. For at the Romans' departure[49] the
Germans – from national habit when free of external fear, and
then from rivalry for glory – had turned weapons against themselves. The tribes' might and their leaders' valour were equal.
But Maroboduus' royal title kept him hateful to his countrymen; Arminius' freedom wars found favour.[50]

45. Accordingly, not only did the Cherusci and their allies –
long Arminius' men – resume warfare, but Suebian tribes from
Maroboduus' kingdom, the Semnones and Langobardi,
defected to him. With these additions Arminius dominated,
except that Inguiomerus and some dependants fled to Maroboduus, his reason simply this: *Obeying a young nephew as an
elderly uncle is undignified.* (2) Battle lines were drawn up with
equal hope on both sides, but not the random incursions used
formerly in Germany or in scattered hordes. Through long soldiering against us they were accustomed to following standards,
having reinforcements for support and taking commanders'
orders.

(3) On that occasion Arminius, making a horseback survey
of the whole, paraded before all he met. *Liberty regained!
Legions slaughtered! And many still hold prizes and weapons
seized from the Romans!* Maroboduus, by contrast, he called a
runaway. *In battle he took no part. The Hercynian hideaway
was his defence. Then, using gifts and embassies, he requested
a treaty. He is a traitor to his country and a courtier to Tiberius,
to be expelled with the loathing you felt while killing Quinctilius Varus.*[51] (4) *Just remember your many battles, in whose
outcome, and recently in the Romans' ejection, lies sufficient
proof of which of us has supremacy in war.*

46. Nor did Maroboduus refrain from boasting about himself or insulting his enemy. Clasping Inguiomerus, he declared:
*In his body is the entirety of Cheruscan glory. From his plans
came our successes. Arminius, a madman ignorant of reality,
appropriates another's glory for the treacherous deception*[52] *of
three straggling legions and a leader ignorant of his stratagem –
to great calamity for Germany and disgrace for himself, since
his wife and son still endure servitude.* (2) *I, however, when
attacked by twelve legions – Tiberius was their leader – kept
Germany's glory undiminished, then disengaged on equal
terms. Nor am I sorry that the decision is in our hands, whether
we prefer a new war against the Romans or unbloodied peace.*

(3) These words were goads, and the armies had their own
provocations, too. For Cherusci and Langobardi it was a contest for ancient glory and recent freedom, on the other side for

dominion's increase. (4) Never before did armies clash with greater impact – or less decisive outcome (there were routs on both right wings). People hoped for fight's renewal, except that Maroboduus took his camp away into the hills. (5) This signified defeat and deserters gradually left him destitute. He withdrew to the Marcomani and sent envoys to Tiberius to beg help. The response? *You have no right to summon Roman arms against the Cherusci, since you gave Romans fighting the same enemy no assistance at all.* But Drusus was sent, as I reported – for peace, a prop.

47. That same year twelve populous cities in Asia collapsed in an earthquake at night,[53] which made the disaster more confounding and grievous. People's customary refuge on such occasions, rushing into the open, was no use. The gaping earth swallowed them. *Huge mountains subsided, flatland is now visible aloft, fires gleamed among the ruins,* they recalled. (2) The harshest affliction was the Sardians', which brought them the most compassion. Ten million sesterces were promised by Tiberius and Treasury payments were remitted for five years. (3) The people of Magnesia on the Sipylus were next in damage and remedy. For Temnians, Philadelphians, Aegaeatans, Apollonidenses and those called Mosteni and Hyrcanian Macedonians, plus Hierocaesaria, Myrina, Cyme and Tmolus – tax relief for the same period was decided, and a senatorial envoy to inspect conditions and provide relief. (4) Ex-praetor Marcus Ateius[54] was chosen, lest – Asia's governor being an ex-consul – rivalry between equals emerge and with it impediments.

48. The splendour of public largesse Tiberius increased by equally gratifying generosity. For he passed the property of Aemilia Musa (wealthy, intestate, and despite Treasury claims) to Aemilius Lepidus; she was from his household, apparently. And he passed the estate of the wealthy equestrian-ranked Pantuleius, although he himself was listed as partial heir, to Marcus Servilius,[55] whom he found named in an earlier valid will. *The noble birth of both men ought to have money's support,* he said beforehand. (2) Tiberius entered into no inheritances but those that were friendship's due. Strangers and testators naming the Emperor[56] out of hostility to others he kept at a distance.

(3) Although for respectable poverty in innocent men he provided relief, the extravagant and depravity-impoverished – Vibidius Virro, Marius Nepos, Appius Appianus, Cornelius Sulla, Quintus Vitellius – he removed from the senate or allowed to withdraw voluntarily.

49. Just then Tiberius dedicated divine temples. They were ruined by age or fire, Augustus' projects: the temple to Liber, Libera and Ceres near the Circus Maximus, vowed by Aulus Postumius as dictator, and in the same location the temple to Flora established by Lucius and Marcus Publicius as aediles, plus the Janus sanctuary built in the Forum Holitorium by Gaius Duillius, who first conducted Roman operations successfully at sea and earned a naval triumph over the Carthaginians. (2) A temple to Hope was consecrated by Germanicus; Aulus Hostilius vowed it in that same war.[57]

50. Meanwhile, the treason law kept maturing. Even Appuleia Varilla,[58] Augustus' sister's niece, was cited by an informer for treason. *She mocked Augustus and Tiberius and his mother with insulting talk, and – Tiberius' kinswoman! – is liable on an adultery charge.* (2) On adultery the Julian law[59] provisions seemed sufficient. Treason? Tiberius demanded distinctions. *She must be convicted if she said anything irreverent about Augustus. Attacks on me I do not want brought into court.* When asked by the consul for his recommendation on the accusation of things said amiss about his mother – silence. At the next meeting he requested in Livia's name, too, that none incur a charge for verbal attacks, whatever their nature, on her (3) and cleared Appuleia of treason. Adultery? He protested against overly severe punishment and urged that, following ancestral example, her kinsmen remove her beyond the two-hundredth milestone. For her adulterer Manlius, Italy and Africa were banned.

51. Over substituting a praetor for Vipstanus Gallus – death took him – a contest arose. Germanicus and Drusus, who were still in Rome, backed Haterius Agrippa, Germanicus' relative. Against this, many contended that, for candidates, the number of children should be decisive, as the law ordered. (2) Tiberius was happy that the senate was arbitrating between his sons

and the laws. Law lost, obviously, but not immediately or with paltry support – just as laws, even when robust, used to be defeated.

52. That same year war began in Africa. The enemy leader was Tacfarinas. By nationality he was Numidian. He had years of auxiliary service in Roman camps but was later a deserter. He first assembled men – nomads accustomed to banditry – to plunder and seize, then arranged them military-fashion in detachments and squadrons. Finally, it was not of a disorganized mob but of the Musulamii that he counted as leader. (2) A strong people near Africa's deserts, still without cities' culture, they took up arms and dragged their neighbours the Moors into the war. These, too, had a leader, Mazippa, and the armies were divided such that Tacfarinas kept picked men armed Roman-fashion in camp and accustomed them to discipline and orders, Mazippa with a mobile force spread fires and slaughter and intimidation. (3) They had forced the Cinithii, too, a significant people, into their cause, when Africa's governor Furius Camillus collected a legion and some allies in his command and led them towards the enemy. A modest force, if you consider the multitude of Numidians and Moors. But Camillus' principal worry was lest fear make the enemy avoid warfare.[60] (4) The legion was positioned in the middle, rapid-deployment infantry and two cavalry units on the wings. Tacfarinas did not refuse the fight. The Numidians were routed, the first time in many years that a Furius gained military glory. (5) (After the Furius who recovered Rome[61] and his son Camillus other families had the praise for victorious generalship, and the Furius mentioned here was considered inexperienced in war.) The more readily, therefore, did Tiberius celebrate his achievements in the senate. Senators decreed an honorary triumph[62] – and this, because Camillus lived moderately, caused him no harm.

53. (18 CE) The following year had Tiberius (third time) and Germanicus (second time) as consuls.

Germanicus entered office in an Achaean city, Nicopolis, which he reached via Illyricum's coast – he visited his brother

Drusus in Dalmatia – after suffering a difficult voyage in
Adriatic and then Ionian waters. (2) He therefore spent a few
days refitting his fleet, and approached the bays renowned for
the Actian victory, the trophies dedicated by Augustus, and
Antony's camp, in remembrance of his forebears. (As I mentioned, his great-uncle was Augustus, his grandfather[63] Antony,
and Actium was a vast canvas of events both sad and happy.)
(3) From there to Athens, where, as a concession to the treaty
of that allied and ancient city, he used just one lictor. The
Greeks' welcome involved far-fetched honours and preliminaries on long-gone deeds and words to give more dignity to their
flattery.

54. Germanicus' next destination was Euboea, then he
crossed to Lesbos, where Agrippina gave birth for the last time:
Julia Livilla. Then he went to Asia's edge, Perinthus and Byzantium, Thracian cities, later inland to the Propontis strait and
Pontus mouth, moved by desire of acquaintance with places
ancient and storied. Equally, he provided relief to provinces
exhausted from internal quarrels and officials' abuses. (2) On
his return, struggling to visit Samothrace's rites, contrary
northerlies turned him away. So after going to Ilium and the
sights there venerable for shifting Fortune and our origin, he
retraced Asia's coast and docked at Colophon to profit from
the Apollo oracle at Claros. ((3) This is not a woman, as at
Delphi, but a priest from specific families, primarily Milesian.
He hears only the questioners' number and names, then
descends into a cave, drinks from a secret spring and, though
generally ignorant of literature and poems, gives responses in
verse on whatever subjects one has in mind.) (4) The priest was
said to have intoned for Germanicus, riddlingly – oracular
habit! – *imminent departure*.

55. Piso, however, to give his plans a quicker beginning,
berated an Athens dismayed by his disruptive entrance in a
brutal speech with grating but indirect attacks on Germanicus
for excessive affability in paying court, contrary to the dignity
of the Roman name, not to Athenians – who were, from numerous calamities, extinct – but to that ethnic bog. *These were*

Mithridates' allies against Sulla, Antony's against Augustus!
(2) Even the past provided charges: the city's failures against
Macedon, her violence against her own. Piso's annoyance at
Athens stemmed from private anger, too, for not letting off a
certain Theophilus, forgery-convicted in Athens' court, at his
request.

(3) Then, after a quick voyage through the Cyclades and
maritime shortcuts, Piso caught up with Germanicus at Rhodes.
Germanicus, though aware of Piso's taunting attack, behaved
with such mildness that, when a sudden storm swept Piso
against some cliffs and his enemy's death could have been credited to chance, he sent warships to assist in his removal from
danger. (4) But Piso was not appeased. Scarcely tolerating even
a day's delay, he left Germanicus and arrived first.

(5) After he reached Syria and its legions there was largesse,
bribery and gratification for the lowest rankers: he removed
long-standing centurions and strict officers and gave their
places to his own dependants or worthless men, and allowed
laxity in camp, licence in cities, and soldiers loose and carousing through the countryside. So far did he go in corruption that
common talk deemed him 'the legions' parent'. (6) Nor did
Plancina limit herself to female decorum. She took part in cavalry exercises and infantry manoeuvres and hurled insults at
Agrippina and Germanicus. Even some good soldiers were disposed to criminal compliance. *These things are not happening
against Tiberius' wishes*, a covert rumour started. Matters
known to Germanicus, but attending to the Armenians was his
more pressing care.

56. These were an unsettled people, from the inhabitants'
ancient character and the country's situation alongside our
provinces for a wide stretch, and reaching a long way towards
the Medes. They exist between two huge empires and are
quite often at odds, hating Romans or resenting the Parthian.
(2) They didn't have a king then, Vonones having been removed.[64]
But national favour inclined to Zenones, son of Pontus' King
Polemo, because from his earliest infancy Zenones adopted
Armenian institutions and style. With hunting and banquets
and other barbarian practices he had formed attachments to

elite and populace alike. (3) So Germanicus – in Artaxata, nobles approving, multitude swarming – placed the royal diadem on his head. The rest, showing reverence, saluted him as King Artaxias, applying a term from the city's name.

(4) The Cappadocians, given provincial organization again, received Quintus Veranius[65] as governor. There was some tribute reduction from royal levels to encourage hope of Roman control being milder. The Commagenians under Quintus Servaeus were first then in a magistrate's jurisdiction.

57. All ally business was successfully settled, but this did not keep Germanicus happy, because of Piso's insolence. Ordered to lead part of his force – himself or through his son – into Armenia, Piso did neither. (2) At Cyrrus, winter quarters of the Tenth, the two met, faces tight, Piso against fear, Germanicus lest he seem to threaten. (He really was, as I mentioned, quite compassionate. But friends clever at kindling grievances exaggerated the truth, heaped up falsehoods, and against Piso, Plancina and their sons made various sorts of allegations.) (3) Finally, with a few associates present, the conversation was begun by Germanicus in the manner generated by anger and its concealment, and responded to by Piso with defiant entreaties. They parted in open hatred. Afterwards, Piso rarely sat on Germanicus' tribunal, and whenever he did so he was ruthless and disagreed openly. (4) People heard him say, too, at a dinner hosted by the Nabataean king when golden garlands of substantial weight were presented to Germanicus and Agrippina and lightweight ones to Piso and the rest: *This is a banquet for the Roman emperor's son, not the Parthian king's.* He cast aside his garland and said much more about extravagance. This was cutting, to Germanicus, but tolerated nevertheless.

58. Amidst this, envoys from the Parthian king Artabanus arrived, sent to speak of friendship and treaty. *Artabanus desires the pledges renewed and will do Germanicus the honour of approaching the Euphrates' bank. He seeks, meanwhile, that Vonones not be held in Syria or send messages from nearby to move local elites to disaffection.* (2) To this Germanicus responded splendidly about the Roman/Parthian alliance, and about the king's arrival and courtesy towards himself with

dignity and modesty. Vonones was removed to Pompeiopolis, a
coastal city in Cilicia. This was a concession not to Artabanus'
entreaties but to spite for Piso, with whom Vonones was hugely
influential owing to gifts and services he had used to attach
Plancina.

59. (19 CE) Marcus Silanus, Lucius Norbanus, consuls.

Germanicus travelled to Egypt to become acquainted with
antiquity. Concern for the province was his pretext. And he did
relieve the price of grain by opening warehouses and gave the
populace much gratification. He circulated without soldiers, san-
daled and dressed just like a Greek, in imitation of Publius Scipio,
who did this in Sicily with the Punic war still raging, we hear.
(2) Tiberius, after grating references, mildly worded, to Germanicus' dress and demeanour, berated him for having entered
Alexandria. *Contrary to Augustus' arrangements! Without my
assent!* (3) For Augustus, among the regime's other mysteries, set
Egypt apart – entrance was barred, without permission, to senators and equestrian-ranked notables – to preclude the pressure of
famine on Italy by anyone holding that province and its land and
sea barriers with even a thin garrison against huge armies.

60. Germanicus, having not yet discovered his journey
rebuked, sailed up the Nile, starting from Canopus, a Spartan
foundation owing to the burial there of the ship's pilot Canopus when Menelaus, returning to Greece, was thrown off
course into a different sea and to Libya. (2) Next, the river
mouth dedicated to Hercules, whom the locals say originated
in their country and was exceedingly ancient. *Other, later, men
of the same type have his name by association.* Then Germanicus visited ancient Thebes' impressive traces. (3) Still present
on massive structures were Egyptian letters tallying former
opulence. He ordered one of the older priests to translate the
native language. *There once lived here 700,000 men of military
age, and with that army King Rhamses conquered Libya, Ethi-
opia, Medes, Persians, the Bactrian, the Scyth, and held in his
power the lands that Syrians, Armenians and the neighbouring
Cappadocians inhabit, and from the Bithynian sea on one side
to the Lycian on the other.* (4) Also read out were the tributes
imposed: the weight of gold and silver, the number of weapons

and horses, temple gifts of ivory and incense, and what quantities of grain and every supply each nation paid, totals scarcely
less splendid than currently ordained by Parthian might and
Roman power.

61. Germanicus examined other marvels, too. Mainly Memnon's stone likeness, which, when the sun's rays hit it, emits a
voice-like sound, and amidst drifting and scarcely passable
sands the mountain-high pyramids erected by royal rivalry and
riches, and the lake excavated as receptacle[66] for the overflowing Nile. (2) Also the Nile's narrows elsewhere, and its profound
depth, which no investigator's rope-lengths can fathom. Then
to Elephantine and Syene. These used to be the limits of the
Roman Empire,[67] which now extends to the Red Sea.

62. While Germanicus spent this summer[68] going province
to province, Drusus sought substantial glory coaxing the Germans into disputes and driving the now-broken Maroboduus
to complete ruin.

(2) Among the Gotones was a nobly born man named
Catualda, a fugitive from Maroboduus' violence earlier and at
present, Maroboduus' situation being precarious, daring revenge.
With a strong force he entered Marcomani territory and, after
bribing the elite to join him, burst into the palace and adjacent
stronghold. (3) Ancient Suebian booty was found there, and from
our provinces camp-followers and traders whom commercial
privileges, then passion for accumulating money and finally for-
getfulness of country had transferred each from his own home to
enemy ground.

63. For Maroboduus, utterly deserted, the only help was
Tiberius' mercy. After crossing the Danube border of Noricum,
he wrote to Tiberius not as fugitive or suppliant but mindful of
his former lot. *Although many peoples were calling me, once a
most illustrious king, to them, I preferred Rome's friendship.*
(2) Tiberius' response: *You will have a safe and honoured home
in Italy, if you stay. But if your advantage is served otherwise,
you will depart under guarantee as you arrived.* (3) In the senate Tiberius said that Philip was not so great a threat to Athens,
nor Pyrrhus or Antiochus to Rome. The speech survives. Maroboduus' majesty, the impetuosity of his subject peoples, how

close an enemy to Italy, and his own policies in destroying him were Tiberius' themes.

(4) Maroboduus was held at Ravenna, on display, in case the Suebi grew insolent, as ready to return to his kingdom. But he didn't leave Italy for eighteen years and grew old with his renown much diminished by excessive attachment to life. (5) Catualda? Same downfall, refuge no different. He was routed soon thereafter by Hermunduri resources under Vibilius'[69] leadership, then welcomed and sent to Fréjus, a colony in Narbonensis. (6) The barbarian followers of each – lest in quiet provinces their diffusion cause disturbance – were settled beyond the Danube between the Marus and Cusus rivers[70] with Vannius of the Quadi as their king.

64. Simultaneous news: a king, Artaxias, for the Armenians by Germanicus' gift.

Senators decreed that Germanicus and Drusus enter Rome to ovations. Arches, too, were built flanking the Mars Ultor temple with likenesses of the Caesars – Tiberius being happier at having used good sense to consolidate peace than had he concluded a war through battles.

(2) Accordingly, he approached Thrace's King Rhescuporis, too, with ingenuity. That whole people had been under Rhoemetalces' control. At his death, Augustus entrusted half the population to his brother Rhescuporis, half to his son Cotys. In this division arable land and cities and places near Greece fell to Cotys, and what was uncultivated, wild and enemy-connected to Rhescuporis. The kings' characters were comparable: Cotys' was mild and pleasant; Rhescuporis' ruthless, grasping and intolerant of partnership. (3) At first they acted with duplicitous harmony. But then Rhescuporis emerged from his territory, appropriated things given to Cotys and attacked him resisting. He acted tentatively under Augustus, whom – *the source of our royal power and, if spurned, its avenger* – he feared. But upon hearing about the Emperor change he dispatched raiding bands and razed strongholds – inducements to war.

65. Nothing kept Tiberius so anxious as avoiding stability's disruption. He chose a centurion to tell the kings not to fight

and Cotys' auxiliaries were immediately dismissed. (2) Rhescuporis, with pretended restraint, asked to meet. *Disputes can be handled by discussion.* There was little delay over time, place or even terms: in one man easy temper, in the other deceit motivated mutual concessions and acceptances. (3) Rhescuporis added a banquet for sanctifying, as he said, the treaty. The rejoicing extended to late night. Amidst feasting and drunkenness Cotys was incautious. After he understood the plot, he kept invoking the sacrosanctity of kingship, their common family gods, hospitality. Rhescuporis weighted him with chains. (4) All Thrace now in his power, he wrote to Tiberius. *A trap was laid for me and the plotter has been forestalled.* Meanwhile, under pretext of war against Bastarnae and Scythians, he acquired new infantry and cavalry reinforcements. (5) Tiberius' response was mild. *If there was no trickery, you can rely on innocence. Neither I nor the senate will discriminate right and wrong without a hearing, so after surrendering Cotys come and dispel the animosity of accusation.*[71]

66. This letter Moesia's governor Latinius Pandusa sent to Thrace with soldiers for Cotys' surrender. Rhescuporis hesitated between fear and anger, but chose to defend a crime complete rather than a crime begun. He ordered Cotys killed. *Took his own life,* he lied. (2) But Tiberius did not alter approved technique. After the death of Pandusa, whom Rhescuporis accused of being hostile, he installed Pomponius Flaccus over Moesia, a veteran campaigner with a close friendship with the king and therefore more suitable for deception – the principal motivation for his appointment.

67. Flaccus crossed into Thrace and with huge promises impelled Rhescuporis, despite his uncertainty and consciousness of crime, to enter the Roman camp. Surrounding the king thereafter – a show of honour! – was a strong contingent. Officers used advice and encouragement and, the further they travelled, more open custody in dragging him, finally recognizing the inevitable, to Rome. (2) Accused before the senate by Cotys' wife, Rhescuporis was condemned to detention far from his kingdom. Thrace was divided[72] between his son Rhoemetalces – who opposed his father's plans, people agreed – and Cotys'

children. These were still young, so the ex-praetor Trebellenus Rufus was given for the interim administration of the realm, on the model of our ancestors, who sent Lepidus to Egypt as guardian for Ptolemy's children. (3) Rhescuporis sailed to Alexandria, where – attempting flight? falsely charged? – he was killed.

68. In this same period Vonones, whose removal to Cilicia I mentioned,[73] bribed his guards and tried to flee to the Armenians, thence to Albani and Heniochi and a Scythian king, his kinsman. Apparently hunting, he left the coast and sought trackless woods. Then he made a swift ride to the Pyramus, whose bridges the locals broke after hearing of the king's flight. Going through at a ford was impossible. (2) Accordingly, Vonones was arrested on the riverbank by the cavalry officer Vibius Fronto. Remmius, a reservist assigned to the king's former guard, acting angry, ran him through. This increased people's belief that Remmius' complicity in crime and his fear of exposure caused Vonones' death.

69. Germanicus, returning from Egypt, discovered all his orders in legions and cities abolished or reversed. This led to serious rebukes for Piso and equally harsh moves by Piso against Germanicus. Piso decided to leave Syria. (2) Germanicus' ill health detained Piso, but then he heard that Germanicus had revived. Vows for Germanicus' safety were being discharged: victims at altars, sacrificial implements, Antioch's people celebrating – all were cleared away by Piso's lictors. Then he left for Seleucia, waiting out the illness that again befell Germanicus.

(3) The brutal violence of disease was augmented by Germanicus' belief in poison given by Piso. And people kept finding in floor and walls disinterred human remains, spells and curses and Germanicus' name scratched on lead tablets, ashes half-burnt and smeared with gore, and other baneful objects supposed to consecrate souls to underworld deities. Piso's emissaries, too, were blamed for probing Germanicus' physical misfortunes.

70. For Germanicus these were causes for anger no less than alarm. *If my threshold is besieged, if I must breathe my last under enemy eyes, what will befall my poor wife? My infant*

children? Poison seems slow. Piso is in a hurry, pressing to have the province and its legions for himself. But Germanicus is not so feeble and murder's rewards will not remain with my killer! (2) He composed a letter renouncing friendship with Piso. (Many say, too, that Piso was ordered to leave the province.) Without delaying further, Piso sailed, setting his course for a short return journey if Germanicus' death left Syria open.

71. Germanicus was briefly roused to hope, but then – his body exhausted, the end at hand – addressed his attendant friends thus: 'If I were succumbing to fate, I would feel justifiable resentment towards gods hurrying me from parents, children and country during my prime with a premature exit. But now, criminally cut short by Piso and Plancina, I leave in your hearts these last entreaties. Tell my father and brother[74] how, tortured by bitter experiences and overcome by plotting, I finished an utterly wretched life with the worst of deaths. (2) Whoever was stirred by my expectations or kindred blood, and even those envious of me alive, will weep that a man once flourishing, the survivor of numerous wars, fell to womanish subterfuge. You will have occasion to complain before the senate, to invoke laws. (3) The special duty of friends is not escorting a corpse with pointless complaint, but remembering his wishes and carrying out his instructions. Even strangers will mourn Germanicus. You will avenge him, if your attentions were for me, not my position. (4) Show the Roman people Augustus' granddaughter – my wife – and tally six children. Pity will be with the accusers. Those fabricating wicked orders will find neither belief nor pardon.' An oath was taken by his friends with the dying man's right hand in their grasp. *We will forgo life before vengeance.*

72. Turning to his wife, Germanicus pleaded, by her memory of him and by their children. *Shed your high spirit, submit to raging Fortune! And when you return to Rome, do not, by contesting power, provoke those stronger than you!* These words were spoken openly, others in private, signifying, people thought, danger from Tiberius. (2) Soon thereafter life failed, to vast lament in the province and surrounding nations. External peoples and kings grieved – so great was his affability

towards allies, his mildness towards enemies. Appearance and speech alike produced reverence, and, despite his preserving the stature and consequence of exalted position, he escaped enviousness and arrogance.

73. Germanicus' funeral, lacking ancestor busts and cortege, abounded in eulogies and the recollection of his virtues. For some, his beauty, age and manner of death, even the nearby location in which he died, resembled Alexander's destiny. (2) *Each had an attractive physique, illustrious birth, and died not much past thirty from an insider plot among foreign peoples. But Germanicus was mild to friends and moderate in pleasures, with just one marriage and acknowledged children, and was no less a warrior, even if he lacked Alexander's rashness and was prevented from pressing into servitude the Germany he felled in numerous victories. (3) Had Germanicus been sole arbiter of affairs, had he had royal prerogative and name, he would have achieved military glory as readily as he excelled in clemency, self-control and virtue's other attainments.*

(4) The corpse, before cremation, was exposed in Antioch's forum, the location chosen for his last rites. Did it manifest signs of poisoning? Unconfirmed. People's inclinations – pity for Germanicus and preconceived suspicion, or favour for Piso – produced divergent interpretations.

74. There followed a discussion among Germanicus' legates and the other senators present. *Who should be put in charge of Syria?* Although the rest made moderate efforts, between Vibius Marsus[75] and Gnaeus Sentius the question was long disputed. Finally Marsus yielded to Sentius' seniority and more vigorous contention. (2) Sentius sent to Rome a woman notorious for poisoning in Syria, a close friend of Plancina, Martina[76] by name, at the request of Vitellius and Veranius and the others preparing charges[77] and prosecution as if defendants were already on trial.

75. Agrippina, exhausted by grief and physically frail but impatient of anything that delayed her revenge, boarded ship with Germanicus' ashes and children, to everyone's pity. *A woman foremost in nobility, with a marriage, until recently, most fine, accustomed to being seen amidst worshipful*

well-wishers, now clasps dead remains, uncertain of vengeance, anxious for herself and, because of her unhappy fecundity, many times over subservient to Fortune.

(2) Piso was at Cos when the news arrived: *Germanicus is dead!* His reaction showed no control. He sacrificed and visited temples without restraining his joy and with still greater insolence in Plancina. (From mourning for a lost sister she changed right then to happy attire.)

76. Officers streamed in with advice. *You have the legions' support. Return to a province wrongly taken and rulerless!* (2) Piso deliberated, accordingly. *What to do?* His son Marcus recommended hastening to Rome. *Nothing unforgivable has occurred so far, nor should feeble suspicions and empty talk cause great alarm. Disputing with Germanicus merited hatred, perhaps, but not punishment, and the confiscation of your province gave your enemies satisfaction.* (3) *But if you return with Sentius resisting, civil war begins. Officers and soldiers won't stay on your side. Memory of their commander is fresh and deep-seated love for the Caesars prevails.*

77. He was opposed by Domitius Celer from Piso's inner circle. *This is an outcome to be exploited! Piso, not Sentius, is Syria's governor. To you the symbols and prerogative of a governor were given, to you the legions. If hostile action threatens, who is more justified in armed opposition than one with a governor's authority and personal orders?* (2) *Leave time for rumours to grow old. Innocent men generally can't compete with fresh animosity. But if you keep an army and increase your strength, much that is unforeseeable will fortuitously turn out better.* (3) 'Or do we hurry to dock with Germanicus' ashes, so that – unheard and undefended – you are caught by Agrippina's wails and an ignorant mob at the first whisper? You have Livia's complicity and Tiberius' support, but in secret. Germanicus' death is most ostentatiously mourned by those who most rejoice.'

78. It took no great pressure to bring Piso, who was given to spirited actions, into agreement. In a letter to Tiberius he berated Germanicus for extravagance and presumption. *Expelled to make room for revolution, I resumed responsibility*

for my army as loyally as I held it before. (2) Celer was given command of a warship. His orders? *Avoid the coast, take a deep-water route past the islands to Syria.* Deserters converged. Piso organized them into units and armed camp followers. After crossing his ships to the mainland he intercepted a detachment of Syria-bound recruits and wrote requesting auxiliary help to Cilicia's princes. Young Piso provided energetic war service despite having spoken against undertaking a war.

79. Coasting along Lycia and Pamphylia they encountered the ships conveying Agrippina. Both sides were hostile, weapons initially ready. Mutual alarm kept them from going beyond abuse. Marsus served Piso with notice: *You must come to Rome to stand trial.* Piso's mocking response was: *I'll be there when the praetor of the poisoning court has announced a date for defendant and prosecutors.*

(2) Meanwhile Celer docked at Syria's Laodicea. Approaching the Sixth's winter quarters, since he thought this the most suitable unit for revolutionary plans, he was blocked by its legate Pacuvius. Sentius disclosed this to Piso by letter, with a warning: *Don't try using bribery-agents on the camp or war on the province.* (3) Everyone whom Sentius knew to be mindful of Germanicus or opposed to his enemies he assembled. *The Emperor's majesty* – his incessant refrain – *and the state are under attack!* He headed a force strong and battle-ready.

80. Nor did Piso, although his attempts kept going wrong, abandon the safest option available. He seized a Cilician stronghold, well fortified, called Celenderis. Mixing in deserters and recently intercepted recruits and slaves belonging to himself and Plancina, he gave the auxiliary forces sent by Cilicia's princes a legion's organization, (2) declaring: *I, Tiberius' representative, am excluded from the province he gave me, not by the legions – for I come at their summons – but by Sentius concealing private hatred with false charges. Stand firm in battle! His soldiers will not fight when they have seen Piso, whom they once called 'parent', as the better choice on legal grounds and strong on military ones.* (3) Then he deployed his troops before the stronghold's fortifications on a steep and broken hillside; the rest was surrounded by sea. Opposite stood veterans drawn

up in lines and reserves. On one side the soldiers were uncompromising, on the other the terrain was, but there was no
courage and no hope, nor even any weapons except farm tools
or emergency manufactures. (4) Upon contact, suspense lasted
only until the Roman cohorts struggled up to level ground. The
Cilicians fled and shut themselves in the stronghold.

81. Meanwhile Piso attacked the fleet waiting nearby, a vain
attempt. Returning then, and visible on the stronghold wall, he
tried – now by striking his breast, now urging individuals by
name, rewards their inducement – to start a mutiny, rousingly
enough that a standard-bearer of the Sixth brought a standard
over. (2) Then Sentius ordered the horns[78] sounded, a siege-
mound assembled, ladders erected. *Let the fastest go up and
others shoot in javelins, rocks and firebrands, a barrage!*
(3) Finally, his obstinacy defeated, Piso pleaded. *Let me surrender my weapons and stay here while Tiberius is consulted: to
whom does he entrust Syria?* His terms were not accepted, nor
was anything else conceded but ships and safe conduct to Rome.

82. In Rome, after Germanicus' sickness was widely known
and everything – coming from afar – was exaggerated for the
worse, there was grief and anger, an outburst of protest. *So this
is why he was banished to the ends of the earth, why the province was entrusted to Piso. This is the result of Livia's secret
conversations with Plancina!* (2) *And the Drusus-talk of our
elders was true. Rulers disapprove of citizen-like character in
their sons, and these men[79] were cut short simply for advocat-
ing equality's protection for the Roman people, their liberty
restored.* (3) Crowd talk was so fired by news of Germanicus'
death that (before the magistrates' edict, before the senate's
decree) official business was suspended. Courts were deserted,
houses shut. Everywhere there was silence and lamentation,
none of it contrived for show. People did embrace the symbols
of mourning, but their internal grief was deeper.

(4) Some traders who had left Syria with Germanicus still
living chanced to bring happier news about his condition. It
was immediately believed, immediately circulated. At each
encounter people passed the news, however baseless, to others
and those to more, accumulating joy. People rushed about the

city, worked open temple doors. Night-time fostered credulity
and it was easier, in the dark, to insist. (5) Tiberius did not
counteract the error until it weakened with time and distance.
The population – as if bereaved again – felt a sharper grief.

83. Honours were devised and decreed according to each
sponsor's love for Germanicus – or his ingenuity. Germanicus'
name was to be sung in the Salian hymn, chairs of office were
to be set up in imperial cult shrines topped by oak-leaf crowns,
Circus processions to be led by an ivory likeness, priests to
replace Germanicus chosen only from the Julian family.
(2) Plus arches at Rome, on the Rhine, and on Syria's Mt
Amanus. The inscription? His achievements and *He died on
public service*. A cenotaph at Antioch where he was cremated,
a monumental bier at Epidaphne where he died. As for statues
and cult sites, it is not easy to reach their tally. (3) At the proposal of a shield distinctive for gold and size amidst the leaders
of eloquence,[80] Tiberius declared that he would dedicate an
ordinary one, equal to the rest. *Distinction in eloquence is not
based on fortune. It is renown enough if Germanicus is ranked
with the ancient writers*. (4) The equestrian order named a
seating section (formerly called 'junior') 'Germanicus' section'[81] and ruled that on 15 July their squadrons would follow
his image. Many measures persist; some were immediately
abandoned or age brought oblivion.

84. Gloom was still intense when Germanicus' sister Livilla,
who was married to Drusus, gave birth to male twins, an
event – rare and happy even in modest households – that caused
Tiberius so much joy that he did not refrain from boasting in
the senate that no earlier Roman of Drusus' eminence produced twinned offspring. (Tiberius used everything, even
chance occurrences, for glorification.) (2) But for the people,
given the situation, this too brought grief. *Strengthened by children, Drusus will be more oppressive to Germanicus' house*.

85. That same year severe senatorial decrees curbed female
wantonness, banning use of the body for profit to any woman
with a grandfather, father or husband of equestrian rank.
(2) For Vistilia,[82] daughter of a praetor's family, had published
with the aediles her availability for illicit sex, an accepted

practice in older generations. *Enough punishment for unchaste women in acknowledging scandal*, they believed. (3) Coercion was also applied to Titidius Labeo, Vistilia's husband. *Why, with an obviously guilty wife, did you neglect the statutory punishment?* Given his excuse – *The sixty-day period for deliberation has not yet passed* – it seemed sufficient to rule on Vistilia and she was relegated to Seriphus.

(4) There was discussion about expelling Egyptian and Jewish rites, and a senatorial decree: 4,000 people of freedman stock infected with that creed and of suitable age were to be conveyed to Sardinia to check the banditry there. *If the oppressive climate causes their demise, a trivial loss.* The rest were to leave Italy unless before a given date they shed unclean rituals.

86. Thereafter, Tiberius proposed obtaining a Virgin to replace Occia, who for fifty-seven years had presided over Vesta's rites with the utmost sanctity. He thanked Fonteius Agrippa and Comicius Pollio for offering daughters, vying in service to the state. (2) Preference went to Pollio's daughter, only because her mother had stayed in her marriage. Agrippa had diminished his household by divorce and Tiberius gave his daughter, though bested, a million sesterces dowry as consolation.

87. With the cruel cost of grain incurring popular protest, Tiberius set the buyers' price. *I will add two sesterces per measure for sellers.* But he did not therefore adopt the title 'father of his country', which had been offered before, too, and sharply rebuked those who called his actions 'divine' and him 'Lord' – a speaker's path was narrow and slippery under an emperor in whom liberty produced fear and flattery hatred.

88. I find in contemporary writers and senators that a letter from Adgandestrius, a Chattan headman, was read in the senate. He promised[83] Arminius' death if poison was sent for the assassination. The response? *Not by guile or subterfuge but openly and armed does the Roman people punish its enemies*, a vaunt whereby Tiberius likened himself to generals of old, who forbade and exposed poisoning aimed at Pyrrhus.[84] (2) When Arminius, after the Romans' withdrawal and Maroboduus' expulsion, tried for kingship,[85] he found his countrymen's

liberty hostile. Under armed attack he fought with varying fortune, but kinfolk plotting killed him. Liberator of Germany – without a doubt – he challenged not the first stages of the Roman people, like other kings and commanders, but the Empire at its height, his record in battles equivocal, in war undefeated. (3) He completed thirty-seven years of life,[86] twelve of power. His story is still sung among the barbarians, although unknown to the histories of the Greeks, who only admire their own, and not duly celebrated by Romans, since we extol antiquity and give to recent times no attention.

BOOK 3

1. (20 CE) With no interruption to her voyage on the winter sea, Agrippina sailed to Corcyra, an island opposite Calabria's coast. There she spent a few days settling her spirit, a woman violent in bereavement and unacquainted with enduring. (2) At word of her arrival every close friend and many ex-soldiers who had served under Germanicus, and many strangers, too, from nearby towns – some thinking it a service to the Emperor, more following them – rushed to Brundisium. For travellers by sea this was the quickest and safest dock. (3) As soon as the fleet was visible out at sea, all spots were filled – not only port and adjacent waters, but also walls and rooftops and wherever the longest view was possible. The crowd was lamenting and asking whether silence or some utterance should greet her landing, and had not yet reached agreement about what suited when the fleet approached gradually, not, as was customary, with the crew brisk, but with all arrayed for sorrow. (4) With two children and holding the funeral urn Agrippina disembarked, eyes down. A single universal groan went up. You could not distinguish relatives and strangers or men's and women's wailing. Except that Agrippina's company, wearied by long sadness, was outdone by those meeting them, fresh to pain.

2. Tiberius sent two Guard cohorts, plus this: *Let the magistrates of Calabria and Apulia and Campania perform a final tribute to my son's memory.* (2) The ashes were carried on officers' shoulders, preceded by tarnished standards and inverted fasces. When they passed through towns, the populace wore black, the equestrian-ranked formal dress. According to the

wealth of each place, so the burnt offerings: clothing, incense
and the other things customary at funerals. Even those residing
elsewhere met the ashes. They set out sacrifices and altars to
the dead, their tears and cries attesting pain. (3) Drusus travelled to Tarracina with Germanicus' brother Claudius and the
children in Rome. The consuls Marcus Valerius and Marcus
Aurelius[1] – they had already commenced their magistracy –
and the senate and a large portion of the people filled the road,
scattered and spontaneously weeping. For there was no obsequiousness, all being aware that in Tiberius the happiness of
Germanicus' death was thinly concealed.

3. Tiberius and Livia stayed away from the public. Was it
beneath their dignity to mourn openly? Or lest – with everyone's eyes scrutinizing their faces – their falsity be perceived?
(2) What about Germanicus' mother Antonia? Neither in historians nor in the daily gazette of events do I find that she
played any significant role. Yet in addition to Agrippina, Drusus and Claudius, Germanicus' remaining relatives, too, are
recorded by name. Perhaps ill health prevented her. Or else,
defeated by bereavement, her spirit did not tolerate seeing the
magnitude of the loss she suffered. (3) My belief inclines more
easily to this, that Tiberius and Livia, who were not going out,
kept Antonia in to give the appearance of equal sorrow and
that the mother's example detained grandmother, too, and
uncle.

4. The day Germanicus' remains were taken into Augustus'
tomb was now echoing in silence, now restless with wailing.
City streets were full. Torches shone in the Campus Martius,
where armed soldiers and rodless magistrates and the people
arranged by tribes kept shouting – *The republic has fallen! No
hope remains!* – quite readily and openly. Were they mindful of
their rulers? You would not have thought so. (2) However,
nothing so pierced Tiberius as people's burning enthusiasm for
Agrippina. *Rome's jewel, the only blood relative of Augustus,*[2]
a unique embodiment of antiquity! they called her, and looked
to heaven and gods. *May her progeny stay intact and outlive
ill-wishers,* they prayed.

5. Some missed a public funeral's pomp and compared

Augustus' magnificent show of respect for Drusus, Germanicus' father. *Augustus himself at winter's harshest went all the
way to Pavia. Nor did he leave the corpse; they entered Rome
together. Surrounding the bier were portraits, Claudii and Julii.
Drusus was mourned in the Forum, eulogized from the Rostra.
Every tribute the ancestors devised, along with posterity's
inventions, was piled high. For Germanicus? Not even traditional honours, those due any nobleman. (2) True, his body,
because of the journey's length, was cremated anyhow in foreign lands. But more lustre later is only fair, since chance denied
it at first. His brother[3] didn't go more than a day's journey to
him, his uncle not even to the gate. Where are the customs of
old? A likeness on the bier, poems recited for virtue's memory
and praises and tears – or performances of grief.*

6. This was known to Tiberius. To repress the crowd's talk,
he gave an admonitory edict. *Many notable Romans have died
on public business, none celebrated with such passionate yearn-
ing. This is exemplary in me and everyone else – if a limit be
applied. For what suits princes and an imperial people is not
what suits middling houses or states. (2) Feeling bereavement is
appropriate to fresh pain, as is finding solace in mourning. But
our character's firmness must now be restored, as once Caesar,
having lost his only daughter, and Augustus, after grandsons
were torn away from him, put away sadness. (3) No need for
more ancient examples, how often the Roman people endured,
steadfast, army disasters, commander deaths, noble families'
complete annihilation. Princes are mortal, the republic, eternal.
So return to your normal pursuits. And since the Megalensia
Festival[4] is at hand, resume pleasures, too.*

7. Official mourning was shed and people returned to business. Drusus set out for the Illyricum armies, with everyone
keen for Piso's punishment and many a complaint. *By pretentious and duplicitous delay among the pleasure-spots of Asia
and Greece Piso is undermining his crimes' proofs!* (2) For
word had spread that the woman sent, as I said,[5] by Sentius,
the infamous poisoner Martina, was extinguished by a sudden
death at Brundisium. *Poison was hidden in her braids, but no
bodily sign of self-destruction was discovered.*

8. Piso, after sending his son[6] to Rome with instructions for appeasing Tiberius, headed for Drusus, whose attitude to him, he hoped, was not grim at his brother's death but, with a rival removed, rather favourable. Tiberius, to show that his verdict was still undecided, received the man affably and with his habitual generosity towards the sons of noble families in gifts. (2) Drusus' reply[7] to Piso: *If the rumours are true, my position is uniquely painful. Better that they be false and empty than that Germanicus' death bring anyone's destruction.* This was said in public, all privacy avoided. No one doubted that these were Tiberius' instructions, seeing that a man otherwise unwary and with youth's easy temper[8] was using an old man's artifice.

9. Piso crossed Dalmatia's waters and left his ships at Ancona. He travelled through Picenum and then along the Flaminian Way, overtaking a legion being led from Pannonia to Rome and from there to garrison Africa. Rumour went to work on how, on the route of march, he often paraded before the soldiers. (2) Starting at Narni he sailed – to avoid suspicion or because frightened men's plans are unstable – down Nera then Tiber, increasing the crowd's wrath because he docked at the imperial family's tomb by day, with crowds on the bank, with a large retinue of dependants himself and Plancina with a company of women, and arrived looking confident. (3) Among antipathy's irritants was his house: overlooking the Forum, arrayed for celebration, guests, a banquet! In that populous location nothing was hidden.

10. The next day Fulcinius Trio[9] charged Piso before the consuls, opposed by Vitellius and Veranius and the rest of Germanicus' retinue. *This is not Trio's business, and we are not accusers but informants and witnesses bringing Germanicus' instructions.* Trio, letting go this case's prosecution, got to accuse Piso's earlier life, and there was a request that Tiberius handle the trial. (2) This even the defendant accepted, fearing bias in people and senate. *But Tiberius is firm in rejecting rumours and involved in his mother's complicity.*[10] *Distinguishing truth from unduly negative interpretations is more easily accomplished by a single judge. Hatred and antipathy prevail among the many.* (3) Obvious, to Tiberius, were the trial's

importance and the talk hacking at him. So in the presence of a
few friends he heard the accusers' threats and the other side's
pleas, then sent the case to the senate undecided.

11. Meanwhile Drusus returned from Illyricum. Although
the senate had voted[11] him an ovation for recovering Maroboduus and the previous summer's achievements, he postponed
the honour and entered the city.

(2) Next, when the defendant asked Lucius Arruntius, Publius Vinicius, Asinius Gallus, Aeserninus Marcellus and Sextus
Pompeius to represent him, they excused themselves variously.
Marcus Lepidus and Lucius Piso and Livineius Regulus
appeared for him.

The whole city was astir. *How loyal are Germanicus' friends?
What does the defendant count on? Will Tiberius succeed in
checking and suppressing his feelings?* Never before so intensely
hostile to the Emperor were the hidden utterances and suspicion-filled silences the people permitted themselves.

12. When the senate met, Tiberius' speech was carefully balanced. *Piso was my father's representative and friend, and an
assistant to Germanicus[12] of my own providing – with the senate's authority – for managing Eastern affairs. Did he provoke
the man by defying and vying with him there, and rejoice at his
death? Or did he use crime to eliminate him? Unbiased minds
must decide.* (2) 'For if my representative shrugged off his task's
definition and deference to his commander, and took the death
of Germanicus and my bereavement as cause for rejoicing, hatred and exclusion from my house will be my response, not
punishing private antagonisms as emperor. But if an action is
revealed for which punishment is due regardless of who was
killed, you must give Germanicus' children and me his parent
justice's solace. (3) Likewise ponder this: did Piso treat the
armies disruptively, seditiously? Did he gain the soldiers' support with favours? Did he return armed to his province? Or are
these lies, exaggerated and spread by his accusers? (4) (At the
excessive partisanship of these men I am justifiably incensed.
Why expose the body and permit the crowd's eyes to paw it?
Why spread it about, among foreigners even, that Germanicus
was taken by poison, when this was still uncertain and needing

investigation?) (5) I mourn my son and always will, but I do not bar the accused from bringing forward whatever can establish his innocence, or, if there was any unfairness on Germanicus' part, prove that. And I beg you not to take, because this case involves my pain, alleged crimes as proven. (6) You whom kinship and good faith have given to Piso for his defence should use all your eloquence and concern to assist the defendant. The same effort, the same constancy I urge upon the accusers. (7) Our one concession to Germanicus beyond the laws will be that the hearing about his death takes place in the senate house, not the Forum, before senators, not judges. Let the rest be done with matching restraint. None should look to Drusus' tears, to my sorrow, or to the fictions fashioned against us.'

13. Decided immediately: two days to present charges, then after a six-day interval the case for the defendant over three. Fulcinius Trio spoke on old and empty matters – ambition and avarice as Spain's governor – that if proven would not harm a defendant cleared of fresh charges, and if refuted would not absolve one convicted of more substantial crimes. (2) After this, Servaeus,[13] Veranius and Vitellius – their zeal being equal and with great eloquence on Vitellius' part – threw down their charges. *From hatred for Germanicus and from revolutionary zeal Piso so corrupted the common soldiers – through licence, to our allies' cost – as to be called, by the worst, 'the legions' parent'. The best men, by contrast, especially Germanicus' companions and friends, were savaged. Finally, using spells and poison Piso committed murder.* Next: *There were rites and unspeakable offerings, his and Plancina's! An armed attack on the state!* and *Bringing him to trial required his military defeat!*

14. The defence was shaky on many counts, for neither corrupting the soldiers nor submitting the province to terrible men nor indeed insulting his commander could be denied. Only of poisoning did the defence seem to clear him. The accusers could not establish it adequately, arguing that at a party at Germanicus' house, with Piso reclining adjacent, Germanicus' food was doctored by Piso's hands. (2) It seemed absurd to risk this amidst another's slaves and within sight of so many, in Germanicus' presence. The defendant offered his own household

and demanded Germanicus' servants for torture. (3) The judges were for different reasons implacable: Tiberius for the attack on a province, senators never fully persuaded that Germanicus' death didn't involve subterfuge. ***[14] demanding what they had written, which Tiberius no less than Piso refused. (4) People's talk outside the meeting was audible. *We will not refrain from action if he escapes the senators' verdict!* Piso's likenesses, dragged onto the Gemonian steps, were being dismantled, but by the Emperor's order were saved and replaced. (5) So Piso was put in a litter and escorted home by a Guard officer, to rumours various. *Is that a security guard – or an executioner – behind him?*

15. For Plancina there was the same antipathy, but more influence. People therefore considered it uncertain how much Tiberius would be permitted against her. She promised herself, while Piso's hopes were middling, as his ally in any fate whatsoever, even, if it came to this, as his companion in death. But when Livia's secret pleas won her pardon she began to move away from her husband and separate their defences. (2) The defendant understood this as fatal for himself. Wondering whether to persist, at his sons' urging he stiffened his resolve and re-entered the senate. Renewed recrimination, hostile senator words, opposition and brutality everywhere caused him pain, but nothing so alarmed him as seeing Tiberius without compassion, without anger, stubbornly closed against any feeling's breach. (3) Conveyed home, Piso wrote a little, as if rehearsing the next day's defence, applied his seal and handed a freedman the document. Then he completed his body-care routine. Late at night, his wife gone from the bedroom, he ordered the doors blocked. At daybreak he was found with neck gouged, a sword on the ground.

16. (I remember hearing from older men about their seeing a notebook quite often in Piso's hands, never published. Friends claimed, they said, that it contained a letter from Tiberius and instructions on Germanicus, and that Piso meant to produce it in the senate and prove the Emperor guilty, except that he was foiled by Sejanus[15] with empty promises. Also: that his death was not voluntary, since a killer was dispatched. Neither story,

in my view, deserves assent, but I ought not conceal something told by men who survived into my youth.)

(2) Tiberius, with a look now of sorrow, said: *Arousing antipathy towards me is the aim of this death*, ***[16] and with numerous lines of questioning he investigated how Piso spent his last day and night. Most of the responses were prudent, but some were ill-advised. Tiberius read out a document like the following, composed by Piso. (3) 'A conspiracy of enemies and animosity based on a false charge have crushed me. Seeing that the truth and my innocence have no place, I swear by the immortal gods that in life, Tiberius, I was loyal to you and likewise devoted to your mother. You both, I pray, will see to my children. Gnaeus has no link to any fate of mine, since during the whole period he was at Rome. And Marcus argued against attacking Syria. If only I had yielded to a son in his prime rather than he to an elderly father! (4) The more unstinting, therefore, are my prayers that an innocent man not suffer punishment for my perversity. Forty-five years of deference! Your colleague in the consulship! I once had your father Augustus' approval and was your friend. As one who hereafter will ask nothing, I ask salvation for my unfortunate son.' About Plancina? Nothing.

17. Thereafter Tiberius cleared Marcus Piso of civil war. *Father's orders, and a son could not refuse*. He expressed sorrow for the family's renown, even for the crushing blow, however deserved, to Piso himself. Concerning Plancina his speech was embarrassed and disgraceful, offering his mother's pleas. (Against Livia covert complaints by men of character grew hotter. (2) *So this is proper in a grandmother, seeing and speaking with her grandson's murderess and snatching her from the senate's grasp? What the laws offer to all citizens only Germanicus has failed to get. In Vitellius' voice and Veranius' is given the lament for a Caesar; from emperor and Livia we get Plancina's defence! Let her next turn her poisons and her arts – so successfully exploited – against Agrippina and Agrippina's children, let her glut a fine grandmother and uncle on the blood of an utterly wretched family!*) (3) Two days were spent on this sham trial, with Tiberius urging Piso's children to defend their mother. Since accusers and witnesses were outdoing one

another's rhetoric, and no one responded, compassion grew in antipathy's place. (4) The first proposal[17] sought was that of the consul Cotta Messalinus (since Tiberius put the question, the magistrates performed this function). *Piso's name should be erased from the list of consuls and half his property confiscated, half granted to his son Gnaeus, who should change his praenomen. Marcus Piso, stripped of his rank and given 5 million sesterces, should be banished for 10 years.* For Plancina, impunity was granted on Livia's pleas.

18. Much of this proposal was mitigated by the Emperor. *Piso's name should not be removed from the list, since those of Antony, who made war on his country, and of Jullus Antonius, who violated Augustus' house, are there.* Marcus Piso he exempted from disgrace and allowed his paternal inheritance, being quite resistant, as I have often recorded,[18] to money, and the more easily appeased then from his embarrassment over Plancina's exoneration. (2) Likewise, when Valerius Messalinus[19] proposed erecting a golden statue in the Mars Ultor temple, and Caecina an Altar of Vengeance, he forbade them. *External victories occasion such offerings. Domestic losses should be shuttered in sadness.* (3) Messalinus also proposed thanks to Tiberius, Livia, Antonia, Agrippina and Drusus, but failed to mention Claudius. And was then asked by Lucius Asprenas[20] in the senate: *Did you bypass him on purpose?* (Only then was Claudius' name appended.) (4) But the more I reflect on events recent and past, the more I am struck by the element of the absurd in everything humans do. For judging by people's talk, expectation and expressions of respect, anyone was more 'destined to rule' than the future emperor Fortune was hiding.

19. A few days later Tiberius initiated the senate's award of priesthoods to Vitellius, Veranius and Servaeus; to Fulcinius Trio he promised a recommendation for office[21] and warned him not to let impetuosity ruin his eloquence. (2) This was the final act in avenging Germanicus' death, bandied about not only among contemporaries but in subsequent ages too by varied rumour, so uncertain are the most significant events when some take hearsay from whatever source as information, others

convert truth into its opposite and both multiply with time's passage.

(3) Drusus left Rome to retake the auspices,[22] then celebrated his ovation. A few days afterwards his mother Vipsania[23] died, the only one of Agrippa's children with a gentle death. That the others were eliminated was either obvious (by sword) or believed (by poison or starvation).

20. That same year Tacfarinas, whose prior-season repulse by Camillus I reported, renewed the war in Africa[24] with scattered depredations at first, which were unpunished because swift. Then he destroyed villages and carried off substantial plunder. Finally near the Pagyda[25] he surrounded a Roman cohort. (2) The stronghold commander was Decrius, a man energetic in action, experienced in warfare. *This blockade is an outrage*, he thought. He encouraged his soldiers and, to enable fighting in the open, arranged his line in front of the camp. When the first assault pushed the cohort back he was there among the weapons, obstructing fugitives, rebuking standard-bearers. *Roman troops turning tail before irregulars and deserters!* He took some hits. With his eye pierced, he faced the enemy nevertheless. Nor did he abandon the battle until, deserted by his men, he fell.

21. When Lucius Apronius,[26] Camillus' replacement, discovered this, he was troubled by his men's disgrace more than by enemy glory and used a procedure rare then but of venerable memory: every tenth man of the sorry cohort, chosen by lot, was clubbed to death. (2) And through severity he was so effective that a veteran detachment numbering no more than 500 routed the same troops of Tacfarinas after they attacked an outpost called Thala. (3) (In this battle Helvius Rufus, a private, earned the 'citizen-saved' distinction and was decorated by Apronius with torques and spear.[27] Tiberius added a citizen crown; Apronius' failure to award this, too, by virtue of his proconsular power, roused Tiberius' protest but no offence.) (4) Tacfarinas, with his cowed Numidians rejecting blockades, fought a scattered war, yielding to pressure but returning to attack from behind. And while this was his strategy, the barbarian mocked the ineffectual and weary Romans with

impunity. But when he changed course for the coast and, tied down by his booty, stuck to a fixed base, Apronius Caesianus, sent by his father with cavalry and auxiliary cohorts plus the legions' swiftest, successfully fought the Numidians and drove them into the desert.

22. In Rome Lepida, who had, in addition to her Aemilian lustre, Sulla and Pompey as forebears, was reported for simulating a birth to the wealthy and childless Publius Quirinius.[28] Additional charges: adulteries, poisonings, consulting astrologers about the imperial household. Her defender was her brother Manius Lepidus.[29] Quirinius, divorce declared, was still hostile, so despite her infamy and guilt, compassion accrued. (2) It would not have been easy to discern the Emperor's intention in that trial, so thoroughly did he overturn and mix anger's signs and clemency's: first, an entreaty to the senate that no treason charges be handled, then encouraging one of the ex-consuls, Marcus Servilius,[30] and other witnesses to promote charges he had wanted (so to speak) to reject. (3) The same man transferred Lepida's slaves, which were then in military hands, to the consuls and forbade their torture-interrogation on matters pertaining to his own house. (4) He also removed Drusus, then consul-designate, from initiating the verdict. Some deemed this citizen-like, freeing others from the necessity of agreeing. Some took it as brutality. *Drusus would not have yielded unless condemnation was the task.*

23. Lepida – a festival interrupting the trial – entered the theatre[31] with illustrious women. Her plaintive lamentation in evoking ancestors and Pompey himself, whose monuments and statues were visible standing there, roused so much pity that the audience, moved to tears, kept shouting brutal curses at Quirinius. *To his old age and childlessness and his utterly obscure house the wife once intended for Lucius Caesar, as Augustus' daughter-in-law, is being surrendered!* (2) Then slave tortures revealed her crimes. This brought acquiescence in Rubellius Blandus' proposal of exile.[32] Drusus assented, although others offered milder recommendations. Next, Mamercus Scaurus,[33] who had begotten a daughter from Lepida, received the concession that her goods not be confiscated. Only then did Tiberius

reveal his discovery, from Quirinius' slaves, that Quirinius was the poisoning target of Lepida's attack.

24. Noble houses' misfortunes – in a brief interval the Calpurnii lost Piso, the Aemilii Lepida – found solace in the restoration to the Junian family of Decimus Silanus, whose disaster I will recall briefly. (2) Augustus' good fortune, though sturdily advantageous to the state, suffered reverses at home through the unchastity of his daughter and granddaughter, whom he expelled from Rome while punishing their adulterers with death or exile. (His application – to a culpability widespread among men and women – of the crushing label 'sacrilege and treason' was a departure from traditional clemency and his own laws.) (3) The ends of the others[34] I will record together with the rest of the Augustan period if, after completing current projects, I prolong life for further works. As for Decimus Silanus, Augustus' granddaughter's adulterer: even though Augustus' rage went no further than excluding him from friendship, Silanus understood that exile was indicated, and not until Tiberius' reign did he dare protest to senate and emperor through the influence of his brother Marcus Silanus,[35] who was conspicuous for eminently noble birth and eloquence. (4) Tiberius responded to Silanus' thanks in the senate. *I, too, rejoice that Silanus' brother is back from distant travels, which is perfectly legal since he was not banished by senatorial decree or law. But I hold against the man my parent's grievances intact, nor does Silanus' return undo Augustus' wishes.* Silanus existed in Rome thereafter, but never attained office.

25. The next business was moderating the Papia/Poppaea law,[36] which an elderly Augustus enacted after the Julian laws to encourage penalties for the unmarried and to increase revenue, without, however, making marriage and child-rearing more common, given the obvious advantages of childlessness. The crowd of defendants grew, since every household was toppled by informers' exposés. Before, crimes brought suffering; now, laws did.

(2) This matter prompts me to speak in more depth about law's origins and how the present infinite number and variety of laws were reached.

26. The earliest humans, since there were as yet no evil appetites, lived without wickedness and therefore without penalty
and punishments. Nor were rewards necessary, since the honourable was pursued because honourable. Where no desires
surpassed the norm, fear produced no prohibitions. (2) But
after equality was shed, and in place of restraint and shame
ambition and violence arrived, out sprang despotisms. In many
nations these were a permanent fixture. (3) But some nations
immediately, others, after kings proved irksome, preferred
laws. At first, given the primitive state of humankind, these
were simple. Particularly famous were the Cretans', with Minos
as author, and the Spartans', with Lycurgus. For the Athenians,
later, more sophisticated and more numerous laws were written by Solon. (4) For us? Romulus' government was arbitrary,
then Numa used religion's obligations and divine law as the
people's shackles, and there were some inventions by Tullus
Hostilius and Ancus Martius.[37] But ahead of the rest was
Servius Tullius, enactor of laws with which even kings were to
comply.

27. After Tarquinius Superbus' expulsion[38] came senatorial
partisanship, against which the people devised many measures
to protect liberty and secure concord. A Board of Ten was
elected and, after this collected what was exemplary anywhere,
the Twelve Tables were composed, the culmination of equity.
Subsequent laws, though occasionally directed against culprits
in response to crime, were more often passed through violence –
in conflict between the orders – to obtain illegal offices or expel
eminent men or for other perverse purposes. (2) Hence men
like the Gracchi and Saturninus, agitators of the populace, and
Livius Drusus, no less lavish a benefactor in the senate's name,
who bribed the allies with expectations and mocked them in
vetoes. Not even during the Italian and later the Civil War was
this activity neglected; indeed many conflicting laws were
adopted, until the dictator Sulla – after abolishing or overturning earlier laws he added more – produced a pause. Not for
long. Immediately thereafter came Lepidus' disruptive bills,
and soon tribunes regained their licence to set the people moving at will. (3) Then courts were instituted not only with general

reference but also against individuals: the most degenerate state and the most laws.

28. Then Pompey,[39] chosen in his third consulship to rectify behaviour, was more oppressive with his cures than the crimes themselves: author of laws and likewise their subverter, what he protected by force he forfeited by force. Then came twenty years of continuous strife – no morality, no law. The worst actions were unpunished and many honourable ones disastrous. (2) Only in his sixth consulship did Augustus, now secure in power, abolish orders issued during the Triumvirate and give us laws to use under a peaceful emperor. (3) The shackles thereafter were more galling. Surveillance was instituted, its agents encouraged by rewards in the Papia/Poppaea law, such that if parental privileges were shirked, the people, 'everyone's parent', should possess what had been vacated. But these agents burrowed too deeply and ruined Rome and Italy and citizens everywhere. Many people saw their status demolished. (4) Terror was assailing everyone, except that Tiberius, to establish a remedy, chose by lot five ex-consuls, five former praetors and a like number from the remaining senators. In their hands many of law's knots were loosened – a modest and temporary relief.

29. In this same period Nero[40] (one of Germanicus' children, now adult) was commended to the senate. *Service on the Board of Twenty should be waived and he should seek, five years before eligible, the quaestorship.* Thus Tiberius' request, to his hearers' amusement. The pretext? *For myself and my brother the same was decreed at Augustus' entreaty.*[41] (2) (No doubt then, too, in my view, people secretly ridiculed that sort of entreaty, yet the Caesars' supremacy was at an early stage then, and long-standing custom was more before their eyes; and between stepsons and stepfather the connection was slighter than a grandfather's to grandson.) (3) A priesthood was added and, on the day of Nero's first Forum appearance, a gratuity to the populace, altogether happy at seeing Germanicus' offspring now mature. The joy was increased by the marriage of Nero and Drusus' daughter Julia. (4) Although these events produced favourable talk, hostility met the news that Claudius' son had Sejanus as future father-in-law. *Defilement of Claudian*

nobility![42] people thought, and for Sejanus, already suspected of excessive hope, *Undue advancement!*

30. To conclude the year: notable men passed away, Lucius Volusius and Sallustius Crispus. Volusius' family was old but had never gone beyond the praetorship. He contributed a consulship, and even exercised the censorial function of reviewing jury-panels. Of the wealth[43] through which that family was immensely potent he was the first accumulator. (2) Crispus, by origin equestrian-ranked, was adopted – being his sister's grandson – and named by Sallust, Roman history's most celebrated author. Crispus, despite having ready access to office-holding, emulated Maecenas: without senatorial rank he outstripped in power many triumph-winners and ex-consuls. He diverged from tradition's mould in style and elegance: his resources and expenditures bordered on dissipation. (3) Yet underneath lay strength of character, equal to huge tasks, at its most vigorous whenever somnolence and inertia were most on display. While Maecenas was still unscathed, Crispus was next in line, and later pre-eminent as a prop for imperial secrets. Though complicit in the killing[44] of Agrippa Postumus, in advanced age he was more conspicuous in the Emperor's friendship than powerful. ((4) This happened to Maecenas,[45] too. Is it inevitable that power is rarely permanent? Or does surfeit seize both those who have given everything and those who have nothing left to desire?)[46]

31. (21 CE) Next, Tiberius' fourth consulship, Drusus' second.

Father and son as colleagues? Striking. (Two years earlier[47] Germanicus and Tiberius had held the same office: no happy occasion for the uncle, and the real connection was not so close.) (2) At the beginning of the year Tiberius ('to improve his health') retreated to Campania;[48] a limited rehearsal, perhaps, for his long and unbroken absence, or so that Drusus, with his father gone, would accomplish the consuls' tasks alone.

By chance a small affair that developed into a substantial quarrel offered Drusus grounds for accruing goodwill. (3) Ex-praetor Domitius Corbulo[49] complained about nobly born young Lucius Sulla in the senate. *At a gladiatorial spectacle*

Sulla did not make way for me! On Corbulo's side were seniority, tradition and the favour of the elders. On the other,
Mamercus Scaurus and Lucius Arruntius[50] and other Sullan
relatives exerted themselves. (4) Competing speeches cited lessons from ancestors who censured youth's irreverence with
their weightiest decrees. Finally Drusus' speech, designed to
moderate tempers. And satisfaction was given to Corbulo by
Mamercus, who was Sulla's uncle and stepfather as well, and
of that age's speakers the most luxuriant. (5) Another protest
from Corbulo: *Most of Italy's roads, what with contractor
fraud and magistrate negligence, are broken and impassable.*
The job of seeing the business through he undertook willingly –
and handled with less benefit to the public than harm to the
many onto whose fortune and reputation, via convictions and
confiscation, he let violence loose.

32. Soon thereafter a letter reached the senate from Tiberius.
Africa is again troubled by Tacfarinas raiding, he explained.
It is your decision:[51] *a governor must be chosen familiar with
military service, physically robust and adequate to the war.*
(2) The occasion was seized by Sextus Pompeius[52] to stir
hatred against Manius Lepidus. *He is idle, impoverished, a disgrace to his ancestors and, accordingly, should be barred from
the allotment even of Asia.* Pompeius' reproaches met senatorial opposition. *Lepidus is mild rather than cowardly, his
poverty is inherited, and noble birth borne without misbehaviour deserves honour, not insult.* So Lepidus was sent to Asia.
The Africa decision? *Tiberius should choose the man for the
mission.*

33. Meanwhile Caecina[53] moved that magistrates allotted
provincial commands should not be accompanied by their
wives. First, an extensive preface. *My consort is congenial to
me and has produced six children. What I will propose for
public affairs is my domestic policy: she has been limited to
Italy despite the many provinces in which I have accomplished
forty years' public service.* (2) *The former rule was justified: no
women to be taken among the allies or external peoples. The
company of females entails obstacles to peace (their dissipation) and war (their fearfulness) and gives Roman marching*

columns the look of barbarian processions. (3) Feeble and unequal to exertion, the sex is also, if licence offers, brutal, ambitious and greedy for power. They march among the soldiers, have centurions to hand. Recently a woman presided[54] *over cohorts drilling, legions parading! (4) Consider: in extortion trials, wives always incur more charges. To them the worst provincials attach themselves, by them business is undertaken and transacted. Two people's public appearances have followings, two headquarters exist, with the more willful and wayward orders being the woman's. Formerly the Oppian and other laws*[55] *held them in, but now, since restraints are undone, homes and public spaces – and soon armies! – are their domain.*

34. Few hearing this agreed. There was a general uproar. *This is not the business at hand and Caecina is not an appropriate censor for something so significant! (2)* Then Valerius Messalinus[56] responded. (Messala was his parent and he possessed a semblance of his father's eloquence.) *Much of antiquity's inflexibility has been exchanged for better and happier ways. Not now, as formerly, is Rome surrounded by wars, nor are provinces hostile. A few concessions are made to female needs without burdening a spouse's patrimony, let alone the allies; in the rest the husband shares, and this is no impediment to peace. Wars, obviously, require a girded approach, but to those returning after their exertion what is more respectable than wifely comfort? (3) True, some women have lapsed into ambition or greed. Well, many officials, too, are subservient to various pleasures, yet this does not result in no one being sent to the provinces. If husbands are often corrupted by their wives' perversities, are all unmarried men sound? (4) In the past the Oppian laws were approved, as the state's circumstances demanded. Afterwards came abatement and easing because that proved useful. Nothing is achieved by applying to our own timidity other labels. It is the husband's fault if his wife exceeds due measure. (5) Furthermore, the weakmindedness of one or two individuals is depriving all husbands of companionship in prosperity and adversity, and at the same time a sex naturally frail is being deserted and left to its own dissipation and to others' appetites. It is difficult, even with*

guards present, to keep wives unscathed. What will happen when for years at a time, as if divorced, they are made irrelevant? Address crimes committed elsewhere with Rome's depravities firmly in mind! (6) Drusus added a few words about his own marriage. *Emperors will often need to visit distant parts of the Empire. How often Augustus travelled to west and east with Livia as his companion! I myself went to Illyricum and, if it serves, will go to other peoples, rarely calm of spirit, however, if torn from my beloved wife, parent of our numerous children.* Thus was Caecina's proposal foiled.

35. At the next meeting, Tiberius, via a letter containing indirect criticism of the senate for referring everything needing attention to the Emperor, nominated Marcus Lepidus and Junius Blaesus[57] from whom to choose the governor of Africa. (2) Both were heard. Lepidus exempted himself with some insistence (physical frailty, children's ages and a marriageable daughter were his excuses) and people understood even what he did not say, that as Sejanus' uncle, Blaesus had the advantage. (3) Blaesus replied with a show of refusal, less emphatic, and was supported by[58] a chorus of flatterers.

36. Next was aired something that, when people complained in private, stayed under cover: the licence increasingly available to worthless individuals for arousing insults and resentment against decent men while holding an emperor's likeness. Freedmen, even, and slaves brandishing words and fists against patron and master caused alarm. (2) This prompted the senator Gaius Cestius'[59] address. *Emperors are on the level of the gods, but the gods give ear only to just prayers, and no one takes refuge in the Capitoline or Rome's other temples for active assistance in misbehaviour.* (3) *Laws are abolished and utterly overturned when in the Forum, on the senate's threshold, Annia Rufilla, whose fraud conviction I secured in court, is brandishing insults and threats at me, and I don't dare exercise my rights because the Emperor's likeness confronts me!* (4) Similar things echoed from others and some had more appalling tales. They pleaded with Drusus to set an example of punishment, until, after summons and conviction, Rufilla was imprisoned by his order.

37. Two equestrian-ranked men, Considius Aequus and Caelius Cursor, who had fabricated treason charges against the praetor Magius Caecilianus, were also punished, on the Emperor's recommendation and by senatorial decree.

(2) From both actions Drusus accrued praise: with him present in Rome and encountering people in gatherings and conversations, the seclusion of his father was felt less keenly. Nor did the man's extravagance altogether displease. *Better this, better to extend days with building projects and nights with parties than, lonely and distracted by no pleasures, to practise gloomy vigilance and evil cares!* 38 For neither Tiberius nor accusers were tiring. Ancharius Priscus had indicted Crete's governor[60] Caesius Cordus for extortion – plus treason, a charge then used as makeweight in every prosecution. (2) And Tiberius brought Antistius Vetus back. One of Macedon's leading men and acquitted of adultery – his jurors felt Tiberius' rebuke – he had to answer a treason charge for being a troublemaker implicated in Rhescuporis' plans when, after killing Cotys, Rhescuporis urged war against us. Exile was decreed for the defendant, plus confinement on an island convenient to neither Macedon nor Thrace.[61]

(3) (Control of Thrace[62] was divided between Rhoemetalces and Cotys' children, who, infants still, had a guardian, Trebellenus Rufus.) Being unfamiliar with us, Thrace manifested disaffection and, accusing Rhoemetalces no less than Trebellenus, refused to leave injuries to her population unavenged. (4) The Coelaletae, Odrusae and Dii, powerful nations, took up arms under different leaders, all equally unknown to one another, which was why they never united for a formidable war. Some disrupted what was nearby, others crossed the Haemus range to rouse distant peoples. Most of them, the most organized, encircled the king and Philippopolis, a city settled by Philip of Macedon. 39 When this became known, Publius Vellaeus, the nearest army's commander, sent cavalry detachments and rapid-deployment cohorts against those who were roving for plunder or to recruit reinforcements. He himself led the infantry's solid might to relieve the blockade. (2) Immediately, there was success everywhere: raiders killed, dissent

among the besiegers, an opportune sally by the king and the legion's arrival. To call it a pitched battle or combat would not be fitting, when half-armed stragglers were slaughtered with no blood of ours shed.

40. The same year.

The communities of Gaul began a rebellion because of the extent of their indebtedness. The most vigorous instigators were, among the Treveri, Julius Florus, and among the Aedui, Julius Sacrovir. Both had noble birth and ancestral deeds and therefore Roman citizenship by a past gift (this happened rarely and only as valour's reward). (2) After secret meetings and recruitment of the most spirited men or those having – from destitution and depravity-induced fear – the greatest necessity of wrongdoing, they arranged that Florus would rouse the Belgae and Sacrovir the nearby Gauls. (3) So in assemblies and gatherings they spoke sedition about unending tribute, galling interest, brutality and arrogance in those in charge. *Rome's soldiers are discordant at news of Germanicus' death: an excellent moment for regaining freedom. Just consider, prosperous yourselves, how barren Italy is, how unwarlike the urban populace. The army's only vigour is foreign!*

41. Nearly every community was infected by the germs of that uprising, but the first to erupt were the Andecavi and Turoni. As for the Andecavi, the legate Acilius Aviola roused the legion garrisoning Lyon and checked them. (2) The Turoni were crushed by legionary troops sent by Visellius Varro, Lower Germany's governor, under the command of Aviola and some Gallic leaders, who provided help in order to conceal their defection and find a better time for its revelation. (3) On show was Sacrovir himself, helmetless, rousing men to fight for the Romans; a display, he said, of valour. But captives claimed that he made himself recognizable to avoid being shot at. Tiberius, consulted about him, rejected the evidence and, by doubting, fostered war.

42. Meanwhile Florus pursued their plan and tempted a cavalry unit – conscripted from the Treveri but held to our military standard and discipline – to slaughter Roman traders and initiate a war. Of the cavalry a few were seduced, most remained

loyal. (2) Another population, debt-slaves and dependants, did arm and was heading for woods called the Ardennes when from each army legions that Visellius and Gaius Silius[63] had sent against their march proved an obstruction. (3) Dispatched with picked men, one Julius Indus – a fellow tribesman at odds with Florus and thereby the greedier for success – scattered further the disorganized multitude. Florus, by shifting refuges, frustrated the victors but eventually, seeing soldiers occupying his escape routes, fell by his own hand. This, for the Treveran uprising, was the end.

43. The Aeduan uprising grew more vast. The community was more opulent, the force to suppress it further away. Their capital Autun was held by Sacrovir with armed troops, as was the elite progeny of Gaul being educated there. Sacrovir's aim was to recruit – with these as hostages – their parents and relatives. He also distributed clandestinely manufactured weapons to fighting-age men. (2) He had 40,000, a fifth with legionary arms, the rest with spears and knives and other hunting weapons. Plus slaves: some trainee gladiators clad, according to native custom, entirely in iron – the 'cruppellarii', awkward at striking but when struck, impenetrable. (3) Additional strength came from the ready enthusiasm of individuals, although neighbouring communities were not yet in open agreement, and from the Roman commanders' rivalry, an ongoing dispute, each claiming the war for himself. Eventually the frail and elderly Varro yielded to a hale Silius.

44. In Rome the rebellion was believed to involve not just Treveri and Aedui but the sixty-four Gallic tribes, with German allies, Spain wavering. Everything, as is the way with rumour, was exaggerated. (2) Good men, concerned about the state, grieved. But in many – from hatred of present conditions and longing for change – even their own peril caused joy and they berated Tiberius for expending effort, during a movement of such magnitude, on accusers' denunciations. (3) *Will Sacrovir, too, face a treason charge in the senate? Men have finally stood forth with weapons to stop blood-stained letters. For a wretched peace even war is a good exchange!* (4) Tiberius' show of unconcern was ever more unstinting: without altering location

or demeanour he spent his days as usual, either from loftiness of spirit or because he had discovered the trouble to be limited and less than people said.

45. Meanwhile Silius, advancing with two legions, dispatched an auxiliary unit and ravaged villages belonging to the Sequani. These, being at the far edge of Aeduan territory and coterminous, were their allies in arms. Then he headed for Autun moving quickly, standard-bearers racing one another, even regulars shouting no to customary halts, no to night-time intervals. *Don't wait! Just let us see the enemy and be seen – that will suffice for victory!* (2) At the twelfth milestone Sacrovir and his forces appeared on open ground. Forward, he had placed the ironclads; on the wings, infantry; behind, the partially armed. He himself approached among the foremost, distinctively horsed, recalling Gaul's ancient glories and reverses inflicted on Romans. *How fine liberty will be for the victors, and more intolerable slavery for those vanquished again!*

46. His words were quickly done, his hearers unhappy: the legionary line was approaching, and disorganized and untrained villagers were no match for the sight or sound.

Opposite him Silius – although having hope within grasp removed his reasons to exhort – kept shouting: *You should be ashamed! Germany's conquerors are being led against Gauls as if against an enemy.* (2) 'One cohort recently routed the rebel Turoni, one cavalry unit the Treveri, a few squadrons from this very army the Sequani. The Aedui? They are rich in money, in pleasures opulent, unwarlike accordingly. Crush them and be ready for runaways!'[64] (3) There was a vast accompanying shout, then envelopment by cavalry, frontal attack by infantry, rapid movement on the wings. Brief delay at the ironclads, whose plate-armour stood up to pikes and swords. But the soldiers grabbed axes and picks and, as if breaching a wall, hacked at covering and body. Some used poles and pitchforks to topple the inert masses. Once prostrate, with no leverage to get up, the ironclads were left for dead. (4) Sacrovir headed first for Autun, then, fearing surrender, to a nearby villa with his most faithful. There he perished by his own hand, the rest by mutual blows. The villa, fired over them, turned all to ash.

47. Then finally Tiberius wrote to the senate that a war had begun and was done, without subtracting from or adding to the truth in saying that his legates had prevailed with dependability and valour, and he by policy. (2) Next, reasons why he and Drusus had not set out for this war: the Empire's size, which he extolled, and the unsuitability of rulers <heading for>⁶⁵ one or another turbulent community and leaving Rome, the source of their control over everything. *Now that fear is not the inducement, I will go⁶⁶ and observe the situation and settle it.* (3) The senate decreed vows for his return and thanksgivings and other honours. Only Cornelius Dolabella,⁶⁷ trying to get ahead, advanced to absurd flattery, proposing that Tiberius, upon returning from Campania, celebrate an ovation. (4) Then came a letter from Tiberius. *I am not so devoid of glory!* he declared. *After mastering the most spirited peoples and holding – in my prime – or declining numerous triumphs, I am not going to seek, at my age, after a suburban sojourn, a meaningless reward.*⁶⁸

48. Around this time Tiberius asked the senate that the death of Sulpicius Quirinius be marked by a public funeral. Quirinius had no connection to the old patrician Sulpicii. His origins were small-town Lanuvium, but with his energy in soldiering and staunch services he gained a consulship under Augustus and then, after capturing Homonadensian strongholds in Cilicia, an honorary triumph. Official adviser to Gaius Caesar when he was Armenia's governor, Quirinius also courted Tiberius on Rhodes. (2) This Tiberius then revealed in the senate, praising attentions received, and attacking Marcus Lollius, the man responsible, he claimed, for Gaius Caesar's perverse disputes. The rest, however, remembered Quirinius without pleasure, for having aimed danger, as I reported, at Lepida,⁶⁹ and for his sordid and vastly powerful old age.

49. To conclude the year: equestrian-ranked Clutorius Priscus, who, after his famous 'Lament on Germanicus Dying', received an honorarium from Tiberius, was in an informer's clutches. During Drusus' illness, it was said, he wrote a poem to circulate, if Drusus died, for a bigger fee. (Clutorius had given a reading at Publius Petronius' house in the presence of

Petronius' mother-in-law Vitellia and many notable women, showing off.) (2) When an informer emerged, the others were terrified into testifying. Only Vitellia insisted: *I heard nothing.* But those speaking for Priscus' ruin were more plausible, and on the motion of consul-designate Haterius Agrippa[70] the defendant was sentenced to death.

50. Opposing the motion, Marcus Lepidus[71] spoke thus: 'If, senators, we only consider how unspeakable the words were with which Clutorius Priscus defiled his mind and people's ears, neither prison nor noose nor even a slave execution would suffice. (2) But although depravities and crimes have no limit, if in punishment and redress the Emperor's moderation, and both ancestral and present examples, apply restraint and differentiate the trivial from the wicked and words from crimes, there is now room for a verdict that does not leave Priscus' offence unpunished, but also leaves us feeling neither too merciful nor too severe. I have often heard[72] our emperor lamenting when someone's suicide forestalls his pity. (3) Priscus still has his life. If saved, he will not become a public danger, nor, if killed, a moral lesson. His writings, though utterly deranged, are inconsequential and ephemeral, and one need not fear anything significant or serious from a man who exposes his own depravity: it was not into the minds of men, but of mere women that he gained entry. (4) Let him leave Rome and, his property forfeit, live an exile. This is my recommendation, treating him as liable to the law of treason.'

51. With Lepidus only the ex-consul Rubellius Blandus[73] agreed. The rest followed Agrippa's motion and Priscus, taken to the prison, was dead directly. Tiberius criticized this with his customary indirection in the senate. While praising their devotion in punishing severely the Emperor's injuries however slight, he protested against such headlong punishments for verbal offences and praised Lepidus without blaming Agrippa. (2) The senate, therefore, decreed that senatorial rulings would be registered only after nine days and that the condemned would have that interval of life as an extension. But the senate lacked freedom to rethink and in Tiberius a time gap produced no softening.

52. (22 CE) Consuls Gaius Sulpicius and Decimus Haterius came next.

An undisturbed year abroad. At home people feared severity against luxury,[74] which had surged beyond measure for anything on which money is squandered. Some expenditures, heavy though they were, were concealed by regularly fictitious prices, but the outlay on gastronomic gluttony, publicized by non-stop talk, caused anxiety. *Will an emperor of old-fashioned parsimony make a firmer response?* (2) For on the initiative of Gaius Bibulus the other aediles, too, had reported neglect of the sumptuary law. *The illegal sums spent on entertaining are constantly growing and cannot be staunched by moderate measures.* The senate, when consulted, passed the matter directly to the Emperor. (3) Tiberius, after much internal deliberation – *Can such widespread appetites be repressed? Will repression do more general damage? How unbecoming engagement without success will be! Yet succeeding will involve ignominy and disgrace for notable men* – finally wrote a letter to the senate. Its gist was this:

53. 'In other matters, senators, it may be advantageous that I be consulted directly and say what I judge to be in the public interest. But with this proposal my eyes' absence was better, so that, when you were observing the fearful expressions of individuals to accuse of shameful extravagance, I didn't myself see and catch them "in the act". (2) If those valiant fellows, the aediles, had consulted me beforehand, I would probably have urged them to ignore vices that are exceedingly strong and fully grown, instead of doing this, exposing depravities we are no match for. (3) But at least they did their duty; I should like other magistrates, too, to fulfil their obligations. For me, however, silence is not right, nor is expression easy, since my role is not that of aedile or praetor or consul. From the Emperor something bigger and grander is required. And although with deeds well done everyone takes some credit, one man earns antipathy for everyone's wrongdoing. (4) Where shall I begin saying no and cutting back to ancient custom? With villas' boundless extents? With households' sizes, or rather populations? With gold and silver quantities? With bronzes and

paintings, artistic wonders? With clothing common to men and women and a vice particular to women, in whose interest – for the sake of gemstones! – our money is shipped to foreign and enemy peoples?

54. 'I am well aware that at parties and gatherings people fault these practices and demand limits. But suppose someone passed a law and established penalties. "Civic life has been turned upside down! This means ruin for society's stars! No one is clear of crime!" will be their cry. In bodies, too, lingering and long-developed illnesses are only checked by tough, harsh measures. In a frail and feverish character, degradation's victim and agent alike, the fires will not be quenched by remedies feebler than the passions with which it burns. (2) Every law devised by our ancestors or passed by Augustus has been nullified, the former forgotten, the latter, more shockingly, scorned. Luxury is now secure. For suppose you want something not yet forbidden: that you might be forbidden it would be a worry. But if you have transgressed prohibitions unpunished, you're left with no fear or decency. (3) Why did thrift prevail in the past? Because everyone controlled himself and we were citizens of a single city. Present temptations didn't even exist when we ruled Italy. Victorious abroad, we learned to devour others' goods; at home, our own, too. (4) What a little thing the aediles rebuke! How trivial, if you consider the rest! And no one, no one brings up *these* problems: "Italy is dependent on foreign goods! The Roman people's subsistence[75] is daily exposed to the uncertainties of sea and storm!" Without the provincial resources on which landowners, slavery and agriculture rely, our own groves and country places will, no doubt, keep us safe. (5) This responsibility, senators, your emperor assumes. If ignored, it will drag the state down to ruin. For the rest, remedies must be sought within. Let decency change us for the better, and necessity the poor, satiety the rich. If a magistrate has the industry and strictness to confront these problems, I praise him and admit to feeling relieved of some of my labours. (6) But if people want to censure vices and then, after earning a name thereby, to start fights and leave them for me – believe me, senators, I have no appetite for grievances, either. I do

incur them, weighty and usually undeserved, in the public interest. But from these, which are empty and inconsequential and unlikely to benefit either of us, I beg, legitimately, to be excused.'

55. After hearing Tiberius' letter the aediles had less anxiety on this account. Table luxury, which was practised from the war ending at Actium to the conflict in which Galba took control through a century of profuse expenditure, has dwindled gradually. The causes of this change? Let's look. (2) Families once wealthy and noble or conspicuous for renown kept toppling in pursuit of magnificence, for then it was still permitted to court and be courted by the public, the allies, kingdoms. And the more someone's wealth, house and trappings made him visible, the more distinction he got from name and dependants. (3) After the outbreak of slaughter – and great renown meant destruction – the rest turned towards greater prudence. And the numerous new men from Italy's municipalities[76] and even provinces in the senate brought along their native thrift, and although many through luck or industry reached a moneyed old age, their earlier character persisted. (4) But the principal instigator of restrained behaviour was Vespasian, a man of old-fashioned dress and diet. From then on, deference to the Emperor and love of emulation proved stronger than legal sanction and fear. (5) Unless, perhaps, in everything there exists a sort of cycle such that as seasons change so do customs. Not everything was better before. Our age, too, has produced much merit, many attainments worthy of imitation by posterity. Long may this honourable competition with our ancestors persist!

56. Tiberius, after earning a reputation for moderation since he had checked the accusers' advance, sent the senate a letter. Tribunician power for Drusus was his request. (2) This label for the highest eminence Augustus devised to avoid 'king' and 'dictator' and yet to overtop in name all other offices. Later Agrippa was his choice as partner in this power, and after Agrippa's death Tiberius, so that his successor would not be in doubt. *Containment thus for other people's perverse hopes*, Augustus thought – he trusted Tiberius' restraint and his own

stature. (3) On this model Tiberius then brought Drusus closer to governing. (While Germanicus lived, Tiberius had kept his verdict between them open.) After starting the letter with a prayer that the gods foster his plans for the state, he gave a sober report about Drusus' character, without exaggeration's falsity. (4) *Drusus has a wife and three children and is the age I myself was*[77] *when summoned by Augustus to undertake this task. Not prematurely but after eight years' trial – seditions crushed, wars settled – is a man with a triumph and two consulships*[78] *being enlisted to share a known burden.*

57. Senators had sensed this speech coming, so the flattery was particularly laboured. But nothing was devised beyond imperial likenesses, divine altars, temples and arches and other routine proposals, except that Marcus Silanus[79] tried demeaning the consulship to honour emperors. He moved that dates on public and private monuments be recorded not with consuls' names as heading but with those of holders of tribunician power. (2) When, however, Quintus Haterius[80] recommended that the day's senatorial decrees be posted in the senate house in letters of gold, he seemed absurd, an old man earning nothing but the infamy of utterly shameful flattery.

58. Meanwhile, after the extension of Junius Blaesus' Africa governorship, the Jupiter-priest Servius Maluginensis[81] asked to be allotted Asia. *It is mistaken, the widespread idea that holders of this priesthood cannot leave Italy. I have the same entitlement as priests of Mars and Quirinus. If they draw for provinces, why is it forbidden to Jupiter-priests? No laws about this exist, no evidence in the records of religious observances. (2) Pontiffs often perform the sacrifices if the Jupiter-priest is prevented by ill health or public business. For seventy-five years*[82] *after Cornelius Merula's death no priest was installed, with no slackening in religious practice. If the priest's selection can be avoided for so many years without harm to ritual, how much easier his absence for a one-year term of provincial command! (3) Private quarrels used to cause chief pontiffs to block priests' provincial tours. But now, by the gods' gift, the foremost pontiff is the foremost of mankind, whom rivalry, hatred and personal considerations do not hold subservient.*

59. In opposition, the augur Lentulus and others spoke variously, then recourse was had to *Wait for the chief pontiff's opinion*. (2) Tiberius, putting off the hearing on priestly entitlement, limited the observances decreed for Drusus' tribunician power, criticizing specifically the unconventional motion and saying that golden letters were contrary to tradition. A letter from Drusus, too, was read, restrained in inflection but deemed exceedingly arrogant. (3) *It has come to this! Not even the youngster, after so signal an honour, will visit Rome's gods, enter the senate, inaugurate his rule on native soil. Drusus is at war, no doubt, or prevented by absence abroad – touring just then Campania's waters!* (4) *Thus the maiden voyage of a helmsman for humankind, this his father's first policy lesson! Antipathy to seeing fellow citizens afflicts the elderly emperor, naturally, and weary age and retirement are his excuses, but what hinders Drusus except arrogance?*

60. Tiberius, though consolidating his position's might, offered the senate a façade of tradition by forwarding provincial petitions for senatorial hearing. A growing problem throughout Greece was cities' unchecked licence for establishing places of sanctuary. Temples were full of the most villainous slaves. The same help beckoned debtors facing creditors and men suspected of capital crimes. No power was strong enough to control the riots of a people shielding human misdeeds as respect for the divine. (2) Therefore it was decided that cities should send their charters and envoys. Some voluntarily abandoned groundless practices. Many relied on long-standing beliefs and services to Rome. (3) The display that day was impressive: the senate examined grants made by our ancestors, agreements with allies, even decrees by kings who ruled before Rome became mighty, and marks of reverence for the gods themselves – with freedom, as formerly, to ratify or alter.

61. First to arrive were the Ephesians. Their story? *Diana and Apollo were not, as people believe, born on Delos. The Cenchreus stream is in Ephesus, as is the Ortygian wood where Latona, heavy with child, leaned on an olive tree – it still exists! – and birthed those gods. At this sign from the gods the grove was consecrated, and there Apollo himself, after the*

Cyclops-killing, avoided Jupiter's wrath. (2) Later father Liber, victorious in war, pardoned suppliant Amazons at its altar. The precinct's sanctity was augmented by a concession from Hercules when he ruled Asia and its entitlement was not reduced under Persian control. Thereafter Macedonians preserved it, as, next and last, did you.

62. The Magnesians[83] relied on rulings by Scipio and Sulla – the former after Antiochus' expulsion, the latter after Mithridates', in honour of their loyalty and valour – that gave Diana Leucophryena an inviolable sanctuary. (2) The Aphrodisians followed, and the Stratonicensians, with a decree of Caesar recognizing long-ago services to his cause, and a new decree of Augustus with praise for enduring a Parthian invasion[84] without altering their constancy towards the Roman people. (Aphrodisias was protecting reverence for Venus, Stratonicea for Zeus and Trivia.) (3) The Hierocaesarienses dug deeper. *Our Diana is Persian. Her temple was dedicated by King Cyrus.* They also named[85] Perpenna, Isauricus and many other generals who accorded equivalent inviolability to the temple and a two-mile radius. (4) Finally the Cypriots spoke for three temples. Of the oldest, that of Venus Paphia, the founder was Aerias. Afterwards his son Amathus established that of Venus Amathusia. The temple of Zeus Salaminius was established by Teucer, exiled by the wrath of his father Telamon.

63. They also heard other cities' delegations, wearisome to the senators for their number, and because the competition was impassioned. So they allowed the consuls to investigate entitlements and whether unfairness was involved and bring the entire matter back. (2) The consuls' report: *At Pergamum –* beyond the cities I mentioned *– there is an Aesculapius sanctuary. The rest rely on age-obscured foundations. (3) Apollo's oracle is cited by Smyrnaeans: on its order they founded their Venus Stratonicis temple. The Tenians, likewise, an Apollo-prophecy by which they were ordered to consecrate a statue and temple to Neptune. The Sardians' evidence is more recent: Alexander's gift, after his victory. Similarly, the Milesians, using King Darius. (For these two the cult is either Apollo's or Diana's.) The*

Cretans, too, are petitioning on behalf of their Augustus statue.
(4) The senate produced decrees by which, despite many signs
of respect, a limit was prescribed. Cities were ordered to affix
tablets in the temples themselves to enshrine the record, and
warned not to lapse into ambition behind religion's show.

64. Around this time an alarming illness of Livia's forced on
Tiberius a hasty return to Rome – genuine, still, the harmony
between mother and son, or else antagonisms were concealed.
((2) Shortly beforehand, upon dedicating a statue of Augustus[86]
near the theatre of Marcellus, Livia inscribed Tiberius' name
below her own and people believed that, since this was inconsistent with an emperor's dignity, he, though making light
of the galling grievance, stored away the matter.) (3) Eventually thanksgivings were decreed by the senate and a full-scale
festival to be staged by the major priesthoods[87] along with
officials of Augustus' cult. (4) A motion by Lucius Apronius[88]
that war-priests, too, supervise the festival was opposed by
Tiberius' speech differentiating the various priesthoods' entitlements, citing precedents. *The war-priests have never had so
much dignity. Officials of Augustus' cult are added because this
priesthood is associated with the family for which the vows are
being paid.*

(65. My policy is to trace proposals in detail only if conspicuously honourable or of noteworthy disgrace, for in my
view the principal obligation of histories is that manifestations
of excellence not go unspoken and, for perverse words and
deeds, to generate fear from posterity and infamy. (2) Those
times were so infected and filthy with flattery that not only the
state's leading men, who had to protect their renown by obsequiousness, but every ex-consul and the majority of former
praetors and even many junior senators stood up jostling with
shameful and excessive proposals. (3) Tradition holds that
Tiberius, leaving the senate house, used to exclaim – in Greek,
but with this purport – 'Those fellows are ready for slavery!'
Clearly even a man opposed to civic liberty found such abject
passivity in his slaves tedious.)

66. Shortly thereafter matters advanced from unbecoming
to pernicious. Gaius Silanus, a governor of Asia indicted for

extortion by provincials, was simultaneously fastened onto by
an ex-consul, Mamercus Scaurus,[89] and by the praetor Junius
Otho and aedile Bruttedius Niger. The charge was offending
Augustus' divinity, belittling Tiberius' majesty. Mamercus
tossed ancient precedents[90] around: Lucius Cotta prosecuted
by Scipio Aemilianus, Servius Galba by Cato the Censor, Publius Rutilius by Marcus Scaurus. ((2) As if Scipio and Cato
were avenging that sort of thing, or the famous Scaurus – his
own forebear! – whom Mamercus, a reproach to his ancestors,
was disgracing with his infamous initiative.) (3) Junius Otho's
former trade was running a primary school. Then through
Sejanus' power a senator, he actively defiled[91] obscure beginnings with daring impudence. (4) Bruttedius,[92] endowed with
honourable attainments, was on his way – were he pursuing a
proper path – to achievements of renown, but haste goaded his
endeavour to outstrip contemporaries, then superiors, and
finally his own hopes. This has destroyed many men, good
men, too. Belittling late and danger-free achievements, people
hurry them on premature, even ruinous.

   67. Augmenting the accusers' number were Gellius Publicola
and Marcus Paconius,[93] the former Silanus' financial official,
the latter his legate. People felt sure that for brutality and taking
money the accused was liable. (2) Then many factors dangerous
even to the blameless accrued, after (in addition to numerous
senatorial opponents) Asia's most eloquent men were selected
for that reason as accusers. Silanus replied alone, unacquainted
with pleading, at personal risk, something that enfeebles even
practised eloquence, and with Tiberius going so far as to press
with words and looks, indeed frequently posing questions himself. Neither rebuttal nor evasion was allowed, and often
confession, too, was obligatory, lest Tiberius question in vain.
(3) Silanus' slaves were acquired by the public executioner for
interrogation under torture. To prevent relatives from assisting
the defendant there were supplementary treason charges, a
shackle that necessitated silence. (4) Therefore, after requesting
a few days' interval, Silanus abandoned his defence. In his mis-
sive to Tiberius resentment and entreaties were mixed.

   68. Tiberius, to give his plans for Silanus a more indulgent

precedent-covered reception, ordered Augustus' letter on Volesus Messala (the same province's governor) and the senatorial decree against him read out. (2) Then he asked Lucius Piso's[94] opinion. Piso, after an extensive preface on the Emperor's clemency, proposed exile for Silanus and banishment to Gyarus Island. Likewise the rest, except Gnaeus Lentulus.[95] *Silanus' maternal inheritance – he is Appia's son – should be detached and given to his son,* he said, with Tiberius' approval.

69. Then Cornelius Dolabella,[96] pursuing flattery further, berated Silanus' character and added that none scandalous in conduct or blanketed by disgrace should draw provinces, the Emperor to judge. *Crimes are punished by laws, but how much easier it will be on us, and better for the provincials, to ensure that no wrongs be done!* (2) He was opposed by Tiberius. *I am aware of the stories circulating about Silanus, but rumour must not be decision's basis. The provincial conduct of many belies expectation or fear. Some are roused to better behaviour by the magnitude of affairs, others dulled. (3) An emperor cannot hold everything within his ken, and it is not expedient for him to be influenced by another's ambition. Laws are established against facts precisely because the future is uncertain. The ancestors' rule was this: if crimes precede, punishments follow. Do not overturn policies founded in wisdom that have found perpetual assent. (4) Emperors have enough burdens, enough power. Rights shrink when government grows and arbitrary power must not be used when legal action is possible.* (5) These popular-sovereignty views, being quite rare in Tiberius, were heard with particular delight. Tiberius, who was capable of restraint if not spurred by personal anger, added: *Gyarus[97] is harsh and uncultivated. Grant the Junian family and a man once of your order Cythnus instead for his retirement. (6) So, too, requests Silanus' sister Torquata, a Vestal of old-fashioned sanctity.* This proposal was approved directly.

70. Afterwards, the Cyreneans were heard and, with Ancharius Priscus prosecuting, Caesius Cordus was found guilty of extortion.[98] Equestrian-ranked Lucius Ennius, treason-charged for treating a likeness of the Emperor as ordinary-use silver, was refused as a defendant by Tiberius, to open protest from

Ateius Capito[99] in a show of independence. (2) *Senators should not be deprived of decision-making power, nor should so serious a crime go unpunished. Tiberius is naturally relenting when the pain is his own, but he must not condone injuries to the state.* (3) Tiberius understood him (more was involved than Capito said) and stood by his veto. Capito was quite conspicuous in his shame: an expert in human and divine law, he brought, people thought, an outstanding career[100] and domestic rectitude into disgrace.

71. Then religion took over. In what sacred space to place the gift vowed to 'Fortuna Equestris' by the equestrian order on behalf of Livia's health?[101] (Although there were many shrines to Fortuna in Rome, none had the name 'Equestris'.) A discovery: there was a temple so called in Antium and all rites in Italy's towns and sacred spaces and divine statues were under Roman jurisdiction and control. So the gift was situated in Antium. (2) Since religious matters were being handled, the recently postponed decision[102] regarding the Jupiter-priest Servius Maluginensis was delivered by Tiberius. He read out a decree of the pontiffs. *When ill health overtakes the Jupiter-priest he may, with the chief pontiff's authorization, absent himself for more than two nights, but not on holidays or more than twice a year.* This ruling from Augustus' principate showed sufficiently that a year's absence and provincial administration were not granted to Jupiter-priests. (3) Tiberius also mentioned the precedent of Lucius Metellus, the chief pontiff who detained the priest Aulus Postumius. The allotment of Asia, accordingly, was conferred on the ex-consul next after Maluginensis.

72. Just then Marcus Lepidus[103] asked the senate that he might, at his own expense, stabilize and adorn the Basilica of Paulus, a monument to the Aemilian family. At that time public generosity was still customary: Augustus did not prevent[104] Taurus, Philippus or Balbus from contributing their enemy spoils and overflowing wealth for the adornment of Rome and their posterity's glory. Following this precedent, Lepidus, though modestly moneyed, renewed his forefathers' tribute. (2) Pompey's Theatre, however, (coincidentally fire-consumed) Tiberius promised to rebuild[105] – *because none of the family is*

capable of its restoration – retaining nevertheless Pompey's name. (3) He also extolled Sejanus. *Through his effort and vigilance the huge calamity was limited to a single loss.* The senate decreed a statue of Sejanus for placement in Pompey's Theatre. (4) Shortly thereafter Tiberius, exalting Africa's governor Junius Blaesus with an honorary triumph, said that his gift was in honour of Sejanus, Blaesus being his uncle.

And yet Blaesus' achievements deserved such a tribute. 73. For Tacfarinas,[106] though repeatedly repulsed, with reinforcements found in Africa's interior had reached such arrogance as to send envoys to Tiberius demanding unasked a homeland for himself and his army or threatening an entangling war. (2) On no other occasion did an insult to himself and the Roman people make Tiberius more aggrieved, people say, than a deserter and desperado acting like an enemy. *Not even Spartacus[107] – torching Italy unavenged after numerous consular army casualties, when the republic was tottering from Sertorius' and Mithridates' vast wars – was granted a negotiated surrender. Much less with the Roman people at its finest peak will the thug Tacfarinas be bought off with a treaty and grant of lands!* (3) He gave the job to Blaesus. *Seduce others into hoping to lay down arms unscathed, but take the leader himself by any method whatsoever.* Many were recovered by this indulgence. Then: war against Tacfarinas' tactics, waged in like fashion.

74. Because Tacfarinas' army, being no match in strength but better at raiding, attacked in bands then slipped away and attempted ambushes, a three-prong invasion with three columns was prepared. (2) The legate Cornelius Scipio led one in the direction of the raiding against Lepcis and the Garamantes' refuges. Opposite, to prevent the district of Cirta from being plundered with impunity, Blaesus' son[108] had a company of his own. In the middle, with picked men, was Blaesus himself. Placing strongholds and fortifications at suitable locations, he made everything cramped and hostile to the enemy: wherever they headed a portion of Roman soldiery was in front, alongside and often behind. Many were thus killed or caught. (3) Then Blaesus spread his three-part army into more units led

by centurions of proven courage. And he did not, as was customary, withdraw his forces when summer was done or settle
them in the old province's winter quarters. With strongholds
arrayed on war's threshold, so to speak, he used unencumbered
teams familiar with the desert to disrupt Tacfarinas' nomadic
movements. Eventually, after capturing Tacfarinas' brother,
Blaesus withdrew – too early for the provincials' good, since he
left behind the agents of war's resurgence. (4) Tiberius, however, considered the war over and even allowed Blaesus the
tribute of an *imperator*-salute[109] by his legions. (This was a
traditional honour for generals acclaimed after successful conduct of state business in a surge of joy from their victorious
army. There used to be several *imperatores* at once, none
beyond the rest in level. Some received the title even from
Augustus. On that occasion, from Tiberius, Blaesus was the
last.)

75. There died that year notable men. Asinius Saloninus:[110]
his grandfathers were Agrippa and Asinius Pollio, and, conspicuous for his brother Drusus, he was the intended husband
of a granddaughter of Tiberius. Plus Ateius Capito,[111] whom I
mentioned: his standing in Rome's civic business was pre-
eminent, yet his grandfather was a Sullan centurion, his father
an ex-praetor. Augustus accelerated Capito's consulship so that
he might have precedence over[112] Antistius Labeo, who was
outstanding in the same field, with that magistracy's status.
(2) The age produced two paragons of peacetime pursuits
simultaneously. Labeo kept his independence unsullied and was
accordingly more celebrated of reputation; Capito's deference
won more approval from despots. For Labeo, who was limited
to the praetorship, plaudits accrued from injury; for Capito,
who had held a consulship, hatred arose from envy.

76. Junia, too, ended her days, in the sixty-fourth year
from the battle at Philippi. With Cato as her uncle by birth, she
was Cassius' wife, Brutus' sister. Her will was the subject of
much popular talk. *Although her resources were huge and she
honoured almost all the leading men by name, she omitted
Tiberius!*[113] (2) This he took citizen-like, not preventing her
funeral's distinction by a eulogy from the Rostra and the other

customary marks of honour. Twenty portrait-masks from the most illustrious families preceded her: Manlii, Quinctii and other names of equal renown. But Brutus and Cassius outshone the rest, precisely because their likenesses were not on display.

BOOK 4

1. (23 CE) Gaius Asinius, Gaius Antistius, consuls.

For Tiberius, it was a ninth year of settled state and flourishing house (he considered Germanicus' death advantageous). But suddenly Fortune began to riot and he himself to let his violence loose or to empower the violent. Start and cause lay with Aelius Sejanus, the Guard commander, whose power I mentioned earlier.[1] Now I shall explain his origin, character, and by what action he advanced to seize mastery.[2]

(2) Sejanus was born at Bolsena to an equestrian-ranked father, Seius Strabo,[3] and in early manhood attended upon Gaius Caesar, Augustus' grandson. (There was also a rumour that he offered perversion for sale to the wealthy spendthrift Apicius.) Later he so attached Tiberius by various arts as to render this man, inscrutable to others, incautious and unguarded with himself alone, less through cleverness – for Sejanus was defeated by the same arts – than through the gods' anger at Rome, for which his floruit and fall proved equally ruinous. (3) His body was tolerant of exertions, his spirit bold. Self-concealing, he was a denouncer of others, a combination of flattery and insolence. Outwardly, calculated decency. Inside? A passion for attaining the heights. To this end he applied occasional largesse and extravagance, and more often industriousness and vigilance – qualities no less harmful when assumed for acquiring rule.

2. He increased his office's power, previously limited, by gathering the cohorts scattered throughout the city into a single station so they would hear orders simultaneously, and so their number, strength and mutual visibility would yield confidence

for them, and in the rest, fear. His pretexts? *Dispersed, the sol-diers are carousing. In sudden threats, coordinated responses provide more assistance. Their behaviour will be more discip-lined if the fortification is located far from city allurements.* (2) When the station was finished, he infiltrated soldier minds by approaching and addressing them; also, he himself chose the officers. (3) Nor did he refrain from senatorial lobbying: bedecking hangers-on with offices and provinces. Tiberius was amenable and so well-disposed as to honour him – *partner of my labours!* – not just in conversation but before senators and populace, and to permit offerings to Sejanus' statues[4] in the-atres and public squares and at legionary headquarters.

3. But his house was full of Caesars: adult son and grown grandsons[5] hindered Sejanus' desires. Since destroying numbers simultaneously was unsafe, Sejanus' plot required intervals between crimes. (2) He decided, however, on an approach still more secret, beginning with Drusus, against whom he was moved by fresh anger. (Drusus, impatient of his rival and rather excitable in spirit, in a chance quarrel had shown Sejanus his fists and slapped his face when opposed.) (3) As Sejanus tested every possibility, the readiest seemed resorting to Drusus' wife Livilla, Germanicus' sister. (Although her looks early in life were unbecoming, she was later surpassingly beautiful.) As if fired by love, Sejanus lured her with adultery and after winning this first depravity – a woman without her purity not being inclined to refuse other things – urged her towards hope of marriage, towards partnership in rule and husband-murder. (4) With Augustus as her great-uncle, Tiberius as her father-in-law and Drusus' children, Livilla befouled self, ancestors and posterity with a small-town adulterer, replacing respectable and present expectations with scandalous and doubtful ones. She took into complicity Eudemus, her friend, physician and, under profession's cover, the frequenter of her seclusion. (5) Sejanus ousted his wife Apicata, who had borne him three children, lest his mistress become suspicious. But the magnitude of the deed brought fear, postponements and occasional changes of plan.

4. Meanwhile, at year's beginning, one of Germanicus' chil-dren, Drusus, donned manhood's toga. The senate's decisions[6]

about his brother Nero were duplicated. Tiberius added a speech containing much praise of his own son for acting with paternal benevolence towards a brother's children. (Drusus[7] – difficult as it is for power and concord to occupy the same spot – was considered fair to the young men, or at least not antagonistic.) (2) Then the long-standing and often advanced plan of a trip to the provinces was raised. The leader's reasons were the multitude of time-expired men and the necessity of levy-replenishment for the armies. *Volunteers are lacking and, where available, do not behave with the same courage and restraint, since mostly poor and vagrant men voluntarily undertake military service.* (3) Tiberius also surveyed quickly the legions' total and the provinces they secured. I think I, too, should track this. What were Rome's military resources then? Who the allied kings? How much narrower the Empire?[8]

5. Italy's two coasts had two fleets at Misenum and Ravenna over them. Gaul's adjacent shore had the warships captured in the Actian victory, which Augustus sent to Fréjus sturdily crewed. But the principal bulwark was beside the Rhine, support simultaneously against Gauls and Germans: eight legions. The recently conquered Spanish provinces were held by three. (2) The Moors, by gift of the Roman people, were in King Juba's hands. The rest of Africa was controlled by two legions, Egypt by the same number, and from Syria's border to the Euphrates – all the lands encompassed in this huge loop – by four, with Iberian, Albanian and other kings as neighbours, protected by our great size against external realms. (3) Thrace was held by Rhoemetalces and Cotys' children, the Danube bank by two legions in Pannonia, two in Moesia. An equal number were posted in Dalmatia, in a location behind the Danube legions and, if Italy needed emergency troops, nearby for summoning. Yet Rome was occupied by its own soldiers: three Urban and nine Guard cohorts, recruited mostly from Etruria and Umbria or ancient Latium and towns long Roman. (4) At suitable provincial locations there were allied warships and cavalry and auxiliary troops of approximately equivalent strength,[9] but following Tiberius' survey is risky since these moved here and there with contemporary needs, and their number swelled and was occasionally reduced.

6. It is fitting, I am inclined to believe, to review the state's remaining elements as well, how they were handled until then, since that year initiated for Tiberius a regime changed for the worse. (2) At first, public business and the most important private business was conducted in the senate. Leading men had permission to speak, and those who lapsed into flattery were checked by Tiberius himself. He conferred office with regard to nobility of forebears, distinction of military service, brilliant civic attainments; it was agreed that no other men were preferable. Consuls looked like consuls, praetors like praetors, and even lesser magistrates exercised their functions. Laws too – the treason court excepted – functioned well. (3) Grain- and money-taxes, plus other public revenues, were managed by associations of equestrian-ranked men. Tiberius entrusted his affairs to the most well-regarded, even to some strangers on account of their reputation. Once established, they were retained indefinitely; many grew old in the same jobs. (4) The populace did suffer under galling grain prices, but not by the Emperor's fault. Indeed he countered the lands' infertility and rough seas with outlay and attention insofar as he could. For the provinces his policy was that no new burdens trouble them, that they bear old ones without officials' greed and cruelty: no corporal punishment, no property confiscation. (5) Land-holding in Italy was a rarity for Tiberius, his slaves were restrained, his household limited to a few freedmen. And for his disputes with individuals he used courtroom and law.

7. All these things Tiberius retained, though in no affable style – he was prickly, rather, and generally alarming – until they were overset by Drusus' death. For while Drusus survived, they remained, since Sejanus, his power still incipient, wanted to be known for beneficial policies and feared an avenger not hiding his hatred but frequently protesting that despite a living son another was called 'assistant in command'. (2) *How long before the word is 'colleague'?*[10] *At first, hope of mastery requires toil, but once embarked you have support and agents. A station has been built at the commander's behest, soldiers are in hand. People see Sejanus' statue in Pompey's edifice. Future grandchildren*[11] *will be shared with the Drusi. One will*

eventually have to plead for restraint, that Sejanus be satisfied.
(3) Such outbursts by Drusus were neither rare nor restricted to
a few hearers, and even his secrets – his wife having been
seduced – were betrayed.

8. Sejanus, thinking haste necessary, chose a poison that,
by gradual infiltration, would produce a fortuitous disease's
appearance. It was given to Drusus by the eunuch Lygdus, as was
discovered eight years later.[12] (2) Tiberius, throughout Drusus'
illness – either unafraid or to display firmness of character – and
even with him dead but still unburied, attended senate meetings.
When the consuls in a show of grief seated themselves with ordinary senators, he reminded them of office and position. To a senate
effusive with tears he, having mastered his groans and with his
speech therefore uninterrupted, provided backbone. (3) *I am
aware that, with my suffering so fresh, I can be faulted for showing myself to the senate. Even relatives' words are hard to tolerate,
even daylight hard to face for most mourners, and they should
not be blamed for frailty. But I seek sturdier consolations in the
commonwealth's embrace.* Bemoaning Livia's extreme age, the
still untried stage of his grandsons, and his own decline, he asked
that Germanicus' children – *the only balm for present ills* – be
brought. (4) The consuls left, spoke bracingly to the youths and
escorted them before Tiberius. Taking hold, he said, 'Senators,
when these boys lost their father I entrusted them to their uncle
and prayed that, despite having progeny of his own, he foster and
raise them no differently than his own line and train them for his
own benefit and posterity's. (5) With Drusus now taken, I turn
my prayers to you. In the presence of gods and fatherland I
beseech you: these great-grandsons of Augustus, descendants of
the most renowned ancestors, raise them up, guide them, fulfil
your role and mine. These men, Nero and Drusus, replace your
parents.[13] Your birth is such that your good and ill are public
concerns.'

9. There was much lamentation, then propitious prayers,
from the audience. Had he stopped his speech, he would have
filled listeners' minds with pity for him, and praise. Returning to
empty and often mocked themes – restoring the republic, and
the consuls or someone else should assume its direction – he

deprived even what was true and honourable of belief. (2) In Drusus' memory the same things were decreed[14] as for Germanicus, with a number of additions, as is later flattery's wont. Drusus' funeral with its parade of likenesses reached celebrity's maximum: the Julian family's source Aeneas, all the Alban kings and Rome's founder Romulus, then the Sabine nobility, Attus Clausus and other Claudian faces in a long row were on view.

10. In relaying Drusus' death I have reported matters recorded in the most numerous and authoritative sources. But I'm inclined to include a contemporary rumour so strong that it has not yet faded, (2) that, after seducing Livilla for crime, Sejanus also secured, by perversion, the allegiance of the eunuch Lygdus, who was dear to his master for age and beauty and among his most prominent attendants. And that, after the accomplices settled poisoning's place and time, Sejanus went so far in audacity as to change course and, using an enigmatic hint to tax Drusus with poison for his father, to warn Tiberius that he must avoid the first drink handed him when dining with his son. (3) The old man, taken in by the trick, they say, after entering the party, handed the cup he received to Drusus, who, by unwitting acceptance and youthful quaffing, increased Tiberius' suspicion. *Are fear and shame causing him to inflict on himself a death contrived for his father?*

11. This widely publicized story – besides the fact that it is confirmed by no reliable authority – you can readily refute. For what man of even middling insight, let alone the vastly experienced Tiberius, would have offered death to a son unheard, and done so by his own hand with no recourse for regret? Would Tiberius not have tortured poison's agent instead and sought the person responsible? Used the innate hesitancy and delay that he applied even to strangers towards an only son discovered in no previous wrongdoing? (2) But because Sejanus was viewed as every crime's inventor – and in line with Tiberius' excessive fondness for him and others' hatred for both – people believed utterly fantastic and monstrous things – the talk is always quite appalling when our masters die. Besides, the crime's sequence, uncovered through Sejanus' wife Apicata, was laid bare by torturing Eudemus and Lygdus. Nor is there a

writer so hostile as to blame Tiberius, despite their investigation and exaggeration of everything else. (3) Why do I relay and challenge rumour? To rebut in a clear instance false hearsay and to request from those into whose hands my work comes that they not give the widespread and incredible – so greedily received! – priority over things true and not tainted with the marvellous.

12. During Tiberius' eulogy for his son from the Rostra, the senate and people adopted the garb and words of grieving more in simulation than sincerely, and rejoiced in secret that Germanicus' house was reviving. This was favour's inception, which, with their mother Agrippina's failure to hide her hopes, accelerated ruin. (2) For Sejanus saw that Drusus' death yielded no vengeance on killers and lacked public sorrow. Impetuous for crimes, and because the first ones prospered, he pondered how to bring down Germanicus' children, whose succession was certain. Three-way poisoning was not possible, given the unusual loyalty of their guards and Agrippina's impenetrable purity. (3) Her defiance, then, he attacked, stirring Livia's long-standing hatred and Livilla's fresh complicity. *Arrogant in her fecundity, confident in popular support, she covets mastery!* – these were the criticisms they should address to Tiberius. (4) Thus went the words of cunning denouncers, among whom Sejanus placed Julius Postumus, whose adultery with Mutila Prisca brought him intimacy with the grandmother and suitability for Sejanus' plans: Prisca, who was influential with Livia, was making an old woman who was inherently anxious about power aloof towards her daughter-in-law.[15] Even people close to Agrippina were enticed in perverse conversations to stimulate her swollen pride.

13. Tiberius' work on public affairs was uninterrupted. Treating business as solace, he handled citizen trials and allies' petitions, and senatorial decrees were made on his proposal to relieve the earthquake-damaged cities of Cibyra in Asia and Aegium in Achaea by a three-year remission of taxes.[16] (2) As for Vibius Serenus,[17] Further Spain's governor, who was condemned for abuse of office, his appalling behaviour earned him

deportation to Amorgos. Carsidius Sacerdos, charged with helping the enemy Tacfarinas with grain, was acquitted; also, on the same charge, Gaius Gracchus.[18] ((3) Exile's companion while still an infant, taken by his father Sempronius to Cercina and raised there among men outlawed and ignorant of cultural attainments, Gracchus later supported himself by trading cheap goods throughout Africa and Sicily. But he didn't escape the dangers of great rank.) Had Aelius Lamia and Lucius Apronius,[19] former governors of Africa, not protected the innocent man, he would have been eliminated by an unlucky family's renown and paternal misfortunes.

14. This year included embassies from Greek communities – the Samians for Juno, the Coans for Aesculapius – seeking confirmation of the temples' ancient right of asylum. The Samians relied on a decree from the Amphictyonies,[20] whose adjudication in all matters was pre-eminent when the Greeks, having founded cities throughout Asia, controlled the sea coasts. (2) The Coans had an antiquity no different, plus the place's merit: they had led Roman citizens into Aesculapius' temple when on King Mithridates' order[21] they were being slaughtered throughout Asia's islands and cities.

(3) Then, after various and usually futile complaints from the praetors, Tiberius finally brought up the excesses of actors. *Their numerous undertakings are disruptive in public and foul in homes. Farces*[22] – formerly Oscan, utterly trivial crowd-pleasers – *have reached such a point of depravity and clout that the senators' authority must check them.* Actors were expelled from Italy[23] at that time.

15. This same year afflicted Tiberius with another bereavement by removing one of Drusus' twins.[24] No less by the death of his friend Lucilius Longus, partner in all sorrows and joys and the sole senator companion of Tiberius' Rhodian retreat. (2) Accordingly, for Longus, though newly noble, a public funeral and a publicly funded statue in Augustus' Forum were voted by senators, by whom all public affairs were still handled at that time. They even heard the defence of the Emperor's Asia representative Lucilius Capito to the province's accusation,

along with the Emperor's loud assertion. *I gave him jurisdiction only over slaves and private finances. If Capito employed a governor's force and used military manpower, my instructions were ignored. Listen to the allies!* (3) Accordingly, the accused, after trial, was condemned. For this vengeance, and also because of Gaius Silanus' punishment[25] the previous year, Asia's cities decreed a temple[26] for Tiberius, his mother and the senate. Permission was even granted to build it and Nero spoke their thanks to senators and grandfather, amidst the delight of his audience, who, with Germanicus' memory still fresh, felt that it was he they were seeing and hearing. In the man's favour were his restraint and leader-worthy looks, while Sejanus' known hatred for him – *dangerous!* – increased their welcome.

16. Around this time, apropos of choosing a new Jupiter-priest in place of the deceased Servius Maluginensis, and also of passing a new law, there was a speech from Tiberius. (2) *Simultaneous nomination of three patricians born from spelt-wed parents,*[27] *from whom one is chosen, is traditional. But the supply is not as before, the practice of spelt-marriage having been discarded or preserved by small numbers.* (He mentioned[28] several reasons for this, especially the disinterest of men and women, plus the inherent difficulties of the ceremony itself, which is deliberately avoided, and because whoever assumes this priesthood and whoever becomes his wife leave paternal control.) (3) *Accordingly, a remedy is required via senatorial decree or law. Thus did Augustus adapt practices of hoary antiquity to present use.* After consideration of religion's impediments, the decision: to the institution of the priesthood, no alteration. But legislation did put the priest's wife under his control 'for ritual purposes'; in other activities she should have the general rights of women. (4) Young Maluginensis was appointed in his father's place. So that the prestige of consecrated individuals grow, and likewise a readier inclination in them for conducting ceremonial, two million sesterces were voted for Vestal Cornelia, who was admitted in Scantia's place, and that whenever Livia was in the theatre her seat be among the Vestals'.

17. (24 CE) Cornelius Cethegus, Visellius Varro, consuls.

When the pontiffs and, on their example, the other priests undertook vows for the Emperor's preservation, they also commended Nero and Drusus to the same gods, less from affection for the youths than from obsequiousness, which in a corrupt age is equally risky if absent or excessive. (2) For Tiberius, hardly ever mild towards Germanicus' house, was at that time intolerably aggrieved by the equal treatment of young men and his old age. He asked the assembled priests whether it was a tribute to Agrippina's entreaties or threats. The priests, despite denying, were criticized – in moderation, for the majority were his kin or community leaders – but in his senate speech Tiberius advised for the future against using premature honours to exalt young men's unstable spirits towards arrogance. (3) For Sejanus was applying pressure. His complaint? *The community is divided as if for civil war! People call themselves 'pro-Agrippina'! Unless resisted, there will be more. The only remedy for the spreading strife is if one or two of the most forward be toppled.*

18. This led to an attack on Gaius Silius[29] and Titius Sabinus. Germanicus' friendship was fatal for each. For Silius, it was also that, as a huge army's manager for seven years and, after earning an honorary triumph in Germany, the Sacrovir War's victor, the greater the crash of his fall, the more fear-spattered were others. (2) Many believed him to have increased grievance by his lack of control, boasting ceaselessly. *My troops remained dutiful when others plunged towards sedition. Tiberius' dominion would not have lasted had my legions, too, possessed a revolutionary urge.* (3) By this, Tiberius felt his position undermined, no match for so great a favour. For benefits are delightful only insofar as they seem capable of being requited. When they far exceed this, the return, in gratitude's place, is hatred.

19. Silius' wife was Sosia Galla, whom Agrippina's affection made hateful to the Emperor. The decision was to destroy these, postponing Sabinus for now.[30] The consul Varro was dispatched. With the excuse of an inherited antagonism[31] he gratified Sejanus' hatred – to his own disgrace. (2) When the

accused requested a brief delay until his accuser left office, Tiberius countered. *Magistrates regularly proceed against private citizens and there should be no weakening of a consul's privilege, since it rests on his watchfulness 'that the republic suffer no harm'.* (Typical Tiberius, concealing new-found crimes in old-fashioned terminology!)[32] (3) Varro quite agreed – as if Silius' trial was legitimate and he was consul and a republic existed – and the senators were assembled. The defendant remained silent, or else, if he began a defence, he exposed whose anger was crushing him. (4) The charges were complicity in war during the long Sacrovir cover-up,[33] a greed-sullied victory, his wife as partner. True, on the extortion charges Silius and Sosia were liable, but everything was handled as a case of treason and Silius forestalled imminent condemnation with a voluntary end.

20. Violence was nevertheless done to Silius' property. Not so provincials[34] might get their money back – none was reclaiming. But Augustus' generosity was stripped away: there was an itemized list of things claimed for the imperial purse! This was the first occasion of Tiberius' attentiveness to others' money. Sosia was exiled on Asinius Gallus'[35] motion. His proposal? *Half her property should be confiscated, half left for her children.* (2) Marcus Lepidus[36] countered, conceding a quarter to the accusers – the legal requirement – the rest to the children.

(This Lepidus, I find, was a consequential and wise man in that period: he steered many matters away from other men's violent obsequiousness into a better course. Nor did he lack balance, if he flourished with authority and Tiberius' favour unchanging. (3) This makes me wonder. Are fate and one's birth-lot the source, as of other things, also of an emperor's inclination towards some and grievance against others? Or is it something in our choices? Can one forge, between craggy defiance and degrading deference, a path clear of favour-seeking and danger? (4) But Cotta Messalinus,[37] whose ancestors were equally illustrious, was differently disposed and recommended making a provision, by senatorial decree, that governors – even those innocent and unaware of another's guilt – suffer for their wives' provincial crimes as if for their own.)

21. The next action concerned Lucius Piso,[38] a well-born and spirited man. He, as I reported, had shouted in the senate that he would leave Rome because of the accusers' divisiveness, and spurning Livia's power dared to drag Urgulania into court and roust her from the Emperor's house. At the time, Tiberius took this citizen-like. But in a mind recycling angry thoughts, although grievance's impact weakened, memory stayed strong. (2) Piso was berated by Quintus Veranius for secret treasonous conversation. Plus: *There is poison in his house and he attends the senate armed!* This was dismissed as too appalling to be true. But on the numerous other charges that accumulated Piso was entered as a defendant – and not tried, owing to timely death.

(3) There was discussion, too, of the exile Cassius Severus,[39] a man of lowly origin and baleful conduct – an effective speaker, however – who through uncurbed antagonisms had achieved a formal senatorial verdict of removal to Crete. By like behaviour there he attracted hatreds fresh and former. Stripped of property and forbidden fire and water, he grew old on rocky Seriphus.

22. In this same period the praetor Plautius Silvanus for reasons unknown sent his wife Apronia into freefall.[40] Dragged into Tiberius' presence by his father-in-law Lucius Apronius[41] he responded in confusion: *I was heavy with sleep and therefore unaware. My wife took her own life.* (2) Without delay Tiberius went to the house, visited the bedroom. The signs of a woman struggling and pushed were discerned. Tiberius reported to the senate and a trial was scheduled. Urgulania, Silvanus' grandmother, sent her grandson a dagger. *On the Emperor's orders*, it was believed, given Livia's friendship with Urgulania. (3) The defendant, after trying blade in vain, held out his veins for release. Soon Numatina, a former wife accused of inducing derangement in her husband by spells and potions, was judged guiltless.

23. This year finally released the Roman people from the long war against the Numidian Tacfarinas.

Earlier commanders, when they believed their achievements sufficient for obtaining an honorary triumph, would ignore him. There were three laurelled statues[42] in Rome then, but

Tacfarinas was still harassing Africa, strengthened by Moorish auxiliaries. (These Moors, Juba's son Ptolemy[43] being young and inattentive, had exchanged royal freedmen and slave dominance for war.) (2) In the Garamantes' king Tacfarinas had a purchaser for plunder and ally in depredation. Not that the king arrived with an army, but mobile troops were sent and distance magnified their reputation. From the province itself came an eager rush of men destitute of fortune, disruptive in character. For Tiberius, after Blaesus' achievements[44] – as if Africa now contained no enemy – had recalled the Ninth, and the year's governor Cornelius Dolabella did not dare retain it, fearing emperor's orders more than war's uncertainties.

24. Therefore Tacfarinas spread a rumour. *The Roman state is being mangled by other peoples, too, and therefore withdrawing gradually from Africa. The remnants can be overcome if everyone who prefers freedom to slavery bears down.* He increased his forces and, camp established, surrounded Thubursicum. (2) But Dolabella, having assembled the available soldiers – such is the terror of the Roman name, and then Numidians cannot face an infantry line – dissolved the siege upon arrival and fortified the area's useful positions. Dolabella also had the Musulamii leaders who attempted defection beheaded. (3) Then, in the knowledge, after numerous campaigns, that one did not hunt down a roving enemy with a heavy or single incursion, he roused King Ptolemy and his population and readied four columns. These were entrusted to legates or officers. Raiding parties were led by select Moors. Dolabella himself was on hand as adviser to all.

25. Soon thereafter came a report. *The Numidians are at a half-ruined stronghold – they applied the torch – called Auzea. Tents pitched, they are settled and confident in their location: vast surrounding scrublands enclose it.* Unencumbered cohorts and cavalry units were sped forward, ignorant of their destination, in a swift column. (2) At daybreak, as horns chorused and the shouting rang harsh, they were on the half-asleep barbarians. The Numidians' horses were hobbled or feeding loose in the distance. On the Roman side: infantry was massed, cavalry distributed, everything battle-ready. The enemy, by contrast,

was utterly unaware: no weapons, no organization, no plan. Like sheep, they were seized, killed, captured. (3) The soldiers, recalling with animosity their exertions and the fight so often desired against an elusive enemy, sated themselves individually with vengeance and blood. Word spread through the units. *Tacfarinas, familiar from so many battles, should be everyone's prey. Without the leader dead, no rest from war.* Tacfarinas, however, his bodyguard down around him, his son in chains, Romans everywhere, rushed the weapons and so avoided captivity by a death not unrequited. This end capped the fighting.

26. Dolabella sought an honorary triumph. Tiberius refused in deference to Sejanus, lest his uncle Blaesus' praise seem bygone. But Blaesus was not therefore more notable, while, for Dolabella, honour's denial gave his glory vigour: with a smaller army he carried off noteworthy captives, the leader's death and credit for the war's completion. (2) Then came envoys from the Garamantes,[45] rarely seen in Rome. They were sent, after Tacfarinas was killed, by a nation shattered and guilt-conscious, to satisfy the Roman people. In recognition of Ptolemy's active support throughout the war a traditional honour was revived and a senator dispatched to give him an ivory staff, an embroidered toga – venerable senatorial gifts – and the appellation *King and Ally and Friend*.

27. That same summer the seeds of slave war germinated throughout Italy; chance smothered them. The uprising's originator was Titus Curtisius, ex-Guardsman. Beginning with clandestine gatherings in Brundisium and surrounding towns, later with notices posted in public, he was summoning to freedom agriculturalists from remote highlands, spirited slaves, when, as if by the gods' gift, three cruisers arrived to meet the needs of travellers in those waters. (2) The quaestor Cutius Lupus was in the same area (he had the traditional 'pasturelands'[46] province). By distributing his marines he demolished the plot then commencing. Quickly, Tiberius sent Staius, a military officer, with a strong force. Staius dragged the leader and those closest in boldness to a Rome already fearful because of the domestic multitude, which was growing huge while the freeborn populace was every day smaller.

28. The same consuls.

Misery and brutality were on appalling display with a father accused, his son the accuser – both named Vibius Serenus[47] – before the senate. Dragged back from exile with a filthy and unkempt exterior and now in shackles, the father was readied for his son's speech. (2) The younger man was quite elegant and confident-looking. *A plot has been formed against the Emperor and subversives sent to Gaul!* said the war's denouncer and witness. And he implicated ex-praetor Caecilius Cornutus. *He supplied funds.*[48] (Cornutus, worry-weary and because danger seemed tantamount to destruction, inflicted a hasty death on himself.) (3) In response, the accused, his spirit not a bit broken, faced his son, shook his chains, called on avenging gods. *Give me back my exile, where I live far from such behaviour! Let my son, sooner or later, meet punishment!* He insisted: *Cornutus was innocent and mistakenly terrified, and you'll understand this easily – see whether others are divulged. For I did not contemplate emperor-murder and revolution with a single associate.*

29. The accuser then named Gnaeus Lentulus and Seius Tubero,[49] to Tiberius' great embarrassment. Rome's leading men, his own intimate friends, Lentulus extremely old, Tubero frail, they were being arraigned for rousing the enemy and disrupting the state. These men at least were immediately cleared. The elder Serenus was investigated via his slaves and the investigation went against the accuser. (2) Crime-deranged and also terrified of the crowd murmuring threats[50] – *The oak! The cliff!* and *Kin-killer punishments!* – the accuser left Rome. Dragged back from Ravenna, he was forced to pursue the prosecution, Tiberius not hiding his long-standing hatred towards the exile Serenus. (3) For after Libo's conviction[51] Serenus had sent Tiberius a letter complaining that his devotion alone had proven profitless, with additional remarks of more bravado than was safe in arrogant and rather offence-prone ears. Tiberius brought this up eight years later with various charges concerning the intervening years, even if the torture – *Slave stubbornness!* Tiberius said – turned out contrary.

30. After opinions were expressed that Serenus should suffer

the traditional punishment, Tiberius, to mitigate antipathy, vetoed it. Asinius Gallus' proposal that Serenus be confined on Gyarus or Donusa he also rejected. *Both islands are water-less and life's necessaries must be given to whoever is permitted life.* So Serenus was returned to Amorgos. (2) And because Cornutus had fallen by his own hand there was a discussion about abolishing accuser-rewards when someone indicted for treason takes his life before his trial is complete. The voting was in favour, except that Tiberius protested bluntly and, con-trary to his own practice, openly on the accusers' behalf. *The laws are impotent, the state heading for disaster! Better to overthrow the justice system than to remove its guardians!* Thus informers – a breed of men demonstrably a public men-ace and never adequately checked even by penalties – were coaxed forth by rewards.

31. Amidst these events, so persistent, so sorrowful, there arose a modest gladness: equestrian-ranked Gaius Cominius, guilty of a poem abusing Tiberius, was surrendered by Tiberius to the entreaties of his senator brother. (2) This made people feel it more remarkable that a man who knew the better, and the reputation attending clemency, preferred the more dismal. For Tiberius' wrongs were not done in idleness and one can discern when an emperor's deeds are celebrated genuinely and when with illusory gladness. He himself, false-fronted at other times, his words practically fighting their way out, spoke with more fluency and ease when bringing relief. (3) But for Publius Suillius,[52] formerly quaestor to Germanicus, who was facing banishment from Italy upon conviction for bribe-taking as judge, Tiberius proposed island exile with so much intensity of feeling that he pledged, on oath, *This is for the good of the state!* (What seemed harsh at the time turned into praise once Suillius was back: the coming age saw him vastly powerful and venal, a man who long used the Emperor Claudius' friendship profitably, but never well.) (4) The same penalty was decreed for the senator Firmius Catus[53] for attacking his sister on false treason charges. Catus, as I reported, had led Libo into a trap and then destroyed him with evidence. With this service in

mind, but using other pretexts, Tiberius entreated against exile; to expulsion from the senate he made no opposition.

32. Many of the things I have reported – and will report – may seem small and trivial in the recording, I am quite aware. But no one should compare my annals with the writing of those who narrated the past history of the Roman people. Huge wars,[54] successful assaults on cities, routed and captured kings, or, when they turned to internal affairs, disputes of consuls against tribunes, land-holding and welfare laws, conflicts between the commons and the 'best men' – these were the things they recorded, free to roam. (2) My work is in a narrow field and inglorious: peace undisturbed or modestly provoked, Rome's sorry affairs, an emperor inattentive to imperial expansion. It is not useless, however, this scrutiny of things at first sight trivial. From these, great events' stirrings often arise.

33. All nations and city-states are ruled by the people or leading men or individuals; the constitution formed by selecting from and conflating these types finds praise more easily than existence and, when it does exist, cannot last long. (2) Therefore, although in the past, with a forceful populace or when senators were in power, one needed to know the nature of the crowd and how it was managed, and those most fully cognizant of the characters of senate and 'best men' were believed canny about their times and wise, now, with the situation changed and the state's only security consisting in one-man rule, there is advantage in assembling and reporting these things: few use insight to distinguish the honourable from the less good, the useful from the harmful, and more are taught by others' outcomes. (3) But though beneficial they bring minimal pleasure. The locations of peoples, vicissitudes of battles and notable deaths of leaders: these things hold and revive readers' attention. I string together brutal orders, serial accusations, deceptive friendships, the ruin of innocents and identical causes of destruction, confronting the material's monotony and glut. (4) Plus this: antiquity-writers have few critics. No one cares whether you give Carthaginian or Roman armies a happier encomium. But for many who under Tiberius incurred punishment or disgrace, descendants survive, and where the

families themselves are gone you will find people who think, their characters being similar, that others' bad behaviour is a reproach to themselves. Even glory and virtue have haters – for too nearly accusing their opposites. But I return to my project.

34. (25 CE) Cornelius Cossus, Asinius Agrippa, consuls.

Cremutius Cordus was indicted on a novel charge, first heard then. *In published annals, after praising Brutus, he called Cassius 'last of the Romans'*. The accusers were Satrius Secundus and Pinarius Natta, Sejanus' men. (2) This was fatal for the defendant, as was Tiberius' grim-faced attention to the defence speech. Cremutius, resolved on leaving life, spoke thus: 'My words, senators, are faulted – that's how innocent of deeds I am. But my words do not target the Emperor or the Emperor's parent, whom the treason law covers. I am said to have praised Brutus and Cassius, whose achievements many have written up and none has recorded without honour. (3) Livy, pre-eminent for eloquence and reliability, presented Pompey in particular with such extensive praise that Augustus called him a Pompeian – and it was no obstacle to their friendship. As for Scipio, Afranius, this very Cassius and Brutus,[55] Livy nowhere dubs them "criminals and killers", the terms now obligatory, but often "eminent men". (4) Asinius Pollio's works transmit an outstanding memory for those same men; Messala Corvinus[56] boasted of "his commander" Cassius and both enjoyed wealth and office to the end. To Cicero's book[57] raising Cato to Olympus what was Caesar's response but to write a rebuttal, as if for judges? (5) Antony's letters and Brutus' harangues contain slurs on Augustus; false, of course, but extremely sharp. The poems of Bibaculus and Catullus, filled with Caesar-insults, have readers. But both Caesar himself and Augustus tolerated these and let them be; hard to say whether with greater restraint or good sense. Ignored, things fade, but if you get angry they seem legitimate. 35. (I'm not alluding to the Greeks, in whom not only freedom but even wantonness went unpunished, or if someone did take notice, he avenged words with words.) The most complete latitude and freedom from critics pertained to accounts about men whom death had removed from hatred or favour. (2) I am not (am I?) – with Cassius and Brutus in armed possession of Philippi's fields – firing the people for civil war with harangues. Is it not rather that those men, dead these seventy years but known from their likenesses,[58] which even the winner did not abolish, likewise retain a portion of memory in writers? (3) Everyone receives due honour from posterity. People there will be, if condemnation encroaches, not only to remember Cassius and Brutus but also to remember me.' (4) He left the senate then and, by food-abstinence, ended his life. *His books must be burned by the aediles!* the senators decreed. But they survived, hidden and spread. (5) All the more pleasurable, then, to mock the witlessness of those who believe that with present power it is possible to extinguish the future's memory. Punished talents' authority grows. Foreign kings and those who employ like brutality have spawned nothing but shame for themselves and, for those men, glory.

36. The year's series of indictments was such that during the Latin Festival the city's superintendent[59] Drusus, standing on a podium for the opening, was approached by Calpurnius Salvianus about Sextius Marius.[60] This, after open criticism from Tiberius, resulted in exile for Salvianus. (2) An official complaint about the Cyzicenes: inattention to ceremonies for Divus Augustus, plus charges of violence against Roman citizens. They lost the freedom earned under siege in the Mithridatic War, when their constancy no less than Lucullus' defence resulted in Mithridates' rebuff.[61] (3) Fonteius Capito, who as proconsul had attended to Asia, was acquitted after it was discovered that the charges against him were fabricated by Vibius Serenus. This, however, did Serenus no harm – the public's hatred made him safer. For unbridled accusers, in proportion, were practically sacrosanct; the lightweight and insignificant got punished.

37. In this same period Further Spain sent envoys to the senate and requested, on Asia's example, to build a temple to Tiberius and his mother. On this occasion Tiberius, who was generally firm in shunning honours, and believed a rejoinder due those critics whose talk accused him of changing course into ambition, began a speech as follows. (2) 'I know, senators, that many feel me to lack constancy, since when Asia's cities asked this earlier I did not resist. (3) Therefore I shall offer both

a defence of my former silence and my decision for the future. A temple to himself and Rome at Pergamum was not forbidden establishment by Augustus, and because I respect his every act and word as law I was ready to follow approved example, the readier since senate-veneration was linked to worship of me. But although one acceptance may win pardon, being consecrated with cult statues throughout the provinces is rivalry and presumption: Augustus' honour will fade if indiscriminate flattery makes it commonplace. 38. As for me, senators, I am a mortal and have human responsibilities, and I am satisfied to fill the first place. For this I invoke you as my witnesses and I want posterity, too, to remember it. They will accord my memory enough and more if they believe me worthy of my ancestors, watchful over your affairs, steadfast in danger and of grievances accrued in the public interest unafraid. (2) These will be my temples in your hearts, these the loveliest statues, and they will last; stone-built structures, if posterity's judgement turns to hatred, are shunned like tombs. (3) Accordingly, I entreat allies, citizens and the very gods and goddesses:⁶² the latter, that they grant me, life-long, a quiet mind cognizant of human and divine law; the former, that when I'm gone, their praise and good remembrance accompany my achievements and my name's renown.' (4) And he persisted thereafter, even in private conversations, in rejecting such worship of himself. To some this was modesty, to many, *He doesn't believe in himself.* And there were people to whom it signified worthless character. (5) *The best mortals have the loftiest desires. This is why Hercules and Liber, of the Greeks, and Quirinus, for us, are numbered among the gods. Better the policy of Augustus, who hoped. All else emperors have immediately to hand. Just one thing needs insatiable preparation: their favourable memory. Scorn for renown means scorning virtues.*

39. Sejanus, heedless from excessive good fortune and by female desire further inflamed – Livilla was demanding the promised marriage – composed a petition to Tiberius. (It was customary then to approach him, even when present, in writing.) (2) In outline it went as follows: *From the benevolence of your father Augustus and then your many marks of esteem, I am accustomed*

*to bring hopes and prayers not to the gods first but to the Emperor's
ears. I never sought offices' dazzle, but preferred guard-duty and
fatigues – as just one of your soldiers – for my emperor's security.
Yet I obtained the finest thing in being thought worthy of a connection with you.*[63] (3) *From this came hope's beginning. I have
heard that Augustus, in placing his daughter, gave some consideration to the equestrian-ranked. So you, if a husband for Livilla
is needed, should think about a friend who will use nothing but
the relationship's glory.* (4) *This is no attempt to shed the responsibilities imposed on me. I judge it enough that your house*[64] *be
reinforced against Agrippina's unwarranted grievances – for the
children's sake. For myself, what years remain will be enough
and more if spent with such an emperor.*

40. In response, Tiberius, after praising Sejanus' devotion
and reviewing, in moderation, his own favours to him, requested
time for fresh deliberation, adding this: *Other mortals' plans
centre on what they think beneficial to themselves. The
emperor's lot is different: in affairs of state our reputation must
rule.* (2) *Therefore I am not resorting to the easy answer that
Livilla herself can decide whether to marry post-Drusus or to
carry on in the same household. She has a mother and grandmother, advice nearer at hand.* (3) *I will deal more frankly.
First, about Agrippina's antagonism: it will burn much more
fiercely if Livilla's marriage effectively splits the imperial household into factions. As it is, the women's rivalry finds vents and
their strife divides my grandchildren. What if the contest is
intensified by this marriage?* (4) 'For you are mistaken, Sejanus,
if you think that you will remain where you are and that Livilla,
the spouse of Gaius Caesar, then of Drusus, is minded to grow
old with someone of equestrian rank. And suppose I give permission, do you think others will let it rest? Those who saw her
brother, her father and our ancestors at the summit of power?
(5) You yourself wish to stay in your place, but the magistrates
and leading men who importune your reluctance and consult
you about everything make it no secret that you have long since
exceeded equestrian standing and far surpassed those my father
befriended. And jealousy of you makes them criticize me, too.
(6) Augustus, you say, contemplated entrusting his daughter to

someone of equestrian rank. Extraordinary, if – when distracted by cares of every sort and foreseeing huge exaltation for whoever he raised above the rest with such a connection – he spoke about Gaius Proculeius and others of notably quiet lives, without public affairs' entanglements! But if we are influenced by Augustus' doubts, how much stronger the argument that he placed her with Agrippa and then me? (7) Out of friendship I have not kept these matters hidden. However, I will oppose neither your intentions nor Livilla's. What I've been turning over in my own mind, what close ties between us I'm preparing, I won't mention now. I'll just reveal this: nothing is too lofty a reward for your virtues and attitude towards me, and when the occasion arises in senate or assembly, I will not be silent.'

41. Sejanus in turn, no longer on the marriage but with more fundamental worries, tried to dispel the unspoken suspicions, the popular talk, the encroaching antipathy. Lest banning the constant gatherings at his house break his power, or accepting them give his critics material, he changed course to urging Tiberius to abide far from Rome[65] in pleasant settings. (2) His expectations were many. *I will control access and decide about most letters since they will travel with soldiers. Tiberius, nearing old age already and unstrung by the location's secrecy, will more easily transfer the responsibilities of rule. Less antipathy to myself without crowds of well-wishers and, with inanities' removal, more real power.* (3) Therefore, increasingly, the chores at Rome, the people thronging, the multitude of visitors were Sejanus' complaint, while he extolled repose and solitude. *Tedious and annoying matters are absent and affairs of state are one's main business.*

42. The chance occurrence, then, of the hearing about Votienus Montanus, a celebrated talent, pushed Tiberius, already on the verge, to believe that he should avoid senatorial company and talk, which was generally true, and galling face to face. (2) For at Votienus' indictment for slandering Tiberius, the witness Aemilius, a soldier type, in his zeal for proof reported everything and, despite the outcry, persisted in loud assertion. So Tiberius heard the insults used for his secret flaying and was so shaken as to exclaim: *I will clear myself either*

immediately or at the trial! And even with friends' entreaties
and everyone's flattery it was hard to regain composure.
(3) Votienus suffered the treason penalty and Tiberius embraced more stubbornly the mercilessness towards defendants
for which he had been faulted. Aquilia, adultery-indicted with
Varius Ligus (although consul-designate Lentulus Gaetulicus
had condemned her under the Julian law), Tiberius punished
with exile.[66] Apidius Merula, for not swearing loyalty to Augustus' acts, he erased from the senatorial roll.

43. Then came audiences for embassies from Lacedaemon
and Messene concerning rights to the Diana Limnas temple. *It
was dedicated by our ancestors in our territory*, affirmed the
Lacedaemonians on the basis of annals' record and poets'
verses, *and taken by force by Philip of Macedon because we
fought him. Afterwards it was restored by a ruling of Caesar
and Antony.*[67] (2) Contrarily, the Messenians adduced the
ancient division of the Peloponnese among Hercules' descendants. *To our king came the Dentheliate territory where the
temple is. Memorials of this fact – stone-carved and in ancient
bronze – survive.* (3) *But if challenged for the testimony of
poets and annals, we have more and better. Philip's decision
was not arbitrary power but based on truth. This was the verdict of Antigonus the king and Mummius the general; thus
decreed the Milesians as official arbiters, and thus, finally,
Atidius Geminus,*[68] *Achaea's governor.* The concession, accordingly, favoured the Messenians.

(4) The Segestans requested that the Venus temple on Mt
Eryx, age-collapsed, be restored. They recalled the familiar
story of its origin, to Tiberius' delight. He undertook the work
willingly as a 'relative'.

(5) The next matter dealt with was the Massiliots' petition.
It was approved on the Rutilius precedent.[69] (When Rutilius
was formally expelled, the Smyrnaeans adopted him as a citizen, which justified the exile Vulcacius Moschus, welcomed by
the Massiliots, in bequeathing his property to that community
as being his homeland.)

44. Passing away that year: nobles Gnaeus Lentulus[70] and
Lucius Domitius. For Lentulus, in addition to his consulship

and honorary triumph over the Getae, glory came from poverty
well-borne, and later from great wealth innocently obtained
and possessed with restraint. (2) Domitius had prestige from
his father, who in the civil war had a sea-command until he
merged with Antony, then Octavian; his grandfather fell at
Pharsalus for the 'best men'. He himself was chosen as husband
for the younger Antonia,[71] Octavia's daughter, after he crossed
the Elbe with his army and penetrated further into Germany
than anyone before and thereby earned an honorary triumph.
(3) Also passing away: Lucius Antonius, of family renown
great but untoward. For after Lucius' father Jullus Antonius[72]
was executed for adultery with Julia, Augustus removed him –
still quite young, and his sister's grandson – to Marseilles,
where, under studies' cover, exile could be concealed. Antonius
was honoured, however, with a funeral and his bones were
deposited in the tomb of the Octavii by decree of the senate.

45. The same consuls.

A shocking crime was committed in Nearer Spain by a peas-
ant from the Termestine tribe. He made an unexpected attack
on the provincial governor Lucius Piso, who was inattentive
owing to the peace, while Piso was travelling: killed him with a
single wound. With a speedy horse he escaped, and after reaching a highland area and dismissing the horse he frustrated those
following him among trackless precipices. (2) He didn't elude
long: with his horse caught and taken around the nearest districts his identity was known. Found and pressed to reveal his
accomplices, he shouted aloud in native tongue that interrogation was pointless. *My associates can stand and watch! No
pain will be strong enough to elicit the truth!* Brought back for
questioning the next day, with a huge effort he burst free of his
guards and dashed his head against a rock: instantaneously
lifeless. (3) But people believed Piso's killing a Termestine plot,
since after public funds were embezzled his collections were
more vigorous than barbarians tolerate.

46. (26 CE) Lentulus Gaetulicus, Gaius Calvisius, consuls.

Decreed: an honorary triumph for Poppaeus Sabinus[73] for
crushing Thracian tribes living high in the mountains with no
civilization and therefore more bravado. The cause of their

uprising, apart from human nature, was compulsory conscription and giving their strongest to our military. They refused, not being accustomed to obey even kings, except capriciously. Or if they did send auxiliaries, they placed their own commanders in charge and engaged in hostilities only against neighbours. (2) (A rumour had gone round. *Split up and mixed with other peoples, we will be conveyed to distant lands!*) Before initiating force they sent envoys to recall their friendship and compliance. *These will persist if we are tested by no new burden. But if slavery is imposed on us as if we were beaten, we have weapons and men and spirits eager for freedom – or death.* (3) Strongholds perched on crags and parents and wives conveyed there, were their boast, and war – baffling, toilsome, bloody – their threat.

47. Sabinus' response, until he could assemble an army, was mild. After the arrival of Pomponius Labeo[74] with a legion from Moesia, and Rhoemetalces with auxiliaries from local peoples of unchanged loyalty, he added his force to these and proceeded against the enemy now established in wooded ravines. Some made a bolder show on open hillsides; these the Roman leader engaged in battle. He routed them easily, with limited barbarian bloodshed owing to nearby refuges. (2) After fortifying a camp there, Sabinus took a strong detachment and occupied a narrow height connected by a level ridge to the nearest stronghold, protected by vast numbers armed and disorganized. Against the most spirited, who were making their customary feints in front of the rampart, chanting and capering, he sent picked archers. (3) In long-range attack these dealt numerous unrequited wounds, but drawing closer were dislodged by a sudden sally. Cover came from reinforcement by a Sugambrian cohort that the Roman commander – since it was as grim as the Thracians in chants and weapon-clash, and positioned nearby – had deployed for battle.

48. Moving camp alongside the enemy, Sabinus left in his former works the Thracians whose presence on our side I reported, with permission to pillage, burn and haul off booty – provided their plundering kept to daylight and they spent a safe and watchful night in camp. This was observed at first. Later,

converted to dissipation and flush with takings, they abandoned their posts for party carousing or succumbed to sleep and wine. (2) The enemy, having discovered this inattentiveness, prepared two columns, one for an attack on the plunderers, the other to assault the Roman camp, not hoping to take it but so that, given the shouting and weapons, men intent on their own danger would not hear the noise of the other battle. Darkness, too, was chosen to increase the alarm. (3) Those attempting the legions' rampart were easily repelled. The Thracian auxiliaries, terrified by the sudden incursion, some positioned beside the defences but more straying outside, were slaughtered with particular animosity for being – so went the accusation – *Turncoats and traitors bearing arms for your own and your country's enslavement!*

49. The next day Sabinus showed his army in a battle-conducive spot. *Will the barbarians, optimistic from night's success, dare battle?* When they didn't descend from their stronghold or the associated earthworks, he began a blockade, starting with guard-posts suitably fortified. Then, with combined ditch and breastworks, four miles in circumference, encirclement. (2) Gradually, for water- and fodder-deprivation, he drew the cordon tighter, narrowed the enclosure and constructed a siege ramp from which to hurl rocks, missiles and fire at the enemy, now close. (3) But nothing troubled them as much as thirst, since a huge crowd of fighters and non-combatants used a single spring. Horses and livestock – they were enclosed alongside, barbarian-fashion – expired from lack of fodder. Also with them were men's bodies dead of wounds or thirst. Everything was fouled by gore, stench, contagion.

50. Onto chaos the ultimate evil – strife – accrued, some thinking surrender, others death and mutual blows. Some, too, urged not unavenged ruin but breakout. (2) It wasn't the obscure, though they were divided of opinion, but one of the leaders, Dinis, advanced in age and from long experience familiar with Roman might and mercy, who said: *Weapons must be downed – the one remedy for our troubles!* He was the first, with wife and children, to entrust himself to the victor. Following him were the weak of age and sex, and those by whom life

rather than glory was desired. (3) Men in their prime were torn between Tarsa and Turesis, each intending to die with his freedom. Tarsa – *Death be quick! Sever hope and fear together!* was his cry – set an example, plunging sword into chest; and some did meet death thus. (4) Turesis and his band waited for night.

Our leader was well aware and accordingly braced guardposts with fuller-strength units. Night came on, stormy, appalling. The enemy, with confused shouting and occasional echoing silence, made the besiegers unsettled. But Sabinus went round, exhorted. *Don't let indistinct noises and an appearance of calm create an opening for plotters. Do your duty, everyone, without panic. No firing at decoys!*

51. Meanwhile the barbarians descended en masse onto the rampart, now hurling fist-size rocks, fire-sharpened stakes and tree limbs, now using brush and bundled branches – and lifeless corpses – to fill the ditches. Some set advance-made gangways and ladders against the breastworks, grabbing and dismantling. Against the defenders there was a hand-to-hand struggle. The soldiers in response used weapons to dislodge, shield-bosses to shove back. They launched wall spikes and masses of piled-up rocks. (2) Spirit accrued for the Romans from sure victory's expectations and, if they yielded, a more conspicuous scandal. For the Thracians, from safety's last chance and the presence of many mothers and wives, and their laments. The night was, for some, conducive to daring, for others to alarm. Blows were unsure, wounds unforeseen. Ignorance – *Who is friend, who enemy?* – and the mountain curvature's echoing of cries – *From behind!* – so confused everything that some defences, as if breached, were abandoned by the Romans. (3) For the enemy, however, there was no escape except for a very few. The rest, since the most energetic were down or wounded and daylight was now approaching, the Romans muscled up into the stronghold, where they forced surrender. The nearest places were recovered on the inhabitants' initiative. For the remainder, so that they were not subdued by assault or siege, the early and brutal Haemus winter provided relief.

52. In Rome, however, the Emperor's household was roused to begin the sequence of Agrippina's eventual destruction: her cousin Claudia Pulchra was indicted. The accuser was Domitius Afer,[75] fresh from his praetorship, moderately eminent, impatient to shine in action, any action. Unchastity, Furnius her adulterer, preparing poison against the Emperor, and curse spells were the charges. (2) Agrippina, always formidable and at that time also incensed by her kinswoman's danger, headed for Tiberius and chanced to find him sacrificing to his father – an opening for resentment. *It is inconsistent for the same man to offer victims to Divus Augustus and to persecute his posterity. Mute statues are not the receptacles of divine spirit. I am his true likeness, sprung from heavenly blood. I see danger and don mourning. It is pointless to foreground Pulchra, the only cause of whose destruction was choosing me, quite stupidly, for her attentions and forgetting Sosia, struck down[76] for this same thing.* (3) Hearing this elicited a rare utterance from that inscrutable breast. Grabbing her, he admonished with a line of Greek verse: *It is no injury, your not ruling.* (4) Pulchra and Furnius were convicted. Afer joined the foremost orators. His talent became known, with a boost from Tiberius' pronouncement labelling him 'genuinely eloquent'. Undertaking accusations, protecting the accused, Afer got a reputation more favourable for eloquence than for character, except that extreme age took much of his eloquence, too: mind exhausted, he remained intolerant of silence.

53. Agrippina, stubborn in anger and gripped by bodily disease, during a visit from Tiberius wept long in silence, then spoke her resentment and entreaties. *Relieve my solitude, give me a husband! I still have my prime and for respectable women only marriage provides ease. The state contains people * * *[77] will deign to accept Germanicus' spouse and children.* (2) Tiberius, aware of the public significance of the request, but not wanting to be obviously aggrieved and alarmed, left her unanswered, though she pressed. (I found this incident, not transmitted by annals-writers, in the notebooks of the younger Agrippina, Nero's mother, who recorded her life and her family's disasters for posterity.)

54. Sejanus caused the grieving and unwary woman a harder fall by dispatching people to warn – through friendship's façade – about poison prepared for her. *You must avoid your father-in-law's table.* Ignorant of deception,[78] when reclining alongside she did not react to looks or words and touched no food, until Tiberius noticed – by chance? Had he heard? For a more incisive investigation, he praised some fruit served just then and handed it to his daughter-in-law. This aroused suspicion in Agrippina and she passed it, untouched by mouth, to her slaves. (2) Tiberius' response – not direct but turning to his mother – *It is no surprise if my decision is rather harsh about a woman who accuses me of poisoning!* From this came rumour. *Her ruin is readying and the Emperor does not dare anything open: secrecy is being sought for the perpetration.*

55. Tiberius, to deflect talk, was a frequent presence in the senate. He listened for several days to Asia's envoys arguing about which city the temple should be constructed in. Eleven were competing, equal in ambition, in resources various. The narratives were not much different concerning their people's antiquity and devotion to the Roman people[79] throughout the wars with Perses and Aristonicus and other kings. (2) The cities of Hypaepa and Tralles were passed over with Laodicea and Magnesia. *Not thriving enough.* Even Ilium, despite citing Troy as Rome's parent, had no clout except antiquity's glory. There was brief hesitation over the Halicarnassians' claim that for 1,200 years their site had never quaked, that the temple's foundations would rest on bedrock. Pergamum, since Augustus' temple was there – this was their claim's basis – was believed to have enough. Ephesus and Miletus seemed taken, the latter by Apollo's rites, the former by Diana's. (3) So the debate was between Sardis and Smyrna.

The Sardians read out a decree from Etruria. *We are blood relatives! Tyrrhenus and Lydus, sons of King Atys, divided their people because of its multitude. Lydus settled in paternal lands, Tyrrhenus' lot was to settle new lands. The leaders' names*[80] *were applied, the former's to those throughout Asia, the latter's to those in Italy. As the Lydians' opulence increased, they sent peoples to the Greece later named for Pelops.*[81]

(4) Likewise mentioned: commanders' letters and treaties with us during the Macedonian war, and their rivers' copiousness, their climate's mildness, and the rich surrounding territory.

56. The Smyrnaeans, after tracing back their age – Tantalus, Jove's son, their founder, or Theseus, himself of divine stock, or one of the Amazons[82] – passed to the material on which they chiefly relied, services to the Roman people: naval resources dispatched not just for foreign wars but also for those suffered in Italy. *We were the first to build a temple to Rome, during Cato's consulship, when the Roman people's affairs were already great but not yet at their peak, with the Punic city still standing and strong kings throughout Asia. (2) Likewise, on Sulla's testimony: in his army's moment of gravest danger from winter's severity and their lack of clothing, when this was announced to Smyrna at an assembly, all present removed their cloaks and sent them to the legions.* (3) Asked their opinion, the senators preferred Smyrna. Vibius Marsus proposed that Marcus Lepidus,[83] to whom the province had been allotted, receive an extra assistant to attend to the temple. Since Lepidus himself refused, through modesty, to choose, Valerius Naso, one of the ex-praetors, was dispatched by lot.

57. Meanwhile, by a long-contemplated and too often deferred plan, Tiberius went to Campania.[84] The pretext was dedicating temples to Jove at Capua and Augustus at Nola; but he had fixed on abiding far from Rome. As for the withdrawal's cause,[85] I have followed most authorities in referring it to Sejanus' doing, but because after Sejanus was killed Tiberius continued six more years equally secluded, I am somewhat troubled. Is referring it to Tiberius himself truer? The brutality and lust divulged in action – was he concealing them by location? (2) Some believed that in old age he was also ashamed of his body's state: exceptionally thin, height stooped, top bare of hair, face scabbed and generally medicine-spotted. Even during his Rhodes retreat his habit was to avoid company and hide pleasures. (3) Also reported: Tiberius was muscled out by the unruliness of a mother he disdained as partner in mastery but could not dislodge, having received that mastery by her gift. For Augustus was undecided – *Shall I impose Germanicus, my*

sister's grandson and praised by all, on the Roman state? – but overcome by his wife's entreaties he linked Germanicus to Tiberius, Tiberius to himself. With this Livia reproached her son, and demanded a return.

58. Tiberius set out with a limited entourage. One consular senator, Cocceius Nerva,[86] with legal expertise. Of the notable men of equestrian rank, besides Sejanus: Curtius Atticus.[87] The rest were men of learning, mostly Greeks, for conversational diversion. (2) The astrologers' report – *Such were the planets' movements at Tiberius' departure that return is denied him* – caused many ruin. *A speedy end to life!* was their conjecture and outcry. For people did not foresee the outcome – so incredible! – that through eleven years Tiberius willingly did without his country. (3) Eventually the narrow boundary between science and sham lay exposed, and in what obscurities truth is cloaked. That he would not return to Rome was no random utterance. But people acted in ignorance of the rest, for he lived out his final age in the countryside or coast nearby, and often up against the city walls.

59. It chanced that Tiberius' encounter just then with a dangerous crisis amplified empty rumour and provided him with evidence for giving Sejanus' friendship[88] and constancy increased trust. They were dining at a villa called The Cave, between the sea off Amyclae and Fundi's hills, in a natural grotto. Its mouth, when the rock suddenly collapsed, crushed some attendants, (2) which produced fear in everyone and flight by the party's crowd. Sejanus propped himself – knee and hand on each side – over Tiberius to block the falling debris and was found like this by soldiers bringing relief. He was more towering thereafter and, although he urged ruinous actions, because he was unconcerned about himself he was heard with greater credence.

(3) Sejanus acted the judge's part against Germanicus' stock, with agents assigned to play accuser and harass Nero in particular, as next in succession and, though a temperate young man, nevertheless somewhat forgetful of what suited present conditions, while freedmen and dependants, impatient to gain power, goaded him to stand tall and confident of spirit. *The*

*Roman people want this, the army longs for it! Opposition will
not be risked by a Sejanus now making free simultaneously
with an old man's passivity and a young man's indolence.*

60. With Nero hearing this and the like, nothing, certainly,
of perverse intention but occasional defiant and injudicious
utterances emerged for guards standing by to catch and amp-
lify. These were reported and Nero got no chance to excuse
them. And various additional worrying appearances arose:
(2) one man would avoid his encounter, some would exchange
greetings, then immediately turn away; many broke off conversations in progress, to the urging and jeering of the
Sejanus-promoters present. But Tiberius was grim or decep-
tively beaming in expression. Speaking or silent, Nero was
blamed for silence or speech. Not even the night was safe: his
wife.[89] Wakefulness, sleep, sighs – she revealed all to her mother
Livilla, and Livilla to Sejanus, who recruited Nero's brother
Drusus, too, for their side, confronting him with hope of
primacy if he removed an older brother already tottering.
(3) Ruthlessness was in Drusus' character, and besides passion
for power and ordinary fraternal hatreds it was fired by jealousy:
their mother Agrippina was partial to Nero. But in promoting
Drusus, Sejanus contemplated the seeds of ruin for him, too,
knowing him high-spirited and the more liable to ambush.

61. To conclude the year: the departures of notable men.[90]
Asinius Agrippa, of ancestry illustrious rather than old, in his
own life not worthless. And Quintus Haterius, of senatorial
family and celebrated eloquence – while alive. The monuments
of his talent do not enjoy commensurate retention. In impact,
no doubt, rather than study lay his potency, and although other
men's thought and effort gain vigour with posterity, Haterius'
melodious and fluent style was extinguished with himself.

62. (27 CE) Marcus Licinius, Lucius Calpurnius, consuls.

Huge wars' casualties were equalled by unexpected harm,
and the beginning coincided with the end. Building an amphitheatre near Fidenae to stage a gladiatorial show, a certain
Atilius, of freedman parentage, neither set its foundations on
solid ground nor used reliable fastenings in erecting its wooden
superstructure: it wasn't from an abundance of money or

municipal ambition but for filthy lucre that he had sought the job. (2) People streamed in, avid for such things and under Tiberius pleasure-deprived, men and women, every age, in greater numbers owing to Fidenae's proximity.[91] This made the disaster the more grievous. The packed structure gave a heave, collapsing inwards and exploding out. An immense quantity of human beings intent on the show or in the vicinity was carried headlong and buried. (3) Those whom the beginning of the wreckage struck dead – granted, their lot was death – avoided agony. More pitiable those, torn of body, whom life had not yet deserted, conscious – during the day, by sight, during the night, by their wails and groaning – of spouses or children. The rest, rumour-summoned, mourned one a brother, another a kinsman, others parents. Even those whose friends and relatives, for various reasons, were absent felt dread. As long as it was unknown whom accident had felled, uncertainty spread the fear.

63. As the rubble-removal began, people converged on the lifeless. There were embraces, kisses, and many a dispute if, when a face was unrecognizable, similar shape or age caused mistaken recognitions. Fifty thousand that disaster maimed or crushed. Precautions for the future, by senatorial decree: no one to put on a gladiatorial show if his holdings were less than 400,000 sesterces, and no amphitheatres to be built except on ground of verified reliability. Atilius was sent into exile. (2) While the disaster was still recent, the houses of the pre-eminent lay open and supplies of bandages and doctors were everywhere. Rome in those days, though sorrowful of face, resembled the institutions of old, when after great battles the wounded were supported with generosity and care.

64. That calamity was still vivid when fire's violence struck the city beyond the norm: the Caelian was completely burnt. People were saying: *It is a deadly year. The omens are unfavourable for the Emperor's plan of absence.* Such is the crowd's habit, seizing chance occurrences for blame – except that Tiberius countered with gifts of money commensurate with the damage. (2) Thanks accrued – among the senate, from notables, from talk among the people – since no lobbying and no friends' entreaties had prompted him, and even strangers,

spontaneously invited, received generous assistance. (3) Plus proposals: *The Caelian should henceforth be called 'Augustan', since with everything roundabout aflame only Tiberius' likeness in the senator Junius' house remained inviolate. This happened before, to Claudia Quinta:*[92] *her statue, which twice escaped the flames, the ancestors consecrated in the temple of the Great Mother. The Claudii are graced and welcomed by the gods and one must augment the sanctity of a place in which the gods have shown such great respect for the Emperor.*

(65. It is not, I think, preposterous to relay that the hill's name, of old, was Querquetulanus because of the oak woods with which it was dense and prolific; that later it was called Caelius from Caeles Vibenna, the Etruscans' leader, who, after bringing assistance was given the site by Tarquinius Priscus – or perhaps another of the kings, for writers disagree about this. The rest is not in doubt: his numerous troops also inhabited the level ground near the Forum, from which 'Etruscan Street' got the newcomers' name.)

66. The attentions of the pre-eminent and the Emperor's largesse eased disaster, but as for accusers – their virulence, increasing daily, was ever more pernicious – there was no relief to their aggression. Ruined: Quinctilius Varus, a wealthy man connected to Tiberius, by Domitius Afer, his mother Claudia Pulchra's[93] sentencer. Nobody was surprised that a man long needy, having misused recent prize money, was girding for more wrongdoing. (2) That Cornelius Dolabella[94] appeared as his associate in the indictment did surprise: Dolabella's ancestors were renowned and as a relative of Varus' he was destroying his own nobility, his own blood. Still, the senate baulked. The vote? *We must wait for the Emperor* – for pressing evils, the one temporary refuge.

67. Tiberius finished dedicating the Campania temples. Despite a decree warning against interrupting his repose, and soldiers stationed to deter the converging locals, he was disgusted by municipalities[95] and everything mainland. He hid himself away on Capri, an island detached by a three-mile strait from the tip of Sorrentum's promontory. (2) Solitude was probably its greatest recommendation. The surrounding sea is

harbourless, and even modest vessels have few resources, nor does anyone put in without the guard's knowlege. The climate in winter is mild: an obstructing mountain deflects the winds' savagery. Summer faces the west wind and, with open sea all around, is utterly delightful. Capri overlooked a lovely bay before Vesuvius' fires changed the place's appearance. Legend reports Greeks holding this area, Capri inhabited by the Teleboi. (3) But now Tiberius established himself on the names[96] and foundations of twelve villas. His former attention to public responsibilities was now equalled by his relaxation into secretive dissipations and baneful leisure. For his rashness in suspicion and belief persisted, and Sejanus, already in Rome accustomed to amplifying it, began to rouse it more vigorously. There was no more concealment for the plots against Agrippina and Nero, (4) who got a military guard, recording – as if for annals! – their communications, visits, public and private affairs. Plus Sejanus' agents urged taking refuge with Germany's armies or, in the crowded Forum, embracing Augustus' likeness and summoning the people and senate to help. Plans that, though rejected, they were accused of readying.

68. (28 CE) Junius Silanus and Silius Nerva, consuls.

The year's beginning came in foul. Dragged off to prison: a notable of equestrian rank, Titius Sabinus,[97] for friendship with Germanicus. (He had persisted in assiduous attentions to Germanicus' spouse and children: a devotee at home, a companion in public, after so many dependants the only one, and, accordingly, praised by good men and troublesome to unfair ones.) (2) His attackers were Latinius Latiaris,[98] Porcius Cato, Petillius Rufus, Marcus Opsius, ex-praetors all, desirous of the consulship. No access to that except through Sejanus, whose goodwill was gained only by crime. Their plan was that Latiaris, who had some acquaintance with Sabinus, would lay the trap, with the others present as witnesses. *Then we'll initiate the accusation.* (3) So Latiaris dropped conversational remarks, random at first, then praising Sabinus' constancy. *Unlike the rest of the household's friends in prosperity, you have not deserted it in affliction.* Latiaris spoke with respect for Germanicus and compassionately towards Agrippina. And after

Sabinus – so yielding are human souls in calamity! – poured
out tears and added his protests, Latiaris, more boldly now,
belaboured Sejanus: *An animal! Arrogant! Ambitious!* Not
even from Tiberius did he withhold abuse. (4) And these conversations, as if sharing forbidden things, produced the
appearance of close friendship. Eventually Sabinus himself
sought out Latiaris, went to his house and reported sorrows as
if to someone completely trustworthy.

69. Discussion among the aforementioned: *How can these
words be captured by more hearers?* (Where they met, the
appearance of solitude had to be preserved.) *Standing behind a
door?* They feared sight, sound and accidental suspicion.
Between roof and ceiling! Three senators squeezed in – their
hiding place no less shameful than their ploy was despicable –
and applied ears to gaps and cracks. (2) Meanwhile Latiaris
found Sabinus in the city and, as if with fresh discoveries to
report, took him home, into his bedroom. Past and pressing
matters, which were abundantly available, and new terrors,
too, were heaped up. The same from Sabinus, at greater length.
(The more sorrowful one's words, once they've broken out, the
more difficult they are to restrain.) (3) Instant accusation: writing to Tiberius they narrated their ploy in order – and their
shame. Never was a community more anxious and fearful,
screening itself against friends. Gatherings and conversations,
ears known and unknown, were avoided. Even mute and lifeless objects – *the roof! the walls!* – were watched.

70. Tiberius, after the traditional New Year prayer – by letter –
on 1 January, rounded on Sabinus. *He bribed some freedmen to
attack me!* Tiberius claimed. *Vengeance, openly!* was his demand.
There was no delay in its decree. Sabinus was dragged off, a
convict. Insofar as he could with head covered and neck noosed,
he cried out: *Thus begins the New Year! These victims fall to
Sejanus!* (2) Wherever Sabinus directed his eyes, wherever his
words landed, there was flight, rout, emptied streets and squares.
Then some returned and showed themselves again, frightened by
precisely this: that they had been afraid. (3) *What day will be
punishment-free, if amidst rites and prayers, when even unseemly
language is habitually avoided, chains and noose are brought in?*

Not inadvertently has Tiberius incurred such antipathy. It is a calculated plan so that he will not be thought an obstacle to new magistrates' opening the execution chamber as they do temples and altars. (4) Next, Tiberius' letter of thanks for their punishment of a man hostile to the state. Plus: *I live atremble, suspect enemy plots.* There were no names in his attack, but Nero and Agrippina – no one doubted – were the target.

71. (My intention was to report events in their own years, but my soul did yearn to anticipate and mention immediately the outcomes for Latiaris and Opsius and this scandal's other inventors, not only after Gaius assumed power but during the lifetime of Tiberius. Although he didn't want his crimes' agents overthrown by others, he generally – once glutted, and with fresh ones on offer for the same services – struck down veterans now irksome. But these and the guilty men's other punishments I will report in time.)

(2) At this, Asinius Gallus,[99] though Agrippina was aunt to his children, proposed asking the Emperor to speak his fears to the senate and allow them to be removed. (3) None of Tiberius' virtues – as Tiberius thought – was so dear to him as dissembling. He was, therefore, particularly aggrieved at disclosures of what he was suppressing. But Sejanus soothed, not from love of Gallus but to wait out the Emperor's delays, knowing that, though slow in deliberating, whenever Tiberius let loose, grim speech and ruthless action came together.

(4) In this same period Julia passed away. This granddaughter Augustus, after adultery was proven, condemned and disposed of on Trimetus not far from Apulia's shores. There for twenty years she endured exile, supported by Livia's money. (Livia, despite overthrowing her stepfamily in their prosperity, displayed compassion for the afflicted.)

72. That same year the Frisians, a people living beyond the Rhine, shed their quietude, more from our greed than because compliance was intolerable. The tribute Drusus had ordered[100] from them was modest, appropriate to their pinched resources: their payment was oxhides for military use. No one paid attention to how sturdy or how big until Chief Centurion Olennius, imposed on the Frisians as ruler, chose aurochs hide as the

standard for acceptance. (2) Difficult, this, even for other peoples, but harder for Germans to bear since – though the woods teem with huge beasts – their domestic livestock is modest. At first whole oxen, then fields, finally wives' and children's bodies were delivered into slavery. (3) This led to rage and protest and, when no help arrived, a remedy in war. They seized the soldiers then present for payment and crucified them. Olennius forestalled his attackers by flight and holed up in a stronghold called Flevum, where a considerable company of citizens and allies presided over Ocean's shores.

73. When Lucius Apronius,[101] Lower Germany's governor, knew, he summoned detachments from the Upper province's legions and picked infantry and cavalry from the auxiliaries, then immediately took both armies down the Rhine against the Frisians, the stronghold blockade having dissolved and the rebels gone off to secure their own. Accordingly, Apronius built up nearby tidal areas with causeways so that heavier columns could cross. (2) Meanwhile, ford found, he ordered Canninefate cavalry and all the German infantry serving in our army to circle behind the enemy, who, already lined up, were pressuring allied squadrons and legionary cavalry dispatched to help. Three rapid-deployment cohorts were sent in, then again two, then, with time intervening, the main cavalry. Strong enough, had they borne down simultaneously; arriving at intervals, they did not increase the constancy of the dismayed and the panic of the fleeing carried them off. (3) To Cethecius Labeo, the Fifth's legate, Apronius handed what remained of the auxiliaries. Labeo, his own troops' situation shaky, faced a crisis and sent a letter to implore the legions' might. The men of the Fifth burst forth ahead of the rest and, after bitter fighting that pushed the enemy back, recovered the auxiliary infantry and cavalry units, exhausted by their wounds. The Roman leader neither retaliated nor buried his dead, although many officers[102] had fallen. (4) It was discovered later from deserters that 900 Romans were killed in 'Baduhenna's Grove' after prolonging the fight into the following day, and that another group of 400 holding a villa belonging to Cruptorix (he was once in our pay), fearing betrayal, succumbed to mutual blows.

74. There was renown, thereafter, among the Germans, for the Frisian name. Tiberius covered up the losses, so as not to hand anyone a war. Nor was the senate concerned about disgrace at the Empire's edges: dread within gripped their minds. And for this a remedy was sought in flattery. (2) Thus, though consulted about other matters they voted an Altar of Clemency and an Altar of Friendship flanked by statues of Sejanus and Tiberius. The entreaties were frequent. *Give us a chance to see you!*

(3) Sejanus and Tiberius did not leave for Rome or the vicinity, however. Enough, they thought, to leave Capri and be seen in nearby Campania. To this place came senators, equestrians and a large part of the populace, anxious about Sejanus. Meeting him was now harder. Accordingly, it was obtained through bribery and plans' alignment. (4) All agreed: *His arrogance is increased by the sight of this shameful and open servility.* In Rome, coming and going is normal and because of the city's size one's object is unknown. In the countryside there, on the shore, they camped without distinctions, and day and night alike doorkeeper favour or contempt made them suffer, until that, too, was forbidden. (5) People returned to the city atremble if not found worthy of a conversation or glance. And some had mistaken enthusiasm: over these an unlucky friendship's grievous result impended.

75. Tiberius, although he personally betrothed his grand-daughter Agrippina, Germanicus' child, to Gnaeus Domitius, ordered the wedding[103] celebrated in Rome. In Domitius, besides the line's antiquity, Tiberius had chosen blood near the Caesars' (Domitius boasted Octavia as grandmother and through her Augustus as great-uncle).

BOOK 5

1 (29 CE) Rubellius and Fufius, consuls (Geminus was the surname for each).

Livia died,[1] her age advanced, her nobility – through the Claudian family and then by adoption into the Livii and Julii – beyond illustrious. First marriage and children were with Tiberius Nero, who, expatriate after the Perusine War, returned to Rome[2] with peace established between Sextus Pompey and the triumvirs. (2) Thereupon Augustus, desirous of her beauty, took her from her husband – against her wish? uncertain – so impatient that without allowing time for the child's delivery he brought her into his household pregnant. She produced no offspring thereafter, but, being linked with Augustus' bloodline through the union of Agrippina and Germanicus, had great-grandchildren in common with him. (3) In the purity of her household she matched former ways, but was more affable than was praiseworthy for women of old. She was an unruly mother but an easy-going wife, well paired with her husband's arts and her son's pretence. (4) Her funeral was modest, her will[3] long unavailing. The eulogy was delivered from the Rostra by her great-grandson Gaius, soon to be in power.

2 Tiberius wrote excusing his absence from his mother's last rites – and no change to the pleasure of his life – with the volume of affairs. Memorial honours abundantly decreed by the senate he reduced, as if from restraint. Only a few were accepted, with the addendum: *No divine cult[4] should be decreed. This was her preference.* (2) Elsewhere in this letter he berated female friendships, a grating but indirect reference to the consul Fufius,[5] who had prospered with Livia's favour,

being well-suited to attracting women's minds and amusing, too, regularly mocking Tiberius with sharp-edged humour – of which, in the vastly powerful, memory lasts.

3 From then on Tiberius' was a sheer and crushing regime. For with Livia alive a refuge remained, since deference to his mother⁶ was Tiberius' habit and Sejanus did not dare outstrip a parent's authority. But now, as if released from harness, they burst forth, sending a letter against Agrippina and Nero. (People believed that it arrived earlier and was withheld by Livia, for it was read out soon after her death.) (2) Its language was unusually harsh, but mentioned neither arms nor revolutionary intent. Love affairs with men and unchastity were the grandson's charges. Against his daughter-in-law not daring that fabrication, Tiberius censured her arrogance of tongue and defiant spirit, producing much panic in the senate, and silence, until a few who had no expectations from probity – and public troubles *are* taken by individuals as an opportunity for favour – demanded a motion. Readiest was Cotta Messalinus,⁷ his proposal ruthless. (3) But other leading men and especially the magistrates were afraid, for Tiberius, despite his hostile invective, had left the rest ambiguous.

4 Present in the senate was one Junius Rusticus, Tiberius' choice for compiling the record of senatorial actions and accordingly credited with insight into his thoughts. Some deadly impulse – there was no earlier show of constancy on his part – or a perverse cleverness combining obliviousness to immediate threats with fear of the unknown made Rusticus intervene as the consuls hesitated and advise them not to initiate a motion. *Trivial causes overturn exalted conditions, and perhaps someday the destruction of Germanicus' line⁸ will cause the old man regret*, he explained. (2) Simultaneously a crowd carrying likenesses of Agrippina and Nero surrounded the senate house with utterances propitious for Tiberius. *The letter is a fake! It is against the Emperor's wishes that destruction is aimed at his house!* they shouted. (3) So, nothing dismal was done that day. There were even circulating under consular names forged motions attacking Sejanus, many people exercising thereby – the more waywardly because in secret – their

heart's desire. (4) From this, Sejanus gained a more violent anger and grounds for allegations. *Disregard in the senate for the Emperor's pain! Defection by the people! Hearing and reading unprecedented speeches, unprecedented decrees! What remains but seizing weapons and choosing those whose images they follow like standards as leaders and commanders?*

5 Tiberius, after renewing reproaches against grandson and daughter-in-law and berating the populace by edict, complained to the senate that a single senator's imposture had publicly flouted imperial majesty.[9] He nevertheless demanded everything for a fresh hearing by himself. Without further discussion a decree was passed – not of death, for that was forbidden – but declaring the senate ready to punish but blocked by the Emperor's might.[10]

BOOK 6

5.6¹ (31 CE) ... forty-four speeches on this matter, of which a few from fear and most from habit ... (2) '... did I think it would bring me shame or Sejanus antipathy. Fortune turned, and the man who took Sejanus as colleague and son-in-law now gives himself a pardon. The rest, after encouraging a person² in disgraceful behaviour, make criminal attacks on him. Is it more pitiable to be accused for a friendship or to accuse a friend? Hard to decide. (3) No man's cruelty or clemency will I test; rather, free and finding favour with myself, I will forestall danger. I implore you, remember me not in sorrow but light-hearted, adding me, too, to those who with fine ends escaped public troubles.'

5.7 Individual friends minded to assist or converse he kept near or sent away, occupying thus part of the day. With a large crowd still present and everyone watching his fearless expression – they believed there was still time before the end – he fell on the sword he had concealed in a fold. (2) Tiberius harassed the dead man with neither accusation nor reproach, although against Blaesus³ he made many a foul complaint.

5.8 Next came a motion about Publius Vitellius and Pomponius Secundus. Vitellius,⁴ witnesses declared, offered Treasury keys – he was prefect – and military funds for revolution. Pomponius was accused by ex-praetor Considius of friendship with Aelius Gallus, who, after Sejanus' punishment took refuge on the estate of Pomponius, apparently his most reliable prop. (2) The only help for the endangered men came from the constancy of their brothers,⁵ who stood as guarantors. After numerous delays, wearied of hope and fear alike, Vitellius requested a knife[6] 'for his studies' and made a light blow to his veins and an end to his life in bitterness of spirit. Not Pomponius,[7] a man of quite refined habit and notable talent. Tolerating misfortune calmly he outlived Tiberius.

5.9 The next decision concerned punishment for Sejanus' remaining children.[8] Yet the crowd's anger was fading, the majority appeased by earlier sanctions. His son was transported to prison conscious of what impended; his daughter so unwitting that she kept asking, *What was my crime? Where am I being taken? I won't do it again and a spanking will teach me my lesson!* (2) Contemporary writers report that because capital punishment for a virgin was thought unheard of, she was taken by the executioner,[9] noose alongside. Necks crushed, those young bodies were thrown onto the Gemonian steps.

5.10 In this same period Asia and Achaea were dismayed by a rumour more vigorous than lasting. *Germanicus' son Drusus was seen*[10] *on the Cyclades, later on the mainland!* A youth of about Drusus' age had been 'recognized' by some imperial freedmen, his companions in the plot, who attracted the ignorant with a celebrated name, Greek minds being eager for novelties and miracles. (2) *After escaping from custody he is proceeding to his father's armies to invade Egypt or Syria*, was their story and belief. Thronged by a gathering of young men and with public support, he enjoyed present circumstances and vain hopes. Then word reached Poppaeus Sabinus,[11] who was primarily concerned with Macedonia, but had Achaea, too, in charge. (3) To forestall rumours true or false, hurrying past the bays of Torone and Therme, then the Aegean island of Euboea and Piraeus on the Attic shore, Sabinus cleared Corinth's coast and the Isthmian narrows and by way of the other sea[12] entered Nicopolis, a Roman colony, where he learned that, shrewdly questioned about who he was, the man said 'Marcus Silanus' son', and that after many followers slipped away he took ship, apparently for Italy. Sabinus reported this to Tiberius. About the affair's beginning or end I found nothing further.[13]

5.11 At year's exit the strife long-building between the consuls erupted. Fulcinius Trio,[14] quick to attract antagonism and Forum-trained, had made a grating but indirect reference to Memmius Regulus as lazy in crushing Sejanus' agents. Regulus, who maintained self-restraint unless provoked, not only beat back his colleague but tried to subject him – *guilty of conspiracy?*[15] – to enquiries. (2) Although many a senator begged them to relinquish potentially disastrous hatreds, they stayed hostile and menacing until leaving office.

6.1 (32 CE) Gnaeus Domitius and Camillus Scribonianus[16] had begun their consulship when Tiberius crossed the narrow waters between Capri and Sorrentum and began skirting Campania, undecided whether to enter the city or, if intending otherwise, feigning a show of arrival. After frequent stops nearby, with visits to the Tiber-side Gardens,[17] he went back to his rocks and the sea's solitude out of shame for his crimes and the unbridled passions with which he was so afire that kinglike he defiled freeborn youth with perversions. (2) Not just beauty and attractive bodies spurred his lust, but in some, chaste boyhood, in others, their ancestors' visage. Terms unknown before[18] were invented then – 'stool-boys' and 'strangling-boys' – from a disgusting location and many-faceted suffering. Slaves were in charge of discovery and delivery, with gifts for the ready, threats for refusal, and if friend or parent kept one back, violent seizure and the exercise of their own desires as if on war-captives.

6.2 In Rome at year's beginning, as if Livilla's wrongdoing[19] was newly known and not long since punished, too, ruthless proposals were uttered against even her likenesses and memory, and Sejanus' property was taken from state treasury into the Emperor's purse, as if it mattered. (2) Such were the recommendations being offered by men named Scipio and Silanus and Cassius, in terms nearly identical or slightly reworded, with great earnestness, when suddenly Togonius Gallus, inserting his obscurity among the great names, was heard amidst ridicule. (3) *Let the Emperor choose senators, twenty of them, lot-selected and armed, to defend his security whenever he enters the senate,* was his plea. No doubt he believed Tiberius' letter[20] requesting one of the consuls as protection so he could travel safely to Rome from Capri. (4) Tiberius, since mixing absurd and serious was his habit, acknowledged the senators' kindness. *But who can be left out? Who chosen? Always the same or one after the other? Ex-magistrates or youngsters? Private citizens or some magistrates? How will it look, donning swords on the senate threshold? Life will be worth less to me*[21] *if it requires armed protection!* (5) Thus he countered Togonius, his wording restrained and not beyond urging the proposal's cancellation.

6.3 Junius Gallio, however, who had proposed that time-served Guardsmen get the privilege of sitting in the fourteen rows,[22] Tiberius berated vehemently, asking repeatedly – as if he were present – what business Gallio had with soldiers. *For soldiers to receive tributes or rewards from anyone but the Emperor is inappropriate!* (2) *Gallio has clearly discovered something not provided by Augustus. Or is strife and sedition, rather, the aim of Sejanus' minion, to mobilize simple souls with nominal honour to the degradation of military custom?* (3) Such was Gallio's reward for purposeful flattery, plus immediate expulsion from the senate, later from Italy. Because of complaints that he would have an easy time of exile in his chosen Lesbos, an island renowned and pleasant, he was recalled and confined in magistrates' houses.

(4) In the same letter Tiberius struck down ex-praetor Sextius Paconianus[23] to the senators' great joy, a bold malefactor who pried into everyone's secrets, Sejanus' chosen assistant for the plot against Gaius. After this revelation, hatreds long-conceived burst forth and a death sentence was in process, except that Paconianus promised evidence.

6.4 When Paconianus started in on Lucanius Latiaris, accuser and accused, equally hated, provided a most welcome spectacle. (Latiaris, as I reported,[24] was prominent in the entrapment of Titius Sabinus, and now the first punished.) (2) Meanwhile Haterius Agrippa[25] attacked the prior year's consuls. *Why, given the accusations exchanged, your present silence? Clearly fear and complicity in guilt makes you allies. But senators must not withhold what they have heard.* (3) Regulus' response? *There is still time for vengeance. I will pursue it with the Emperor.* Trio's? *Collegial rivalry and anything uttered in disputes is better suppressed.* When Haterius kept insisting, ex-consul Sanquinius Maximus[26] begged the senate not to increase the Emperor's responsibilities by devising additional stringencies. *The Emperor is equal to establishing remedies.* Thus were obtained for Regulus, security, and for Trio, destruction's postponement. ((4) Haterius was the more hated because, being wasted by sleep and libidinous late nights, and too indolent to fear the Emperor, however cruel, he planned distinguished men's destruction amidst gluttony and perversions.)

6.5 Next, Cotta Messalinus[27] – author of all the most brutal proposals, a source of persistent antipathy – was accused, when opportunity first offered, of repeatedly attacking Gaius for dubious masculinity and for labelling a dinner on Livia's birthday, when priests, too, were in attendance, a 'funeral feast'.[28] Also of adding, after complaints about the power of Marcus Lepidus and Lucius Arruntius,[29] with whom he had a financial dispute, 'They will have the senate for protection, but I my dear old Tiberius.' (2) The accusations were all upheld against him by leading citizens, under pressure from whom he appealed to the Emperor. A letter soon arrived, defence-like, with the friendship between himself and Cotta reviewed from its beginning and Cotta's frequent services recalled. *Words perversely twisted and the frankness of convivial sayings must not occasion accusations,* Tiberius demanded.

6.6 Note was taken of the opening of Tiberius' letter, for he began with these words: 'What am I to write to you, senators, or how or indeed what am I not to write on this occasion? May the gods and goddesses send me worse perdition than my present daily lot if I know!' So thoroughly had his crimes and depravities become his own torment. (2) It is quite cogent, the most outstanding philosopher's regular affirmation[30] that, if tyrants' minds were laid open, one would be able to see gashes and bruises, since, like bodies by blows, the soul is torn by brutality, passion and bad decisions. Neither position nor isolation protected Tiberius from acknowledging the torments in his breast and the penalty he paid.

6.7 Offered the authority to rule on the senator Caesilianus, who had made the most disclosures about Cotta,[31] senators

decided to invoke the punishment used on Aruseius and San-
gunnius, Arruntius' accusers. No greater honour accrued to
Cotta – nobly born indeed, but impoverished through dissipation and for his depravities notorious – than being equated in
the status of 'avenged'[32] to Arruntius' sterling attainments.

(2) Thereafter Quintus Servaeus[33] and Minucius Thermus
were brought in. Servaeus was an ex-praetor and formerly Germanicus' companion; Minucius equestrian in rank. Both men
were restrained in the use of Sejanus' friendship, which brought
greater compassion for them. But Tiberius, berating them as
pre-eminent in crime, advised the elder Gaius Cestius[34] to tell
the senate what he had written to him. Cestius undertook the
accusation. ((3) This was the most pernicious development of
those times: leading senators practising the vilest delation,
some openly, others in secret. It was impossible to separate outsiders from connections, friends from strangers, recent events
from those obscured by time. Accordingly, whatever people
said in the Forum or at parties led to censure, so that everyone
hurried to get ahead and target a defendant. Some aimed to
help themselves, but more were infected, so to speak, by sickness and contagion.) (4) Minucius and Servaeus, once
condemned, joined the informers. Drawn into the same plight
were Julius Africanus from the Gallic Santones and Seius
Quadratus, whose origin I didn't discover.

(5) I am aware that most writers omit the full tally of perils
and punishments. They flag at the supply, and fear that material they found excessive and grim may affect readers with like
fatigue. But many matters worth knowing have come to my
notice, even if unheralded by others. 6.8 For at that period,
when Sejanus' friendship was shed by everyone else, dishon-
estly, the equestrian-ranked Marcus Terentius, standing trial
for it, dared embrace it in a senate speech like this: 'For my
future, to acknowledge the charge may perhaps be less expedient than to deny it, but however it turns out I will confess both
that I was Sejanus' friend, and that I sought to become his
friend and after succeeding rejoiced. (2) I had seen him, his
father's colleague, in control of Guard cohorts, later assuming civic and military duties simultaneously. His friends and

connections were raised to magistracies. The more intimate one was with Sejanus, the stronger one's access to Tiberius' friendship. But those to whom he was hostile were harried by fear and humiliation.[35] (3) I make an example of no one. Rather, I will defend all of us who have no part in his latest plan at my peril alone. Our ministrations were not for Sejanus of Bolsena but for part of the Julio-Claudian household, where he took hold by marriage: your son-in-law, Tiberius, your consular ally, handling your state duties. (4) It was not ours to judge who you raise above the rest or on what grounds. To you the gods have given the supreme adjudication of affairs, leaving for us the glory of obedience. Besides, we pay attention to things overt: who has wealth and office from you? Who has the greatest power for help or harm? These Sejanus had, none would deny. About the Emperor's hidden feelings and what he plans in some secrecy, investigation is forbidden and risky; accordingly, you wouldn't succeed. (5) It's not Sejanus' final day, senators, you should consider, but his sixteen years. Even Satrius and Pomponius got our reverence. Sejanus' freedmen, too, and porters – having their acquaintance was tantamount to grandeur! (6) What then? Will this defence be offered without discrimination, wholesale? Instead, let the separation be on just terms. For plots against the state and murderous plans involving the Emperor, let there be punishment. For friendship and services? The same endpoint[36] should absolve both you, Tiberius, and us.'

6.9 The speech's constancy, and the fact that someone was found to utter what everyone was thinking, had such an impact that Terentius' accusers, their earlier misdeeds accruing, received punishments of exile or death.

(2) Next arrived Tiberius' letter against ex-praetor Sextus Vistilius, whom, as a favourite of his brother Drusus, Tiberius had transferred into his own entourage.[37] The cause of his grievance against Vistilius was either that he wrote works attacking Gaius as shameless, or else credence was given to a fib. Barred as a result from the Emperor's company, Vistilius tried a blade with elderly hand. Then he bound up his veins, dispatched a petition and, at the merciless response, released them.

(3) In a heap thereafter came the treason indictments of Annius Pollio and Appius Silanus along with Mamercus Scaurus and Calvisius Sabinus (and Vinicianus was coupled with his father Pollio),[38] all eminent by birth and likewise[39] high office. There was trembling in the senate – how few had no share of kinship or friendship with so many illustrious men? – except that Celsus,[40] an Urban officer and currently among the informants, removed Appius and Calvisius from danger. (4) Tiberius postponed the cases of Pollio and Vinicianus, and of Scaurus, so he could hear them with the senate. He did, however, provide against Scaurus some grim remarks.

6.10 Not even women lacked peril's lot. Unable to be charged with handling public business, they were censured for their tears. The aged Vitia, Fufius Geminus' mother, was murdered because she lamented her son's murder.[41]

(2) Thus with the senate. Similarly with the Emperor. Vescularius Flaccus and Julius Marinus were driven to death, some of Tiberius' oldest intimates: they followed him to Rhodes, were inseparable at Capri. Vescularius was the go-between in Libo's entrapment, while with Marinus'[42] help Sejanus crushed Curtius Atticus. It was happy news that their own examples had redounded onto the devisers.

(3) In this same period Lucius Piso the pontifex[43] – this was a rare occurrence for such great eminence – passed away. No servile proposals were voluntarily authored by him, and whenever necessity pressed he was wisely restraining. That his father was censor, I reported; his age advanced to the eightieth year; he won triumphal honours in Thrace. But his principal glory came from this: as city prefect with a power newly permanent and more oppressive because obedience was unaccustomed, he exercised remarkable sobriety.

6.11 Earlier, when kings and eventually magistrates left Rome, lest the city lack government someone was selected[44] temporarily to dispense justice and remedy emergencies. They say that Romulius Denter was installed by Romulus, later Marcius Numa by Tullus Hostilius, and Spurius Lucretius by Tarquinius Superbus. Next, the consuls delegated their authority (a semblance still exists whenever an overseer is appointed for the Latin Festival[45] to handle the consul's task). (2) During the civil wars Augustus put the equestrian-ranked Maecenas in charge of everything in Rome and Italy. Then, when he was himself in power, because of the populace's size and the laws' slow assistance, he appropriated one of the ex-consuls to discipline slaves and a citizen element boldly disruptive unless fearing force. (3) The first, Messala Corvinus, accepted the power and, within a few days, its termination, as if ignorant of its exercise. Then Statilius Taurus, though of advanced age, supported the power well. Next, Piso did so for twenty years with consistent approval. A public funeral by senate decree was his tribute.

6.12 Then there was a motion before the senators by the plebeian tribune Quintilianus concerning a Sibyl's book.[46] Caninius Gallus from the Fifteen[47] had demanded its acceptance among that seer's other books and a senatorial decree on the subject. After the decree (made by division)[48] Tiberius sent a letter with tempered criticism of the tribune as ignorant of ancient ways owing to his youth. (2) Gallus he reproached: *Though a veteran of lore and ritual, you acted in a thinly attended senate on dubious authority, before the Board's decision, and not, as is customary, after the oracle was read and assessed by officials.* Likewise he reminded them – since many meaningless oracles were circulating under the famous name – *Augustus set a deadline for delivering Sibylline oracles to the urban praetor. Private possession became unlawful.* (3) (This was also decreed by our ancestors after the Capitoline burned[49] in the Social War. There were searches in Samos, Ilium, Erythrae, throughout Africa even, and Sicily and Italian settlements for 'the Sibyl's' oracles, whether she was one or several, and priests were given the task of distinguishing, insofar as human ability could, the genuine.) Therefore on this occasion, too, the book was submitted to the Fifteen's scrutiny.

6.13 The same consuls.

Trouble in the grain supply resulted in near sedition. There was much importuning over many days in the theatre, with more licence than usual against the Emperor. Shaken, Tiberius censured magistrates and senators for not using state authority to discipline the people; he also reported what provinces he imported grain from and how much more than Augustus. (2) Accordingly, to chastise the populace, there was a senatorial decree composed with former severity, and the consuls issued edicts equally vigorous. Tiberius' silence was interpreted not (as he had thought) as citizen-like, but as arrogance.

6.14 To conclude the year: the equestrian-ranked men Geminius, Celsus and Pompeius perished, conspiracy the charge. Geminius, exorbitant of wealth and soft of life, was Sejanus' friend – to no serious purpose. The officer Julius Celsus[50] was fettered; loosening and looping the chain, he pulled back and broke his own neck. (2) Rubrius Fabatus – on the grounds that, as if, having given up on Rome, he would seek refuge in Parthian pity – was placed under guard. True, when discovered at the Sicilian strait and hauled back by a centurion, Fabatus gave no acceptable explanation for his distant travels. Nevertheless, he remained unscathed – from forgetting rather than clemency.

6.15 (33 CE) Servius Galba, Lucius Sulla, consuls.

After a long search for husbands for his granddaughters,[51] Tiberius, since the girls' age was now pressing, chose Lucius Cassius and Marcus Vinicius. Vinicius' stock[52] was municipal: born at Cales, father and grandfather consular, but the family otherwise equestrian, a mild character of neat eloquence. Cassius was from Rome, his stock plebeian but ancient and honoured. Despite the strict paternal discipline of his education Cassius[53] was praised more often for easy temper than for exertion. Tiberius joined him to Drusilla, Vinicius to Julia Livilla, Germanicus' daughters,[54] and wrote to the senate about it with faint praise for the men. (2) After more explanations, quite vague, for his absence, he turned to weightier matters and grievances incurred on public business. His request was that Guard commander Macro[55] and a few officers come in with him whenever he entered the senate. (3) But despite a broadly worded senatorial decree without stipulation of officer number or type, Tiberius never approached even the roofs of Rome, let alone a public meeting, generally circling his country on remote roads, then diverging.

6.16 Meanwhile a great host of accusers assailed men who
grew their money by lending it, contrary to the law of Caesar
regulating the nature of loans and property ownership in Italy –
a law long since neglected, private profit taking precedence
over public good. True, the evil of moneylending was inveter-
ate at Rome. It was seditions' and disputes' most frequent
cause, and therefore restricted, even under ancient and less
degraded mores. (2) First, a Twelve Tables rule that no one lend
at more than one-twelfth. (Exactions were formerly made at
the whim of the rich.) Later the rate was reduced to half that by
tribunician law. Finally, paying interest was forbidden.[56] There
were many laws providing obstruction to chicanery – so often
checked but rising again in astounding practices. (3) On this
occasion Gracchus, the praetor to whom the relevant court was
allotted and overwhelmed by the number of defendants,
brought it before the senate. The senators, alarmed since from
this guilt none was exempt, sought the Emperor's indulgence –
granted. The next year and a half were given for everyone to
arrange their finances in accordance with the law.

6.17 The result was a money shortage, given the simultaneous disturbance to everyone's debts and the fact that, with so
many convictions and foreclosures, cash was detained in state
and imperial treasuries. In addition, the senate had stipulated
that people invest two-thirds of their capital in Italian land, (2)
but creditors demanded full payment and it was not respectable for those dunned to fail their pledge. Thus, first, there
were scrambling and entreaties, then a clamour at the praetor's
tribunal.[57] What had been devised as a remedy, selling and buy-
ing, turned into the opposite, since lenders had placed all their
cash in land purchases. (3) With depreciation following the
glut of selling, the more someone owed the more he was subject
to distraint. Many were toppled from riches. The overturning
of fortunes sent statuses and reputations headlong until Tiberius
brought help: 100 million sesterces banked for three-year,
interest-free loans if the borrower gave the people twice the
value in estates as guarantee. (4) Thus was credit re-established,
and gradually private lenders, too, were found. Nor was the

sale of land conducted to the requirements of the senatorial decree – vigorous the beginnings, as so often in such matters, careless the end.

6.18 Former fears then returned with the treason indictment of Considius Proculus, who – unapprehensive, celebrating his birthday – was hurried before the senate and immediately convicted and killed. His sister Sancia was exiled on the accusation of Quintus Pomponius.[58] Restless of character, Pomponius claimed that this deed and its like were done by him in order to win the Emperor's favour and remedy the peril of his brother Pomponius Secundus. (2) Pompeia Macrina was also sentenced to exile. Her husband Argolicus and father-in-law Laco, leading Greeks, were previously struck down by Tiberius. Her father, too, a notable of equestrian rank, and her ex-praetor brother,[59] condemnation upon them, killed themselves. The charge was that 'their forebear Theophanes of Mytilene[60] was Pompey's intimate' and that after Theophanes' death divine honours were Greek flattery's tribute.

6.19 Next came Sextus Marius,[61] Spain's wealthiest man. He was reported for incest with his daughter and thrown from the Tarpeian rock. No doubt the size of his fortune turned to harm: Marius' mines,[62] though state-confiscated, Tiberius took for himself. (2) Roused by punishment, Tiberius ordered killed all prisoners charged with association with Sejanus. The wreckage lay immense: every sex, every age, the notable, the unknown, scattered or heaped. (3) For connections and friends there was no opportunity for assistance, tears or more than a glance. Instead, the surrounding guards, alert to anyone's grief, accompanied the rotting bodies being dragged to the Tiber; floating or ashore, no cremation, no contact. The human capacity for fellowship perished from fear's violence, and as brutality grew stronger compassion was kept at bay.

6.20 Around this time Gaius, companion to his uncle's departure for Capri, received Marcus Silanus' daughter Claudia[63] in marriage. His monstrous soul he concealed with sly self-control: at his mother's condemnation and his brothers' destruction not a sound escaped him. Whatever outlook Tiberius adopted, his was the same, and practically identical his words. Whence later the witty saying of the orator Passienus:[64] *Never was there a better slave or worse master.*

(2) I must not omit Tiberius' prediction about Servius Galba, then consul, to whom, after summoning and testing him in various discussions, Tiberius eventually addressed in Greek the statement, 'You, too, Galba, will one day taste dominion,' signifying Galba's late and brief power from his own knowledge of astrology. For learning this Tiberius had had leisure at Rhodes and Thrasyllus as teacher, after discovering Thrasyllus' skill in the following way.

6.21 For his investigations in this business Tiberius used a lofty section of his house and the complicity of a single freedman, illiterate but strongly built. This man would lead over trackless precipices – the house overhung a cliff – anyone whose skill Tiberius had decided to test, and on the way back, if suspicion of inanity or imposture had arisen, would send him headlong into the sea below so none survived to disclose the secret. (2) Thrasyllus, led up these same crags, after exciting his questioner by shrewd revelation of Tiberius' dominion and future, was asked whether he had cast his own horoscope. *What sort of year are you having? What sort of day?* After measuring the stars' positions and distances Thrasyllus first hesitated, then grew anxious and, as he kept looking, more and more atremble with wonder and fear. *A dangerous and perhaps fatal crisis is at hand!* he finally exclaimed. (3) Then came an embrace from Tiberius and congratulations for a man foreknowing danger. *You will remain safe.* Treating whatever Thrasyllus said as oracular, Tiberius kept him among his most intimate friends.

6.22 As I hear these things and their like my verdict is uncertain: do human affairs turn on fate and immutable necessity? Or chance? The wisest of the ancients and those who now emulate their path differ, you will find. In many, fixed opinion is that neither our beginnings nor our end – or indeed humanity – concern the gods, so that dismal things very often befall good men, happy things worse men. (2) Others, however, think that fate matches circumstances. Not because of wandering stars, but rather on the principles and interconnection of natural causes. These philosophers allow us a choice of life, but once you've chosen, events' succession is fixed. Their evil and good are not as the crowd thinks. Many men visibly struggling with adversity they deem blessed, and still more, although wealth persists, they deem utterly wretched – if the former bear painful fortune with constancy or the latter use prosperity injudiciously. (3) But most people cling to this: that at birth one's future is determined, even if some things turn out other than predicted, from the falsehoods of those telling things unknown and thus spoiling the credibility of an art clear proofs of which both antiquity and our age have produced. (4) Indeed, Thrasyllus' son foretold[65] Nero's dominion – the account later, lest I digress too far from my beginning.

6.23 The same consuls.

Word of Asinius Gallus'[66] death spread. That starvation killed him was certain. Whether it was voluntary or by necessity was unknown, people thought. Tiberius, consulted for burial permission, did not blush to allow it, or to blame circumstances for removing a defendant prior to his conviction before himself – in the intervening three years, of course, there hadn't been a moment to undertake a trial for an aged ex-consul, parent of so many ex-consuls. (2) Then Drusus was eliminated, although with pitiable sustenance (by chewing mattress stuffing) he lasted eight days. Some reports say that Macro's instructions, if Sejanus tried weapons, had been to take the Palace-detained youth from prison and install him as the people's leader. Later, since a rumour travelled that Tiberius would reconcile with daughter-in-law and grandson, Tiberius chose brutality over regret.[67]

6.24 Indeed, after levelling insults at the dead man's physique, he reproached his character as destructive to kin and hostile to state, and ordered a recitation[68] of Drusus' deeds and words, recorded day by day. Was anything more appalling? *At Drusus' side for years there have been people to catch his expressions, groans and even secret mutterings. His grandfather was capable of hearing the reports, reading them, publishing them!* It was scarcely credible, except that the centurion Attius and freedman Didymus in letters provided the name of every slave who beat and terrorized Drusus whenever he left his room. (2) The centurion even included his own words – full of brutality, as if a fine thing – and the dying man's expressions. At first, since Drusus pretended mental derangement, these were (from apparent insanity) gloomy about Tiberius. Later, despairing of life, they were purposeful and elaborate curses. *Daughter-in-law, nephew, grandsons! As you have filled our house with deaths, so must you pay retribution to ancestral name and family, and to posterity!* (3) There was uproar from the senators in a show of abhorrence. But panic penetrated, and amazement. *Has Tiberius, formerly canny and, concealing his crimes, inscrutable, become so confident as to display, as if with walls removed, his grandson under a centurion's lash, amidst slave blows, begging in vain for life's last sustenance?*

6.25 This grief had not yet faded when people heard about Agrippina.[69] After Sejanus was killed she lived on, I suppose, hope-sustained, but when brutality received no remission chose death – unless by deprivation of sustenance her end was made to look like one voluntarily taken. (2) For Tiberius blazed out with utterly foul charges. Unchastity was the accusation and Asinius as her lover. *His death made her weary of life.* But Agrippina – intolerant of equality, greedy for mastery, masculine her concerns – had shed women's vices. (3) *She died on the same date as Sejanus two years earlier*, Tiberius added as something worthy of record. His vaunt? *She was not noose-strangled or cast onto the Gemonian steps.* Thanks were given for this[70] and a decree that on 18 October, the death-date for each, a gift be yearly consecrated to Jupiter.

6.26 Soon thereafter Cocceius Nerva, who was always alongside the Emperor, an expert in all divine and human law, status intact and body undamaged, made plans to die. Tiberius, on discovery, approached, asked his reasons, added pleas, and finally said: *It weighs heavily on my conscience, heavily on my reputation if my closest friend, having no reason to die, flees life.* (2) Refusing conversation, Nerva continued abstinence from food. Those cognizant of his thoughts reported that from increasingly close acquaintance with public ills came, in anger and alarm, his wish, while intact and untroubled, for an honourable end.

(3) Agrippina's ruin – it is hard to believe – brought down Plancina.[71] The wife, formerly, of Gnaeus Piso, she was openly happy at Germanicus' death. When Piso fell, the pleas of Livia and, no less, the antagonism of Agrippina saved her. After hatred and favour departed, justice prevailed. Under attack on familiar charges, by her own hand came late but not undeserved her punishment.

6.27 In a city gloomy with so many losses, part of the sadness was that Drusus' daughter Julia,[72] once Nero's wife, married into the house of Rubellius Blandus, whose grandfather many remembered as an equestrian-ranked denizen of Tibur.

(2) At year's close Aelius Lamia's[73] death was honoured with a public funeral. Finally released from his sham administration of Syria, he had been made urban prefect. His birth was estimable, his old age vigorous, and being denied a province added prestige. (3) Next, at the death of Pomponius Flaccus, Syria's governor, a letter was read out from Tiberius complaining that the best men suitable for controlling armies were refusing the task, and that he was being driven by this dearth to entreaties for moving some ex-consuls to take up provinces. He forgot Arruntius,[74] prevented for ten years now from setting out for Spain. (4) That same year died Marcus Lepidus,[75] about whose restraint and good sense I assembled enough in earlier books. His noble birth requires no very long demonstration: the Aemilian clan is fecund of good citizens, and even that family's degraded characters had notable lives.

6.28 (34 CE) Fabius Paulus, Lucius Vitellius, consuls.

After a centuries-long cycle, the phoenix came to Egypt and provided the most learned natives and Greeks with matter for many a disquisition on this miracle. It is a pleasure to publish what they concur on, and the more numerous things uncertain but not preposterous to know. (2) That the creature is sacred to the Sun, and in head and plumage-markings different from other birds, is agreed by those who have rendered its appearance. On the number of years reports vary. (3) The most common year-interval is 500; some insist that 1,461 intervene, and that earlier phoenixes flew into the city named Heliopolis[76] during the reigns of Sesosis, first, and later Amasis, then Ptolemy, who ruled third of the Macedonians – with a great company of other birds admiring its strange appearance. (4) Antiquity is inscrutable, but between Ptolemy and Tiberius were fewer than 250 years. So some believed the current phoenix a fake not of Arabian origin and with none of the attributes fixed in long-standing memory. (5) *Its cycle complete, when death approaches it builds a nest in its native land and infuses the vital spirit from which its offspring arises. The grown bird's first concern is to bury its father, not casually but – after bringing a quantity of myrrh and attempting a long journey to see whether it is equal to burden and distance – shouldering its father's corpse, carrying it to the altar of the Sun, and consecrating it in flames.* (6) These things are unverified and fable-augmented. But the occasional sightings of this bird in Egypt are not in dispute.

6.29 In Rome there was continued carnage. Pomponius Labeo,[77] whom I mentioned as Moesia's governor, discharged blood through ruptured veins, a model followed by his wife Paxaea. This manner of death was opportune for those who feared the executioner, and because the condemned had their property confiscated and were denied burial. For those who made their own decisions the bodies were interred, the wills stood – expeditiousness' reward. (2) Tiberius sent the senate a letter. *It is ancestral custom, when breaking off friendships, to bar someone from one's house and end favour thus. This measure I took with Labeo, but Labeo, since a poorly administered province and other charges were pressing, screened guilt with antipathy.*[78] *His wife shared his terror without warrant, guilty but nevertheless danger-exempt.* (3) Then Mamercus Scaurus[79] was arraigned again, a man eminent for noble birth and pleading cases but in conduct scandalous. It wasn't friendship with Sejanus that toppled him but – equally strong for destruction – Macro's hatred. Practising the same arts in greater secrecy, Macro cited the plot of a tragedy written by Scaurus, together with the verses applicable to Tiberius. (4) From the accusers

Servilius and Cornelius, however, adultery with Livilla[80] and magical rites were the charges. Scaurus, as was worthy of the Aemilii of old, forestalled condemnation with the encouragement of his wife Sextia, death's spur and partner.

6.30 Accusers, too, felt punishment if opportunity arose. Thus Servilius and Cornelius, infamous after Scaurus' destruction, were banished to island exile for accepting money from Varius Ligus[81] for abandoning an indictment. (2) And ex-aedile Abudius Ruso, who imperilled Lentulus Gaetulicus, under whom he had headed a legion, for intending Sejanus' son as his son-in-law, was himself condemned and expelled from Rome. Gaetulicus was then responsible for Upper Germany's legions and had accrued astonishing affection. His clemency was lavish and he was restrained in severity and favoured by the neighbouring army, too, because of his father-in-law Lucius Apronius.[82] (3) From this came constant talk that he had dared to write to Tiberius. *My marriage connection with Sejanus was initiated not by me but on your advice. I am as capable of error as you, and a mistake shouldn't count simultaneously as blameless for you and disastrous for others. My loyalty is intact and will, if not waylaid, remain. A successor will simply point me towards death. We should ratify a pact, so to speak: the Emperor to control everything else, I to retain my province.* (4) These words, though astonishing, gained credence from the fact that alone of all Sejanus' connections Gaetulicus remained secure and quite influential, with Tiberius contemplating public hatred of himself, and his advanced age. *Reputation is a stronger prop than force for my affairs.*

6.31 (35 CE) Gaius Cestius, Marcus Servilius, consuls.

Parthian nobles came to Rome unbeknownst to King Artabanus.[83]

Loyal to the Romans from fear of Germanicus, and fair towards his own, Artabanus later adopted arrogance against us and brutality against his countrymen, reliant upon the wars he had waged successfully against surrounding nations and scorning Tiberius' old age – *disarmed*, he thought. He was greedy for Armenia, over which after King Artaxias' death he placed Arsaces, oldest of his children – an insult, as was sending men to reclaim the treasure Vonones[84] left in Syria and Cilicia, as well as the former boundaries between Persians and Macedonians. *I will invade Cyrus' possessions, then Alexander's!* – thus in empty talk and threats he boasted.

(2) The Parthian initiative of sending secret messengers came most forcefully from Sinnaces, who was equally distinguished in family and wealth, followed by Abdus, whose manhood had been removed. (This causes no disrespect among the barbarians, but rather power.) They had other leading men, too, as associates. Because there was no Arsacid to place atop the government – most had been killed by Artabanus or were still children – they requested Phraates, son of King Phraates, from Rome. *Only a name and beginning are needed for the Arsacid family to be seen at Tiberius' behest on the Euphrates' bank.*

6.32 Just what Tiberius wanted. He equipped and girded Phraates for his father's eminence, holding to his intention of handling foreign affairs with plans and ingenuity, keeping weapons away. Meanwhile, the plot discovered, Artabanus moved slowly from fear, then in a passion for revenge took fire. To barbarians, hesitation seems servile, immediate execution royal. (2) Expediency, nevertheless, prevailed so that Abdus, having been invited to dinner with a show of friendship, was ensnared by slow poison, and Sinnaces was kept busy through pretence and presents. Phraates, in Syria, abandoned the Roman living to which he had been accustomed for so many years and adopted Parthian practices. Unfit for ancestral ways, he was taken by disease. (3) But Tiberius did not abandon his undertakings. He chose[85] Tiridates, a man of the same blood, as Artabanus' rival, and Iberian Mithridates to recover Armenia, and he reconciled Mithridates to his brother Pharasmanes, who held their birthright power. All Eastern plans he put under the charge of Lucius Vitellius. (4) (About this man, I realize, talk at Rome is unfavourable, and many foul things are on record.[86] But in governing provinces he acted with old-fashioned merit. After returning, he converted – from fear of Gaius and friendship with Claudius – to base servitude, an example to posterity of flattering disgrace. His first period yielded to his last, and to the good deeds of his prime a scandalous old age brought oblivion.)

6.33 Of the minor kings, Mithridates first forced Pharasmanes to aid his initiatives of guile and violence. Corruption's agents, once found, drove Arsaces' attendants (with much gold) to crime. Simultaneously the Iberi with a large force burst into Armenia and took Artaxata. (2) After Artabanus learned this he readied his son Orodes as avenger, giving him Parthian troops and sending people to make auxiliaries with money. Pharasmanes, however, attached Albanians and summoned Sarmatians. (Sarmatian rulers, taking gifts from each side by national habit, donned diverse loyalties.) (3) The Iberi, advantageously positioned, rapidly poured Sarmatians against the Armenians along the Caspian road. Those arriving for the Parthians were easily repulsed. Their opponent had closed all entrances but one lying between the Caspian and Albania's mountain flanks, which summer blocked. (The fords were swollen by Etesian winds. Winter's south wind reverses the waves and, driving the sea inwards, lays bare the shallows.)

6.34 Meanwhile Orodes, who lacked allies, received from an auxiliary-strengthened Pharasmanes calls to fight and, upon avoidance, pressure: forays against his encampment, attacks on his supplies, and often siege-like encircling guard-posts. Finally the Parthians, unaccustomed to insults, surrounded Orodes and demanded battle. And yet their only strength was in cavalry; Pharasmanes also had infantry power, for (2) the Iberi and Albani, highland dwellers, were more habituated to hardiness and endurance. (Their story was that their origin was Thessalians, from when Jason, after Medea's voyage and her childrens' birth, claimed Aeetes' newly empty palace and the rulerless Colchians. They revere many things in Jason's name, including Phrixus' oracle, nor would anyone make sacrifice with a ram, which was believed – whether animal or ship-emblem – to have conveyed Phrixus.) (3) With both sides aligned, the Parthian spoke of Oriental dominion and Arsacid renown and, by contrast, the Iberian unknown with his mercenary manpower. Pharasmanes said to his men: *Unsullied by Parthian mastery, the more we seek, the greater our honour if victorious and, if we flee, our shame and danger.* He also pointed out their own rugged line and the gold-bedecked columns of Medes. *Here are men, there is booty.*

6.35 Among the Sarmatians the leader's voice was not alone. They exhorted themselves. *Don't leave the battle to arrows! Advantage must be seized with onset, rather, and close quarters!* Hence the combatants' various displays. The Parthian, accustomed to pursue and flee with equal skill, deployed squadrons and sought shot room. The Sarmatians, abandoning their shorter-range bows, charged with pikes and swords. Sometimes there were cavalry battle reversals of front and rear; occasionally a close-up battle of bodies and weapons' impact, driving forward and being driven back. (2) Soon the Albani and Iberi were pressing, unhorsing, doubling the enemy's fight, with the cavalry harrying from the air[87] and the infantry with closer wounds. Among these, Pharasmanes and Orodes, encouraging the valiant and relieving the hesitant, were conspicuous and therefore recognized. A shout. Horses! Weapons! They converged, Pharasmanes with more vehemence: he drove home through Orodes' helmet. But he couldn't repeat, having ridden past and with the most valiant of Orodes' retinue protecting the wounded man. However, talk of Orodes' death, mistakenly credited, terrified the Parthians; they yielded victory.

6.36 Artabanus retaliated with the whole muster of his realm. Familiarity with the terrain gave the Iberi battle superiority, but this didn't make Artabanus leave, except that Vitellius, having assembled his legions and spread a rumour that he would invade Mesopotamia, caused fear of a Roman war. (2) Armenia was abandoned and Artabanus' government undone, Vitellius encouraging desertion of a king brutal in peacetime and with his misfortunes in battle ruinous. Thus Sinnaces (he was already hostile, as I mentioned) drew his father Abdagaeses and others who were conspiring in secret – and after continuous disasters more openly – to defect. There gradually accrued men kept down by fear rather than benevolence, who, finding leaders, took heart. (3) Nothing now remained to Artabanus but his foreign bodyguards, exiles from their own countries, with no understanding of the good or concern about

evil, cash-nurtured agents of crime. (4) Taking these he fled to
the distant Scythian border, hoping for aid because of his marriage connection with the Hyrcani and Carmanii. *Meanwhile
the Parthians, who favour the absent and are fickle to the present, may change course to regret.*

6.37 Vitellius, with Artabanus now fugitive and the population's attention turned to a new king, urged Tiridates to grasp
what was waiting, and led the solid might of legions and allies
to the Euphrates bank. (2) At the sacrifice, one offered, Roman
fashion, boar, ram and bull; the other had arrayed a horse to
placate the stream. A report came in from the locals. *The
Euphrates, without any quantity of rain – spontaneously! – is
rising huge and coiling diadem-like circles in bright foam, a
presage of prosperous crossing.* Some interpreted more cannily.
*There will be initial successes for the undertaking, short-lived
ones, since portents of land and sky have surer reliability, while
waters' unstable nature simultaneously reveals signs and
removes them.* (3) A bridge of boats was made; the army taken
across. Ornospades was the first, with many thousands of cavalry, to enter the Roman camp. (Formerly an exile and to
Tiberius, when he was completing the Dalmatian war,[88] a con-
federate of no little glory; Roman citizenship was his reward.
Later, having regained the Parthian king's friendship and much
honoured by him, he governed lands encircled by the Euphrates
and Tigris – famous streams – and therefore called Mesopotamia.) Soon thereafter Sinnaces increased Tiridates' forces,
and the pillar of the cause Abdagaeses added treasure and royal
trappings. (4) Vitellius, thinking a show of Roman arms sufficient, advised Tiridates and the leading men: him, to remember
his grandfather Phraates and foster-father Tiberius and the
splendours of both, them, to preserve obedience towards the
king, respect towards us, and each his honour and word. Then
he returned with the legions to Syria.

6.38 Two summers' action[89] I have combined here to give
the mind relief from domestic evils. For in Tiberius, despite the
three years since Sejanus' killing, the things that generally
soften others – time, entreaties, surfeit – caused no reduction
in his punishing doubtful or forgotten matters as if terribly

troubling and fresh. (2) Fearing this, Fulcinius Trio avoided accusers' attacks. In his will he wrote many shocking things against Macro and Tiberius' foremost freedmen – and against Tiberius himself. *His mind has gone with age and his extended absence is virtual exile!* was the reproach. (3) These things, concealed by Trio's heirs, Tiberius ordered read. Displaying tolerance of another's freedom he was a despiser of his own infamy – or perhaps, long ignorant of Sejanus' crimes, he preferred publicity for any sort of statement, and to know the truth, which flattery blocks, even if via shame. (4) Just then the senator Granius Marcianus, treason-indicted by Gaius Gracchus,[90] did himself violence, and ex-praetor Tarius Gratianus was condemned to summary punishment under the same law.

6.39 No different were the departures of Trebellenus Rufus and Sextius Paconianus, for Trebellenus died by his own hand; Paconianus was strangled in prison for poems composed there about the Emperor. (2) These things Tiberius heard not while separated by the sea, as formerly, or via long-distance messengers. He was near Rome so as to reply to the consuls' letter the same day or with a night intervening – a spectator, practically, for blood flooding people's houses and executioner hands.

(3) To conclude the year: Poppaeus Sabinus passed away. Middling in origin, with the friendship of emperors he achieved consulship and honorary triumph. He headed huge provinces[91] through twenty-four years for no outstanding skill but because adequate to the task and no more.

6.40 (36 CE) Consuls Quintus Plautius and Sextus Papinius came next.

In that year neither the fact that Lucius Aruseius *** were killed[92] was regarded, from habituation to evils, as an atrocity. Terror, however, arose when the equestrian-ranked Vibullius Agrippa, after his accusers' peroration, took poison from a fold and drank it in the senate house itself. He collapsed dying and was hurried by hasty lictor hands to prison. On his neck – he was already lifeless – was inflicted the noose. (2) Not even Tigranes, once Armenia's ruler and now accused, avoided citizen punishments[93] with his royal name. Ex-consul Gaius Galba and the two Blaesi[94] fell by voluntary ends. A sour letter from

Tiberius barred Galba from provincial assignment. As for the Blaesi, their priesthoods – intended for the house when it was intact, postponed when riven – he now bestowed as if unassigned on others, which the Blaesi understood, and executed, as a signal for death. (3) Aemilia Lepida,[95] whose marriage to young Drusus I reported, harassed her husband with frequent accusations. Though infamous, she continued, unpunished, while her father Lepidus survived. Thereafter informers got her for a slave adulterer. There was no doubt about the scandal, so, forgoing defence, she ended her life.

6.41 In this same period the Cietae,[96] a people subject to Archelaus of Cappadocia, because they were compelled in Roman fashion to declare property and endure taxation, withdrew into the heights of the Taurus range and used the nature of the terrain to secure themselves against the king's unwarlike forces, until Marcus Trebellius, a legate sent by Syria's overseer Vitellius with 4,000 legionaries and select auxiliaries, surrounded the two barbarian-occupied mountains – the lower was called Cadra, the other Davara – with siegeworks, and used sword on those who dared a sally and thirst on the rest to force surrender.

(2) Tiridates,[97] as the Parthians wished, took Nicephorium and Anthemusias and other Macedonian-established cities with Greek names, and the Parthian towns Halus and Artemita. There was competition in rejoicing among those who, detesting Scythian-raised Artabanus for his brutality, hoped for an affable character in Tiridates with his Roman ways.

6.42 Flattery's extreme was adopted in Seleucia,[98] a powerful city wall-protected and not degraded into barbarism but retentive of its founder Seleucus. Three hundred men chosen for wealth or wisdom served as senate; the people had its role. (2) When they were in agreement, the Parthian was rebuffed; when they differed, since each invited support against rivals, the Parthian summoned against part prevailed over all. As recently happened under King Artabanus, who consigned the populace to the leading men – in self-interest, for control by the people was practically liberty, and mastery by the few was closer to a king's heart. (3) Upon Tiridates' arrival they extolled

him with ancient kings' honours and the more generous discoveries of a recent generation, simultaneously pouring insults on
Artabanus. *Arsacid on his mother's side, otherwise worthless.*
Tiridates entrusted city affairs to the people. (4) Consulting,
then, on when to adopt kingship's ceremonial, he received a
letter from Phraates and Hiero, who controlled the strongest
districts,[99] begging brief delay. His decision was to await these
potentates. Meanwhile Ctesiphon, power's seat, was his destination. But they kept postponing, so in the approving presence
of many the Surena[100] crowned Tiridates in traditional fashion
with the royal emblem.

6.43 Had he visited the interior and his other peoples, the
uncertainty of the hesitant would have been crushed – everyone
acquiescing in his sole rule. By besieging the stronghold where
Artabanus stored money and concubines he provided an opening for shedding accords. For Phraates and Hiero and others
who had not joined the coronation-day celebrations – part from
fear, others from jealousy towards Abdagaeses, potent then over
court and new king – went over to Artabanus, (2) who was
found among the Hyrcani with a filthy exterior and deriving sustenance from his bow. At first – *Is this a trick?* – he was terrified,
but after receiving assurance that they had come to restore mastery, his spirits lifted and he asked why the sudden change.
(3) Then Hiero berated Tiridates' youth. *The descendant of
Arsaces has no control, just an empty name in an unwarlike man
of foreign softness! Power is in Abdagaeses' house.*

6.44 The veteran ruler[101] perceived that the false in affection
were not faking hatred. Not delaying except to raise Scythian
auxiliaries, Artabanus proceeded quickly, outstripping his
enemies' schemes and his friends' regret. Nor did he shed his
squalor – for the crowd's compassionate notice. No impos-
tures, no pleas were omitted, nothing whereby to attract the
undecided and confirm the ready. (2) He and a large band were
already approaching Seleucia's vicinity, while Tiridates, upset
by rumour and by Artabanus himself, was divided in counsel.
Face him? Or drag the war out with delay? (3) Those in favour
of battle and hastening a decision said: *Artabanus' men, scattered and tired from their journey's length, are not even in spirit*

sufficiently unified for obedience, being recent traitors to and enemies of the man they now support. (4) Abdagaeses, however, proposed: *We must retreat into Mesopotamia, so that with the river in the way and the Armenians, meanwhile, and Elymaei and others rearwards roused, we may try our fortune strengthened by allied troops and those sent by the Roman commander.* This opinion prevailed, authority resting principally with Abdagaeses, and Tiridates being cowardly in the face of dangers. (5) But their departure had the appearance of flight and, following the lead taken by the Arab nation, the remainder went off home or into Artabanus' camp, until Tiridates rode back to Syria with a few and released all from shame in betrayal.

6.45 The same year afflicted Rome with a grievous fire. Burned were part of the Circus touching the Aventine, and the Aventine itself, damage that Tiberius turned to glory by paying the houses' and tenements' cost. A hundred million sesterces was the outlay for this munificence, the more acceptable to the crowd given that he was restrained in private building and in public constructed two works only, the temple to Augustus and the stage-building of Pompey's theatre. The finished works – from scorn for favour-seeking or perhaps through old age – he did not dedicate. (2) To assess individual losses were chosen Tiberius' granddaughters' husbands: Gnaeus Domitius, Lucius Cassius, Marcus Vinicius, Rubellius Blandus, plus, on the consuls' nomination, Publius Petronius. Everyone in character devised and proposed honours for the Emperor. Which ones he refused or accepted was unclear: life's end was near.

(3) (37 CE) Soon thereafter, Tiberius' last consuls, Gnaeus Acerronius and Gaius Pontius, took office.

Macro's power was already excessive, and Gaius' favour, never neglected, he nurtured more vigorously day by day. After the death of Claudia, whom I reported as Gaius' wife,[102] Macro urged his own wife Ennia to attract the youth by acting enamoured, and to bind him with a marriage agreement. Gaius refused nothing, provided he secure mastery. Though excitable by nature, he had learned simulations' deceits in his grandfather's lap.

6.46 Tiberius knew this, was therefore undecided about
consigning the state. Between his grandsons,[103] first. Drusus'
offspring, by blood and affection nearer, had not yet entered
maturity. Germanicus' son had manhood's vigour, the crowd's
support – the very things that produced hatred in his grandfather. Tiberius even considered Claudius:[104] age settled,
desirous of virtue's attainments; impaired mind an obstacle.
(2) A successor chosen from outside the household? *Augustus'
memory and the Caesars' name will be exposed to derision and
insult*, he feared. Tiberius' concern was not contemporary
goodwill but rather seeking posterity's favour. (3) Eventually,
uncertain in mind, tired of body, he left the decision to which
he was unequal to fate, after making some utterances to let it
be understood that he foresaw the future. (4) To Macro he
gave, with a riddle of no obscurity – *You desert a setting sun
and look to one rising* – a reproach. To Gaius, who mocked
Sulla in casual conversation, a prediction: *You will have all of
Sulla's vices, and nothing of his virtue*. Also, embracing with
many a tear the younger of his grandsons while the other
looked grim: 'You will kill him,' he said, 'and another, you.'
(5) As ill health weighed heavier, he gave up none of his
debauches, finding in endurance a semblance of sturdiness. (He
habitually mocked medical arts and anyone who after his thir-
tieth year needed another's advice to distinguish things useful
and harmful for his own body.)

6.47 Meanwhile at Rome the seeds of post-Tiberius carnage
were being sown. Laelius Balbus had reported Acutia, once
Publius Vitellius'[105] wife, for treason. After her condemnation,
when the accuser's prize was being decided, the plebeian tribune
Junius Otho vetoed it, which led to their hatred and eventually
Otho's destruction. (2) Next, Albucilla – notorious for numerous love-affairs; she had been married to Satrius Secundus,[106]
the conspiracy's informant – was indicted for impiety towards
the Emperor. Linked as accomplices and adulterers[107] were
Gnaeus Domitius, Vibius Marsus, Lucius Arruntius. Domitius'
renown I mentioned earlier. Marsus, too, had inherited honours
and was notably accomplished. (3) The witness interrogation
and slave torture were overseen by Macro, as records sent to the

senate reported. The absence of a hostile letter from the Emperor roused suspicion that in his frailty and (perhaps) ignorance much was fabrication resulting from Macro's known antagonism towards Arruntius.

6.48 Therefore Domitius, who was planning a defence, and Marsus, whose intention, apparently, was starvation, prolonged life. Arruntius, when friends urged tarrying and delays, replied, *The same things do not suit everyone. My span is sufficient. My only regret is that I endured an anxious old age amidst absurdity and danger, long hated by Sejanus, now by Macro, always by one of the powerful, not for guilt but because I am intolerant of depravities.* (2) *No doubt the few days until the Emperor's last can be survived, but how to escape the vigorous age of the one looming? If Tiberius, with his vast experience of affairs, was riven and remade by the power of mastery, will Gaius, his boyhood scarcely ended, himself utterly ignorant and evilly raised, manage better under the guidance of Macro, who, as a worse man than Sejanus and therefore chosen for his suppression, has harried the state with more numerous crimes? The prospect now is sharper servitude, so I am simultaneously fleeing things done and coming.* (3) Speaking thus, prophet-like, he released his veins. What followed will be proof that Arruntius put death to good use. (4) Albucilla, self-wounded by an ineffectual cut, was taken on the senate's orders to prison. Decreed for her perversions' assistants: that ex-praetor Carsidius Sacerdos be deported to an island, that Pontius Fregellanus lose senatorial rank. There were identical punishments for Laelius Balbus,[108] this at least to senatorial rejoicing: Balbus was viewed as grimly eloquent, eager against the innocent.

6.49 Just then Sextus Papinius,[109] whose family was consular, chose a sudden and ugly exit, hurling himself bodily headlong. Responsibility was assigned to his mother, who – earlier rejected[110] – allegedly used flatteries and extravagance to push the youth into actions from which he found no escape except death. (2) Accused, therefore, in the senate, although she fell at his father's knees and spoke at length about their joint bereavement and women's minds being weaker in such a plight, with other sorrowful and pitiable things showing the same pain, she was banned nevertheless for ten years from Rome, until her younger son left youth's slippery ground.

6.50 Body and strength now abandoned Tiberius, dissimulation not yet. Firmness of mind remained: in conversation and mien alert, he sometimes summoned affability to hide his nevertheless obvious decline. After frequent place-changing he finally settled in a villa on Misenum's promontory (Lucullus was a former proprietor). (2) That he was nearing his last was discovered there thus. There was a doctor, professionally eminent, Charicles by name, whose role was not to govern the Emperor's health but to provide nevertheless a supply of advice. He, apparently going about his business, and with a show of courtesy, took Tiberius' hand, felt his pulse – and was caught. (3) For Tiberius – annoyed and therefore repressing anger the more? unknown – ordered the banquet spread and reclined longer than usual, as if doing honour to a departing friend. Charicles nevertheless assured Macro: *Breath is leaving him and will not last beyond two days.* (4) This brought hurried action with meetings among those present, and messengers to generals and armies.

On 16 March, breathing now stopped, Tiberius was believed to have consummated mortality,[111] and with a great gathering of well-wishers Gaius was embarking on rule's first stages when word suddenly arrived: *Speech and sight are returning to Tiberius and people are being summoned to bring strengthening food!* (5) Panic filled everyone. The others scattered in every direction, each feigning himself gloomy or unaware. Gaius, stuck in silence, after hope's heights expected the worst. Macro was fearless. *Smother the old man under a heap of blankets!* he ordered, and *Get away from the door!* Thus ended Tiberius, in his seventy-eighth year.[112]

6.51 Tiberius' father was a Nero. His origin[113] on both sides was in the Claudian family, although his mother passed into the Livian and then Julian families via adoptions. His situation from earliest infancy was unsettled. When his father was proscribed, he followed him into exile.[114] After entering Augustus' household[115] as stepson he contended with numerous rivals while

Marcellus and Agrippa and later Gaius and Lucius Caesar were flourishing; even his brother Drusus had the citizens' love to greater advantage. (2) But he lived on slippery ground,[116] especially after accepting Julia in marriage, enduring his wife's shamelessness or turning away. Back from Rhodes[117] he secured the Emperor's now deserted household gods for twelve years, then control of Rome's affairs for nearly twenty-three. (3) Of character, too, there were different phases. One phase was excellent in conduct and reputation, as a private citizen or a commander under Augustus. One was secretive and sly at feigning virtues, while Germanicus and Drusus survived.[118] The man was a mixture between good and evil with his mother alive.[119] He was infamous for brutality – but his debaucheries were concealed – so long as he loved, or feared, Sejanus.[120] Finally he burst forth into crime and with it disgrace, after shame and fear were removed and he was simply himself.

BOOK 11

1. (47 CE, continued) . . . for Messalina believed that Valerius Asiaticus, twice consul, had been Poppaea Sabina's[1] lover. Coveting likewise the Gardens, begun by Lucullus, that Asiaticus was improving with notable magnificence, she dispatched Suillius[2] to accuse both. Suillius' associate was Sosibius, Britannicus' tutor, his job to warn Claudius, with well-meaning façade, to beware power and wealth hostile to rulers. (2) *Asiaticus, chiefly responsible for killing Gaius, was not afraid to admit the deed in an address to the Roman people, and to assert glory's claim. He is renowned in Rome for it and talk in the provinces says he is preparing an approach to forces in Germany, since as a native of Vienne with many strong ties there he will find it easy to disrupt kindred populations.* (3) Claudius, investigating no further, swiftly sent soldiers, as if for war's suppression, with the Guard commander Rufrius Crispinus.[3] Asiaticus was found at Baiae and, after shackling, rushed to Rome.

2. Given no access to the senate, he was heard in Claudius' chamber, with Messalina present and Suillius accusing. Corruption of soldiers was alleged – *ensnared with money and sex for every kind of crime* – then adultery with Poppaea Sabina; finally, a soft physique. At this, his silence broken, the defendant burst out with 'Ask your sons, Suillius![4] They will say that I am a man!' He began his defence. Claudius was profoundly moved and even Messalina's tears were stirred. (2) Leaving to wipe them dry, she warned Vitellius:[5] *Do not let the accused slip away.* She herself hurried to destroy Poppaea; her agents used execution's terror to propel the woman towards voluntary

death. Claudius was so unaware that days later, when Poppaea's husband Cornelius Scipio[6] came to dinner, Claudius
asked why he was there without his wife. *She passed away*, was
Scipio's reply.

3. When Claudius asked, however, about acquittal for
Asiaticus, Vitellius, weeping, mentioned their long-standing
friendship and how they had both honoured the Emperor's
mother Antonia. After reviewing Asiaticus' services to the state
and his recent campaign against Britain and whatever else
would elicit compassion, he granted Asiaticus free choice of
death. Then came Claudius' verdict showing the same mercy.
(2) People urged fasting and a gentle death. *I decline the favour*,
said Asiaticus. He exercised as usual, bathed, had a cheerful
dinner, then, after saying, *I would have died more honourably
through Tiberius' cunning or a push from Gaius than brought
down by female subterfuge and Vitellius' shameless mouth*, he
opened his veins – not, however, before seeing his pyre and
ordering it moved elsewhere lest the trees' shade cover suffer
from the fire's heat. So carefree was his end.

4. After these events the senate was summoned. The next
step for Suillius was to indict equestrian-ranked notables, Petra
their surname. The cause of their murder was providing their
house to Mnester and Poppaea[7] for encounters. (2) But an
apparition from night-time repose was the charge against one:
he saw Claudius with his grain-crown inverted and on this
vision's basis spoke of trouble for the grain supply. Other versions: the vision was a vine-leaf crown with pale foliage,
interpreted as showing the Emperor's death at autumn's end.
About this there was no doubt: from some dream or other
Petra and his brother incurred destruction. (3) A million and a
half sesterces and an honorary praetorship were voted to
Crispinus. Vitellius added a million to Sosibius for assisting
Britannicus with his teachings and Claudius with advice. Even
Scipio was asked his opinion. 'Since I feel as everyone does
about Poppaea's crimes, suppose that I pronounce as everyone
does' – a well chosen compromise between conjugal love and
senatorial necessity.

5. Suillius was now relentless and brutal in accusations and

had many rivals in daring. For with all of the laws' and magistrates' functions now in his grasp the Emperor had revealed sources for plunder. (2) No public commodity was more saleable than lawyers' treachery. One result was that Samius, an equestrian-ranked notable, after giving 400,000 sesterces to Suillius and then learning of the man's collusion, fell on his sword at Suillius' house. (3) Accordingly, starting with the consul-designate Gaius Silius[8] – whose power and destruction I will record in time – senators stood and demanded a Cincian law,[9] from which of old there was security against anyone accepting cash or gift to plead cases.

6. Amidst protests from this insult's targets, Suillius' antagonist Silius pressed on vigorously with examples of the past's orators, who thought fame and posterity the rewards of eloquence. *The finest and foremost of virtue's attainments, in other conditions, now have a sordid, menial taint. Nor will good faith remain dependable when profit's extent is considered. (2) If no one's wages are riding on cases heard,[10] cases will be fewer. At present, antagonisms, accusations, hatreds and injuries are fostered. Just as a quantity of diseases brings profit to healers, so the Forum's sickness brings lawyers money. Remember Asinius Pollio, Messala Corvinus, and, more recently, Arruntius and Aeserninus,[11] men carried to the heights by unsullied life and eloquence!* (3) With the consul-elect speaking thus and others agreeing, a proposal for liability to the extortion law was in preparation. Then Suillius and Cossutianus Capito[12] and the rest, seeing the groundwork not for a trial – since their guilt was manifest – but for punishment, surrounded Claudius, excusing past actions.

7. With his assent, they began. *What man is so arrogant as to stake hope on an eternity of fame? Utility and affairs are served[13] by ensuring that no one, for want of a lawyer, be subject to the powerful. Nor does eloquence come without cost: neglect of family concerns while exerting oneself for another's business. For many the military, for some agriculture is a livelihood; people only pursue things with profits they foresee. (2) Easy for Pollio and Corvinus, bloated with gain from the wars between Antony and Augustus, or rich families' heirs like*

Aeserninus and Arruntius, to act magnanimous. For us, pre-
cedents are readily available: how much were the customary
fees for Clodius or Curio[14] *when they addressed the crowd?*
(3) *We are ordinary senators in quiet times, seeking only the*
advantages of peace. Consider the commoner splendid in his
toga: if arts' rewards are removed, arts themselves will perish.
(4) Although less estimable, these arguments were not unavailing to Claudius' mind. For taking money,[15] a limit of 10,000
sesterces was his decision; beyond that, liability to the extortion law.

8. Around this time Mithridates – who was Armenia's ruler,
and then, on Gaius' order, imprisoned, as I recorded – at Claudius' recommendation returned to his kingdom[16] reliant on
Pharasmanes' might.

Pharasmanes, king of the Iberi and Mithridates' brother,
sent reports of Parthians discordant and government unsettled.
Lesser matters[17] *do not concern them.* (2) For Gotarzes, among
many brutal acts, had rashly murdered his brother Artabanus
and Artabanus' wife and son. This generated fear among the
rest, who summoned Vardanes.[18] (3) Vardanes, always ready
for great daring, in two days penetrated 3,000 stades.[19]
Gotarzes, unaware and dismayed, was ousted. Vardanes
quickly seized nearby districts; only the Seleucenses refused
him mastery. Against them, anger – *They were defectors from*
my father, too! – rather than present need fired him, and he
became entangled in the siege of a city strong and, given the
protection of an adjacent river,[20] and their wall and provisions,
confident. (4) Meanwhile Gotarzes, strengthened by the might
of the Dahae and Hyrcani, renewed the war, forcing Vardanes
to abandon Seleucia and decamp to Bactria.

9. With the East's forces distracted and the outcome uncertain, now came Mithridates' chance to seize Armenia, using the
power of Rome's soldiers to destroy strongholds on high, while
in the plains the Iberian army ran rampant. He met no resistance from Armenia after the rout of one who dared battle, the
district-head Demonax. (2) There was a little delay from Lesser
Armenia's[21] King Cotys – some of the elite had turned to him.
A letter from Claudius curbed him, and everything converged

on Mithridates, who was more ruthless than suited a new reign. (3) Parthia's rulers, preparing a fight, suddenly agreed to a truce upon learning of a popular plot (Gotarzes revealed it to his brother). They met, hesitantly at first then clasping hands. At an altar they pledged to punish their enemies' imposture and make concessions one to the other. (4) Vardanes seemed more capable of retaining royal power. Gotarzes, to prevent any rivalry arising, withdrew deep into Hyrcania. Upon Vardanes' return, Seleucia surrendered in the seventh year post-defection, to the discredit of Parthians so long foiled by a single city.

10. Vardanes immediately inspected his strongest districts, avid to recover Armenia, except that Vibius Marsus[22] – Syria's governor, threatening war – produced restraint. Meanwhile Gotarzes, regretting the forfeit of royal power and summoned by the nobility – on whom peacetime servitude is harder – gathered troops. (2) He was met at the Erind.[23] In the much-contested crossing Vardanes overcame him. Battle successes against the intervening peoples led to subjugation as far as the Sind, the boundary between Dahae and Arii. There Vardanes' successes ended, for the Parthians, despite their victories, disdained distant campaigns. (3) Monuments were built attesting Vardanes' might. *No earlier Arsacid won tribute from these peoples.* He returned hugely glorious and therefore the more spirited and to subjects unbearable. These, in a pre-arranged plot when he was unwary and intent on the hunt, killed him in his prime – but in renown the peer of few long-lived kings, had he but sought equally love among his population and fear in the enemy. (4) The murder of Vardanes disturbed the Parthians' affairs, producing division over whom to take as king. Many inclined to Gotarzes, some to Meherdates, a descendant of Phraates sent to us in pledge.[24] Gotarzes prevailed, took the throne, then by brutality and extravagance compelled the Parthians to send to Claudius in secret. *Give Meherdates leave to reach his ancestral eminence,* was their plea.

11. The same consuls.[25]

Century Games in the eight hundredth year after Rome's foundation,[26] the sixty-fourth from Augustus' show, drew a crowd. The two rulers' rationales I omit: they are sufficiently

told in my books[27] on the history of the Emperor Domitian.
(He, too, presented Century Games, which I attended the more
actively for being holder of a quindecimviral priesthood[28] and
concurrently praetor, something I mention not to boast but
because these priests have had the responsibility from of old,
and magistrates performed most of the ceremony's duties.)
(2) Claudius was in the audience at the Circus[29] when noble
boys entered on horseback for the 'Game of Troy'. Among
them were Britannicus, the Emperor's son, and Lucius Domitius, soon admitted to power and the Neronian name by
adoption. The favour of the populace, stronger for Nero,
seemed prophetic. (3) Word spread – *His infancy was attended
by serpent guardians!* – a fable assimilated to foreign wonders.
As Nero himself, no self-detractor, used to tell it: *Only one
snake*[30] *was seen in my chamber.*

12. Popular preference was a survival from the memory of
Germanicus (Nero was his last male descendant). For Nero's
mother Agrippina, compassion gained strength from Messalina's
brutality. Always pernicious, Messalina was now particularly
roused. But she deployed no charges, no accusers, being by a
new love – near madness! – preoccupied. (2) So ablaze was she
for Gaius Silius[31] – of Roman manhood the loveliest – as to evict
the noblewoman Junia Silana from her marriage to him and take
possession of a vacant lover. To Silius both depravity and danger
were apparent, but, with death certain if he refused, and some
hope of escaping notice, and the rewards being great, he found
in letting the future be and enjoying the present sufficient solace.
(3) Messalina – not furtively, but with a numerous entourage –
visited his home, accompanied his excursions, lavished wealth
and position. Finally, as if fortune had already gone over, the
Emperor's slaves, freedmen and trappings were seen at her lover's
house.

13. From Claudius, who was ignorant of his marital situation, and doing censorial duty, the licence of theatre crowds
earned harsh edicts' rebuke because the former consul Pomponius Secundus[32] – he supplied poems for the stage – and
distinguished women had been insulted. (2) By legislation Claudius curbed creditor brutality. *No more 'payable on parent's*

death' loans to minors.[33] The water of springs on the hills of
Simbruvium he channelled into Rome.[34] And three new letter
shapes were supplied and publicized after he discovered that
the Greek alphabet, too, was incomplete when new.

14. At first animal shapes were used by Egyptians to express
ideas – these exceedingly ancient monuments of human memory
are visible on stone – and Egyptians claim to be letters' inventors.[35] *From Egypt the Phoenicians, dominant on the seas, took
letters to Greece and gained glory for having devised what they
merely acquired.* (2) There is indeed a story that Cadmus, who
voyaged with his Phoenician fleet while Greek peoples were still
primitive, was the art's inventor. Some record that Athenian
Cecrops or Theban Linus or during Trojan times Argive Pala-
medes devised sixteen letter shapes. Later other men, especially
Simonides, devised the rest. (3) In Italy Etruscans learned from
Corinthian Demaratus, native populations from Arcadian
Evander. Latin letter shapes were like the oldest of the Greek.
For us, too, they were few at first, with later additions. Following this precedent Claudius added three. In use while he was in
power, afterwards forgotten, they are seen even now on the official bronzes used for publishing senatorial decrees to the
populace and affixed in public squares and temples.

15. Claudius then consulted the senate about a haruspical
priesthood,[36] lest Italy's most venerable lore disappear through
laxity. *Haruspices are often summoned during the state's misfortunes. By their advice rituals are renewed and in the future
more properly conducted. Etruria's foremost men voluntarily,
or prompted by the Roman senate, preserve the science
and reproduce it in their families, with greater indolence now
from public inaction concerning virtue's attainments, and
because foreign beliefs*[37] *are flourishing.* (2) *Conditions are
happy at present, but for the gods' kindness thanks should be
given. Sacred rites tended during equivocal times should not be
forgotten in prosperity.* (3) A senatorial decree resulted: the
pontiffs[38] must determine what to preserve and support in
haruspicy.

16. That same year the Cherusci[39] requested a king from
Rome. They had lost their nobility in internal wars and one last

survivor of royal stock was detained in Rome, Italicus by name.
His father's family derived from Arminius' brother Flavus, his
mother was a descendant of Actumerus, a Chattan headman.
The man himself was in appearance attractive, in weaponry
and horsemanship trained in native ways and ours. Claudius,
having strengthened him with money and bodyguards, too,
urged brave acceptance of the family crown. *Born at Rome, no
hostage, you go a citizen to rule abroad.* (2) At first the Germans welcomed his arrival: he was fêted and attended because,
steeped in no disputes, he treated all with equal favour. Sometimes he practised affability and self-control, which nobody
dislikes, more often drinking and debauches, which please barbarians. He was distinguishing himself among peers and further
afield, when men mistrusting his power – they had prospered in
division – departed for adjacent peoples and attested the loss of
Germany's ancient liberty and Roman might's rise. (3) *Is there
really no one born in Germany to fill the leader's position
unless the spy Flavus' offspring is raised above everyone? He
touts Arminius in vain. If a son of Arminius was raised on
enemy soil and came to power one might indeed worry that he
was infected by dependence, servitude, upbringing, everything
foreign. But if Italicus has his father's character? No man bore
arms against country and ancestral gods with more hostility
than his parent.*

17. With these and like words a great force was mustered.
Italicus' followers were no fewer. *I did not come as an invader
against your wishes,* he reminded them. *I was invited because
in noble birth I outstrip the rest. Test my valour. Am I worthy
of my uncle Arminius, my grandfather Actumerus?* (2) *My
father is no cause for shame: loyalty to the Romans, taken up
with German assent, he never abandoned. It is a sham, the
banner of 'liberty' raised by men – worthless individuals, community's bane – who have no hope except in disputes.* (3) He
got cheers from an animated crowd. In a great battle between
barbarians, the king won. After Fortune's favour reduced him
to arrogance he was driven out, then reinstated by Langobard
might. In happy times and misfortunes alike Italicus was, for
the Cherusci, an affliction.

18. In this same period the Chauci,[40] given a lack of dissension at home and Sanquinius' death,[41] were optimistic until Corbulo arrived.[42] Lower Germany was overrun under the leadership of Gannascus, a Canninefas by tribe, an auxiliary serviceman[43] and later a deserter. Roving with light vessels he ravaged especially the Gauls' riverbank, knowing them rich and unwarlike. (2) Corbulo, entering his province with great designs and soon glory – this tour was his beginning – sent warships up the Rhine channel, and other boats according to capacity into estuaries and canals. With the enemy's skiffs sunk and Gannascus evicted, present conditions were now sufficiently settled. The legions, however, were lazy at works and working, while plunder made them happy. Corbulo brought them back to old ways. *No one leaves a column or enters a fight without orders.* (3) Sentry duty, night watches, daytime and night-time tasks were carried out under arms. People say that a soldier digging the rampart unarmed and another armed with dagger only were punished with death. Exaggerated, and unclear whether falsely spread, these reports nevertheless originated in the commander's strictness: he was in earnest and for significant offences inexorable, you can see, if such harshness even towards trivial matters found credence.

19. The terror Corbulo aroused affected soldiers and enemy differently. Our valour grew, the barbarians' spirit broke. The Frisian nation,[44] which was hostile and unreliable after the rebellion that began with Lucius Apronius' disaster, sent hostages and settled in territory defined by Corbulo, who imposed a senate, magistrates, laws. (2) To prevent his orders' repudiation, he fortified the garrison and sent men to induce the Greater Chauci[45] to capitulate; also for a stealthy attack on Gannascus. Neither unsuccessful nor unworthy was this ambush against deserter and oath-breaker. (3) But his slaughter shifted the mood of the Chauci and Corbulo supplied rebellion's seeds. Though he was celebrated by most people, some criticized. *Why rouse the enemy? Misfortune may befall Rome, and if your actions are successful an eminent man is a threat to peace and to a cowardly emperor utterly galling.* Claudius, therefore, banned any

new use of force against Germany. *Send the garrisons back to our side of the Rhine,* was his order.

20. A fort in enemy territory was already being built by Corbulo when the letter arrived. In this crisis, though overwhelmed by many considerations at once – danger from emperor, contempt from barbarians, mockery among allies – with only *Rome's former generals were lucky men!* as preface, he signalled retreat. (2) To relieve soldiers of idleness, however, Corbulo drove a canal twenty-three miles long between Maas and Rhine for avoiding, by this route, Ocean's uncertainties. An honorary triumph Claudius granted. A war, however, he refused.

(3) Soon afterwards Curtius Rufus[46] obtained the same honour for opening a shaft in the territory of the Mattiaci in which to mine silver. Its profits were slight and short-lived. For the legionaries, however, it was a costly effort: they were excavating rivercourses and endeavouring below ground tasks difficult on the surface. Overcome, the soldiers – in many provinces their sufferings were similar – secretly composed a letter on the armies' behalf with an entreaty for the Emperor. *When you are going to give people armies, give them their honorary triumphs first!*

21. About the origin of Curtius Rufus[47] – a gladiator's son by some accounts – I am reluctant to publish falsehoods, yet tracking the truth brings shame. As an adult in the retinue of the quaestor allotted Africa, while walking alone at midday in a deserted portico in Hadrumetum, he saw a female apparition of superhuman size and heard a voice: 'You are one, Rufus, who will enter this province as governor.' (2) An omen like this excited him to hope and he left for Rome. With his friends' largesse, and likewise a vigorous nature, he obtained a quaestorship and soon, among nobly born candidates, a praetorship with the Emperor's backing. Tiberius veiled the disgrace of his birth thus: 'Curtius Rufus seems to me his own parent.' (3) Thereafter he had a long old age. Towards superiors he used irksome obsequiousness; he was arrogant to inferiors, among equals difficult. Consular power, honorary triumph, and finally Africa were his. When he died there the fateful prophecy was fulfilled.

22. Meanwhile at Rome, for no reason visible then or learned later, the equestrian-ranked Gnaeus Nonius was discovered armed among the company of the Emperor's callers. Torture-wracked, he made no denial[48] about himself but revealed no associates. Was he hiding something? Unclear.

(2) The same consuls.

Cornelius Dolabella[49] proposed the annual staging of a gladiatorial show at the expense of those who had gained quaestorships. (3) Traditionally, office was virtue's reward. Every citizen was permitted, if confident in his attainments, to seek magistracies. Even age was no bar to entering consulships and dictatorships in first youth. (4) Quaestors were instituted when kings still ruled, as is evidenced by the law revived by Lucius Brutus.[50] The consuls kept the power of choosing, until the people began bestowing the quaestorship, too. The first elected, Valerius Potitus and Aemilius Mamercus in the sixty-third year[51] from the expulsion of the Tarquins, were to accompany the military's money. (5) As affairs multiplied, two were added with responsibilities at Rome. The number was soon doubled; Italy now made payments and provincial taxes accrued. (6) Later, under Sulla's law,[52] twenty were elected to stock the senate, to which he had transferred the lawcourts. And although the equestrian class recovered the lawcourts, quaestorships were freely granted in accordance with a candidate's worth or the electorate's easy temper until, on Dolabella's recommendation, they were practically put up for sale.

23. (48 CE) Aulus Vitellius, Lucius Vipstanus, consuls.

During a discussion about stocking the senate, the leading men of the part of Gaul called 'Long-haired',[53] long since recipients of treaties and Roman citizenship, requested eligibility for office-holding at Rome. This led to much and various talk.[54] (2) Different opinions were contested before the Emperor, with some insisting that Italy was not too feeble to supply a senate for her city. *Natives sufficed for kindred populations in the past and the old Republic causes no regret. Indeed people still cite the models for valour and glory that Roman character with its former ways produced. (3) Is it not enough that Veneti and Insubres[55] burst into the senate, without ushering in a host of*

*foreigners for our captivity, so to speak? What offices are there
for the nobility's remnants or for impoverished senators from
Latium,* (4) *with all filled by wealthy men whose grandfathers
and great-grandfathers – enemy nations' generals! – slew our
armies with violent sword and besieged Caesar at Alesia? These
are recent events. What if memory arise of those felled by Gallic
hands on the Capitoline,*[56] *in Rome's citadel? Gauls should certainly enjoy the title 'citizen', but the senate's distinctions and
the honours of office should not be made common property.*

24. These words and their like did not persuade the Emperor.
He countered immediately, and, after summoning the senate,
began thus:[57] 'My ancestors, the most ancient of whom,
Clausus,[58] Sabine in origin, was simultaneously admitted into
Roman citizenship and patrician families, urge me to apply
equivalent policies in managing the state by transferring here
anything that is excellent anywhere. (2) I am aware that the
Julii of Alba, the Coruncanii of Camerium, the Porcii of Tusculum, and, not to delve into antiquity, men from Etruria and
Lucania and all Italy have been called into the senate, and that
Italy itself was finally advanced to the Alps so that not only
individuals one-by-one but lands and peoples might amalgam-
ate into our name. (3) At that time there was continuous
domestic calm and against foreign powers we prospered once
the Transpadanes were received into citizenship, once our
weary empire obtained relief – although it looked like settling
legions[59] throughout the world – from the addition of the
strongest provincials. What cause for regret that Balbi came
over from Spain or equally eminent men from Narbonensis?
Still here, their descendants yield no precedence to us in loving
this country. (4) What else undid Lacedaemonians and Athenians, powerful militarily though they were, than excluding the
defeated as foreigners? But our founder Romulus so surpassed
them in wisdom as to regard several peoples as enemies and
then, on the same day, as fellow citizens. Newcomers have been
kings here. Bestowing magistracies on freedmen's sons is not,
as some mistakenly believe, a recent practice but our predecessors'.[60] (5) "But we fought the Senones!" Did Vulsci and Aequi
never align forces against us? "We were the Gauls' prisoners!"

We also gave hostages to Etruscans and suffered the Samnites' yoke. (6) Yet if you review all of our wars, none was completed in a shorter span than that against the Gauls. From then on, there has been unbroken and loyal peace. Since they have now mingled with our customs, attainments and marriages, let them contribute their gold and resources rather than keep them separate. (7) Everything, senators, that is now believed most ancient, was once new: plebeians as magistrates after patricians, Latins after plebeians, men from Italy's other peoples after Latins. Time's sanction will accrue to this, too, and what we defend with examples today will be one of the examples later.'

25. The Emperor's speech was followed by a senatorial decree. Aedui were the first to obtain senatorial rights at Rome – benefiting from their ancient treaty, and because, of Gauls, only they have a name for brotherhood with the Roman People.[61]

(2) About now Claudius admitted to patrician ranks[62] the most senior senators and those of renowned parentage, there being few now left of the families that Romulus named the 'Greater' or Lucius Brutus the 'Lesser', and exhausted, too, those that Caesar with the *lex Cassia*, and Augustus with the *lex Saenia*, substituted. These were glad tasks and to public benefit, undertaken to the censor's great enjoyment. (3) As for men notorious for misconduct: *How do I expel them from the senate?* worried Claudius. Mild and modern and not consonant with former severity was the method he applied,[63] advising each to consider his own case and request the right to leave the order. *It is easily had, this concession. And I will post simultaneously the names removed from the senate and those excused, so that the verdict of the censors and the decency of those voluntarily withdrawing, combined, eases the ignominy.* (4) For this, consul Vipstanus proposed the title 'Father of the Senate' for Claudius. *The appellation 'Father of the Country' is everywhere and new services to the state should be honoured with unconventional expressions.* Claudius himself checked the consul as too flattering. (5) He also closed the census: 5,984,072 citizens were counted.

Here ended Claudius' ignorance about his household. Soon

afterwards he acknowledged and punished his wife's crimes under duress – which set him ablaze for nuptials incestuous.

26. Messalina, since their easiness had produced an aversion to adulteries, was coursing towards unheard-of appetites when Silius himself urged dissimulation's rupture – from deadly infatuation or thinking for impending perils peril itself a remedy. (2) *We are in no position to await the Emperor's old age. While the harmless have wholesome plans, those manifest in scandal must seek audacity's support. We have associates, equally afraid. I am unmarried, childless – ready for marriage and adopting Britannicus. Your power will remain unchanged, with a gain of security if we forestall Claudius, careless of plots but quick to anger.* (3) Inaction met his words. Not from love for her husband, but lest Silius, having gained the heights, reject an adulteress and assess a crime approved in uncertainty at its eventual real cost. Yet she aspired to 'marriage' with its vast infamy – for voluptuaries, the final pleasure. Waiting only until Claudius set out for a sacrifice at Ostia, she staged a complete and traditional nuptial.

27. I know it will seem incredible that any mortal possessed such recklessness in a community that knows all and hushes nothing, let alone that a consul-elect and the Emperor's wife – day pre-announced, witnesses present to sign – were joined for the ostensible purpose of begetting children; that she listened to the priests' words, undertook vows,[64] sacrificed to the gods; that there was a banquet with guests, kisses, embraces and, finally, a night passed with conjugal licence. But nothing has been fabricated to amaze. The stories and writings of the older generation I pass on.

28. The Emperor's household was horrified, especially those with power and, if the situation changed, alarm. They protested, no longer in hidden conversations but openly. *When the actor[65] made free with the Emperor's bedroom, disgrace, certainly, accrued, but annihilation was remote. Now a nobly born youth with dignity of form, force of mind and an upcoming consulship is girding for greater things. His next step, after such a marriage, is obvious.* (2) Fear entered, no doubt, as they reflected that Claudius was doltish and attached to his wife and

that many deaths were done by Messalina's order. Yet the
Emperor's easy temper gave confidence. *If we prevail because
of the crime's shock value, she can be suppressed, convicted
before trial. The danger lies in her being heard: his ears must be
closed even to her confession.*

29. At first Callistus, who was present earlier in my narrative of Gaius' murder, and Narcissus, the contriver of Junius
Silanus' killing, plus the man with the most potent influence at
that time, Pallas,[66] discussed whether they should dislodge
Messalina from her love for Silius with secret threats and conceal everything else. (2) Then, from fear lest they, too, be
dragged to ruin, they desisted[67] – Pallas, that is, from cowardice, and Callistus with previous palace experience of power
being held more safely with cautious plans than vigorous ones.
Narcissus persisted, with this one change: *Not a word to give
Messalina foreknowledge of charge and accuser.* (3) He stayed
alert to opportunity. With Claudius' long delay at Ostia, he
impelled two concubines – Claudius had grown particularly
accustomed to their bodies – by largesse and promises, and by
showing their power greater after a wife's overthrow, to undertake the denunciation.

30. Straightaway Calpurnia – this was one concubine's
name – got Claudius alone and fell at his knees. *Messalina has
married Silius!* was her cry. Immediately Cleopatra, who stood
waiting nearby, was asked if she had heard the same. At her
nod, Narcissus' summons was requested.[68] (2) He begged pardon for the past, for concealing men like Titius, Vettius and
Plautius.[69] *I am not now going to bring an adultery charge.
Don't reclaim house, slaves and fortune's other trappings – let
Silius have those, but he must return the wife and destroy the
marriage documents.* 'It's divorce! Don't you recognize it? Silius' marriage has been seen by populace and senate and soldiers.
Unless you act quickly, Rome belongs to her husband.'

31. Claudius' chief friends were called. First the grain-supply
overseer Turranius, then Lusius Geta, the Guard commander,
were questioned.[70] At their acknowledgement there was jostling
clamour from the rest. *Go to the barracks! Secure the Guard
cohorts! Think of safety before revenge!* All accounts show

Claudius so overwhelmed by panic that questions kept coming. *Am I the Empire's master? Is Silius my subject?*

(2) Messalina, however, was never more adrift in dissipation. Autumn now ripe, she staged a mock vintage at home. Presses were worked, vats overflowed. Skin-girt women capered about like celebrants or raving Bacchants. She herself, hair loose, held a thyrsus. Beside her Silius was ivy-crowned. They wore tragedy boots, tossing their heads to the noisy accompaniment of a chorus untrammelled. (3) Vettius Valens, they say, who as a lark had struggled up an enormous tree, when people asked what he could see, responded, 'A formidable storm from Ostia' – either a storm was visible or a random utterance turned prophetic.

32. Then arrived not rumour but messengers from all directions. *Claudius knows all and is en route ready for vengeance.* Messalina left for Lucullus' Gardens, Silius – to conceal fear – for his duties in the Forum. The rest were all slipping away when centurions arrived with chains for anyone found in public or in various hiding places. (2) Messalina, although misfortune was undoing her plan,[71] nevertheless determined with alacrity to meet and be seen by her husband; this had often helped her before. She sent word that Britannicus and Octavia should go to their father's embrace. She also begged Vibidia, the senior Vestal, to obtain the chief pontiff's ear and plead for clemency. (3) Meanwhile, with just three companions – such was her sudden solitude – she traversed Rome's breadth on foot. On a cart for garden-refuse removal she started down the Ostia road with no pity from anyone: her depravities' ugliness was overpowering.

33. Fear afflicted Claudius, too, however. In Geta, the Guard commander, they had little confidence, as being equally mobile towards the honourable and the perverse. Therefore Narcissus, along with those similarly concerned, declared to Claudius: *Your only hope of safety lies in transferring military command for today onto one of your freedmen. I will undertake it*, was his offer. Lest during the carriage journey to Rome Claudius be turned to remorse by Lucius Vitellius or Caecina Largus, Narcissus requested and took a seat in the same conveyance.

34. It was frequently said thereafter that during the Emperor's varied outbursts – sometimes he condemned his wife's depravities, but occasionally reverted to the memory of their marriage and their children's infancy – Vitellius uttered nothing but 'Oh the deed!' and 'Oh the crime!' Narcissus pressed him to open up his obscurities and make truth available, but succeeded only in getting equivocal responses tilting in any given direction. And Vitellius set an example for Caecina Largus. (2) Then Messalina was in sight, crying: *Hear the mother of Octavia and Britannicus!* The accuser shouted back: *Silius! The wedding!* Narcissus also handed over documentation of her debauches, which diverted Claudius' eye. (3) Soon, at Rome's gate, their common children were on offer – except that Narcissus had ordered them removed. Vibidia he was unable to deter from her antipathy-arousing demand. *Claudius must not destroy his wife unheard.* Narcissus therefore replied: *The Emperor will listen, there will be opportunity to clear herself. Meanwhile, go tend your Vestal rites.*

35. There was remarkable silence throughout from Claudius. Vitellius tried to affect ignorance. Everything was in the freedman's hands. *Open the adulterer's house, take the Emperor there,* was his order. First, in the vestibule, he pointed out a likeness of Silius' father,[72] banned by senate decree, then ancestral possessions of the Nerones and Drusi, Silius' wages for wickedness. (2) Incensed and bursting with threats, Claudius was taken to the barracks; an assembly of soldiers was ready. To them, after prefatory remarks by Narcissus, Claudius spoke little[73] since his displeasure, however just, was obstructed by shame. Continuous came the cohorts' outcry demanding offenders' names and punishment. Brought before the tribunal, Silius attempted no defence, no delay. He prayed that death be hastened. (3) Eminent men of equestrian rank behaved with the same constancy.[74] Titius Proculus – Silius had given him to Messalina as guardian – offered evidence and Vettius Valens confessed. They and their associates Pompeius Urbicus and Saufeius Trogus were handed over for execution by his order.[75] Also the Watch commander Decrius Calpurnianus, a gladiatorial

school supervisor Sulpicius Rufus, and a senator Juncus Vergilianus: same punishment for them.

36. Only Mnester[76] gave pause, tearing open his garments, shouting. *Observe the whips' traces, remember the command by which you subjected me to Messalina's orders. Others' guilt arose from largesse or huge hopes, mine from necessity. And none would have had to perish sooner were Silius in power.* (2) Shaken by this and inclined to pity, Claudius was driven by his freedmen not to consider an actor after killing so many eminent men. *Whether wrongdoing so great was voluntary or coerced makes no difference.* (3) The defence of equestrian-ranked Traulus Montanus was not accepted, either. (Possessed of youth's modesty, but a notable body, he was summoned at Messalina's behest, then within a single night ousted, she being equally capricious in desire and aversions.) (4) Suillius Caesoninus and Plautius Lateranus[77] were excused death, the latter for his uncle's outstanding service. Caesoninus was protected by his vices: in that foulest of companies he had suffered the woman's lot.

37. Meanwhile Messalina, in Lucullus' Gardens, prolonged life and composed pleas. Some hope she had, and occasionally anger, so great was her arrogance at the end. If Narcissus had not hastened her killing, ruin would have recoiled upon the accuser. (2) For Claudius, back home, was soothed by an early dinner. Once heated by wine, he gave an order. *Go tell the poor woman* – his expression, they say – *to be here tomorrow to speak her case.* At this, there was alarm. *His anger is flagging, his love returning. And if we delay, there will be night's arrival and the memory of his wife's chamber.* Narcissus broke free and signified to the officers present to accomplish the killing. *Thus your emperor orders.* As guard and enforcer went one of the freedmen, Euodus. (3) Quickly going ahead to the gardens, he found her sprawling with her mother Lepida[78] alongside. During her daughter's prime, Lepida was little sympathetic, but at the inevitable end was won to compassion. She urged her not to await the killer. *Your life's course is complete, and for death, honour should be your only aim.* (4) But a mind degraded by

debauches contained nothing honourable. Tears were coming and useless complaints, when at the arrivals' thrust the gates burst and the officer stood there in silence. The freedman, however, berated Messalina with many a slavish insult.

38. Only then did she perceive her situation and accept a blade. This she applied in vain to throat and breast, trembling the while; the officer's blow ran her through. The body was given to her mother, (2) and an announcement to Claudius, dining: *Messalina is dead* – no distinction whether by her hand or another's. Nor did he enquire. He asked for his cup and put on the usual party. (3) He gave no sign, on subsequent days, of hatred, joy, anger, sorrow, indeed of any human emotion, not when her accusers, rejoicing, caught his eye, or her children, grieving. Assistance in forgetting was given him by the senate decreeing removal of her name and likenesses from places public and private. (4) Decreed for Narcissus: an honorary quaestorship – a trifle to the conceit of one superior to Pallas and Callistus. Worthy deeds, origin of much worse.[79]

BOOK 12

1. (48 CE, continued) Messalina's killing produced dislocation in the Emperor's household. A contest arose among the freedmen over who would choose a wife for Claudius, a man impatient of unmarried life and obedient to wives' commands. In lobbying, the women burned equally hot: noble birth, beauty and wealth were held up and shown worthy of a marriage so important. (2) The principal dilemma was between Lollia Paulina, a descendant of the ex-consul Marcus Lollius, and Agrippina,[1] Germanicus' daughter. The latter had Pallas, the former Callistus, as supporter. Aelia Paetina[2] of the Tubero family was encouraged by Narcissus. Claudius, now here, now there inclined after hearing each backer, summoned the disputants to a council and ordered each to offer an opinion and give reasons.

2. Narcissus spoke of a former marriage, a common daughter, for Antonia was Paetina's. *There will be no novelty in your halls if a familiar wife returns, one unlikely to regard with stepmotherly hatred Britannicus and Octavia, children so close to her own.* (2) Callistus: *Scorned during a long separation, Paetina will be, if restored, domineering for this very reason. Much better to bring in Lollia. Having borne no children she will be devoid of rivalry and will fill a parent's place for her stepchildren.* (3) Pallas praised especially this in Agrippina: *She brings Germanicus' grandson. Her noble birth is clearly worthy of imperial fortune, and links Julian and Claudian posterity.*[3] *Plus, a woman of proven fecundity, with her youth intact, must not convey the Caesars' renown into another house.*

3. This argument prevailed, assisted by Agrippina's allure-ments: under cover of the family connection she visited frequently, so enticing her uncle that, once she was given pref-erence, though not yet a wife she exercised wifely power. (2) When sure of her own marriage, she laid greater plans. Matrimony between Nero, her son by Gnaeus Domitius, and Octavia, Claudius' daughter, was her contrivance. This could not be accomplished without crime, since Claudius had betrothed Octavia to Lucius Silanus,[4] a man already renowned, whom Claudius, by an honorary triumph and gladiatorial games' magnificence, had displayed to public enthusiasm. But nothing seemed difficult with an emperor who had no opinion and no hatred except by dictation and order.

4. So Vitellius – a man who used censorial office to cover slavish lies and foresaw impending regimes – in order to earn Agrippina's gratitude involved himself in her plans. He brought charges against Silanus, whose quite lovely and wayward sister Junia Calvina[5] was lately Vitellius' daughter-in-law. (2) In her was the accusation's starting-point: sibling love – not incestu-ous, but unguarded – Vitellius stretched to infamy. And Claudius lent his ears, the readier to admit suspicions against a son-in-law from affection for his daughter. (3) Silanus, unaware of plots and, as it happened, praetor that year, was suddenly, by Vitellius' edict, removed from the senate's ranks, although the senate review had occurred earlier and the census period ended. Simultaneously Claudius broke the marriage connection; Sila-nus was forced to abdicate office and the remaining day of his praetorship was transferred to Eprius Marcellus.[6]

5. (49 CE) Gaius Pompeius, Quintus Veranius, consuls.

The marriage pact between Claudius and Agrippina was soon being confirmed by rumour and illicit love. They did not yet dare celebrate the wedding. There was no precedent of niece being married to uncle. Incest was a worry, and that it might – if the worry be dismissed – erupt into public harm. (2) Hesitation lasted until Vitellius, using his regular tactics, undertook the accomplishing. He asked Claudius: *Will you yield to the people's orders, to the senate's authority?* Claudius' response: *I am a single citizen, no match for consensus.* Whereupon

Vitellius ordered him to wait in the Palace. (3) Vitellius entered the senate and, insisting that the government was at issue, demanded permission to speak first. He began: *The Emperor's weighty tasks, world-encompassing, require some support, so that he serve the public interest free of domestic care. And what more respectable relief is there for a censor's mind than taking a spouse, an ally in prosperity and uncertainty, to whom his intimate thoughts, his little children may be transmitted? For he is unaccustomed to dissipation and pleasures, law-abiding, rather, from early manhood on.*

6. After this favour-winning speech's preliminaries, which were followed by much senatorial approbation, he started over. *Since everyone urges that the Emperor marry, it is necessary to choose a woman notable for nobility, childbearing and purity. Nor must we look far. Agrippina is peerless in eminence of birth. Proof exists of her fertility and she is Claudius' match in probity. (2) But the best is this: by divine providence a widow[7] will be joined to an emperor familiar only with his own wives. You have heard from your parents and have yourselves seen wives abducted for Caesars' lusts. A long way, that, from present restraint. Indeed you must document the fact that an emperor is receiving a wife from the senate. (3) Yes, it is a novelty for us, matrimony with a niece. But elsewhere it is regular, where there is no legal ban. Even cousin marriage – long unknown – over time became frequent. Custom adapts itself to convenience and this, too, will soon become something done.*

7. Some senators burst from the meeting vying to declare: *If Claudius delays, we will apply force!* A mixed crowd massed, shouting: *The Roman people's prayer is the same!* (2) Claudius, without any further wait, offered himself to congratulations in the Forum and, entering the senate, requested a decree legalizing weddings to brothers' daughters even for the future. (But only one man was found to covet such a marriage: equestrian-ranked Alledius Severus, who most say was impelled by Agrippina's influence.)

(3) A reorientation followed in the city. All things served a woman, and it wasn't through caprice, as with Messalina, that Agrippina made a travesty of Rome: hers was a strict and

practically manly servitude. In public there was austerity and quite often arrogance. At home, nothing unchaste unless it aided mastery. Her vast desire for gold seemed explicable. *Props for a regime are being readied.*

8. On the wedding day Silanus put himself to death. Either he maintained hope of life until then, or the day was chosen to increase antipathy. His sister Calvina was banished from Italy. Claudius supplemented with rites based on King Tullus' laws,[8] and expiations pontiff-performed in Diana's Grove – to general mockery, given the pursuit of punishment and atonement for incest just then. (2) Agrippina, lest she be known for evil deeds only, obtained remission of exile for Seneca[9] and simultaneously a praetorship – *A happy event for the community on account of his literary renown* – so that Nero's boyhood would mature under such a teacher and they would have his advice in their aspiration for mastery. Seneca was believed faithful to Agrippina, remembering her favour, and hostile to Claudius, resenting his injury.

9. The next decision: without further delay consul-elect Mammius Pollio was induced by huge promises to advance a motion begging Claudius to engage Octavia to Nero. *At their ages it is apt and will open greater possibilities.* (2) Pollio used practically the same words as Vitellius' recent recommendation, and Octavia was engaged. Now, in addition to his previous connection, fiancé and son-in-law, Nero equalled Britannicus through his mother's pursuits and the artfulness of those in whom, owing to their accusation of Messalina, her son's vengeance roused fear.

10. In this same period the Parthian envoys, who were sent, as I reported,[10] for Meherdates, entered the senate and commenced their task thus. *We are here neither ignorant of the treaty nor in defection from the Arsacid family. Indeed Vonones' son, Phraates' grandson, is with us against Gotarzes' regime, to nobility and populace alike intolerable. Already our brothers, kin and more distant connections have been lost to slaughter, with the addition now of pregnant wives and little children, while Gotarzes, idle at home and unlucky in war, conceals his cowardice with cruelty. (2) Our friendship with you is*

long-standing and official. Relief should be sent to allies in
strength equal, deferential through respect. Rulers' children are
given as hostages, so that if internal power rouses impatience,
recourse exists to emperor and senate. From these a better king,
one habituated to their ways, can be adopted.

11. After they presented these and like arguments, Claudius
began a discourse on Rome's height and Parthian compliance,
likening himself to Augustus with reference to the request of a
king[11] – forgetting Tiberius, though he, too, sent one. (2) He
added instructions, for Meherdates was present. *Contemplate*
not mastery and slaves but guide and citizens, and strive for
clemency and justice. These are unknown to barbarians and
therefore the more welcome. (3) Turning, then, to the envoys
he extolled Rome's nursling. *He is of proven restraint so far.*
Nevertheless, royal ways should be borne with. There is no
benefit to frequent changes. Rome, from a surfeit of glory, has
reached the place of wanting calm for foreign peoples, too. The
assignment thereafter for Gaius Cassius, Syria's governor, was
to escort the man to the Euphrates' bank.

12. (At that period Cassius overtopped the rest in legal
expertise. Military skills are in idle times unknown, and peace
keeps energetic men and cowardly ones level. Nevertheless,
insofar as was possible without war, Cassius revived former
ways,[12] drilled his legions, and acted with the care and foresight consistent with an enemy presence – behaviour worthy of
his ancestors and the Cassian family, which was famous among
those peoples, too.)

(2) Cassius roused those through whose recommendation the
king was requested and established camp at Zeugma, where
the Euphrates crossing is easiest. After Parthian nobles and the
Arabs' King Acbarus arrived, Cassius warned Meherdates. *Bar-*
barian impulses, though sharp, flag with delay or change into
betrayal, so keep pressing this start. (3) Advice that Meherdates
spurned, tricked by Acbarus, who detained the man – he was
ignorant and supposed that exalted position meant dissipation –
for many days at the town of Edessa.[13] And despite Carenes'[14]
summons – *Everything is ready,* he showed, *if you arrive*
swiftly – Meherdates did not head for Mesopotamia nearby but

detoured for Armenia, which was inconvenient just then with winter beginning.

13. Snow- and mountain-weary they approached the plains. After they joined forces with Carenes' and crossed the Tigris, they passed through the Adiabeni, whose King Izates wore alliance with Meherdates openly, although he was secretly and more reliably inclined to Gotarzes. (2) The city Ninos[15] was captured in passing, Assyria's most ancient seat and a stronghold known to fame: at the final battle between Darius and Alexander, Persian might collapsed there. (3) Meanwhile, at the mountain called Sanbulos, Gotarzes was undertaking vows to the local gods. (There is particular reverence for Hercules, who at set times instructs sleeping priests to station horses arrayed for hunting beside the temple. The horses receive full quivers and, after roaming the woods at night, return, panting, quivers empty. And again with a night-time vision the god shows his route through the forests and slain animals are discovered everywhere.)

14. Gotarzes, his army still too weak, used the River Corma as a defence and, despite taunting messages summoning him to battle, wove delays, changed location and, after sending seducers, got his enemies to shed loyalty for a price. Among them departed Izates with the Adiabene army, and later Acbarus with the Arabs' – with the characteristic fickleness of these nations, and because experience shows that barbarians prefer seeking kings from Rome to having them. (2) Meherdates, stripped of their powerful support and suspecting betrayal by the rest, chose the one thing left, to hand the matter to chance: trial by battle. Nor did Gotarzes refuse a fight, showing spirit now that his enemies were fewer. The conflict produced great carnage and ambiguous result until Carenes, having routed his opponents, rode too far and was beset by a fresh band from behind. (3) All hope lost, Meherdates, following the promises of Parraces, a dependant of Meherdates' father, was taken by guile and delivered to the victor. Gotarzes berated him not as kinsman and Arsacid by birth, but as foreign-born and Roman, and – after shearing off his ears – ordered him to live: a demonstration of his clemency and, for us, humiliation. (4) Gotarzes

then sickened and died, and Vonones was summoned to king-ship, the Medes' current ruler. He had no successes or misfortunes by which to be remembered. His reign was brief and inglorious, then Parthia's government passed to his son Vologaeses.

15. Mithridates of Bosporus[16] was roving resourceless. After learning that the Roman commander Didius and the core of his army had departed, leaving in the new kingdom the youth-ful and thus inexperienced Cotys and a few cohorts with equestrian-ranked Julius Aquila, Mithridates scorned both. He started rousing peoples and attracting refugees. Eventually, after mustering an army, he evicted the Dandarid king and took his power. (2) When this became known, and Mithridates was thought near to invading Bosporus, Aquila and Cotys dis-trusted their manpower. Since Zorsines, king of the Siraci, had resumed hostilities, they, too, sought foreign influence, sending envoys to Eunones, foremost of the Aorsi. It was no trouble to win an alliance, since they offered Roman power against rebel Mithridates. The terms: cavalry battles to be Eunones' fight, city sieges the Romans' undertaking.

16. They assembled a column and advanced. At front and back were the Aorsi; the middle was secured by cohorts and Bosporans in our gear. The enemy was driven back and they reached Soza, a Dandarid town abandoned by Mithridates because of the population's uncertain temper. To hold it, leav-ing a garrison, was the decision. (2) Continuing immediately against the Siraci, they crossed the river Panda and surrounded the city of Uspe, lofty in position and fortified by wall and ditch, except that the wall, made not of rock but of wicker-work twigs with a core of dirt, was feeble against invaders. Towers raised above it, along with torches and spears, evicted the besieged. Had night not sundered combat, the city's capture would have been begun and accomplished within a day.

17. Finally, they sent envoys begging pardon for free per-sons: they offered 10,000 slaves. This the victors rejected, since slaughtering the surrendered seemed brutal, and guarding a great multitude toilsome. *Better they fall to the law of war.* The soldiers, who had gone up via ladders, were given the order to

kill. (2) The annihilation of Uspe struck fear into the rest. *Nothing is safe when weapons and fortifications, locations obstructed or elevated, rivers and cities alike succumb.* Accordingly, Zorsines, weighing long whether to serve Mithridates' final crisis or his ancestral kingdom, after national advantage prevailed, gave hostages and bowed before Claudius' likeness, to the great glory of the Roman army, which, unbloodied and victorious, is agreed to have been a three-day journey from the Don.[17] (3) On the return, their fortune was different. Some ships – for they sailed back – were carried onto the Taurian shore and beset by barbarians, with cohort commander and many auxiliaries killed.

18. Meanwhile Mithridates, lacking military support, considered whose mercy to try. His brother Cotys, who first betrayed then fought him, was alarming. Of the Romans, none present had the authority to make his promises count much. He turned to Eunones: no personal hostilities caused offence and the recently concluded alliance with us gave strength. (2) With dress and expression suited to his present fortune, therefore, he entered Eunones' residence and fell at his knees. 'Mithridates am I,' he said, 'Rome's quarry over land and sea for numerous years, here of my own volition. Use as you will great Achaemenes' issue,[18] my lineage being the one thing the enemy has not taken.'

19. To Eunones the man's renown, change of circumstance and not unworthy plea were persuasive. He raised the suppliant, praised him for choosing the Aorsi and for choosing his own protection when seeking forgiveness. Envoys and a letter were sent immediately, as follows. (2) *The Roman people's rulers and great nations' kings possess, from like fortune, friendship, but you and I also have community in victory.* (3) *Wars are best ended by arranging pardons. Defeated Zorsines has suffered no expropriation; for Mithridates, who deserves worse, I seek not power or kingdom, but that he be led in no triumph and not pay with his life.*

20. Claudius, though mild towards foreign nobles, hesitated nevertheless. *Is it better to receive him as captive with a guarantee of safety or to pursue him under arms?* Towards the latter

he was inclined by the grievance of harm suffered and the desire for revenge. The arguments against were: undertaking a war where travel follows no roads and the sea has no harbours. Plus, spirited kings, nomadic populations, soil poor in crops; delay's annoyance, haste's risks; modest the victors' praise, but quantities of infamy if repulsed. *Instead, I should seize what is offered and keep Mithridates an exile. The longer he lives in need, the greater his punishment.* (2) Thus persuaded he wrote to Eunones. *Mithridates deserves extreme measures and I am strong enough to apply them, but the Roman way is to match persistence against enemies with kindness towards suppliants. Triumphs come from peoples and kingdoms still strong.*[19]

21. Mithridates was surrendered thereafter and conveyed to Rome by Pontus' governor Junius Cilo. They say he spoke before Claudius with more spirit than his fortune warranted. The taunt spread through the crowd as follows: 'It's not that I was sent back to you; I returned. You don't believe me? Let me go, then have a look!' His expression, too, was undismayed as he stood there near the Rostra surrounded by guards, on display to the people. An honorary consulship was decreed for Cilo, an honorary praetorship for Aquila.

22. The same consuls.

Agrippina, a formidable hater and hostile to Lollia for vying with her over Claudius' marriage, contrived crimes and an accuser to charge Lollia with astrologers, fortune-tellers and consulting the Apollo oracle at Claros about the Emperor's wedding. (2) Claudius, without hearing the accused, addressed the senate. His preamble contained much on Lollia's renown:[20] she was Lucius Volusius' sister's daughter, Cotta Messalinus was her great-uncle and she was Memmius Regulus' wife once upon a time. (About her marriage to Gaius he maintained silence.) Then: *Her plans harm the state, and crime should be deprived of means. Accordingly: property confiscation. Then she must leave Italy.* Five millions from a vast fortune were left to the exile. (3) (Calpurnia,[21] too, a woman of note, was overset. The Emperor had praised her beauty, not lustfully but in casual conversation, so Agrippina's wrath stayed within bounds.) Lollia was sent a military tribune to drive her deathwards. Another person convicted, for extortion, was Cadius Rufus,[22] with the Bithynians accusing.

23. Narbonensis, in return for its surpassing reverence for the senate, was given a privilege: the province's senators could visit their estates without first seeking the Emperor's permission, as applied for Sicily. The Ituraeans and Judaeans, their kings Sohaemus and Agrippa[23] having died, were added to the province of Syria. The senate decided to revive the 'Divination of Well-being',[24] a ritual neglected for twenty-five years, and to perpetuate it. (2) And the city's sacred boundary was lengthened by Claudius.

Ancient custom permitted those who had extended the Empire to expand the city's limits as well. Of Rome's commanders, however, despite the conquest of many great nations, none had used it but Sulla and Augustus.[25] 24. About the kings' ambition or renown in this connection various stories circulate. To learn the origin of its foundation, however, and what boundary Romulus established, is not, I think, preposterous. The furrow outlining the city was begun at the cattle market where we see a bronze bull's likeness, since this sort of animal is harnessed to the plough. It goes around the Great Altar of Hercules, and from there, with boundary-stones placed at regular intervals, along the foot of the Palatine to Consus' Altar, the old Assemblies and the Lares' Shrine. (2) The Forum and the Capitoline, people believe, were added to the city not by Romulus but by Titus Tatius. The boundary was later lengthened in proportion to our fortune. The limits established by Claudius are easily seen, and described in public records.

25. (50 CE) Gaius Antistius, Marcus Suillius, consuls.

Adoption for Nero was set in motion with Pallas as its sponsor. Linked to Agrippina as marriage broker, then secured by her debauchery, he urged Claudius: *Consider the public good! Buttress Britannicus' boyhood with strength. Thus it was in Augustus' household that, despite its basis in grandsons, stepsons flourished. And Tiberius brought Germanicus in over his own offspring. You, too, should gird yourself with a young man ready to handle a share of your concerns.* (2) Overcome by these arguments Claudius gave Nero, three years the older, precedence over his son, after a senate speech styled on the freedman's. Experts noted: *No earlier adoption is on record among patrician Claudii,*[26] *who have lasted continuously from Attus Clausus.*

26. Next, there were expressions of gratitude for the Emperor, with more studied flattery of Nero.[27] A law was introduced permitting his passage into the Claudian family and its name. Agrippina, too, was strengthened by the title Augusta. After these measures no one was so devoid of pity as not to feel Britannicus' sad lot. Gradually forsaken even by slave attendants, the boy mocked his stepmother's untimely kindnesses, knowing them false. They say he had a lively nature. Perhaps it was true, or else favour won from perils preserved the tale untested.

27. Agrippina, to demonstrate her power to allied peoples, too, obtained permission to found a veteran colony in the Ubian capital, where she was born; it was named for her.[28] (The Ubii, after moving across the Rhine, also happened to have been received under the protection of her grandfather Agrippa.)

(2) Just then in Upper Germany fear arose at the approach of marauding Chatti. Pomponius Secundus, the governor, dispatched auxiliaries[29] plus cavalry, with instructions to forestall the raiders or, if they slipped past, to encircle them unsuspecting.

(3) The soldiers' exertion followed the leader's plan. They divided into two columns. Those who took the left-hand route surrounded the Chatti soon after they turned back in dissipated enjoyment of their booty, heavy with sleep. Roman joy was augmented by releasing some men – forty years after the Varian disaster![30] – from servitude. 28. Those who went right, taking the closer, shorter path, were confronted by the enemy, who risked battle. These did more damage and returned burdened with booty and fame to the Taunus,[31] where Pomponius waited with his legions in case the Chatti, desiring revenge, offered a chance to fight. (2) Afraid of being surrounded by the Romans on one side and the Cherusci, with whom they were perpetually at odds, on the other, they sent envoys to the city, and hostages. An honorary triumph was decreed for Pomponius,[32]

a modest contribution to his fame with posterity, where his poems' glory gives distinction.

29. In this same period Vannius,[33] the ruler imposed on the Suebi by Drusus, was expelled. During his rule's first period he was illustrious and accepted by the population. With time he changed to arrogance and was beset by both his neighbours' hatred and domestic disputes. Those responsible were Vibilius, the Hermunduri king, and Vangio and Sido, sons of Vannius' sister. (2) Nor did Claudius, though often entreated, intervene militarily in the barbarian struggle. Safe refuge he did promise to Vannius, if expelled, and he wrote to Palpellius Hister, Pannonia's governor: *A legion and auxiliaries raised from the province must be arrayed along the Danube to support the defeated and as deterrent to the victors, lest exalted by Fortune they trouble our peace, too.* (3) For uncountable numbers were arriving, the Lugii and other peoples. Such was the reputation of the wealthy kingdom that Vannius had grown through thirty years of raids and taxes. Since Vannius' troop – infantry, plus cavalry from the Sarmatian Iazuges[34] – was unequal to the enemy multitude, he had decided to protect himself with strongholds and protract the war.

30. The Iazuges – impatient of blockade, they went roving in nearby territories – made fighting a necessity after the Lugii and Hermunduri encroached. Leaving his strongholds, Vannius was routed, but praised, despite his misfortunes, for taking part in the fight and receiving frontal wounds. (2) The fleet waiting at the Danube was his refuge. His dependants soon followed. With a gift of territory they were settled in Pannonia. Vannius' kingdom Vangio and Sido[35] split. Towards us their loyalty was excellent. From their subjects – owing either to that people's nature or to slavery's – they had much affection while they were aiming at mastery, and more hatred after they gained it.

31. In Britain[36] the governor Publius Ostorius was met by turbulent conditions, the enemy having overrun allied territory the more forcefully for thinking the new commander, with an unknown army and winter beginning, unlikely to oppose. (2) Ostorius, aware that initial events yield fear or confidence,

quickly gathered cohorts and, after killing those who stood fast, chased down the scattered. Lest they mass again, lest an unfriendly and insincere peace allow neither leader nor soldier rest, he prepared to confiscate the arms of the suspect and to control with forts everything up to the rivers[37] Trisantona and Sabrina. (3) This the Iceni, first, refused – a powerful people not yet battle-bruised since they had sought our alliance voluntarily. Influenced by these, nearby nations chose for the fight a place encircled by a crude rampart with a narrow approach to prevent cavalry passage. (4) These fortifications the Roman commander, though – lacking the legions' strength – leading allied forces, approached for breaching. With cohorts arrayed and cavalry squadrons readied even for infantry tasks, at his signal they shattered the rampart and dismayed men impeded by their own barrier. With awareness of rebel status and escapes blocked, their deeds were many and fine. In this battle the governor's son[38] Marcus earned citizen-saving distinction.

32. The calamity of the Iceni brought calm to those hesitating between war and peace. The army was led against the Decangi. Their territory was ravaged, pillaging widespread. The enemy did not venture battle or, if they tried harrying the column from hiding, their stealth was punished. The sea situated near Ireland had nearly been reached when disputes among the Brigantes recalled a commander fixed in his intention of avoiding new undertakings unless earlier ones were secured. (2) The Brigantes, after the few who initiated the fighting had been killed and the rest pardoned, subsided. But for the Siluran people neither ruthlessness nor clemency caused alteration. They prosecuted the war and had to be kept down by legionary forts. To expedite this, the colony[39] of Camulodunum was settled with a strong company of veterans on captured territory – to help against rebels and for habituating allies to the laws' obligations.

33. The next move was against the Silures, who relied, in addition to their own spirit, on Caratacus' might. Outcomes both equivocal and successful had exalted him to overtop the other British commanders. Ahead then in ingenuity and position-ploys but in soldier numbers inferior, he transferred the

war to the Ordovices. After the accession of those who feared our peace, he wagered all. A battlefield was chosen with approaches and exits – everything! – inconvenient for us and better for his men. On one side there were lofty mountains, and wherever access was smooth Caratacus spread a rampart-like barrier of boulders. In front he had a river of variable depth and masses of armed men stationed as fortifications.

34. Plus, the peoples' captains circulated and exhorted and braced men's spirits by diminishing fear, by kindling hope, and with other spurs to war. Indeed, Caratacus stopping here and there affirmed: *This day, this battle will yield freedom's recuperation or initiate perpetual servitude!* He called out the names of forebears. *These men repelled Caesar! By their courage, and clear of axe*[40] *and tax, we have our wives' and children's bodies undefiled.* As he spoke these and like words the crowd cheered. Every man pledged by his native rite: *Neither weapons nor wounds will make me yield.*

35. This enthusiasm stunned the Roman general. Likewise terrifying were river obstacle, rampart reinforcement, heights overhanging, nothing but ruthlessness everywhere and crowds of defenders. But his soldiers demanded battle, shouting: *Valour is all-vanquishing!* Officers[41] speaking equivalent words intensified the army's ardour. (2) Ostorius, after discovering which routes were impassible and which permeable, led the attack and easily passed the river. At the earthwork the battle of projectiles occasioned more wounds for us and much carnage. Shields locked overhead, the rocks' rude and formless fabric was undone. When the hand-to-hand battle drew even, the enemy withdrew to mountain heights. (3) But this location, too, both lance- and heavy-armed soldiers invaded, the former making armed feints, the latter marching in formation. There was disruption in the Britons' facing lines, which did not have the protection of breastplate or helmet. If they tried to resist the auxiliaries they were slain by legionary swords and pikes, and if they turned to the legions, by auxiliary blades and spears. It was an illustrious victory. The wife and daughter of Caratacus were captured, his brothers were surrendered.

36. Caratacus – such, generally, is the insecurity of

misfortune – after entrusting himself to the Brigantes' queen Cartimandua, was bound and delivered to the victors. It was the ninth year[42] since the start of war in Britain, the source from which Caratacus' fame was carried beyond the islands and overran the nearest provinces. Throughout Italy, too, it was celebrated and people longed to see who he was, that man who for so many years defied our might. (2) Not even in Rome was his name obscure, and Claudius, while exalting his own honour, increased the glory of the vanquished. The populace was summoned for a striking spectacle. The Guard stood at arms in the open in front of their barracks. (3) The king's dependants filed in, then a train of military decorations and the gains of foreign wars, then brothers, wife and daughter, finally himself on display. The others' pleas were unworthy from fear. But it was not for Caratacus, by downcast glance or words, to seek pity. Standing before Claudius' tribunal he spoke thus:

37. 'Had I had as great a measure of success as of noble birth and good fortune, I would have entered this city a friend rather than a captive, nor would you have disdained – given my descent from illustrious forebears and control of numerous peoples – to welcome me with treaty and peace. (2) My present lot is disfiguring for me; for you, however, splendid. I had horses, men, weapons, wealth. What wonder if I lost them unwilling? If you desire to control everyone, does it follow that everyone accepts slavery? (3) Had immediate capitulation preceded extradition, neither my fortune nor your glory would have grown illustrious. My execution will be followed by forgetting, but if you keep me safe I will be an everlasting example of your clemency.' (4) At this, Claudius pardoned Caratacus and his wife and brothers. From these, freed of their chains, Agrippina, too – she was conspicuous nearby on another platform – was venerated with the same praise and thanks as the Emperor's. (It was a novelty, unlike long-standing custom, that a woman preside over Roman standards. But she conducted herself as partner in an empire won by her forebears.)

38. The senators summoned thereafter gave many a splendid speech about Caratacus' captivity. *It is no less illustrious than Scipio's display of Syphax and Paulus'*[43] *of Perses and whoever*

else displayed chained kings to the Roman people. (2) They decreed for Ostorius an honorary triumph.

His successful outcomes to that point soon turned equivocal. Perhaps, with Caratacus removed – as if the war was done – the campaigning on our side was less intent, or perhaps the enemy, from compassion for so great a king, burned the more sharply for revenge. (3) The camp superintendent and legionary cohorts that were left to establish garrisons among the Silures were encircled. And without swift action[44] – thanks to messengers from the closest strongholds – in relief of the besieged troops, they would have succumbed. Still, the commander and eight centurions and the readiest regulars fell. And soon thereafter our foragers and cavalry units sent to assist were routed.

39. Ostorius then set unencumbered cohorts as a barrier. But he was not stopping the rout – if his legions had not taken up the battle. With their strength, the fighting drew even, then better for us. (2) The enemy escaped with little damage since the sun was setting. Thereafter, there were frequent battles, generally raid-like: in the woods and marshes as opportunity or bravery offered, reckless or planned, moved by anger or booty, on orders or with leaders unaware. The Silures were particularly persistent, fired by circulation of the Roman commander's statement: *Just as the Sugambri[45] were once excised or transferred into Gaul, so now the Silures' name must be utterly extinguished!* (3) Accordingly, they intercepted two auxiliary cohorts that, owing to their commanders' greed, were ravaging quite heedlessly. With outlays of plunder and captives the remaining peoples were being induced to defect when Ostorius, careworn and tired, passed away. To enemy rejoicing: war, if not battle, had annihilated a leader not to be despised.

40. Claudius was informed of his representative's death. Lest the province lack a guide, he made Aulus Didius[46] the replacement. Didius sailed quickly, but found the situation worse for the combat misfortune of the legion with Manlius Valens in charge. This event's rumour was exaggerated both among the enemy, to alarm the newcomer general, and with Didius himself amplifying what he heard, so that greater praise

for a settlement would accrue, or, if the enemy proved obdurate, fuller exoneration. (The Silures inflicted that damage, too,
and ran rampant until driven off by Didius' incursion.)

(2) After Caratacus' capture, the man paramount in military
expertise was Venutius of the Brigantes, as I mentioned above.[47]
He was long loyal and was protected by Roman arms while he
held Queen Cartimandua in matrimony. Later, there was a split
and immediately a war, and he adopted hostilities against us,
too. (3) But at first the contest was between themselves only,
and with artful cunning Cartimandua cut short the lives of
Venutius' brother and kin. The enemy was then on fire, with
shame a goad. *We must not succumb to a woman's rule!* A
strong and combat-ready force invaded her kingdom. We foresaw this, and the cohorts sent to assist fought a hard battle
whose equivocal beginning made its conclusion the happier.
(4) There was a fight with similar outcome by the legion with
Caesius Nasica in charge. (Didius, who was heavy with age and
plentifully supplied with honours, acted through subordinates
and deemed it sufficient to parry the enemy.)

I have combined[48] the achievements of two governors over
several years, lest, divided, they produce a less effective memorial. To the regular sequence I now return.

41. (51 CE) Tiberius Claudius (5th time), Servius Cornelius
Orfitus, consuls.

Nero's 'adulthood'[49] was celebrated early so he would seem
fit for public business. Claudius yielded gladly to senatorial
flattery: at twenty, Nero was to enter the consulship; in the
meantime, as consul-designate, he was to have proconsular
power outside Rome and be called 'first of the youth'. Plus cash
gifts were made in Nero's name to the military and the populace.
(2) At the Circus games given to win the crowd's enthusiasm,
Britannicus paraded in purple-edged toga, Nero in triumphal
garb. (The people, it was thought, should see the one dressed as
emperor, the other as boy, and infer a comparable future for
each.) Officers who lamented Britannicus' lot were removed on
false grounds; some were even apparently promoted. And
freedmen, those with unsullied loyalty, were displaced owing to
occurrences like the following.

(3) In an encounter, Nero used 'Britannicus', Britannicus 'Domitius' as greeting. Agrippina reported this to her husband as the beginning of strife, greatly protesting. *It is a rejection of the adoption! The senate's decree and the people's order are nullified among the household gods! If the perversity of those teaching such hostility is not parried, it will burst forth for public ruin.* Shaken, and taking these as criminal charges, Claudius inflicted on his son's best teachers exile and death, and put a stepmother's men in charge of Britannicus' custody.

42. Not yet were the heights of contrivance within Agrippina's daring, unless Guard responsibility be detached from Lusius Geta and Rufrius Crispinus,[50] whom she believed mindful of Messalina and attached to her children. *The cohorts are being undone by the lobbying of two. If ruled by one, discipline will be tighter*, Claudius' wife insisted. Control was transferred to Afranius Burrus,[51] a man of outstanding military fame and aware of who willed his command. (2) Her own eminence, too, Agrippina heightened. She went up the Capitoline in a carriage. This distinction, a concession of old for priests and sacred objects, increased veneration for the woman: victorious general's daughter, sister of a man who ruled the world and spouse and mother – a pattern unique to this day. (3) Meanwhile her chief champion Vitellius, exceedingly strong of influence, fell prey at life's end – so uncertain is the situation of the powerful! – to a denunciation by Junius Lupus, a senator. The charges were treason and a passion to rule.[52] Claudius would have paid attention, except for the alteration induced by Agrippina's threats – not pleas – so that he banished Lupus, just as Vitellius wanted.[53]

43. Numerous portents occurred that year: Capitoline occupied by ill-omened birds, houses collapsing in frequent earthquakes and, as fear spread, the weak getting crushed by the crowd's panic. A dearth of grain and the consequent famine were also taken for a portent. People protested, and not just under cover. Claudius, giving judgements, was swarmed by a noisy disturbance, forced to the edge of the Forum and threatened with violence until in a mass of soldiers he penetrated the hostile crowd. (2) *Fifteen days' food supply, no more, remains,*

people knew. The gods' kindness and winter's forbearance in this extremity provided relief. (But, heavens! Italy once transported her legions' provisions into distant provinces. Even now she does not suffer from infertility, but instead we work Africa and Egypt, and the survival of the Roman people is entrusted to shipping's hazards.)

44. The same year.

A war between Armenians and Iberians, newly arisen, caused between Parthians and Romans, too, grave disturbances. (2) The Parthian nation's ruler was Vologaeses.[54] His maternal origin being a Greek concubine, he gained kingship by his brothers' concession. The Iberi were in Pharasmanes' control by long-standing ownership, the Armenians[55] in his brother Mithridates', through our might. (3) Pharasmanes had a son, Radamistus: handsome stature, striking in physique and trained in traditional attainments. His local reputation was brilliant. *The Iberian kingdom is unremarkable*, he would say. *And kept so by my father's longevity!* A protest too spirited and too frequent to keep desire hidden. (4) Pharasmanes, whose own years were now in decline, feared a younger man ready for power and girded with popular favour. He drew him to another hope, indicated Armenia. *After the Parthians were expelled, I myself gave it to Mithridates. But violence should be deferred. A trick is better for crushing him, unwary.* (5) Accordingly, Radamistus, offering strife with his father as an excuse – *I can't take my stepmother's hatred*, he claimed – went to his uncle. Treated with great affability, in appearance one of Mithridates' children, he enticed Armenia's leading men to revolution, with Mithridates unaware and still doing him honour.

45. With a show of reconciliation, Radamistus returned to his father, announcing: *What can be accomplished by imposture is ready. The rest requires weapons.* Pharasmanes fabricated war causes. *When I was at war with the king of the Albani, my brother opposed a request for Roman reinforcements, an injury I intend to avenge with his annihilation.* He then handed his son substantial forces. (2) Radamistus, invading unforeseen, forced a terrified Mithridates from the field into the stronghold Gorneas, defended by its position and a garrison with the

auxiliary officer Caelius Pollio and the centurion Casperius[56] in
charge. (3) Nothing is so unfamiliar to barbarians as the engines
and stratagems of assault. For us, however, this aspect of warfare is thoroughly familiar. Accordingly, Radamistus, after
frustration and loss in an attempt on the fortifications, began
a blockade. (4) Force meeting disregard, he purchased the
auxiliary officer's greed, though Casperius objected. *Neither
an allied king nor Armenia – the Roman people's gift – should
be overthrown by criminal money!* Finally, with Pollio pleading enemy numbers, Radamistus his father's orders, Casperius
arranged a truce and left to deter Pharasmanes from war or, if
not, to inform Syria's governor Ummidius Quadratus about
Armenia's situation.

46. With the centurion's departure Pollio, as if released from
his keeper, urged Mithridates to ratify a treaty. Brotherhood's
tie, Pharasmanes his senior, and other kinship terms were the
arguments: the other's daughter was his wife; he himself was
Radamistus' father-in-law. *The Iberi do not refuse peace,
though presently the stronger; Armenian perfidy is well known
and your only prop is an ill-provisioned stronghold. Do not
prefer*[57] *doubtful attempts afield to bloodless terms!* (2) At
Mithridates' delay – Pollio's advice was suspect: he had defiled
a royal concubine and was thought to have his price for every
appetite – Casperius went again to Pharasmanes. *The Iberi
must withdraw from the blockade*, was his demand. (3) Pharasmanes, his open responses non-committal and usually mild,
sent secret messengers to warn Radamistus: *You must somehow hasten the assault.* Wrongdoing's fee went up and Pollio,
keeping corruption hidden, urged his soldiers to insist on
peace, to threaten abandoning the garrison. Under this necessity Mithridates accepted a date and place for the treaty and
left the stronghold.

47. At first Radamistus, rushing to his embrace, feigned deference and called him father-in-law and parent. Adding an
oath – *By no blade or poison will I do you violence* – he drew
Mithridates into a nearby grove. *The preparations for a sacrifice are ready there*, he said, *so that the gods' witness confirms
the peace.* (2) It is customary for kings, when they join in

alliance, to clasp right hands, bind thumbs together and fasten with a knot. When fluid suffuses the tips, with a slight nick they ease out some blood and take turns licking. This is a mystical bond, they believe, with exchanged blood as its sanction. (3) On that occasion, however, the man applying the fastenings, feigning a fall, went for Mithridates' knees and tripped him. Then there was a general rush and chains were heaped. In fetters – dishonouring, in barbarian eyes – Mithridates was dragged away. (4) Then the crowd, having been under harsh rule, plied insult and fist. This met some opposition – people pitied a change of fortune so great – and the arrival of Mithridates' wife and small children brought lamentation to the full. In separate closed conveyances they were removed while Pharasmanes' orders were sought. (5) In him, passion for rule outweighed brother and daughter; also a crime-ready mind.[58] To his eyes, however, he gave consideration: the killing was not done in his presence. Radamistus, claiming oath-observance, deployed no blade, no poison against sister and uncle. He killed them sprawling in the dirt under a vast and heavy pile of clothing. Mithridates' sons, too – for crying over their parents' killing – were slain.

48. Quadratus, learning of Mithridates betrayed and that his kingdom was in the killers' possession, summoned his advisers and reported events. *Shall I avenge?* A few cared about Rome's honour; the majority spoke of safety. (2) *Every foreign crime is cause for rejoicing. Indeed, seeds of hatred should sometimes be supplied, as Roman emperors have repeatedly offered this very Armenia in a show of largesse to unsettle barbarian minds. Let Radamistus have his ill-gotten gains, hated and hissed. It is more to our advantage thus than had he won with glory.* So decided. But lest they seem to have assented to crime – and Claudius' orders were otherwise – messengers were sent to Pharasmanes: *Leave Armenia and remove your son.*

49. Cappadocia's governor was Julius Paelignus, a man despicable for both cowardly spirit and clownish body, but very close to Claudius, for whose useless leisure, when an ordinary citizen, the conversation of jokesters provided amusement. Paelignus, having assembled local forces – *for recovering*

Armenia, he said – plundered allies more than enemies. At the
departure of his men, with barbarians invading, he needed protection and went to Radamistus. Gifts won Paelignus over.
Indeed, he urged Radamistus to take up the royal insignia and
then stayed as sponsor and attendant. (2) When word spread
with this shameful report, to prevent the rest being deemed like
Paelignus, the legate Helvidius Priscus[59] was sent with his
legion to attend duly to the turbulent situation. Quickly crossing the Taurus range, Priscus had used more moderation than
force to produce quiet when he was ordered back to Syria, lest
the beginning of war with Parthia result.

50. For Vologaeses, thinking that an occasion for invading
Armenia – *It was my forebears' possession and a foreign king
has wrongly taken hold* – was at hand, assembled troops and
prepared to escort his brother Tiridates into the kingdom, so
that no part of his household lack dominion. With the Parthian
arrival the Iberi were driven off without battle, and the Armenians' cities Artaxata and Tigranocerta took the yoke. (2) Then
fearful winter and inadequate provisions and sickness consequent on both drove Vologaeses to abandon present attempts.
With Armenia rulerless again, Radamistus invaded, more cal-
lous than before, as facing defectors who would seize an
opportunity to fight. The Armenians – though accustomed to
servitude – their patience ruptured, took arms and beset the
palace.

51. Radamistus' only support was his horses' speed, with
which he got himself and his wife away. (2) She was pregnant
and tolerated flight's first phase from enemy-fear and fondness
for husband, but later, when prolonged hurry left her womb
shaking and innards aquiver, begged for honourable death as
exemption from captivity's insults. (3) He at first caressed,
comforted, encouraged, now admiring her fortitude, now sick
with worry lest, left behind, she be someone else's. Finally, with
love's impetuosity – and being no stranger to crime – he drew
his knife. Wounded her, dragged her to Araxis' bank, gave her
to the river so even her corpse would be removed. He himself
went headlong to the Iberi, his ancestral realm.

(4) Zenobia – this was the woman's name – was in a quiet

wash, still breathing and showing life, and was noticed by shepherds. From the respectability of her looks thinking her a worthy, they bandaged the wound, applied rustic remedies and, learning her name and case, carried her to Artaxata. From there she was escorted in official custody to Tiridates, affably received, and kept in royal style.

52. (52 CE) Cornelius Sulla, Salvius Otho, consuls.

Furius Scribonianus was exiled on grounds of using astrologers to investigate the Emperor's end. Implicated in the crime was his mother Vibia, impatient of her previous situation (she had been banished). (2) Scribonianus' father Camillus had roused war[60] across Dalmatia, a fact that Claudius included in his 'clemency'. *I am preserving enemy offspring for a second time.* The exile's life thereafter was not long. Was he eliminated by accidental death? Or through poison? People spread the version they believed. (3) As for the astrologers, the senatorial decree of expulsion from Italy was ruthless – and ineffectual.

In a speech by the Emperor there was praise for men who, in financial straits,[61] left the senatorial order voluntarily, and removal for those who, by staying, added impudence to poverty.

53. Claudius also put before the senate the punishment of women cohabiting with slaves. Decided: women who had fallen so far without a master's knowledge should be deemed in servitude to him, but if he consented, his freedwomen. (2) For Pallas, whom Claudius had announced as the measure's inventor, an honorary praetorship and 15 million sesterces were proposed by consul-designate Barea Soranus. Plus, from Cornelius Scipio, a public thanksgiving that a descendant of Arcadian kings[62] ranked exceptionally ancient nobility behind public utility and permitted himself to be considered among the Emperor's assistants. (3) Claudius' statement: *Pallas, content with honour, will stay impoverished, as before.* A senate decree whereby a freedman possessing 300 million sesterces received abundant praise for antique thrift was set in official bronze.

54. His brother, Felix by name, did not have equivalent moderation. Long since atop Judaea, he thought his every misdeed done with impunity (Pallas' great power was his prop).

The Jews did give the appearance of revolt when sedition arose after [they were ordered by Gaius to place his likeness in the temple. And although][63] once his murder was manifest there had been no compliance, concern continued that some emperor might give the same command. (2) Felix with untimely 'remedies' kept provoking offences and was rivalled for the worse by Ventidius Cumanus, in whose charge lay part of a province divided so that Galileans were to obey Cumanus, Samaritans Felix. These were peoples long inimical, and now, from contempt for their rulers, their hostility was less restrained: (3) there were mutual raids, robber bands dispatched, ambushes arranged and occasional encounters in battle, with spoils and booty accruing to the Emperor's agents.[64] These rejoiced at first, but soon, as damage multiplied, they interposed arms. Soldiers were killed. The province was aflame with war, had Quadratus, Syria's guide, not provided relief. (4) There was little delay over Jews who had broken free to murder soldiers: they paid with their lives. Cumanus and Felix gave pause, for Claudius, hearing the rebellion's causes, had given Quadratus authority to decide even about imperial agents. But Quadratus displayed Felix among the judges,[65] welcome on his tribunal – thus to deter accuser enthusiasm. Cumanus was condemned for outrages committed by the two and the province's calm restored.

55. Soon thereafter some peoples from the Cilician countryside – Cietae[66] was their name; they were often roused before – with Troxoborus as leader, seized rugged mountains as a base from which, in descents on coastline or city, they dared violence against farmers and town-dwellers, especially towards merchants and shipowners. (2) The city of Anemurium[67] was blockaded. The cavalry sent from Syria to help – their commander was Curtius Severus – were confounded: harsh surroundings, suitable for infantry fighting, did not permit equestrian battle. Then the coastal king Antiochus,[68] using allurements for the populace and subterfuge against the leader, fractured the barbarians' forces. After executing Troxoborus and a few leading men, he used clemency to reconcile the rest.

56. Around this time the ridge between the Fucine Lake and

the Liris[69] was penetrated. So that more people would see the work's magnificence, a naval battle was staged on the lake, following Augustus, who had once given a show in a pool built near the Tiber, but with lighter boats and smaller numbers. (2) Claudius equipped triple- and quadruple-banked warships and 19,000 men. The shoreline was ringed with boats, lest there be widespread escapes, and yet the area encompassed suited rowers' power, captains' skill and boats' momentum – battle routine. On the boats stood Guard units and squadrons. In front, there were defences from which catapults and ballistas could be fired. The rest of the lake was controlled by 'marines'[70] in decked ships. (3) Lakeshore and hills and mountain heights were filled, theatre-like, by a countless multitude from the nearest towns and others from Rome itself, desirous of seeing, or dutiful towards, the Emperor. He himself, in a striking military cloak, and Agrippina nearby in a mantle of gold, presided. The fighting, though between convicts, showed brave men's spirit and after numerous wounds they were exempted from the killing.

57. At spectacle's end the watercourse was opened. The work's carelessness was manifest: it was not sunk deep enough into the lake's depths or even the middle. Accordingly, over time the conduits were dug deeper and to muster the multitude again there was a gladiatorial show with platforms laid for foot-battle. (2) Also, a dinner party sited at the lake's outflow, which caused everyone great alarm, since the waters' force bursting out carried off everything near. Even further away things were toppled or terrified by the crash of sound. Agrippina cited the Emperor's fright in censuring the work's manager, Narcissus, for cupidity and looting. Nor was he silent. *Female unruliness and her excessive hopes!* were his charges.

58. (53 CE) Decimus Junius, Quintus Haterius, consuls.[71]

At sixteen Nero took Octavia, Claudius' daughter, into matrimony. And in order to shine with respectable pursuits, too, and oratory's glory, he took up Ilium's cause. *A Roman is an offshoot of Troy, Aeneas was founder of the Julian line,* and other old matters, practically fables, he detailed eloquently, effecting the city's release from every public obligation. (2) With

him again as speaker the colony of Bononia,[72] consumed by
fire, received as relief an outlay of 10 million sesterces. To the
Rhodians was restored a freedom often stripped or confirmed,
depending on their foreign-war service or, at home, seditious
offences. And the Apameans, uprooted by an earthquake, got a
five-year remission of taxes.

59. Claudius, however, was driven to promulgate extreme
brutality. This, too, was Agrippina's doing. She overset Statilius
Taurus, a man notable for his wealth – she coveted his gardens – with an accusation from Tarquitius Priscus. One of
Taurus' legates while he ruled Africa with proconsular power,
Priscus indicted him after their return on a few extortion
charges, also magical beliefs. (2) False accuser and undeserved
humiliation did not make Taurus suffer long: he did violence to
his life before the senate's verdict.[73] Priscus was nevertheless
driven from the meeting, because senators with their hatred of
informers won out[74] against Agrippina's lobbying.

60. That same year people heard quite frequently an imperial utterance. *There must be equal force in matters adjudicated
by my agents*[75] *as if I myself decided.* And, lest this seem an
accidental lapse, provision was made by senatorial decree,
fuller than before and more comprehensive.

(2) Augustus' orders had been that legal business was to be
done before the equestrian-ranked governors of Egypt, and
their rulings were to count as if given by Roman magistrates.
Later throughout the other provinces and in Rome itself authorization was given for many things praetors used to adjudicate.
(3) Claudius delivered up every prerogative[76] so often contested
through sedition and combat, as when Gaius Gracchus' bills
placed the equestrian order in possession of the courts, or when
Servilius' laws restored courts to the senate. And Marius and
Sulla once did battle especially over this. (4) The equestrian
and senatorial orders back then had divergent ends, and each
victory strengthened their public position. Oppius and Balbus
were the first empowered by Caesar's might[77] to handle negotiations for peace and decisions for war. Men like Matius
thereafter and Vedius and other prepotent equestrian names

are pointless to mention, since Claudius made freedmen – those in charge of his finances – equal to himself and to laws.

61. He next proposed granting tax immunity to the Coans, making many a reference to their antiquity. *Argives, especially Latona's father Coeus, were the island's most ancient inhabitants. Then with Aesculapius' arrival the healing art was imported and celebrated especially in his posterity's hands.* Claudius gave individuals' names and the eras when they flourished, plus this: (2) *Xenophon,*[78] *whose skill I myself used, originated in that family and his prayers should be granted. Free in future from all taxation, let the Coans inhabit an island sacred and subservient only to the god.* Certainly their many services to the Roman people and their conjoined victories could have been mentioned, but Claudius, with his customary easy temper, did not veil his concession to one man with any extraneous props.

62. The Byzantines, however, given opportunity to speak when requesting of the senate relief from their taxes' weight, reviewed everything, beginning with the treaty struck with us when we were warring against the Macedonian king – dubbed, for his worthlessness, Pseudophilip[79] – then the troops sent against Antiochus, Perses and Aristonicus, and in the pirate war their assistance to Antony, their contributions to Sulla and Lucullus and Pompey, and then recent services to the emperors. *We occupy locations convenient for leaders and armies crossing by land and sea, and for conveying provisions.*

63. A very narrow split between Europe and Asia is where the Greeks established Byzantium at Europe's edge. (Asking Pythian Apollo where to found the city, they got an oracle: *Seek a site opposite the territory of the blind.* (2) In this riddle the Chalcedonii were meant, who sailed there first and, seeing the two sites' utility, selected the worst.) Byzantium's soil is fertile, its sea productive. A vast quantity of fish bursts free of the Black Sea and, terrified by crosswise underwater cliffs, leaves the opposite shore's curve and is carried into Byzantium's harbours. (3) Accordingly, the Byzantines were at first acquisitive and opulent. Then, under pressure from taxes' weight, they

begged for either cessation or limitation, with the Emperor's support. *Fresh from Thracian and Bosporan wars, they are weary and deserve aid.* For their tax, therefore, a five-year remission.

64. (54 CE) Marcus Asinius, Manius Acilius, consuls.[80]

A change for the worse, it was recognized, was signified by many portents: military standards and tents ablaze with fire from the sky; Capitoline summit occupied by bee swarm; biform human births; sow litter with hawk talons. Counted among the prodigies was the diminution in all magistrate numbers: quaestor, aedile, tribune, plus praetor and consul dead inside a few months. (2) A particular panic, however, gripped Agrippina. An utterance by Claudius, made while drunk – *I am fated to suffer, then punish, my spouses' wrongdoing!* – was her concern. She decided to act speedily, but after destroying Domitia Lepida.[81] Female reasoning: Lepida, a daughter of the younger Antonia with Augustus as her great-uncle, cousin-once-removed to Agrippina and sister to Agrippina's husband Gnaeus, believed her birth equally illustrious. (3) In beauty, age and wealth quite close, and each being shameless, shocking and rash, they vied in vice no less than in Fortune's gifts. Their sharpest contest, however, was whether aunt or mother prevail with Nero. Lepida used allurement and outlay to attach a young mind, a contrast to the harsh and menacing Agrippina, who could give dominion to her son, but not tolerate his dominance.

65. The charges: *Lepida attacked the Emperor's spouse with curse tablets and disturbs Italy's peace with a host of slaves insufficiently controlled in Calabria.* For these, death was the sentence, to strong opposition from Narcissus. More and more suspicious of Agrippina, he told those closest – so goes the story – *My ruin is certain whether Britannicus holds power or Nero, but Claudius deserves from me a life expended for his benefit. (2) Convictions were obtained for Messalina and Silius, but equivalent causes for accusation will repeat if Nero becomes dominant. With Britannicus as successor, however, Claudius has nothing to fear.*[82] *The whole household is now riven by stepmotherly plots, a scandal greater than if I left Messalina's*

shamelessness unspoken. And yet shamelessness is present now,
with Pallas as Agrippina's adulterer. Everyone should under-
stand her to hold honour, shame, body – everything! – more
paltry than rule. (3) With these and like words he embraced
Britannicus. *May the vigour of age mature soon, very soon!*
was his prayer, hands stretched now to gods, now to the boy.
Drive out your father's enemies and punish your mother's kill-
ers,[83] *too!*

66. Under this great burden of cares Narcissus fell prey to
illness. To restore his forces through climate's gentleness and
waters' healthfulness he went to Sinuessa.

Agrippina was long since resolved on crime and – if occasion
offered – quick and well supplied with agents. She took advice
on poison type. *Something sudden and abrupt will reveal*
wrongdoing, she worried. *If I choose a slow and wasting type,*
Claudius, facing the end and perceiving the plot, will return to
loving his son. She decided on something special, to confound
intellect and defer death. (2) An artist in such matters was
chosen, Locusta[84] by name, a woman earlier condemned for
poisoning and long retained among the instruments of rule. By
her cleverness a toxin was prepared. Its agent was one of the
eunuchs, Halotus, who routinely served Claudius' meals and
tested them by taste.

67. Everything was so soon known that it is already attested
in contemporary writers' accounts: poison infused[85] into a
choice mushroom, the drug's power not immediately seen –
was Claudius too sluggish or too drunk? – and loosened bowels
apparently providing relief. (2) Dismay filled Agrippina and
with finality threatening she dismissed present antipathy and
deployed the doctor Xenophon's pre-arranged complicity. He,
as if assisting Claudius' struggles to vomit, sent down his throat
a feather coated with quick-acting poison, so it is believed, perfectly aware that the greatest crimes are begun dangerously but
accomplished profitably.

68. Meanwhile the senate was summoned. Vows for the
Emperor's preservation were undertaken by consuls and priests,
while Claudius, already lifeless, was buried beneath blankets
and bandages until the props for Nero's power were

assembled. (2) To begin, Agrippina – as if overcome by grief
and seeking comfort – held Britannicus in embrace. *A true likeness of his father*, she called him, while artfully delaying his
exit from the chamber. (3) She detained Antonia, too, and
Octavia, his sisters. After closing and manning all approaches,
she circulated frequent notices that Claudius' condition was
improving, intending that the soldiers remain hopeful and the
moment pronounced advantageous by astrologers arrive.

69. At midday on 13 October the palace doors suddenly
opened. Accompanied by Burrus, Nero approached the cohort
present by military routine on patrol duty. At their commander's prompting they found propitious words of greeting. Then
he was put in a litter. Some hesitated, they say, looking back.
Where, where is Britannicus? Eventually, with no alternative
authorized, they followed what was offered. (2) Nero was
brought to the barracks and, after some words suited to the
occasion and the promise of a donative on the model of paternal largesse, hailed as emperor. The soldiers' opinion was
followed by the senators' decrees. There was no hesitation in
the provinces, either. (3) Divine honours were voted for Claudius and his funeral was celebrated like the deified Augustus',
since Agrippina rivalled her great-grandmother Livia's magnificence. Claudius' will, however, was not read, lest its placement
of stepson before son – injury and insult! – trouble the crowd's
mood.

BOOK 13

1. (54 CE, continued) The new regime's first death – Junius Silanus,[1] Asia's governor; Nero was unaware – was set up by Agrippina's plotting. Not by impetuosity of character did Silanus provoke ruin: he was indolent and despised under other rulers, indeed Gaius used to call him a 'golden sheep'. But Agrippina, having contrived the murder of his brother Lucius, feared an avenger. Widespread public opinion was that Silanus was preferable to a Nero just out of boyhood holding power acquired by crime: a man of settled age, innocent, noble-born and – something that would count then – from the Caesars' line. (Silanus, too, was Augustus' great-great-grandson.) (2) Hence his murder. Its agents were the equestrian-ranked Publius Celerius and the freedman Helius,[2] the men responsible for imperial property in Asia. They gave the governor poison at a banquet, too openly to escape notice. (3) Equally hastily was Narcissus, a freedman of Claudius' whose conflicts with Agrippina[3] I reported, driven to death by harsh imprisonment and the inevitability of the end, against the wishes of the Emperor, whose still-hidden vices Narcissus' greed and exorbitance suited marvellously.

2. The plan was to kill, except that Burrus and Seneca blocked it. Guides for the imperial youth and – something rare in a partnership of power – concordant, these men were equally potent with different arts: Burrus had military responsibilities and austerity of character; Seneca instruction in eloquence and estimable affability. They cooperated to facilitate tethering the Emperor's slippery phase, if he rejected virtue, to licensed pleasures. (2) Their united campaign was against Agrippina's

temerity. Aflame with an evil regime's every desire, she had in her camp Pallas, on whose advice Claudius, by incestuous marriage and disastrous adoption, had overthrown himself. But not even Nero's spirit submitted to slaves, and Pallas with his irksome arrogance exceeded a freedman's measure and roused impatience. (3) In public, however, every honour was heaped on Agrippina, and when an officer, following military protocol, asked for the password, Nero gave 'best of mothers'. By senatorial decree she was given two public attendants,[4] a cult office and a public funeral for Claudius, followed by consecration.

3. At the funeral the Emperor began Claudius' eulogy. So long as Nero was reckoning the family's antiquity and its ancestral consulships and triumphs, he himself was earnest, as were others. References to intellectual attainments, too – and *During Claudius' reign nothing grim befell the state from outside* – were humoured in the hearing. When he turned to Claudius' foresight and wisdom, no one refrained from laughter, although the speech, written by Seneca, displayed much elegance, given that Seneca's character was pleasant and suited to the age's ears. (2) The elderly, their leisure spent comparing past and present, remarked: *Of those who have come to power, Nero is the first to need someone else's eloquence.*

(Caesar rivalled the best speakers, and Augustus' eloquence was ready and fluent and fit for an emperor. Tiberius was also skilful at the art of weighing words, and therefore effective with meaning or deliberately ambiguous. Even Gaius' disturbed mind did not impair forcefulness of speech. And when Claudius spoke prepared words you would not have missed elegance. (3) Nero from boyhood on diverted his lively mind elsewhere: metalwork, painting, songs and the control of horses were his pursuits. Occasionally in writing verse he showed that he possessed the beginnings of an education.)

4. Grief's performance complete, Nero entered the senate. Senatorial authority and military consensus formed his preface, then he stated: *I have advice and models for excellent rule, and my youth was not steeped in civil conflicts or domestic disputes. I bring no hatreds, no hurts and no desire for revenge.*

(2) Then he laid out the pattern of the coming principate, deviating especially from what recently roused resentment. *I will not be every trial's judge: with accusers and defendants sequestered in one house[5] the power of a few runs riot. Nothing in my household is venal or bribery-permeable. Home and state are separate. Let the senate retain its ancient tasks. At the consuls' tribunal let Italy and the senatorial provinces make their pleas, and let consuls give access to the senate. I will look after the armies in my trust.*

5. Credibility was not absent. Much *was* decided at the senate's behest,[6] including: no one should be hired with gifts or fee to plead a case, and there should be no necessity for quaestors-designate to sponsor gladiatorial games. Though Agrippina opposed – *Claudius' enactments are undone!* – the senate got their way.

(The senate used to convene on the Palatine[7] so Agrippina could attend – a doorway having been added at the back – separated by a curtain to prevent sight but not eliminate hearing. (2) Indeed, when Armenia's envoys were pleading their nation's case before Nero, Agrippina was preparing to ascend the Emperor's dais and preside with him, except that, when everyone else was panic-rooted, Seneca advised: *Go meet your mother.* Nero's show of filial devotion blocked disgrace.)

6. To conclude the year: troubling rumours. *The Parthians[8] have burst out again! Armenia is being ravaged after the expulsion of Radamistus, who keeps taking control of the kingdom then running away, and has again abandoned the fight.* (2) In gossip-greedy Rome: *How will an emperor scarcely seventeen years old be able to shoulder or parry that burden? What help is there in a man ruled by a woman? Can battles, too, and sieges and war's other elements be run by teachers?* (3) On the other side: *This is a better outcome than if Claudius, ineffective by age and cowardice, was summoned to warfare's rigours, a man obedient to slave orders. Burrus and Seneca are reputed to have much experience of affairs. And how much can the Emperor's strength be lacking, when Pompey in his eighteenth year and Octavian in his nineteenth undertook civil wars?* (4) *In exalted positions achievements are generally based on*

auspices and advice rather than weapons and combat. Nero
will give clear proof of the friends he will employ – are they
respectable or otherwise? – if for commander, with jealousy set
aside, he chooses someone outstanding rather than someone
wealthy or influence-reliant who uses bribery.

7. With these and like words circulating, Nero gave orders.
Find men in nearby provinces, move them forward to fill the
East's legions. The legions themselves must be placed nearer
Armenia. Two long-standing kings, Agrippa and Antiochus,[9]
were to deploy troops for an offensive into Parthian territory,
and bridges were to span the Euphrates. Lesser Armenia Nero
consigned to Aristobulus, the Sophene region to Sohaemus,[10]
with royal insignia for both. (2) There arose a timely challenger
for Vologaeses, his son Vardanes, and the Parthians left Armenia,
war apparently postponed.

8. In the senate every tribute was exaggerated in the proposals of those who voted thanksgivings and triumphal garb, on
days of thanksgiving, for the Emperor. *He should celebrate an*
ovation! Plus, a statue of him equal in size and in the same temple as Mars Ultor. Beyond their customary flattery, senators
were happy that he charged Domitius Corbulo[11] with securing
Armenia and that opportunity for excellence looked open.
(2) Eastern forces were divided thus: part of the auxiliary and
two legions stayed with Syria and its governor Ummidius
Quadratus, and Corbulo had an equal number of citizens and
allied troops, plus the infantry and cavalry that wintered in
Cappadocia. Allied kings were ordered to obey according to
the war's needs, but their support was readier for Corbulo.
(3) To press rumour's advantage – strongest in new undertakings – Corbulo travelled quickly and encountered Quadratus at
Aegaeae, a city in Cilicia; Quadratus having come that far, lest, if
Corbulo enter Syria to receive his forces, he turn all eyes to himself: body vast, splendid of speech, Corbulo possessed, besides
experience and good sense, also showy nothings' strength.

9. Each sent messengers advising King Vologaeses to prefer
peace to war and, giving hostages, to continue his predecessors'
customary reverence for the Roman people. Vologaeses, either

to prepare for war conveniently, or so that suspected rivals could be removed under the label 'hostage', handed over the most princely of the Arsacid family. (2) They were received by the centurion Insteius, Quadratus' emissary, who by chance was earlier to make contact with the king on the matter. When Corbulo learned this he ordered the auxiliary officer Arrius Varus[12] to go and retake the hostages. The quarrel ensuing between officer and centurion, lest it offer outsiders a longer spectacle, was submitted to the decision of the hostages and their own leaders. They preferred Corbulo, the man of recent glory and a certain favour even from foes. (3) From this came disaffection between generals. Quadratus' complaint: *Commandeering gains made by my policy!* Corbulo's contrary declaration: *The king did not decide to offer hostages until I was chosen the war's general and turned his hope to fear.* Nero, to settle the opponents, ordered notice given: for the successes of Quadratus and Corbulo, laurels were added to the Emperor's fasces.[13] (Events that went on[14] into other years I have annexed here.)

10. That same year Nero asked the senate for a statue of his father Gnaeus Domitius and an honorary consulship for Asconius Labeo, who had been his guardian; for himself statues of solid silver or gold, when offered, he prevented. And although senators voted that the beginning of the year start in December, the month in which Nero was born, he preserved the old ritual of beginning the year on 1 January. (2) Indictments were rejected concerning the senator Carrinas Celer, whom a slave accused, and the equestrian-ranked Julius Densus, charged with favouring Britannicus.

11. (55 CE) Claudius Nero, Lucius Antistius, consuls.[15]

When the magistrates were swearing to uphold the emperors' actions, Nero forbade his colleague to swear to uphold his. Great was the senators' praise, so that the youthful spirit, excited by even insubstantial matters' glory, might pursue praises greater. (2) There followed leniency towards Plautius Lateranus:[16] expelled for adultery with Messalina, he was restored to the senate by Nero, who pledged clemency in many a speech that

Seneca – to prove how estimable his teaching was or to show off his talent through the Emperor's voice – published.

12. The power of Nero's mother was gradually dismantled after he fell in love with a freedwoman named Acte and recruited as co-conspirators Otho and Claudius Senecio,[17] attractive young men; Otho from a consular family, Senecio son of an imperial freedman father. (2) With Nero's mother unaware, then vainly resisting, Acte crept far in through extravagance and equivocal secrets. The Emperor's older friends made no opposition, given that the young woman, with no injury to anyone, was satisfying the Emperor's desires; and since his wife Octavia – nobly born indeed and of proven worth – by some fate or because the forbidden prevails, seemed repulsive. Their worry? *He will break free for illicit affairs with women of rank if forbidden that desire.*

13. Agrippina protested, female-fashion – *A freedwoman rival! A slave-girl daughter-in-law!* and other such things – without waiting for either regret from her son, or surfeit. The more foul the reproaches, the more fired Nero was, until, mastered by love's power, he shed mother-obedience and put himself in Seneca's hands. (One of Seneca's dependants, Annaeus Serenus, simulating love for the same freedwoman, veiled Nero's first passions and provided a name, so that the Emperor's furtive tributes to the young woman were, in public, Serenus' generosity.) (2) Then Agrippina, changing tactics, used attentions to approach Nero: her own chamber and retreat were on offer now for concealing what first manhood and exalted position were after. Indeed, she confessed that her austerity was untimely and surrendered some possessions, hers being scarcely less than the Emperor's – excessive formerly in checking her son, then unduly humble. (3) The change did not fool Nero, and his closest friends were worried. *Beware the plots of a woman always formidable, now false, too,* they begged. (4) It chanced that Nero just then, after inspecting the trappings with which emperors' spouses and relatives dazzled, chose a garment and jewellery and sent the gift to his mother, not stinting: he offered choice pieces coveted by others, spontaneously. But Agrippina protested. *This does not stock my*

wardrobe, but deprives it of the rest! My son is dividing a whole he had from me! 14. And there was no lack of people reporting worse.

Nero, hostile to those propping up the woman's arrogance, removed Pallas from responsibility for affairs. Placed in charge by Claudius, Pallas once wielded practically regal sway.[18] They say that when Pallas was departing with a multitudinous escort, Nero remarked aptly that 'Pallas was going to lay down his office.'[19] (Pallas had indeed stipulated that no past action be investigated and that his accounts with the state be considered balanced.) (2) Then Agrippina rushed headlong to terror and threats. Not even the Emperor's ears were spared. Indeed, she declared: *Britannicus is now grown, the true stock, worthy to take up his father's power, which is now exercised – thanks to your mother's injustices![20] – by a grafted-on adoptee.* (3) *I do not reject revealing all the unhappy house's wrongs, my marriage especially, my use of poison. Only one precaution have the gods and I taken: my stepson lives. I will go with him to the barracks! Let them hear Germanicus' daughter on this side, on that the cripple Burrus and the exile Seneca, who with hacked-off hand and professorial tongue claim control of humankind!* Arms high, heaping shame, she invoked Claudius the god and the underworld shades of the brothers Silanus[21] and those many fruitless crimes.

15. Troubled by this and by the proximate day when Britannicus would complete his fourteenth year,[22] Nero pondered now his mother's impetuosity, now Britannicus' character, recently discovered in an experience trivial indeed, but productive of wide favour. (2) At the Saturnalia, in one of the games when his fellows were drawing lots for 'Jest's king', the lot went to Nero. To others went various tasks, none raising a blush, but Nero ordered Britannicus to rise and come forward to begin a song. Laughter was his aim, at a boy unacquainted with even sober parties, let alone drunken ones. Britannicus, steadfast, spoke a poem of which his toppling from ancestral seat and power's summit was the point. This generated compassion, which became more obvious once night-time carousing stripped away dissimulation. (3) Nero, perceiving others'

antipathy, intensified his own hatred. He was under pressure from Agrippina's threats, but lacked a charge, and the order for a brother's open killing seemed too bold. So he moved in secret[23] and ordered poison prepared. His helper was Julius Pollio, a Guard officer, in whose custody was a condemned poisoner named Locusta[24] with crimes' considerable renown. (That those close to Britannicus had no care for law or loyalty had already been seen to.) (4) The first poison was given by his caretakers. It passed with loosened bowel; it was too weak, or else diluted to rouse no immediate violence. (5) Nero, impatient at slow crime, threatened the officer, ordered the poisoner's execution. *Taking rumour into consideration, preparing defences, you are delaying my safety!* They then promised murder as quick as if by sword to throat. Near Nero's chamber they brewed a toxin from previously tried poisons, swift-acting.

16. Custom was that children of the imperial family sit with others of the same age, noble-born, to eat in sight of their relatives, but at their own more frugal table. There Britannicus dined. Accordingly – since his food and drink were taste-tested by a designated servant – lest routine be forsaken or the death of two expose the crime, the following ruse was devised. (2) Harmless still but overly hot and already tasted, a beverage was handed to Britannicus. This was rejected for temperature. Cold water was added, and in it a poison that so possessed his every limb that both speech and breath were taken. (3) There was alarm among those near, flight by the unwise. Those with deeper insight stayed in place and watched Nero. He, remaining at ease and as if unwitting, said: *This is normal for the alarming disease*[25] *that from his first infancy has afflicted Britannicus. Sight and feeling will return gradually.* (4) For Agrippina, such panic, such consternation – although their expression was repressed – flashed out that people agreed she was as ignorant as Octavia, Britannicus' sister. Indeed, she saw her last support removed, and the family-killing precedent. Octavia, too, though of raw youth, had learned to hide grief, affection – every emotion. Thus, after a short silence, there was a return to the party's gaiety.

17. A single night held both Britannicus' murder and his pyre. Funeral preparations had been seen to earlier; they were modest. But he was buried on the Campus Martius, during rainstorms so tempestuous that people believed them a portent of the gods' anger at a deed that most humans condoned, deeming brotherly disputes an ancient matter and royal power indivisible. (2) Most historians of the period report that on many a day before the elimination Nero molested Britannicus' boyhood. Accordingly, the death could not seem either premature or brutal, even if hurried on amidst hospitality's sacrament, without time for sisters' embrace, under enemy eyes, against the last bearer of Claudian blood, incest-tainted before the poison. (3) The obsequies' hurry was defended by Nero's edict. *It is ancestral practice to remove unseasonable fatalities[26] from sight, not to delay for praise and pomp. Having lost a brother's help, my remaining hopes are placed in the state, and senators and populace must cherish all the more their emperor, lone survivor of a family born to the highest eminence.*

18. Next, there was largesse to aggrandize his chief friends. Some people criticized men who professed moral seriousness for then apportioning houses and villas like spoils. Others believed it a necessity imposed by an emperor conscious of crime and hoping for forgiveness if he put the strongest under obligation. (2) His mother's anger no generosity assuaged. Instead, she embraced Octavia and often met her own friends in secret. Beyond Agrippina's innate greed, laying hold of money from everywhere as if in reserve, she entertained military officers companionably and honoured the names and qualities of the nobly born, who still existed then, as if seeking leader and party. (3) When Nero realized, he ordered the departure of the sentries kept for her as emperor's wife formerly and then as mother and, also of a comparable honour, the recently added German bodyguard. So that she wouldn't be frequented by a company of callers, he separated their domicile and transferred his mother into the house that had been Antonia's.[27] He always went there surrounded by a crowd of centurions and departed after a brief kiss.

19. Of all things mortal none is so baseless and fluid as the

fame of power reliant on force not its own. People retreated instantly from Agrippina's threshold. There was no one to comfort her, no one to visit except a few women – from love or hatred? Unclear. (2) Amongst them was Junia Silana,[28] whose expulsion by Messalina from her marriage to Gaius Silius I reported above, a woman notable for birth, beauty and a wild life – long Agrippina's darling. Later there were hidden grievances, mutual: Sextius Africanus,[29] a man of noble birth, was deterred from wedding Silana by words – *Unchaste! Of declining years!* – that Agrippina used not to reserve Africanus for herself, but lest Silana's wealth and childlessness accrue to her husband's control. (3) Silana took this opportunity for revenge and readied accusers from her dependants: Iturius and Calvisius. The denunciation relayed not old and often heard tales – Agrippina mourning Britannicus' death and publicizing the wrongs done Octavia – but this: *Agrippina intends to rouse Rubellius Plautus – who through his mother possesses descent from Augustus equal to Nero's – to revolution! With marriage and an emperor's power she will again assail the state.* (4) Thus the revelation made by Iturius and Calvisius to Atimetus, a freedman of Nero's aunt Domitia. Atimetus, delighted with the offering – between Agrippina and Domitia a hostile rivalry was exercised – urged the actor Paris,[30] himself Domitia's freedman, to hurry and give the crime an alarming denunciation.

20. It was late night and Nero was prolonging it with drink when Paris entered. Normally at this hour Paris' role was to intensify the Emperor's dissipations, but on that occasion he was arrayed for gloom. When he had presented the indictment fully, Paris so terrified his audience that not only were Agrippina's and Plautus' deaths planned but also Burrus' removal from the Guard: *Advanced by Agrippina's favour, he is now repaying it.*

((2) Fabius Rusticus relates that a document was drawn up entrusting Caecina Tuscus with Guard responsibility, but that with Seneca's help Burrus' office was preserved. Pliny and Cluvius[31] report no doubt about the prefect's loyalty. Of course, Fabius tends to praise Seneca, by whose friendship he prospered.

My plan is to follow the sources' consensus; where their accounts diverge I will give them by name.)

(3) Nero, atremble and avid for mother-killing, could not be deterred until Burrus promised her murder if she was proven guilty. *But everyone, and certainly a parent, should get a defence. No accusers are present, just one person's word, and that from an enemy house. Think about the shadows and the night sleepless with revelry and everything bordering on the rash and foolish.*

21. The Emperor's fear thus assuaged and day having come, people went off to Agrippina. *She must hear and clear the accusation or pay the penalty.* Burrus carried out these instructions with Seneca; also present were some freedmen as witnesses to the conversation. Burrus' conduct, after he laid out the charges and those responsible, was menacing. (2) Agrippina, characteristically spirited: 'It is no surprise that Silana, never having given birth, is unfamiliar with a mother's feelings. Parents don't change their children as readily as a slut does her seducers. If Iturius and Calvisius, having completely consumed their fortunes, undertake this accusation as a last service for the old bag's compensation, that is no reason for me to incur the infamy of kin-killing – or Nero its guilt! (3) For Domitia's antagonism I would be grateful if benevolence to my Nero were the issue of our contest. But with bedmate Atimetus and actor Paris it's practically stage plays she's composing. She was making improvements to pools in her beloved Baiae when by my plans adoption, proconsular privileges, designation to a consulship, and the other preparations for assuming power were made. (4) Let someone come forward with *this* accusation: city troops tampered with, provincial loyalty undermined, slaves or freedmen seduced for crime! (5) Could I live if Britannicus took control of affairs? And with Plautus or anyone else, once he has seized the state, as my judge? There will certainly be accusers to indict me, not with the occasional word incautiously uttered from affection's impetuosity, but with crimes of which I can be absolved only by my son.' (6) Shaken, those present undertook to calm her defiance. She demanded a meeting with her son.

There, her words did not defend innocence, as if she had misgivings, or mention benefits, as if she was reproaching, but won punishment for her denouncers and rewards for her friends.

22. The assignments were: prefecture of the grain supply to Faenius Rufus; oversight of games Nero was preparing to Arruntius Stella; Egypt to Claudius Balbillus. Syria was intended for Publius Anteius.[32] Baulked by various designs at first, he was in the end kept in Rome. (2) Silana was exiled. Calvisius, too, and Iturius were banished, Atimetus executed. Paris was too influential in the Emperor's pleasures to be punished. Plautus, for now, was silently overlooked.

23. Next denunciation: *Pallas and Burrus conspired for Cornelius Sulla to be called to power*. (Sulla[33] was renowned by birth and related to Claudius, to whom, owing to his marriage with Antonia, he was son-in-law.) This accusation's source was a certain Paetus, notorious for his speculative activities at the Treasury. Now he was obviously inventing. (2) Pallas'[34] innocence, however, was not as welcome as his arrogance was galling. When his freedmen were named as, it was alleged, accomplices, he replied: *At home I only ever use nods and hand signals to communicate, or, if more explanation is needed, writing; no spoken exchanges*. Burrus, though himself accused, gave his verdict among the judges. Exile for the accuser was the sentence, and his debt documents were burned. (Paetus used to pursue debts forgiven[35] by the Treasury with them.)

24. To conclude the year: the guard-post of a cohort formerly a presence at the games was moved elsewhere[36] for a greater show of freedom, and so that the soldiery, untainted by theatre's licence, would be less decadent, and the populace demonstrate whether, without guards, restraint would be preserved. (2) Rome the Emperor purified following haruspical advice.[37] (Jupiter's temple and Minerva's had been lightning-struck.)

25. (56 CE) Quintus Volusius, Publius Scipio,[38] consuls.

There was calm abroad, at home shameful carousing.[39] Nero used to wander the city's streets, brothels and bars arrayed in slave garb to disguise his identity, with companions to grab the wares on display and attack passers-by, who were so unwitting that Nero himself took a blow to the face and flaunted it.

(2) When people knew that Nero was behind the assaults, and injuries multiplied against eminent men and women – some men, once licence was given, under Nero's name got away with the same things using their own bands – it was like a captured city at night. Julius Montanus, who was senatorial in rank but had not yet held office, met the Emperor by chance in the dark. Because Montanus resisted the attempted violence sharply and then upon recognition uttered pleas that were in effect reproaches, he was forced to die. (3) Nero, however, more fearful from then on, surrounded himself with soldiers and many gladiators. In fights they were supposed to allow limited beginnings, one-on-one. But if injured parties reacted too vigorously, they used their weapons. (4) At shows, too, licence and the actors' fans were turned practically into battles by the absence of punishment, the rewards, and Nero himself looking on hidden, and sometimes openly. Eventually, with populace divided and an alarming prospect of more serious upheaval, the one remedy discovered was to expel actors from Italy and have soldiers again a presence in the theatre.

26. In this same period there was a senate discussion about freedman duplicity and an importunate demand pertaining to the undeserving. *Give their patrons the right to revoke freedom!* People supported this, but the consuls, not daring to take a vote with the Emperor unawares, drafted a 'senatorial opinion'. (2) Nero, looking to issue a decision * * *[40] among a small number with divergent views. Some raged. *The irreverence born of freedom has burst bounds to such an extent that freedmen take advice on whether to employ force or their legal equality with their patrons. Indeed they threaten physical violence and impudently recommend their own punishment. What recourse remains to an outraged patron other than banishing his freedman to beyond the hundredth milestone – to Campania's beaches? (3) Other legal proceedings are equally available to both. Some weapon should be provided, one not to be despised. It is not burdensome for the freed – retaining liberty[41] by the deference through which they obtained it. But the manifestly guilty deserve to be dragged back into slavery, so they may be controlled by fear if benefits have not altered them.*

27. Arguments against: *The fault of a few ought to ruin them, but nothing should be subtracted from everyone's rights. That collective body is of wide extent: from it voters, civil servants, staff for magistrates and priests, and even police units are recruited. Most men of equestrian rank and many senators draw their origin from here. If freedmen are segregated, we will see the paucity of the freeborn.* (2) *Not for nothing did our ancestors, when distinguishing the marks of rank, make freedom shared. Also, two types of manumission were instituted so that there would remain room for regret or a new favour. (Those whose patron did not free them in court remain in a kind of bondage.) Everyone must consider merits well and grant slowly what once given cannot be removed.*

(3) The latter opinion prevailed and Nero wrote to the senate: *Weigh individually the cases of freedmen accused by their patrons, but make no universal subtraction.* Soon thereafter the freedman Paris was detached from Nero's aunt: 'civil rights' were the pretence, not without shame for the Emperor, who ordered a finding of freebirth.[42]

28. There remained, nonetheless, a façade of public business. Between the praetor Vibullius and plebeian tribune Antistius[43] a conflict arose: actors' unruly fans, arrested by the praetor, the tribune ordered released. The senate upheld the arrest and condemned Antistius' overstepping. (2) At the same time tribunes were barred from depriving praetors and consuls of their rights and from summoning people from Italy[44] to enable lawsuits. The consul-elect Lucius Piso[45] added that inside their residences tribunes not take official cognizance, and that fines imposed by them not be entered by Treasury officials into the public accounts for four months, leaving the intervening period for appeals to be decided by the consul. There were tighter restrictions on aediles' power, too: statutory amounts for what aediles could seize as security or impose as fine. (3) Also, the plebeian tribune Helvidius Priscus brought a personal complaint against the Treasury official Obultronius Sabinus.[46] *Sabinus is using his power to auction mercilessly against the moneyless.* Later, the Emperor transferred responsibility for public accounts from elected to appointed officials.

29. This office was variously configured, often changed. Augustus allowed the senate to choose the officials. Later – bribery being suspected in the selection process – they were chosen by lot from the year's praetors. This didn't last long, either, since the lot ended up at the unsuitable. (2) Claudius reimposed quaestors and – so that fear of giving offence wouldn't encourage lax administration – promised early advancement. But maturity's firmness was wanting in men undertaking their first magistracy. Therefore Nero chose former praetors, who were experience-tested.

30. Condemned that year: Vipsanius Laenas for greedy government of his province, Sardinia. Acquitted: Cestius Proculus, of extortion; the Cretans were his accusers. Clodius Quirinalis, commander of rowers at Ravenna, having harassed Italy – as if it were a country of no importance – with extravagance and brutality, took poison, forestalling condemnation. (2) Caninius Rebilus, a man at the forefront for legal expertise and pecuniary amplitude, tortured by a frail old age, escaped by releasing his veins' blood. People didn't credit him with constancy sufficient for choosing death, he being, for his appetites, a notorious effeminate. Lucius Volusius[47] passed away with an outstanding reputation: he had ninety-three years of life and considerable wealth used with rectitude and without incurring the many emperors' malice.

31. (57 CE) Nero (second time), Lucius Piso, consuls.

Little memory-worthy occurred, unless one wants to fill bookrolls praising the substructures and beams of the massive amphitheatre Nero built on Mars' field, when it suits the dignity of the Roman people that significant events be entrusted to historical record, such things to the city's daily gazette.

(2) The settlements at Capua and Nuceria[48] were reinforced by an addition of veterans. The City populace received a handout of 400 coins per person, and 40 million were added to the Treasury to sustain public credit. The 4 per cent tax on slave sales was abolished, in appearance if not effect: what the seller used to be required to pay always accrued to the buyer's price. (3) And Nero decreed that no magistrate or imperial agent put on a show of gladiators, beasts or others in his province.

Earlier such 'generosity' was as much an affliction to their subjects as was revenue collection, since the sponsors were devising
for appetite's crimes bribery's protection.[49]

32. A senatorial decree pertinent to revenge and security was
made: if someone was killed by his slaves, the freedmen freed
by his will who remained in his household were to be punished
with his slaves. (2) Restored to the senate: the ex-consul Lurius
Varus, earlier expelled on charges connected with greed. Pomponia Graecina, a woman of eminence and married to Aulus
Plautius,[50] whose ovation over Britain I reported, was charged
with a foreign creed[51] and consigned for trial to her husband.
Using an old-fashioned procedure, in the presence of his friends
he conducted a trial involving his wife's fate and fame, and
found her innocent. (3) This Pomponia had a long life – and
continuous grief. After Drusus' daughter Julia was killed[52] by
Messalina's plotting, Pomponia lived for forty years exclusively
in garments of mourning and gloom of spirit. Under Claudius
she got away with it. Later it turned to glory.

33. The year saw several on trial. The trial of Publius
Celerius, accused by Asia, Nero drew out, since he was unable
to acquit him, until age caused Celerius' death. In the case of
Celerius, the killer of the governor Marcus Silanus,[53] as I
recorded, his crime's magnitude was his other transgressions'
shield. (2) Cossutianus Capito[54] was indicted by the Cilicians.
Blighted and foul, he believed that audacity had the same privileges in a province as in Rome. But he was contending with a
persistent accusation, and finally gave up his defence and was
convicted of extortion. (3) On behalf of Eprius Marcellus, from
whom the Lycians sought restitution, bribery was so effective
that some of his accusers were punished with exile for having
endangered an innocent man.

34. (58 CE) Nero (third time) consul.

Valerius Messala, too, entered the consulship. His great-
grandfather, the orator Corvinus, as a few now elderly
remembered, was colleague in the same office to the deified
Augustus,[55] Nero's great-great-grandfather. The noble family's
honour was increased by the offer of 500,000 sesterces annually as assistance to Messala's guiltless poverty. For Aurelius

Cotta, too, and Haterius Antoninus, annuities were established by the Emperor, although they had squandered their family money through luxury.

(2) At year's onset, the war between Parthians and Romans[56] over possession of Armenia, prolonged by its gentle initial phases, was now taken up vigorously. Vologaeses would not allow his brother Tiridates to be deprived of the kingdom he gave or to hold it as a gift from another power, and Corbulo thought it worthy of the Roman people's greatness to recover gains made by Lucullus and Pompey. In addition, the Armenians, whose loyalty was uncertain, welcomed both forces. By territorial situation and cultural similarity they were quite close to and intermarried with the Parthians, and – liberty being unknown – inclined their way.

35. Corbulo's charge weighed heavier in countering his soldiers' cowardice than in facing enemy perfidy. Transferred from Syria, the legions, lax from long peace, had scant tolerance for the routine of a Roman camp. Fact was, some veterans in that army had undertaken no sentry duty, no night watches. Rampart and ditch they regarded as marvellous novelties. Lacking helmets, lacking breastplates, they were sleek and acquisitive from military service completed in town. (2) After discharging those struggling with age or ill health, Corbulo requested reinforcement. Throughout Galatia and Cappadocia there were levies, and a legion was added from Germany with auxiliaries of horse and foot. (3) The entire army was kept 'under canvas',[57] yet the winter was so severe with ice cover that the ground had to be excavated to provide a place for tents. Many men had frostbitten limbs from the cold's violence, and some expired on guard duty. A soldier carrying a bundle of wood was noticed whose hands froze so stiff that they clung to their burden and fell from his arm stumps. (4) Corbulo himself, with lightweight clothing and his head bare, was often present in their column and at their labours. Praise for the hard-working, consolation for the frail, and an example for all were on display. Subsequently, since given the rigours of climate and service many refused and deserted, a remedy was sought in severity. In other armies, first and second offences are prosecuted leniently.

Not here. Whoever left the standards suffered capital punishment directly. This was a measure wholesome in practice and
better than mercy, evidently: fewer deserted Corbulo's camp
than those in which pardon is given.

36. Corbulo, with his legions confined to camp until spring
matured and his auxiliary cohorts distributed to suitable positions, directed: *Do not dare initiate a fight.* Responsibility for
the garrisons he gave to Paccius Orfitus,[58] a former chief centurion, in trust. (2) Orfitus had written: *The barbarians are
unwary and an opportunity for success offers.* But he was
ordered to keep to his fortifications and await larger forces, a
command that was broken: after a few cavalry units from
nearby strongholds arrived and invited a fight with their incompetence, Orfitus met the enemy and was routed. Dismayed by
his losses, those who should have brought reinforcements
returned to base in terrified flight. (3) This news was galling to
Corbulo. After berating Orfitus, he ordered him and his officers and men to encamp outside the rampart. In this insulting
position they remained, released only by the entire army's
pleas.

37. Tiridates, who had the assistance, beyond his own
dependants, of his brother Vologaeses' resources, was no longer
furtive in waging war, but open: he ravaged peoples he believed
loyal to us, dodged if troops were led against him, and with his
random descents caused dismay more by rumour than by fight.
(2) Corbulo, though he long tried for battle, was thwarted.
Enemy example forcing him to spread war out, he divided his
forces so that legionary and cavalry commanders could hit different places with simultaneous incursions. (3) King Antiochus
he advised to attack nearby districts. Pharasmanes, having
killed his son Radamistus – *Traitor!*[59] – to demonstrate loyalty
to us, was already working his long-standing hatred of the
Armenians. Then, first were the Moschi drawn in. An outstanding Roman ally,[60] they invaded Armenia's trackless parts.
(4) Thus Tiridates' plans went awry and he sent spokesmen to
protest in his and the Parthians' name. *Why, after the recent
exchange of hostages and friendship's renewal, which ought to
open opportunities for new favours, am I being driven from*

long-standing possession of Armenia? Vologaeses himself is not yet in motion, because he prefers action by argument to force, but if you persist in war the Arsacids will not be short of courage – or of the luck so often manifested in Roman disaster![61] (5) At this, Corbulo, having learned that Vologaeses was detained by the Hyrcanian defection, urged Tiridates to petition Nero. *You can get a stable realm and unbloodied possessions, if, letting go of a hope distant and late-arriving, you pursue one present and better.*

38. The next plan, since the exchange of messengers produced no progress towards overall peace, was for a meeting of principals, time and place to be determined. *A thousand-rider guard will attend me*, Tiridates said. *For you, Corbulo, I do not specify how many you should have alongside or what type, provided you come without breastplates and helmets and with peaceful mien.* (2) To anybody, let alone a veteran and discerning commander, the barbarian's 'ingenuity' would have been obvious. Why a restricted number for the one as a limit, a greater offered to the other? To prepare a trap: if unprotected bodies were exposed to riders trained to shoot, their multitude would not help. (3) Pretending not to understand, Corbulo responded: *It is better to argue matters of public concern with whole armies present.* He chose a place with, on one side, gently rising hills to accommodate infantry ranks; the other stretched flat for the deployment of cavalry units. (4) On the agreed day, Corbulo arrived earlier. He put allied cohorts and the kings' auxiliaries on the wings, in the middle the Sixth. To this he had added, after summoning them by night from a different camp, some 3,000 of the Third, mixing them in with the Sixth under a single eagle, as if a single legion was on view. Tiridates, when day was already waning, stopped at a distance, more visible than audible. So without a meeting the Roman commander ordered his soldiers back to base.

39. The king, either suspecting subterfuge, since the departure was for several directions at once, or to intercept our supplies en route via the Black Sea and the town of Trabezus, left quickly. But he was unable to attack the supplies because they were routed through mountains occupied by our garrisons.

Corbulo, lest the war drag on without result, and to force the Armenians to defend their possessions, prepared to raze their strongholds. For himself he took the district's strongest, Volandum. Lesser places he entrusted to the legate Cornelius Flaccus and camp superintendent Insteius Capito. (2) After reconnoitring fortifications and providing necessary assault equipment, he exhorted his soldiers: *A vagabond foe, ready for neither armistice nor arms, but confessing perfidy and cowardice by flight – strip him of his bases and keep glory and booty alike in view!* (3) The army was divided in four. He sent some, massed under locked shields, to undermine the rampart, others he ordered to place ladders against the walls, many to the engines to hurl firebrands and spears. Slingers were assigned a distant position from which to whirl their bullets. His intention was that no one portion of the enemy relieve others in difficulty, fear being equal everywhere. (4) So great was the ardour of the army as it fought that within four hours walls were denuded of defenders, gate obstacles were overthrown, fortifications taken by ascent and all of fighting age slaughtered. Not a soldier was lost, very few were wounded. The non-combatant crowd was sold into slavery, the remaining booty went to the victors. (5) Legionary and cavalry commanders had equal good fortune, and after three strongholds were stormed in one day the rest were surrendered by a terrified, and sometimes willing, population.

(6) This gave Corbulo confidence to attack the country's capital, Artaxata. But the legions were not taken by the most direct path. If they used the bridge to cross the Araxes, which washes Artaxata's walls, they would be under fire, so distant and broader fords were used to go across.

40. Tiridates, shamed and fearful – *If I permit a siege, people will see in me no help; if I try to prevent, I will entangle myself and my cavalry in difficult terrain* – decided to show his line and, if occasion was given, to begin battle, or else to simulate flight and adopt a stratagem. Accordingly, he suddenly surrounded the Roman column. Our leader was not caught unawares: he had disposed his army for travel and combat alike. (2) The Third marched on the right flank, the Sixth on

the left. In the middle were picked men of the Tenth. Baggage was contained within the lines. The rear was protected by a thousand cavalry with orders to resist attackers who engaged, but not follow them in flight. On the wings were infantry archers and the remaining cavalry. The left wing was longer along the hills' base, so that, if the enemy penetrated, it would be simultaneously met and encircled. (3) There were feints on different sides from Tiridates, not to within range, but now threatening, now with a show of fear, in case he could relax the lines and pursue the dispersed, but they met no temerity, no loosening, nothing more than a cavalry officer advancing too boldly and arrow-pierced. And his example confirmed the rest in obedience. Near nightfall Tiridates departed.

41. Corbulo took camp measurements where he was and considered. *Shall I continue to Artaxata with legions unencumbered, by night? Surround it with a siege? That is where Tiridates has withdrawn*, he thought. After scouts reported that the king was travelling far – *unclear whether he is heading for Medes or Albani* – Corbulo waited for day, sending ahead rapid-deployment troops to encircle the walls meantime and begin the blockade at a distance. (2) But the townspeople opened the gates voluntarily and entrusted themselves and their possessions to the Romans. That saved them. In Artaxata fire was loosed and the town demolished, razed to the ground. (It could not be held without a strong garrison owing to the wall's magnitude, and we lacked the manpower to divide between securing the garrison and prosecuting the war. Or: *If Artaxata is left whole and undefended, there is no utility or glory in its capture*.) (3) There was also a remarkable occurrence,[62] seemingly heaven-sent: everything was sunlit when suddenly what the walls girded was so covered by black cloud and threaded by lightning – *as if the gods are attacking!* was what people believed about the town's consignment to ruin.[63]

(4) In consequence, Nero was hailed victorious. By senate decree thanksgivings were held, and statues and arches and consecutive consulships for the Emperor decreed, and that among holidays henceforth should be the days on which the victory was accomplished, announced and discussed. Plus

other decrees in the same mould, so beyond measure that Gaius Cassius,[64] after assenting to the other honours, maintained: *If the thanks given to the gods are matched to Fortune's kindness, a whole year will not suffice for thanksgivings, and therefore days must be apportioned: some holy, some business. Then we can worship the divine without hindering the human.*

42. Then came the trial of a man tossed by chance's changes, who had earned the hatred of many – but considerable antipathy towards Seneca accrued from his condemnation. This was Publius Suillius,[65] who under Claudius had been frightening and venal, and with time's alterations was less humbled than his enemies desired. *Better to seem guilty than suppliant,* he thought. (For his ruin, it was believed, was revived the senatorial decree and the Cincian law's[66] punishment aimed at lawyers paid for pleading.) (2) Suillius indulged in complaint and rebuke, being spirited by nature and, in extreme old age, free, berating Seneca as hostile to the friends of Claudius, under whom he suffered an exile entirely just. (3) *With useless pursuits and young men's ignorance as his habitat, Seneca is spiteful towards those who exercise in defence of fellow citizens a vigorous and unsullied eloquence. I was Germanicus' quaestor; Seneca was that house's adulterer. Or should it be deemed worse to obtain, at the litigant's pleasure, a reward for honest labour than to sully the bedchambers of imperial women?* (4) *What wisdom, what philosophers' teachings has Seneca used to acquire, in four years' royal friendship, 300 million? At Rome inheritances and the childless, as in a hunt, are Seneca's prey. Italy and the provinces have been emptied by Seneca's vast loans. My wealth has been earned by effort and is moderate. The charge, the forfeit – I will endure it all rather than abase a long-standing and self-generated reputation before sudden prosperity.*

43. People reported this in Suillius' words, or worse, to Seneca. Prosecutors, once found, reported Suillius for plundering the allies when he governed Asia and for embezzlement of public money. When they were given a year for the investigation it seemed quicker to begin with his urban crimes,[67] whose witnesses were nearby: (2) by Suillius' prosecutorial harshness

Quintus Pomponius reduced to the extremity of civil war; Drusus' daughter Julia and Poppaea Sabina driven to death; Valerius Asiaticus, Lusius Saturninus and Cornelius Lupus beset; and a host of equestrians condemned. All of Claudius' brutality was laid to Suillius' charge. (3) *None of this was undertaken voluntarily. I obeyed the Emperor*, was the defence, until Nero cut that speech short: *I know from my father's records that no one's accusation was compelled by him.* (4) Then Suillius used *Messalina's orders* as a shield, a shaky defence. *Why was no one else chosen as that shameless madwoman's mouthpiece? There must be punishment for atrocities' agents when, possessed of crimes' rewards, they impute the crimes themselves to others!* (5) Half his wealth was confiscated, half ceded to son and granddaughter; an inheritance from mother and grandmother was also exempted. Suillius was sent to the Balearic Islands. Neither at the trial nor after conviction was he broken in spirit. Report held that he endured his seclusion with a monied and soft existence. When prosecutors attacked his son Nerullinus out of antipathy to Suillius, using an extortion charge, the Emperor interceded: *Vengeance is satisfied.*

44. In this same period Octavius Sagitta, a plebeian tribune, was deranged by love of the married woman Pontia. With huge presents he purchased infidelity, and soon: *I will leave my husband.* He promised marriage and fixed the date. But the woman, once free, wove delays, blamed her father's opposition, and – hope accruing of a wealthier spouse – shed her promises. (2) Sagitta in response wailed and threatened, protesting: *My reputation is ruined, my money exhausted. My life – all that remains to me – is in your hands.* Rejected, he requested a single night's solace: *Soothed by this I will control myself in the future.* (3) The night was set and Pontia charged a maidservant accomplice with guarding the chamber. Sagitta, accompanied by a freedman, brought a blade hidden in his clothing. As happens in love and anger, there was squabbling, pleading, reproaches, excuses, and half the night devoted to pleasure. Seemingly afire, he ran her through, unsuspecting. When the maid ran up he scared her off with a wound and

burst free of the chamber. (4) Next day, murder was manifest, with no uncertainty about the killer, for he was proven to have been with her. But the freedman insisted: *The crime was mine! I avenged the harm done my patron.* And he persuaded some people – *magnificent example!* – until the maid, recovered from her wound, revealed the truth. (5) Sagitta was arraigned before the consuls by the victim's father and after leaving office was convicted by a senatorial verdict in accordance with the statute on murderers.

45. Equally notable that year was a shamelessness that was the beginning of huge evils for the state. There was at Rome one Poppaea Sabina,[68] daughter of Titus Ollius. (She had taken the name of her maternal grandfather,[69] the ex-consul Poppaeus Sabinus, brilliant with a triumph's honour. Ollius, before he reached office, was ruined by Sejanus' friendship.) (2) This woman had everything but respectable character. Her mother, surpassing women of her day in loveliness, gave as much glory as beauty. Poppaea had resources appropriate to her family's renown, companionable conversation and apt intelligence. (3) Restraint was her façade, carousing her life. She made rare appearances in public and always with face partly veiled, lest she satiate observation – or because it suited her. Reputation was never a worry; between lovers and husbands she made no distinction. Nor did affection – hers or anyone else's – rule her. Wherever she saw advantage, there her passion was transferred. (4) When she was married to the equestrian-ranked Rufrius Crispinus,[70] from whom she had a son, Otho seduced her with youth and dissipation, and because Nero's friendship for him was thought to burn extremely hot. Infidelity was soon succeeded by matrimony.

46. Otho would praise his wife's beauty and elegance when with the Emperor, either heedless from love or so as to inflame. *If we possess the same woman, that bond, too, will increase my dominance.* He was often heard, rising from a party at Nero's, saying he was off to Poppaea. *They are mine to enjoy, her noble birth, her loveliness – everyone's prayers and the lucky ones' delights,* he would insist. (2) With these and like provocations the delay was short. Poppaea granted an approach and used

artful flattery to gain strength. *I am helpless with desire and your beauty's captive,* she pretended. The Emperor now painfully in love, she turned to arrogance. If kept more than a night or two: *I am a married woman and can't leave my marriage. I am bound to Otho by his manner of life, equalled by none. He is splendid in spirit and style, and in him I see things worthy of fortune's heights. But you, bound by your maidservant lover and her familiarity, you get nothing from cohabitation with a slave except the low and sordid.* (3) Otho was ousted from his customary intimacy and later from congress and companionship. Finally, lest in Rome he act the rival, he was made governor of Lusitania,[71] where, until the civil wars, his actions were not according to his earlier disrepute, but honest and just. He was wayward when idle, in power quite sober.

47. Hitherto[72] Nero tried to mantle his depravities and crimes. He was very suspicious of Cornelius Sulla,[73] taking the man's idle character for its opposite. *A clever disguise,* he thought. This fear Graptus intensified. (Graptus was one of the imperial freedmen, a man with experience and age – from Tiberius onwards! – thoroughly knowledgeable about the imperial household.) (2) The Mulvian Bridge those days was packed with nocturnal allurements. Nero used to go there, so as to have, outside the city, more freedom to run wild. *For your return along the Flaminian Way an ambush was arranged, and avoided by chance since you took a different route and went to Sallust's Gardens. The plot's source was Sulla,* Graptus lied. For it chanced that the Emperor's attendants, homeward-bound, had been given an empty fright by people acting with youthful licence; it was everywhere then. (3) None of Sulla's slaves or dependants was recognized, and his contemptible nature, capable of no daring, was utterly incompatible with the charge. Directly, however, as if convicted, he was ordered to leave the country and stay within the walls of Marseilles.

48. The same consuls.

There was a hearing for Puteoli's opposing delegations. Councillors and citizens were sent to the senate, the former berating the populace's violence, the latter the magistrates' and leading men's greed. This unrest, which had progressed to stone-throwing and arson threats and might, people worried, elicit armed slaughter, Gaius Cassius[74] was chosen to remedy. His strictness was deemed intolerable, so at his request the task was transferred to the brothers Scribonii,[75] with a Guard unit. From fear of this, and a few executions, the townspeople recovered harmony.

49. I mention an utterly commonplace senatorial decree permitting Syracuse to exceed the size limit for gladiatorial shows only because Thrasea Paetus[76] opposed it and provided detractors matter for criticizing his position. (2) *Why, if you believe the state needs a free senate, are such trivialities targeted? Why no war or peace, no taxation and laws and other matters pertinent to the state in your speeches pro and con? Senators are free, when exercising their right to state a position, to expound anything they like and demand a vote.* (3) *Is only this in need of correction, that Syracuse's spectacles not be too lavish? Is everything everywhere in the Empire so wonderful? As if not Nero but Thrasea was holding the reins? Or if extensive suppression leaves issues disregarded, surely the insignificant should be avoided.* (4) Thrasea countered, when friends asked his reasoning: *Not in ignorance of the present do I criticize such decrees, but to increase senatorial prestige. Obviously senators will not suppress concern for major affairs when they attend to even the most trivial.*

50. That same year, after repeated popular outcry protesting tax-farmers' excesses, Nero contemplated ordering the cessation of all indirect taxes.[77] *Shall I give this loveliest of gifts to the human race?* (2) His impulse, after much praise of his magnanimity, was checked by senators. *It means the Empire's dissolution if the revenues on which the state depends are reduced. If tariffs go, next will come a demand for tribute's abolition!* (3) *Most tax-farming companies were formed by consuls and tribunes when the Roman people's liberty still had vigour. For the rest, later, provision was made[78] that the account of profits and the imposition of demands matched. Relief is certainly needed from tax-farmers' cravings, lest what was for years tolerated without complaint becomes, with new rigours, resentment.*

51. So Nero decreed that the rules for each tax, hidden till then, were to be published: uncollected claims were not to be reissued after a year; at Rome the praetor (and in the provinces, governors) was to give priority to suits against tax-farmers; for soldiers tax-immunity was to be preserved except for sales; plus other measures, equally equitable. They were observed briefly, then futile. (2) What did last was the abolition of the 2.5 per cent and 2 per cent charges, and of other categories of illegal fees that tax-farmers had devised. Relief was given in overseas provinces to grain transport, and a rule established that ships not be listed as traders' property or incur tax.

52. Africa took to court her former governors Sulpicius Camerinus and Pompeius Silvanus. Nero acquitted them. Camerinus faced a few individuals, their charge more brutality than extortion. (2) Silvanus a great host of accusers surrounded, demanding time for summoning witnesses. The defendant requested immediate defence. He prevailed owing to monied childlessness and age, which he extended beyond the lifetimes of those whose lobbying got him off.

53. Germany's affairs[79] were calm until now, from the character of its commanders, who, once honorary triumphs became commonplace, used to expect a greater honour from maintaining the peace. (2) At this period Pompeius Paulinus and Lucius Vetus[80] headed the army. Lest the soldiers they managed grow slack, Paulinus completed an earthwork designed to control the Rhine, begun sixty-three years earlier by Drusus. Vetus was planning to link Moselle and Saône with a canal, so that goods conveyed by sea, then via the Rhône and Saône, then along the canal and via the Moselle, might descend to the Rhine and from there to the sea. *With the journey's difficulties removed, boat communications will exist between western and northern shores!* (3) Opposition to the task came from Aelius Gracilis, Belgica's governor, warning Vetus: *Do not to bring legions into another's province and chase popularity in Gaul. It is fear-inducing for the Emperor*, he insisted. Thus are prevented[81] most honourable undertakings.

54. From the armies' sustained inactivity came talk. *The right to lead against the enemy has been stripped from Nero's*

governors. Therefore the Frisians,[82] sending their men via forests and swamps, their non-combatants over lakes, moved up to the Rhine and settled on territory empty and set aside for military use. Those responsible were Verritus and Malorix, who ruled that people – insofar as Germans are ruled. (2) They had planted houses, sown crops – as if using ancestral ground – when Dubius Avitus, after taking over from Paulinus, threatened Roman force unless the Frisians went away to their old sites or obtained a new home from Nero, thereby forcing Verritus and Malorix to petition. (3) They set off for Rome. Awaiting Nero, who was intent upon other responsibilities, they entered Pompey's theatre – it was among the sights shown to barbarians – to see the size of Rome's population. They had nothing to do there, since the ignorant take no pleasure in plays. Enquiring about the general seating, the distinctions of rank – *Who is equestrian-ranked? Where is the senate?* – they noticed people in foreign garb in the senators' seating. Asking who they were, they heard that this honour was given to envoys of nations distinguished for valour and Roman friendship. *No one in the world*, they cried, *precedes Germans in arms or trustworthiness!* They went down and sat among the senators. (4) This received a friendly reception, as being of old-fashioned assertiveness and fine rivalry. Nero awarded citizenship to both, but ordered the Frisians to leave the territory. When they refused, auxiliary cavalry, dispatched suddenly, imparted necessity. Anyone too stubbornly resisting was captured or slain.

55. The territory was then seized by the Ampsivarii, a stronger race owing not only to their own capacity, but also to neighbouring peoples' compassion. Having been expelled by the Chauci[83] and now homeless, a safe exile was their prayer. Speaking on their behalf was a man renowned throughout those tribes and loyal to us, too, one Boiocalus. His story: *I was taken prisoner in the Cheruscan rebellion*[84] *by Arminius' order. Thereafter I saw army service under Tiberius and Germanicus. To fifty years' obedience I am adding this, too, the subjection of my race to your authority.* (2) *How much land lies idle,*[85] *to receive sometimes the soldiers' flocks and cattle! We should certainly keep an abode for herds, when humans are starving!*

*Unless you prefer waste and empty land to friendly peoples.
The Chamavi once held those fields, then the Tubantes, and
later the Usipi. As is the sky to gods, so is the earth a gift to
humankind. Vacant lands are common property.* (3) Then
looking up at the sun and invoking the other stars he asked
them, as if present, a question: *Do you wish to look upon barren ground? It would be preferable to discharge the sea against
land's thieves!*

56. Roused by these words, Avitus said: *You must submit to
your betters' command. It is the will of the gods you implored
that decision rests in Roman hands about what to give, what to
take. And Romans submit to no other judges than themselves.*
This was the public response to the Ampsivarii. To Boiocalus
himself: *In view of our friendship, I will give you lands.* Boiocalus rejected this as betrayal's price, adding, 'We can be
deprived of land on which to live, but not on which to die.'
With hostility on both sides, they parted. (2) The Ampsivarii
summoned Bructeri, Tencteri and more distant tribes to join in
war. Avitus, after writing to Curtilius Mancia, Upper Germany's legate, to cross the Rhine and show force from the rear,
led his legions into Tencteri territory, threatening them with
annihilation unless they made their cause separate. (3) When
these withdrew, an equal fright dismayed the Bructeri. Since the
rest, too, abandoned dangers not their own, the Ampsivarii
withdrew alone to the Usipi and Tubantes. Driven out from
there, they approached Chatti, then Cherusci, after long wandering, as guests in need. As enemy invaders their men were
slaughtered; non-combatants became booty's shares.

57. That same summer there was conflict between Hermunduri and Chatti, a great battle over a river fertile for salt
production, their common border. They tried to seize it by
force. Beyond their desire to decide everything by arms was
their settled belief that this place was closest to heaven. *Mortal
prayers are nowhere heard by the gods from closer at hand.
That is the reason for divine generosity to the river, so that in
these forests salt comes forth – not as among other nations
from the overflow of drying sea – from water poured over a
blazing heap of timber. It is a compound of mutually opposed*

elements, fire and water! (2) The war was a success for the Hermunduri. For the Chatti, it was quite ruinous, since they consecrated the enemy army to Mars and Mercury, if victorious. In this vow horses, men – every living thing! – are given over for killing and their hostile threats were turned against them.

(3) The Ubii,[86] a people allied to us, suffered unexpected harm. A fire that emerged from the earth was destroying farmhouses, fields and villages in every direction, and moving onto the newly founded colony's fortifications. It could not be extinguished, not if rain fell, not if doused by river water or any other liquid, until some rustics, desperate and infuriated by the calamity, hurled rocks from a distance, and then, as the flames slowed, came closer and by hitting it with clubs and other flails frightened the fire, beast-like, away. Finally they tore off their clothing and piled it on. The more unclean and use-tainted it was, the better for fire suppression.

58. That same year the 'Ruminal' tree in the assembly place, which 830 years earlier shaded Remus and Romulus as infants, was reduced to dead brush and drying trunk. This was considered a portent, until it revived with new growth.

BOOK 14

1. (59 CE) Gaius Vipstanus, Gaius Fonteius, consuls.

A crime long contemplated, Nero deferred no longer. Audacity maturing with power's age, he was daily more ablaze with love of Poppaea.[1] She, hopeless of marriage for herself and divorce for Octavia with Agrippina alive, kept scolding the Emperor with frequent accusations and occasional mockery, calling him a puppet. *Subservient to another's orders, you lack not only power but even freedom.* (2) *Why is my wedding being deferred? My body, no doubt, displeases, or my laurelled ancestors, my fertility, my true heart. Is there concern lest as wife I expose the senate's sufferings, the people's anger at your mother's arrogance and greed? But if Agrippina can only tolerate a daughter-in-law pernicious to her son, let me be restored to marriage with Otho! I will go anywhere, so long as I only hear of insults to the Emperor instead of seeing them and sharing your danger.* (3) These and like words, with tears and adultery's art, hit home. Nobody opposed them, since everyone desired the mother's power broken, and none thought the son's hatred would extend to murder.

2. Cluvius records that, desirous of retaining power, Agrippina went so far – at midday, when Nero was heated by wine and dining – as to offer herself more than once, he being drunk, she groomed and ready for incest. Already wanton kisses and caresses signalling depravity were noticed by insiders, Cluvius says,[2] when Seneca sought a woman's help against female allurements. The freedwoman Acte, anxious about her own danger and Nero's shame, was dispatched with a denunciation: *Incest talk is widespread – your mother's boasting! – and*

soldiers will not tolerate an unclean emperor's rule. (2) Fabius
Rusticus reports the impulse as not Agrippina's but Nero's, and
as thwarted by the same freedwoman's ingenuity. Cluvius'
story other authors, too, recount and reputation inclines this
way: either Agrippina did intend this enormity or contemplation of strange lust seemed perfectly believable in one who as a
girl defiled herself with Lepidus in hope of mastery, and from
the same impulse submitted to Pallas' desires and trained for
every disgrace by wedding her uncle.[3]

3. Nero avoided private concourse and when Agrippina left
for her park or her estates in Tusculum or Antium he commended her for relaxing. Eventually finding her insufferable
wherever she was housed, he decided to kill her, deliberating
only as to poison, sword or other method. (2) He favoured poison first. But if given at the Emperor's table it could not be
ascribed to chance, Britannicus already having died thus. And
it seemed toilsome to test the servants of a woman alert, from
criminal experience, to plots. Plus, by taking antidotes in
advance she had fortified her body. How sword and slaughter
might be hidden no one discovered, and the possibility that
someone selected for so momentous an action might defy
orders was frightening. (3) The freedman Anicetus,[4] commander of the Misenum fleet, offered an idea. He was Nero's
boyhood tutor and was hated – the feeling was mutual – by
Agrippina. He explained: *A ship can be built such that, at sea,
part will come loose by design, disgorging her unawares. Nothing contains as many accidents as the sea, and if she is cut short
by shipwreck, who is so unjust as to assign to crime damage
done by wind and wave? The Emperor will give the deceased a
temple, plus altars and other signs of devotion.*

4. The cleverness was pleasing, and the date helped: Minerva's festival[5] was spent at Baiae. Nero lured his mother there,
repeating, *Parental ill-humour must be endured and my own
temper calmed*, in order to generate a reconciliation rumour
that Agrippina would accept, women being gullible for happy
report. (2) Meeting her at the shore – she was coming from
Antium – with hand clasp and embrace, he took her to Bauli.
(This is the name of a sea-washed villa on an inlet between

Cape Misenum and Baiae's lagoon.) (3) Among the boats stood one more ornate – this, too, apparently, in his mother's honour; she had been used to conveyance by trireme[6] and fleet rowers. Then she was invited for dinner, so that night would help conceal crime. (4) There was clearly a traitor. Agrippina, either after hearing about the boat plot or uncertain whether to believe it, went to Baiae in a chair. Attentiveness alleviated fear: she got a friendly reception and a seat next to Nero. There was much conversation, sometimes with youthful intimacy on Nero's part, then again reserved, as if sharing serious matters. The party went on long and he escorted her out, clinging fast to eyes and person, either to complete the illusion or else the last sight of his doomed mother checked a spirit however bestial.

5. A night star-bright and, with sea calm, quiet – practically proving the crime! – was provided by the gods. The boat did not go far. (Two of Agrippina's household accompanied her: Crepereius Gallus, standing near the tiller, and Acerronia, leaning back near the foot of Agrippina's couch, speaking happily of the son's penitence, the mother's recovered influence.) At a signal, the canopy collapsed from a heavy load of lead. Crepereius, crushed, expired immediately. Agrippina and Acerronia, the couch's projecting ends being by chance too strong to succumb to the weight, were protected. (2) Nor did the ship's dissolution result, since there was universal confusion and the plotters were hampered by the many unaware. The rowers' next plan was to tilt the boat to one side and sink it that way. But not even they reached quick consensus in the crisis, and the others, opposing, made an easier opportunity for going overboard. (3) Acerronia, crying out unwisely, *I am Agrippina! Help the Emperor's mother!* was killed by naval weaponry, poles and oars and whatever chance offered. Agrippina was silent and therefore less visible; she did, however, receive a shoulder wound. By swimming, then encountering rowboats, she found conveyance to Lake Lucrinus and was taken to her villa.

6. Pondering the purpose behind the invitation – *Deceitful letter!* – and the particularly honorific reception, the fact that the boat – *near shore, no wind pushing, not on the reef –* collapsed top-down like a structure on land; observing, too, the

murder of Acerronia and considering her own wound, Agrippina realized that the trap's only remedy lay in not being understood. (2) She sent her freedman Agermus to report to her son: *By the gods' kindness and your good fortune I escaped grave accident. I beg you, however frightened you are by your mother's danger, to defer your intention of visiting. At present I need repose.* (3) Meanwhile, simulating unconcern, she applied medicines to her wound and bandages to her body. She ordered Acerronia's will found and her property sealed – this alone without pretence.

7. Nero, awaiting word of deed complete, was informed: *She got away, lightly wounded but having come close enough to danger to be sure about[7] its source.* (2) He was unstrung by panic, insisting: *Soon, soon she will arrive quick to avenge! She'll arm slaves or rouse soldiers, or else approach senate and people – and blame me for shipwreck and wound and murdered friends! What prop do I have against her, unless Seneca and Burrus have something?* (Reviving, he had summoned them immediately. It is unclear whether they were ignorant earlier, too.) (3) A long silence from both ensued, lest they dissuade in vain. Or else they believed matters so far deteriorated that unless Agrippina was forestalled Nero must perish. Seneca was the readier in that he turned to Burrus and asked whether the soldiers should get the order to kill. (4) *Guardsmen pledged to the whole house of the Caesars and, remembering Germanicus, will venture no atrocity against his progeny*, Burrus replied. *Let Anicetus finish what he promised.* (5) Anicetus, unhesitating, demanded crime's culmination. At this, Nero declared: *Today, finally, I am being given power. The source of so great a gift? A freedman! Anicetus, go quickly and take the men readiest to orders.* (6) Hearing that the messenger Agermus had come from Agrippina, Nero himself set the stage for incrimination: as Agermus relayed his message, Nero threw a sword between his feet and, as if Agermus had been caught in the act, ordered chains – to pretend that his mother, having contrived the Emperor's exit and from shame at crime apprehended, took her own life.

8. News of Agrippina's accident spread – as if it had happened

by chance! When people heard, they went to the shore. Some mounted embankments, some nearby boats, others went as far as body permitted into the sea, some stretched up hands. With protests, prayers and shouts from people, questioning variously and replying uncertainly, every shore was full. There streamed in a huge crowd with lights. At knowledge of her safety people hurried as for congratulation, until deflected by sight of an armed and menacing column. (2) Anicetus surrounded the villa with sentries. He demolished the gate and seized the slaves he encountered, eventually reaching Agrippina's bedroom door. A small number stood there, the rest having been dismayed by terror at the invaders. (3) In the bedroom there was a modest light, a single slave girl. Agrippina was more and more anxious at there being no one from her son, not even Agermus. *A happy outcome would look otherwise than solitude and sudden noises and indications of the worst.* (4) When the girl started to leave, 'You too desert me?' she cried. And turned to see Anicetus, accompanied by ship captain Herculeius and fleet centurion Obaritus. *If you are paying a call, report me recovered. But if you intend to accomplish the deed – I don't believe it of my son. No order has been given for kin-murder!* (5) The killers surrounded her couch. First was the captain, with a club to the head. To the centurion, then drawing sword for death, she thrust forward her middle and cried, 'Hit the belly!' Many wounds finished her.

9. Reports agree so far. Did Nero inspect his lifeless mother, praise her body's beauty? Some relate, others deny. She was cremated that night with a dining couch for bier and paltry offerings. (Nor, while Nero held power, did earth cover or enclose her. By her household's care she received an insignificant mound near the Misenum road and Caesar's lofty villa looking out on bays below.) (2) The pyre ablaze, a freedman of hers, Mnester by name, ran himself through – unclear whether from fondness for his benefactress or fear of destruction. (3) This was the finale that for many years Agrippina saw and scorned. Consulting astrologers about Nero, she was told that he would rule – and kill his mother. 'Let him kill me,' she said, 'provided that he rule.'

10. Nero only realized the crime's magnitude when it was complete. The rest of the night, sometimes in silence, rooted, more often panic-spurred and witless, he awaited daylight thinking it would bring ruin. (2) At Burrus' instigation early obsequiousness from Guard officers determined him to hope. They clasped his hand and congratulated him on escaping from danger unforeseen and from his mother's deed. Friends then visited temples and, after their example, nearby Campanian towns attested joy with sacrifice and deputation. Nero's pretence was the opposite. He was gloomy, apparently angry at his own safety, in tears over his parent's death. (3) Since, however, unlike the human countenance, the look of places does not alter, and the troubling sight of that sea and shore accosted him – some even believed that a trumpet sounded from surrounding heights and wailing from his mother's tomb – he withdrew to Naples and sent the senate a letter whose gist was this: *An armed assassin was discovered – Agermus, one of Agrippina's most trusted freedmen – and retribution has been given in consciousness of guilt by the woman who devised the crime.*

11. He added far-fetched accusations.[8] *She hoped for partnership in power and Guards swearing obedience to a woman, and for an equivalent disgrace for senate and people. Frustrated and in anger at soldiers, senate and populace, she discouraged largesse to citizens and soldiers and contrived perils for notable men. How I exerted myself to ensure that she not invade the senate or pronounce on foreign nations!* (2) The Claudian era, too, offered indirect attack. He transferred all of that regime's crimes onto his mother, accounting her elimination Rome's good fortune. For he even told the shipwreck story. But who could be found so doltish as to believe it an accident? Or that a shipwrecked woman sent a single armed man to break through the Emperor's cohorts and fleets? (3) Not Nero – whose monstrousness exceeded all complaint – but Seneca was criticized[9] for this production: it was a confession, what he had written.

12. There was remarkable competition among the preeminent: thanksgivings were decreed for the regular temples;

Minerva's festival, during which the plot was uncovered, was
to be celebrated with annual games; a gold statue of Minerva,
and beside it the Emperor's likeness, was to be placed in the
senate house; Agrippina's birthday was to be inauspicious.
Thrasea Paetus, though accustomed to dismiss earlier flatteries
with silence or terse assent, left the senate then, causing danger
for himself without initiating freedom for the rest. (2) Portents,
meanwhile, were frequent and vain: woman birthing snake;
woman dead by lightning during conjugal relations; sun suddenly obscured;[10] bolts from heaven in Rome's fourteen regions.
So devoid of heavenly concern were events, that for years afterwards Nero united command and crime.

(3) To accumulate antipathy to his mother and – with her
removed – prove his own mildness increased, he restored to
their family seats the notable women Junia and Calpurnia[11]
and the ex-praetors Valerius Capito and Licinius Gabolus,
Agrippina's exiles. Permission was granted that Lollia Paulina's ashes[12] be returned and a tomb built. Men that he himself
recently relegated, Iturius and Calvisius, were released.
(4) Silana[13] had met her end after returning from a more distant
exile to Tarentum when Agrippina, whose antagonism brought
her down, was already tottering – or relenting nevertheless.

13. Nero lingered in Campania's towns, anxious. *How shall
I make my entrance into Rome? Will I find the senate compliant, the people supportive?* He was answered by the vicious, of
whom no palace produced more: *Agrippina's name was hated;
her death fired the people's favour. Go fearless and experience
veneration for yourself firsthand. Let us lead the way!* (2) They
found everything readier than promised: citizen groups met
him, the senate in festal garb, their wives and children mar-
shalled by sex and age. Viewing stands were built along his
route, as at triumphs. Accordingly, the proud conqueror of
public servility approached the Capitoline, rendered thanks,
and poured himself into every barely checked debauch that
mother-respect, such as it was, had delayed.

14. He had a long-standing desire to mount a racing chariot, and an eagerness no less foul for singing to the lyre
competitively. *To race horses is royal*[14] *and was practised by*

commanders of old, he maintained. *It is celebrated by poets'
praises and done in the gods' honour. And songs are sacred
to Apollo. The god stands in singer's garb not only in Greek
cities but also in Roman temples, foremost and foreknowing.*
(2) Nero could not be stopped. So Seneca and Burrus decided,
lest he win both, to concede the former. An area in the Vatican
valley was enclosed for his racing, with limited seating. Soon,
the Roman people were invited and exalted him with praise: so
pleasure-hungry is the crowd, and if the Emperor inclines that
way, so happy! (3) But public knowledge of his shame did not
so much sate – as his advisers expected – as spur. Thinking that
the disgrace was mitigated if he sullied more people, Nero
brought noble families' descendants – mercenary from need –
onto the stage. (These men, now dead, I will not name, in due
deference to their ancestors. For the offence is his who gave
money for wrongdoing rather than to stop it.) (4) Well-known
men of equestrian rank, too, Nero compelled to promise their
services to the arena – with huge gifts, except that cash from
one who can command has the force of necessity.

15. Postponing disgrace on the public stage, Nero instituted
'Youth Games'[15] for which there was widespread enlistment.
Noble birth barred no one – nor did age or office – from practising the actor's art in Greek or Latin, including gestures and
music scarcely manly. (2) Even notable women gave unseemly
performances. Bazaars were put up in the grove that Augustus
planted around the Battle Pool,[16] with foodstands and luxury's
provocations on sale. 'Pocket money' was provided for the virtuous to spend out of necessity, the rowdy with flair. (3) From
this came a multiplication of scandal and shame: nothing beleaguered behaviour, already degraded, with more debauchery
than that bog.[17] It is hard to retain decency in respectable
attainments, and it was much harder in competitions of vice for
modesty and restraint and anything of sound character to be
preserved. (4) Finally Nero himself went on stage, tuning carefully and giving a prelude[18] to attendant music teachers. There
was also a cohort of soldiers there, with officers and Burrus
mourning – and praising. (5) Then for the first time were men
of equestrian rank enlisted as 'Augustiani', conspicuous for

youth and strength, some natural libertines, others hoping for power. These made day and night ring with applause, labelling the Emperor's form and voice with gods' names – as if this were virtue, and they themselves eminent and honoured.

16. The Emperor, lest only his competition pieces be known, also took up poetry as a pursuit, assembling whoever had talent for writing but not yet[19] a distinctive reputation. They would sit down and weave together verses brought with them or invented on the spot, and supplement Nero's words, whatever their metre. As the poems reveal: there is no momentum, no inspiration and no unified voice to their flow. (2) Philosophers got Nero's time after dinner, and so that the clash of contrary positions might entertain. (There were indeed people who wanted to be seen dismal of countenance amidst royal amusements.)

17. About now, from a trivial beginning there arose fearful carnage among colonists of Nuceria and Pompeii at a gladiatorial show given by Livineius Regulus, whom I reported[20] earlier as removed from the senate. It was small-town carousing: mutual provocation, with insults, then rocks, finally swords as weapons. The Pompeian crowd was stronger and their amphitheatre was the show's venue. Many Nucerians were conveyed to Rome maimed and the majority had either child or parent to mourn. (2) Nero asked for a ruling from the senate. The senate left it to the consuls. When the matter was again referred to the senate the Pompeians were banned for ten years from gatherings of that sort and the clubs they had formed illegally were disbanded. Livineius and others who had encouraged the riot received exile as punishment.

18. Also removed from the senate was Pedius Blaesus,[21] accused by the Cyreneans. *Aesculapius' temple treasury was plundered by him and military recruitment impaired by cash and favours!* (2) The Cyreneans also indicted Acilius Strabo, an ex-praetor sent by Claudius to resolve disputes about properties that were once the inheritance of King Apion and then bequeathed to the Roman people[22] with his kingdom. (Neighbouring landowners had moved in, long-standing licence in wrong now serving them as right and equity. (3) When the properties were repossessed, antipathy to the judge arose.) The

senate replied: *Claudius' instructions are unknown. The
Emperor should be consulted.* Nero wrote: *Despite approving
Strabo's decision, I am nevertheless providing relief to the allies
and granting them their appropriations.*

19. Next came the deaths of notable men, Domitius Afer
and Marcus Servilius,[23] who flourished in high office and great
eloquence, the former celebrated as a trial lawyer, Servilius for
a long courtroom career and later for writing Roman history,
and for his life's refinement. These made Servilius more
renowned: equal in talent but for character distinct.

20. (60 CE) Nero (fourth time), Cornelius Cossus, consuls.

A quinquennial festival[24] was instituted at Rome according
to the pattern of Greek contests – with mixed reception, as
practically everything new.

(2) Some reported: *Pompey, too, was censured by the older
generation for giving theatre a permanent site. Earlier, plays
were presented in temporary stands with purpose-built stage,
or, if you look further back, people watched standing, lest sitting in the theatre they continue days-long in idleness.* (3) *In
the show itself, at least, antiquity's rule should be upheld: in
the praetor's presence, no citizen is obliged to compete.*
(4) *Ancestral ways, gradually decayed, are being utterly overthrown with imported frivolity. Accordingly, anything capable
of suffering or causing degradation is now seen in Rome. The
able-bodied are sinking to foreign pursuits – gymnasia, leisure
and shameful love are their training – authorized by emperor
and senate, who do not just license vice but apply force, under
pretext of oratory and song, to defile Rome's pre-eminent on
stage. What remains but to bare body, don gloves and practise
boxing instead of soldiery and weapons?* (5) *Will justice
increase, will equestrian panels fill their judicial role with distinction if they listen to warbles and dulcet voice as experts?
Nights, too, are added to disgrace lest time remain for decency,
with promiscuous gatherings in which whatever the most reckless aspires to by day he may venture in the shadows!*

21. More found licence itself agreeable, but applied respectable labels. *Our forebears,[25] too, embraced shows as amusements,
in proportion to conditions back then. For this purpose actors*

were imported from Etruria, horse races from Thurii, and after
the acquisition of Greece and Asia Minor plays were presented
more lavishly. No Roman of respectable birth has sunk to theat-
rical pursuits in the 200 years since Mummius' triumph, which
first offered shows of this type in Rome. (2) Moreover, thrift is
served in establishing a permanent seat for the theatre, rather
than the huge expense of yearly erection and demolition. And
magistrates won't so exhaust personal fortunes, nor will the
people have cause to importune them for Greek contests, when
the state meets this expense. (3) For orators and poets, victory
will be a spur to talent, nor is it burdensome for judges to give
respectable pursuits and permissible pleasures a hearing. To
gaiety, not frivolity, are given these few nights out of an entire
quinquennium. And such is the blaze of illumination that noth-
ing illicit can be concealed.

(4) In fact no signal humiliation transpired during that show.
The populace did not burn with even moderate enthusiasm,
since pantomime, though now permitted on stage, was excluded
from sacred contests.[26] No one won the prize for eloquence,
but Nero was pronounced the winner. Greek costume, in which
many appeared during that period, became obsolete.

22. Concurrently a comet[27] blazed, popularly believed to
portend a change in kings. As if Nero were already dislodged,
therefore, people tried to discover who was the chosen one. On
everyone's lips: *Rubellius Plautus*.[28] He had noble birth through
his mother from the Julian family. He himself upheld traditional
values: austere demeanour, chaste and private household. The
more fear induced concealment, the greater became his reputation. (2) There was more talk, equally baseless, from the
interpretation of a thunderbolt. *Since, when Nero was dining*
near the pools of Simbruvium, in the villa called 'Lakeside',
dishes were struck and the table was smashed, and since this
occurred in Tiburtine territory, which is Plautus' paternal ori-
gin, Plautus is the man marked out by divine sign, so people
believed, gladly, many of them, in whom ambition is eager to
court early the new and uncertain – and usually disappoints.
(3) Troubled, Nero wrote to Plautus: *Protect Rome's calm and*
remove yourself from people spreading perverse rumours. You

have ancestral lands in Asia in which to enjoy a safe and undisturbed prime. To Asia, accordingly, with his wife Antistia[29] and a few close friends, Plautus withdrew.

(4) During these same days dissipation's boundless desire brought Nero infamy – and danger. He entered the source of the city's Aqua Marcia for a swim, visibly defiling sacred springs and the sanctity of the place by bathing, and there followed a critical illness declaring divine wrath.

23. Corbulo, after Artaxata's demolition,[30] thought the recent panic should be put to use for seizing Tigranocerta, so that with that city razed he might intensify the enemy's fear, or, if he spared it, win fame for clemency. As he advanced, his army was not aggressive, lest he remove hope of pardon, but his attention was taut. *Armenians are changeable, as slack in the face of danger as they are untrustworthy if opportunity offers.* (2) The barbarians all acted in character: some sent entreaties, others abandoned villages and left for trackless parts, and some hid in caves along with their dearest. The Roman general therefore used different methods – mercy for the suppliant, speed for the fugitive – and was obdurate towards those in hiding: the caverns' mouths and exits were filled with brushwood and fired. (3) As he was travelling past their territory the Mardi attacked, experienced raiders, mountain-defended against invasion. These Corbulo pillaged, dispatching the Iberi:[31] enemy audacity was avenged with foreign blood.

24. Corbulo and his army, although free of battle's damage, were weary with want and exertion, forced to ward off starvation with meat from livestock. This, plus lack of water, scorching weather and lengthy marches, was eased only by the endurance of a general bearing what the common soldier bore, and more. (2) Cultivation was reached, harvests reaped, and of the two strongholds to which the Armenians had fled one was captured by assault; those who repelled the first attack were subdued by siege. (3) Crossing into Tauronitan territory Corbulo escaped an unexpected danger: hard by his tent a barbarian nobleman was caught armed. Under torture he divulged the plot's plan – *I am its author* – and his allies. Those who under friendship's guise were preparing a trap were convicted and

punished. (4) Soon envoys from Tigranocerta reported the walls open, the population ready for orders. They also delivered a gift of welcome: a golden circlet. Corbulo accepted it, and did them honour: the city was deprived of nothing, so that, unscathed, they would more readily remain compliant.

25. The bastion Legerda,[32] sealed by a spirited force, was taken only after a struggle: the Armenians even risked battle outside the walls, and, once driven within, succumbed at last to ramp and the invaders' weapons.

(2) These developments found easier success owing to Parthian preoccupation with the Hyrcanian war.[33] (The Hyrcani had sent the Roman emperor a plea for alliance, arguing that distracting Vologaeses was their pledge of friendship. Upon the envoys' return Corbulo, lest across the Euphrates they be caught by enemy patrols, supplied a guard as escort to the Red Sea coast.[34] From here, skirting Parthian territory, they returned to their native land.)

26. When Tiridates went through Median territory and entered furthest Armenia, Corbulo sent ahead his legate Verulanus[35] with auxiliary troops, and came himself with legions moving quickly, thereby forcing Tiridates to depart to a distance and discard war's hopes. Those Corbulo found opposed to[36] us he ravaged utterly with slaughter and flame, and he was establishing possession of Armenia when Tigranes[37] arrived, Nero's choice for taking power.

Tigranes was one of Cappadocia's nobility, a descendant of King Archelaus.[38] But having long been a hostage at Rome, he was reduced to slavish passivity. (2) Nor was there consensus in his welcome. In some people favour for the Arsacids endured, but the majority detested Parthian arrogance and preferred a king supplied by Rome. Tigranes was given a guard: a thousand legionaries, three cohorts from the allies and two cavalry units. To facilitate the new kingdom's protection, parts of Armenia were placed under the orders of the nearest rulers, Pharasmanes and Polemo,[39] plus Aristobulus and Antiochus.

Corbulo headed for Syria,[40] which had lacked a governor since the death of Quadratus and was now released to him.

27. This same year one of Asia's notable cities, Laodicea,

after collapsing in an earthquake, revived without our assistance, using its own resources. In Italy the ancient town of
Puteoli[41] acquired from Nero colony status and his name.
(2) The veterans enrolled as citizens at Tarentum and Antium,[42]
however, did not relieve the depopulation there: most scattered
into the provinces where they had served and – unused to marrying and the raising of children – left their houses childless,
without posterity. ((3) No longer, as formerly, were legions settled entire, with officers and soldiers in their own units, to
make a community from fellow-feeling and love. Rather, strangers from different units, without guide, without mutual
affections, practically from different branches of humankind,
were abruptly gathered into one location – a quantity rather
than a colony.)

28. The election of praetors,[43] customarily decided by the
senate, was ablaze with unusually vigorous lobbying. This was
calmed by the Emperor assigning three candidates – those surplus to available offices – to legionary commands. He also
increased the senate's honour by ruling that litigants appealing
from civil courts to the senate must pay the same earnest-
money[44] as those appealing to the Emperor. (Earlier, the
procedure was open and risk-free.)

(2) To conclude the year: equestrian-ranked Vibius Secundus, accused by Mauretania, was found guilty of extortion and
banished from Italy. That his penalty was not more severe was
owing to his brother Crispus'[45] resources.

29. (61 CE) Caesennius Paetus, Petronius Turpilianus,
consuls.

A grievous calamity accrued in Britain, where Aulus Didius
as governor had merely retained possession, as I reported, and
his successor Veranius,[46] after modest excursions to ravage the
Silures, was prevented by death from advancing the war. (Veranius was renowned for austerity during his lifetime, but his
last, testamentary, words revealed ambition. After much Nero-
flattery he added: *I would have rendered the province subject
to you had I lived another two years.*) (2) Then Suetonius Paulinus[47] governed the Britons. In military expertise and popular
talk, which leaves no one without a rival, he was Corbulo's

competitor, desirous of matching the honour from Armenia's recovery by mastering the foe. (3) Therefore he prepared to attack Anglesea, an island stronghold for inhabitants and a haven for deserters. He constructed flat-bottom boats for the shifting shoals. With these the infantry crossed, the cavalry via ford or, in deeper waters, swimming alongside their horses.

30. Standing shore-front was a various formation, thick with weapons and men. There were women running among them, Fury-like in funereal dress, hair loose, brandishing torches. And Druids around them, pouring forth curses, hands heavenward. A strange sight, they dismayed the soldiers, so that, as if paralysed, these exposed motionless bodies to wounds. (2) Then, at their leader's exhortations and indeed their own goading – *Don't be scared by a column of females and fanatics!* – they advanced and felled their opponents, wrapped them in their own flames. (3) A garrison was set over the defeated, and groves sacred to cruel beliefs were cut down. (Using captive blood to anoint altars and human innards to consult gods was, they held, lawful.) When Suetonius was thus engaged his province's sudden mutiny was announced.

31. The king of the Iceni,[48] Prasutagus, a man renowned for long opulence, had made Nero his heir with his two daughters, thinking by such deference to keep both kingdom and household apart from harm. The opposite occurred. Indeed his kingdom was pillaged by centurions, his household by slaves, like war spoil. His wife Boudicca was beaten, his daughters raped. The Iceni elite – as if the entire region was included in the gift! – were stripped of ancestral possessions and the king's relatives enslaved.[49] (2) At this insult and fearing worse, being now in a provincial framework, they took arms, rousing to insurrection the Trinovantes and others not yet broken to servitude, and secretly pledged to regain freedom. The bitterest hatred was for veterans. (3) Recent settlers[50] at Camulodunum were driving people from their houses and evicting them from their fields, calling them prisoners and slaves. Support for the veterans' unruliness was given by current soldiers: their lives were similar and they hoped for the same licence. (4) In addition, a temple of Claudius the god was regarded as an altar to

eternal enslavement and the chosen priests, with religion as pretext, squandered entire fortunes. It seemed easy to exterminate a settlement that lacked a fortification ring – this owing to our generals' inadequate foresight, planning for pleasure instead of utility.

32. For no obvious reason a Victory-statue at Camulodunum slipped from position and turned its back, as if yielding to the enemy. Women, agitated to frenzy, intoned: *Ruin is at hand! Foreign cries were heard in the assembly! The theatre rang with wails! A reflection in the Thames estuary showed a town overthrown!* The ocean looked bloody and at tide's ebb human body shapes were left behind. To the Britons, these were signs for hope; to the veterans, for dread. (2) In Suetonius' absence they sought help from the imperial agent Decianus Catus. He sent no more than 200 and these lacked full gear. A modest band of soldiers was already there. People counted on the temple's protection. Disrupted in their efforts by covert partisans of rebellion, the veterans neither fortified it with ditch or rampart nor removed old men and women so the able-bodied could resist alone. As unwary as if surrounded by peace, they were beset by the barbarians' throng. (3) In the onslaught everything was pillaged or burnt except the temple where the soldiers massed. That was besieged for two days and taken. The victorious Briton met Petillius Cerialis,[51] legate of the Ninth, coming up in support. He routed the legion and killed all the infantry. Cerialis and the cavalry escaped to their base and found safety inside its defences. The province's calamity and its hatred – a province driven to war by his greed – made Catus tremble. He crossed to Gaul.

33. Suetonius, admirably steady, headed into the enemy's midst, to London, a place not distinguished by the title 'colony', but with its quantity of traders and goods hugely busy. There, uncertain whether to choose that seat for war but observing the paucity of soldiers and having sufficient evidence in Cerialis of temerity checked, he decided to save the whole at the cost of one town. The tearful lamentation of people seeking help did not deflect him from giving the signal for departure and opening to fellow travellers his train. Anyone detained by

unwarlike gender, weary age or the location's lure was overcome by the enemy. (2) The same calamity befell Verulamium.[52]
Ignoring forts and garrisons, the barbarians went after the military stores, a rich prize for the taker and undefended. (They
rejoice in booty, but hard work finds them slack.) Some 70,000
citizens and allies, it is agreed, perished in the places I mentioned. No prisoners were taken or sold. There was none of
war's commerce, but sword and gibbet, fire and cross – as if
they were aware of coming punishment, but meanwhile
avenged – in a hurry.

34. Suetonius had the Fourteenth, a detachment from the
Twentieth, and auxiliaries from nearby, about 10,000 in arms,
when he prepared to end delay and join battle. He chose a
place narrow of approach, blocked behind by a forest. There
were no enemies except in front, he ascertained, and an open
plain, no fear of ambush. (2) Legionaries stood in close-packed
ranks, rapid-deployment troops on either side, massed cavalry
as wings. British forces rioted everywhere in swarms and
troops, in numbers as never before, and with such spirit that
they brought their wives, too, to witness victory and set them
in wagons circling the battlefield's edge.

35. Boudicca, in a chariot with her daughters before her,
went from tribe to tribe, declaring: *It is British custom to fight
under female leadership, but on this occasion I am not, though
offspring of great ancestors, after kingdom and wealth. Instead,
I am one woman from the crowd seeking retribution for liberty
lost, for body beaten, for daughters' purity violated. The
Romans' lusts are so excessive that they leave no bodies – not
aged, not virgin – undefiled. (2) But the gods side with just vengeance. A legion that dared battle has perished and the
remaining men are hiding back at base and looking for escape.
The din and shouting of so many thousands will not be
withstood, let alone onset and combat. If you weigh troop
numbers and war's reasons with me, we should either win on
that field or perish. This is a woman's intention. You men may
survive – enslaved!*

36. Nor was Suetonius, given the emergency, silent. Despite
confidence in his men's valour, he mixed exhortation and plea.

*Scorn the barbarians' noise, their empty threats! More women
than warriors are visible. The non-combatant and unarmed
will yield immediately when the steel and valour of victors is
recognized by men so often routed. (2) Even with many legions
present, small numbers break battles. It will be to your glory's
credit if this small band acquires a whole army's renown.
Together, then, and, after spear-cast, with shield and sword
persevere in rout and slaughter, to spoils oblivious. Victory
gained, everything will be yours!* (3) Such enthusiasm followed
the general's words, so ready for hurling spears were the veteran soldiers with much battle experience, that Suetonius was
certain of victory as he gave the battle signal.

37. Initially the legion stood fast, using the position's narrowness as a defence. As the enemy approached, spears were
loosed with sure aim until spent, then the legion burst out,
wedge-like. The auxiliaries had a similar impact. The cavalry,
lances out, shattered the strength facing them. The rest offered
their backs and flight was difficult since the circled wagons
barred outlets. The troops did not refrain even from slaying
women; they impaled animals, too, and augmented the body
heap. (2) Illustrious, and ancient victories' equal, was the praise
won that day. Some record that just under 80,000 Britons fell,
with only about 400 soldiers killed and a few more wounded.
(3) Boudicca ended her life with poison. Poenius Postumus,
camp-commander of the Second, heard of the successes of the
Fourteenth and Twentieth. Having cheated his own legion of
equal glory and refused – contrary to military usage – his general's orders, he used a sword to run himself through.

38. Assembled at last, the entire army was kept under canvas to finish the war. Troop strength was increased by Nero:
2,000 legionaries from Germany, eight auxiliary cohorts, a
thousand cavalry. With their arrival the Ninth's tally of legionaries was filled. (2) Auxiliary troops were placed in new winter
bivouacs. Of the tribes, the undecided or opposed were pillaged with fire and sword. But no scourge matched hunger for
a people unconcerned with sowing, all ages turned to war,
intending our provisions for themselves. (3) These high-spirited
peoples inclined the more slowly to peace because Julius

Classicianus, Catus' successor and antagonistic to Suetonius, impeded public good with private quarrels, putting this about: *You should wait for a new governor, one without combatant-anger and victor-arrogance, who will tend gently those who have surrendered.* He also sent to Rome: *Expect no end to battles unless Suetonius is replaced.* Misfortunes he ascribed to the man's perversity, successes to Fortune.

39. Accordingly, one of the freedman, Polyclitus, was sent to inspect Britain's state. With grand aspirations on Nero's part. *Polyclitus' authority will permit not only harmony between governor and imperial agent to develop, but also the barbarians' rebellious spirits to be settled in peace.* (2) Certainly Polyclitus, who with his huge train was a burden on Italy and Gaul, after crossing the sea was frightening to our soldiers, too. But to the enemy he was a joke – liberty being still vivid to them then and freedmen's power not yet known – and they marvelled that the commander and army responsible for so signal a victory obeyed slaves. (3) Polyclitus' whole report to Nero was nevertheless rather mild. Suetonius was kept on to administer affairs, but because he lost a few ships and crews against the shore he was ordered to hand over his army – as if war were ongoing! – to Petronius Turpilianus, who had just left the consulship. Turpilianus, without provoking the enemy and unchallenged, imposed the honourable name of peace on lazy inactivity.

40. That year at Rome noteworthy crimes were committed, one with a senator's audacity, in the other, servile.

Ex-praetor Domitius Balbus, owing both to long old age and to childlessness and wealth, was exposed to plots. (2) His relative Valerius Fabianus, aiming for political office, forged a false will, assisted by equestrian-ranked Vinicius Rufinus and Terentius Lentinus. (They had made Antonius Primus[53] and Asinius Marcellus their allies. Antonius was reputed ready of audacity, Marcellus renowned for his great-grandfather Asinius Pollio and worthy of character, except that he believed poverty the chief evil.) (3) Fabianus got the will sealed in the presence of those I mentioned and others less eminent, as was proved before the senate. Fabianus and Antonius with Rufinus and

Terentius were condemned under the *lex Cornelia*.[54] As for
Marcellus, the memory of his forebears and Nero's plea
exempted him from punishment, not shame.

41. That day overthrew Pompeius Aelianus, too, a young
ex-quaestor, for knowing Fabianus' enormities. He was banned
from Italy and Spain, his place of origin. Equal disgrace befell
Valerius Ponticus because he denounced defendants to the
praetor[55] to prevent their accusation before the urban prefect,
intending first under laws' pretext then by collusion to cheat
vengeance. An addition was made to the senate's decree: that
whoever pays or is paid for such a service is to be liable to the
same penalty as those guilty of false accusation in a criminal
court.

42. Soon afterwards the urban prefect Pedanius Secundus
was killed by his own slave. Either liberty was denied the slave,
despite an agreed-upon price, or he was hostile from love for a
man-whore and found having his master as rival unbearable.
(2) Since ancient custom required that the entire household
under that roof be taken to execution, from a hasty assemblage
of a populace offering protection – *so many innocents!* – a real
riot ensued and the senate was besieged. In the senate itself
there were passionate rejections of excessive severity, while the
majority's view was that nothing should be changed. One of
them, Gaius Cassius, at his turn, spoke as follows:

43. 'Often, senators, have I been in this company when
novel senatorial decrees contrary to our ancestors' institutions
and laws have been demanded. I did not oppose them, not
because I doubted that in every matter former provisions were
better and truer and that changes were for the worse, but lest I
seem, with excessive love of ancient custom, to be promoting
my own calling.[56] (2) Whatever authority I possess should not
be destroyed by frequent rebuttals, I judged, so that it stay
sound in case the state ever needed my counsel. This moment
arrived today, with a consular killed at home through a slave's
plot that no one blocked or betrayed, although the law was not
yet reeling, the law that threatens execution for the entire
household. (3) Go ahead and decree – heavens! – impunity.
Whom will position defend when for the urban prefect it

proved useless?[57] Whom will numbers keep safe, when Secundus' 400 did not protect him? To whom will a household give help, if even with cause for fear it does not notice our danger? Or, as some are not ashamed to pretend, was it injuries the killer avenged? Had he used ancestral assets to make a deal? Was he deprived of a family possession? Let us, then, announce that we think the master lawfully killed!

44. 'Shall we seek rationales for something weighed by wiser men? Even if now were the first time we needed to decide this, do you believe that a slave resolved to kill his master without a threat escaping, uttering nothing rashly? Suppose he did hide his plan, did ready a weapon without others' knowledge; surely he couldn't pass through the guards, open the bedroom door, bring forward the light and accomplish the killing with everyone unaware! (2) Many indications precede a crime. If our slaves give them away we can live as individuals among many, safe among the wary, and finally, if perish we must, not unavenged among aggressors. (3) Our ancestors distrusted the character of slaves, even when born in the same countryside or house and from the start possessing affection for their masters. But now that we have entire peoples in our households, with different rites and foreign gods – or none! – your rabble can only be ruled by fear. Some innocents will perish? (4) So, too, in a routed army, when one in ten is clubbed to death, even the valiant draw lots. Some unfairness lies in every important lesson compensating individuals' cost with public benefit.'

45. Cassius' motion no one dared oppose alone, but a confusion of voices countered. *So many! Children! Women!* And the undoubted innocence of most roused pity. Those for punishment prevailed, however. But compliance was impossible, since a multitude had massed, brandishing rocks and torches. (2) Nero berated the populace with an edict and hedged the entire route along which the condemned were led to punishment with soldiers, guarding. Cingonius Varro[58] had moved that the freedmen, too, in the house be deported from Italy. This the Emperor blocked,[59] lest ancient custom – which pity had not attenuated – be intensified by brutality.

46. That year Tarquitius Priscus[60] was condemned for

extortion, Bithynians bringing the action, senators rejoicing greatly: they remembered his prosecution of the governor Statilius Taurus, his own superior. (2) The census in Gaul was conducted by Quintus Volusius and Sextius Africanus, with Trebellius Maximus.[61] Volusius and Africanus were rivals for nobility of birth, but Trebellius, disdained by both, outshone them.

47. That year Memmius Regulus[62] met his end. Authority, constancy and name – insofar as the Emperor's overshadowing eminence permitted – made him renowned. Indeed, Nero, when ill of body and surrounded by flatterers saying that the Empire's end was at hand should he succumb to fate, replied: *The state has reserves.* When they asked *In whom, particularly?* he added, *In Memmius Regulus.* Regulus nevertheless lived on thereafter, protected by his quietude and because his family's renown was new, his wealth not invidious. (2) A gymnasium was dedicated by Nero that year, with oil provided for equestrian-ranked and senators – Greek laxity!

48. (62 CE) Publius Marius, Lucius Afinius, consuls.

The praetor Antistius, whose unruly action as plebeian tribune I reported,[63] produced abusive poems against the Emperor and divulged them at a well-attended party, while dining at Ostorius Scapula's house. And was immediately denounced by Cossutianus Capito (a man recently restored to senatorial rank at the request of his father-in-law Tigellinus)[64] on a treason charge, the first revival of that law. (2) Capito's aim, people believed, was less Antistius' destruction than Nero's glory. *After a senate condemnation Nero will use his tribunician veto to exempt the man from death.* And although Ostorius, giving evidence, denied hearing anything, belief went to hostile witnesses. The consul-designate Junius Marullus moved that the defendant be stripped of his praetorship and executed according to ancestral custom.[65] (3) The rest were assenting, until Thrasea Paetus, with much praise of Nero and after sharply berating Antistius, said: *Whatever the defendant deserves to suffer, we are not required – not under an outstanding emperor, in a senate bound by no necessity – to impose it.* (4) *Executioners and nooses have long since been abolished and penalties are*

set by laws. Punishments are decided in accordance with these,
without brutality from the judges and infamy for the times.
Why not an island and property confiscation? The longer
Antistius drags out a guilty existence, the greater the misery of
the individual and a powerful example of our community's
clemency!

49. Thrasea's freedom broke others' servility and when the
consul permitted a vote, people supported his motion, with
some exceptions. (Of these, readiest with flattery was Aulus
Vitellius,[66] harrying good men with abuse and silenced by
retort, as the timid generally are.) The consuls, not daring to
finalize the senate's decree, wrote to Nero about the verdict.
(2) Hesitating between shame and anger, he finally replied: *Pro-*
voked by no injury, Antistius uttered grave insults against the
Emperor. Retribution was requested from you senators. That
the penalty be matched to the size of the offence would have
been fitting. But I, who would have blocked the judges' severity,
do not prevent their moderation. You should decide as you
please, licensed even to absolve. (3) When these words and their
like were read out, his vexation visible, the consuls did not on
that account change the motion, nor did Thrasea retreat from
his proposal or others desert their vote, some lest the Emperor's
exposure to animosity seem their fault, the majority safe in
numbers, Thrasea with customary firmness of character – and
lest his glory lapse.

50. Fabricius Veiento contended with a similar charge for
having composed much abuse of senators and priests in the
books he titled *Codicils*. Plus, from the accuser Tullius Geminus: *Veiento offered for sale favours from the Emperor and*
eligibility for office. (2) This led Nero to handle the trial. After
the conviction he expelled Veiento from Italy and ordered
his books burnt. (They were collected and read while there
was peril in the purchase; later, licence to possess brought
forgetting.)

51. As public woes weighed ever more heavily, the props
dwindled. Burrus passed away – unclear whether from ill health
or poison. Ill health was inferred from the fact that, throat swelling gradually inwards, passage blocked, he stopped breathing.

The majority asserted: *He died by Nero's order. As if in medicine's application, Burrus' mouth was smeared with a noxious drug. Burrus understood the crime. When the Emperor called, Burrus avoided his glance and replied just this to his questions: 'I am well.'* (2) Rome missed him greatly, through memory of his virtue and, in his successors, the one's indolent innocence, the other's utterly open depravity. (Nero imposed two men on the Guards. Faenius Rufus[67] was favoured by the crowd because he handled the grain supply without profiteering. As for Ofonius Tigellinus,[68] his long-standing shamelessness and infamy were the attraction. (3) These men turned out as per known traits. Tigellinus was more influential with the Emperor, in intimate desires his accessory. Rufus was prosperous of reputation with populace and military, and so with Nero experienced the opposite.)

52. Burrus' death shattered Seneca's power. Rectitude did not have the same strength with one of its two 'guides' removed, and Nero was inclining to worse men. (2) With various accusations these attacked Seneca: huge wealth, beyond private measure and still increasing; turning the citizens' favour towards himself; in the pleasure of his parks and his villas' magnificence practically surpassing the Emperor. (3) Another reproach: *Seneca wants eloquence's palm for himself alone and produces poems more frequently now that you have become passionate about poetry. For he is openly opposed to his emperor's amusements: he disparages your power commanding horses and ridicules your voice when you sing.* (4) *How long will there be nothing renowned in the republic except Seneca's 'discoveries'? Certainly your boyhood is over, manhood's vigour at hand. Shed your tutor, sufficiently equipped as you are with impressive teachers in your ancestors.*

53. Seneca was aware of his accusers; they were exposed by people who cared about probity. Since Nero increasingly shunned his companionship, Seneca begged an opportunity for conversation, which was granted. He began thus:

(2) 'This is now the fourteenth year, Nero, from when I was associated with your potential, the eighth of your rule. Meanwhile, you have so heaped me with offices and wealth that

nothing is lacking to my prosperity except moderation. (3) The impressive parallels I will cite suit not my fortune but yours. Your ancestor Augustus permitted to Agrippa retirement in Mytilene, and to Maecenas nearly a visitor's leisure in Rome itself. The one was his partner in wars, the other active in Rome's many tasks, and they had received rewards ample indeed but proportionate to huge services. (4) Myself, with what could I prompt your generosity except teachings trained up, so to speak, in the shade, now in bright renown, because I am seen as having been attendant to your youth's beginnings – a magnificent reward. (5) You have surrounded me with immense influence, uncountable riches, so much that I often ponder: "Am I, with my equestrian, indeed provincial, origin, counted with Rome's pre-eminent? Among noblemen boasting trains of honours does my new rank shine out? Where is that soul content with the middle? Does it lay out urban parks like this, tread these suburban estates, run riot with fields so extensive, revenues so vast?" One defence only is at hand: I was not to resist your gifts.

54. 'Both of us have reached capacity, you of what emperor can bestow upon friend, I of what friend can accept from emperor; surplus grows envy. This, like all mortal concerns, is beneath your majesty, but it weighs on me. I need relief. (2) Just as if weary from warfare or travel I were begging a prop, so in this journey of life, an old man unfit for even the lightest cares, unable any longer to sustain my wealth, I seek support. Order my property administered[69] by your agents and received into your fortune. (3) I will not be reducing myself to poverty. Relieved of things whose flash dazzles, I will reclaim time now devoted to parks and villas for my soul. You have abundant strength and many years of rule at the highest eminence. We your older friends can seek repose. This, too, will tend to your glory: that you carried men to the top for whom even the middle was bearable.'

55. To this Nero replied approximately thus: 'My prompt rebuttal to your prepared speech is the first of your gifts, you who taught me to expound not only set pieces but also extempore. (2) My ancestor Augustus granted leisure's employment

to Agrippa and Maecenas after their labours, but when he was at an age whose authority would defend his tributes, whatever they be. Still, he stripped neither of his rewards. (3) They had earned them through war and perils, for in these Augustus' youth was occupied. I would not have lacked your weapon and hand, had I been in arms, but with what circumstances then demanded – reason, advice, instruction – you nurtured my boyhood and youth. (4) Your gifts to me, while life lasts, will be eternal. The things you have from me – parks and revenues and villas – are subject to chance. Granted, they seem numerous. But many men scarcely your equal in attainments have had more. (5) I am abashed to mention the freedmen we see wealthier. Indeed it is a reproach to me that though pre-eminent in my affection you do not yet outstrip all in fortune.

56. 'Your age, too, is sound and adequate to both affairs and their emoluments, while I am but in the first phase of my rule. Unless, perhaps, you rate yourself behind Vitellius,[70] consul three times, and me behind Claudius? The sum Volusius[71] acquired with long-continued thrift, can my generosity not top it up for you? Wherever youth's slippery ground sends me sliding, won't you call me back and provide, to vigour equipped with your assistance, a more unstinting guidance? (2) Not your moderation, if you return your money, or your "repose", if you abandon your emperor, but my greed and my cruelty's terror will be on everyone's lips. However great the praise for your self-command, it would not become a philosopher to accept glory for himself that produces infamy for his friend.' (3) To these words Nero added an embrace and a kiss, a man fashioned by nature and trained by habit to veil hatred with deceptive charm. Seneca – this was the conclusion of every conversation with the ruler – thanked him. But the practices of his former power he changed: he forbade assemblies of callers, avoided escorts and was rarely in Rome. *Health prevents me*, he said, or *Philosophical pursuits keep me home*.

57. Once Seneca was overthrown, weakening Faenius Rufus[72] was simple: Agrippina's friendship for him was the allegation people made.

Tigellinus grew stronger by the day. Thinking that attainments in wickedness – his only source of power – would give more pleasure if he ensnared the Emperor with complicity in crime, he ferreted out Nero's fears. Learning that Plautus and Sulla[73] caused the greatest alarm, Plautus having recently been removed to Asia, Sulla to Narbonensis, he brought up their noble birth and the fact that near the one were the armies of the East, near the other, those of Germany. (2) *I myself, unlike Burrus,[74] look to no other hope than your safety. That is being secured – somewhat – against city-based plots by my effort here, but how can distant disturbances be suppressed? Gaul is awake to the dictator's name, and Asia's peoples are equally expectant at the renown of Plautus' grandfather Drusus. (3) Sulla, lacking resources, is all the more daring: he is simulating indolence until temerity's chance turns up. Plautus with his vast resources is not even feigning a desire for retirement. He is flaunting, rather, his imitations of the Romans of old, with an addition of Stoic arrogance and a sect that makes men disruptive and eager for action.* (4) Nero delayed no longer. Sulla was murdered on day six – his killers reached Marseilles by boat, before fear or rumour – while taking his couch for dinner. They brought back his head. Nero ridiculed its premature grey: *Hideous.*

58. Plautus' murder plot was less well hidden. More people had his safety as a concern and the distance travelled by land and sea, plus the intervening time, stirred talk. (2) People imagined: *He has sought out Corbulo, a man in charge of large armies, and, if renowned and innocent men are getting killed, particularly at risk.* Further: *Asia has armed in Plautus' favour. The soldiers sent for the crime were neither strong in number nor ready of spirit. When they proved unable to carry out orders, they crossed to revolutionary hopes.* (3) These empty words, as is talk's way, were multiplied by the idleness of their believers.

A freedman of Plautus, wind-sped, arrived before the military with a message from Plautus' father-in-law Lucius Vetus.[75] (4) *Avoid a passive death while recourse exists.[76] Pity for a great*

name will find you good men, you will unite the bold. For now,
no assistance should be spurned. If sixty soldiers, which is the
number en route, are parried – while a message goes to Nero
and another unit travels – much will follow that may strengthen
even into war. Finally, either safety accrues from such a plan or
no worse awaits the daring than the coward.

59. The message did not stir Plautus. Either no help was in
prospect – he being unarmed, an exile – or from impatience
with a doubtful future. Or perhaps from love of wife[77] and
children, towards whom he thought the Emperor would be
more readily appeased if disturbed by no worry. Some say that
other messengers from Vetus reported no atrocity impending
and that his philosophical advisers – Coeranus, a man of Greek
stock, and Musonius,[78] of Etruscan – urged constancy in
expectation of death, instead of uncertain and fearful life.
(2) He was certainly found at midday stripped for exercise. Just so
the centurion slew him, in the presence of the eunuch Pelago.
(Nero had put him in charge of centurion and troops, as if they
were attendants and Pelago a royal minister.) (3) The victim's
head was brought back. At its appearance – let me give the
Emperor's own words – 'Why,' he said, 'did Nero . . .' * * *[79] . . .
and after he let go his fear, Nero prepared to accomplish Poppaea's wedding,[80] which had been delayed by panics of this
sort, and to remove his spouse Octavia. However retiring her
life, she was, given her father's name and the people's favour,
an encumbrance. (4) Nero wrote to the senate about the killing
of Sulla and Plautus. It was not a confession. *The character of*
each was disruptive and state security received my careful
attention. A thanksgiving was accordingly decreed, and that
Sulla and Plautus be removed from the senate – more galling
now the absurdity than the wrong.

60. With news of the senate's decision, when Nero saw his
every crime received as extraordinary, he evicted Octavia –
Barren, he insisted – and was immediately joined to Poppaea.

(2) Long his concubine, and holding Nero as both lover and
husband in her power, Poppaea urged one of Octavia's attendants to accuse her of an affair with a slave. The intended
offender was one Eucaerus, an Alexandrian expert at playing

the flute. (3) In consequence, inquisitions were conducted among the maids. By their torments' violence some were prevailed upon to affirm lies, but more stood fast to protect their mistress' purity. One woman, with Tigellinus pressing, replied: *Octavia's female parts are cleaner than your mouth.*[81] (4) Octavia was removed. At first it looked like an ordinary divorce: she got Burrus' house and Plautus' estates – ill-omened awards! She was later banished to Campania under military guard. (5) Then came frequent protests, openly, among the crowd, which has less prudence and, owing to their condition's insignificance, fewer dangers. At these, although Nero, repenting his offence, recalled his wife Octavia***.[82]

61. Joyous they climbed to the Capitoline and at last did homage to the gods. Poppaea's statues were toppled and Octavia's likenesses shouldered, flower-strewn, and placed in Forum and temples. There was even praise for Nero, with rivalry among those doing homage.[83] The Palatine, too, was full of crowd and clamour when military units were sent in: with beatings and sword point they dismayed people and dispersed them. And reversed what people had altered through sedition: Poppaea's honour was restored.

(2) Poppaea was always formidable for hatred, now also for fear. *The crowd's violence may press home or Nero be changed by popular predilection.* She fell at his knees. *At issue here are not my affairs – the competition for matrimony, although that matters more to me than life – but my very life, which is on the brink now owing to Octavia's hangers-on and slaves, who call themselves 'the populace' and dare in peacetime what would scarcely occur in war. (3) These weapons are lifted against the Emperor! Only a leader is lacking, something easily found once things are in motion. All Octavia has to do is leave Campania and make for Rome herself, she at whose nod, even absent, sedition is astir. (4) In any case, what is my offence? What reason for anyone's grievance? That I am about to give a true descendant to Nero's household? Do the Roman people prefer an Alexandrian flute-player's offspring raised to imperial eminence? Finally, if this will help, summon a mistress of your own accord, not coerced. Or else look to your safety! By just*

punishment and moderate remedies the first disturbances were
settled, but if people despair of Nero's wife being Octavia, they
will give Octavia a husband.

62. Poppaea's words, mixed to suit fear and anger, simultaneously terrified her listener and incited him. But the slave
allegation was feeble and foiled by the maids' interrogation. Better, therefore, that confession be sought from someone against
whom a charge of revolution, too, could be fabricated. (2) A
suitable candidate was Anicetus,[84] engineer of mother-murder
and commander, as I mentioned, of the Misenum fleet. (After
this crime he had received scant gratitude, then ever heavier hatred, since evil deeds' agents are viewed as a standing reproach.)
(3) He was summoned and reminded by Nero of his earlier service. *You alone supported the Emperor's security against a*
plotting mother! Opportunity for no less gratitude awaits if you
dislodge a hostile wife. No need for hands or weapons: admit
adultery with Octavia. Nero promised rewards – secret, naturally, at present – but great ones, and a pleasant retreat. Or, if
Anicetus refused, instant murder. (4) With innate infatuation
and the ease of earlier enormities Anicetus fabricated more than
was ordered and admitted all in the presence of friends brought
in as 'advisers' by the Emperor. He was banished to Sardinia,
where he enjoyed a wealthy exile and passed away.

63. Nero made a public announcement. *The fleet com-*
mander was seduced to aspire to an alliance for the fleet! And,
forgetting the recent complaints about barrenness: *Offspring*
were aborted in cognizance of debauchery. And: *I found out.*[85]
He shut Octavia away on Pandateria.[86]

(2) No other exile[87] moved the watching crowd to greater
pity. Some still remembered Agrippina under Tiberius. The
more recent memory of Julia Livilla was also before their eyes
(she was expelled by Claudius). But those women had the benefit of adulthood; they saw happy times and alleviated current
brutality by recollection of a better fortune. (3) Octavia had,
first, a wedding day tantamount to a funeral: she was married
into a household where she had nothing but hurt, since poison
deprived her of father and soon brother. Then a slave more
influential than her mistress, and Poppaea a bride – necessarily

ruinous for Nero's wife. Finally, an accusation more crushing than any fatality.

64. She was a girl of twenty[88] among officers and soldiers. A presentiment of evil already estranged her from life, but she did not yet acquiesce in death. After a few days' interval she was ordered to die, still insisting: *I am not married now, a sister only*. She invoked common parentage[89] and, finally, named Agrippina, during whose lifetime she had endured a marriage unhappy indeed but not fatal. (2) Octavia was tied down, the veins of every limb opened. And because her blood, panic-staunched, ran out too slowly, she was finished off by the heat of a suffocating sauna. A sequel of more appalling brutality: her head was cut off, taken to Rome, viewed by Poppaea. (3) Gifts decreed to temples – what point recording them? Whoever comes to know the events of that age from me or another authority must assume that whenever the Emperor decreed exile or killing, the gods got thanks and every former emblem of good fortune. (At that time, they were emblems of public disaster.) I will not, however, mute senatorial decrees novel in flattery or in compliance extreme.

65. That year Nero was thought to have killed the chief freedmen, too, with poison: Doryphorus for opposing Poppaea's wedding; Pallas[90] because of immense wealth sequestered by longevity. (2) In secret accusations Romanus complained that Seneca was Gaius Piso's[91] associate, but fell harder to Seneca wielding the same charge. The result was alarm in Piso, and a plot arose against Nero, vast in size and unavailing.

BOOK 15

1. (62 CE continued) Parthia's king Vologaeses learned of Corbulo's deeds. *And a king, foreign-born Tigranes, has been imposed*[1] *on Armenia! Likewise, with the concomitant expulsion of my brother Tiridates, Arsacid pre-eminence has been slighted!* He wanted to take revenge, but such were Rome's might and Vologaeses' respect for the still-valid treaty that he was drawn to different tasks, being innately hesitant, and occupied with the defection of the Hyrcani, a mighty tribe, and numerous resulting wars.

(2) Vologaeses, undecided, found fresh news of insult provoking: Tigranes quit Armenia and pillaged the Adiabeni, a bordering people, ranging too widely and too long to be after plunder. Local leaders were outraged. *Are we now so contemptible as to be invaded not only under Roman leadership but by the temerity of a hostage for years considered a slave?* (3) Their grievance was inflamed by Monobazus, Adiabene's ruler. *What protection do we have, where shall we look? Armenia? It has been conceded, and neighbours are being dragged along. If Parthians offer no protection, servitude to Romans will come on easier terms from surrender than defeat!* (4) Tiridates, a refugee from his own kingdom, in silence or moderate complaint also carried weight. *Cowardice does not preserve great empires. Men and arms must be risked! At the heights, might determines right. To retain one's own possessions is praise for private houses, but for kings it is contending for what others have.*

2. Roused, Vologaeses summoned his council. Placing Tiridates alongside he began: 'This man, my own father's

son – being younger, he yielded to me the highest title – I placed in possession of Armenia, third place in power; Pacorus already had the Medes. I seemed, countering long-standing fraternal hostility and aggression, to have reconciled our family's household gods. (2) The Romans thwart me, rupturing even now – to their own destruction! – a peace never yet disturbed to their advantage. (3) Granted, I would have preferred to retain ancestral possessions by right rather than by bloodshed, by argument rather than by arms. If I erred with delay, I will set things straight with valour. Your might and glory are intact, and a reputation for restraint has accrued; something not to be scorned by the greatest mortals, and indeed esteemed by the gods.' (4) At this he encircled Tiridates' head with a diadem, handed to the nobleman Monaeses the available cavalry – his regular escort – along with Adiabene auxiliaries, and charged Monaeses with evicting Tigranes from Armenia. He himself, after settling his disputes with the Hyrcani, stirred his country's forces, a very colossus of war, to threaten Roman provinces.

3. Reliable word reaching Corbulo about these matters, he sent two legions under the command of Verulanus Severus and Vettius Bolanus[2] to support Tigranes, with secret instructions to act with composure, not haste. Corbulo wanted to have a war available rather than to fight one. He had written to Nero: *Armenia's defence needs its own commander. Syria, with Vologaeses encroaching, faces increasingly acute dangers.* (2) Corbulo placed his remaining legions along the Euphrates, armed an emergency band of provincials and obstructed enemy incursions with garrisons. The region being meagre in water, strongholds were built at springs; he also buried some streams with piled sand.

4. While Corbulo was preparing thus for Syria's defence, Monaeses, though pushing his troops rapidly to forestall word, did not find Tigranes ignorant or off guard. (2) Tigranes held Tigranocerta, a city strong in defender numbers and rampart size. Also, the Nicephorius, a river of not inconsiderable width, protected a portion of the walls and a huge moat ran where the river was not trusted. Inside were soldiers and provisions. (In the conveyance of these a few soldiers, having ranged too

greedily, were trapped by Monaeses' sudden arrival; this fired the rest more with anger than fear.) (3) The Parthian lacks daring in close combat for executing sieges: with his occasional arrows he causes no terror inside and frustrates himself. When the Adiabeni advanced ladders and siege engines, they were easily repulsed, then cut down by our sally.

5. Corbulo, thinking good fortune to be used with restraint, however favourable his circumstances, sent to Vologaeses to protest the aggression against his province. *An allied and friendly king, and Roman cohorts, are surrounded! Abandon the siege or else I, too, will establish camp in enemy territory.* (2) The centurion Casperius[3] chosen for the mission met the king at Nisibis, thirty-seven miles from Tigranocerta, and presented Corbulo's instructions with spirit.

(3) Vologaeses' long-standing and settled policy was to avoid Roman arms and the situation was not developing to his advantage: siege ineffective; Tigranes secure with manpower and supplies; those who attempted to take the city put to flight; legions sent to Armenia; legions on Syria's border ready to invade. His own cavalry was weak from scarcity of fodder. (With the arrival of a host of locusts every grass and leaf was gone.) (4) Repressing his fear, Vologaeses offered rather mild terms. *I will send envoys to the Roman emperor about my claims to Armenia and securing peace.* He ordered Monaeses to abandon Tigranocerta and himself withdrew.

6. These developments many exalted as a splendid consequence of the king's fearfulness and Corbulo's threats. Others assumed a secret agreement that, with the cessation of war on both sides and Vologaeses' departure, Tigranes, too, would leave Armenia. (2) *Why was the Roman army withdrawn from Tigranocerta?[4] Why a peacetime desertion of what we defended in war? Is it better to winter in furthest Cappadocia in hastily erected shelters than in the capital of a kingdom recently secured? Combat was postponed, clearly, so that Vologaeses would engage with someone other than Corbulo, and Corbulo avoid further risk to glory earned over so many years!* (3) For, as I reported, Corbulo requested a commander assigned to

protect Armenia and there was talk that Caesennius Paetus was on the way.

And then Paetus was present. Their forces were divided: the Fourth and Twelfth obeyed Paetus, together with the Fifth, which was recently removed from the Moesians, and likewise auxiliary troops from Pontus and the Galatians and Cappadocians, while the Third, Sixth and Tenth, as well as Syria's troops, remained with Corbulo. The rest they shared or divided according to utility. (4) But Corbulo was not tolerant of rivals, and Paetus – glory enough for him in being second to Corbulo! – belittled Corbulo's achievements. *There was no carnage or booty and the cities were taken in name only*, Paetus kept saying, *I will impose on the conquered, in place of a royal cipher, taxes and statutes and Roman law*.

7. Then Vologaeses' envoys[5] – sent, as I mentioned, to the Emperor – returned unsuccessful and the Parthians made open war. Nor was Paetus reluctant. He entered Armenia with two legions. The commanders were: for the Fourth, Funisulanus Vettonianus;[6] for the Twelfth, Calavius Sabinus. There was a grim omen. (2) In crossing the Euphrates by bridge, the horse carrying the consul's insignia, upset for no obvious reason, escaped to the rear. And a sacrificial animal in the winter camp then under construction burst free of the half-finished works and took itself outside the defences. Also, the soldiers' javelins appeared to be on fire, a more significant portent in that the enemy fought with airborne weapons.

8. Scorning omens, leaving winter camp inadequately secured, without arranging provisions, Paetus hurried his army across the Taurus to – his words! – recover Tigranocerta and pillage regions Corbulo had left unscathed. (2) Some strongholds were indeed captured, some glory and booty won, if he he had taken possession of glory temperately or booty carefully. He ranged far over untenable territory. The provisions he captured had spoiled and winter was already pressing when he brought his army back and wrote to Nero: *The war is finished* – splendid words, but empty of substance.

9. Corbulo invested the never-neglected Euphrates with

more garrisons. He was superimposing a bridge, and to prevent enemy squadrons from obstructing him – they were already much in evidence roaming nearby – he moved enormous ships connected by decks and made taller by towers across the river, and ousted the barbarians with catapults and ballistas. (Their stones and spears penetrated the enemy's ranks further than could be matched by arrows shot in return.) (2) The river was bridged and the hills opposite occupied by auxiliary cohorts, and later by a legionary camp. Such was Corbulo's speed and show of strength that the Parthians abandoned preparations for the invasion of Syria and turned all hope to Armenia, where Paetus, ignorant of the imminent, had let the Fifth stop in far-off Pontus and weakened his remaining legions with indiscriminate leaves, until he heard that Vologaeses was on the way with a large and hostile force.

10. The Twelfth was summoned. Paetus had hoped that it would cause talk – *His army has grown!* – but its ranks proved thin. With it, however, the camp could have been secured and the Parthian dodged by delaying, had Paetus been steadfast in either his plans or others'. But first military men would make him resolute against pressing dangers, then, lest he seem to need other men's advice, he would pass to different plans, and worse. (2) At last he abandoned winter camp, exclaiming: *My wherewithal against the enemy is not ditch and rampart, but bodies and arms!* He took command as if to decide the issue in battle. Losing a centurion and a few soldiers that he had sent ahead to inspect the enemy forces, he returned, trembling.

(3) Since Vologaeses' advance was proving rather feeble, Paetus, vain confidence resurgent, placed 3,000 picked infantrymen on the nearest Taurus ridge to prevent the king's passage. He also placed Pannonian horsemen, his cavalry's core, on the plain. His wife and son were hidden in a stronghold called Arsamosata with a cohort for guard. (The soldiers were dispersed, although they would have been better able to oppose the roving enemy if kept together.) (4) Paetus was forced – with difficulty, they say – to report to Corbulo the enemy threat. Nor did Corbulo make haste, so that growing

dangers might augment help's merit, too. He did, however, order march-ready a thousand men from each of his three legions and 800 cavalrymen, plus an equal number of auxiliaries.

11. Vologaeses, though informed that his way was blocked here with infantry, there with cavalry, maintained his plan: with violence and threats he frightened off Paetus' cavalry and crushed the legionaries. Only one centurion, Tarquitius Crescens, dared to defend the tower where he was in command, with frequent sallies and by slaughtering barbarians who approached too near, until he was overcome by the launching of flames. (2) Foot soldiers, if unharmed, sought distant and trackless parts; the wounded sought the camp, exalting, in their fright, the king's valour and his peoples' brutality and manpower – everything! – and finding easy belief in those who feared these same things. (3) Not even their commander struggled against misfortune. Paetus deserted all military responsibilities and sent another entreaty to Corbulo: *Come quickly and protect the standards and eagles and remaining reputation of an unhappy army! We, meanwhile, will retain loyalty as long as life.*

12. Corbulo, undismayed, and leaving part of his force in Syria to secure the Euphrates defences, set out by the shortest provisioned route: Commagene, then Cappadocia, finally Armenia. Accompanying the army, in addition to things customary for war, was a large host of camels laden with grain for repelling both enemy and hunger. (2) From the stricken forces Corbulo first came upon Paccius,[7] a chief centurion, then many soldiers. These, offering various explanations for their flight, he advised: *Return to your units and test Paetus' clemency. I am merciless to all but victors!* (3) His own legions he approached and roused, reminding them of former achievements,[8] displaying fresh glory. *No Armenian towns or villages are your goal and the reward for your exertions, but a Roman camp and two legions. If an individual soldier receives a civic crown from the imperial hand for a fellow citizen's preservation, what great honour will be yours, considering the equal number of those bringing aid and those receiving it?* (4) Animated as a group by

these and like words – and some driven by the more personal stimulus of danger to brothers or kin – they hastened day and night.

13. Harder and harder did Vologaeses press the besieged, attacking now the legions' rampart, now the stronghold in which non-combatant generations were protected, approaching more closely than Parthian custom, hoping by this presumption to draw the enemy into battle. (2) But the Romans, extracted with difficulty from their tents, fought for nothing but the fortifications, some by the commander's order, others from their own cowardice or waiting for Corbulo. They had in view, in case the enemy's might encroached, truce precedents, Caudium and Numantia.[9] *And the Samnites, an Italic people, did not have the might of the Parthians, rivals to Rome's empire. Even antiquity, strong though it was and admired, whenever Fortune turned contrary, took thought for safety.*

(3) His army's despair compelled Paetus to write to Vologaeses, not a grovelling letter this first one, but rather a complaint: *You are engaging in hostilities over Armenia, which has always been a Roman possession or subject to a king chosen by the Emperor. Peace serves both sides equally. Do not look only to the present. You confront two legions with your entire kingdom's forces, but we Romans have the rest of the world to assist our wars!*

14. Vologaeses' response contained nothing relevant: *I must wait for my brothers Pacorus and Tiridates. That is the time and place for planning our decision about Armenia. The gods have granted that Arsacids – as is our due! – will simultaneously be deciding about Roman legions.* (2) Messengers were then sent by Paetus, a conversation with the king requested. Vologaeses ordered his cavalry commander Vasaces to go.

Paetus evoked commanders like Lucullus, Pompey, and whatever the emperors had done to hold or bestow Armenia. Vasaces said that we had the illusion of keeping Armenia or giving it away, but the Parthians had the power. (3) After a lengthy back-and-forth argument they brought in Adiabenian Monobazus the following day as witness to the terms: legions released from siege, every soldier leaving Armenian territory, strongholds and provisions to the Parthians. *With these things settled, Vologaeses will have an opportunity to send envoys to Nero.*

15. The river Arsanias – it bordered his camp – Paetus bridged, apparently making march preparations, but the Parthians had ordered it as proof of victory. They used it, our men went another way. (2) Rumour added that legions were sent under the yoke and other things consistent with misfortune. An illustration was provided by the Armenians: they entered the fortifications before the Roman column left and filled the roads, identifying and seizing captured slaves and livestock. Garments were pulled away and weapons grasped and the frightened soldiers yielded, lest cause for fighting arise.

(3) Vologaeses had the weapons and bodies of the slain heaped up as evidence of our disaster, but refrained from watching the legions' flight: a reputation for moderation was his aim after satisfying pride. The king forced his way across the Arsanias on elephant-back, his relatives by the strength of their horses, for a rumour had arrived that the bridge would collapse under its burden by a plot of its builders. But those who dared to start learned that it was sound and trustworthy.

16. The besieged Romans, it is agreed, had food in such abundance that they fired their grain stores. Corbulo, by contrast, would have it[10] that the Parthians lacked supplies and, fodder exhausted, intended to abandon the siege. He himself was less than three days distant. (2) He adds that assurances were given by Paetus, under oath and before the standards, alongside the king's witnesses, that no Roman would enter Armenia until Nero's letter arrived about whether he agreed to peace. (3) Granted that these things were fabricated to increase Paetus' infamy, the rest are public knowledge: that in a single day Paetus covered forty miles, leaving the wounded along the way, and that the panic of those fleeing men was as ugly as if they had turned tail in battle.

(4) Corbulo with his troops met them at the Euphrates with no show of standards and weapons, so as not to shame their contrast. His regulars, sorrowful and commiserating with comrades, even wept. There was scarcely a salute, such was the lamentation. Gone were competition in valour and ambition

for glory, the passions of fortunate men. Only pity flourished, and principally at the lower ranks.

17. The leaders conversed briefly. Corbulo lamented achievement nullified: *The war could have ended with Parthian flight!* Paetus: *We each have resources undiminished. Let us reverse the eagles and invade together an Armenia weakened by Vologaeses' departure.* (2) Corbulo: *These were not the Emperor's instructions. Roused by pity for the legions' danger, I left my province, but since the Parthians' moves are unknown I will return to Syria. Even so, I will have to pray for good luck, if an infantry force exhausted by the distance it has marched is to overtake a fresh cavalry outstripping them thanks to an easy route across the plains.*

Paetus winter-quartered his troops in Cappadocia. (3) Vologaeses' messengers to Corbulo said: *Pull down strongholds beyond the Euphrates and make the river, as before, the dividing line.* Corbulo demanded: *Armenia, too, must be emptied of enemy garrisons.* Eventually the king yielded, the fortifications Corbulo built across the Euphrates were destroyed and the Armenians were left to themselves.

18. In Rome, victory monuments 'Over the Parthians'[11] were set up, including an arch halfway up the Capitoline hill. They were decreed by the senate with the war still undecided and work continued while appearances were being maintained, common knowledge notwithstanding. (2) In another attempt to mask foreign worries, Nero threw public grain – rotten with age – into the Tiber[12] to bolster confidence in the grain supply. There was no price increase, either, although a violent storm had consumed nearly 200 ships already in port, and an accidental fire a hundred others towed up the Tiber. (3) He put three ex-consuls – Lucius Piso, Ducenius Geminus and Pompeius Paulinus[13] – in charge of taxation, criticizing earlier emperors for exceeding total revenue with heavy expenditures: *I myself bestow annually 60 million sesterces on the state.*

19. Widespread at that period was a crooked practice: with the approach of elections or provincial sortition, childless persons – many! – possessed themselves of children by fictitious adoptions, then, having drawn for praetorships or provinces

among the fathers, immediately released the adoptees. (2) People approached the senate indignantly, weighing nature's due and the labours of bringing up children against the imposture and artifice and brevity of adoption. *The childless are rewarded enough! In complete security, unburdened, they have ready to hand influence, marks of distinction, everything! As for us, the laws' promises, long awaited, are becoming a mockery, when some worry-free parent, childless without bereavement, is suddenly the equal of fathers with their long-continued aspirations.*[14] (3) A senatorial decree resulted: fictional adoptions[15] should provide no help towards any office and should not give advantage, even for obtaining legacies.

20. Crete's Claudius Timarchus was put on trial, the charges being those regularly brought against domineering provincials excited by excessive wealth to the abuse of those below. But one boast went so far as to insult the senate. *It lies in my power whether official thanks are decreed to Crete's governors.* (2) The occasion was turned to public advantage by Thrasea Paetus, who, after recommending the defendant's expulsion from Crete, added this:[16]

(3) 'Experience shows, senators, that outstanding laws and moral lessons are generated among good men from others' offences: advocates' licence produced the Cincian bill,[17] candidates' corruption the Julian laws, magistrates' greed the Calpurnian decrees. For crime comes before penalty, and remediation after wrongdoing. (4) Therefore in the face of this unprecedented provincial insolence, let us adopt a policy appropriate to Rome's good faith and constancy, whereby nothing is subtracted from our responsibility to our allies, but we stop thinking that a man's reputation is decided anywhere other than in the judgement of fellow citizens. 21. In the past, we sent not only magistrates but even private citizens to visit provinces and report on their deference. Nations trembled at the assessment of individuals. But now we court and flatter foreigners, and indictments come even more readily at their behest than official thanks. (2) Indictments should be brought, and such demonstrations of their power[18] should be secured to provincials, but so should false praise extracted by entreaty be

curbed, and likewise malice and cruelty. (3) Wrongdoing more often occurs when we are obliging than when blunt. Indeed, some virtues foster hostility: resolute strictness and a disposition unmoved by influence. (4) Our terms of office generally begin well and go downhill at the end as we seek approval like candidates. But if these practices are banished the provinces will be governed more equitably and steadily. For just as rapacity is crippled by fear of extortion proceedings, so will the currying of favour be curbed by a ban on official thanks.'

22. Great accord greeted this proposal. No decision could be taken, however. According to the consuls: *The issue is not before us*. Soon, on the Emperor's authority, they ruled that no one should propose to provincial assemblies that official thanks to governors be expressed in the senate and that no one should carry out such a mission.

(2) The same consuls.

A lightning-struck gymnasium burned down,[19] its statue of Nero melting into a shapeless mass. And in an earthquake much of the populous Campanian town of Pompeii collapsed. The Vestal Virgin Laelia passed away. Cornelia, of the Cornelii Cossi, was taken into her place.[20]

23. (63 CE) Memmius Regulus and Verginius Rufus,[21] consuls.

A daughter born to Nero by Poppaea Sabina exalted him to the heavens with happiness. He called her Augusta and gave Poppaea the same title. The birthplace was Antium, a Roman colony where Nero himself was born. (2) The senate had already commended Poppaea's womb to the gods and undertaken public vows;[22] these were multiplied and discharged. Thanksgivings were added, a temple to Fecundity decreed, likewise games modelled on the Actian.[23] Also, that gilded statues of the goddesses of Fortune[24] be placed on the throne of Capitoline Jupiter, and that there be Circus games for the Claudian and Domitian families at Antium like those for the Julian family at Bovillae.[25] (3) It was all transitory: the infant was dead within four months. Then came the flatteries of men proposing divine honours: couch, temple, priest. Nero was as immoderate in lamentation as in rejoicing. (4) It was observed that when the entire senate streamed down to Antium after the birth, Thrasea, excluded, calmly took the insult as signalling imminent death. Nero is said to have boasted later to Seneca that he was reconciled to Thrasea, and Seneca to have congratulated Nero. From then on, glory grew for outstanding men – and danger.

24. At spring's beginning Parthian envoys arrived with instructions from King Vologaeses. A letter had the same purport: *I omit my earlier and often advanced claims to Armenia, since the gods, arbiters of peoples however powerful, have delivered possession to the Parthians, not without Rome's disgrace. (2) When Tigranes was trapped recently, and later Paetus with his legions, I could have crushed them, but let them go unharmed. Having amply demonstrated my power, I tried leniency, too. Tiridates would not have refused to come to Rome for his crown if not prevented by priestly scruple.*[26] *He will approach military standards and the Emperor's image to inaugurate his rule in the legions' presence.*

25. Thus Vologaeses' letter. Paetus had written otherwise: *My situation is unchanged.* A centurion who came with the envoys, questioned about conditions in Armenia, replied: *All Romans have left.* (2) Then people saw the barbarians'[27] mockery, asking for what they had seized. Nero consulted the community's leading men about whether they preferred unpredictable war or dishonourable peace. *War, immediately! And Corbulo should lead, a man familiar for years with troops and enemy, lest mistakes again arise from someone else's ignorance!* (They were irked about Paetus.) (3) The envoys were sent back unsuccessful, but with gifts, so that Tiridates would hope to succeed at the same request if he petitioned in person. Governance of Syria was entrusted to Gaius Cestius, her troops to Corbulo, reinforced by the Fifteenth, which Marius Celsus was to bring from Pannonia. Written instructions went out to princes, kings and governors of neighbouring provinces to obey Corbulo. His power was amplified to practically the same level as that given by the Roman people to Pompey[28] for the pirate war. (4) When Paetus returned fearing worse, Nero contented himself with a witty attack.[29] *I pardon you directly, lest a man so prompt to panic grow ill with prolonged worry.*

26. Corbulo, transferring to Syria the Fourth and Twelfth as
unfit for battle after the loss of their bravest men and the others'
fright, led Syria's Sixth and Third into Armenia, troops both
fresh and, owing to numerous successful exercises, ready.
(2) He added the Fifth, which in its Pontus posting kept clear of
calamity, and likewise the recently arrived Fifteenth, and select
detachments from Illyricum and Egypt, plus auxiliaries of horse
and foot and royal forces collected at Melitene, where he
intended to cross the Euphrates. (3) His army, duly purified and
assembled, he addressed with splendid words about the
Emperor's potency and his own achievements, deflecting misfortunes onto Paetus' incompetence – all with great authority,
which in a military man counts as eloquence.

27. He travelled the route once pierced by Lucullus,[30] clearing what time had blocked. Peace envoys from Tiridates and
Vologaeses were made welcome and they went back with centurions bearing a mild message: *Nothing yet necessitates all-out
battle.* (2) *The Romans have had their successes, some, too, the
Parthians – a contraindication to arrogance! Accordingly, it is
in Tiridates' interest to accept the gift of a kingdom unscathed,
and Vologaeses will serve the Parthian people better with a
Roman alliance than with reciprocal hurt. He knows[31] how
much internal discord he rules over, what unconquered and
high-spirited peoples. My own commander, by contrast, has
undisturbed peace everywhere, and this one war.* (3) Corbulo
supplemented advice with intimidation: he expelled Armenian
magnates – the first to defect from us – and destroyed their
strongholds, filling equally plains and hills, strong and weak
with fear.

28. Corbulo's name was not considered hostile or hateful to
the barbarians. They therefore believed his advice trustworthy.
Vologaeses was not ruthless in principle, and sought a truce for
certain districts. Tiridates set the date and place for talks.
(2) The time was soon. The place chosen by the barbarians –
where Paetus and his legions were recently besieged, for the
reminder of their own happy outcome – was accepted by Corbulo.
Dissimilarity of outcome will increase my glory. Paetus' shame
was no concern of his, as became quite clear when he ordered

Paetus' son, an officer, to lead units charged with burying defeat's leavings. (3) On the set day there came to Tiridates' camp Tiberius Alexander, an equestrian-ranked notable deputed to assist in the war, and Annius Vinicianus,[32] Corbulo's son-in-law, who, though not yet of senatorial age, commanded the Fifth – a sign of respect for Tiridates and to ensure with such a pledge that he not fear a trap. Each side brought twenty riders. When Corbulo was spotted, the king dismounted first, nor did Corbulo hesitate. Approaching on foot, they clasped hands.

29. The Roman opened with praise for the young man's pursuit, after desisting from rash courses, of security and advantage. Tiridates' lengthy preface concerned his noble birth. The remainder was circumspect. *I will go to Rome and bring Nero an unusual honour: with Parthia thriving, a Parthian prince[33] suppliant!* The agreement was that Tiridates place his royal emblem before the Emperor's likeness, and resume it only from Nero's hand. The meeting ended with a kiss. (2) After a few days' interval there was an impressive display on both sides: there, cavalry drawn up by squadrons with traditional heraldry; here, a legionary column on foot; eagles and standards shining; and statues of gods as in a temple; a dais in between holding a chair of office, the chair a likeness of Nero. (3) Tiridates approached and after the customary sacrifices placed the diadem from his head before Nero's likeness. In everyone there were powerful emotions, heightened by the slaughter and siege – stamped in memory! – of Roman forces. But now the situation had changed. *En route Tiridates will be a spectacle to the world, how little different from a captive?*

30. Corbulo increased the occasion's lustre with convivial entertainment. The king, struck by each new thing, asked its origin: watch changes announced by a centurion; banquet dismissed with a horn; an altar that had been constructed in front of the commander's tent kindled and burnt. Magnifying it all, Corbulo roused wonder at ancient custom. (2) The following day Tiridates begged an interval in which to visit brothers and mother, before embarking on so considerable a journey. He gave his daughter as hostage, meanwhile, and a letter of entreaty to Nero.

31. Setting out, he found Pacorus[34] among the Medes, and at Ecbatana Vologaeses solicitous of his brother. He had sent his own request to Corbulo: *Tiridates must suffer no semblance of servitude: not surrender his sword, not be kept from governors' embrace or denied entrance to their houses. At Rome he must enjoy the consuls' distinctions.* Accustomed to foreign hauteur, Vologaeses was naturally unfamiliar with our ways, where what counts is an office's power – empty signs are passed over.

32. This same year Nero promoted the peoples of the Maritime Alps[35] to Latin status. In the Circus he placed equestrian-ranked in front of plebeian seating. (Until this point they attended without distinctions, since the Roscian law[36] stipulated nothing except about the theatre's fourteen rows.) Gladiatorial shows were as magnificent as ever this year, but in the arena more noble women and senators were sullied.[37]

33. (64 CE) Gaius Laecanius, Marcus Licinius, consuls.

Nero was impelled by an ever sharper desire to frequent the public stage. So far he had performed[38] in palace or park at the 'Youth Games', which he now despised as too thinly attended and limited for so big a voice. (2) Not daring to start at Rome, he chose Naples, a city practically Greek. *Debuting there, I will cross to Greece and acquire the famous and ancient festival crowns, so as to win citizen support with reputation enhanced.* (3) An assemblage of locals and residents of nearby towns,[39] motivated by word of the event, and those who kept company with Nero for show or service – even companies of soldiers! – filled Naples' theatre.

34. It ended grimly in most people's view, but in Nero's, providentially and with divine favour: after the crowd's departure, without harm to anyone, the empty theatre collapsed. Nero wrote and performed songs of thanksgiving on the happy outcome of the recent collapse.

Intending to cross the Adriatic, Nero stopped temporarily at Beneventum,[40] where Vatinius was giving well-attended gladiatorial games. (2) (Vatinius was among the foullest of that court's monstrosities: raised in a cobbler's shop, twisted of body, scurrilous of wit. Adopted first as humour's butt, he later grew so powerful by attacking excellence that he overtopped even evil men in influence, money and the power to do ill.)

35. Attending these games, even amidst pleasures, Nero didn't discontinue his crimes: Torquatus Silanus[41] was forced to die just then, because, in addition to the renown of the Junian family, he displayed as great-great-grandfather Augustus. (2) On orders his accusers said: *He is lavish of outlay, revolution his only hope. Moreover, he has secretaries of 'Correspondence' and 'Petitions' and 'Finance' – labels and plans for a government!* (3) With his most trusted freedmen bound and carried off and condemnation upon him, Torquatus dissevered arm veins.[42] Then came Nero's regular speech. *Although guilty and duly distrustful of his defence, Torquatus would nevertheless have lived had he awaited his judge's clemency.*

36. Greece was dropped for the moment – for reasons unclear – and Nero revisited Rome. But eastern provinces, especially Egypt, occupied his reveries. Promising that his absence would not be long, and that all matters of state would remain untroubled and prosperous, he visited the Capitoline temple on the subject of his trip (2) and paid respects to its gods.[43] When he entered Vesta's temple,[44] too, he began to tremble in every limb, either because the divinity frightened him or because recollection of crimes left him perpetually fearful. He abandoned the undertaking, claiming that all of his projects weighed less with him than love of country. (3) *I have seen my fellow citizens' gloomy faces. I can hear their hidden lament about my embarking on so long a journey when they scarcely survive even my limited departures, being accustomed to find comfort against the unexpected in the sight of their emperor. Just as in private relationships one's nearest prevails, so the Roman people is supremely powerful and must be obeyed if it holds me back.* (4) These and like words gratified a crowd passionate for pleasures and – their especial concern – fearing food shortage if he were absent. The senate and leading men were uncertain whether Nero was more alarming far or near. Thereafter, as is natural in frightening circumstances, they believed that what happened was worse.

37. Nero, to gain credence that no place made him so happy, entertained in public and used the whole city as his home.[45] The party most celebrated for luxury and notoriety was prepared by Tigellinus. For example – so as not to have to narrate the same exorbitance too often – (2) in Agrippa's Pool[46] he built a raft on which he set a banquet. This, towed by other boats, was to be mobile. The boats were styled with gold and ivory; the rowers were perverts arranged by age and sexual expertise. He requisitioned bird and beast from lands remote, and sea creatures all the way to Ocean. (3) Near the pool's fringes stood brothels stocked with noble women. Opposite, naked whores had visitors. First, there were obscene gestures and movements, then, as dark arrived, the adjacent groves and surrounding buildings rang with song and grew bright with lamplight. (4) Nero himself, befouled by things licit and illicit, left untried no outrage by which to increase his degradation – unless it was that a few days later he wed one of that flock of filth, Pythagoras by name, in a ceremony like regular marriage. The Emperor put on the wedding veil and priests were present. Dowry, conjugal bed, nuptial torches and, finally, things that even for a woman night covers – all were on display.

38. Next came a calamity.[47] Whether by accident or by the Emperor's plotting is uncertain – authorities give both accounts – but it was more harmful and fearful than any others that have befallen the city through fire's violence. (2) Originating first in the Circus where it abuts the Palatine and Caelian hills, among shops stocked with combustibles, the blaze was strong as soon as it started. Sped by the wind it took hold the length of the Circus, for neither dwellings hedged with masonry nor temples girded by walls nor any other delay was in its path. (3) With a rush the fire overran level areas, then surging to the heights and again ravaging lower zones it outpaced remedies. So swift was the evil, and the city was vulnerable with its narrow streets bending this way and that, its shapeless neighbourhoods – Rome of old. (4) Plus, the cries of frightened women, the elderly, or those of youthful inexperience, some people saving themselves, others saving others – tugging invalids along, or waiting – one delaying, one hurrying, everything

got in the way. (5) And often, while looking behind, people were trapped from sides or front. Or if they found refuge nearby, when that, too, caught fire they discovered even distant parts – as they thought – in the same situation. (6) Finally, uncertain what to avoid, what to seek, they filled streets and scattered through fields. People perished, even though escape lay open: some because they had lost everything, livelihood even, some out of affection for family they had been unable to rescue. (7) Nor did any dare fight the fire, what with threats from many who prohibited quenching, and because others were openly throwing firebrands and claiming authorization, either to pillage more freely or, in fact, under orders.

39. Nero was in Antium. Nor did he return to Rome until the fire neared the residence by which he had joined the Palatine to Maecenas' Gardens.[48] The fire could not be stopped. Palatine and residence and everything roundabout were consumed. (2) As relief for the displaced and refugee populace, he opened the Campus and the Agrippa buildings and even his own park, and put up temporary buildings to receive the needy multitude. Supplies were brought from Ostia and nearby towns and the price of grain was reduced to three sesterces.[49] (3) These were popular measures, but fruitless, since rumour spread. *With the city aflame Nero mounted his domestic stage and performed a 'Sack of Troy', likening present ills to ancient calamities.*

40. Finally on day six a stop was put to the fire at the base of the Esquiline, buildings having been demolished over a vast area so that flat ground and, as it were, vacant air might block the relentless rampage. But before fear was shed or hope returned to the populace[50] the fire attacked again in the city's more open areas, where there was less human wreckage, but more temples and pleasure-giving colonnades succumbed. (2) This blaze incurred more shame: it erupted from Tigellinus' Aemilian estate, and Nero seemed to be seeking the glory of founding a new city and naming it for himself.[51] (Rome has fourteen regions, of which four remained whole and three were destroyed down to the ground; in the other seven a few traces of buildings remained, mangled and charred.)

41. The number of houses and apartment blocks and temples lost would be difficult to reckon. But of the oldest religious foundations, those burnt were Servius Tullius' for Luna, the great altar and shrine that Arcadian Evander consecrated to 'Hercules Present'; the temple of 'Jupiter the Stayer' vowed by Romulus; the royal residence of Numa; and the sanctuary of Vesta with Rome's tutelary deities. Also, treasures won in many a victory, and glories of Greek art, plus ancient and unsullied works of genius. However great the beauty of the reborn city, the older generation remembered much that could not be replaced. (2) Some noted that the outbreak of this fire occurred on 19 July, the day on which the Senones burned captive Rome. Others' inquisitiveness has gone so far as to enumerate the equal number[52] of years, months and days between the two fires.

42. Nero exploited the national disaster and built a residence[53] whose marvels were less gemstones and gold – things customary long since and widespread by luxury – than fields and pools and, as in a wilderness, forests here, there open spaces and vistas. (It was planned and built by Severus and Celer, whose character and audacity were such as to attempt by art what nature denied – and to trifle away the Emperor's resources. (2) They promised to dig a navigable canal from Lake Avernus to Ostia, along barren coast or else through mountain barriers, with nothing to generate water except the Pomptine marshes; the rest was steep and dry, and, if pierceable, the effort was unendurable and the reason insufficient. Nero, however, coveting the incredible, endeavoured to excavate the ridge nearest Avernus. Traces of his vain hope remain.)

43. The parts of Rome beyond Nero's residence were not, as after the Gallic fires, built abutting or everywhere, but with streets laid out, major roads wide and buildings restricted as to height, supplied with courtyards and fronted with colonnades as protection for the blocks. (2) These colonnades Nero promised to finance; also to clear sites before releasing them to owners. He added incentives proportional to class and resources, and set a deadline by which to claim them with completed houses and apartment blocks. (3) He assigned Ostia's

marshes for the rubble: ships ferrying grain up the Tiber were to go downstream rubble-laden. The buildings themselves were to be supported in fixed measure by Gabian or Alban stone – impervious to fire – not timbers. (4) To ensure that water, formerly waylaid by individuals' licence, flow for public use more abundantly and in more places, there were to be overseers. And everyone was to have available fire-fighting supplies. No more party-walls: each building was to be enclosed by its own. (5) The measures adopted for utility's sake brought beauty, too, to the new city. Some people, nevertheless, believed the old configuration more healthful, since narrow streets and tall buildings were less penetrable to the sun's combustion, whereas now wide openings protected by no shade sweltered in more oppressive heat.

44. Such were the provisions of human design. Later, atonements were sought, with consultation of the Sibyl's books.[54] From which came supplications addressed to Vulcan, Ceres and Proserpina, and Juno was propitiated by matrons, first at the Capitoline, thereafter at the closest shore. (Water from here was sprinkled on the temple and the goddess's statue, and ritual banquets and vigils were enacted by those still married.)

(2) But it was not within human power, either by princely outlay or divine appeasement, to remove the shame. *The fire was ordered*, people believed. To destroy this rumour Nero supplied as perpetrators, and executed with elaborate punishments, people popularly called Christians, hated for their perversions. (3) (The name's source was one Christus, executed by the governor Pontius Pilatus when Tiberius held power. The pernicious creed, suppressed at the time, was bursting forth again, not only in Judaea, where this evil originated, but even in Rome, into which from all directions everything appalling and shameful flows and foregathers.) (4) At first, those who confessed were arrested. Then, on their evidence, a huge multitude was convicted, less for the crime of fire than for hatred of humankind. Their deaths were accompanied by derision: covered in animal skins they were to perish torn by dogs, or affixed to crosses to be burnt for nocturnal illumination when light faded. (5) Nero offered his park for the show and staged

games in the Circus, mixing with the crowd in the garb of a driver or riding a chariot. This roused pity. Guilty and deserving of extreme measures though they were, the Christians' annihilation seemed to arise not from public utility but for one man's brutality.

45. The collection of monies caused havoc in Italy and ruin for provinces, allied peoples and so-called 'free cities'. Even gods became booty. Rome's temples were stripped, emptied of the gold that every generation of the Roman people had consecrated, in triumphs and in vows, when thriving or in fear. (2) Across Asia and Greece, however, not offerings only but the gods' statues themselves were hauled away. (To these provinces were sent Acratus and Secundus Carrinas. The former was a freedman ready for any enormity; the latter, trained in Greek philosophy so far as talk went, had not clothed his soul in rectitude.) (3) Seneca, it was said, pleaded for a distant country retreat to deflect antipathy for the sacrilege. This not being granted, with a fiction of ill health – a muscular complaint – he kept to his chamber. According to some sources, Seneca escaped a poison prepared for him by his own freedman Cleonicus on Nero's order, owing either to the freedman's perfidy or to habitual fearfulness. (Seneca supported life with a very plain diet: wild fruit and, if thirst prompted, spring water.)

46. In this same period gladiators at Praeneste, attempting a breakout, were checked by their military guard. Spartacus[55] and other troubles of old were the subject of popular talk: revolution was both desired and feared. (2) Soon thereafter the navy suffered a calamity. Not in wartime – hardly ever was peace so untroubled. Nero had ordered the fleet to return to Campania by a fixed day, without provision for the sea's uncertainties. The pilots, therefore, despite a wild ocean, moved out from Formiae. Driven against the coast near Cumae by a hard south-westerly as they strove to pass Cape Misenum, they lost many warships and a host of lesser vessels.

47. To conclude the year: widespread portents announced impending evils. There was lightning's violence in unwonted frequency, plus a comet, something always expiated by noble blood.[56] Two-headed human and other animal births were

exposed or discovered during rites in which it is the custom to sacrifice pregnant victims. (2) Near Placentia a calf born beside the road reportedly had a head on its leg. (Subsequent interpretation by haruspices was: *Another head is being readied for human affairs, neither strong nor secret, since the creature was quashed in the womb and birthed by the roadside.*)

48. (65 CE) Then began the consular year of Silius Nerva and Vestinus Atticus, with a quick-growing conspiracy in which senators, equestrian-ranked, soldiers and even women vied to enlist, from both hatred of Nero and favour towards Gaius Piso.

(2) By birth a Calpurnius, and including in his lineage many eminent families through his father's noble birth, Piso was a popular celebrity for his virtue – or qualities that looked like virtues: (3) eloquence in defence of fellow citizens, generosity towards friends, and even for strangers a friendly word and presence. He had Fortune's gifts, too, being tall and good-looking. Seriousness of character and thrift in pleasure were absent: he favoured leniency and magnificence and occasionally dissipation. This was widely approved: so sweet are their vices that people want a government neither disciplined nor overly severe.

49. The conspiracy did not begin from Piso's desire. Nor would I find it easy to record who caused or at whose instigation was roused what so many sustained. (2) The most stalwart were Subrius Flavus, a Guard officer, and the centurion Sulpicius Asper, as their deaths' constancy showed. (3) Lucan and Plautius Lateranus wielded lively hatreds. Lucan's grievance had personal causes: Nero was limiting his poems' fame and had forbidden their display, vainly thinking to match him. Not injury but love of country made consul-designate Lateranus an ally. (4) Flavius Scaevinus and Afranius Quintianus, senators both, and contrary to their reputations, headed the momentous act. Scaevinus' intellect was slack with dissipation, his life languid with sleep. Quintianus, notoriously soft and vilified by Nero's abusive poem, intended to avenge the insult.

50. The Emperor's crimes, his rule's end, the necessity of choosing a champion for a weary world – airing such things amongst themselves or with friends, they recruited Claudius

Senecio, Cervarius Proculus, Vulcacius Araricus, Julius Auguri-
nus, Munatius Gratus, Antonius Natalis, Marcius Festus,
equestrian-ranked all. (2) Of these, Senecio was particularly
intimate with Nero[57] – he kept up the appearance of friendship
even then – and for this reason hounded by many dangers.
Natalis shared Piso's every secret. The rest had expectations
from revolution. (3) Enlisted, too, was military support in addition to the aforementioned Subrius and Sulpicius: Gavius
Silvanus and Statius Proxumus, Guard tribunes, and Maximus
Scaurus and Venetus Paulus, centurions. But the stoutest prop
appeared to be the Guard commander Faenius Rufus. Celebrated in conduct and repute, he was losing ground to
Tigellinus'[58] brutality and shamelessness in Nero's esteem. Tigellinus belaboured Nero with accusations and often left him
scared. *Rufus was Agrippina's lover and, missing her, is intent
on revenge.*

(4) Trusting from Rufus' own repeated utterance that even
the Guard commander was on their side, the conspirators considered more readily the time and place for killing. Subrius
Flavus was said to have urged attacking as Nero was singing on
stage or when he was making nocturnal excursions[59] unguarded.
The latter's attraction was solitude, the former's the crowd
itself, a most beautiful witness to so glorious an act – except for
the restraint imposed by the desire to avoid punishment, which
always blocks great undertakings.[60]

51. The conspirators were hesitating and postponing hope
and fear. A woman named Epicharis – how she found out is
uncertain; she never before cared about probity – began to
incite and chide. Finally, impatient with their slowness, and
being in Campania, she attempted to undermine the top men of
the Misenum fleet and to involve them in complicity, beginning
as follows.

(2) A fleet captain, Volusius Proculus,[61] having assisted in
dispatching Nero's mother, had not, he thought, been promoted
in accordance with that crime's magnitude. He was either
known to Epicharis before, or newly a friend. He divulged what
he did for Nero and how useless it proved, adding complaints
and an intention of revenge should opportunity arise. This gave

hope that he could be set moving and win others over. And the fleet would be useful, its opportunities numerous, since Nero liked to enjoy the sea at Puteoli and Misenum. (3) Therefore Epicharis went further, listing all the Emperor's crimes. *The senate has no resources left, but provision has been made to punish Nero for ruining the state, if only you gird yourself to the task and bring your staunchest soldiers onto our side. You can expect suitable reward.* She did not, however, name the conspirators. (4) Proculus' evidence was therefore useless, although he reported to Nero what he had heard. Epicharis, summoned and confronted with the informer, easily refuted him. *He is sustained by no witnesses!* But she was kept in custody, Nero suspecting that Proculus' words were not false, though not proven true.

52. Troubled by fear of betrayal, the conspirators decided to achieve the killing at Baiae in Piso's villa, the pleasure of which often made Nero a visitor. And frequenting bath and banquet he did without retinue and imperial trappings. But Piso refused, alleging antipathy if the inviolable custom of the table and the gods of hospitality were bloodied by the killing of an emperor, however bad. *Better at Rome in that hateful house built on citizen spoils, or in public, to accomplish a deed undertaken on public behalf.* (2) Thus in meetings. Privately he worried, lest Lucius Silanus, a man raised to the highest renown by noble birth and Gaius Cassius'[62] upbringing – he was educated in Cassius' house – seize power. *People will offer it readily, those not involved in the conspiracy, pitying a Nero criminally killed.* (3) Many believed that Piso shunned the consul Vestinus, too, an unbending man, lest he rise for freedom or choose another emperor and bestow the state on him. For Vestinus had no part in the conspiracy, although Nero used this charge, too, to satisfy a long-standing hatred for an innocent man.

53. Finally they set a day of Circus games in honour of Ceres for accomplishing their design. Nero, rarely emergent and closeted in house and park, did attend competitions in the Circus and was easier of access because of his happiness at the show. (2) The plot was to proceed thus: Lateranus, ready with a plea, ostensibly for financial assistance, would fall at the Emperor's

knees, trip and pin him unsuspecting. (The man was stout of heart and huge.) As Nero was lying caught, officers and centurions, whoever dared, would run up and strike. Scaevinus demanded the lead. He had retrieved a dagger from the Temple of Well-Being – or, in other accounts, from the Temple of Fortune at Ferentum – and treated it as if consecrated to a great task. (3) Meanwhile Piso would be waiting at the Temple of Ceres, from where the Guard commander Rufus and others would summon and escort him to the barracks. Claudius' daughter Antonia would go along to win the crowd's favour, so Pliny says. (4) (My intention is not to conceal anything with any authority, even if it seems preposterous[63] that Antonia lent her name to vain hope or danger, or that Piso, known for love of his wife, committed himself to a new marriage – unless desire for rule is of all emotions the most devouring.)

54. It was remarkable how, with reticence among a group diverse by rank, age and sex, rich and poor, everything was kept close, until betrayal began in Scaevinus' household. The day before the ambush Scaevinus conversed long with Antonius Natalis, then returned home and sealed his will. Taking from its sheath the aforementioned dagger and complaining that it was blunt with age, he ordered it sharpened. *The point must shine!* The job was entrusted to his freedman Milichus. (2) Scaevinus' dinner that night was more lavish than usual. Favourite slaves were given, some of them, freedom, others money. He himself was gloomy and visibly engrossed in thought, although with wandering talk he feigned happiness. (3) Finally, he ordered[64] the preparation of wound-bindings and what would staunch bleeding, and gave the instructions to this same Milichus, a man either aware of the plot and hitherto trustworthy, or ignorant and only then conscious of suspicion, as most say. For when the servile mind calculated the rewards of perfidy – he envisaged vast sums and power – propriety succumbed, as did his patron's well-being and the memory of freedom received. Milichus sought his wife's advice, too, which was female and worse, in that she also excited fear: *Many freedmen and slaves are present and see the same things. The*

silence of one will serve no purpose, but one will have the
rewards – the one who arrives first with information.

55. At dawn Milichus went to the Servilian Gardens. Turned
away at the door, he insisted that his news was important and
alarming, and was escorted by doorkeepers to Nero's freedman
Epaphroditus[65] and from there quickly to Nero. He told of
pressing danger, powerful conspirators and the rest of what he
had heard or conjectured. He showed the weapon prepared for
Nero's assassination and ordered that the defendant be summoned. (2) Scaevinus, abducted by soldiers, spoke his defence:
The weapon of which I am accused is an object of family cult
stored in my bedroom, stolen for the freedman's fabrication.
The tablets of my will are sealed quite often, without reference
to particular days. Money and freedom, too, have been given to
slaves before. I do so more generously now because, with
scanty holdings and creditors pressing, I don't trust testament-
ary arrangements. (3) *I always spread a generous board: it is a*
pleasant life, viewed by harsh judges with some disfavour.
Bandages? Not by my order. Since the other, public, imput-
ations are baseless, Milichus has attached a charge with himself
as equally informer and witness. (4) Words that Scaevinus reinforced with constancy, scolding – *Useless! Scoundrel!* – with so
much confidence of voice and mien that the indictment would
have foundered except for Milichus' wife's reminder: *Antonius*
Natalis often spoke secretly with Scaevinus, and both are Piso's
intimates.

56. Natalis was therefore summoned and each was interro-
gated separately. *What was that discussion of yours, what*
about? Suspicion arose when their answers weren't congruent.
Shackled, with torture in view and threatened, they capitulated,
(2) Natalis first, who was the more knowledgeable about the
whole conspiracy and therefore a cleverer accuser.[66] He spoke
first about Piso, then added Seneca. (Perhaps Natalis was a go-
between for Seneca and Piso, or perhaps he was after thanks
from Nero, who was hostile to Seneca and looking for any tac-
tic to crush him.) (3) Learning of Natalis' indictment, Scaevinus,
too, being equally feeble, or, believing that everything was

revealed and there was no advantage in silence, exposed the rest. (4) Of these, Lucan, Quintianus and Senecio long denied. Afterwards they were seduced by promised impunity and in order to excuse their tardiness Lucan named his own mother Acilia, Quintianus named Glitius Gallus, and Senecio named Annius Pollio, their closest friends.

57. Nero, remembering Epicharis detained on Proculus' evidence and thinking a woman's body unequal to pain, ordered torture. But neither whips nor fire nor the ever sharper anger of her tormentors – *We will not be scorned by a woman!* – overcame her denial. Thus was the inquisition's first day flouted. (2) When she was being dragged back the next day for the same torments – she was conveyed by carrying-chair, unable to stand on limbs undone – tying the band from her chest like a noose to the chair's frame, she inserted her neck and by applying her body's weight blocked her now scanty breath. She was an example all the brighter, a freedwoman in such straits, aiming to protect people not hers, practically strangers, when freeborn men[67] of equestrian and senatorial rank, untouched by torture, betrayed each his dearest ties.

58. Lucan, too, and Senecio and Quintianus kept exposing accomplices everywhere, and Nero was more and more frightened, although he surrounded himself with multiplied guards. (2) Indeed Rome herself – with walls held by military units, sea and river occupied – was practically his prisoner. Rushing everywhere through city squares, through houses, fields and the nearest towns, were soldiers on foot and horse, Germans included, whom the Emperor trusted as outsiders. (3) Shackled columns were dragged without cease to lie at the Gardens' gate. When they entered to speak, the 'charges' were not only support for conspirators,[68] but also chance conversations and unforeseen encounters, or if they were at a party or entered a show together. In addition to cruel questions put by Nero and Tigellinus, Faenius Rufus, too, made violent attacks. Not yet named by informants, and to create belief in his ignorance he was ruthless towards his allies. (4) With Subrius Flavus at his side and signalling – *Shall I draw my sword during the trial itself and accomplish the killing?* – he shook his head and

checked Flavus' impulse when he was already moving hand to hilt.

59. After the conspiracy was betrayed, while Milichus was being heard and Scaevinus hesitated, some urged Piso to head to the barracks or mount the Rostra and test the support of soldiers and populace. *If people aware of your attempt muster, even strangers will follow. An uprising's rumour is vast and rumour is of great avail to revolutionary plans.* (2) *Nero has no provision against these. Even brave men panic at the unexpected. Surely that thespian, along no doubt with Tigellinus and his whores, won't rouse weapons against you! Many things are accomplished by trying, toilsome though they seem to the indolent.* (3) *It is misguided to hope for silence and loyalty of mind and body among so many conspirators. With torture or reward, everything is permeable. Men are coming to bind you, too, and later, to inflict a humiliating murder. With how much more praise will you perish while embracing the public good, while summoning help for liberty! Soldiers may fail you, the plebs may forsake you, provided that your death – if life be taken early – wins approbation from your ancestors and your descendants.* (4) Piso was unmoved by these words and stayed only briefly in public. Afterwards, hidden at home, he braced his mind against the end until a group of soldiers arrived. (Nero chose recruits or recent servicemen, fearing veterans as favour-tainted.)[69] (5) Piso died with his arm veins ruptured. His will, with its shameful flatteries of Nero, was a concession to love for his wife, whom he had detached, worthless and recommended by bodily beauty alone, from marriage to a friend. (The woman's name was Satria Galla, her former husband's, Domitius Silus. He by passivity, she being shameless spread Piso's disrepute.)

60. As the next murder Nero arranged Plautius Lateranus', the consul-elect, in great haste: no embracing of children, no free and quick choice of death was permitted. Hurried to the place of slave execution, Lateranus was slain by the hand of the officer Statius Proxumus. Replete with steadfast silence, Lateranus did not charge him with like complicity.

(2) Next came the killing of Seneca, a great happiness to the

Emperor, not because he knew him a conspirator, but to get at him with sword, poison having disappointed.[70] (3) Only Natalis divulged Seneca's name, and only so far. *I was sent to visit an ailing Seneca and remonstrate: 'Why do you keep Piso away? Better to exercise friendship with familiar concourse!' Seneca responded that conversational exchange and frequent discussion served neither man, but that his own well-being depended on Piso's safety.* (4) The Guard officer Gavius Silvanus was ordered to take this statement and ask whether Seneca acknowledged Natalis' words and his own replies. By chance, or perhaps well-knowing, Seneca had returned from Campania that day, stopping in a suburban property four miles from Rome. Silvanus arrived near evening and surrounded the villa with groups of soldiers. Seneca was at dinner with his wife Pompeia Paulina and two friends when Silvanus revealed Nero's instructions.

61. Seneca's response: *Natalis was sent to me and remonstrated on Piso's account that he was kept from visiting me, and I gave considerations of health and love of repose as excuse. I have no reason to privilege a private person's safety over my well-being, nor is my character inclined to flattery, as is familiar to no one more than Nero, who has more often experienced from me liberty than servility.* (2) At this report, given in the presence of Poppaea and Tigellinus – innermost council for an emperor infuriate – Nero asked whether Seneca was preparing voluntary death. Silvanus: *There were no signs of panic, nothing gloomy was detected in word or look.* He was ordered back to dictate death. (3) Fabius Rusticus reports that the return route was different; that Silvanus detoured to Rufus, his commander, and having revealed Nero's orders asked whether to obey. And was advised by Rufus to carry on – inevitable and universal cowardice. (4) For Silvanus, too, was one of the conspirators and augmented the crimes to whose punishment he had agreed.[71] Silvanus spared himself, however, speech and sight of Seneca, sending in one of the centurions to announce the inevitable end.

62. Seneca, undismayed, called for his will. At the centurion's refusal he turned to his friends. *Prevented from rendering*

*thanks for your services, I leave you my one last – and most
beautiful! – possession: the cast of my life. Mindful of this, you
will have rectitude's renown as reward for so constant a friendship.* (2) Their tears he recalled to firmness, now by conversation,
now more forcefully, like someone applying the bit. *Where are
philosophy's teachings, where is reason's response to the future
looming, pondered over so many years? Who is not familiar
with Nero's brutality? Nothing remains after murdered mother
and brother but to add the slaughter of teacher and guide to the
heap!*

63. After these and like words for the world, so to speak, he
embraced his wife and, relenting a little from present fortitude,
asked and pleaded that she refrain from a burden of perpetual
grief.[72] *In contemplation of a well-lived life, endure your longing for your husband with honourable consolations.* She
answered, *Death is my intent, too,* and demanded the killer's
stroke. (2) Seneca, who was not opposed to her glory and was
also moved by love – he did not want to abandon to harm a
woman singularly esteemed – said: 'To life's comforts I would
have pointed you, but you prefer death's honour. I will not
begrudge you a name. In this brave death, constancy may
belong equally to both, but in your end there is more renown.'

Thereafter, with a single stroke of the sword, they let flow
their arms. (3) Seneca, since his aged body, attenuated by scanty
diet, gave slow release to blood, ruptured his shin and knee
veins, too. Worn out by cruel pains, lest he damage his wife's
courage with his suffering or himself lapse into intolerance in
the presence of her torments he persuaded her to withdraw into
another room. Eloquence was at his disposal even in his final
moments. Summoning scribes, he imparted to them much that,
given to the public in his own words, I forbear to recast.

64. Nero, having no hatred for Paulina, and lest antipathy
for his cruelty grow, kept her from death. At the soldiers' urging, slaves and freedmen bound her arms and stopped the
blood – she perhaps unconscious. (2) People being inclined to
the worse, some believed that as long as she feared Nero
implacable, she sought the fame of a death allied to her husband's, but was later – gentler hope on offer – overcome by

life's allurements. She added a few years in praiseworthy remembrance of her husband, face and limbs white to a pallor that showed much of her vital spirit to have been removed.

(3) Seneca, with death still dragging and slow, requested that Statius Annaeus, a man long valued for loyal friendship and medical art, supply the poison prepared earlier – *The poison by which those condemned in Athens' court*[73] *are deprived of life.* It was brought, but Seneca took it in vain, cold already in limb, his body closed to poison's power. (4) Finally he entered a hot bath. Sprinkling the nearest slaves, he added: *This liquid is libation to Jupiter Liberator.* Conveyed thence to a sauna, he expired in its heat and was cremated without funeral. Thus he prescribed in his will, for even when vastly wealthy and vastly powerful he took thought for his end.

65. Word was that Subrius Flavus and his centurions planned in secret, but with Seneca's knowledge, that after Nero was dispatched with Piso's help, Piso, too, would be killed and power handed to Seneca. With his virtues' renown Seneca was the choice of innocent men, they thought, for the highest eminence. Indeed there was even a saying of Flavus': *It makes no difference to our shame if a lyre-player is removed and a tragic actor succeeds him.* (Nero sang to the cithara, likewise Piso in tragic costume.)

66. The military conspiracy, too, eventually came to light, once informants were provoked to betray Faenius Rufus. It was intolerable to have the same man as accomplice and inquisitor! As Rufus pressed and threatened, Scaevinus, smiling back, said: *No one knows more than you!* And urged: *Repay our fine emperor's favour!* (2) Neither speech nor silence was Rufus' response to this – he kept swallowing his words and was obviously afraid. Since the rest, especially the equestrian-ranked Cervarius Proculus, were pressing to show him guilty, at a word from Nero to Cassius, a soldier present for his remarkable strength, Rufus was seized and shackled.

67. On information from these same people the tribune Subrius Flavus was overset. At first he adduced character difference in defence: *A man of arms would not ally himself to unarmed effeminates for a deed of such enormity!* Under pressure, he

embraced confession's glory. (2) Questioned by Nero about what led him to forget his oath: 'I hated you. No soldier was more faithful while you deserved to be loved. I began to hate you when you revealed yourself as killer of mother and wife, charioteer and actor and incendiary.' (3) (I have related Flavus' own words, since unlike Seneca's they have not been made public, and it is equally proper that a military man's sentiments be known, uncouth and strong. Clearly nothing in that conspiracy fell harder than this on the ears of a Nero ready for criminal action, but unaccustomed to hearing how he was acting.) (4) Flavus' execution was entrusted to the officer Veianius Niger. In a nearby field Niger ordered a pit dug, which Flavus criticized as shallow and narrow. 'Not even this,' he said to the surrounding soldiers, 'is according to code.' Advised to extend his neck bravely, he said, 'May you strike as bravely!' Niger was shaking. Since it took him two blows to behead Flavus, barely, he boasted to Nero of his brutality, declaring Flavus killed with a blow-and-a-half.

68. The next example of constancy was offered by the centurion Sulpicius Asper. Nero asked why he conspired to kill him and Asper replied briefly: *For transgressions so numerous it was the only possible relief*. Punishment was then ordered and met. Nor did other centurions prove decadent in suffering. But Faenius Rufus' courage was no match. He piled his lamentations even onto his will.

(2) Nero expected the consul Vestinus to be drawn into the allegations, thinking him violent and hostile. But the conspirators had not involved Vestinus in their plans, some owing to long-standing disputes, more because they believed him impetuous and aloof. (3) (Nero's hatred for Vestinus began in close companionship, Vestinus knowing well and despising the Emperor's cowardice; Nero afraid of his friend's spirit, having often been the butt of sharp-edged humour, which when largely grounded in truth leaves a painful memory. An additional reason recently was that Vestinus married Statilia Messalina,[74] though aware that her adulterers included even Nero.)

69. There being neither charge nor accuser, Nero was unable to don the appearance of a judge. Turning, accordingly, to the

power of mastery, he dispatched the officer Gerellanus with a cohort of soldiers. He ordered him to anticipate the consul's attempts, to seize his 'citadel', to crush his 'picked men'. (Vestinus had a residence overlooking the Forum and attractive slaves all of an age.) (2) Vestinus had completed all consular duties that day and was hosting a party, either fearing nothing or to conceal fear. Then soldiers entered and said he was summoned by their commander. Not delaying, he rose and everything happened at once: bedroom door shut, doctor present, veins cut. Vestinus was carried to the bath still living and sunk in hot water. Not a word of self-pity was uttered. (3) Surrounded meanwhile by a guard, his guests were held until late at night, when their panic – they expected destruction after dinner and Nero laughed to imagine it – was, Nero said, *Sufficient punishment for dining with a consul*.

70. Next Nero commanded Lucan's killing. Blood was flowing, and Lucan perceived his feet and hands cold and life leaving his extremities, while his core was still warm and lucid. Remembering a poem in which he had related a wounded soldier dead by a death like this, he spoke the very verses[75] and these were his last words. (2) Senecio perished next, and Quintianus[76] and Scaevinus, quite unlike their former soft lives, and soon the rest of the conspirators, without deed or word needing record.

71. Rome was replete with deaths, the Capitoline with offerings. Some had had a son killed, others a brother or relative or friend, yet they thanked the gods, trimmed their houses with laurel, fell at Nero's knees and wearied his hand with kisses. Believing this to be joy, he repaid the swift evidence of Natalis and Proculus with a grant of impunity. Milichus, enriched by his rewards, adopted the name 'Saviour', using the Greek term.[77] (2) Of the tribunes, Gavius Silanus, though absolved, fell by his own hand. Statius Proxumus, obtaining pardon from the Emperor, spoiled it by the nullity of his end.[78] Officers relieved of duty were Pompeius * * *,[79] Cornelius Martialis, Flavius Nepos, Statius Domitius; though not hostile to Nero, they were thought to be. (3) Novius Priscus, on account of his friendship with Seneca, and Glitius Gallus and Annius Pollio,[80]

who were both impugned rather than convicted, were granted exile. Priscus was accompanied by his wife Artoria Flaccilla, Gallus by Egnatia Maximilla. (Maximilla's property – great at first and untouched, later confiscated – twice increased her glory.) (4) Removal of Rufrius Crispinus,[81] too, was occasioned by the conspiracy. Nero hated him because of his former marriage to Poppaea. Verginius Flavus and Musonius Rufus were banished for their renown. (Verginius encouraged the enthusiasms of the young with his eloquence; Musonius with his philosophical teachings.) To fill out the column, so to speak,[82] Cluvidienus Quietus, Julius Agrippa, Blitius Catulinus, Petronius Priscus, Julius Altinus, were allotted Aegean islands. (5) Caedicia, Scaevinus' wife, and Caesennius Maximus were simply banned from Italy, only discovering the charge from the sentence. Lucan's mother Acilia – with no acquittal and no punishment – was ignored.

72. After these matters were settled and Nero had addressed the soldiers, he distributed 2,000 coins per man[83] to the regulars, plus free grain. (Formerly they got the subsidy.) Then, as if to expound deeds of war, he summoned the senate and awarded honorary triumphs to Petronius Turpilianus, an ex-consul, Cocceius Nerva,[84] a praetor-designate, and Tigellinus, a Guard commander, so exalting Tigellinus and Nerva that in addition to triumphal statues in the Forum he placed their likenesses on the Palatine. An honorary consulship was decreed for Nymphidius.

((2) He comes up first now. I will go back briefly: he, too, will be part of Rome's disasters. Born from a freedwoman mother who shared an attractive body among the imperial household's slaves and freedmen, Nymphidius claimed descent from Gaius. Either he was built tall and grim-faced[85] by chance, or Gaius, lusting even after whores, molested this man's mother, too.)

73. Nero, after his senate speech, combined a public announcement with evidence collected in book form and the confessions of the condemned. He was galled by popular talk that out of envy and fear he was eliminating even innocent men. (2) But there was no doubt about the conspiracy's beginning,

growth and substantiation – at least for anyone concerned to learn the truth – and it was affirmed by those who returned to Rome after Nero's death. (3) In the senate, with all the most grief-stricken stooping to flattery, Junius Gallio, frightened by his brother Seneca's death and pleading for security, was berated by Salienus Clemens – *Public enemy! Parricide!* – until senatorial consensus deterred Clemens. *Don't give the impression of turning public misfortune into an opportunity for private hatred, or reverse matters settled or suppressed by the Emperor's mildness into new brutality.*

74. Gifts and thanksgivings to the gods were decreed, with particular honour to Sol, for whose ancient temple in the Circus the crime was planned. *By his divine power the conspiracy's secrets were revealed.* There were more horse races for the Circus games at the Cerealia; the name 'Neroneus' for the month of April; a temple to 'Well-Being' to be erected where Scaevinus got his dagger. (2) Nero himself dedicated the dagger in the Capitoline temple with inscription *to Jupiter Vindex (the Avenger)* – something hardly noticed at the time, but after Vindex' war[86] it was taken as sign prophetic of future vengeance. (3) I find in the senate's records that the consul-designate Anicius Cerealis recommended that a temple to 'Nero the god' be established at public expense as soon as possible, which he proposed 'for one who has exceeded mortal limit and deserves men's veneration',[87] but that Nero blocked it lest in the interpretation of some it become an omen of his end, since divinity is not applied to the Emperor until his life among men has ceased.

BOOK 16

1. (65 CE continued) After this, Fortune toyed with Nero, aided by his vanity and the promises of Caesellius Bassus. Carthaginian in origin, of troubled mind, Bassus turned a vision from night-time repose into hope bordering on certainty. He went to Rome, bought access to the Emperor, told his story: *A discovery on my property! A cave, immensely deep, with a great quantity of gold inside, not in money form but of clumsy ancient mass.* (2) *Heavy gold bars are lying there, with rods of gold standing elsewhere, objects long concealed to increase present prosperity! Phoenician Dido* – this was his supposition – *a refugee from Tyre, once Carthage was founded, hid those resources lest the new people riot with excessive wealth, or the kings of Numidia, already hostile on other grounds, from greed for her gold be roused to war.*

2. Nero, instead of scrutinizing the reliability of teller or tale, and sending no one to verify, himself magnified the rumour and sent men to bring him 'his' prize. He supplied warships and chosen oarsmen to improve their speed. People talked of nothing else in those days, the crowd crediting the story, the insightful taking a different line. (2) It chanced that the festival celebrating Nero's second five-year period was then under way. For speakers this was panegyric's principal theme. *The earth is yielding not only ordinary crops and ore-encumbered gold, but is bountiful with novel fertility! The gods set wealth before your feet!* and so on, with slavish fictions of the highest eloquence and equal flattery from men confident of their listener's easy belief.

3. Nero's extravagance meanwhile multiplied from vain

hope. Present funds were being spent as if funds in prospect would allow many years' prodigality. Indeed, he was already spending freely from these: the expectation of riches contributed to state impoverishment. (2) Bassus' property and wide fields around it were dug up, while he was asserting that here or there was the promised cave. Nero's soldiers followed him, as did a crowd of country folk hired for digging. Eventually, after shedding his delusion and surprised that his dreams, heretofore reliable, had now deceived him, Bassus fled shame and fear by voluntary death. Some sources said he was arrested and soon released, his property confiscated in place of royal treasure.

4. The senate, to avoid shame at the upcoming festival contests, offered Nero victory for song, and added the crown for eloquence, hoping to veil competition's degradation.[1] (2) But Nero insisted: *I require from the senate neither backing nor clout. I am on equal footing with my rivals and will gain due praise from the judges' integrity.* Then he delivered a poem from the stage. (3) When the crowd urged him to make his every endeavour known – these were their words – he entered the theatre obedient to music's rules: no sitting when tired, no wiping sweat except with one's garment, no visible excretions from mouth or nose. (4) Knee bent, he saluted the audience and awaited the judges' decision with pretended anxiety. The city populace, accustomed to cheering the performances even of actors, responded noisily with their regular acclamations and pre-arranged applause. You would have thought them enjoying themselves – and perhaps they *were* enjoying themselves, careless of public disgrace.

5. People from distant towns and parts of Italy still austere and retentive of ancient custom, and people from far provinces – unfamiliar with frivolity, they had come for public embassies or private profit – found the spectacle intolerable and failed at their dishonourable task: they grew weary of clapping unpractised hands, disrupted seasoned spectators and earned blows from the soldiers stationed in the seating to prevent a moment's time passing with half-hearted cheering or lazy silence. (2) Persons of equestrian rank, it was known, were

crushed, struggling through the narrow entrances with the
advancing multitude. Others, joining day to night in their seats,
fell prey to fatal illness: the dread of missing the show weighed
heavier, since there were people – many openly, more hidden –
scrutinizing names and faces, also enthusiasm or gloom. (3)
Punishments were immediately ordained for the less prominent. Hostility to notables was ignored for the moment, but
eventually discharged. People used to say that Vespasian,
berated by the freedman Phoebus for nodding off, and shielded
with difficulty by superiors' pleas, escaped imminent ruin by
his greater fate.

6. After the festival's conclusion Poppaea met her end from
a chance outburst of her husband's rage: though pregnant, she
felt his foot strike. I am not inclined to believe in poison, as
some writers transmit – more out of hatred than reliably. For
Nero wanted children and was smitten with his wife. (2) Her
body was not cremated the Roman way, but in the practice of
foreign royalty was embalmed and placed in the Mausoleum.
She did receive a public funeral, however. Nero himself pronounced the eulogy from the Rostra, praising her beauty and the
fact that she was the parent of a divine child, plus other things –
Fortune's gifts rather than virtues.

7. Poppaea's death was, in public, a sad event. A happy one,
however, in view of her shamelessness and brutality. Nero
brought hatred to full measure by excluding Gaius Cassius
from her funeral, a first indication of danger. This was not long
delayed, and Lucius Silanus was added. There was no crime,
except that Cassius, for old money and sober character, and
Silanus, for family renown and disciplined vigour, stood out.
(2) In a speech sent to the senate Nero argued that both should
be removed from public life. His accusation? *Cassius venerates
among his ancestor masks a portrait of Cassius inscribed
'leader of his party'! Seeds of civil war and defection from the
house of the Caesars are obviously his aim, and lest he have
only a hated name's memory to produce disaffection he has
recruited Silanus – a man noble in birth, uncompromising in
spirit – as revolution's figurehead.*

8. Nero berated Silanus as he had Silanus' uncle Torquatus.[2]

*You are arranging imperial concerns and appointing freedmen
to secretariats of accounts, petitions and correspondence!*
Empty accusations and false, for fear made Silanus quite alert
once he was terrified by his uncle's destruction into precaution.
(2) People were brought in as 'witnesses' to fabricate charges
against Lepida – Cassius' wife, Silanus' aunt – incest with her
brother's son, and ghastly rites. (3) Incriminated as accomplices
were Volcacius Tertullinus and Cornelius Marcellus, both senators, and equestrian-ranked Calpurnius Fabatus.[3] These
avoided instant condemnation by appealing to the Emperor,
and since Nero was preoccupied by major offences they got off
as insignificant.

9. Cassius and Silanus were exiled by senatorial decree.
About Lepida? *Nero should decide.* Cassius was transported to
Sardinia – they counted on old age. Silanus was taken to Ostia
as if for a voyage to Naxos, later imprisoned in an Apulian
town called Bari. (2) There he endured undeserved misfortune
philosophically, until taken charge of by the centurion sent to
kill him. Urged to rupture his veins, he replied: *I intend to die,
but I refuse to spare my killer the glory of his task.* The centurion, seeing Silanus, though unarmed, very strong and more
angry than frightened, ordered his soldiers to hold him. Silanus
kept struggling and striking back, insofar as he could bare-
handed, until he fell to the centurion with frontal wounds, as in
battle.

10. Almost immediately Lucius Vetus,[4] his mother-in-law
Sextia and his daughter Antistia Pollitta[5] succumbed to slaughter. They were hated by Nero: *By living they reproach me with
the murder of Rubellius Plautus.*[6] (Plautus was Vetus' son-in-
law.) (2) Occasion for disclosing Nero's brutality came from
Vetus' freedman Fortunatus: after pocketing his patron's property he turned accuser. (Fortunatus' associate was Claudius
Demianus, imprisoned for depravity by Vetus when governor
of Asia. Nero released him as accusation's reward.) When the
defendant saw himself and a former slave arrayed on equal
terms, he left for his estate at Formiae. Soldiers established a
secret cordon. (3) With him was his daughter, a formidable
woman, above and beyond the approaching danger, with her

long sorrow from seeing her husband Plautus' killers. (She had embraced his bleeding trunk and still preserved the bloodied clothing, a widow unkempt from constant grief, no food but to keep death at bay.) (4) Now she went to Naples at her father's urging. Prevented from approaching Nero, she beleaguered his sorties – *Hear an innocent man! Don't put your consular colleague into freedman hands!* – sometimes with female wailing, occasionally exceeding her sex and shouting abuse, until the Emperor showed himself equally unmoved by entreaties and resentment.

11. She told her father to discard hope and make use of the inevitable. Word arrived that a senate trial was being arranged, and a stern verdict. Some advised Vetus: *Name Nero your principal heir[7] and thereby provide for your grandchildren from the remainder*. Scorning this, lest he stain a life lived very nearly in liberty by terminal servility Vetus bestowed his ready money on his slaves and ordered each to take for himself whatever could be carried away, leaving only three small couches for the end. (2) Then – same room, same blade – they cut their veins and were quickly carried to the bath wearing each a single garment, modesty's due. Father gazed upon daughter, grandmother on granddaughter, she upon both. They vied in praying for a swift exit for their departing souls, and to leave their loved ones as survivors soon to die. Fortune kept order: the older failed soonest, then she whose life began the last. (3) Accusation followed burial, as did a decree of punishment according to ancestral custom. Nero interceded, permitting voluntary death. These mockeries accrued with the killing already accomplished.

12. The equestrian-ranked Publius Gallus was banished from Italy as an intimate of Faenius Rufus[8] and a connection of Vetus. Vetus' freedman prosecutor received as reward[9] for his work a theatre seat with the tribunes' staff. (2) The months following April – it was also called 'Neroneus'[10] – were changed in name: May to 'Claudius', June to 'Germanicus'. Claudius Orfitus, the proposal's author, declared: *'June' is being transferred because the execution of two criminal Junii Torquati[11] has made the name Junius unlucky.*

13. A year ugly with so many wrongs the gods, too, marked with storm and sickness. Campania was devastated by a whirlwind that wrecked villas, orchards and crops, and brought its violence to Rome's vicinity. In Rome a virulent pestilence[12] ravaged all manner of people, although there was no atmospheric anomaly to see. (2) Houses were filled with lifeless bodies, roads with funerals. No sex or age was danger-free. Slaves and freeborn alike failed suddenly amid the laments of spouses and children, who, while attending, while mourning, were often cremated[13] on the same pyre. The deaths of men of equestrian and senatorial rank, though indiscriminate, were less tearful. *By commonplace mortality they are forestalling imperial brutality.*

(3) This same year levies were held throughout Narbonensis, Africa and Asia to replenish the legions stationed in Illyricum, from which soldiers worn out by age or ill health were being discharged. A disaster at Lyon[14] was alleviated by the Emperor's gift of 4 million sesterces to restore the city's losses, a sum the people of Lyon had earlier bestowed on Rome's misfortunes.[15]

14. (66 CE) Gaius Suetonius, Luccius Telesinus, consuls.

Antistius Sosianus, whose abusive poems against Nero led to punishment, as I mentioned, by exile,[16] heard of the preferment for informants and the Emperor's eagerness for killing. A troublemaker at heart, alert to opportunity, he used similarity of misfortune to befriend a fellow exile, Pammenes, famous as an astrologer[17] and therefore supported by many a friendship. Sosianus thought that frequent messages and consultations signified something, and learned that Publius Anteius provided Pammenes an annuity. Also known: *Nero is hostile to Anteius[18] because of Agrippina's affection, and Anteius' wealth is a particular inducement to desire. The same cause has destroyed many.* (2) Accordingly, intercepting one of Anteius' letters, he stole notebooks, too, in which Anteius' birthday and future were hidden amidst Pammenes' secret lore. Sosianus also found writings on Ostorius Scapula's[19] origin and life. He wrote to the Emperor: *I will bring you important information pertaining to your security if granted brief respite from exile. Anteius and Ostorius are a danger to the state and are enquiring after their*

own destiny and yours. (3) Boats were sent at once,[20] Sosianus
swiftly brought. With the denunciation's publication, Anteius
and Ostorius counted as condemned rather than as on trial, so
much so that no one would put his seal to Anteius' will until
Tigellinus stepped forward after warning Anteius not to delay
the final document. Anteius, having taken poison and disgusted
by its slow action, cut through his veins to hasten death.

15. Ostorius was on a distant estate near Liguria's border. A
centurion was sent to accomplish his killing. (The reason for
speed was that Ostorius – a man of considerable military glory
and recipient of the civic crown[21] in Britain, gigantic of physique and a weapons-expert – frightened Nero. Would he not
attack one perpetually afraid and now, having recently discovered a conspiracy, more terrified still?) (2) The centurion,
after stopping up the villa's escapes, revealed Nero's orders to
Ostorius. The fortitude Ostorius had often displayed against
enemies he turned on himself. When his veins, though gaping,
emptied themselves of insufficient blood, he used a slave's help
only to this extent, to hold the dagger still: he seized the man's
hand and ran it to his throat.

16. Were I recording with such similarity of event foreign
wars and deaths on state service, surfeit would have mastered
even me, and I would expect impatience in others, too, spurning fellow citizens' ends, however honourable, as dismal and
unending.[22] As it is, slavish passivity and the volume of blood
squandered at home weary the spirit, hobble it with sorrow.
(2) My defence[23] – the only one I would ask from those who
come to know these words – is that I must not hate men perishing so slackly. It was divine anger at Rome, not, like disasters
to our armies or the capture of cities, to be simply announced
and passed over! Let us grant this to the legacy of notable men:
just as they are distinct in their funerals from common burial,
so let them receive in the record of their final hours, too, lasting
possession of a particular remembrance.[24]

17. Within days there died in single file[25] Annaeus Mela,
Anicius Cerealis, Rufrius Crispinus, Titus Petronius. Mela and
Crispinus were men of equestrian rank with senatorial stand-
ing. (2) Crispinus,[26] formerly Guard commander and honorary

magistrate, latterly driven to Sardinia by a conspiracy charge, when he got word of the death order, killed himself. (3) Mela, born from the same parents as Gallio and Seneca,[27] had held aloof from pursuit of office with his perverse ambition that a man of equestrian rank equal ex-consuls in power. He believed, moreover, that the shorter road to wealth was by administering the Emperor's affairs. (4) Mela fathered Lucan, a substantial addition to his renown. Upon Lucan's death[28] he went after Lucan's property vigorously, provoking an accuser, Fabius Romanus, from Lucan's intimates. *Knowledge of the conspiracy was shared between father and son*, it was alleged, and there was a forged letter from Lucan. Upon seeing this, Nero ordered it taken to Mela. (He coveted the man's wealth.)[29] (5) Mela opened his veins – death's readiest road – after updating his will with substantial sums to Tigellinus and his son-in-law Cossutianus Capito,[30] so that the other arrangements would stand. (6) Onto the codicils themselves was appended a statement, as if Mela had written to protest the injustice of his death: *While I am dying without grounds for punishment, Rufrius Crispinus and Anicius Cerealis are enjoying life, though hated by Nero*, words written about Crispinus, people thought,[31] because he had already been killed, and about Cerealis so that he would be killed. And Cerealis soon did violence to himself, less pitied than others, because people remembered that he betrayed a conspiracy to Gaius.[32]

18. On Petronius, brief background is warranted. His days were spent in sleep, his nights with work and life's amusements. Other men reached renown through exertion, he through indolence. Unlike many who swallow their fortunes, he was considered not a glutton and wastrel, but a man 'of refined dissipation'. The freer his words and deeds, and the more they displayed a certain nonchalance, the more welcome they were for apparent candour. (2) Nevertheless, as governor of Bithynia and later as consul[33] he showed himself vigorous and equal to affairs. Then, relapsing into vices – or imitations of vice – he was taken into Nero's inner circle as arbiter of elegance, at least while Nero deemed nothing pleasant or expensively delicate[34] unless Petronius commended it to him. (3) Hence Tigellinus'

resentment against a rival more potent in the science of pleas-ures. Tigellinus, accordingly, addressed himself to the Emperor's cruelty – other appetites yielding ground to this one – and accused Petronius of friendship with Scaevinus,[35] after bribing a slave for evidence, vacating the defence, and arresting most of Petronius' household.

19. It chanced that Nero had just then gone to Campania. Petronius reached Cumae,[36] where he was detained. He aban-doned fear's delay – and hope's – without hurrying to banish life. (2) Veins were slit and bound up as he fancied. Then he opened them again and spoke to friends, but not on serious topics or ones by which to pursue constancy's glory. He listened, too, not to talk about the soul's immortality or philosophical doctrine but to lightweight songs and easy verses. Some slaves got largesse; a few got beatings. He began a meal and enjoyed a nap so that compulsory death might nevertheless seem for-tuitous. (3) Not even in his will – unlike most victims – did he flatter Nero or Tigellinus or anyone influential. Indeed he cata-logued the Emperor's enormities under the names of partners male and female, including each perversion's novelty. The list he sealed and sent to Nero, and broke his seal ring so it could not later be used to manufacture trouble.

20. To Nero, wondering how his nocturnal ingenuity was known, Silia came to mind, a woman of note for marriage to a senator, his own associate in every debauch – and Petronius' close friend. Silia was exiled for not keeping silent about things seen and suffered. She had earned Nero's hatred. (2) The ex-praetor Minucius Thermus, however, Nero surrendered freely to a quarrel with Tigellinus, against whom one of Thermus' freedmen had laid slanderous charges. The freedman paid with torture's agonies, his patron with execution undeserved.

21. With so many eminent men slain, Nero finally aspired to excise virtue itself with the murder of Thrasea Paetus and Barea Soranus.[37] He was long hostile to both, and new reasons[38] accrued against Thrasea: he left the senate when it was con-sulted about Agrippina, as I reported, and provided too little help at the Youth festival. (The latter grievance penetrated more deeply in that Thrasea performed in tragic costume in his

hometown Padua at games established by Trojan Antenor.)[39] (2) Furthermore, when praetor Antistius was condemned to death for scandalous compositions against Nero, Thrasea proposed and won a milder sentence. And when Poppaea's divine honours were decreed, he absented himself and did not attend her funeral. (3) None of this was suppressed by Cossutianus Capito, a man headlong for depravities but also biased against Thrasea, by whose authority he was felled when Thrasea supported Cilician envoys calling him to account for extortion.[40]

22. Indeed Cossutianus' charges continued: *At the new year Thrasea avoids the loyalty oath and misses vows to the immortal gods,*[41] *despite holding a public priesthood. He has never offered sacrifice for the Emperor's health or divine voice. Formerly constant and tireless,*[42] *a man who even in ordinary senate business would declare his position for or against, he has not entered the senate for three years, and quite recently, with senators vying to be first to check Silanus and Vetus, Thrasea instead found time for his dependants' affairs.* (2) *This is secession and faction and, if many dare as much, it is war!* 'Formerly,' Cossutianus said, 'Caesar and Cato were the talk of a strife-hungry citizenry. So now are you, Nero, and Thrasea. And he has followers, or rather "attendants", who adopt, if not yet his defiant stance, at least his port and mien: unbending and grim, thereby to reproach you with frivolity. (3) He alone gives your security no thought, your artistry no honour. The Emperor's good fortune he disdained. Do even Nero's bereavement and suffering give no satisfaction? Thrasea's position is consistent: he will not believe Poppaea a goddess if he doesn't swear to uphold the enactments of the gods Augustus and Julius. He rejects religion and nullifies laws. The report of state business is now read with unusual care in province and army – to know what Thrasea has not done. (4) Let us either go over to his teachings, if they are better, or remove from those who desire revolution their leader and cause! That sect of his produced men like Tubero and Favonius, inimical even to the republic of old. To undermine power they raise freedom's standard, but if they bring power down they will attack freedom herself. (5) In vain did you remove a Cassius if you suffer

to grow and flourish those who emulate men named Brutus. To conclude: you yourself need write nothing about Thrasea. Leave the senate to decide between us!' (6) Nero exalted Cossutianus' ready spirit and reinforced it with Eprius Marcellus'[43] biting eloquence.

23. Barea Soranus had already been indicted by the equestrian-ranked Ostorius Sabinus for his governorship of Asia,[44] during which Soranus had multiplied the Emperor's grievances by just and industrious administration: he both attended to clearing Ephesus' port and left unpunished a Pergamene riot that tried to prevent the Emperor's freedman Acratus from carrying off statues and paintings. But the charges were friendship with Rubellius Plautus[45] and ambition to recruit the province for revolutionary hopes.

(2) As occasion for their condemnation, Nero chose Tiridates' arrival[46] to receive the kingdom of Armenia, so that with talk turned to external affairs domestic crime might be overshadowed, or else to display imperial majesty by killing notable men, a right royal action.

24. When all Rome poured out to welcome the Emperor and see the king, Thrasea was barred from approach. Undaunted, he composed a petition to Nero asking the complaint. *I will clear myself if given notice of the charges and opportunity for exculpation,* he insisted. (2) Nero snatched up the tablets, hoping that a fearful Thrasea had written to exalt the Emperor's renown and disgrace his own reputation. Not so, and since the look, defiance and independence of the man even innocent caused him dread, he ordered the senate assembled.

25. Thrasea consulted with his nearest: *Shall I attempt defence or reject it?* Different plans were offered. Some favoured appearing in the senate. *We trust your constancy: you will say nothing except to increase your glory. (2) Indolent and timid men surround their final moments with secrecy. Let the populace watch a man encounter death, let the senate hear words as if from some divine source, practically superhuman! Possibly even Nero will be moved from very astonishment. But if he persists in cruelty, with posterity, at least, the memory of an honourable end is different from perishing in cowardly silence.*

26. Those who recommended waiting at home said the same about Thrasea himself, but also that derision and insult threatened. *Withdraw your ears from slanders and slurs.* (2) *Not only Cossutianus and Marcellus are ready for crime. There are also some who may, from savagery, dare physical attack; and even good men follow from fear. Avert from the senate, which you so graced, outrage's infamy. Let it remain uncertain – with Thrasea charged – what senators were going to decide.* (3) *That shame might seize Nero at these outrages is floated in vain. Much more to be feared is Nero infuriate against your wife, household and others held dear. Inviolate, undefiled, continue to the end in the glory of those by whose example and precept you steered your life.*[47]

(4) Present at this discussion was Arulenus Rusticus,[48] a vehement youth. Ardent for praise he offered to veto the senate's decision. (Rusticus was tribune.) (5) Thrasea reined in his defiance: *Do not initiate something meaningless and unprofitable to the defendant but fatal for the veto's author. My own span is complete and a pattern of life unbroken for so many years is not to be forsaken, but your career is beginning, your future uncompromised. Consider well beforehand – engaging in public affairs at such a time!*[49] *– the road you are embarking on.* Whether attending the senate was fitting, Thrasea left to his own reflections.

27. Next morning two armed cohorts occupied the temple of Venus Genetrix.[50] The senate's approach was beset by a group in civilian dress – with swords perfectly visible – and detachments were scattered throughout the city's squares and public buildings. Through their looks of menace the senators entered and heard the Emperor's quaestor read the address. (2) Without attacking anyone by name, Nero denounced the senate for deserting public responsibilities. *With your example, men of equestrian rank are turning to indolence. No surprise at scarce attendance from distant provinces, when many who have held the consulship and priesthoods devote themselves rather to the pleasure of their parks!* Accusers took this up like a weapon.

28. Cossutianus began, then with greater force Marcellus exclaimed: *The government is at stake! With defiance in*

subjects, a ruler's mildness dwindles. Heretofore senators have been too gentle: Thrasea withdrawing, Helvidius Priscus his son-in-law equally raving, likewise Paconius Agrippinus, heir to his father's emperor-hatred, and Curtius Montanus[51] *composing abhorrent poems – all have been permitted to deride with impunity!* (2) *I look for an ex-consul in the senate, a priest at sacrifices, a citizen at the oath-taking – unless Thrasea opposes ancestral practices and rituals and wears the mantle of declared traitor and public enemy. Finally, a man habitually playing senator and protecting the Emperor's critics should attend meetings and state his opinion about what he wants corrected or changed. You will more easily tolerate him berating particulars than the silence of wholesale censure.* (3) *Does he dislike universal peace, the army's bloodless victories? When a man sorrowful at public prosperity considers city squares, theatres and temples a desert, when he threatens exile, you should not grant his perverse ambition. To Thrasea, decrees, magistracies – Rome! – seem as nothing. Let him sunder his life from the community from which he long ago stripped his affection and now even his presence.*[52]

29. While with these words and their like Marcellus' intensity – he was a pitiless, menacing man – showed in his words, face and eyes, in the senate there was not that familiar misery, habitual now from perils' frequency, but a new and deeper dread as they eyed the soldiers' hands, the weapons. (2) Thrasea's venerable image confronted them and some pitied Helvidius, too, likely to pay for a blameless marriage. *What is alleged against Agrippinus but his father's sad fate? For he, too, equally innocent, was felled by Tiberius' brutality. And Montanus – youth commendable, verse not insulting – is banished for display of talent!*

30. Ostorius Sabinus, Soranus' accuser, arrived meanwhile and began on Soranus' friendship with Rubellius Plautus, saying also: *As Asia's governor he acted with more advantage to his own renown than to public welfare by fostering cities' restiveness.*[53] (2) Old matters, these. A fresh charge, one by which he tied Soranus' daughter to her father's danger: *She spent money on fortune-tellers.*[54] (This was certainly due to the filial

devotion of Servilia – that was the girl's name – who from affection for her father and the folly of youth had simply asked about her family's security. *Can Nero be placated, can a senate trial have a result other than appalling?*) (3) She was summoned into the senate. They stood separately before the consuls' dais, aged parent opposite his daughter, who was not yet twenty, recently left widowed and desolate by the banishment of her husband Annius Pollio.[55] She did not look at her father, whose danger she had clearly aggravated.

31. When the accuser asked whether she sold her trousseau – *The necklace from your throat!* – to amass funds for magical rites, she fell to the ground and wept long in silence, then clasped the altar. 'No impious gods did I invoke with my unhappy prayers, no curses, nor anything except that you, Nero, and you, senators, preserve[56] this best of fathers unharmed! (2) Yes, I gave them my jewels and my garments and the tokens of my status, as I would have given my blood and life had they demanded those. It's their affair – those wretches hitherto unknown to me – what they are called, what art they practise![57] I did not mention the Emperor except among divinities. And my most unhappy father knows nothing. If this is a crime, I alone did wrong.'

32. With his daughter still speaking, Soranus took the floor and cried out: *She did not go to my province with me! She cannot, given her age, have known Rubellius Plautus! She is not implicated in her husband's crimes! Set aside one charged only with excessive devotion. Let me undergo whatever is my lot.* He rushed to his daughter's embrace, except that interposed lictors obstructed. (2) Time, then, for witnesses. The pity aroused by the accusation's brutality equalled the anger at Publius Egnatius[58] as witness: (3) Soranus' protégé, bribed to crush his friend. (Egnatius paraded obedience to Stoic doctrine and was practised at displaying probity of manner and expression, but in character he was perfidious and sly, his greed and lust hidden. When money brought these to light he became a cautionary exemplum. As one must beware men engaged in chicanery or stained by depravity, so, too, those deceptive with a façade of rectitude, traitors to friendship.)

33. The same day also provided the worthy example of Cassius Asclepiodotus, pre-eminent among Bithynians for his wealth. Having honoured with attentiveness Soranus prospering, he did not desert him in his fall. He was stripped of his entire fortune and banished,[59] such was the gods' evenhandedness with instances of good and evil. (2) Thrasea, Soranus and Servilia were given free choice of death. Helvidius and Agrippinus were expelled from Italy; Montanus pardoned as a favour to his father, provided he did not engage in public service. The accusers Marcellus and Cossutianus were awarded 5 million sesterces each, Ostorius 1,200,000 sesterces and an honorary quaestorship.[60]

34. Thrasea being then at his city estate, a quaestor[61] was sent when day was already turning to evening. Thrasea had assembled a great company of notable men and women, and paid particular attention to Demetrius, a teacher of Cynic doctrine, enquiring – as one could conjecture from the intensity of his gaze and what was audible when the conversation grew more emphatic – about the nature of the soul and the separation of spirit and body. Then one of his closest friends, Domitius Caecilianus, arrived and revealed the senate's decision. (2) Thrasea urged the weeping and protesting company to act quickly and avoid dangerous contact with the fate of a man condemned. Arria, ready to share her husband's end and mother's example, he encouraged to hold onto life, and not to remove their daughter's one support.[62]

35. Thrasea was in the portico when the quaestor found him, happy on the whole, having learned that his son-in-law Helvidius was merely banned from Italy. He listened to the senate's decree and took Helvidius and Demetrius into his chamber. He held out the veins of each arm, and after the blood was flowing began shaking it onto the ground and called the quaestor closer. 'A libation to Jupiter Liberator,' he said. 'Watch, young man! I hope the gods block the omen – but you have been born into times when it is useful to brace the mind with examples of constancy.' Death's slow pace brought agony, so turning to Demetrius[63]

Appendix

The following is a list of places where the text underlying the translation diverges from that of Heubner's edition. I indicate briefly the text I translated, the manuscript evidence and Heubner's reading. On my use of the abbreviation 'M' and Heubner's edition see my Note on the Translation (p. liv).

1.8.3 Reading *ex quis† maxime insignes visi* with M (Goodyear supplies the crux). Heubner reads *ex quis maxime insignes [visi]*.

1.20.2 Reading *intentus* for M's *intus,* with Goodyear. Heubner reads *vetus*, which also makes sense.

1.27.2 Reading *digredientem eum <a> Caesare* with Goodyear. Heubner reads *digredientem [eum Caesare]*.

1.32.1 Reading *sexagenis* with Goodyear. Heubner follows M in reading *sexageni*.

1.63.1 Reading *omnis*, with Goodyear (following Andresen), for M's *romanis*. Heubner reads *Romanus*.

2.1.1 Reading *Tauro* with M. Heubner deletes the extra cognomen.

2.9.2 Reading *permissu progressus salutatur* with Goodyear. Heubner reads *permissu<m> progressusque salutatur*.

2.23.3 Reading *tumidis* with M. Heubner reads *humidis*.

2.37.4 Reading *florente aetate*, an emendation. Heubner accepts M's *florente te*.

2.43.4 Reading *ei*. Heubner accepts M's *et*.

2.61.2 The translation renders Goodyear's emendation *inquiren<ti res>tium spatiis*. Heubner prints M's *inquirentium spatiis*.

3.12.2 The translation is based on the emendation *non ut princeps* for M's *noui principis*. Heubner reads *no<n> ui principis*.

3.13.2 Reading *post qu<a>e* for M's *postque*. Heubner reads *post que<m>*.

3.43.1 Reading *<et> nobilissimam ... ut eo*. M has *nobilissimam ... ut eo*. Heubner reads *<ut> nobilissimam ... et eo*.

3.49.1 Reading *legerat* with M. Heubner reads *iecerat*.

3.61.2 Reading *proximos. Magnetes*, an emendation of M's *proximosnagnetes* that attaches *proximos* to *nos*. Heubner reads *proximi <hos> Magnetes*, taking *proximi* with *Magnetes* in the following sentence.

3.63.3 Reading *rege uti*, an emendation for M's *regi uti*. Heubner reads *rege niti*.

3.67.4 Reading *missis*, an emendation for M's *ausis*, which Heubner accepts.

4.26.2 Rendering Lipsius' emendation *et culpae conscia*. Heubner accepts Halm's emendation *sed culpae nescia*. M has *ed culpae nescia*.

4.28.1 Reading *praeparatur* with M. Heubner reads *<com>paratur*.

4.33.1 Reading *conflata*, Kiessling's emendation for M's *consciata*. Heubner reads *cons<o>ciata*.

4.38.3 Reading *deos et deas ipsas* with the correction in M. Heubner reads *[deos et] deos ipsos*.

4.50.2 Reading *quamvis* with M. Heubner accepts Madvig's emendation *tantum his*.

4.59.2 Reading *utroque* with Martin and Woodman. Heubner accepts M's *vultuque*.

6.26.1 Reading *omnis* with M. Heubner accepts the emendation *comes*.

6.49.2 Reading *patris* with M. Heubner reads *patri<bu>s*, others read *patrum*. The expressions 'his father's knees' and 'their joint mourning' make the mother address her appeal for pity directly to her son's father; either of the commonly accepted emendations would make her speak instead to the senate at large ('the fathers') and require a more general 'mourning's fellow-feeling' for *luctum ... communem*.

Patris, besides being the transmitted text, intensifies the picture of familial disarray.

11.4.2 Reading *dixisset* with M. Heubner reads *<prae>dixisset*.

11.14.3 Reading *publicandis plebi* SC*tis* with Grotius. Heubner excises the corrupt phrase.

11.23.3 Reading *coetus* with M. Heubner reads *coetu*.

11.24.2 Reading *accitos* with M. Heubner reads *adscitos*.

11.25.3 Reading *exeundi* with M. Heubner reads *exuendi*. For transitive *exire* see 6.49.2.

11.33 Reading *assumitque* (i.e., *adsumitque*) with M. Heubner reads *adsumit<ur>que*.

12.10.1 Reading *et* and *accedere* with M. Heubner brackets *et* and reads *accersere*.

12.15.2 Reading *praecellebat* with M. Heubner reads *praesidebat*.

12.17.1 Reading (for the first word in the sentence) *postremo* with M. Heubner reads *postero* (sc. *die*).

12.22.1 Reading *simulacrum* with M. Heubner reads *oraculum*.

12.26 Reading *fortunae maeror* with M. Heubner reads *fortuna maeror<e>*.

12.33 Reading, with M, *astu locorum fraude*. Heubner reads *astu <et> locorum fraude*.

12.36.1 Reading *insulas* with M. Heubner reads *insulam*.

12.37.1 Reading *foedere et pace*, Becher's emendation. Heubner reads *foedere <in> pacem*.

12.37.3 Reading *traderer* with M. Heubner reads *traherer*.

12.38.3 Reading *nuntiis e castellis proximis subventum foret copiarum obsidioni*, which is the text of M except for the final word, where M has *obsidione*. Heubner reads *nuntiis e castellis proximis <missis> subventum foret, [copiarum obsidione]*.

12.39.1 Reading *exposuit* with M. Heubner reads *opposuit*.

12.41.3 Reading *ac* with M. Heubner reads *aut*.

12.45.3 Reading, with M, *at nobis ea pars militiae maxime gnara est*. Heubner brackets the clause, perhaps rightly, since it is a feeble and unnecessary addition to the assertion about the barbarians. But *nobis* prevents one from seeing it as in origin a gloss.

12.50.2 Reading *bellaturos* with M. Heubner reads *<re>bellaturos*.

12.57 In the first two sentences of this chapter I follow M's admittedly awkward text. Heubner reads *<cum> apertum* and [*vel media*].

13.1.2 Reading *Celerius* with M. Heubner has *Celer*. For the name, see W. Eck, 'P. *Celerius, procurator Asiae*, und Tac. *Ann.* 13.1' in *Splendidissima civitas: études d'histoire romaine en hommage à François Jacques* (Paris: Publications de la Sorbonne, 1996).

13.6.1 Reading *tum quoque bellum* with M. Heubner emends to *tum bellum quoque*.

13.30.2 Reading *malitia* with M. Heubner prints the emendation *amicitia*. *Alii alia*.

13.35.1 Reading *castrorum Romanorum*. M has *Romanorum*. Heubner reads *castrorum*. The text translated here captures Tacitus' double antithesis: Syria/Rome, peace/war.

13.41.1 Reading *praemissa[que] levi armatura*. Heubner reads *praemissaque levi<s> armatura*.

13.44.3 Reading *et quasi incensus* for M's *et quastim census*. Heubner reads *ea quasi incensus*.

13.50.2 Reading *senatores* with M. Heubner reads *seniores*. Neither word is quite apt for the context.

13.56.3 Reading *defendentibus* with M. Heubner reads *deserentibus*.

14.2.2 Omitting (with M) Lepidus' praenomen, which will have been familiar from the earlier narrative. Heubner supplies *<M.>*.

14.7.2 The text is difficult here. Nero's concluding clause lacks a verb, and the participle *expergens* is both rare and oddly placed. The translation takes *expergens* as being in pointed antithesis with *exanimis* ('unstrung') and therefore displacing *quos* to second position in its clause. Heubner, instead, deletes it. Others convert the participle into a verb meaning 'discover' in Nero's last clause 'except what Seneca and Burrus might discover'. Woodman suggests *quos experiens*.

14.7.2 Reading *et ante* with M. Heubner accepts the normalization *an et ante*.

14.7.6 Reading *exitum* with M. Heubner emends to *exitium*.

14.10.3 Emending M's *qua* to *quae*. Heubner emends to *quasi*. *Alii alia*.

14.12.4 Reading *vel tamen mitigata* with M. Heubner deletes *tamen*.

14.13.1 Reading *cunctari* with M. Heubner reads *cunctari tamen*, moving to this spot the *tamen* deleted from the previous sentence.

14.18.3 Reading *scripsit* with M. Heubner emends to *<re>scripsit*.

14.20.5 Reading *munus expleturos* with M. Heubner adds *<melius>*.

14.26.1 Reading *amittere* with M. Heubner emends to *omittere*.

14.26.2 Reading *accedit* with M. Heubner emends to *abscessit*.

14.31.4 Reading *ara* with M. Heubner emends to *arx*.

14.42.1 Reading *infensus* with M. Heubner emends to *incensus*.

14.54.3 Reading *visum <summi> fastigii* with Halm. Heubner replaces *visum* with *summi*.

15.13.2 Reading *ac* for M's *aut* and assuming that *paenis* is a (corrupt and) intrusive gloss. Heubner prints *aut <Hispanis quam> Parthis*. *Alii alia*.

15.19.2 In M this sentence lacks both subject and verb. The translation follows the emendation that converts M's *adeuntibus* to *adeunt <qui> ius*. Heubner adds *<igitur qui filios genuerant>* at the beginning of the sentence and reads *adeunt, ius* for *adeuntibus*.

15.34.1 The translation 'in the view of' leaves open the question of the verb's tense. M has a present tense; editors, including Heubner, generally change to imperfect *arbitra<ba>ntur*.

15.36.3 Heubner prints a feeble addition in this sentence, *in re publica*, which I did not translate.

15.37.4 Omitting the modifier for *auspices*, of which the text is uncertain. M has *misit*. Heubner reads *missi*. *Alii alia*.

15.41.2 Reading *numerent* with M. Heubner reads *numer<ar>ent*.

15.45.2 Reading *induerat* with M. Heubner reads *imbuerat*.

15.45.3 Reading *persimplici victu* with M. Heubner reads *per simplice<m> victu<m>*.

15.49.3 Reading *lenitate* with M. Heubner reads *levitate*.

15.51.3 Reading *senatui* with M. Heubner accepts the emendation *sancti*.

15.54.3 Taking *de consequentibus* as a gloss. Heubner reads *de consequentibus <consentitur>*.

15.61.3 Reading *reditum* with M. Heubner reads *red<isse> t<ribun>um*.

15.63.1 Reading *dolorem aeternum* with M and accepting the emendation of M's *susciperet* to *suscipere*. Heubner reads *dolori <neu> aeternum susciperet*.

15.64.1 Accepting Pichena's emendation of M's *inhiberi* to *inhibet*. Heubner reads *<iubet> inhiberi*.

15.65 Reading *insontibus* with M. Heubner accepts Acidalius' emendation to *insonti et*. The point of *quasi insontibus* is that they would look innocent (of conspiracy) in killing the conspiracy's head and placing a worthy man on the throne.

15.68.2 Reading *in crimina traheretur* with M. Heubner reads *in crimen traheretur*.

15.72.1 Ending the sentence at *Nymphidio*, beginning the next with *qu<i>a*. Heubner reads *Nymphidio <Sabino decreta, de quo> q<u>ia*.

15.73.1 Reading *viros et insontes* with M. Heubner reads *viros <claros> et insontes*.

15.74.1 Reading *eo loci ex quo* with M, though without strong confidence that it is correct. The words mean 'in that place whence', which seems odd since 'that place' was already a temple of Salus (see 15.53). Heubner reads *eius loco ex quo*.

16.2.1 Reading *parta* with M. Heubner accepts the emendation *parata*.

16.14.1 Reading *innixum* with M. Heubner accepts the emendation *innexum*.

16.22 2 Deleting M's *et* as dittography before *ex-* at the beginning of the following word (*expectabilem*). Heubner deletes *et* and changes *expectabilem* to *spectabilem*.

16.24.2 Reading *venit* with M (see 12.32.2 *id quo promptius veniret*, 14.43.2 *quod hodie venit*). Heubner reads *<e>venit*.

16.26.2 Reading *auderent*, Grotius' emendation for M's obviously corrupt *augusti*. Heubner reads *ingest<ur>i <sint>*. Other editors emend otherwise.

16.26.2 Reading, with M, *perornavisset*, rather than, with Heubner *<sem>per ornavisset*. *Perornavisset* is a neologism, but *semper* is inaccurate, given that Thrasea had abandoned the senate three years earlier.

16.26.3 Reading, with M, *familiam*, rather than *filiam* with Heubner and other editors.

16.28.2 Reading *increpantem* in place of M's non-word *increpatium* (corrected by a later hand to *increpantium*, but corrupt even so). Heubner reads *increpanti<s> v<oce>m*.

Notes

BOOK 1

1. *The city of Rome*: This opening paragraph provides a thumbnail sketch of Rome's various forms of government from the city's foundation in 753 BCE to the battle of Actium in 31 BCE, with an emphasis on the nature of the dominant authority.

2. *first citizen*: This expression renders the Latin term *princeps*, a euphemism based on various Republican-era expressions for 'primacy among equals', and adopted by Augustus to make his autocratic power less offensive to the political elite. Tacitus uses this and other terms for the Emperor's position interchangeably in his narrative and all are hereafter rendered 'emperor', unless the context requires more precision.

3. *without anger or favour*: Tacitus' characteristic brevity renders this famous disclaimer capable of various constructions: a promise of active resistance to bias ('whose causes I keep at a distance'); a statement of fact ('I am far removed from the causes of bias'); or, as in the text above, a statement of belief.

4. *a republic*: Or 'the Republic', a more specific reference to Rome under the political system in place before Augustus' accession.

5. *Sallustius Crispus*: Tiberius later asked Crispus to deal with the false Agrippa Postumus (2.40). For Crispus' death in 20 CE see 3.30.

6. *into the Julian family and Augustus' name*: i.e., Livia's official name became Julia Augusta. Tacitus uses a variety of appellations for her (see the Index of Names). For ease of identification she is 'Livia' everywhere in this translation.

7. *Gallus . . . Arruntius . . . Messala*: All three men are prominent in Tacitus' narrative of Tiberius' principate as representatives of elite behaviour, usually bad (see the Index of Names for specific

passages). Arruntius is the best of the bunch: for his death scene see 6.48.1–3.

8. *against a republic*: The interpretation of this phrase (*in rem publicam*) is disputed. Some take it as 'for the republic'.

9. *the same date*: 19 August: the date on which Augustus took up his first consulship in 43 BCE, and on which he died in 14 CE.

10. *and Vedius Pollio's extravagance*: The beginning of this sentence is garbled in the manuscript. It presumably named one or more associates whose actions brought reproach on Augustus.

11. *the first names ... Piso*: Like Gallus and Arruntius, who were introduced earlier (see 1.8.3), Lepidus and Piso are prominent in Tiberius' principate. Lepidus wins Tacitus' praise for his balance (4.20.2–3; see the Index of Names for further references). Piso demonstrates a more uncomfortable mix of arrogance and devotion to the emperors, and dies under a cloud of suspicion for his opposition to Germanicus.

12. *Anxious about resentment*: The underlying Latin can be construed variously. Tacitus communicates the presence of resentment without specifying who felt it or what caused it.

13. *Junius Blaesus*: He gains notoriety later in the *Annals* for being the uncle of Sejanus. For a creditable military success see 3.73–4.

14. *Sejanus*: This is the first reference to Sejanus, the evil genius of Tiberius' principate (see 4.1 and the notes below).

15. *underage sons*: This is an efficient but slightly misleading rendering of *filii familiarum*, a Latin phrase that refers to legal status rather than to biological age. (In 14 CE Drusus was about twenty-eight.) In many aspects of life a Roman's status depended on whether or not his or her father was alive. If so, his children, regardless of age, lacked certain powers (for an example see 11.13.2) and could therefore seem *underage* until well into middle age. English has no good equivalent.

16. *Gnaeus Lentulus*: See 4.29.1.

17. *horns*: Tacitus names two types of horn here. A Roman reader would associate different sounds with the different instruments, but neither has an exact English equivalent. Since the point of the passage is the noise, I have given a simplified rendering instead of cluttering up the scene with unhelpful specificity. Likewise at 1.68.3 and 2.81.2.

18. *The Upper army*: This was upstream of the Lower army and closer to Italy. The men mentioned here, Gaius Silius and Aulus Caecina, appear frequently in military roles in the Tiberian books (see the Index of Names). Silius was driven to suicide in

24 CE (4.18–19); his like-named son married Claudius' wife Messalina and shared her fall in 48 CE (11.26–35). Caecina's last appearances are in the senate (3.18, 3.33–4).

19. *have our name by association*: The last was true of their own commander Germanicus and of his father Drusus, whose victories with the legions of Germany were reflected in the name (see Suetonius, *Claudius* 1.3).

20. *Septimius . . . Cassius Chaerea*: Presumably centurions.

21. *he set out quickly*: Germanicus goes first to the legions of the more restive Lower army. See 1.37.3.

22. *designated for destruction*: The alarmist nature of these reports is conveyed by their overwrought language. The Ubian capital was later Cologne, and is henceforth referred to by that name.

23. *back at Cologne*: Germanicus is back with the Lower army, which he left for the Upper at 1.37.3. The delegation was dispatched at 1.14.3.

24. *the senatorial decree*: This is either a hitherto unmentioned decree authorizing the delegation to Germanicus or the decree that the soldiers fear will annul the concessions they have won. The latter is a figment of their imagination, of course.

25. *Little Boot*: The Latin for 'little boot' is Caligula, a name that stuck to the future emperor Gaius.

26. *a place called Vetera*: It was at the sixtieth milestone downstream (north-west) from Cologne, near modern Xanten.

27. *the first to mutiny*: See 1.31.3, 1.37.1.

28. *the men should still have time*: The men in question are those of the Fifth and Twenty-first. The narrative picks up from the end of 1.45.

29. *allied infantry cohorts*: The size of auxiliary units varies, but here it is clear that the allied forces outnumber the legionaries.

30. *the town of the Regini*: Rhegium, modern Reggio di Calabria.

31. *her lengthy exile*: Julia was exiled in 2 BCE.

32. *did not yet dare*: For later episodes showing Tiberius' attitude towards such entertainments see 1.76.4, 1.77, 4.14.3, 4.62.2.

33. *Lucius Apronius*: For his military record see 1.72.1 and 3.21.1–4, 4.73, 6.30. He also appears in various senatorial roles, particularly in connection with trials (2.32.2, 4.13.3, 4.22.1).

34. *I will report*: This promise is not fulfilled in the extant books. Arminius' son seems to have died before 47 CE (11.16).

35. *priesthood*: In the Latin this word has a modifier, but the text is corrupt and has not yet been convincingly emended.

36. *rods and axes and toga*: These stand for Roman provincial

administration, the first two being the instruments of punishments decreed by the governor, the toga being the dress of Roman civic life.

37. *Lucius Domitius*: Consul in 16 BCE and Nero's grandfather, he died in 26 CE. Tacitus gives his obituary at 4.44.2.

38. *horns*: See note 17 above.

39. *Pliny*: For Tacitus' rare references to sources, see p. xxvii.

40. *Publius Vitellius*: He appears frequently in the first three books of the *Annals* as Germanicus' legate and friend (see the Index of Names). For his suicide in 31 CE see 5.8.

41. *Cassius Severus*: He was exiled. The senate increased the strictness of his exile under Tiberius (4.21.3).

42. *theatre-related licence*: For the previous episode see 1.54.2. The problem requires renewed attention at 4.14.3.

43. *Haterius Agrippa*: His subsequent appearances trace his rise through the *cursus honorum* (2.51.1, 3.49.2, 6.4.2) and end with a very unflattering character sketch (6.4.4).

44. *1 per cent sales tax*: The tax issue is raised again at 2.42.4 and 13.50–51.

45. *municipal delegations*: Tacitus mentions two types of Italian municipality here – indigenous towns and citizen colonies – but the distinction is unimportant in the context, so I use the shorthand *municipal* here and *towns* below, where he speaks (inaccurately) only of colonies. The fundamental contrast here is between Italy's towns and Rome. Likewise at 15.33.3. See also 3.55.3 and 4.67.1 .

46. *the best arrangements . . . are nature's*: The outlet was in fact man-made. See Cicero, *Letters to Atticus* 4.15.5.

47. *Piso*: As the text stands it is unclear who this Piso is (of many men so called in the *Annals*). Presumably a distinguishing praenomen has fallen out.

48. *Poppaeus Sabinus*: Tacitus gives a detailed narrative of one of Sabinus' subsequent military campaigns at 4.46–51; see also 5.10.2–3. His obituary appears at 6.39.3.

BOOK 2

1. *Phraates*: His military successes dated to the invasion of Mark Antony in 36 BCE. Returning the Roman standards lost by Antony and Crassus (in 53 BCE) was one of the 'forms of homage' Phraates employed (20 BCE). This paragraph and the three

NOTES
367

that follow it supply the Augustan background to the troubled
situation in the east mentioned at 2.1.1 and 2.5.1. Tiberius'
countermeasures begin at 2.43.1.

2. *Artabanus*: Subsequent developments in Artabanus' Parthia are
narrated at 6.31–7, 6.42–4.

3. *untrustworthy*: For other analyses of Armenian foreign policy
see 2.56.1, 13.34.2.

4. *Creticus Silanus*: For the end of his tenure see 2.43.2.

5. *where due*: At 2.68.

6. *building a fleet*: Germanicus was himself handling the Gallic
census in 14 CE when news of Augustus' demise arrived (1.31.2).
All of the officers mentioned here except Antius and Anteius
appeared earlier in the narrative (see the Index of Names).

7. *the Chatti*: For other incursions against the Chatti see 1.55–6,
2.25. Germanicus celebrates a triumph over this and other German tribes in 17 CE (2.41.2).

8. *Germanicus*: For his earlier operations in this area see 1.60.
Thirty years later, under Corbulo, a naval campaign here is no
longer labelled venturesome (11.18.2).

9. *a mistake*: The text of this passage is corrupt and its interpretation disputed. The only certainty is that Tacitus here criticizes
Germanicus' decision about the landing.

10. *laying out defences*: Tacitus' brevity leaves it unclear where these
defences were (at 2.9.1 Germanicus is already on the Weser, east
of the Ems) and when the Angrivarii (who at 2.19.2 seem to be
based east of the Weser) came under Roman control. Textual
corruption and authorial error have also been suspected here.

11. *Stertinius*: For his other special missions see 1.60.3, 1.71.1, 2.22.2.

12. *Arminius*: For similar scenes contrasting Arminius with other
Germans see 1.58–59 and 2.45–6.

13. *Your wife*: Arminius' wife was captured at 1.57.4; she gave birth
to a son in captivity (1.58.6).

14. *Follow Rome's birds*: An allusion to legions' eagle-topped standards.

15. *auxiliary cohorts opposed*: Literally, 'Raetian, Vindelican and
Gallic cohorts opposed.' The precise origins of these troops
mean little to a modern reader and are therefore elided in the
translation. A Roman reader would understand that what they
had in common was the non-citizen status of their soldiers, a
characteristic for which *auxiliary* is a useful shorthand.

16. *slingers*: Tacitus names two types of slinger here. A Roman
reader would have different associations for the two types

(different equipment, different tactics, different impact), but the distinction is lost on modern readers. Since this battle narrative emphasizes Germanicus' rapid response to developments on the ground I have given a simplified rendering instead of cluttering up the scene with unhelpful specificity.

17. *a thousand ships*: The text of this sentence is suspect; no emendation has won general acceptance.

18. *a triumph has been decreed*: At 1.55.1 (15 CE).

19. *internal strife*: This ensued at 2.44.2.

20. *a second consulship*: In the event, Germanicus' entire second consulship was served abroad (18 CE: 2.53.1 to 2.59.1) and Drusus was sent first to Illyricum, not Germany (2.44).

21. *Firmius Catus*: He is himself brought to trial at 4.31.4.

22. *Vescularius Flaccus*: His end is reported at 6.10.2.

23. *Fulcinius Trio*: His role here is a prelude to his involvement in the prosecution of Gnaeus Piso (3.10.1, 3.19.1) and other contentious actions (see 5.11, 6.4.2, 6.38.2).

24. *Vibius Serenus*: He was himself a defendant later (see 4.13.2, 4.28.1, 4.29.2–3).

25. *an official*: He was called a 'public agent'; the nature of his job is not known.

26. *Publius Quirinius*: For his personal connection to Tiberius see 3.48.

27. *Libo's property was divided*: The distribution of Libo's entire estate to his successful accusers is anomalous; the statutory award was a quarter of the estate (see 4.20.2). One of the accusers, Vibius Serenus, later claims that he got no reward (4.29.3).

28. *Libo's likeness*: On ancestor likenesses at Roman funerals see 3.5.1, 3.76.2, 4.9.2. For other appearances by the many senators named here and in the following sentences see the Index of Names. Plancus' name is restored by conjecture where the manuscript has a gap. Other names have also been proposed.

29. *the cliff*: For this punishment see 4.29.3. The phrase *an ancient punishment* refers to death by scourging. Tacitus uses other expressions for this at 4.30.1, 14.48.2 and 16.11.3.

30. *Lucius Piso*: For a reprise of these events and Piso's sudden death in 24 CE see 4.21.1–2. For his defence of his brother Gnaeus Piso in the interim see 3.11.2; for his father see 2.43.2; for his son 4.45.1.

31. *sent a summons*: The more negatively coloured report at 4.21.1 suggests that Piso delivered the summons himself and that Urgulania was at Livia's house at the time (see Goodyear's commentary).

32. *Piso ... Gallus*: For an earlier pairing of the two see 1.13.2–3.

33. *Italy's assembly and the provinces' converging*: These phrases allude in non-technical language to the fact that Italians and provincials came to Rome for trials and senatorial hearings. Juries for the former were equestrian.

34. *magistrates . . . be elected*: Starting in 14 CE magistrate 'elections' were effectively decided in the senate on the basis of the Emperor's recommendations (see 1.14.4 to 1.15.1). It is unclear whether Gallus' proposal was intended as an ad hoc measure or as a permanent arrangement. In either case the immediate consequence for Tiberius would have been an obligation (or opportunity) to name five years' worth of praetors and thereby create sixty praetors-designate.

35. *on the senate-house threshold*: More precisely, in the library situated in the portico of the Palatine temple of Apollo, which adjoined Augustus' house. The speaker's grandfather Hortensius was a former owner of the house.

36. *winning pity*: Hortalus presumably means that his pitiful plight might rouse antipathy against the (unspecified) persons or circumstances that caused it. Brevity renders the expression elliptical.

37. *Agrippa's murder*: The murder of Agrippa Postumus in 14 CE was reported at 1.6.1 as *the first action of the new regime*. His killers presumably used military transport. The words *had rescue not been quick* are somewhat puzzling, since Clemens was not caught until 16 CE, but presumably they refer to the short period between his arrival in Ostia and execution in Rome.

38. *Bovillae*: At 15.23.2 Tacitus refers to another honour for the Julian family at Bovillae, the Julian Games.

39. *Germanicus celebrated a triumph*: As Goodyear notes ad loc., 'Arminius . . . must have been conspicuous by his absence.' The geographer Strabo gives a fuller account of the procession (7.1.4).

40. *increased onlooker attention*: The Latin underlying this awkward expression is quite anomalous.

41. *the 1 per cent tax*: The burden of this tax was mentioned earlier (1.78.2) and the issue of taxation more generally is addressed at 13.50–51.

42. *what I reported above*: At 2.1–4.

43. *governors*: Tacitus names the two most senior categories of provincial governor here, those *chosen by lot or sent by the Emperor*. The glossing necessary to convey the meaning of these terms and of the lesser governorships that they subsume would unduly clutter the text and obscure the central point that Germanicus' authority in the east was superior to that of everyone but Tiberius.

44. *Creticus Silanus*: For an earlier reference to Silanus see 2.4.3. Piso made a number of earlier appearances (1.13.3, 1.74.5, 1.79.4, 2.35.1) and is a central figure in the narrative from this point until the conclusion of the trials held in connection with the death of Germanicus (3.19.2).

45. *Plancina*: 'The most unpleasant female in Tacitus' pages' (Goodyear, ad loc.). For her appearances see the Index of Names.

46. *female rivalry!*: The position of the Latin phrase underlying *female rivalry!* leaves it unclear whether Tacitus meant it to characterize Livia's motivation or Plancina's (subsequent) behaviour. It suits both situations and Tacitus would have found either unbecoming.

47. *Drusus*: He was born in 13 BCE and was therefore around thirty in 17 CE.

48. *given to . . . carouses*: For another perspective on Drusus' carousing see 3.37.2.

49. *at the Romans' departure*: The narrative picks up from 2.26.3.

50. *found favour*: Arminius later incurred the same sort of hostility as Maroboduus (see 2.88.2).

51. *killing Quinctilius Varus*: The events Arminius refers to here occurred during Augustus' principate (6 and 9 CE), before the beginning of the *Annals*.

52. *treacherous deception*: For Tacitus' narrative of this event see 1.63–8; for the capture and captivity of Arminius' wife and son see 1.57–8. The term *straggling* here renders the emendation *vagas* for the manuscript's *vacuas*. Others emend otherwise.

53. *an earthquake at night*: For other earthquakes see 4.13.1, 12.58.2, 15.22.2.

54. *Marcus Ateius*: The name of the senate's representative is not secure. Other emendations have been suggested for the garbled form in the manuscript.

55. *Marcus Servilius*: For a later episode involving Servilius see 3.22.2.

56. *testators naming the Emperor*: For other passages featuring bequests (or their absence) to the Emperor see 3.76.1, 16.11.1, 16.17.5.

57. *that same war*: i.e., in the first Punic War, 264–241 BCE. All of the temples mentioned here traced their origins to early centuries of the Republic.

58. *Appuleia Varilla*: The precise relationships between Varilla and Augustus and Tiberius are not clear.

59. *the Julian law*: The Julian law (or laws) of 18 BCE, which

regulated and rewarded marriage in the upper echelons of society, also established a complicated set of punishments for
adultery, one of which was banishment, as Tiberius recommends
to the informal court of her kinsmen just below.

60. *lest fear make the enemy avoid warfare*: At this spot the manuscript contains a feeble epigram that editors have excised from
Tacitus' text as an interpolation: 'By hope for victory they were
led on to their own defeat.'

61. *the Furius who recovered Rome*: Tacitus alludes (somewhat
inaccurately) to Furii from the 4th century BCE, best known now
from Livy's history.

62. *an honorary triumph*: This war, like that *finished* by Germanicus
(2.41.2), was not over. For subsequent episodes see 3.20–21,
3.32, 3.73–4, 4.13.2 and 4.23–6.

63. *his great-uncle . . . his grandfather*: For Germanicus' lineage see
2.43.5.

64. *Vonones . . . removed*: See 2.4.3.

65. *Quintus Veranius*: He is prominent among Germanicus' supporters in the sequel: 2.74.2, 3.10.1, 3.13.2, 3.17.2, 3.19.1.
Likewise Servaeus (mentioned in the next sentence): 3.13.2,
3.19.1.

66. *a receptacle*: i.e., Lake Moeris, its ancient name, or Birket Qarun,
its modern.

67. *the limits of the Roman Empire*: Tacitus' geography here, as
often, is imprecise and hard to square with modern maps. The
narrows are the Nile's southern cataract; Germanicus would
have reached Elephantine and Syene before the cataract. More
significant problems arise from the imprecision of his expression
now extends (*nunc patescit*) and the multiplicity of reference
possible in *to the Red Sea* (*rubrum ad mare*; see 14.25.2), because
scholars have elicited from this statement of *present extent* and
its relationship to real conditions during the reign of Trajan
information about the date at which Tacitus was writing. If, as
some argue, this bit of Book 2 was written *c.* 116 CE, after Trajan's conquest of Parthia and before Hadrian's cession of it in
117, then the bulk of the *Annals* was written under Hadrian. For
discussion see Goodyear's commentary.

68. *Germanicus spent this summer*: Only Egypt has been mentioned,
however, for the summer of 19 CE. This discrepancy and others
involving the ovation Drusus was awarded for these achievements (see 2.64.1, 3.11.1) incline some to place chapters 62–7
immediately after chapter 58, thereby moving the events here

described to 18 CE, the year of Germanicus' journey from Rome
to his eastern command.

69. *Vibilius*: He is called king of the Hermunduri at 12.29.1 (50 CE),
where he is involved in the expulsion of Vannius (mentioned in
the text below).

70. *the Marus and Cusus rivers*: The Marus is the modern Morava;
the Cusus has been variously identified.

71. *dispel the animosity of accusation*: This phrase is as cryptic in
English as is the underlying Latin (*transferret . . . invidiam crim-
inis*). It is unclear whether this accusation is the 'trap' by Cotys
alleged by Rhescuporis or the 'trickery' on Rhescuporis' part
mentioned by Tiberius. Likewise unclear is whose animosity is
involved. Presumably but not certainly Tiberius', given the paragraph's opening reference to his anxiety.

72. *Thrace was divided*: For the sequel in Thrace see 3.38–9,
4.47–51.

73. *whose removal . . . I mentioned*: At 2.43.2.

74. *tell my . . . brother*: Germanicus mentions one brother (presumably Drusus), but had two; Claudius doesn't count in this
narrative (see 3.5.2, 3.18.3–4).

75. *Vibius Marsus*: Unlike the other associates of Germanicus mentioned here, after a brief reference at 2.79.1 Marsus disappears
until much later in the narrative of Tiberius' principate: 4.56.3,
6.47.2 to 6.48.1.

76. *Martina*: She died en route in suspicious circumstances: 3.7.2.

77. *preparing charges*: For the eventual proceedings against Piso and
Plancina and their sons and associates see 3.10–19.

78. *horns*: See note 17 to Book 1.

79. *these men*: The crowd here refers to Drusus and his son Germanicus. For their republican sentiments see 1.33.2.

80. *a shield . . . amidst the leaders of eloquence*: Such 'shields' bore
likenesses of the honorand; a series honouring orators adorned
the senate house. Augustus had one, too.

81. *Germanicus' section*: This seating section was a portion of the
fourteen rows reserved for the equestrian order at public shows
(see 15.32).

82. *Vistilia*: Her father may be the ex-praetor Sextus Vistilius mentioned at 6.9.2.

83. *He promised*: The text of this sentence is suspect in two separate
places, but the meaning is clear.

84. *poisoning aimed at Pyrrhus*: A story from the 3rd century BCE
most easily accessible in Plutarch, *Life of Pyrrhus* 21.

85. *Arminius ... tried for kingship*: Earlier, Arminius' policy fostered liberty: see 2.44.2.
86. *He completed thirty-seven years of life*: Arminius' death seems to have occurred in 21 CE, at any rate several years after his last effective action against a Roman opponent; see 11.16 for more on the sequel in Germany. Using Adgandestrius' letter as a pretext, Tacitus relates it here (under 19 CE) for maximum effect.

BOOK 3

1. *consuls Marcus Valerius and Marcus Aurelius*: Tacitus here names these men using the form traditional in official contexts such as dates. Elsewhere he refers to the former with other elements of his name (see the Index of Names under Cotta Messalinus). The traditional form of the names makes the anomalous year-beginning formula all the more striking (see the Introduction, p. xxxix).
2. *the only blood relative of Augustus*: Their enthusiasm for Agrippina blinds these speakers to the existence of another granddaughter (Julia, in exile since 8 CE: 4.71.4) and to Livia's pretensions to old-fashioned virtue (5.1.3).
3. *His brother*: Germanicus had two brothers: Drusus (by adoption) and Claudius.
4. *Megalensia Festival*: This annual civic festival at Rome included official events such as religious observances honouring the Great Mother goddess and theatrical performances. The festival took place in April, which helps to date the upcoming trial. Germanicus died in October 19 CE and the final verdicts on his trial were not published until December 20 CE.
5. *as I said*: At 2.74.2.
6. *after sending his son*: Piso sent his younger son Marcus, whose part in eastern events is recounted at 2.76.2–3; for his role in the trial of his parents and for the post-trial fate of both of Piso's sons see 3.16–18.
7. *Drusus' reply*: The studied ambiguity of Drusus' expression is faithful to the Latin.
8. *youth's easy temper*: Drusus was in his thirties (born in 13 BCE).
9. *Fulcinius Trio*: For Trio as accuser see 2.28.2–3 and 5.11.1 and the accompanying notes. Of the members of Germanicus' retinue, Vitellius and Veranius were mentioned by name earlier, too (1.70.1, 2.56.4, 2.74.2).

10. *his mother's complicity*: See esp. 2.43.4, 2.77.3, 2.82.1. For the consequences of Livia's alleged complicity see 3.17.4, 6.26.3.

11. *the senate had voted*: See 2.64.1. The vote involved parallel honours for Germanicus (then still alive) and Drusus. For the military successes here acknowledged see 2.62–3.

12. *an assistant to Germanicus*: The narrative background to this speech begins with the appointments of Germanicus and Piso (2.42–3), continues with their arrival and early actions (2.53–61, 2.64) and ends with their final quarrels, Piso's departure, Germanicus' death and funeral, and Piso's return and defeat in battle (2.68–81). Light is shed on the whole episode by a large inscription that reports 'the senate's decision about the elder Piso' (*Senatus consultum de Cn. Pisone patre* or *SCPP*).

13. *Servaeus*: His connection with Germanicus is illustrated at 2.56.4 and remembered during his trial at 6.7.2–4.

14. ***: Some text has been lost at this point.

15. *foiled by Sejanus*: An ominous but passing reference to Sejanus, who was introduced earlier (1.24.2), appears occasionally in Book 3 and dominates Books 4 and 5 (see 4.1.1 and the Index of Names).

16. ***: Some text has been lost at this point.

17. *The first proposal*: Meaning the function of speaking first, which usually went to consuls-designate (if any) when the consuls themselves were presiding.

18. *as I have often recorded*: For Tacitus' prior references to Tiberius' resistance to other people's money see 1.75.2 and 2.48; at 4.20.1 he marks a change.

19. *Valerius Messalinus*: It is unclear whether this is the Valerius active earlier and later in Tiberius' principate (consul in 3 BCE: 1.8.4, 3.34.2–5) or his son, the present year's consul (3.2.3), who is not otherwise mentioned. For Caecina (consul in 1 BCE) see 1.31.2 and 3.33.

20. *Lucius Asprenas*: See also 1.53.6.

21. *a recommendation for office*: Trio reached the consulship only in 31 CE (5.11.1).

22. *retake the auspices*: This renewed the foreign command that Drusus laid down to attend the trials in Rome (3.11.1).

23. *Vipsania*: See 1.12.4. The deaths of her five siblings and half-siblings are noted in the extant books of the *Annals*: Gaius and Lucius Caesar (1.3.3), Agrippa Postumus (1.6.1), Julia (4.71.4) and the elder Agrippina (6.25.1).

24. *renewed the war in Africa*: For the earlier episode (from 17 CE)

see 2.52. The war against Tacfarinas continues until 24 CE:
3.32–5, 3.72–4, 4.23–6.

25. *the Pagyda*: The modern name of this river is unknown.

26. *Lucius Apronius*: See 1.56.1 and 4.13.3; Camillus was in command at 2.52.3–5.

27. *torques and spear*: The military decorations mentioned in this passage – *torques, spear* and (in the next sentence) *civic crown* – are widely depicted on Roman *officer* tombstones; the civic crown is much the rarest.

28. *Publius Quirinius*: He was last mentioned at 2.30.4, in connection with a trial strikingly similar to Lepida's. For his death and social obscurity (adduced below) see 3.48.1–2.

29. *Manius Lepidus*: He appears again at 3.32.2.

30. *Marcus Servilius*: He benefited financially from a ruling of Tiberius at 2.48.1.

31. *entered the theatre*: Pompey's theatre, dedicated in 55 BCE as a monument to his military achievements.

32. *exile*: Literally, 'exclusion from fire and water'. For this punishment, usually applied to those convicted of treason, see 3.38.2, 3.50.4, 3.68.2, 4.21.3, etc. For another of Rubellius Blandus' proposals see 3.51.1. For Blandus' own marriage connections to the imperial household see 6.27.1, 6.45.2.

33. *Mamercus Scaurus*: He may be the man mentioned at 1.13.4; see further 3.31.3–4 (new marriage connections), 3.66.1–2 (involvement in another trial) and 6.29.3–4 (his own trial and death).

34. *the ends of the others*: Tacitus has already described the fate of one of them, Sempronius Gracchus, in some detail (1.53.3–6) and alluded to that of another, Jullus Antonius (1.10.4 and 3.18.1; see also 4.44.3).

35. *Marcus Silanus*: See also 3.57.1 and 6.20.1.

36. *the Papia/Poppaea law*: This was named for the consuls of 9 CE, the year it became law; Augustus (born 63 BCE) was past seventy. The Julian laws (or law) of 18 BCE, named after Augustus himself, regulated and rewarded marriage in the upper echelons of society.

37. *Romulus . . . Numa . . . Tullus Hostilius . . . Ancus Martius*: This list of Rome's kings omits the Tarquinii (Priscus and Superbus), but Superbus is mentioned at the start of chapter 27.

38. *After Tarquinius Superbus' expulsion*: This paragraph runs through Roman history at a rapid pace and with significant gaps (all dates are BCE): Superbus' expulsion (509); various

liberty-protecting measures (early 5th century); Board of Ten and Twelve Tables (451–450); Gracchi (130s and 120s); Saturninus (tribune in 103 and 100); Drusus (tribune in 91, or perhaps his father in the 120s); Italian War (91–88); Civil War (88–86); Sulla (dictator in 82–81); Lepidus (consul in 78); restoration of tribunician powers (complete in 70). New courts were established on various occasions during the last two centuries of the Republic; perhaps most salient here (given their position in the list) are the laws passed by Clodius resulting in Cicero's exile in 58.

39. *Then Pompey*: The historical survey continues with Pompey's third consulship (52 BCE) and military defeat at Pharsalus (48 BCE); Augustus' sixth consulship (28 BCE); and the Papia/Poppaea law (9 CE). It then returns to the narrative present of Tiberius' principate (20 CE).

40. *Nero*: The eldest of Germanicus' sons, this Nero was born around 6 CE and was now in his early teens. This is his first adult appearance in the *Annals*. His public career and eventual removal by Sejanus constitute a leitmotif in the remaining books on Tiberius' principate (see 4.4, 4.8, 4.15, 4.17, 4.59–60, 4.67, 4.70, 5.3–4, 6.27).

41. *Augustus' entreaty*: Augustus' promotion of his stepsons resulted in quaestorships at age nineteen for Tiberius (24 BCE) and Drusus (19 BCE).

42. *Defilement of Claudian nobility!*: By Tiberius. Other reactions evoked by the prospect of this marriage are mentioned at 4.7.2 and 4.39.2.

43. *the wealth*: The family's wealth is mentioned again in the obituary of Volusius' son (13.30.2); the Volusii were still prominent during Tacitus' lifetime (consuls in 87 and 92).

44. *complicit in the killing*: For Crispus' role in Agrippa Postumus' death see 1.6.3 and 2.40.2.

45. *Maecenas*: His loss of influence is used by Tacitus' Seneca as an argument for retirement (14.55.2).

46. *those who have nothing left to desire*: Tacitus' equestrian minister Sejanus has much in common with Maecenas and Sallustius.

47. *Two years earlier*: The reference is to 18 CE (2.53.1), three years before. It is not clear whether the mistake is the historian's or a scribe's. With *the real connection* Tacitus reminds the reader that Germanicus was both Tiberius' nephew and his adopted son.

48. *retreated to Campania*: For Tiberius' return see 3.64.1. His absence is made present to the reader when he communicates with the senate via letter (3.32.1, 3.35.1, 3.47.1, 3.52.3, 3.56.1).

49. *Domitius Corbulo*: The reputation of Corbulo's like-named son eclipses his own (see the Index of Names). This Lucius Sulla may be the future consul of 33 (6.15.1).

50. *Scaurus ... Arruntius*: For Scaurus see 3.23.2; for Arruntius see 1.8.3 and 3.11.2.

51. *It is your decision*: Most militarily active provinces were governed by the Emperor's appointees, but the senate selected governors for Asia and Africa from its own ranks, usually by lot. The reference to Tacfarinas connects this episode with those at 2.52, 3.20–21, 3.72.4–3.74, and 4.23–6.

52. *Sextus Pompeius*: See his other appearances as consul of 14 CE (1.7.1) and declining to defend Gnaeus Piso (3.11.2).

53. *Caecina*: His most recent appearance was at 3.18.2.

54. *a woman presided*: The reference is most directly to the behaviour of Plancina in Syria (2.55.6), but also, obliquely, to that of Agrippina, especially in Germany (see 1.69.1–2).

55. *the Oppian and other laws*: The reference to the Oppian law points the reader to the debate over its repeal in 215 BCE, which was narrated by Livy (34.2–4) and dominated by Cato the Elder.

56. *Valerius Messalinus*: For Messalinus see 1.8.4; his father Messala (who outshone his son in Tacitus' view) is mentioned at 4.34.4, 6.11.3, 11.6.2, 13.34.1.

57. *Lepidus ... Blaesus*: For Lepidus see also 1.13.2, 3.11.2 and 3.50–1; for Blaesus see also 3.73–4 and 1.16.2. At 3.72 the pair are shown together earning praise in different spheres.

58. *was supported by*: The underlying Latin text is corrupt.

59. *Gaius Cestius*: He is forced to do Tiberius' bidding at 6.7.2 and appears as consul at 6.31.1 (35 CE).

60. *indicted Crete's governor*: The outcome of this trial is reported at 3.70.1.

61. *Thrace*: The situation in Thrace, summarized below, was explained in some detail at 2.64.2 to 2.67.

62. *Control of Thrace*: The brevity of this summary renders the meaning obscure; the text is also suspect.

63. *Gaius Silius*: Governor of Upper Germany, he plays the dominant role in the suppression of the Sacrovir revolt, and he paid the price of success by attracting Tiberius' hostility: 4.18–20.

64. *opulent, unwarlike ... be ready for runaways!*: The text and interpretation of this passage are disputed.

65. *<heading for>*: A word or more has fallen out of the text here.

66. *I will go*: He did not go.

67. *Cornelius Dolabella*: For other attention-seeking moves by

Dolabella, who would be the senate's appointee as governor of Africa in 24 CE (4.23.2), see 3.69.1, 4.66, 11.22.2.

68. *a meaningless reward*: Tiberius celebrated full triumphs in 7 BCE (Germany) and 12 CE (Pannonia), and the more modest triumph called an 'ovation' in 9 CE (Pannonia).

69. *Quirinius . . . at Lepida*: This episode is reported at 3.22.1. Quirinius' power may derive from his combination of wealth and childlessness.

70. *Haterius Agrippa*: See 1.77.3.

71. *Marcus Lepidus*: He was introduced at 1.13.2, see note 11 to Book 1. The present passage illustrates the balance that Tacitus credits him with at 4.20.2, particularly in its combination of arguments used by Caesar (for clemency) and Cato (for severity) in Sallust's famous debate over the punishment of the Catilinarian conspirators.

72. *I have often heard*: See, for example, 2.31.3.

73. *Rubellius Blandus*: For another trial involving Blandus see 3.23.2 and note 32 to Book 3.

74. *luxury*: This episode resumes the theme of luxury and its repression introduced at 2.33.

75. *subsistence*: For Tiberius' attention to the food supply see 2.87.1, 4.6.4.

76. *Italy's municipalities*: Tacitus mentions two types of Italian municipality here – indigenous towns and citizen colonies – but the distinction is unimportant in the context, so I use the shorthand *Italy's municipalities*. For the modern reader, the irrelevant constitutional detail would obscure the more important pairing of Italy and the provinces.

77. *the age I myself was*: Tiberius was thirty-six in 6 BCE when he was given tribunician power; Drusus (born 14 or 13 BCE) was thirty-five or thirty-six in 22 CE. The *eight years' trial* mentioned in the next sentence began in 14 CE when Tiberius became emperor.

78. *a triumph and two consulships*: For Drusus' triumph in 20 CE see 3.19.3; he was consul in 15 CE (1.55.1) and 21 CE (3.31.1).

79. *Marcus Silanus*: See also 3.24.3–4 and 6.20.1.

80. *Quintus Haterius*: For his obituary notice see 4.61. His son has just been mentioned as one of the year's consuls (3.52.1).

81. *Blaesus . . . Maluginensis*: For Blaesus' appointment to Africa in 21 CE see 3.35. For Maluginensis see also 3.71.2–3 and 4.16.1.

82. *seventy-five years*: Conflicting evidence makes both seventy-five (an emendation) and seventy-two (the transmitted text) possible

numbers here. The gap in the series of Jupiter-priests covered much of the 1st century BCE; Merula died amidst civil conflict in 87 BCE, Maluginensis seems to have been chosen by Augustus at some point around 11 BCE.

83. *The Magnesians*: There were (at least) two cities in Asia Minor called Magnesia. The temple belongs to Magnesia on the Mae-ander, but the second of the stories about Magnesia's loyalty to Rome under duress may, instead, pertain to Magnesia in Sipylus. If so, Tacitus must have added it erroneously to the claim made by the Magnesians themselves during their hearing before the senate. The dates are 190 BCE (Scipio/Antiochus) and 88 BCE (Sulla/Mithridates).

84. *a Parthian invasion*: The invasion alluded to here occurred in 40 BCE.

85. *They also named*: Cyrus 'the Great' ruled Persia in the 6th century BCE. The Roman generals came later: Perpenna as victor over Aristonicus in 130 BCE; Isauricus as governor of Asia under Caesar's dictatorship in 46–44 BCE.

86. *dedicating a statue of Augustus*: Tiberius, who had been absent from Rome for more than a year at this point (see 3.31.2 for 21 CE), obviously missed the dedication ceremony.

87. *the major priesthoods*: Specifically, 'by the pontiffs and the augurs and the boards of 15 and 7 and the Augustales'. The *war-priests* mentioned at the end of this paragraph are the fetials.

88. *Lucius Apronius*: See 1.56.1. His reason for promoting the war-priests is unknown.

89. *Mamercus Scaurus*: See 3.23.2.

90. *ancient precedents*: These trials took place in 138, 149 and 116 BCE, respectively; only in the first was the charge certainly extortion. All three prosecutions failed.

91. *actively defiled*: This renders the otherwise unattested verb *pro-polluebat*; scholars often emend.

92. *Bruttedius*: He was, among other things, a historian; only a few fragments of his work survive.

93. *Marcus Paconius*: His later career is alluded to indirectly at 16.28–9, when his son is said to possess his father's hatred for emperors and he himself to have perished through Tiberius' brutality.

94. *Lucius Piso*: This Piso has been plausibly identified as *the pontifex*, on whom see 6.10.3.

95. *Gnaeus Lentulus*: See 4.29.1. The name of Silanus' mother is a conjecture; the manuscript reads *alia*. For his son see 6.9.3.

96. *Cornelius Dolabella*: For more flattery from Dolabella see 3.47.3 and note 67 to Book 3.

97. *Gyarus*: See also 4.30.1.

98. *Cordus was found guilty of extortion*: His trial commenced at 3.38.1.

99. *Ateius Capito*: For his normally deferential behaviour see his obituary at 3.75.

100. *outstanding career*: These words render an uncertain text on the basis of the antithesis with *domestic rectitude*.

101. *Livia's health*: For Livia's *alarming illness* in 22 CE see 3.64.1.

102. *postponed decision*: See 3.58–9.

103. *Marcus Lepidus*: See 1.13.2. He and Blaesus (see note 108 below) were shown as rivals for the governorship of Africa at 3.35.

104. *Augustus did not prevent*: In fact, Augustus encouraged such munificence (see Velleius Paterculus 2.89.4; Suetonius, *Augustus* 29). The buildings here alluded to were dedicated in the early part of his principate.

105. *Tiberius promised to rebuild*: On Tiberius' reputation for stingy contributions to the adornment of Rome see also 6.45.1. Here his generosity is connected with his promotion of Sejanus, for which see 4.2.

106. *For Tacfarinas*: The Africa narrative resumes from 3.21.

107. *Not even Spartacus*: Spartacus' rebellion and the wars against Sertorius and Mithridates took place in the 70s BCE. All three figured prominently in Sallust's *Histories*.

108. *Blaesus' son*: Blaesus' sons are also mentioned at 1.19.4 and 6.40.2.

109. *an imperator-salute*: The terminology here resists translation. The point is that when victorious legions saluted their commander with the title *imperator* they were using a term that later became synonymous with emperors (*imperatores*).

110. *Asinius Saloninus*: His name preserves the memory of a military exploit by one of his grandfathers: Pollio's capture of Salonae in 39 BCE. His *brother Drusus* was Tiberius' son, who himself dies young (4.8); Agrippa's daughter Vipsania, Tiberius' first wife, was mother to both. His intended wife was presumably one of Germanicus' daughters. His father Asinius Gallus (on whom see 1.13.2) is not mentioned.

111. *Ateius Capito*: For his involvement in *civic business* see 1.76.1, 1.79.1, 3.70.1–3. The term is generally understood more precisely as a reference to his expertise as jurist, which Labeo shared, but as often Tacitus uses an expression with wider resonance.

112. *have precedence over*: This phrase is an inadequate rendering of
     Tacitus' etymological play with Antistius' name (literally, 'one
     who stands in front') in connection with the status rivalry
     between the two men, which is echoed in the following sentence
     in the expression rendered here, again inadequately, 'limited to
     the praetorship' (literally, 'standing no higher than the praetor-
     ship'). Antistius wrote a treatise on etymology (Aulus Gellius,
     Attic Nights 13.10.1–2).

113. *she omitted Tiberius!*; For the issue of bequests (or the absence
     thereof) to the Emperor see 2.48.2.

BOOK 4

1. *whose power I mentioned earlier*: See especially 1.24.2 and
    3.66.3 (for other mentions see the Index of Names); Sejanus is
    omnipresent in this book and the surviving fragment of Book 5.

2. *by what action he advanced to seize mastery*: The reference here
    is presumably to the poisoning of Tiberius' son Drusus (see
    4.8.1).

3. *Seius Strabo*: He was a very distinguished member of the eques-
    trian order: commander of the Guard (see 1.7.2, 1.24.2) and
    subsequently governor of Egypt. Gaius Caesar died in 4 CE (see
    1.3.3) and was replaced as heir presumptive by Tiberius (see
    6.51.2).

4. *Sejanus' statues*: For a recently erected statue (and a good illus-
    tration of Tiberius' favour for Sejanus) see 3.72.3.

5. *adult son and grown grandsons*: Drusus (born c. 14 BCE) was in
    his thirties; the grandsons (Germanicus' sons Nero, Drusus, Gaius
    and Drusus' twins) ranged in age from late teens to quite young.

6. *The senate's decisions*: For the honours voted to Nero see 3.29.1.

7. *Drusus*: This is Tiberius' son, uncle to the Drusus mentioned
    earlier in the chapter.

8. *How much narrower the Empire?*: A contrast with Tacitus' own
    day is implicit in the following survey.

9. *approximately equivalent strength*: Equivalent, that is, to regular
    army numbers.

10. *colleague*: Sejanus became Tiberius' consular colleague in 31 CE,
    just before his fall.

11. *Future grandchildren*: For the betrothal of Sejanus' young
    daughter to a short-lived son of Tiberius' nephew (and future
    emperor) Claudius see 3.29.4; Sejanus boasts of it at 4.39.2.

12. *eight years later*: Drusus died in July of 23 CE; the fact of his death is curiously understated here. Details of his murder came to light after Sejanus' fall.

13. *replace your parents*: Their mother, the elder Agrippina, was still alive, however.

14. *the same things were decreed*: For (some of) Germanicus' honours see 2.83.

15. *grandmother ... daughter-in-law*: The terms used of Livia's relationships with Germanicus' sons and their mother skip a generation here: she was the boys' great-grandmother and mother to Agrippina's husband's father.

16. *remission of taxes*: For more earthquake relief see 2.47 and note 53 to Book 2.

17. *Vibius Serenus*: The prequel to this brief notice was given at 2.30, an extended sequel at 4.28–30, with *appalling behaviour* all around.

18. *Sacerdos ... Tacfarinas ... Gracchus*: For Sacerdos' eventual exile on a different charge see 6.48.4; for Tacfarinas see 2.52.1. This Gracchus may be the Gracchus mentioned in an unflattering light at 6.38.4; for his father's misfortunes see 1.53.3–6.

19. *Lamia ... Apronius*: For Lamia's obituary see 6.27.2 (33 CE); the precise date of his governorship of Africa is not known. On Apronius in Africa see 3.21; he is also mentioned at 4.22.1 (another trial) and 4.73 (a military debacle) and in more minor senatorial and military roles earlier (see the Index of Names).

20. *Amphictyonies*: These councils ruled on religious matters involving Greek city-states.

21. *on King Mithridates' order*: The slaughter of Romans and Italians in Asia Minor was ordered by Mithridates in 88 BCE to initiate war with Rome.

22. *Farces*: The entertainment known as the Oscan (or Atellane, from the Oscan town of Atella) farce was presumably no longer performed (if it ever was) in Oscan; hence Tacitus' rather pedantic 'formerly'.

23. *expelled from Italy*: Actors were expelled again, after their return under Gaius, in 56 CE (see 13.25.4). For earlier stages of the problem see 1.54.2, 1.77.

24. *Drusus' twins*: For the twins' birth in 19 CE see 2.84.1.

25. *Gaius Silanus' punishment*: The story is told in considerable detail at 3.66–9.

26. *a temple*: For more on this temple see 4.55–6; Livia is not mentioned in connection with either punishment.

27. *spelt-wed parents*: Spelt-marriage or *confarreatio* takes its name from the (obscure) role played by the grain spelt (*far*) in this archaic form of wedding. As *pontifex maximus*, Tiberius would choose the priest of Jupiter.

28. *He mentioned*: Tacitus' other passages on Maluginensis describe in some detail the career impediments faced by holders of this priesthood (3.58.1–3, 3.71.2–3).

29. *Gaius Silius*: He was in command of Upper Germany's legions at the tempestuous beginning of Tiberius' principate in 14 CE and stayed there until 21 CE (1.31.2, 2.6–7, 2.25, 3.42–6); for the honorary triumph of 15 CE see 1.72.1, for victory in the Sacrovir War of 21 CE see 3.46.

30. *postponing Sabinus for now*: For Sabinus' eventual trial in 28 CE see 4.68–70.

31. *inherited antagonism*: For the enmity Varro inherited from his father see 3.43.3.

32. *old-fashioned terminology*: Tiberius adopts the wording of a now-defunct institution, the 'final decree of the senate' or SCU (*senatus consultum ultimum*).

33. *the long Sacrovir cover-up*: For the 'cover-up' allegations see 3.44.3.

34. *provincials*: This word is a gloss rather than a translation for Tacitus' *stipendiariis*, which literally means 'payers of tribute'. Tribute refers to taxes assessed on provincials and used (so the theory went) to pay for the armies that protected them. In this period Roman citizens did not pay this tax. Extortion charges such as those on which Silius and his wife were 'caught' were normally brought by provincials reclaiming (the verb is *repetere*) the property extorted, but those charges do not seem to have gone forward.

35. *Asinius Gallus*: See 1.8.3.

36. *Marcus Lepidus*: See 1.13.2.

37. *Cotta Messalinus*: His bad behaviour (occasionally with reference to his illustrious ancestors) is also pilloried at 2.32.2, 3.17.4, 6.5.1, 6.7.1.

38. *Lucius Piso*: This Piso, who also appears at 3.11.2, is often called 'the augur' to distinguish him from his homonymous contemporary 'the pontifex' (on whom see 3.68 and 6.10.3); for his outburst and the indictment of Urgulania see 2.34. For his father see 2.43.2, for his son see 4.45.1.

39. *Cassius Severus*: He had been in exile since sometime late in Augustus' principate (see 1.72.3). The phrase *removal to Crete*, like

Tacitus' Latin, eschews standard terminology: exile without property confiscation was normally called 'relegation' or 'banishment'.

40. *into freefall*: Tacitus' Latin is as vague as the English here; only later does one discover, via Tiberius' investigation, that Silvanus pushed his wife out of a bedroom window.

41. *Lucius Apronius*: See 4.13.3 and note 19 above.

42. *three laurelled statues*: For the war's earlier phases see 2.52, 3.20–21, 3.32, 3.73–4.

43. *Juba's son Ptolemy*: In the survey of the Empire as of 23 CE, Ptolemy's father Juba was still king (4.5.2). Ptolemy's execution in Rome in 40 CE (Dio 59.25.1) may have been mentioned in the lost books of the *Annals*.

44. *Blaesus' achievements*: For Blaesus (Sejanus' uncle) see 1.16.2. His governorship of Africa began under a cloud, at least in Tacitus' account (3.35). Dolabella, too, attracted dispraise in earlier appearances (3.47.3–4, 3.69); for the sequel see 4.66.2 and 11.22.2–6.

45. *from the Garamantes*: For their contribution to the war see 4.23.2.

46. *pasturelands*: This province was one of several that involved responsibilities exercised in Italy. They rarely surface in the historical record.

47. *both named Vibius Serenus*: For Serenus *père*, a former governor of Spain, see 4.13.2; the son returns as accuser at 4.36.3.

48. *He supplied funds*: Presumably in connection with Sacrovir's revolt (3.40–46).

49. *Lentulus . . . Tubero*: For Lentulus' other appearances see 1.27.1, 2.32.2, 3.68.2, 4.44.1 (his obituary); for Tubero see 2.20.1. Both men were sent with Tiberius' sons to counter the mutinies of 14 CE.

50. *murmuring threats*: *The oak* refers to some element of pre-execution confinement in the execution chamber; *the cliff* to the Tarpeian cliff, from which traitors were thrown to their deaths; and *kin-killer punishments* to a much-feared form of execution: a parricide was flogged, enclosed in a sack with various biting animals, and submerged in water.

51. *after Libo's conviction*: For the entrapment and trial of Libo see 2.27–32 with 2.30.1 for Serenus' role and 2.32.1 for the other accusers' rewards.

52. *Publius Suillius*: For what survives of Tacitus' account of Suillius' career under Claudius see 11.1–2, 11.4–7, 13.42–3.

53. *Firmius Catus*: For his role in Libo's destruction see 2.27.1.

54. *Huge wars*: Tacitus catalogues in brief the typical material of histories of the Republic, a period characterized (according to this summary) by vigorous military exertion abroad and, at home, conflicts between magistrates (consuls, tribunes) and interest groups (the commons, the *best men*) for control of public business, such as legislation concerning the distribution of public land and food assistance. With the expression *best men* Tacitus adopts, no doubt ironically, a political slogan used in the Late Republic for those who favoured senatorial control over what was in their view demagoguery. Once Augustus had taken into his own hands *the business of the senate, the magistrates, and the laws* (1.2.1), not to mention control of the army, the nature of the historical record was bound to be very different.

55. *Scipio, Afranius . . . Cassius and Brutus*: These men fought on the Pompeian side in the civil war; the first two died as Pompeians; Brutus and Cassius joined Caesar after Pharsalus.

56. *Messala Corvinus*: See also 3.34.2, 6.11.3, 11.6.2, 13.34.1.

57. *Cicero's book*: Cicero's *Cato* is lost, but left traces in the biographical tradition; of Caesar's rebuttal, the *Anticato*, some fragments survive.

58. *known from their likenesses*: Tacitus drew attention to the absent likenesses of Brutus and Cassius in his account of a descendant's funeral (3.76.2).

59. *the city's superintendent*: This phrase renders the title of a temporary office to which dignitaries were occasionally appointed. This Drusus is the son of Germanicus, and as *superintendent* he conducted rituals associated with the Latin Festival. For the regular official with a very similar title in Latin, normally rendered 'Urban Prefect', see 6.11.

60. *Sextius Marius*: Acquitted here, he was successfully prosecuted later (6.19.1).

61. *Mithridates' rebuff*: Cyzicus, a port city on the Sea of Marmara, survived a long siege by Mithridates, king of Pontus, in the 70s BCE, when Lucullus was in command of the war against him.

62. *the very gods and goddesses*: The reference to female divinities seems an apposite reminder of Livia's involvement in the proffered cult, which Tacitus' Tiberius otherwise studiously ignores.

63. *a connection with you*: For the connection, which was fairly distant as yet (Sejanus was future father-in-law to a great-nephew of Tiberius), but even so aroused ill-feeling, see 3.29.4 and 4.7.2.

64. *your house*: The Latin does not specify whose house is meant or which children. Some assume Sejanus is speaking about the

advantage to his own current household (three children; see
5.9.1) from this connection to the imperial house; the translation
here leaves open the possibility of a reference to Tiberius' bloodline (Livilla's present children, the surviving twin and a daughter
called Julia, were Tiberius' grandchildren; see 2.84.1, 3.29.4).
Agrippina's grievances were directed more against Tiberius'
descendants than against Sejanus' (see 4.12.3 and 4.40.3).

65. *far from Rome*: For different explanations of Tiberius' eventual
withdrawal from Rome see 4.57.

66. *punished with exile*: The Julian law penalty was banishment (see
2.50.2–3); exile also involved property confiscation. For more
on Ligus and Gaetulicus see the juxtaposed notices at 6.30.1 and
6.30.2–4.

67. *Philip ... Caesar ... Antony*: Philip II, Alexander's father, controlled the Peloponnese after 338 BCE; Caesar and Antony in the
40s BCE.

68. *Antigonus ... Mummius ... Milesians ... Geminus*: Antigonus
III's involvement in the area came in the 220s BCE, Mummius
governed the area for the Romans after 146 BCE, the Milesian
arbitration took place in 135 BCE. Atidius Geminus seems to
have been a governor of early Augustan date.

69. *the Rutilius precedent*: Publius Rutilius Rufus was a notable
Roman statesman who fell victim to corrupt politics in the early
1st century BCE. His 'precedent' is mentioned very allusively
here: he was banished and abandoned Rome for good in the late
90s BCE, and wrote memoirs (which Tacitus mentions as a precedent for his own *Agricola*; see *Agricola* 1) in exile.

70. *Gnaeus Lentulus*: For his brief appearances earlier see 4.29.1
and note 49; his career was mostly Augustan.

71. *the younger Antonia*: Tacitus has confused Octavia's two daughters by Antony: Domitius was married to the elder Antonia.
Similarly at 12.64.2. Domitius' German campaign was alluded
to at 1.63.4.

72. *Jullus Antonius*: A son of the famous Antony, he was raised in
the imperial household and executed for adultery (or committed
suicide) in 2 BCE.

73. *Poppaeus Sabinus*: He was governor of Moesia (1.80.1). The
variety of peoples in Thrace was sketched on the occasion of an
earlier uprising at 3.38.3–4. The term rendered here as *no civilization* (*incultu*) has been thought intolerably harsh in its syntax
and variously emended.

74. *Pomponius Labeo*: He is not mentioned again in the extended

narrative of Sabinus' success, but reappears at 6.29.1–2, where
he commits suicide after Tiberius ends their friendship. There are
earlier references to Rhoemetalces at 2.67.2, 3.38.3 and 4.5.3.

75. *Domitius Afer*: He is involved in another prosecution at 4.66.1
and receives a brief obituary at 14.19.1.

76. *Sosia, struck down*: See 4.19–20.

77. ***: In the manuscript there is a blank space in this sentence into
which a few words would fit, probably a relative pronoun,
'who', and a description of 'Germanicus' spouse'.

78. *Ignorant of deception*: The ambiguity of this phrase – unaware
of being deceived or incapable of employing deceit? – reflects the
ambiguity of the Latin.

79. *devotion to the Roman people*: The services mentioned in this
paragraph and the next are connected with Rome's wars in the
2nd and 1st centuries BCE: wars against Perses (171–168, also
referred to as the Macedonian war) and Aristonicus (131–129);
the external wars also include the war with Antiochus (191–
188); the wars in Italy include the Social and civil wars (91–88
and much of the period between 88 and 31); Sulla led Rome's
armies in the war against Mithridates (88–84). The consulship of
Marcus Porcius (Cato the Elder) was in 195 BCE. For a comparable review of relations between Byzantium and Rome see 12.62.

80. *the leaders' names*: Tyrrhenia is another name for Etruria; the
adjective form 'Tyrrhenian' is more common.

81. *named for Pelops*: The Peloponnese, 'Pelops' island'.

82. *one of the Amazons*: i.e., the original Smyrna.

83. *Marsus . . . Lepidus*: For Marsus see also 2.74 and 6.47–48.1;
for Lepidus see 4.20.2–3 and 1.13.2.

84. *went to Campania*: The main verb of this sentence, representing
an action that coloured the remaining eleven years of Tiberius'
principate, was either omitted by Tacitus (possibly) or lost in
transmission (probably). I have supplied a minimal *went* on the
basis of the prepositional phrase *to Campania*.

85. *withdrawal's cause*: The plan is first mentioned at 3.31.2. For
Sejanus' role see 4.41; another cause is described in 4.42.

86. *Cocceius Nerva*: For the death of Nerva (grandfather of the
future emperor) by voluntary starvation see 6.26.1–2.

87. *Curtius Atticus*: He eventually fell victim to Sejanus' intrigues
(see 6.10.2).

88. *Sejanus' friendship*: The senate later proposed erecting an 'Altar
of Friendship' for the pair (4.74.2).

89. *his wife*: For Nero's marriage to Livilla's daughter Julia see 3.29.3.

90. *notable men*: Agrippa was consul the preceding year (4.34.1),
     but earns no other mention from Tacitus; his grandfathers were
     Augustus' ally Agrippa and the historian Asinius Pollio. Haterius
     belonged to an earlier generation (consul in 5 BCE); his behav-
     iour in earlier appearances (1.13.4–6, 3.57.2) wins him even less
     credit than his oratorical style.

91. *Fidenae's proximity*: The town is about five miles up the Tiber
     from Rome.

92. *Claudia Quinta*: The praise silently alters the history of Claudia
     Quinta's statue to suit the occasion: her statue commemorated a
     public demonstration (in 204 BCE) of the gods' approval of her
     as Rome's most chaste woman, and that statue *subsequently* sur-
     vived two fires in 111 BCE and 3 CE.

93. *Claudia Pulchra*: For her condemnation see 4.52.

94. *Cornelius Dolabella*: He last appeared in a successful military
     campaign against Tacfarinas (4.23–6).

95. *municipalities*: See 1.79.2.

96. *established himself on the names*: The expression is unusual and
     the text suspect. But the idea that a ten-year imperial residence
     on Capri obliterated the earlier names of the twelve villas is not
     far-fetched.

97. *Titius Sabinus*: His danger was announced at 4.18.1, postponed
     at 4.19.1.

98. *Latinius Latiaris*: He might be the man mentioned, under the
     name Lucanius Latiaris, at 6.4.1.

99. *Asinius Gallus*: See 1.8.3. Two of his sons appear as consuls in
     Book 4 (4.1.1, 4.34.1).

100. *the tribute Drusus had ordered*: Tiberius' brother Drusus' dispos-
     itions on the lower Rhine were made in 12 BCE.

101. *Lucius Apronius*: See 1.56.1. The consequences of this debacle
     are mentioned at 11.19.

102. *many officers*: Tacitus lists three different grades of officer, but
     the point lies in *many*, not in the specification of these as opposed
     to other grades of officer, so I give a simplified rendering.

103. *the wedding*: The Emperor Nero was one result of this marriage.
     For Domitius' family see 4.44.1–2.

BOOK 5

1.   *Livia died*: She must have been in her eighties; Tiberius was now
     seventy.

2. *returned to Rome*: In 39 BCE. Suetonius gives the story (*Tiberius* 4).

3. *her will*: Her great-grandson Gaius eventually made the distributions she desired (Suetonius, *Caligula* 16.3).

4. No *divine cult*: Twelve years later Livia *was* deified shortly after the accession of her grandson Claudius.

5. *the consul Fufius*: He is dead at his next mention (6.10.1); according to Dio, he and his wife Mutila Prisca – one of Livia's female friends (see 4.12.4) – committed suicide (58.4.5–6).

6. *deference to his mother*: For an example see 2.34.3.

7. *Cotta Messalinus*: His other appearances also earn adverse comment (2.32.2, 3.17.4, 4.20.4, 6.5.1, 6.7.1).

8. *Germanicus' line*: From here to the end of the sentence the text is corrupt and variously restored.

9. *flouted imperial majesty*: Tiberius seems to assume that Rusticus' action signified a loyalty to Germanicus' family that in his own agent made a mockery of his majesty.

10. *the Emperor's might*: Book 5 breaks off here. In the two-year gap before the text resumes Agrippina, Nero and Nero's brother Drusus are exiled and Nero dies. See also the first note to Book 6.

BOOK 6

1. *5.6*: The beginning of Book 6 is lost. The traditional numbering system followed here reflects a now-abandoned view of the book divisions. Also lost is some two years' worth of narrative that included additions to Sejanus' power (e.g., the consulship of 31 CE and the prospect of marriage into the imperial family) and his dramatic fall from favour. The narrative resumes with a fragment on an unspecified matter that provoked a remarkable number of speeches, presumably before the senate, in the aftermath of Sejanus' execution. The continuous text begins in the midst of one such speech by an unknown associate of Sejanus.

2. *a person*: Commentators and translators differ on whether *a person* refers to the speaker (my view) or to Sejanus.

3. *Blaesus*: Like the unknown suicide, Quintus Junius Blaesus was an associate of Sejanus; his uncle, in fact. Earlier, this worked to Blaesus' advantage (see 3.35, 4.23.2, 4.26.1 and especially 3.72–4). Later, Tiberius' manifest displeasure drove Blaesus' sons to suicide (6.40.2).

4. *Vitellius*: Formerly legate and friend to Germanicus (see the

Index of Names); what caused his disaffection here is not known. His wife was later accused of treason (6.47.1). The Emperor Vitellius was his nephew.

5. *their brothers*: Publius Vitellius had three brothers, Aulus, Quintus and Lucius, the last being the most prominent (see the Index of Names, and Suetonius, *Vitellius* 2 for all four brothers). For Pomponius Secundus' brother Quintus see 6.18.1. *Guarantors* promised that the accused would appear at the trial and often provided the house for house arrest.

6. *a knife*: It was presumably used for sharpening pens or working with papyrus.

7. *Pomponius*: He appears again in the Claudian books, where he is credited with military success and, especially, literary glory (11.13.1, 12.27–8).

8. *Sejanus' remaining children*: See 4.3.5; one son was punished with his father. Their mother committed suicide before these final punishments.

9. *taken by the executioner*: They reported, that is, that she was raped. Tacitus uses the suggestive *taken*, rather than a legalistic or crude expression.

10. *Drusus was seen*: The whereabouts of the real Drusus must have been reported in the missing portion of Book 5: from sometime in 30 CE he was under close guard, presumably in Rome. For his fate see 6.23.2.

11. *Poppaeus Sabinus*: He was a long-time governor of the Danube province of Moesia, to which Macedonia and Achaea were added in 15 CE (1.80.1). For his obituary see 6.39.3; for his granddaughter, the future Empress Poppaea Sabina, see 13.45. An earlier episode shows him a competent commander (4.46–51).

12. *the other sea*: i.e., in the Ionian sea. The expression is awkward here, the text suspect and variously emended.

13. *I found nothing further*: Dio, however, mentions 'Drusus'' arrest and delivery to Tiberius (see 58.25.1), whether correctly or not we do not know.

14. *Fulcinius Trio*: Trio's enmity-producing ways were on display earlier: 2.28–30, 3.10.1, 3.19.1. His dispute with Regulus continues at 6.4.3. For his fate see 6.38.2–3. The grounds (if any) for the charge against Regulus were presumably given in the missing portion of the narrative. For Regulus' obituary and the quietism mentioned in the next sentence see 14.47.

15. *guilty of conspiracy?*: According to Dio, Trio had aligned himself with Sejanus (Dio 58.9.3).

16. *Domitius ... Scribonianus*: Domitius married the younger Agrippina (4.75, 6.45.2), fathered the Emperor Nero and was accused of adultery (6.47–8). Scribonianus, who was related to Galba's short-lived heir Piso, rebelled against Claudius (see 12.52.1–2).

17. *Tiber-side Gardens*: See 2.41.1.

18. *Terms unknown before*: For *stool-boys* the location in question was the latrine (*sellarium*). The rendering *strangling-boys* is quite uncertain. The etymology of the Latin term involves 'cinching up' or 'drawing tight', whence *strangling*.

19. *Livilla's wrongdoing*: See 4.3. Livilla's death seems to have come shortly after Sejanus' (Dio 58.11.7), but association with her is still the subject of accusations in 34 CE (6.29.4). The *state treasury* was in theory under the control of the senate and its appointees, while the Emperor's *purse* (*fiscus*, whence 'confiscate') was managed in his household. But as Tacitus suggests, the Emperor used Treasury funds as freely as his own.

20. *Tiberius' letter*: According to Suetonius and Dio, this was the letter in which Tiberius denounced Sejanus to the senate (Suetonius, *Tiberius* 65; Dio 58.10.2, 58.13.3).

21. *Life will be worth less to me*: An assertion soon belied by his request for a bodyguard (6.15.2–3).

22. *sitting in the fourteen rows*: This was a mark of distinction formerly reserved for citizens of equestrian rank.

23. *Sextius Paconianus*: His eventual death is reported at 6.39.1.

24. *as I reported*: For the earlier episode see 4.68–71.1. There, however, the man is called Latinius Latiaris. Either the manuscript or Tacitus is wrong.

25. *Haterius Agrippa*: He behaves equally badly in two earlier appearances (see 1.77.3, 3.49). For his political career see also 2.51 and 3.52.

26. *Sanquinius Maximus*: For his death see 11.18.1, a passage suggesting military achievements in Germany that would have been narrated in the lost books.

27. *Cotta Messalinus*: See 2.32.1; for a recent 'brutal' proposal see 5.3.2.

28. *a funeral feast*: An indirect allusion to Tiberius' refusal to permit her deification (5.2.1).

29. *Lepidus ... Arruntius*: See 1.13.2 and 1.8.3, respectively.

30. *the most outstanding philosopher's regular affirmation*: Either Socrates (the speaker) or Plato (the author) at *Gorgias* 524E.

31. *disclosures about Cotta*: This accusation must have been reported in the lost portion of the Tiberian narrative.

32. *in the status of 'avenged'*: That is, the accusers of both men were punished.
33. *Quintus Servaeus*: He is mentioned as praetorian governor of Commagene at 2.56.4; as Germanicus' associate at 3.13.2 and 3.19.1.
34. *the elder Gaius Cestius*: See also 3.36.2 and 6.31.1; for the younger Cestius see 15.25.3.
35. *humiliation*: This renders *sordes* (more literally, 'the clothing of suppliants'), a rare word also used at 12.59, where the context suggests more clearly that the humiliation took the form of a false prosecution.
36. *the same endpoint*: i.e., the fact that others, including Terentius, ended their friendship with Sejanus when Tiberius did.
37. *transferred into his own entourage*: Presumably after Drusus' death in 9 BCE. If so, Tiberius had known Vistilius for more than three decades.
38. *Scaurus ... Sabinus ... Vinicianus ... Pollio*: Scaurus first attracts Tiberius' ill will at 1.13.4; for another round of accusation and his death see 6.29.3–4. The others survived Tiberius (see the Index of Names).
39. *and likewise*: The underlying text is corrupt and emended variously.
40. *Celsus*: For his death see 6.14.1.
41. *murder*: This is Tacitus' verdict. For Vitia's manner of death no information survives, but according to Dio her son committed suicide (see 5.2.2).
42. *Vescularius ... Marinus*: On Vescularius' role in the case against Libo see 2.28. Tacitus's account of the attack on Curtius Atticus (on whom see 4.58.1) is lost.
43. *Lucius Piso the pontifex*: His only earlier appearance is at 3.68.2; the title *pontifex* distinguishes him from the other famous Lucius Piso of Tiberius' reign, who was an augur (see 2.34.1). His father's censorship (see just below in the text) is not mentioned in the surviving books; that his father was also Julius Caesar's father-in-law apparently did not merit a mention.
44. *someone was selected*: Tacitus' account moves rapidly from the regal period (Romulus, Tullus Hostilius, Tarquinius Superbus) through the Republic (*the consuls*) to the triumviral and Augustan periods. Maecenas was Rome's superintendent twice in the 30s BCE, Messala Corvinus held the new office of urban prefect in 26 BCE, Statilius Taurus in 16 BCE. Piso's appointment must have come during Augustus' last years, *c.* 13 CE.

45. *an overseer . . . for the Latin Festival*: For an instance see 4.36.1.
46. *a Sibyl's book*: Such books contained oracles written in Greek verse. They were subject to careful imperial control administered by the Board of Fifteen (see note 47 below). In crises such as natural disasters it was often proposed that they be consulted: see, for example, 1.76.1 (flood) and 15.44.1 (fire).
47. *the Fifteen*: This was a board of priests charged with (among other things) oversight of Century Games and foreign cults naturalized at Rome, and with preservation of the Sibylline books. Tacitus was a member (see 11.11.1).
48. *made by division*: This traditional voting procedure required senators to separate into different areas of the senate house, following the man whose motion they supported. However, the expression can also refer to decrees made without discussion, which would suit the occasion here, since Tacitus reports none.
49. *the Capitoline burned*: The temporal connection between the Capitoline fire of 83 BCE and the Social War (91–88 BCE) is erroneous. The temple burned down during the subsequent civil war, as Tacitus says in the *Histories* (3.72.1).
50. *Julius Celsus*: See also 6.9.3.
51. *his granddaughters*: Drusilla and Julia Livilla were in their mid-teens.
52. *Vinicius' stock*: For Vinicius' father see 3.11.2.
53. *Cassius*: He is perhaps the person alluded to in general terms at 6.2.2; he appears again with Vinicius at 6.45.2. His brother gets a more favourable treatment from Tacitus (12.12).
54. *Germanicus' daughters*: The first marriage of the girls' sister Agrippina was reported with special prominence at the end of Book 4 (4.75). For the marriage of their brother Gaius see 6.20.1.
55. *Guard commander Macro*: He replaced Sejanus as commander of the praetorian guard, a grim figure during Tiberius' final years: see 6.29.3, 6.38, 6.45–50.
56. *First . . . Later . . . Finally, paying interest was forbidden*: These measures date to the 5th and 4th centuries BCE. Tacitus' language is too vague for firm conclusions about the actual rates of interest involved.
57. *first . . . then a clamour at the praetor's tribunal*: That is, people who needed to pay back current loans made the rounds of potential lenders, pleading for a new loan, and then ended up in court, presumably having failed to obtain one.
58. *Quintus Pomponius*: At 5.8 Tacitus mentioned both a senator

named Considius and Pomponius Secundus (see note 5 above), but the connection between that incident and this is obscure.

59. *her ex-praetor brother*: For an earlier incident involving Pompeia's brother Quintus Pompeius Macer and Tiberius see 1.72.3.

60. *Theophanes of Mytilene*: Among other signs of Pompey's favour, Theophanes received Roman citizenship and thus the family name Pompeius also borne by his descendants. Divine honours were a traditional expression of thanks for public benefactions in the Greek world.

61. *Sextus Marius*: For an earlier incident involving Marius and Tiberius see 4.36.1.

62. *Marius' mines*: A corruption in the text prevents us from knowing what kind of mines, besides gold mines, Marius possessed. Copper is a strong possibility.

63. *Claudia*: The daughter of Tiberius' friend and flatterer Marcus Junius Silanus (on whom see also 3.24.3–4, 3.57.1 and perhaps 5.10.3). There is conflicting evidence about the year in which this marriage took place. She is dead by 37 CE (6.45.3).

64. *Passienus*: Suffect consul under Tiberius in 27 CE, Passienus survived Gaius' principate to serve as consul again under Claudius in 44 CE. As the younger Agrippina's second husband, he was stepfather to the future Nero.

65. *Thrasyllus' son foretold*: The prediction is reported at 14.9.3 without credit to Thrasyllus' son.

66. *Asinius Gallus*: See 1.8.3. His arrest three years before the date of the present passage was presumably reported in the missing portion of Book 5.

67. *chose brutality over regret*: A remarkably compact expression, signifying that Tiberius chose brutality in the present over future regret if he happened to change his mind again about this grandson.

68. *ordered a recitation*: Tiberius' insults, too, were conveyed by a letter read out in the senate. The vague expression 'insults at the dead man's physique' (*probra corporis*) serves as foil for more specific criticisms about Drusus' attitude towards family and country; people read into it a variety of objectionable practices. His younger brother Gaius incurred similar abuse (6.5.1). For Drusus' Sejanus-inspired plot to remove his older brother Nero see 4.60.3.

69. *Agrippina*: She had been living in exile on Pandateria since 29 CE.

70. *Thanks were given for this*: The Latin leaves it unclear whether

for this refers to Tiberius' refraining from execution or to her death.

71. *Plancina*: She appears frequently in Tacitus' account of the two years of Germanicus' life in Books 2 and 3 (see the Index of Names). For her husband Piso see 1.13.2.

72. *Drusus' daughter Julia*: For her well-received first marriage see 3.29.3.

73. *Aelius Lamia*: He has not appeared in the surviving books since 4.13.3, when he was governor of Africa. He must have succeeded to the post of urban prefect in 32 CE upon Lucius Piso's death (6.10.3).

74. *Arruntius*: On Lucius Arruntius, and the grounds for Tiberius' worries about him, see 1.13.1–2.

75. *Marcus Lepidus*: See especially 1.13.2 and 4.20.2 (for other passages see the Index of Names).

76. *Heliopolis*: The 'City of the Sun' is where the *altar of the Sun* mentioned later in this paragraph is located.

77. *Pomponius Labeo*: For his governorship see 4.47.

78. *screened guilt with antipathy*: Tacitus' expression is very condensed. The reader must understand Tiberius' thought thus: Labeo's suicide seemed forced, and Tiberius seemed responsible, and the resultant antipathy towards Tiberius prevented people from seeing Labeo's crimes. All this in four Latin words (*illum . . . culpam invidia velavisse*).

79. *Mamercus Scaurus*: For an earlier threat to Scaurus see 6.9.3–4. For his oratory see 3.31.3–4 (for the defence) and 3.66.1–2 (an accusation); in the latter passage Tacitus' verdict on Scaurus is consonant with *in conduct scandalous*.

80. *Livilla*: See 4.3 and 6.2.1.

81. *Varius Ligus*: See also 4.42.3.

82. *Lucius Apronius*: At last mention he had suffered a costly and embarrassing defeat in Germany (4.73). For his earlier career see 1.56.1. Gaetulicus was mentioned earlier (4.42.3), again in conjunction with Varius Ligus (see note 81 above).

83. *King Artabanus*: He had been the Parthians' ruler for longer than Tiberius the Romans'; for his accession see 2.3.1. The reference to Germanicus in the next sentence points the reader back to 2.56.3.

84. *Vonones*: See 2.58.2 and 2.68.

85. *He chose*: Tiberius here sets in motion a conflict that plays out brutally under Claudius (see 11.8–9 and 12.44–8).

86. *many foul things are on record*: Tacitus' Claudian books contain a sufficient sample: see 11.2–4, 11.33–5, 12.4–5, 12.9, 12.42.

87. *harrying from the air*: The weapons of the Sarmatian cavalry included arrows (see 6.35.1).

88. *when he was completing the Dalmatian war*: Tiberius commanded Augustus' troops in the Balkans from 6 to 9 CE and in 12 CE celebrated a triumph for his success there.

89. *Two summers' action*: The Parthian narrative will resume at 6.41.2.

90. *Gaius Gracchus*: This may be the Gracchus whose history is given at 4.13.2–3.

91. *huge provinces*: For Sabinus' provinces see 1.80.1.

92. *neither the fact that Lucius Aruseius *** were killed*: Both *neither* and the plural verb indicate that text is missing after Aruseius' name. Aruseius may be the man mentioned at 6.7.1, whose actions must have been reported in a portion of the *Annals* now missing.

93. *citizen punishments*: This means execution. The identity of this Tigranes (a name borne by several Roman-backed rulers of Armenia) is uncertain.

94. *two Blaesi*: The Blaesi were connected to Sejanus: their father Quintus Junius Blaesus (see 5.7.2) was Sejanus' uncle; their house was riven by Sejanus' fall in 31 CE.

95. *Aemilia Lepida*: Tacitus' report of her marriage to Germanicus' son is lost; Lepidus' death was reported at 6.27.4.

96. *the Cietae*: On this restive people see also 12.55. Archelaus may be the son of the same-named ruler mentioned at 2.42 (for 17 CE).

97. *Tiridates*: The Parthian narrative resumes where the story left off at 6.37 with Tiridates arriving in Parthia and Artabanus in exile among the Scythians.

98. *Seleucia*: This city was founded by Seleucus Nicator *c.* 300 BCE on the west bank of the Tigris; it lies opposite the Parthian capital Ctesiphon (on which see just below in the text) and just downstream from modern Baghdad. In the mid-first century CE Pliny estimates its population as 600,000 (*Natural History* 6.122). For a later episode involving the city and its relationship with eastern kings see 11.8–9.

99. *the strongest districts*: *Districts* are the large constituent units of the Parthian Empire, comparable to Roman provinces.

100. *the Surena*: He was the Parthian second-in-command.

101. *the veteran ruler*: Artabanus became king in 10/11 CE.

102. *whom I reported as Gaius' wife*: For the marriage see 6.20.1.

103. *his grandsons*: Tiberius Gemellus was born in 19 CE (2.84.1); Gaius in 12 CE.

104. *Claudius*: He was born in 10 BCE.

105. *Publius Vitellius*: See 5.8.

106. *Satrius Secundus*: He must have laid information about Sejanus' alleged conspiracy in 31 CE; their association is attested at 4.34.1 and 6.8.5.

107. *accomplices and adulterers*: On Domitius see 4.75 (marriage with Agrippina), 6.1.1 (consul), 6.45.2 (fire commission); Marsus was mentioned at 2.74.1. For Arruntius see the Index of Names.

108. *Carsidius ... Balbus*: For Carsidius see also 4.13.2; for Balbus 6.47.1.

109. *Sextus Papinius*: He is assumed to be the son of the previous year's consul (6.40.1).

110. *rejected*: This expression may indicate divorce from a husband, but need not be so understood.

111. *consummated mortality*: The possibility of immortality implicit here was never realized; unlike his mother (see note 4 at 5.2.1) and the other 1st century CE emperors who died in their beds, Tiberius was not deified.

112. *his seventy-eighth year*: Tiberius' birth date was 16 November 42 BCE.

113. *His origin*: For Tiberius' parentage see 5.1.1.

114. *exile*: The family was in exile from 42 to 39 BCE during the triumviral period.

115. *entering Augustus' household*: Tiberius joined Augustus' household after his father's death in 33 BCE; he was about nine years old.

116. *he lived on slippery ground*: His rivals died: Marcellus (23 BCE), Agrippa (12 BCE), his brother Drusus (9 BCE), Lucius Caesar (2 CE) and Gaius Caesar (4 CE). This catalogue echoes the review of Augustus' dynastic plans at 1.3.

117. *Back from Rhodes*: Tiberius withdrew to Rhodes in 6 BCE and stayed there until 2 CE. He was adopted by Augustus in 4 CE, increasingly dominant from then until Augustus' death in 14 CE, and emperor from 14 to 37 CE.

118. *One phase was ... One was*: From early manhood onwards Tiberius held numerous civil and military positions under Augustus (for details see 1.4.4). Germanicus died in 19 CE; Tiberius' son Drusus died in 23 CE.

119. *with his mother alive*: Livia died in 29 CE.

120. *so long as he loved, or feared, Sejanus*: Sejanus' influence ended with his fall in 31 CE.

BOOK 11

1. *Messalina ... Asiaticus ... Sabina*: The names are supplied from the context and are absent in the text, which resumes here after a gap of ten years.

2. *Suillius*: He was convicted of giving a corrupt verdict in 24 CE (4.31.3), but was banefully influential under Claudius (as is shown in this and the following six chapters). He was tried again and exiled under Nero (13.42–3).

3. *Rufrius Crispinus*: He would later become the first husband of Poppaea Sabina's daughter (the future Empress Poppaea): see 11.4.3, 12.42.1, 13.45.4 and, for his death, 15.71.4.

4. *Ask your sons, Suillius!*: One of Suillius' sons, Marcus Suillius Nerullinus, would become consul in 50 CE (see 12.25.1 and, also on this son, 13.43.5). For the other son, Caesoninus, see 11.36.4. Dio's account of this trial (60.29.5–6) offers different circumstantial details.

5. *Vitellius*: Consul and censor with Claudius in 47 CE (the narrative's present), he was the father of the future Emperor Vitellius, who, according to Tacitus, owed his elevation entirely to his father's renown (*Histories*, 3.86.1 and also 3.66.3–4). Here he is Messalina's agent (for which connection see also 11.33–5), but he is best known for persuading Claudius to marry Agrippina (12.4–5). Tacitus gives a brief assessment of Vitellius' long career shortly after his first consulship (6.32.4; see also 6.28.1 for the consulship); there is no obituary.

6. *Claudius ... Scipio*: For their interactions see also 11.4.3 and 12.53.2.

7. *Mnester and Poppaea*: A connection between Messalina and Mnester was presumably established in the missing books. For Mnester's death shortly after hers see 11.36.1–2.

8. *Gaius Silius*: See further 11.12.2 and 11.26–35.

9. *a Cincian law*: The *lex Cincia* (also alluded to at 15.20.3) was a law from the Middle Republic (3rd century BCE) that prohibited the acceptance of payment or gift for legal representation. Its basic provisions were reiterated by Augustus. The underlying principle is debated here. Claudius' eventual ruling (see 11.7.4) is overturned by Nero in 54 CE (13.5.1).

10. *If no one's wages are riding on cases heard*: The wording of the conditional clause is uncertain, but the sense of the sentence as a whole is clear.

11. *Pollio ... Corvinus ... Arruntius ... Aeserninus*: On Asinius Pollio see 1.12.4; on Messala Corvinus see 3.34.2. Both were active during the transition from Republic to Principate and under Augustus. For the Tiberian-age orators Arruntius and Aeserninus see 1.8.4 and 3.11.2, respectively.

12. *Cossutianus Capito*: See 14.48.1.

13. *Utility and affairs are served*: Brevity obscures the meaning of the first part of this sentence in Latin. Translators render variously.

14. *Clodius or Curio*: These men were demagogic speakers of the Late Republic. The *fees* they received are usually considered bribes for political favours.

15. *For taking money*: The issue of payment for legal representation is revisited early in Nero's principate (13.5.1).

16. *Mithridates ... returned to his kingdom*: For background for this section (through to 11.10) see 6.31–44; for the sequel see 12.10–21. Tacitus' narrative of the episode from Gaius' principate is lost. The events, though difficult to date precisely, cover much more than a year. The vast scale of territory involved (from Armenia and the Caspian Sea in the north to the lower Tigris to far-eastern Bactria) is best appreciated by consulting a map. The phrase *on Gaius' order* is a conjecture (based on information from other sources) to fill a gap in the manuscript, where only 'Caesar's' is present.

17. *Lesser matters*: Control of Armenia was one of these *lesser matters*.

18. *Vardanes*: It appears from 11.9.3 (and perhaps earlier, in a lost episode) that he was a brother of the Parthian king Gotarzes. The text of this sentence is corrupt, leaving it unclear where Tacitus meant the emphasis to lie. Its strung-together structure as translated (following Heubner's text) is alien to Tacitus' normal style.

19. *3,000 stades*: Roughly 350 miles, a prodigious feat if true.

20. *an adjacent river*: Seleucia's river is the Tigris (see 6.42.1).

21. *Lesser Armenia*: This was a separate kingdom west of Armenia, but the two had in the past been jointly ruled. In Tacitus' time it formed part of a Roman province together with Cappadocia, to its west.

22. *Vibius Marsus*: He served in Syria earlier under Germanicus (2.74, 2.79). Tacitus also shows him exposed to the dangers of

eminence in Rome under Tiberius: 4.56, 6.47–8. The governorship here mentioned seems to have occurred sometime between 42 and 45 CE.

23. *the Erind*: This and *the Sind* in the sentence after next are rivers whose location and modern identification are uncertain.

24. *sent to us in pledge*: i.e., as a pledge of Parthian friendship. Tacitus' expression here is unique for this common practice (see 2.1.2).

25. *The same consuls*: i.e., Claudius and Lucius Vitellius. The beginning of the year 47 CE, where these names would have been given to label the year, is missing.

26. *the eight-hundredth year after Rome's foundation*: The traditional date for the foundation was 753 BCE; Augustus' *Century Games* (also referred to as the Secular Games) were held in 17 BCE. The *rationales* mentioned in the next sentence concern the definition of *century*.

27. *my books*: i.e., the *Histories*. The books on Domitian are lost.

28. *a quindecimviral priesthood*: For the quindecimviri or Board of Fifteen see 6.12.1.

29. *at the Circus*: The three-day festival involved a variety of events, including some in the Circus. *The Game of Troy* was an equestrian spectacle; some idea of its nature is given in Virgil's *Aeneid* (5.545–603). *Britannicus*, mentioned in the next sentence, was six; the future *Nero* was nine. The name *Nero* signified a member of the Claudian *gens*.

30. *Only one snake*: According to Suetonius' *Nero* (6.4), Nero wore a bracelet containing the snake's skin as a protective charm.

31. *Gaius Silius*: He was old enough to be on the verge of a consulship, and was presented in a different light at 11.5–6. Silana's story is continued at 13.19–22.

32. *Pomponius Secundus*: He was mentioned at 5.8 and returns to the narrative as governor of Upper Germany (and poet) at 12.27–8.

33. *minors*: This is an efficient but slightly misleading rendering of *filii familiarum*. In money matters (but not civic matters) a Roman's status depended on whether or not his father was alive. If so, his son, regardless of age, could own no property. Therefore a man could remain a 'minor' in this sense until well into middle age. See also 1.26.2.

34. *he channelled into Rome*: Tacitus refers to (but does not name) the famous Aqua Claudia.

35. *letters' inventors*: Claudius wrote a treatise on the history of alphabets (Suetonius, *Claudius*, 41).

36. *a haruspical priesthood*: Haruspicy, the art of divining the future from animal entrails, originated in Etruria (about which Claudius wrote a twenty-volume history, which may have served Tacitus as a direct or indirect source; see references to other Claudian works at 11.14, 11.22, 11.24 and 12.23–4 with Appendices 40–41 in Syme's *Tacitus*). Practitioners were consulted by Roman officials (see 13.24.2 and 15.47.2) and private citizens alike, but until this period they were not organized in an official priesthood.

37. *foreign beliefs*: See also 12.59.1, 13.32.2 and 14.30.3.

38. *the pontiffs*: For these priests, who were already organized in an official priesthood, see 1.10.5.

39. *the Cherusci*: The background for this and the following paragraphs on Germany is given at 1.55–71, 2.9–27 and 2.88; the sequel at 12.27–8 and 13.53–7.

40. *the Chauci*: For the Chauci, whom Tacitus calls 'Germany's noblest people' (*Germania* 35), see earlier 1.60.3 and 2.17.5.

41. *Sanquinius' death*: Sanquinius, a former consul last mentioned at 6.4.3, was presumably governor of Lower Germany; his death must have been reported in the missing books, and Corbulo was his successor.

42. *Corbulo arrived*: The long and distinguished military career of Gnaeus Domitius Corbulo begins here in the *Annals*. For further episodes see 13.8–9, 13.34–41, 14.23–6, 14.29, 14.58, 15.1, 15.3–17, 15.25–31. Corbulo's suicide in 67 CE (ordered by Nero) occurred after the end of the *Annals*' extant books. Corbulo left an account of his campaigns (his *Commentarii*) which Tacitus seems to cite at 15.16.1 and may well have drawn on elsewhere (see the Introduction p. xxvii). Corbulo's daughter Domitia Longina, wife to the Emperor Domitian, survived into the period of the *Annals*' composition.

43. *auxiliary serviceman*: The text underlying *auxiliary serviceman* is quite uncertain, but the general meaning is clear.

44. *The Frisian nation*: On this transrhenane tribe see 1.60 and, for the rebellion, 4.72–4. Their relationship to Rome is renegotiated at 13.54.

45. *the Greater Chauci*: There was also a group called the Lesser Chauci, separated from the Greater by the Weser river.

46. *Curtius Rufus*: He was governor of Upper Germany. On the Mattiaci see 1.56.4.

47. *the origin of Curtius Rufus*: For another version of this story see the younger Pliny's *Letter* 7.27. Some believe this Curtius Rufus

to be the author of the extant *History of Alexander*, but if so Tacitus does not make his literary credentials evident.

48. *he made no denial*: There is a gap in the text of this sentence filled here by the word *denial*, an emendation based on 3.14.1.

49. *Cornelius Dolabella*: See 3.47.3. His proposal was apparently adopted, but short-lived: see 13.5.

50. *the law revived by Lucius Brutus*: Tacitus' expression is elliptical. Lucius Brutus, one of the first pair of consuls after the expulsion of the kings (*the Tarquins* mentioned two sentences later) in 509 BCE, used the legal formula that formerly empowered a new king to empower the magistrates who replaced the king under the Republic. Among the powers conferred by this formula, apparently, was appointing quaestors. This digression on the development of the quaestorship may reflect a treatise on the subject by Claudius. For this and other instances where Tacitus might be using Claudius as a source see 11.15.1.

51. *the sixty-third year*: The date is 447 BCE.

52. *Sulla's law*: Sulla's law on quaestors was passed in 81 BCE.

53. *the part ... called 'Long-haired'*: i.e., Gallia Comata. It was brought into the Roman Empire by the conquests of Julius Caesar in the 50s BCE. 'Long-haired' distinguishes this part of Transalpine Gaul from 'the Province', later Provence, which was considered more civilized and had been under Roman control much longer.

54. *much and various talk*: The discussion will have been initiated in connection with the ongoing census, one function of which was to determine the senate's membership. 'Long-haired' Gaul is a common antithesis for 'toga-wearing' Gaul; the notional location of the border between the two parts changed over time.

55. *Veneti and Insubres*: These peoples lived in the Gallic territory between the Alps and the Po, which was made 'Italian' by Caesar.

56. *Gallic hands on the Capitoline*: The reference is to the sack of Rome by the Gauls in 390 BCE. The text of this sentence is corrupt. *Arise* and *felled* are conjectures.

57. *He ... began thus*: Much of Claudius' original speech is preserved on an inscription erected in Lyon, presumably to commemorate the success of the Gauls' petition ('the Lyon tablet' *Corpus Inscriptionum Latinarum* 13.1668, *Inscriptiones Latinae Selectae* 212; translations are widely available in sourcebooks on Claudius' principate).

58. *Clausus*: See 4.9.2.

59. *settling legions*: This is an allusion to the practice of settling dis-
     charged veterans in colonies (see 12.27.1, 12.32.2, 13.31.2,
     14.27.2, 14.31–2). These colonies were generally effective recruit-
     ment centres.

60. *our predecessors'*: Literally, 'the earlier people's'. Claudius refers
     here to what we call the Republic. At 1.1.2 a similar formula is
     made clearer by the addition of the adjective *Roman*.

61. *brotherhood with the Roman People*: Tacitus substitutes an
     abstract expression for the familiar title 'Brothers of the Roman
     People'.

62. *Claudius admitted to patrician ranks*: The antiquarian informa-
     tion here, which differs from other accounts, may have been
     taken from Claudius' own researches (see 11.15.1).

63. *the method he applied*: Tiberius used a similar procedure (2.48.3)
     and the issue recurs under Claudius (12.52.3).

64. *undertook vows*: The object of *undertook* is missing in the
     manuscript; *vows* is one conjectural supplement among many,
     all based on different aspects of the traditional wedding cere-
     mony.

65. *the actor*: Mnester, on whom see 11.4.1. The text underlying
     made free with is corrupt.

66. *Callistus ... Narcissus ... Silanus ... Pallas*: This is Callistus'
     first appearance in the extant books (for his last see 11.38–12.2);
     other sources attest to his prominence in Gaius' court. Narcissus
     and Pallas, too, appear here for the first time in the *Annals*, mid-
     course in careers of unprecedented power (see the Index of
     Names for references). Junius Silanus was murdered at Messa-
     lina's behest in 42 CE.

67. *they desisted*: Tacitus' focus on the discreditable in this episode
     (see just above in the text for *secret threats* and the concealment
     of crimes) obscures the sequence of thought. He omits to men-
     tion any discussion of the obvious (and eventually adopted) plan
     of denouncing Messalina to Claudius, which is what Pallas and
     Callistus here desist from and Narcissus (in the following sen-
     tence) persists in.

68. *was asked ... was requested*: Tacitus leaves the identity of the
     person asking and requesting unclear: it could be either Calpur-
     nia or Claudius.

69. *men like Titius, Vettius and Plautius*: This is a generalizing
     plural based on the names of some of Messalina's lovers; for
     their stories see the following chapters. The first name is an
     emendation of a corrupt text.

70. *were called ... were questioned*: Tacitus leaves the identity of the person calling and questioning unclear: it could be either Narcissus or Claudius. For the prominence of these two offices see 1.7.3 and note that Turranius was already in charge of the grain supply in 14 CE. For Geta see also 11.33 and 12.42.1.

71. *although misfortune was undoing her plan*: Tacitus' brevity permits various interpretations for this clause: the words can be construed more abstractly ('although adversity was taking away her discernment') or *plan* can refer to the future instead of the past ('although the disaster prevented planning').

72. *a likeness of Silius' father*: For the condemnation of Silius' father see 4.18–20.

73. *Claudius spoke little*: Suetonius (*Claudius* 26.2) has Claudius promising never to marry again.

74. *behaved with the same constancy*: The text is disturbed here by an intrusive gloss, which, together with a misunderstanding of *with the same constancy*, has led some editors to suspect that the names of the equestrians have fallen out and that Titius, Vettius, Pompeius and Saufeius represent a separate list. But *with the same constancy* means 'with no constancy', since Silius' abject capitulation is not likely to count as constancy for Tacitus (compare his scathing remarks on other eminent Romans' deaths at 16.16).

75. *by his order*: Again Tacitus leaves the agent unclear: does the order come from Claudius or Narcissus?

76. *Mnester*: See also 11.4.1.

77. *Caesoninus ... Lateranus*: For Caesoninus see 11.2; for Lateranus see 13.11.2; for Lateranus' uncle Plautius Silvanus see 13.32.

78. *her mother Lepida*: On Domitia Lepida see also 12.64–5. Lepida's husband Appius was mentioned as Narcissus' victim at 11.29.1.

79. *Worthy deeds, origin of much worse*: The book's last sentence in the manuscript is corrupt and may be an intrusive gloss.

BOOK 12

1. *Agrippina*: This is Agrippina the younger, mentioned earlier as Germanicus' daughter (4.75.1) and Nero's mother (11.12.1). She begins her ascent to power here. For more on her rivalry with Lollia Paulina see 12.22 and 14.12.3.

2. *Aelia Paetina*: She was Claudius' wife before his marriage to Messalina in the late 30s CE; the mother of his daughter Antonia, she was divorced for 'trivial offences', according to Suetonius (*Claudius* 26.2).

3. *links Julian and Claudian posterity*: Corruption in the text of this sentence obscures its precise meaning, but Narcissus' emphasis on the dangerously distinguished birth of both Nero and Agrippina is clear. Editors restore and translators translate variously.

4. *Lucius Silanus*: His renown came from his relationship to Augustus (great-great-grandson). His brothers, too, fell victim to their rulers' crimes (see 13.1.1, 15.35.1); for the next (and last) generation of the family see 16.9.

5. *Vitellius . . . Calvina*: For Vitellius see 11.2.2. For more on Junia Calvina see 12.8.1 and 14.12.3.

6. *Eprius Marcellus*: Marcellus is presented in a dubious light in this his first appearance and even more so in his second at 13.33.3. The harm he did as a *delator* is suggested at 16.22 and 16.28–9; he survived into Vespasian's principate.

7. *a widow*: Agrippina's two previous husbands, Gnaeus Domitius Ahenobarbus (see 4.75) and Gaius Sallustius Crispus Passienus (see 6.20.1), were deceased.

8. *King Tullus' laws*: The king was Tullus Hostilius, the occasion the murder of a sister by a brother (see Livy 1.26.13). *Diana's Grove* in the same sentence may refer to her precinct near Lake Nemi. Calvina was released from her sentence after Agrippina's death (14.12.3).

9. *Seneca*: This is the first mention in the extant books of Seneca the Younger, Nero's future tutor and adviser. His loyalty to Agrippina was limited, as his role in her eventual murder showed (see 14.2–11). The *injury* mentioned in the next sentence is a reference to the sentence of exile imposed by Claudius soon after his accession for reasons that remain unclear. Tacitus presumably treated the episode in a lost book, and likewise Seneca's literary renown.

10. *as I reported*: For the earlier episode see 11.8–10 (under the year 47 CE).

11. *the request of a king*: For the kings supplied to Parthia by Augustus and Tiberius see 2.1–2 and 6.31–2.

12. *Cassius revived former ways*: Tacitus alludes to events of a century earlier, when a homonymous ancestor of Cassius secured Roman Syria after the crushing defeat of Crassus' army at Carrhae (53 BCE).

13. *Edessa*: The capital of Acbarus' kingdom in upper Mesopotamia.

14. *Carenes*: He appears only here, but was presumably familiar to the reader from an earlier appearance as a person of authority in Mesopotamia.

15. *the city Ninos*: Presumably a stronghold in the vicinity of Gaugamela, where the decisive battle took place in 331 BCE.

16. *Mithridates of Bosporus*: He is identified as 'the Bosporan' to distinguish him from the Iberian king of the same name active earlier and later in Claudius' reign (see 11.9, 12.45–8). The background to the present episode was presumably given in the lost books: Mithridates' brother Cotys (to be distinguished from the homonymous king of Thrace under Tiberius) has replaced him as king of Bosporus. For Aulus Didius, governor (perhaps) of Moesia, see 12.40. The Dandarids were a people subordinate to the Bosporan king.

17. *the Don*: This river seemed a far edge of the Graeco-Roman world.

18. *Achaemenes' issue*: Achaemenes was the founder of the dynasty that ruled Persia in an earlier age (6th–4th centuries BCE).

19. *Triumphs come from peoples and kingdoms still strong*: The concluding sentence is meant to explain the renunciation of military action against the suppliant Mithridates implicit in Claudius' statement about 'the Roman way'. But the logic is sufficiently loose that translators render variously.

20. *Lollia's renown*: The renown of Lollia's family is visible in the *Annals*: Volusius gets a brief obituary at 13.30.2; Cotta Messalinus was introduced at 2.32.1; Memmius Regulus' obituary is given at 14.47.1. See also 12.1–2, where Tacitus (like Claudius just below), maintains silence about her marriage to Gaius (attested to in Suetonius' *Caligula* 25 and Dio 59.12.1). Her ashes are returned to Italy at 14.12.3.

21. *Calpurnia*: For her restoration see 14.12.3; there, too, her fate is connected with that of Lollia.

22. *Cadius Rufus*: Tacitus had recorded his restoration to the senate in *Histories* 1.77.3.

23. *Sohaemus and Agrippa*: This Sohaemus is not mentioned elsewhere; Agrippa, a long-standing associate of the Roman imperial family, presumably appeared in the lost *Annals* books on Gaius and Claudius.

24. *the 'Divination of Well-being'*: In this ritual, permission was requested from the gods for a prayer for the Roman people's

well-being; permission being granted, the prayer would be made on a day when no Roman army anywhere in the world was engaged in conflict. Such days were rare. If the number 25 is correct, the ritual was most recently performed in 25 CE, a year whose events Tacitus recounts in Book 4. The ritual is not mentioned there, so the number has been doubted. The senate's decision that the ritual should be *perpetuated* expresses confidence in the continuation of current peaceful conditions. The next event Tacitus mentions, however, is the adoption of Nero (12.25.1).

25. *none had used it but Sulla and Augustus*: Tacitus seems to be mistaken about Augustus having extended the sacred boundary (an achievement not mentioned in his *Res gestae*). The long digression on the subject that follows may be indebted to Claudius' own antiquarian researches (see 11.15.1). Extentions by later commanders (up to the time of Tacitus) are recorded for Nero, Vespasian, Titus and Trajan.

26. *patrician Claudii*: On the Claudian family see 4.9.

27. *Nero*: Up to this point in the *Annals* Tacitus refers to the future Nero by his birth name of Domitius. To minimize confusion I use the name Nero throughout this translation. Here, where Tacitus mentions Nero's acquisition of the Claudian cognomen 'Nero', this policy proves undeniably awkward.

28. *it was named for her*: This colony in lower Germany (modern Cologne) received from Agrippina the last part of its variously transmitted name: Agrippinensis or Agrippinensium. Agrippina's own name recalls that of her grandfather Agrippa, whose connection to the Ubii is mentioned in the next sentence. Their resettlement took place around 38 BCE.

29. *auxiliaries*: Tacitus specifies that the auxiliaries belonged to tribes named Vangiones and Nemetes. Since neither is mentioned elsewhere in the *Annals*, the names seem superfluous for the modern reader.

30. *Varian disaster!*: This refers to the annihilation of a Roman army under the command of Publius Quinctilius Varus by German tribes in 9 CE. See 1.3.6.

31. *the Taunus*: A mountain near Wiesbaden, which earlier, too, served as a base of operations against the Chatti (see 1.56.1).

32. *Pomponius*: For his literary achievements see also 5.8.2 and 11.13.1.

33. *Vannius*: For his installation in 19 CE see 2.63.6, where Vibilius (mentioned in this paragraph) is also introduced.

34. *Sarmatian Iazuges*: Tacitus mentions the excellence of Iazugan cavalry in the *Histories* (3.5.1) in close conjunction to another reference to Sido (see following note).

35. *Sido*: He was still king of the Suebi in 69 CE; Tacitus mentions him as a Flavian ally and his people as 'more tolerant of loyalty than orders' (*Histories* 3.5.1, 3.21.2).

36. *In Britain*: The British narrative, which runs to 12.40, presumably picks up from an earlier panel on events in Britain in the lost books; Ostorius' governorship began in 47 CE. The narrative continues at 14.29–39 under the year 61 CE.

37. *everything up to the rivers*: The text is corrupt here and the meaning (starting from *to control*) uncertain. The rivers here mentioned are variously identified (Trent, Tern or Avon; and Severn).

38. *the governor's son*: The younger Ostorius will later fall victim to Nero: see 14.48 and 16.14–15.

39. *the colony*: For the local reaction to the colony and *the laws' obligations* see 14.31.

40. *clear of axe*: The axe was a symbol of Roman authority and the instrument of capital punishment.

41. *Officers*: Tacitus specifies that the officers were prefects and tribunes, which means they were in command of auxiliary and legionary troops, respectively. But for the modern reader the specificity gets in the way of seeing the more important antithesis between soldiers and their officers. So I simplify with *officers*.

42. *the ninth year*: The ninth year (by Roman inclusive counting) from the invasion in 43 CE was 51 CE.

43. *Scipio's . . . Paulus'*: Scipio's triumph over Syphax is dated to 201 BCE; Paulus' over Perses to 167 BCE.

44. *And without swift action*: The text of this sentence is corrupt in several places (for details see the Appendix).

45. *the Sugambri*: See 2.26.3.

46. *Aulus Didius*: He held a command in the east in 49 CE (see 12.15) and seems to have become governor of Britain in 52 CE. He served there until his death in 57 or 58 CE (see 14.29).

47. *as I mentioned above*: The earlier *Annals* passage (if there was one) is lost, but Tacitus also refers to Venutius and Cartimandua in *Histories* 3.45.1.

48. *I have combined*: This panel on events in Britain covers some eleven years and extends into Nero's principate, a significant departure from both the annalistic and the regnal structural principles (see Introduction).

49. *Nero's 'adulthood'*: Nero was thirteen, an unusually young age for the Roman coming-of-age ceremony.
50. *Geta ... Crispinus*: For Geta see 11.31 and 11.33; for Crispinus see 11.1 and note 3 to Book 11.
51. *Afranius Burrus*: This is the first appearance of the Guard commander who would help Seneca manage Nero upon his accession to power. He plays a prominent role in the Neronian books until his death in 62 CE (see 14.51). Like Seneca, he was more loyal to Nero than to Agrippina (see 14.7).
52. *Vitellius ... passion to rule*: His son Aulus Vitellius briefly fulfilled this passion as emperor in 69 CE.
53. *just as Vitellius wanted*: This is Vitellius' last appearance. No obituary from Tacitus marks his death soon hereafter.
54. *Vologaeses*: He was introduced as the new Parthian ruler at the end of 12.14. 4; he is a frequent presence in the remaining books of the *Annals* (see the Index of Names). His brothers are Tiridates and Pacorus; see 15.1–2.
55. *The Iberi ... the Armenians*: For the background see 11.8.
56. *the centurion Casperius*: He reappears, again intransigent, at 15.5 (see note 3 to Book 15).
57. *Do not prefer*: Starting here the text is corrupt and variously emended; the antithesis between fighting (*afield*) and negotiation (*terms*) is sound.
58. *a crime-ready mind*: Pharasmanes' readiness for crime eventually extends to killing Radamistus: see 13.37.3.
59. *Helvidius Priscus*: This is later the name of a man prominent in the early Flavian period (see the Index of Names); whether the two are identical is disputed.
60. *Scribonianus' father Camillus had roused war*: An elliptical reference to an episode from 42 CE, an armed insurrection spearheaded by Camillus (consul in 32 CE; see 6.1.1), the then governor of Dalmatia, against Claudius early in his principate; Tacitus' account is lost. The *clemency* for which Claudius claims credit is presumably a pardon granted to Camillus' son on that occasion; Camillus' death at the hands of his own side is mentioned by Tacitus in the *Histories* 2.75.
61. *in financial straits*: On the issue of impoverished senators see also 11.25.3.
62. *a descendant of Arcadian kings*: The name 'Pallas' is treated as a link between Claudius' adviser and the Pallas made famous by the *Aeneid*, whose father Evander came to Italy from Arcadia.
63. *[they were ordered ... And although]*: The material within

square brackets is supplied by conjecture (based on *Histories* 5.9.2) to fill a lacuna in the manuscript. Tacitus presumably treated this infamous incident in the lost books.

64. *to the Emperor's agents*: i.e., to Felix and Cumanus, who were both *procuratores* or 'financial administrators' in the area, which was at this time under the overall authority of the governor of Syria (see 12.23.1). The precise division of responsibilities among the three is represented differently by Josephus, a contemporary source.

65. *Quadratus displayed Felix among the judges*: Showing thereby Felix' earlier confidence justified.

66. *Cietae*: Their restiveness was illustrated at 6.41.1; on that occasion, unlike the present (see the following sentence in the text), the governor of Syria sent legionary soldiers and auxiliary troops against them. Cilicia and Judaea lie on opposite sides of the province of Syria, and their juxtaposition here, combined with the Armenia narrative of 12.44–51, shows how that governor's authority stretched over a wide area.

67. *Anemurium*: Located on a cape at the south-west corner of Asia Minor, facing Cyprus.

68. *the coastal king Antiochus*: Antiochus Epiphanes IV, king of Commagene, was an appointee, most recently, of Claudius. His father, also named Antiochus, died early in Tiberius' principate (2.42.5). Antiochus himself had earlier been installed as king by Gaius and then deposed. In the Neronian books he is shown subject to Roman orders (13.7, 13.37, 14.26); he figures similarly in Tacitus' account of 69 CE (*Histories* 2.81.1, 5.1.2).

69. *the Fucine Lake and the Liris*: The modern names for lake and river are Celano and Garigliano; the ridge that separates them is Monte Salviano. Pliny the Elder (*Natural History* 36.124), Suetonius (*Claudius* 20–21) and Dio (60.11) supply information about the engineering challenges and labour involved in this eleven-year undertaking; Tacitus focuses on the concluding spectacle(s). Augustus includes his spectacle among the achievements catalogued in the *Res gestae* (23).

70. *by 'marines'*: i.e., by the prisoners (see the rest of this passage) punished by participation in this spectacle, who were equipped as soldiers of the fleet.

71. *Decimus Junius, Quintus Haterius, consuls*: For the consular dating formula Tacitus uses the traditional praenomen/nomen form of the names. Junius is called Torquatus Silanus at 15.35 and Torquatus at 16.8; Haterius is called Haterius Antoninus at 13.34.

72. *Bononia*: Modern Bologna.

73. *the senate's verdict*: Presumably a guilty verdict and therefore a victory for the accuser, which explains *nevertheless* in the next sentence.

74. *senators . . . won out*: Priscus' eventual conviction for extortion is mentioned at 14.46 with a back reference to this passage.

75. *my agents*: The term *agents* (*procuratores*) covers a wide range of imperial functionaries, from governors of militarily unimportant provinces to financial officers in larger provinces, and down to property managers for imperial estates.

76. *Claudius delivered up every prerogative . . . Sulla*: The dates for the bills of Gracchus and the laws of Servilius are 122 and 106 BCE, respectively. The wars of Marius and Sulla (which were *not* primarily concerned with equestrian and senatorial roles) occupied much of the following two decades. The issue remained hotly contested through to the end of the Republic.

77. *empowered by Caesar's might*: Oppius, Balbus and Matius were associates of Caesar; Vedius (Pollio) of Augustus.

78. *Xenophon*: His next and final appearance in the surviving books comes at 12.67.2, where he is a party to Claudius' murder. From inscriptions set up in his honour on Cos we also know that he received signal rewards for his attendance on Claudius during the expedition to Britain, Tacitus' account of which is lost.

79. *Pseudophilip*: The real name of the 'false-Philip' was Andriscus; he was defeated by a Roman army in 148 BCE. The other campaigns mentioned here were fought in the 2nd and 1st centuries BCE; the order is not quite chronological, since Rome faced Antiochus and Perses before Andriscus.

80. *Marcus Asinius, Manius Acilius, consuls*: For the consular date Tacitus uses the traditional form of Asinius' name. At 14.40 he calls this man Asinius Marcellus.

81. *Domitia Lepida*: She was introduced at 11.37–8 as Messalina's mother; here she is Nero's aunt. Her sister Domitia, equally Nero's aunt, was also viewed as a rival by Agrippina (see 13.19, 13.21, 13.27). The genealogy given here is mistaken (Lepida's mother was the elder Antonia); Tacitus also confused the two Antonias at 4.44.

82. *Claudius has nothing to fear*: It is hard to make sense of the text of this sentence as transmitted, and Narcissus' reasoning is hard to follow even when emended (as it is here, reading with Heubner *metum* for M's *meritum*). The central point seems to be that Claudius' probable fate was different, depending on whether

Nero or Britannicus was marked as his successor: plots like that of Messalina and Silius could be expected in the one case, security in the other.

83.   *punish your mother's killers*: Narcissus' final plea communicates his wish for Claudius' safety even at the expense of his own punishment (as, in effect, Messalina's killer).

84.   *Locusta*: She is later used by Nero to poison Britannicus (13.15–16).

85.   *poison infused*: The text from *mushroom* to *sluggish* contains several corruptions that deny us certainty about (1) whether Tacitus mentioned a mushroom, and (2) whether sluggishness characterized Claudius or those watching him.

BOOK 13

1.   *Junius Silanus*: i.e., Marcus Junius Silanus, consul in 46. For his brother Lucius (mentioned in the following sentence) see 12.8.

2.   *Celerius . . . Helius*: Celerius reappears at 13.33; Helius' future prominence as regent of Italy during Nero's long tour of Greece (67–8 CE) comes after the end of Tacitus' narrative as we have it.

3.   *conflicts with Agrippina*: See 12.57.3 and 12.65.

4.   *public attendants*: These officials, called lictors, accompanied persons of importance (usually magistrates) in public; Tiberius refused them for Livia (see 1.14.2). Agrippina's 'cult office' was a priesthood charged with worship of the soon-to-be-deified Claudius.

5.   *sequestered in one house*: The problem of closed-door trials under Claudius is vividly illustrated at 11.2–4.

6.   *at the senate's behest*: For the Claudian precedents of these measures see 11.5.3 and 11.22.6.

7.   *convene on the Palatine*: See 2.37.2.

8.   *The Parthians*: The report from Parthia continues the story from 12.51.

9.   *Agrippa . . . Antiochus*: Herod Agrippa received kingships over parts of Syria and Judaea from Claudius (in 48 and 52 CE) and Nero (in 54 CE), and supported Vespasian in 69 CE (*Histories* 2.81.1, 5.1.2). For Antiochus of Commagene see 12.55.2.

10.   *Aristobulus . . . Sohaemus*: Aristobulus figures again in Roman arrangements for this area at 14.26.2. Tacitus links a king named Sohaemus with Agrippa in providing support for Vespasian in 69 CE (see note 9 above), but it is not known whether that Sohaemus is the king mentioned here.

11. *Domitius Corbulo*: For the beginning of Corbulo's story see 11.18–20. It continues from here to beyond the end of the *Annals* as we have them; he was driven to suicide in 67 CE.

12. *the auxiliary officer Arrius Varus*: He outranks Insteius.

13. *laurels were added to the Emperor's fasces*: The *fasces* were insignia of power (consisting of the rods and axe of corporal punishment); the laurel decoration signified military success and was often the prelude to a triumph.

14. *Events that went on*: The tale resumes, in 58 CE, at 13.34.

15. *Claudius Nero, Lucius Antistius, consuls*: In the consular dating formula Tacitus refers to the Emperor as *Claudius Nero* and uses the traditional praenomen/nomen form to refer to his colleague, a man he elsewhere calls Lucius Vetus. This joint consulship is mentioned in an attempt to save Vetus from Nero at 16.10.4.

16. *Plautius Lateranus*: For Lateranus as adulterer see 11.30.2, 11.36.4; in 65 CE he will join Piso's conspiracy against Nero from *love of country* (15.49.3).

17. *Acte ... Otho ... Senecio*: For Acte see further 14.2.1. Otho (the future emperor) reappears as crony at 13.45–6; Senecio as crony *and* Pisonian conspirator at 15.50.1–2.

18. *regal sway*: For Pallas' influence see 11.29.1.

19. *lay down his office*: This expression alludes to the resignation formula used by a magistrate at the conclusion of his term. Pallas, of course, held no magistracy; indeed, as a freedman he was ineligible to do so.

20. *to your mother's injustices!*: Or 'to your mother's cost'.

21. *the brothers Silanus*: See 13.1.1.

22. *his fourteenth year*: At fourteen Britannicus would be ready to enter his maturity by putting on the 'toga of manhood'. Nero did so, early, aged thirteen (12.41.1).

23. *he moved in secret*: Suetonius (*Nero* 33) tells the story with more circumstantial detail.

24. *Locusta*: See 12.66.2.

25. *the alarming disease*: Epilepsy is the disease in question, but Tacitus does not use its clinical name. *Alarming disease* renders *comitialis morbus* (literally, 'assembly-related disease'), where the connection with assemblies lies in the fact that epileptic seizures were taken as a sign of divine displeasure and therefore functioned as an alarm causing the dissolution of public assemblies.

26. *unseasonable fatalities*: An elevated expression for 'children's deaths'.

27. *the house that had been Antonia's*: Several Antonias are men-
    tioned in the *Annals*; the best known was probably Agrippina's
    paternal grandmother, on whom see 3.3.2. Her house, where the
    Emperor Gaius lived as a child (Suetonius, *Caligula* 10), may
    have figured in the lost books.

28. *Junia Silana*: The first phase of Silana's story is told at 11.12; the
    last at 14.12.

29. *Sextius Africanus*: On Africanus' noble birth see also 14.46.2.

30. *the actor Paris*: See further 13.27.3, where Paris seems to be
    rewarded by Nero with a fictional status of *freeborn*. Nero had
    him killed in 67 CE; the surviving sources allege artistic jealousy
    (Suetonius, *Nero* 54; Dio 63.18.1).

31. *Fabius . . . Pliny . . . Cluvius*: On Tacitus' literary sources see the
    Introduction. The citation-by-name policy exemplified here and
    promised for the future just below is, in fact, followed only occa-
    sionally.

32. *Faenius . . . Anteius*: Two of these friends of Agrippina reappear
    in the narrative: Faenius at 14.51 and 14.52 and in the Pisonian
    conspiracy (15.50 ff.); Anteius at 16.14.

33. *Sulla*: Faustus Cornelius Sulla remained a source of worry for
    Nero and was eventually executed: 13.47, 14.57, 14.59. For
    Claudius' daughter see also 15.53.

34. *Pallas*: See also 13.2 and 13.14.

35. *forgiven*: Or 'forgotten'. The Latin can mean either and both
    would yield notoriety, the former more so.

36. *a guard-post . . . was moved elsewhere*: The sequel comes at the
    end of the next chapter.

37. *haruspical advice*: For the haruspices see 11.15.

38. *Publius Scipio*: At his earlier appearances this man was called
    Cornelius Scipio (see the Index of Names).

39. *shameful carousing*: On the carousing in Rome the reports of
    Suetonius (*Nero* 26) and Dio (61.8) have more circumstantial
    detail.

40. ***: There is a gap, probably small, in the text here. The whole
    passage shows textual corruption and many emendations have
    been proposed.

41. *It is not burdensome . . . retaining liberty*: The Latin syntax here
    is unusually awkward (in aid of brevity, unless the text is cor-
    rupt), but the point of this sentence is clear from its antithesis
    with the following one.

42. *a finding of freebirth*: The legal details, which Tacitus replaces
    with abstractions, are known from *Digest of Justinian* 12.4.3.5.

43. *plebeian tribune Antistius*: He next appears as a praetor himself: 14.48–9.
44. *from Italy*: i.e., from beyond Rome; tribunician power was traditionally limited to the city and its immediate vicinity.
45. *Lucius Piso*: See further 15.18.3.
46. *Priscus ... Sabinus*: On Priscus see further 12.49.2. Tacitus mentioned Sabinus' subsequent execution in the *Histories* 1.37.3.
47. *Lucius Volusius*: Nero cites Volusius' remarkable wealth at 14.56.1.
48. *settlements at Capua and Nuceria*: For more on veteran settlements in Italy see 14.27.2.
49. *for appetite's crimes bribery's protection*: The concluding epigram is built around two complicated antitheses (criminal offence/military defence, and satisfying oneself/gratifying others). In translating its five Latin words I have privileged brevity over clarity. What Tacitus means is that officials who sponsor shows to gratify the provincials are currying favour as protection against future charges arising from their own licentiousness. But it takes a lot of words to say that.
50. *Aulus Plautius*: He led Claudius' invasion of Britain in 42 CE and governed the province until 47 CE, the year of his ovation. His services are alluded to at 11.36.4, but Tacitus' narrative is lost.
51. *a foreign creed*: This is generally taken to refer to either Judaism or Christianity. Tacitus' phrase privileges evaluation over identification.
52. *Drusus' daughter Julia was killed*: Another incident from early in Claudius' principate, from 43 CE (see Dio 60.18.4 and Suetonius, *Claudius* 29). Four decades of mourning would bring Pomponia into Tacitus' adulthood.
53. *the killer of ... Marcus Silanus*: Silanus' death was *the regime's first* (see 13.1). For the form of Celerius' name see 13.1.2.
54. *Cossutianus Capito*: For his equally foul future see 14.48.1.
55. *colleague ... to the deified Augustus*: The year was that of Actium, 31 BCE. Messala, one of the Republic's last great figures, is also recalled at 3.34.2, 4.34.4, 6.11.3 and 11.6.2. His great-grandson Tacitus mentions only here.
56. *war between Parthians and Romans*: The Parthian narrative picks up from 13.9.
57. *under canvas*: Roman tents were, of course, made of animal hides, not canvas.
58. *Paccius Orfitus*: He returns to the narrative at 15.12.2.

59. *Traitor!*: The grounds for the treachery accusation are, it seems, provided in 13.6.

60. *outstanding Roman ally*: Tacitus' praise may refer to services during Trajan's Parthian campaign of 114–17 CE, rather than to the incursions mentioned here; if so, it is an allusion contemporary with the composition of the *Annals*.

61. *Roman disaster!*: An allusion, at a minimum, to costly defeats suffered at Parthian hands by Roman armies led by Crassus in 53 BCE and by Antony two decades later. There were perhaps others.

62. *a remarkable occurrence*: The text of this sentence from *everything* to *so* is very uncertain, but the weather miracle's basic elements are clear.

63. *the town's consignment to ruin*: The narrative of events in Armenia continues at 14.23.

64. *Gaius Cassius*: His next appearance in the senate (14.42–4) is given even more prominence. For his character see 13.48; for his eventual disgrace and exile see 15.52 and 16.7–9.

65. *Publius Suillius*: On Suillius' power under Claudius see 11.1–5; for his disgrace earlier see 4.31.3.

66. *the Cincian law*: The revival mentioned here occurred under Claudius (see 11.5–8); on lawyer's fees under Nero see 13.5.1.

67. *his urban crimes*: Quintus Pomponius was introduced at 6.18.1. Most prominent immediately after Gaius' assassination, when he called for restoration of the Republic, he was probably involved in Camillus Scribonianus' rebellion early in Claudius' principate (see 12.52.2); Tacitus' narratives are lost. On Drusus' daughter see 13.32.3; she was the mother of Rubellius Plautus. On Poppaea Sabina and Valerius Asiaticus see 11.1–2.

68. *Poppaea Sabina*: In the *Annals* Poppaea, future wife of Nero, appears first here. Tacitus gives a different account of the Otho/Poppaea/Nero triangle in the *Histories* 1.3.

69. *her maternal grandfather*: For the grandfather's career under Tiberius see 1.80, 4.46–51; for his obituary see 6.39.3.

70. *equestrian-ranked Rufrius Crispinus*: On Crispinus (whose labelling here belittles: he was Guard commander under Claudius) see 11.1.3, 12.42.1 and, for his death, 15.71.4.

71. *governor of Lusitania*: At twenty-six Otho was very young for a governorship. He stayed in Lusitania, modern Portugal, for a decade.

72. *Hitherto*: The unstated antithesis is 'but now he ceased to do so'.

73. *Cornelius Sulla*: See 13.23.

74. *Gaius Cassius*: See 13.41.4.
75. *the brothers Scribonii*: They succumbed to delation in 67 CE; Tacitus' narrative does not survive, but he alludes to their destruction in the *Histories* (4.41.3).
76. *Thrasea Paetus*: This is the first appearance in the narrative of Thrasea Paetus, a senator whose actions figure prominently in Tacitus' analysis of the role of the senate in the principate. For the rest of his story see 14.12, 14.48–9, 15.20–21, 15.23 and 16.21–35.
77. *the cessation of all indirect taxes*: Taxation was an issue in the narrative of Tiberius' reign as well: see 1.78.2 and 2.42.4.
78. *provision was made*: Tacitus employs so many abstract nouns here (*ratio, quaestus, necessitas, erogatio*) that his meaning is unclear. The translation aligns his words with the traditional complaint against tax-farmers, namely, that their exactions greatly exceeded the sums the state was trying to raise. This would be remedied by the publication (see 13.51) of the rules for each tax. Other translations give the expression a broader application.
79. *Germany's affairs*: Germany was last mentioned at 12.27 (50 CE). In this and the next four chapters Tacitus brings the situation up to date (and therefore relates events of more than one year; see Introduction, p. xl).
80. *Paulinus ... Vetus ... Drusus*: The army in Germany was divided between two provinces (Upper and Lower), each with its own governor. Belgica (one of the provinces of Gaul) faced Lower Germany across the Rhine. For Tiberius' brother Drusus, who died in 9 BCE, and his engineering projects in the area see 2.8; Tacitus gives a somewhat fuller description of the earthwork mentioned here in the *Histories* (5.19.2). For Paulinus see also 15.18.3, for Vetus see 13.11. For the army's employment in construction projects see also 11.20.
81. *Thus are prevented*: For the same bitter generalization expressed somewhat differently see 15.50.4.
82. *the Frisians*: For prior arrangements see 11.19.
83. *the Chauci*: See 11.18–19.
84. *the Cheruscan rebellion*: This was an uprising in 9 CE, prior to the *Annals*' beginning. On Arminius see 2.88. For Tiberius' campaigns in Germany see 2.26.3; Germanicus' campaigns dominate Books 1 and 2.
85. *How much land lies idle*: Tacitus' language here is somewhat obscure, but the following sentence makes it clear that Boiocalus

is protesting (with whatever precise inflection) Roman plans for or use of the land in question.

86. *The Ubii*: On the colony of the Ubii (modern Cologne) see 12.27.1.

BOOK 14

1. *Poppaea*: For Poppaea Sabina and the various qualities mentioned below see 13.45–6.

2. *Cluvius says*: Cluvius Rufus and Fabius Rusticus (mentioned just below) are two of the literary sources noted by Tacitus; see p. xxvi. For Acte see 13.12.

3. *Agrippina ... Lepidus ... Pallas ... wedding her uncle*: The story of Agrippina and her brother-in-law Lepidus belongs in the narrative of her brother Gaius' reign; Tacitus' version is lost. For her association with Pallas see 12.25; for the marriage to Claudius see 12.5.

4. *Anicetus*: See also 14.62.2.

5. *Minerva's festival*: Literally, 'the festal days of the Quinquatrus', a holiday celebrated from 19 to 23 March.

6. *conveyance by trireme*: A privilege perhaps stripped with the others mentioned by Tacitus at 13.18.3.

7. *to be sure about*: The translation here relies on a commonly accepted but fairly implausible double emendation (<*ne*> dubitaret<*ur*>).

8. *far-fetched accusations*: For these charges see 13.5.

9. *Seneca was criticized*: On Seneca as Nero's ghostwriter see also 13.3.1. Quintilian (8.5.18) quotes a phrase from this letter echoed by Tacitus' narrative at 14.10.2: 'That I am safe – even now I hardly believe it, nor do I rejoice.'

10. *sun suddenly obscured*: The solar eclipse occurred on 30 April 59 CE.

11. *Junia and Calpurnia*: For the two women (exiled under Claudius) see 12.4.1 and 12.8.1 and 12.22.3, respectively.

12. *Lollia Paulina's ashes*: For Agrippina and Paulina see 12.22.

13. *Silana*: For Silana's dispute with Agrippina, in which Iturius and Calvisius played a role, see 13.19–21.

14. *To race horses is royal*: The text in the first clause of this sentence is uncertain, but a reference to racing seems required by the context.

15. *'Youth Games'*: The name seems to have referred to Nero's

youth (the occasion of the first festival, anyway, was the first shaving of his beard: Dio 61.19.1), not that of the performers. For later phases of performance see 15.33 and 16.4.

16. *the Battle Pool*: This was Augustus' *Naumachia*; see 12.56.1.

17. *beleaguered ... bog*: The Latin is as thickly censorious as the English here.

18. *giving a prelude*: After *prelude* the text is very uncertain.

19. *but not yet*: After *but not yet* the text is very uncertain.

20. *whom I reported*: The earlier report does not survive.

21. *Pedius Blaesus*: For his restoration to the senate see the *Histories* 1.77.

22. *bequeathed to the Roman people*: The bequest was made in 96 BCE, accepted in 74 BCE.

23. *Domitius ... Servilius*: For Domitius see 4.52. Servilius Nonianus, whose consulship under Tiberius was noted at 6.31.1 (35 CE), was one of Tacitus' predecessors in writing the history of the Julio-Claudian dynasty. He is mentioned by Tacitus' contemporaries Pliny and Quintilian, but his historical writings are entirely lost. The text in the final part of the sentence is disputed, but the antitheses are secure.

24. *a quinquennial festival*: The Neronia (Dio 61.21, Suetonius, *Nero* 12.3); see further 16.4. Nero's earlier consulships were in 55 CE (13.11.1), 57 CE (13.31.1), and 58 CE (13.34.1).

25. *Our forebears ... Mummius*: Actors came to Rome from Etruria in 364 BCE; Rome 'possessed' Greece from 146 BCE on; Asia Minor from 129 BCE; Mummius' triumph celebrated a victory of 146 BCE.

26. *excluded from sacred contests*: For earlier restrictions see 13.25.4.

27. *a comet*: Another is reported in 64 CE (15.47.1).

28. *Rubellius Plautus*: For more on Plautus' predestination see 13.19.3; for his death see 14.57–9.

29. *Antistia*: See further 16.10–11.

30. *Artaxata's demolition*: For the capture and destruction of Artaxata in 58 CE see 13.41.1–3; the narrative picks up from there.

31. *the Iberi*: For the Iberi and their king Pharasmanes see 11.8, 12.44, 13.37.3.

32. *Legerda*: The name of this bastion is uncertain owing to textual corruption here (*Legerda* is a reasonable suggestion based on a geographical text: see the note in Furneaux's commentary), but the exemplary nature of the episode comes across regardless.

33. *the Hyrcanian war*: See 13.37.5.

34. *the Red Sea coast*: What Tacitus means by the *Red Sea* is

uncertain: possibilities include the Indian Ocean, the Persian Gulf and the Red Sea (see 2.61.2). But since the Hyrcani lived near the Caspian, both authorial error and textual corruption have been suspected here.

35. *Verulanus*: He is sent on another mission for Corbulo at 15.3.1.

36. *opposed to*: This phrase captures the general sense of a passage in which the text is corrupt.

37. *Tigranes*: For Tigranes see 15.1–6.

38. *King Archelaus*: For Archelaus see 2.42.

39. *Pharasmanes . . . Polemo*: The first names listed here are corrupt in M. The connectives suggest that there should be four names altogether; the first two are a plausible but not certain suggestion.

40. *Corbulo headed for Syria*: For the peculiar situation in Syria see 13.22.1.

41. *the ancient town of Puteoli*: For earlier troubles in Puteoli (modern Pozzuoli) see 13.48. The new colony's name was Colonia Claudia Augusta Neronensis Puteolanorum.

42. *Antium*: This was Nero's birthplace (15.23.1). Marriage was illegal for legionaries at this period, a restriction not removed until the 3rd century CE, although its consequences were gradually eased over the course of the 2nd century.

43. *The election of praetors*: For earlier passages on election procedure see 1.14.4–15.1 and 2.36.1.

44. *earnest-money*: This was a substantial deposit that the appellant forfeited if he lost his case.

45. *his brother Crispus*: For the talented, wealthy and influential orator and *delator* Vibius Crispus see Tacitus' *Dialogus* (8, 13) and the *Histories* (2.10, 4.42–3).

46. *Didius . . . Veranius*: For Didius in Britain see 12.40; for the Siluri 12.32–3; for Veranius see Tacitus' *Agricola* (14.3).

47. *Suetonius Paulinus*: He is mentioned here for the first time in the extant *Annals*, but some account of his earlier career was presumably given in the lost books. For his record in Britain see *Agricola* 14–17. He is also prominent in the surviving books of the *Histories*.

48. *the Iceni*: See 12.31.

49. *stripped . . . enslaved*: Tacitus gives a similarly searing account of provincial administration at *Agricola* 15.

50. *Recent settlers*: Veterans were settled in colonies in areas behind the current front. At Camulodunum (modern Colchester) there had been a Roman fort, and before that a native stronghold.

51. *Petillius Cerialis*: His later military achievements are prominent in the *Histories* and *Agricola*.

52. *Verulamium*: St Albans.

53. *Antonius Primus*: After conviction (see just below in the text) Primus was restored to senatorial rank by Galba; his prominent role in the Flavian bid for power is detailed in the *Histories*.

54. *lex Cornelia*: A law of Sulla's that set penalties for interference with wills, including exile, property confiscation and expulsion from the senate.

55. *he denounced defendants to the praetor*: Trials arranged by the urban praetor followed an elaborate procedure governed by rules and precedents going back to the Republic. For the urban prefect's court, a new institution, see 6.11.2–3.

56. *my own calling*: As a jurist, Cassius was much engaged with legal precedent and, more generally, law's foundations. For a previous appearance in the senate see 13.41.4.

57. *Whom will position defend . . . proved useless?*: The garbled syntax in the manuscript here is emended variously. The speaker's rhetoric comes through clearly, even if its details are unreliable.

58. *Cingonius Varro*: He was summarily executed early in the confused period that followed Nero's death; see *Histories* 1.6.1.

59. *the Emperor blocked*: Nero ignores the senate's earlier ruling that resident freedmen as well as slaves be punished in such cases (see 13.32.1).

60. *Tarquitius Priscus*: For his prosecution of Taurus see 12.59.1.

61. *Trebellius Maximus*: He was governor of Britain in 69 CE, and is painted rather black by Tacitus in the *Histories* (1.60, 2.65.2) and *Agricola* (16.4).

62. *Memmius Regulus*: His only other important appearance in the *Annals* is much earlier: 5.11.1 (31 CE), but see also 12.22.2.

63. *whose unruly action as plebeian tribune I reported*: For the earlier incident see 13.28; Antistius reappears in connection with Scapula at 16.14. Scapula's military command in Britain is treated at 12.31, his forced suicide at 16.15.

64. *Capito . . . Tigellinus*: For Capito's extortion conviction see 13.33.2; for an earlier dubious associate see 11.6.3. For Tigellinus' appointment as Guard commander see 14.51.2. On the pair see further 16.17.5 and the narrative of Thrasea Paetus' undoing, starting at 16.21.3. On the treason law under Gaius and Claudius see note at 12.42.3.

65. *executed according to ancestral custom*: By scourging; see 2.32.3 and note 29 to Book 2.

66. *Aulus Vitellius*: The future emperor, prominent in *Histories* 1–3.
67. *Rufus*: Rufus, mentioned earlier at 13.22.1, will play a leading role in the Pisonian conspiracy; see 15.50–68.
68. *Tigellinus*: Tacitus gives an overview of Tigellinus' career and describes his death in the *Histories* 1.72.
69. *Order my property administered*: At the beginning of this sentence the text is uncertain but the sense clear.
70. *Vitellius*: For his influence see 11.2–4 and 12.5.2.
71. *Volusius*: See 13.30.2.
72. *Rufus*: See 14.51.2.
73. *Plautus and Sulla*: For Plautus see 14.22; for Sulla 13.47.
74. *Burrus*: Like Faenius Rufus he had had ties to Agrippina; see 12.42.1.
75. *Lucius Vetus*: Nero's victim at 16.10–12.
76. *while recourse exists*: The text underlying *while recourse exists* is very uncertain.
77. *love of wife*: For Plautus' wife Antistia, who was with him in Asia Minor, see 16.10–11.
78. *Musonius*: For the Stoic Gaius Musonius Rufus see also 15.71.4. Tacitus paints an unflattering portrait in the *Histories* (3.81.1, 4.10.1, 4.40.3).
79. ***: Some text is missing here. According to Dio (62.14.1) Nero mocked Plautus' large nose.
80. *Poppaea's wedding*: For Nero's marriage to Octaria in 53 CE see 12.58.1. Nero's relationship with Poppaea is first mentioned at 13.45 (58 CE).
81. *cleaner than your mouth*: In Dio's version (62.13.4) the woman, Pytheas, reinforces her point by spitting at Tigellinus.
82. ***: The lacuna signals the absence of a main clause in this sentence. In light of 14.61.2 editors also suspect *recalled*; in 14.61 the populace may be reacting to a rumour rather than reality.
83. *with rivalry among those doing homage*: The text of the second part of this sentence is very uncertain.
84. *Anicetus*: See 14.3.3 and 14.8.
85. *I found out*: Readers who hear an echo of Cicero's much-mocked 'I have found out' boast about his discovery of the Catilinarian conspiracy will get extra pleasure from this scene. (For the boast, see Cicero, *Against Catiline* 1.10, 1.27, 3.3, 3.4; for the mockery, Cicero, *Letters to Atticus* 1.14.5, on a public meeting where he says that Clodius 'only accused me of "having found out" everything'.)
86. *Pandateria*: This served earlier as an island prison for Augustus'

daughter Julia (1.53.1) and Agrippina the elder (Suetonius, *Tiberius* 53).

87. *No other exile*: The exile of Agrippina the elder came in 29 CE, that of Germanicus' daughter Julia Livilla in 39 CE; Tacitus' accounts (presumably there were such) came in books now missing.

88. *a girl of twenty*: In fact, Octavia was somewhat older than twenty; by how much is not known.

89. *common parentage*: This phrase renders *communes Germanicos*, which refers to her descent from Tiberius' younger brother Drusus through Drusus' younger son Claudius (her parent), and Nero's through Drusus' older son, the man familiarly known as Germanicus (his mother's parent), and also, of course, by adoption, through Claudius. All three ancestors bore the cognomen Germanicus.

90. *Pallas*: See 11.29.

91. *Romanus . . . Piso*: Romanus cannot be identified; the text is suspect. For Piso and the conspiracy of 65 CE see 15.48–74.

BOOK 15

1. *a king . . . imposed*: For these events see 14.26; for the treaty 12.10.1. The extended narrative of war with Parthia that opens Book 15 begins back in 61 CE; for Tacitus' adaptation of the 'annalistic' narrative structure to imperial conditions see p. xl.

2. *Severus . . . Bolanus*: For Severus see also 14.26.1. Bolanus enjoyed success later in Nero's principate (consul in the late 60s CE), in the civil war of 69 CE (governor of Britain) and under the Flavians (governor of Asia in the late 70s CE). Two of his sons held consulships when Tacitus was engaged on his historical works.

3. *Casperius*: See also 12.45.3–4.

4. *Why was the Roman army withdrawn from Tigranocerta?*: This withdrawal is not mentioned in the narrative. The reader is thus even more in the dark than were Corbulo's critics, whose suspicions about secret negotiations are given voice here. The narrative has now moved into 62 CE; the overwintering mentioned below is that of 61/62 CE.

5. *Vologaeses' envoys*: For the projected embassy see 15.5.4.

6. *Funisulanus Vettonianus*: Here mentioned at the start of what would be a distinguished military and political career under the Flavians. Descendants were consuls in 100 and 121.

7. *Paccius*: He was also responsible for an earlier defeat: see 13.36.
8. *former achievements*: See, for example, 13.39 and 14.23.
9. *Caudium and Numantia*: These are place names referring to infamous capitulations of Roman armies in 321 and 137 BCE, respectively; Caudium is in Samnite territory.
10. *Corbulo ... would have it*: Corbulo's viewpoint is probably taken from his memoirs; on Tacitus' use of this source see p. xxvii.
11. *Over the Parthians*: This phrase (*de Parthis* in Latin) echoes the inscriptions on such monuments.
12. *into the Tiber*: With this manoeuvre compare 16.23.2.
13. *Piso ... Geminus ... Paulinus*: Only for Piso's consulship is the date known (13.31.1: 57 CE). For Paulinus see also 13.53.2.
14. *fathers with their long-continued aspirations*: A lovely phrase in Latin, hard to render: *longa patrum vota*.
15. *fictional adoptions*: On the restrictions to inheritance by the childless see 3.28.3.
16. *Thrasea Paetus ... added this*: For the direct quotation form used by Tacitus here – one of only two speeches by senators so presented in the Neronian books of the *Annals* – see p. xxxv.
17. *the Cincian bill*: For this law of 204 BCE see 11.5.2–3. Neither the Julian laws (18 and 8 BCE) nor the Calpurnian decrees (149 BCE) are mentioned elsewhere in Tacitus.
18. *demonstrations of their power*: The text is very difficult here. The translation extrapolates the subject of *should be secured* from *ostentandi*; for similarly elliptical genitive gerunds see *vitandi* (15.5.3) and *retinendi* (13.26.3). But this passage is more difficult.
19. *A lightning-struck gymnasium burned down*: The reference is presumably to the gymnasium in Rome, whose construction – a novelty – is mentioned at 14.47.2.
20. *taken into her place*: For the procedure see 2.86.1.
21. *Verginius Rufus*: This is the first of Verginius Rufus' three consulships (the others 69 CE and 97 CE). As suffect consul in the year of Rufus' death (97 CE), Tacitus wrote his eulogy (Pliny, *Letters* 2.1).
22. *public vows*: The vows were for Poppaea's well-being.
23. *games modelled on the Actian*: Literally, 'following the model of the Actian ritual', i.e., of the quinquennial games instituted by Augustus at Actium in commemoration of his victory there.
24. *goddesses of Fortune*: A pair of sisters worshipped at Antium, goddesses of the fortunes of peace and war (Suetonius, *Caligula* 57.1; Macrobius, *Saturnalia* 1.23; Martial 5.1.3).

25. *those for the Julian family at Bovillae*: The institution of honours for the Julian family at Bovillae is mentioned at 2.41.1; games are not specified.

26. *priestly scruple*: According to Pliny the Elder (a contemporary), the priests known as *magi* (of which Tiridates was one) opposed the discharge of human waste into the sea (*Natural History* 30.16). For Tiridates' eventual arrival in Rome in 66 CE see 16.23.2.

27. *the barbarians'*: The plural presumably refers to Vologaeses and his puppet Tiridates (mentioned later in this passage). Their request is here simplified, by implication, to *possession of Armenia*, whereas above (15.24.2) Vologaeses is shown fussing over where Tiridates will receive Nero's formal recognition of that possession. The slippage shows an outraged people's disregard for detail.

28. *given by the Roman people to Pompey*: In 67 BCE by the *lex Gabinia*. A closer parallel is the position of Germanicus in 20–22 CE (2.43.1).

29. *a witty attack*: For Nero's jokes see further 13.14.1, 14.57.4, 14.59.3 and, more sinister, 16.11.3.

30. *pierced by Lucullus*: In 69 BCE.

31. *He knows*: Or possibly 'Corbulo knows' (Tacitus omits the subject).

32. *Annius Vinicianus*: Tacitus emphasizes Vinicianus' unusual distinction with the information that he commanded *pro legato*, 'with a legate's authority', rather than 'as legate'. 'Legate' was the regular title of a legionary commander, and such posts regularly went to senators. Rapid advancement is also attested by Dio (62.23.6: suffect consul in 66). Late in Nero's principate there was a conspiracy, called the *coniuratio Viniciana* (Suetonius, *Nero* 36), that may perhaps have involved this young man. By then his father-in-law Corbulo was disgraced and dead (Dio 63.17.5–6).

33. *a Parthian prince*: Literally, 'a descendant of Arsaces'.

34. *Pacorus*: He was king of the Medes; see 15.2.1.

35. *the Maritime Alps*: The area, a province since the time of Augustus, became in effect part of Italy and its magistrates Roman citizens.

36. *the Roscian law*: By this law of 67 BCE the first fourteen rows of seating in theatres were reserved for members of the equestrian order (senators sat even closer to the stage, in the orchestra).

37. *noble women and senators were sullied*: For earlier instances see 14.14–15.

38. *he had performed*: See 14.15 for the Youth Games; 16.4 for an eventual appearance in Rome.

39. *towns*: See 1.79.2.

40. *Beneventum*: This was the hometown of Vatinius (Juvenal, *Satires* 5.46), a Neronian of interest to Tacitus' contemporary satirists (Martial and Juvenal) and to Tacitus himself (*Dialogus* 11.2; *Histories* 1.37.5).

41. *Torquatus Silanus*: Consul in 53 CE (see 12.58.1, where Tacitus uses the other two parts of his name, Decimus Junius).

42. *dissevered arm veins*: The awkwardness of this English expression reflects the Latin. Tacitus has at least a dozen different ways of saying that someone has slit their veins, and some of his variants are necessarily far-fetched.

43. *paid respects to its gods*: i.e., he prayed to the gods of the Capitoline triad for a sign of their support for (or opposition to) his plans. He seems to have received such a sign at the next temple he visited, Vesta's.

44. *he entered Vesta's temple*: Suetonius, *Nero* 19.1 has a more matter-of-fact description of these same events.

45. *used the whole city as his home*: Suetonius, *Nero* 27.2–3 offers another version of these events, including a detail relevant here: Nero encouraged his friends to provide similar entertainments.

46. *Agrippa's Pool*: This was an ornamental water feature connected to the baths Agrippa had built in the Campus Martius.

47. *a calamity*: For other narratives of the fire see Suetonius, *Nero* 38 and Dio 62.16–17.

48. *Maecenas' Gardens*: These lay on the Esquiline. The conjunction of the two hills was accomplished by what Suetonius calls a 'passageway residence' (*Nero* 31: *domus transitoria*) that was later replaced by the Golden House. *The Agrippa buildings* mentioned in this same section are presumably in the Campus Martius. On Nero's park see 14.14.1.

49. *three sesterces*: Its price more than a century earlier (Cicero, *Against Verres* 3.174).

50. *But before fear . . . to the populace*: The translation here depends on emendations to a corrupt text.

51. *naming it for himself*: For 'Neropolis' see Suetonius, *Nero* 55.

52. *Senones . . . equal number*: Rome was captured and burned by the Senones, a Gallic tribe, in 390 BCE, some 454 years (or 418 years, months and days) earlier; see the note in Furneaux's commentary. For an earlier reference to the Senones see 11.24.4.

53. *a residence*: The Golden House or Domus Aurea. Suetonius' *Nero* (31) gives a fuller description.
54. *Sibyl's books*: For the Sibylline books (their usual name) see 6.12.
55. *Spartacus*: See 3.73.1.
56. *expiated by noble blood*: See, for example, the comet at 14.22, which prepares the way for Rubellius Plautus' elimination (14.57–9).
57. *Senecio . . . intimate with Nero*: See 13.12.1.
58. *Rufus . . . losing ground to Tigellinus*: They held the Guard command jointly (14.51.2).
59. *nocturnal excursions*: See 13.25, where, however, a military guard is mentioned. The manuscript's puzzling phrase 'with his house ablaze', which Heubner and others excise and is therefore not given in the text above, may refer not to the occasion of the fire (which causes puzzlement) but rather to brightly lit parties in the palace, which was now so big that Nero could 'make excursions' in his own home, unguarded. See further 15.53.1.
60. *blocks great undertakings*: For the same bitter generalization expressed somewhat differently see 13.53.3.
61. *Volusius Proculus*: Tacitus does not mention Proculus in the narrative of Agrippina's murder (14.1–9).
62. *Silanus . . . Cassius*: Silanus' exile and death are recounted at 16.7–9. For Cassius, who was exiled at the same time, see the same passage and, earlier, 12.11–12.
63. *it seems preposterous*: The danger, at any rate, was real: Antonia was executed on charges of rebellion (Suetonius, *Nero* 35).
64. *Finally, he ordered*: The text of this sentence suffers from corruption, but its sense is nevertheless clear.
65. *Epaphroditus*: This is Tacitus' only extant reference to Epaphroditus, who figures largely at Nero's death (Suetonius, *Nero* 49.3; *Domitian* 14.4).
66. *a cleverer accuser*: The expression is somewhat puzzling, which has led to emendations for the phrase, such as Woodman's *purgandi imperitior*: 'unskilled in exculpation'. Natalis' cleverness, however, may lie in offering only two names, one of which Nero would have been delighted to hear, and concealing the rest, perhaps in the hope that the Guard conspirators, who would be involved in the coming arrests and interrogation, might still rise against Nero, if only to save their own skins. In fact, their names are not revealed to Nero for some time (see 15.66.1).
67. *a freedwoman . . . freeborn men*: The contrast is reinforced in

Latin by a sound effect not reproducible in English: pro*tegendo* ('to protect') ... pro*derent* ('betrayed').

68. *not only support for conspirators*: The text is corrupt here: *support for* is an emendation.

69. *favour-tainted*: Tacitus' expression *favore imbutus* leaves open the question of who was favoured: Piso or Nero? The former can be supported by reference to Tacitus' words at the beginning of the conspiracy narrative (15.48.1 *favour towards Gaius Piso*), the latter by more distant Tacitean passages (e.g., *Histories* 1.5.1: *miles ... longo Caesarum sacramento imbutus*, with notes in Damon's commentary).

70. *poison having disappointed*: For the poison episode, perhaps only a rumour, see 15.45.3.

71. *the crimes to whose punishment he had agreed*: i.e., Nero's crimes.

72. *a burden of perpetual grief*: The text is corrupt, but the sense is clear.

73. *those condemned in Athens' court*: Socrates, most famously.

74. *Statilia Messalina*: Nero would later marry her himself (Suetonius, *Nero* 35).

75. *the very verses*: Perhaps Lucan 3.635–46.

76. *Quintianus*: See 15.49.

77. *using the Greek term*: Soter.

78. *spoiled it by the nullity of his end*: Tacitus' reproach here is vague to the point of obscurity, and we have no other information about Proxumus' end.

79. *****: There is a gap in the text after *Pompeius*. This long list of names can be compared with that given at the beginning of the conspiracy narrative (15.50.1).

80. *Cornelius ... Pollio*: Tacitus' lists of conspirators, though tedious where (as here) we know nothing else about the persons named, allow us to see that more than half of the upper officer echelons of the Guard were (or were regarded as) connected to the plot: one of two prefects, seven of twelve tribunes (six named here; Subrius Flavus was the seventh).

81. *Rufrius Crispinus*: See 11.1.3, 13.45.4 and 16.17.6.

82. *the column, so to speak*: The military simile here is used as a metaphor in another list of victims at 16.17.1 (*in single file*).

83. *2,000 coins per man*: Officers got more in proportion. Suetonius in *Nero* (10.1) associates the free grain provision with Guards only; whether the legionaries received benefits at this time is not clear. For the grain subsidy see 1.2.1.

84. *Cocceius Nerva ... Nymphidius*: This is the future emperor. The text here and at the end of the next paragraph seems incomplete (Nymphidius' *cognomen* is lacking, for a start), as if Tacitus planned to insert a character sketch of Nymphidius Sabinus (who figures importantly, if briefly, in the transition of power from Nero to Galba: see the *Histories* 1.5 and Plutarch, *Life of Galba* 13) but did not finish the job. Nymphidius replaced Faenius Rufus as co-commander of the Guard with Tigellinus.

85. *tall and grim-faced*: The details of Nymphidius' appearance align with those of the parent he claimed: see Suetonius, *Caligula* 50 for Gaius' height and his menacing brow.

86. *Vindex' war*: The armed rebellion started by Julius Vindex in the spring of 68 CE led eventually, after Vindex' own defeat, to Nero's fall later that year (see Suetonius, *Nero* 40 and Dio 63.22–4).

87. *men's veneration*: From *veneration* to *some* the text is very uncertain.

BOOK 16

1. *competition's degradation*: For earlier competitions see 14.15 and 15.33; for the institution of this particular festival, the Neronia, see 14.20.

2. *Silanus' uncle Torquatus*: For the uncle see 15.35.

3. *Calpurnius Fabatus*: He was later the grandfather-in-law and correspondent of Tacitus' contemporary, Pliny.

4. *Lucius Vetus*: He was governor of Asia in 64/65 CE (see volume 1 of Syme's *Tacitus*, p. 21) and he was consul with Nero (see just below in the text) a decade earlier (13.11.1: 55 CE).

5. *Antistia Pollitta*: She appeared earlier at 14.22.3.

6. *Rubellius Plautus*: See 14.57–9.

7. *Name Nero your principal heir*: For the issue of bequests to the Emperor see 2.48.2.

8. *Faenius Rufus*: For his end see 15.66–8.

9. *Vetus' freedman prosecutor received as reward*: The compensation for his associate Claudius Demianus is specified above: release from prison. On seating by rank in Roman theatres see 15.32 and note 36 to Book 15.

10. *'Neroneus'*: See 15.74.1; 'Germanicus' and 'Claudius' are also parts of Nero's name: Nero Claudius Caesar Augustus Germanicus.

11.   *two criminal Junii Torquati*: For Decimus Junius Silanus Torquatus see 15.35; for Lucius Junius Silanus Torquatus see 16.7–9.

12.   *a virulent pestilence*: Suetonius' *Nero* (39.1) attributes 30,000 deaths to this pestilence.

13.   *were often cremated*: Brevity omits the fact that they died while sitting in attendance and mourning.

14.   *A disaster at Lyon*: A fire: see Seneca, *Letters* 91.14.

15.   *Rome's misfortunes*: i.e., the fire at Rome in 64 CE (see 15.38–45).

16.   *punishment . . . by exile*: See 14.48.4 to 14.49.3.

17.   *as an astrologer*: Literally, 'at the Chaldaeans' art'.

18.   *Nero is hostile to Anteius*: Nero's distrust of Anteius was manifest already in 56 CE: see 13.22.1.

19.   *Ostorius Scapula*: See 14.48.1–2. His son was Tacitus' colleague as suffect consul in 97 CE.

20.   *Boats were sent at once*: Sosianus was sent back to his island in 70 CE (*Histories* 4.44.2).

21.   *the civic crown*: See 15.12.3.

22.   *Were I recording . . . dismal and unending*: A difficult sentence. The modifiers *with such similarity of event* and *dismal and unending* fit the deaths that Tacitus is describing, but the syntax refers to hypothetical subject matter.

23.   *My defence*: Brevity obscures Tacitus' meaning here. By *defence* he seems to mean 'protection against the imputation of malice towards Nero's victims' (for his rejection of hostility more broadly construed see also 1.1.4). With *ask from those* he seems to encourage his readers, impatient at the dismal series of deaths, to remind themselves that the historian is not to blame for the events he records.

24.   *a particular remembrance*: This need not be a flattering remembrance; Tacitus reminds readers of the historian's power (see 3.65) and declares, once again, that he himself uses this power without malice (see 1.1).

25.   *in single file*: For the opening metaphor see note at 15.71. Anicius was last seen proposing a temple to Nero (15.74.3).

26.   *Crispinus*: For an incident in which he earned honorary office see 11.4; there the award is an honorary praetorship, here Tacitus speaks of an honorary consulship. Either Tacitus has made a slip or there was another award unknown to us. For the conspiracy see 15.71.4.

27.   *Mela . . . Gallio . . . Seneca*: For Lucius Junius Gallio see 15.73.3; Seneca is omnipresent in the Neronian books until his death at

15.64. Mela held the procuratorships of the equestrian career ladder.

28. *Upon Lucan's death ... Romanus*: See 15.70.1. Romanus may be the man referred to at 14.65.2, but textual problems there prevent certainty.

29. *He coveted the man's wealth*: The implication is that the mere sight of the 'evidence' will suggest suicide to Mela. As it did.

30. *Tigellinus ... Capito*: For this pair see also 11.6, 14.48 and 16.20–28.

31. *words written about Crispinus, people thought*: Tacitus leaves unsaid who was thought to have written them. If Mela, it was seen as posthumous vengeance against Cerealis (for reasons unknown to us), bolstered by reference to a 'known' enemy of the ruler, Crispinus. If Nero, it was seen as justification for the execution of Crispinus and preparation for the execution of Cerealis. No doubt different people believed different things, and Tacitus, here as elsewhere, evokes the murk of suspicion.

32. *betrayed a conspiracy to Gaius*: The betrayal would have been related in the now lost *Annals* books on Gaius.

33. *governor of Bithynia and later as consul*: Petronius was suffect consul in 62 CE; the date of his governorship is not known.

34. *expensively delicate*: The syntax of the word rendered here *expensively* (*adfluentia*) is disputed. I take it as an ablative of respect qualifying *delicate* (*molle*); others take it as causal ablative 'from extravagance', modifying the verb 'deemed'.

35. *Scaevinus*: See the narrative of the Pisonian conspiracy, beginning at 15.48.

36. *Petronius reached Cumae*: Presumably seeking a personal interview with Nero. Hence, Tigellinus' precaution above (*vacating the defence*).

37. *Paetus ... Soranus*: Paetus was last mentioned at 15.23.4 in 63 CE; Soranus at 12.53.2 in 52 CE. Paetus' offence in connection with the Youth festival seems to have been a refusal to display his talents on Nero's stage (thus Dio 62.26.4).

38. *new reasons ... Poppaea's divine honours*: See the narrative at 14.12 (senate meeting on Agrippina), 14.15 (Youth Games, no mention of Thrasea), 14.48.4 to 14.49.3 (Antistius' trial), 16.6 (Poppaea's honours, no mention of Thrasea).

39. *Antenor*: The 'founder' of Padua. *Games* has a modifier in the Latin, but scholars disagree about what it should be. Rather than translate any of the (variously unsatisfactory) proposals, I omit

it. Dio says the festival was celebrated once every thirty years
(62.26.4).

40. *calling him to account for extortion*: On the trial see 13.33.2;
Thrasea is not mentioned there.

41. *vows to the immortal gods*: These annual vows were on behalf
of the state (1 January) and of the Emperor's continued good
health (3 January; see 4.17.1). Thrasea was a member of the
'Board of Fifteen for Religious Rites', a priestly body of which
Tacitus became a member under Domitian (11.11.1; for the
board's duties see 3.64.3 and note 47 to Book 6).

42. *Formerly constant and tireless*: Historical allusions in Capito's
speech: *ordinary senate business* (e.g., 13.49.1); Silanus (16.7–
9); Vetus (16.10–11); Poppaea's divine honours (16.6); *that sect*
is Stoicism; Tubero and Favonius (opponents of the Gracchi and
Caesar respectively); Cassius (16.7.1; his name an allusion to
Caesar's assassin); *men named Brutus* (Caesar's assassin and his
forebear, who brought in freedom and the consulship (1.1.1)).

43. *Eprius Marcellus*: See 12.4.3.

44. *his governorship of Asia*: Soranus' governorship was three or
four years earlier; the precise date is uncertain. Ephesus' port
needed clearing of the silt brought down by the Cayster river. For
a subsequent 'art-collecting' mission see 15.45.2. (Or else Tacitus has mixed up the proconsuls, ascribing to Soranus charges in
fact laid against Antistius Vetus in 65 CE.)

45. *Rubellius Plautus*: For his death in Asia see 14.59.1.

46. *Tiridates' arrival*: For the background on Tiridates' visit see
15.29–31; for the manoeuvre of exchanging external and internal preoccupations compare 15.18.2.

47. *Inviolate, undefiled ... steered your life*: A difficult passage.

48. *Arulenus Rusticus*: He was 'tribune of the people': *tribunus
plebis*. Tacitus reverses the formula: *plebi tribunus*.

49. *at such a time!*: Rusticus became praetor in 69 CE, suffect consul
in 92 and fell foul of Domitian soon thereafter. He was the
author of a biography of Thrasea Paetus (*Agricola* 2.1).

50. *the temple of Venus Genetrix*: Presumably the senate's intended
meeting place.

51. *Priscus ... Agrippinus ... Montanus*: For Priscus see 12.49.2
and 13.28.3; Tacitus introduces him to posterity in the *Histories*
4.5–6. Agrippinus was a senator and Stoic; for his fate see
16.33.2; for his father, a senator under Tiberius, see 3.67.1. For
Montanus' poems see 16.29.2; for his punishment 16.33.2; for
his activity as a senator under Vespasian see the *Histories* 4.40.1

and especially 4.42, where Tacitus puts a long speech in his mouth.

52. *Let him sunder ... now even his presence*: In the *Histories* (4.8.3) Tacitus shows Marcellus trying to exculpate himself for this speech: 'Thrasea was brought down less by my speech than by the senate's verdict.'

53. *fostering cities' restiveness*: See 16.23.1.

54. *fortune-tellers*: On these and their illegal services see 2.32.3.

55. *Annius Pollio*: He was killed soon after his banishment, for which see 15.71.3.

56. *except that you, Nero, and you, senators, preserve*: Dio 62.26.3 has different, but equally innocuous, details.

57. *what they are called, what art they practise!*: Servilia is alluding to 'Chaldaeans' and the Chaldaean art: astrology (see 16.14.1).

58. *Publius Egnatius*: In the *Histories* (4.40.3) Tacitus reports his trial and condemnation in 70 CE. Egnatius' 'bad example' is also mentioned in the *Histories* (4.10) and in Juvenal's *Satires* 1, 3 and 6.

59. *stripped of his entire fortune and banished*: Presumably for giving evidence in Soranus' favour (thus Dio 62.26.2).

60. *an honorary quaestorship*: This gave him senatorial status.

61. *a quaestor*: His identity is not known, but his role in the immediate sequel, as the recipient of pointed advice from Thrasea Paetus (16.35.1), suggests that his future was significant.

62. *Arria ... and mother's example ... their daughter's one support*: Tacitus alludes here to three women whose stories were told by his contemporary Pliny: *Letters* 3.16 (on the elder Arria), 7.19 (on the younger Arria – Thrasea's wife – and their daughter Fannia).

63. *so turning to Demetrius*: The text ends here, mid-sentence, mid-death.

Index of Names

Personal names are listed under the fullest form used in the translation. If more of the name is known from other sources, the full known version is given in parentheses immediately after the lemma. Where a variant form is used in the translation or in the Latin, it is given in parentheses after the reference, unless the variant is simply the cognomen of a person recently introduced by nomen and cognomen or the nomen of a person introduced with praenomen and nomen. The name of a person alluded to but not named is given in square brackets.

Individual references are not made to the various emperors' appearances in the books covering their reigns. So references to Claudius during the principates of Tiberius (Books 1–6) and Nero (Books 13–16) are listed individually, but not those during his own principate (Books 11–12).

The names of peoples are listed here as well as in the Index of Places, since Tacitus refers to entities such as cities or countries both by the name of the inhabitants (Athenians, Armenians, etc.) and by the name of the place (Athens, Armenia, etc.). My translation uses the form that best suits the situation.

Marcius see also under Barea,
 Philippus
Marcius Festus 15.50
Marcius, Publius 2.32
Marcius Numa 6.11 (Numa
 Marcius)
Marcomani 2.46, 2.62
Mardi 14.23
Marinus see under Julius
Marius (Gaius Marius) 1.9,
 12.60
Marius, Publius (Publius Marius
 Celsus) 14.48
Marius, Sextus 4.36, 6.19
Marius Celsus (Aulus Marius
 Celsus) 15.25
Marius Nepos 2.48
Maroboduus 2.26, 2.44–6,
 2.62–3, 2.88, 3.11
Mars 2.22
Mars Ultor 2.64
Marsi 1.50, 1.56, 2.25
Marsus see under Vibius
Martina 2.74, 3.7
Massiliots 4.43
Matius (Gaius Matius) 12.60
Mattiaci 1.56, 11.20
Maximus see also under
 Sanquinius
Maximus Scaurus 15.50
Mazippa 2.52
Medea 6.34
Medes 2.4, 2.56, 2.60, 6.34
Meherdates 11.10, 12.10–14
Mela see under Annaeus
Memmius Regulus (Gaius
 Memmius Regulus, cos. 63)
 15.23
Memmius Regulus (Publius
 Memmius Regulus) 5.11, 6.4,
 12.22, 14.47
Memnon 2.61

Menelaus 2.60
Messala see also under
 Vipstanus, Volesus Messala
Messala Corvinus (Marcus
 Valerius Messala Corvinus)
 3.34 (Messala), 4.34 6.11
 11.6–7 (M. Messala), 13.34
 (Corvinus)
Messalina 11.1–2, 11.12,
 11.25–6, 11.28–32, 11.34–8,
 12.1, 12.42, 12.65, 13.11,
 13.19, 13.32, 13.43
Messalinus see under Cotta,
 Valerius
Messenians 4.43
Metellus, Lucius 3.71
Milesians 3.63, 4.43, 4.55
Milichus 15.54–5, 15.59, 15.71
Minos 3.26
Minucius Thermus 6.7
Minucius Thermus 16.20
Mithridates (king of the Iberi)
 6.32–3, 11.8–9, 12.44–8
Mithridates (Mithridates VI
 Eupator, king of Pontus) 2.55,
 3.62, 3.73, 4.14, 4.36
Mithridates Bosporanus
 12.15–16, 12.18–21
Mnester 11.4, 11.36
Mnester 14.9
Monaeses 15.2
Monobazus 15.1–2
Montanus see under Curtius,
 Julius
Moors 2.52, 4.23–4
Mostenes 2.47
Mummius, Lucius 4.43, 14.21
Munatius Gratus 15.50
Munatius Plancus (Lucius
 Munatius Plancus) 1.39, 2.32
Murena see under Varro
Musonius Rufus 14.59, 15.71

Index of Places

The names of peoples are listed here as well as in the Index of Names, since Tacitus refers to entities such as cities or countries both by the name of the inhabitants (Athenians, Armenians, etc.) and by the name of the place (Athens, Armenia, etc.). In the translation I use whichever form suits the situation best. For places shown on one or more of the maps included in this volume the relevant map is noted in parentheses. (RE = Roman Empire, NE = Near East, AM = Asia Minor, IT = Italy, LC = Latium and Campania, GE = Germany, BR = Britain, BA = Balkans, RO = Rome).

PENGUIN CLASSICS

THE ANALECTS
CONFUCIUS

> 'The Master said, "If a man sets his heart on benevolence,
> he will be free from evil"'

The Analects are a collection of Confucius' sayings brought together by his pupils shortly after his death in 497 BC. Together they express a philosophy, or a moral code, by which Confucius, one of the most humane thinkers of all time, believed everyone should live. Upholding the ideals of wisdom, self-knowledge, courage and love of one's fellow man, he argued that the pursuit of virtue should be every individual's supreme goal. And while following the Way, or the truth, might not result in immediate or material gain, Confucius showed that it could nevertheless bring its own powerful and lasting spiritual rewards.

This edition contains a detailed introduction exploring the concepts of the original work, a bibliography and glossary and appendices on Confucius himself, *The Analects* and the disciples who compiled them.

Translated with an introduction and notes by D. C. Lau

PENGUIN CLASSICS

THE RISE OF THE ROMAN EMPIRE
POLYBIUS

> 'If history is deprived of the truth,
> we are left with nothing but an idle, unprofitable tale'

In writing his account of the relentless growth of the Roman Empire, the Greek statesman Polybius (*c*. 200–118 BC) set out to help his fellow-countrymen understand how their world came to be dominated by Rome. Opening with the Punic War in 264 BC, he vividly records the critical stages of Roman expansion: its campaigns throughout the Mediterranean, the temporary setbacks inflicted by Hannibal and the final destruction of Carthage in 146 BC. An active participant in contemporary politics, as well as a friend of many prominent Roman citizens, Polybius was able to draw on a range of eyewitness accounts and on his own experiences of many of the central events, giving his work immediacy and authority.

Ian Scott-Kilvert's translation fully preserves the clarity of Polybius' narrative. This substantial selection of the surviving volumes is accompanied by an introduction by F. W. Walbank, which examines Polybius' life and times, and the sources and technique he employed in writing his history.

Translated by Ian Scott-Kilvert

Selected with an introduction by F. W. Walbank

THE STORY OF PENGUIN CLASSICS

Before 1946 ... 'Classics' are mainly the domain of academics and students; readable editions for everyone else are almost unheard of. This all changes when a little-known classicist, E. V. Rieu, presents Penguin founder Allen Lane with the translation of Homer's *Odyssey* that he has been working on in his spare time.

1946 Penguin Classics debuts with *The Odyssey*, which promptly sells three million copies. Suddenly, classics are no longer for the privileged few.

1950s Rieu, now series editor, turns to professional writers for the best modern, readable translations, including Dorothy L. Sayers's *Inferno* and Robert Graves's unexpurgated *Twelve Caesars*.

1960s The Classics are given the distinctive black covers that have remained a constant throughout the life of the series. Rieu retires in 1964, hailing the Penguin Classics list as 'the greatest educative force of the twentieth century.'

1970s A new generation of translators swells the Penguin Classics ranks, introducing readers of English to classics of world literature from more than twenty languages. The list grows to encompass more history, philosophy, science, religion and politics.

1980s The Penguin American Library launches with titles such as *Uncle Tom's Cabin*, and joins forces with Penguin Classics to provide the most comprehensive library of world literature available from any paperback publisher.

1990s The launch of Penguin Audiobooks brings the classics to a listening audience for the first time, and in 1999 the worldwide launch of the Penguin Classics website extends their reach to the global online community.

The 21st Century Penguin Classics are completely redesigned for the first time in nearly twenty years. This world-famous series now consists of more than 1300 titles, making the widest range of the best books ever written available to millions – and constantly redefining what makes a 'classic'.

The Odyssey continues ...

The best books ever written

PENGUIN CLASSICS

SINCE 1946

Find out more at www.penguinclassics.com